Business & Legal Primer for Game Development

Legal Disclaimer

Business & Legal Primer for Game Development

S. Gregory Boyd

Brian "Psychochild" Green

Charles River Media

A part of Cengage Learning

COURSE TECHNOLOGY
CENGAGE Learning™

Australia • Brazil • Japan • Korea • Mexico • Singapore • Spain • United Kingdom • United States

COURSE TECHNOLOGY
CENGAGE Learning™

**Publisher and General Manager,
Course Technology PTR:**
Stacy L. Hiquet

Cover Designer: Tyler Creative

For product information and technology assistance, contact us at
Cengage Learning Customer & Sales Support, 1-800-354-9706
For permission to use material from this text or product,
submit all requests online at **cengage.com/permissions**
Further permissions questions can be emailed to
permissionrequest@cengage.com

All trademarks are the property of their respective owners.

Library of Congress Control Number: 2006030732

ISBN-10: 1-58450-492-7
ISBN-13: 978-1-58450-492-4

Course Technology, a part of Cengage Learning
20 Channel Center Street
Boston, MA 02210
USA

Cengage Learning is a leading provider of customized learning solutions with office locations around the globe, including Singapore, the United Kingdom, Australia, Mexico, Brazil, and Japan. Locate your local office at:
international.cengage.com/region

Cengage Learning products are represented in Canada by Nelson Education, Ltd. For your lifelong learning solutions, visit **courseptr.com**
Visit our corporate website at **cengage.com**

Printed in the United States of America
3 4 5 6 7 12 11 10 09

To Laura, my wife and favorite violinist.
—Greg

To Kat, my constant support.
—Brian

Contents

About the Authors xiii

Acknowledgments xvii

Chapter 1 Introduction 1

Why Write This Book? 1

What You Will Find In This Book 3

Enjoy the Book! 4

Chapter 2 So You Want to Start a Game Company? 5

Spencer Zuzolo

Before the Paperwork 6

Company Formation 10

Money 16

The Daily Grind 23

More Tasty Business Tasks! 30

Government: The Horror and Insanity 32

Human Resources 34

A Word About Health and the "Other" Insurances 35

Change: The Real End Game 36

Conclusion 38

Checklist for Starting a Business 39

Chapter 3 Business Operations 41

Matthew B. Doyle

Employee Management 41

The Dreaded Crunch 45

Who Does What 49

The Prospective Employee 55

Company Culture 63

Rewards and Punishment 64

Staying in the Black 66

Measuring Your Success 69

Beware of Pitfalls! 69

How to Save Money 69

Seeking Out Opportunities 71

Networking—How and Where 71
Maintaining Your Company's Independence 72
Knowing When to Expand 73
Conclusion 74

Chapter 4 Contracts—A Brief Overview **75**

Matthew Hector

Contracts Basics 75
Overview of Common Contract Terms 78
Controlling Legal Fees Associated with Contracts 84
Non-Disclosure Agreements 85
Employment Contracts 88
Intellectual Property Licensing and Assignments 91
Publishing and Developer Contracts 93
Conclusion 99
Endnotes 99

Chapter 5 Marketing Is a Game, Too **101**

Roxanne Christ

Marketing versus PR 101
Marketing Your Game versus Marketing Your Company 102
Ad Dollars 102
Developing Your Marketing Strategy 102
Knowing Your Audience 109
Live Advertising: Trade Shows 112
Print Marketing 114
Traditional Television, Radio, and Movie Marketing 116
In-Game Advertising (Product Placement) 117
Other Internet Options 121
Measuring Marketing Success 124
Marketing Mistakes and How to Avoid Them 127
Conclusion 130
Endnotes 130

Chapter 6 PR Plans and Programs for the Game Developer **133**

Ted Brockwood

The Question Everybody Asks: What Is PR? 133
Do It Yourself versus Hiring Someone 134
PR Planning 134

Crafting a Press Release 136

Fact Sheet Development 140

Asset Development.. 142

The Story Pitching Process 145

The Demo Process 147

Online Communities 148

Press Tours 150

Industry Events 152

Viral Marketing 153

Contents... 154

A Sample PR Program for Galaxy Dynamo............................... 155

Contingency Planning... 157

Conclusion... 158

Chapter 7 Intellectual Property

S. Gregory Boyd

The Importance of IP 161

Copyright 163

Common Questions about Copyright 171

Trade Secret 172

Trademark 176

Patents... 181

Rights of Publicity.. 187

IP Strategy 101.. 188

Three Important Points.. 190

Conclusion... 191

Sources of Further Information 191

Endnotes 191

Chapter 8 Licensing Intellectual Property 193

Gary S. Morris and Richard A. Beyman

The Nature of Intellectual Property 193

Intellectual Property Rights 194

Elements of a License... 198

Licensing for Rights in Literary Works 200

Licensing for Rights in Musical Works 204

Licenses for Rights in Audiovisual Works.................................. 207

Licensing for Rights to Name, Image, Likeness, and Indicia Rights
of Individuals 208

Conclusion... 212

Endnotes 213

Chapter 9 Intellectual Property Litigation (Avoiding It, But Winning If You Have to Fight). 215

John Flock

Litigation—Forced Dispute Resolution. 215
Before the Suit Begins 216
Where Does the Fight Occur? 218
When the Lawsuit Is Filed. 219
The Quick Knockouts 220
The Markman Ruling on Patent Claim Scope. 222
Discovery 226
Trial. 232
Alternative Dispute Resolution 237
Conclusion. 239
Endnotes 241

Chapter 10 Selling Internationally 245

Kellee McKeever

Considerations for Selling Internationally. 245
Sales Agent versus Employee 246
Considering Potential Revenue 247
Finding an International Partner 248
Types of International Deals. 248
Selecting a Partner in Smaller Territories. 250
Partnering with the Competition? 251
Local Manufacture and Pricing 253
Game Type Can Determine Deal Type 254
Do You Trust Your Partner?. 255
Legal Issues in Other Territories 257
Controlling Piracy 258
Localization 259
Payment. 260
Let's Make a Deal 262
Conclusion. 264

Chapter 11 Taxation 267

Peter H. Friedman

Entity Selection 267

State Selection 272

Accounting. 273

Employees or Independent Contractors. 278

Payroll Tax Compliance 281

Depository Tax Requirements 283

Fringe Benefits 285

Stock Option Plans 286

Tax Incentives 290

Other Tax Issues 292

Conclusion. 295

Endnotes 296

Chapter 12 Exit Strategies 299

Greg Costikyan

Why Exit? 299

How to Exit?. 300

Preparing for Purchase. 303

Downside Exits 309

Conclusion. 310

Chapter 13 Virtual World Law. 311

James Grimmelmann

Virtual Worlds Have Five Kinds of Rules. 312

EULAs as Contracts 317

Terms Ensuring that Players Play by the Rules 322

Terms Giving You the Power to Set the Rules 337

Terms Staving Off Legal Trouble from Third Parties 347

Further Horizons 358

Conclusion. 359

Endnotes 359

Chapter 14 I Wish I Knew 361

Dave Ahl 361

Ralph Baer 364

Richard Bartle 366

John Erskine 369

Matt Esber 370

F. Randall "Randy" Farmer. 371

Scott Foe 374

     Steve Goldstein 376

     Brian Green 378

     William Leverett. 380

     Alexander Macris. 381

     Jessica Mulligan 383

     Jeff Vogel 387

     Gordon Walton. 388

     Andrew S. Zaffron 392

Chapter 15 HUSTLE & FLOW: The Intangibles of Running a Game Company 395

Peter Lee and Eric Zimmerman

     First Things First: Make Everyone an Author 396

     Playing at Work: A Research-Focused Company Culture. 398

     The Flow of Flow: Encouraging an Open Process. 401

     The World Outside: Becoming an Honest Hustler 403

     Conclusion. 405

Chapter 16 Game Development Agreement Analysis. 407

S. Gregory Boyd and Erik Smith

     Conclusion. 454

Chapter 17 Wrapping It All Up 455

For Further Reading 457

     Contracts 457

     Virtual World Law 457

     Intellectual Property 458

     Public Relations. 458

     Business Management 458

Glossary 459

Index 473

About the Authors

Richard A. Beyman

Richard A. Beyman is a partner at the law firm of Franklin, Weinrib, Rudell, & Vassallo, P.C. in New York (*http://www.fwrv.com/*). His practice focuses on all facets of the entertainment industry, including the license, acquisition, and exploitation of intellectual property rights for motion pictures, television, music, book publishing, character licensing, and a variety of digital, new media, and Internet applications. Mr. Beyman is a graduate of Cornell University (with Distinction) and Fordham University School of Law.

S. Gregory Boyd (Editor)

Greg Boyd is an attorney with Kenyon & Kenyon LLP in New York. He has represented some of the most prominent game companies in the world; his practice includes IP counseling and litigation for both publishers and developers. As a member of the International Game Developers Association IP Rights Committee, he was an author and editor on the International Game Developers Association IP Whitepaper. Dr. Boyd has spoken at several national conferences, including AIPLA, GDC, Austin Game Conference, and State of Play. His commentary on business and law in the game industry has appeared in national publications, including *Fortune*, *Forbes*, *Game Developer Magazine*, and *Gamasutra*. He sits on the Board of Advisors for Mobygames. Dr. Boyd obtained MD and JD degrees from the University of North Carolina at Chapel Hill.

Ted Brockwood

Ted Brockwood is the owner of Calico Media Communications (CMC). CMC has done a variety of work for an equally diverse number of customers, ranging from CDV Software Entertainment and Buena Vista Games to EA Sports' "Big" label. Currently, Mr. Brockwood is heavily involved in CDV's 2006 product lineup, contributing to the PR, marketing, Web site content development, and product analysis. Some of the front-page features he has helped secure have appeared on game networks such as IGN, GameSpot, and GameSpy. Print features he has contributed to have appeared on the pages of *Maximum PC*, *GameInformer*, *PC Gamer*, *Playboy*, and others. You can find more information about CMC at *http://www.calico-media.com/*.

Roxanne Christ

Roxanne Christ is a partner at the Los Angeles office of the law firm of Latham & Watkins LLP (*http://www.lw.com/*). Ms. Christ's practice focuses on general intellectual property transactions for companies and investors in the video game industry and on other forms of entertainment and technology. She received her BA in Economics and History from the University of California, Los Angeles, and her JD from Loyola Law School. She is an Adjunct Professor of Video Game Law at Loyola Law School in Los Angeles.

Greg Costikyan

Greg Costikyan is a distinguished game developer, having designed more than 30 commercially published board, role-playing, computer, online, and mobile games, including five Origins Award winners. He has written many articles on games and the industry, four novels, and multiple short stories. In 2000, he co-founded Unplugged Games, one of the first North American mobile game startups. He later joined Nokia as a full-time games researcher, but left them in 2005 to found Manifesto Games (*http://www.manifestogames.com/*) with Johnny Wilson. Manifesto Games works to build a vibrant, innovative, and viable independent game industry. Mr. Costikyan also coordinates the New York City chapter of the International Game Developers Association. His blog containing information about the game industry can be found at *http://www.costik.com/weblog/*.

Matthew Doyle

As of this writing, Matthew Doyle works as a designer at the Midway office in sunny Los Angeles, California, developing next-gen console titles. He is a loving father and husband, having worked in the industry now for six years as an artist and designer on high-profile projects, including MMOs, shooters, and fighting games. His career began in 2000 when he started his own studio, Plutonium Games in Houston, Texas, working on a first-person horror RPG entitled *Cleric*. He ran Plutonium Games for nearly three years and has been interviewed and featured in and on many gaming magazines and Web sites throughout his career. His competencies include game design, art, writing, business operations, and marketing. For more insight into his thought processes, visit his blog at *http://rocketjumping.blogspot.com/*.

John Flock

John Flock is a partner at the law firm of Kenyon & Kenyon LLP. Mr. Flock is an experienced trial lawyer with nine years of service as an Assistant District Attorney in New York City. In addition to his trial work, Mr. Flock has argued appellate cases, advised attorneys on trial tactics, and given demonstrations of trial techniques. He also has particular expertise and hands-on experience in computer technology, including design and implementation of mainframe and personal computer programs, supervision of a computer programming staff, and service as court-appointed receiver for a software company.

Peter H. Friedman

Peter Friedman is the Managing Partner of Sales Tax Collector LLC, a software company helping software and e-commerce companies resolve international and U.S. taxation issues regarding indirect taxation, and is an owner of the accounting firm Peter H. Friedman CPA. Mr. Friedman is also a frequent speaker and author on the topic of U.S. multistate tax compliance for e-commerce businesses. He has attended the annual U.S. Securities and Exchange Commission Government-Business Forum on Small Business Capital Formation since 1992.

He was an expert witness at the U.S. Government E-Commerce Tax Advisory Commission public forums and contributed to the Independent Game Developers Association 2003, 2004, and 2005 Online Game White Papers on legal, tax, and financial issues of wireless gaming. He has frequently lectured in front of various State Bar and CPA Societies on multistate and international tax issues of electronic commerce and the Sarbanes-Oxley Act of 2002, and testified in front of the North Dakota Senate regarding the economic and tax impact of legalizing online poker. Mr. Friedman is licensed as a CPA in the States of New Hampshire and New York, and is registered with the Public Company Accounting Oversight Board. He can be contacted at *peter@peterfriedmancpa.com*.

Brian "Psychochild" Green (Editor)

Brian "Psychochild" Green is the co-editor of this book. He is best known for his work on *Meridian 59* and for his popular industry blog, which can be found at *http://www.psychochild. org/*. Full biographical information can be found in Chapter 14, "I Wish I Knew."

James Grimmelmann

James Grimmelmann is a Fellow of the Information Society Project at Yale Law School and an Adjunct Professor of Law at New York Law School. After graduating with a degree in Computer Science from Harvard College, he worked as a programmer for Microsoft and then attended law school at Yale. His work bridges law and computer science; his goal is to help programmers and lawyers speak intelligibly to each other. His publications include *Virtual Borders, First Monday* (February 2006), *Regulation by Software*, 114 Yale L.J. 1719 (2005), and *Virtual Worlds as Comparative Law*, 49 N.Y. L. Sch. L. Rev. 147 (2005). He has been blogging since 2000 and playing video games since the early 1980s. His home page is at *http://james.grimmelmann.net/*.

Matthew Hector

Matthew Hector is a practicing transactional attorney focusing on contract and license drafting. He is also attending The John Marshall Law School, completing his Master of Laws (LL.M.) in Information Technology & Privacy Law. In the early 1980s, he bought an Intellivision at a garage sale. In the late 1990s, he was a volunteer customer service manager for a popular MMO title. In an attempt to make use of a lifetime as a gamer, Mr. Hector has applied his gaming and legal experience to his articles published at *The Escapist* (*http://www.escapistmagazine.com*) and at *Grimwell Online* (*http://www.grimwell.com*), addressing topics including real money trading of virtual assets, the privacy risks of a life online, and decoding enduser license agreements for popular MMOs. He believes that legal writing should be accessible to the layperson and that complex contracts can be effectively drafted in plain language. He received his BA in English and German from the University of Alabama and his JD (cum laude) from The John Marshall Law School.

Kellee McKeever

Kellee McKeever is a 12-year veteran of the game industry. She is currently the Director of International Sales for NCSoft in the United States. She has worked for Virgin Interactive, Interplay, and Encore Software. She has been involved with the international sales of titles such as *Command & Conquer*, *Baldur's Gate*, and *Guild Wars*. Ms. McKeever has a BS in Geography from California State University at Fullerton and a Master's in International Business from Thunderbird. She has lived and worked in France, Switzerland, and Japan.

Gary Morris

Gary Morris is a partner at the law firm Kenyon & Kenyon LLP. He has over 20 years of experience in the field of information technology, including computer and network security, cryptography, and telecommunications. His legal expertise encompasses both intellectual property law and European competition law. Mr. Morris has a postgraduate diploma in EC Competition law from the University of London, Kings College, and has advised the European Commission on the effects of the concentration of patent rights by corporate acquisition. He has helped negotiate development contracts for computer game developers and publishers and has negotiated patent licenses, employment contracts, and other agreements that implicate intellectual property. He has also counseled clients regarding open source software and other technology-related copyright issues.

Erik Smith

Erik Smith has been playing video games for nearly 20 years, and is excited about the burgeoning field of video game law. He is a third-year law student at Duke University School of Law and has a BS in Bioengineering from the University of California, San Diego and an MS in Mechanical Engineering from the University of California, Los Angeles. He is looking forward to a rewarding career in intellectual property law, and hopes to make video game law a major part of his practice.

Spencer Zuzolo

Spencer Zuzolo entered the game industry as the managing partner of Ninjaneering, a massively multiplayer online game studio located in Austin, Texas. Five years later, he started a new company, GameCamp!, which focuses on educating students about careers in the game development and digital media industries. GameCamp! brings together middle and high school students with game industry professionals and academia to help students create successful career paths from secondary school through college. Spencer is also currently the president at the newly formed nonprofit called 3-D Squared. He can be reached at *spencer@gamecamp.org*.

Acknowledgments

Any book is the result of the hard work of many people. We deeply apologize to anyone we missed. The editors and chapter authors would like to thank the following people for their assistance in helping to make this book a reality:

Michael Emmons
Kat Foley
Monica Awadalla
Grant Yang
Cecilia Stiber
Tom Makin
Vincent Rubino
Umar Arshad
Tom Lavery
The IGDA IP Rights Special Interest Group

CHAPTER 1

Introduction

You hold in your hands hundreds of thousands of dollars' worth of advice. Advice from lawyers who are highly respected in their field. Advice from business owners who have experienced mistakes and triumphs, and who want to share. Perhaps it is a bit crude to put a price on all this knowledge; it might be better to say that it is priceless. Or, worth at least whatever the price says on the cover.

The co-editors of this book are recognized experts in their respective fields. S. Gregory Boyd is a bright intellectual property attorney who has extensive experience in the game industry. Brian "Psychochild" Green is a recognized expert on game development, working professionally as a game developer since 1998 and as an amateur several years before that. He has owned his own business, Near Death Studios, Inc., since 2001 according to his toe-tag shaped business cards.

Together, they asked some of the most experienced and knowledgeable people they know to write chapters about the important business and legal issues someone planning to start up a game development studio should know. From business operation, management, and taxation to intellectual property, licensing, and litigation, it is all in this book. All the information some of the lawyers and business owners wish they had known back in the day.

Why Write This Book?

This is perhaps the most important question in your mind right now. It also answers the question, "Why should you buy this book?"

To put it plainly, we want to address the needs of people making games. Few resources are as complete as this one. We might even modestly say that there has never been such a quality introductory book on business and law in the game industry before now. We wanted all this information in one convenient reference, something we wish had been done previously.

In addition, we want you to succeed. Too often, people get into game development without considering the vital business and legal issues that are part of running a business. Unfortunately, if you ignore these issues, your chances of success are greatly diminished, and that means your great idea will never have the chance to become a great game. Why? Let us talk about some specific problems a business owner will face.

Business Issues Are Unavoidable

It is a great dream to build your own game company and bring your wonderful idea to life. It can be very exciting to think that your game will be in the hands of thousands of players, bringing them great amounts of fun and cementing your reputation as a great game developer.

Unfortunately, that is *only* a nice dream at this point, and it is not easy to realize this dream. Running a game development studio means running a business, and no amount of denial can change that. If you ignore things like payroll taxes or minimum wage laws, you will soon find yourself out of business and in trouble with the government. It is hard to make a hit game when you have to spend your time in tax audits.

You also need to learn things about management to keep the company running smoothly and to keep your employees happy. Disorganized employees are inefficient employees, and you will have trouble keeping people on the job if you do not manage them well. Even something as simple as hiring a new employee can become a complicated process once you have to do all the business work to support that employee.

Finally, you also have to learn how to manage a business to attract investment. Just because you have a great idea does not mean the publishers will give you a great contract. You have to show that you can manage the money they are investing in your company and that you will return a profit on that investment. Even when you are self-funded, learning how to keep your books and how to track your expenses and cash flow are important to knowing what you can spend money on and what will simply have to wait.

All that business stuff you hoped you could ignore is vital to the process of making a good game. You need to learn it, and this book was written to be a great introduction.

Legal Problems Can Ruin Your Company

Just as business issues affect your company, legal issues play an important part in game development. Every game is based on the concept of intellectual property. Stories, characters, gameplay, technology, and every other part of the game can be described in terms of intellectual property.

To get your game into the hands of your players, you will encounter other legal issues. End-user license agreements, developer/publisher contracts, and other forms of agreement are governed by the legal system. Knowing what is important in these different legal agreements can save you time and money when you have to consult your own lawyer.

Finally, being ignorant of the legal issues can hurt your business just as much as not understanding the business issues discussed before. Using an unlicensed song seems innocent enough because the game is small, but a lawsuit from the owner of that song can literally destroy your company. Knowing how to license this type of song, or knowing what kind of agreement you need to get original music done for your game can help save you time, money, and legal headaches in the future.

What You Will Find in This Book

As stated previously, the co-editors of this book have assembled a group of talented and experienced writers for each chapter. The people who contributed chapters on business have practical knowledge of what it takes to run a small business. The legal experts we asked to write the chapters dealing with law have years of experience dealing with the issues at hand. Some even had small teams of experts working to help them write the best possible chapter.

Information You Can Use

Our goal is to give you practical information on every subject important to starting and running a game business. This is not an abstract tome filled with theory; it contains information and anecdotes from people who have done, and are still doing, some of the dirty work of running a game company.

In addition, most of these authors have been in the same position most aspiring game developers find themselves in: they are enthusiastic people who wanted to strike out on their own. Perhaps they were self-funded, and perhaps their companies did not get funding, but they learned from their experiences and are sharing the lessons learned, perhaps the hard way, with you.

Finally, we have tried to give you the latest information we could find. For example, we have included a detailed chapter on legal issues for virtual worlds (MMORPGs). Games have evolved over the years, and these online games are at the forefront of change. You have the latest legal information about virtual worlds at the time of the writing of the chapter.

Legal Information without Paying Hourly

In some ways, this might be one of the most expensive books ever written in the game industry. Some of the authors in this book are partners at respected law firms that charge several hundred dollars per hour for their services. They spent literally hundreds of hours writing these chapters. Yet, this book will cost you less than one tenth of one hour if they were actually billing you for legal advice.

This book will also save you money on your own legal bills. After reading this book, you should understand the basics of the legal framework surrounding the game industry and how that will affect you. This means that you can ask the intelligent questions necessary to get information from your lawyer, reducing the time you have to pay for it.

Finally, this book has what every game developer needs: an example contract with detailed and occasionally funny annotations from an attorney. You get to study in detail something that has been kept out of reach of most developers. Although the names have been changed and the agreement is a sample created from many different agreements, you will see what an agreement between a developer and a publisher really looks like. Use this to learn what is important in your own negotiations.

Advice from Industry Leaders

One of the most exciting chapters is Chapter 14, "I Wish I Knew." In this chapter, we asked highly respected leaders in video game development what they wish they had known at the beginning of their careers. The entire chapter is a series of brief bits of advice from these industry legends.

In addition, we have an entire chapter written by Eric Zimmerman and Peter Lee, co-founders of the successful independent game developer Gamelab. At the time of this writing, the Gamelab title *Diner Dash* is one of, if not the most, successful independent games of all time. They detail what they consider the biggest contributor to their success: the intangible aspects of the company. This section is a must-read for anyone wishing to create a successful independent company.

Enjoy the Book!

This book represents thousands of hours of hard work by more than two dozen people over a period of nearly two years. Behind all that hard work was the even harder work of creating businesses, studying legal issues, and learning from successes and failures. The editors and chapter authors hope this book gives you the information you need to create the business that will create wonderful hit games. Reading this book is the right first step in that process.

S. Gregory Boyd
Brian "Psychochild" Green

CHAPTER 2

So You Want to Start a Game Company?

Spencer Zuzolo

spencer@gamecamp.org

When I was asked to write a chapter for this book, I thought, "This is really exciting!" Then I realized I needed to write about starting a company and thought I was stuck with the most boring part of the book. Then I realized that someone else had to write about intellectual property and contracts and I was back to "this is really exciting." In any event, I tried to make this fun and in no way should any of the bitter and disagreeable passages be taken as anguish about starting a game company. It is just an attempt to add some comic relief to what can be some normally dry reading.

This chapter is more oriented to individuals and small groups that are trying to bootstrap their way into the game industry. If you have $10 million already and you are starting a game company, then you can afford to hire a lawyer to do all this work for you.

The information in this chapter is based on information about the game company Ninjaneering. It originally started as a partnership between two friends who were going to develop and market 3D products and services for the game industry and the Web. Then, some standard game industry volatility led to the cancellation of *Ultima Online*™ *2* at Origin/Electronic Arts and the addition of the lead designer, lead server programmer, some 3D graphics gurus, and a couple of highly recommended game developers to the company. Finally, a newly formed, massively multiplayer online game development company was born.

The pain of starting *one* game company was not enough, however, so I recently embarked on developing two new startups. The first is called "GameCamp!" and focuses on educating students about careers in the videogame industry, and the second is a nonprofit called "3-D Squared." But, all the punishment endured over the years is condensed in this chapter for your benefit.

Before the Paperwork

OK, before you pour your savings into your own game venture, make sure you can pass a simple test. Gather your friends and family and see if you can convince them that you are sincere and truthful when you utter these phrases:

- "I am not in this for the money, but for the love of making games!"
- "I love paperwork and it loves me!"
- "Unpaid royalties are my GOD!"
- "Eighteen-hour days are like a walk in the park . . . if the park is made of hydrochloric acid."
- "Nine straight meals of a 'meat product' pizza are awesome!"
- "Why can't they make a Mountain Dew® in the gallon size with more caffeine?" (OK, this one is more of a request, but it shows the kind of internal fortitude necessary for starting your own game company.)
- "Why yes, I would love to bring you, the 'almighty investor/publisher/owner/ producer/team lead/guy next to you in your cubicle' a rock! Oh, not that rock that took me six weeks to carry here? Well, sure I will bring you another rock that looks just like that one but is imperceptibly different based on your whims."
- "I love playing games . . . I just wish I had time to play them!"

Do you still want to start a game company? Well then, we should run through some of the things you will need to deal with before the actual game development begins:

- Creating a legal business entity
- Determining your core business owners
- Creating legal documentation
- Creating organizational rules/bylaws
- Getting office space
- Purchasing office equipment
- Setting up your accounting system
- Setting up your project management tools
- Hiring staff
- Building your vendor/contractor/publisher/distributor relationships
- Acquiring game development hardware and software
- Product and market analysis
- Raising capital
- Creating the game, game product, or game service . . .

All of the preceding cost time and money, and all can be made easier by asking yourself some simple questions:

Why Do I Want To Start a Game Development Company?

It may seem like a silly idea to ask this question after you bought a book to help you start a game development company, but it is actually the most important question you can ask yourself and your partners. For me, it was something exciting to do with some of my friends. Having spent a long time working for the Texas State Legislature and then for a large corporation, doing something independent was appealing. It was a life change and a very exciting and creative industry. For you, the answer may be different, but whatever the answer is you do need it to be a good one. If you cannot answer this question and be reasonably satisfied, then, do not start a game company.

What Kind of Game Company Do You Want to Start?

One "that makes cool games" is not a very good answer. A good answer might include the types of games you want to make, but it should also be more about the type of company you want to create. What are your near- and long-term goals? Money? Security? Challenge? Masochism?

 Note of Introspection: If your answer to this question is, "You know, we will develop AAA titles that go gold and then we will retire on our millions!" you are doomed to failure more than likely.

Even the largest game companies started somewhere small, so understanding the type of company you want to become is important. Most of you are probably going to be independent developers working on your own title and then searching for a publishing and distribution solution or self-publishing/distributing. This is all good, but what if you want to become part of a particular company or develop games for a certain console platform?

Not everyone wants to navigate the indy waters his whole life, and other types of game companies can be aspired to, including third-party and in-house developers. The former is more of a single game contract where a publisher hires you to complete a game for them and they will foot the bill. Your freedom is limited to the agreed upon milestones and the ability to convince the publisher that your design choices are worthy of the money it will take to build them. The in-house developers are owned partially or fully and often have more freedom than third-party developers. They may work on one or more titles for their parent company, have access to cool intellectual property (IP), and in some cases can retain their original corporate branding identity and culture.

Who Will Be Involved in Your Game Company?

Is it just you at the top and then your employees? Or is it you and some friends who will partner up to run the company *and* develop the game? Are you looking for an investor or possibly merging into another small group to form a more stable startup? Whatever the answer is, you must make sure you can achieve what you want with the people involved, and that requires a lot of soul searching and asking of the right questions.

Working with friends can be particularly difficult without the proper understanding of roles and procedures. It is very important to have everyone's expectations understood and codified through legal documentation; contracts and corporate bylaws are good places to start. Revisit and update these documents regularly to make sure everyone is still on board.

Team chemistry is vital, and you may feel that your potential partners are just right for the company. The last thing you want is to be approached by a publisher and find out a couple of people in your group are completely opposed to anything but self-publishing your title. Suffice it to say that the first test of team chemistry is the agreement by everyone to get the legal documents completed so that when individuals change their plans, there is a process in place to handle it. It is not unique to the game industry for friendships to be dissolved along with the company, so it behooves you to explore many potential scenarios for your company, from total failure to unbelievable success, *before* you start.

Who Is in Charge of the Company?

It is crucial to know who will be in charge and what specifically their authority and power will entail. If you are working with partners, this should be spelled out long before you spend any real money putting the company together. Once your company is formed, you should codify your decisions about who is in charge.

How Are You Going to Fund the Company?

Even the least expensive companies (sole proprietorships) cost money to start. There is paperwork, legal consultations, financial advisement, market analyses, office supplies and equipment, software, letterhead, and so forth. How are you paying for all of this? Once it is paid for, how do you continue to pay ongoing costs as you are developing the game? How are your employees' salaries and benefits paid? There are a variety of funding answers out there and you should explore them all before you start your company.

It's a nice dream to think that you can work in your garage making a hit game, but the problem is that those days are gone. Game development might still seem in its infancy as an industry, but it has grown up enough so that most games require serious money to build them. This is true even with the low-end casual games where you might think the programming and art requirements seem minimal.

For example, say you are making a Web-based casual game clone. It seems easy technically, but then you realize that you will spend a good chunk of money and time marketing it as "unique" to get people to play it rather than the other 50 games that have identical gameplay. Then again, if you are making an original title, you will be building everything from scratch and spending time and money to get publishers to buy into it as a viable product. Often, you will create throwaway art and code so you can meet the minimum "demo requirements" just to get into the publishers' view.

Then there is the serious stuff, like buying intellectual property and building a game around it. It is still possible to purchase untapped IP; however, the time and investment to find it can be expensive and you may be better off just building your game without it. The point is simple: modern game development is all about money, so plan accordingly.

What Is Your Exit Strategy?

OK, so the game industry thumped your head a little and everything is not all it is cracked up to be. How do you get out gracefully? You need to think about that long before you decide to leave. Not having an exit strategy is a classic mistake in forming a business. Chapter 12, "Exit Strategies," covers exit strategies in detail. However, as an introduction, there is a variety of ways to structure an exit strategy:

- Sell or merge your company
- Buyout by a partner, investor, or another entity
- Transfer the company to someone in your family
- Dissolve your company
- Change entity to nonprofit

 Reality Check: It is important to remember that the exit strategy isn't just for you personally. Investors will want in clear detail an exit strategy that explains when and how they exit as well. They will want to know how they will recoup their investment, how much profit they stand to make, and how much risk they might incur over the investment period.

Right and Wrong Reasons to Start a Game Company

Right Reason
You have a vision, team, passion, organization, market opportunity, funding, distribution model, and the tenacity to succeed.

Wrong Reasons

- "You are an avid game player so you think you can build the ultimate game company and then create the ultimate game."
- "You have made a few of your own games and they work pretty well."
- "You think it would be great to have a job where you play games all day."

A Bit of Research Goes a Long Way

Take some time to do a little research before you completely jump into the "startup" waters. There are two Web sites that you should go to and thoroughly investigate. The first is the Small Business Administration's page on startups at *http://www.sba.gov/ starting_business/*; the second is the Internal Revenue Service's page at *http://www.irs. gov/businesses/small/article/0,,id=99336,00.html*. Both of these Web sites will give you most of the information you need, but if you desire a more human interface, try your city's Chamber of Commerce or regional economic development agency.

Company Formation

Companies are formed, bought, regulated, sold, and dissolved every day. If you get one thing out of this section, it should be that no matter how cool, revolutionary, unique, or marketable your game product is, it still must exist inside a legal business entity that is recognized by your state and federal government. This section is a brief explanation of the various business entities, their advantages and disadvantages, and some considerations for how you choose your particular entity.

Now, the choice of that entity can be endlessly debated until all your seed money runs out and you are left with no entity and no game company. If the Internet was built for anything, it was for researching this type of mind-numbing but essential information. There are five primary business entities that will be covered in this section: *Sole Proprietorship, Partnership, Limited Liability Company (LLC), S Corporation,* and *C Corporation*. All of them require that you register with your state and federal agencies in varying degrees, and produce a number of documents that legally organize and place obligations on the company participants. We strongly suggest that the choice of business entity and organization be the topic of a conversation with a business lawyer, and that you only hold the editors liable for any factual errors or omissions. The biggest impact your choice of entity will affect is taxes; details about different entities and the tax implications are covered in Chapter 11, "Taxation."

When Ninjaneering went from a two-person partnership to a seven-person Limited Liability Company, we spent a substantial amount of time researching and consulting a lawyer to determine what type of entity was right for us. Some of the questions you want to ask yourself when confronted with this issue include the following.

Who Owns and Controls the Business?

In our case, it was a Limited Liability Partnership that would be controlled by senior stakeholders. Partners were responsible for full consultations and votes on important business issues. You may have other requirements, especially if you bring in a large amount of outside investment, or depending on your future plans and exit strategy.

Is What You Are Doing in the Game Space Legal?

Our lawyer made us put this in here for liability reasons. For instance, games that involve gambling or sweepstakes are common startup ideas. They are also tightly regulated and often prohibited in the United States. So, try to run a game company instead of a gaming (or gambling) company.

Who Has Responsibility If the Company Loses Money or Fails?

We chose an LLC mostly for the liability protection it afforded each member and simple organization structure. Liability means that if the company owes money, it generally cannot be collected from the owners.

There are several exceptions to liability, however. If you sign an agreement personally (such as any credit card offers, read the fine print), you can be held personally liable for the debt. If you intentionally break the law, courts may ignore limits on liability. Also note that the IRS is not covered by these liability protections, and they have their own army to squeeze every last penny you owe out of you!

How Long Does the Company Exist?
How Can You Sell the Company?

Our company existed "in perpetuity," and honestly, we never really talked about getting the company sold other than that our initial stakes in the company represented a rough percentage of our individual post-sale value. Putting together a *Buy/Sell Share Agreement* is a good way to protect everyone if something changes drastically between the principals in your company. This type of agreement spells out in detail what it means if someone is fired, dies, or just wants out of the company. Even if you're working with your closest friends, make sure you get this type of document made.

Now that we know why you want to start a company and what type of company it will be, we will start with one of the easier steps.

Naming Your Company

Ninjaneering was the coolest name for a game company! Our lead 3D guy came up with it under what had to be questionable conditions, but we did not care. The name rocked and rolled off the tongue. Ninjas, games, and engineering—who could not love that? Indeed, people remembered it and commented on how cool it was all the time. Now this fantasy love affair with how cool our name was ended the first time it had to be told to someone important over the phone. If you were there, you might have heard this conversation in its third go round . . .

Customer Service Worker 1: NinjaENGINeering . . . cool name!

Spencer: No, man, NINJANEERING! N . . . I . . . N . . . J . . . A . . . like in ninja, man. Yeah, yeah, a ninja, that is right . . . little dudes with knives and poison coming out of toilets to kill emperors and stuff . . . Yeah, exactly . . . Ninja and "NEERING" . . . no . . . no . . . not engineering, just NEERING . . . Yes, a hybrid of sorts. Yep, NINJA-NEERING. Now spell it back to me.

Customer Service Worker 1: N . . . I . . . N . . . J . . . A . . . E . . . N . . . G . . . I . . . N . . .
<Sound of Spencer's hand slapping his head>.

Spencer: AHHHHHHHHHH . . . I just want to get some printer ink shipped to me <sobbing>, just some printer ink, man.

And no, the bank will not cash a check written to your "cool" but misspelled company name, even with the "come on, it is clearly just a typo" argument. To banks, it is all just whining and cutting in on their rightful duty to subject you to their control over your money whether they have it or not.

What lesson can be learned from this? From our experience, company names should meet the following requirements:

- Memorable
- Easy to spell
- Domain name available
- Not owned by someone else
- Not offensive

Serious Tip: Businesses that are using a fictitious name to do business may have special legal registration requirements for that name. Also, as discussed in Chapter 7, "Intellectual Property," being certain that the company name is not used by someone else can be critical down the road when registering trademarks and avoiding litigation.

Choosing and Registering a Business Entity

So, how does one go about choosing a business entity? Dice rolls and dartboards work, of course, but are not recommended. Different entities offer different protections and liabilities to their owners. For this reason, it is good to know what your company is and what it will turn into so you can make the most informed choice possible. Table 2.1 is designed to help you figure out your business entity; however, you should consult a lawyer before legally establishing your business.

TABLE 2.1 Types of Business Entities

Entity	Cost	Advantages	Disadvantages
Sole Proprietorship	Very inexpensive	Centralized decision making, profits and tax benefits to owner, operating capital needs less	Personal liability, hard to raise capital
Partnership	Inexpensive	Extra sources of capital available, management and oversight, less regulation	Personal liability, divided decision-making, finding good partners
Limited Liability Company	Inexpensive	Limited liability, partner determined organization and structure, pass through taxation	Increased administration for taxes, partnership agreements, organization, and compensation
S Corporation	More expensive to start and maintain	Ownership can be transferred, limited liability, central authority in board of directors, easier to raise capital	Highly regulated, heavy record-keeping burden
C Corporation	Most expensive to start and maintain	Ownership can be transferred, limited liability, central authority in board of directors, easier to raise capital	Highly regulated, double taxation, heavy record-keeping burden

Now we have an entity. You have chosen <insert entity, applause>. This is really exciting, so let us dive right into the legal and regulatory parts to cool down our buzz the old-fashioned way . . . with paperwork.

Standard Business Formation Documentation

Depending on your state and entity of choice, you will be required to have some of the following documents:

Federal Tax Identification Number: This is so the IRS knows how to tax you. For example, this is your Social Security Number for Sole Proprietorships, or an Employer Identification Number (EIN) issued by the IRS after you fill out Form SS-4 for corporations.

State Comptroller Registration: Each state will require certain information and fees for your business to operate legally. This information should be easily accessible on the state government's Web site; however, we recommend going personally and talking to real people to get the information and to answer questions.

Franchise Tax Registration: Some states require a franchise tax to be paid on corporate income above a certain level. Again, check the Web site of your state comptroller (or equivalent).

Articles of Incorporation: These are documents required by various state agencies that outline the type of company, officers, and types of business your company will be conducting in that state.

Operating Agreement/Bylaws: These types of documents are internal to the company and describe how the company operates in relation to the stakeholders.

Company Leaders: Who Is in Charge?

You would be surprised at how resistant people can be to direction, even when they agree that you are the decision maker. We have no idea why this is, but it is important to make sure all the people on your team understand who is in charge, and to have the tools in place for dealing with transgressions against the company or the team. You must make it clear that abuse of the rules and corporate culture will have consequences.

 Morale Note: Never use the word transgressions to describe employee behavior at a company meeting—very bad mojo.

Well-defined leadership is a must to keep the development ball rolling. Good leaders will know when enough data is collected to make a decision and will make smart adjustments when certain decisions turn out to be less than optimal.

Conversely, if you are in charge, it is important for you to do the work to earn the respect of your team. How do you earn that, you ask? You put them first by doing everything you can to make sure they have the tools, direction, and compensation to complete their tasks. A good leader makes the company as transparent as possible so employees know the struggle for success goes all the way to the top. Work hard to create clear lines of communication so that goals, expectations, and process are all known quantities.

Also, listen to other people. People are working for your company, sometimes earning barely enough money to buy ramen noodles, simply because they love games. They want to have a say on what the game is, but more than likely they will respond to reason about certain features and game aesthetics being limited or denied as long as the logic rings true within the corporate processes you have consistently applied. True, you need strong leadership to make sure the projects are done on time, but in my opinion it's best not to rule by fiat and make other people feel they are not important to the game development process.

It can also help to have other leaders to help you lead. How do you pick your senior people, team leaders, and regular working staff? You look for self-starters with an iron will to achieve greatness. You bring together the greatest minds in design and art to implement the greates. . . . errrttt! Hold on, you have no funding, so start again with an excerpt from your memoirs entitled *When My Game Sold a Billion Units*.

your business, if they are not interested in the specifics of your vision, they probably have their mind elsewhere and will not learn enough about the industry to help you do what you need to accomplish.

Accounting

Many people dread accounting, and unless you are an accountant, you may find it boring. An easy way to get around this is to think of accounting in the same way you might play a character in your favorite online RPG. After all, you are all about accounting when you are saving every single gold piece for the "Lemon Blade of Paper Cuts" or "Greasy Hairpiece of Evasion." You've practiced your finance skills by working the auction house like a pro, cashing in on the inability of players to price their "rare" items, and thus making a killing. You also make appropriate purchases for your upcoming quests and maybe borrow a little now and then to keep your tavern and spice bread habits fixed. All of this is done with the future in mind, saving enough gold so you can buy your mount and stop running everywhere! Why? Because running is like accounting. It stinks, but sometimes it is the only way out of being eaten or pummeled.

So, why is real-life accounting so complicated? Mostly because the tools you use are not cool like an MMO, and the only other people who care about numbers besides your accountant are your programmers. There are also fewer quests that pay out enormous rewards in accounting. But, how does someone who wants to start a company solve this lack of accounting skill problem? First, figure the cost of an accountant into your startup budget. Good accountants are essential and will save you money in the long run. They also *like* to talk about financial issues in general. Get a good accountant to help and you will reap the benefits of insurance, investment, loan, entity structuring, employee benefits, and many other bits of good advice that will only cost you your time and a cup of coffee.

So, what if you do not have enough money for an accountant and are really bad at accounting? First, one of the owners of the company better get good at it! Understanding your cash flow at a minimum is crucial to your survival. Also, being able to identify your costs over time will allow you to plan your company's growth better. Plus, learning how to balance a checkbook and use your credit cards properly cannot be a bad idea for you personally, right?

Second, get some accounting software like Simply Accounting by Sage or Intuit's QuickBooks®. These are not very expensive, often starting at a couple hundred dollars. They are simple enough to set up and can be exported into formats used by just about every tax and general accountant. Third, get an intern from your local university or community college business department. Students are always looking for opportunities to get business experience, and the mere mention that you are a game company will likely attract a worthy accounting intern.

Our accountant has us using a simple Excel® spreadsheet for our records. We identify our income from clients and our payments to vendors and contractors. Once we deliver the spreadsheets to her, she takes care of everything, unless there was a question about how something was purchased or someone was paid. Although one time we did get a call asking us to identify the food item that covered an amount on a receipt. (Our guesses: 47% chance pizza, 9% chance Chinese food, 39% chance not food at all, and a bunch of people who did not respond to the receipt survey. Look, we make games here, not pie charts.)

When you can afford an accountant, it is inevitable as a Chinese proverb that he or she might suggest check processing companies to automate your payroll and tax system. This of course would be done from a remote set of servers using proprietary software on par with what the military uses to calculate "collateral damage" that you see on the nightly news stories about "Foreignwaristan." Anyway, there are only two solutions to this type of suggestion. If your accountant suggests that "we should" consider getting a payroll service, you should: (a) fire your accountant on the spot. It is probably a calculated (that is what an accountant does) power move to outsource what you are paying that person to do. Not good for a small company and you are the sole outsourcer. Or (b) Give your accountant an immediate raise!

Now, let us say you open your check and discover that it has been "processed by Meglocheck Inc." Well, you suddenly realize that you can afford this service because you are heading a giant game company named <insert game> and you have become a billion unit seller of *CMSW* for the <insert platform> and *CMSW: Wee Ones in Orbit: THE DOMINATION*, again for the <insert platform>. This reminder of your game greatness makes you think that your accountant *has* the budget to outsource (as authorized by you) *and* took the initiative (that you cultivated through incredible leadership) to modernize your accounting department. Good work! Now back to crunching.

Like everything else, this kind of service is dependent on your cash flow and whether it actually allows you to add more value to your game by allocating more man-hours to the development team. In other words, if you have a person who does all your accounting and he or she is not going to help on the development side even if you free up some of his time, why waste the money on a service if that person can do it in a normal work day? However, if one of your designers or artists can be freed of that responsibility and your cash flow allows it, then by all means investigate some of the payroll companies that cater to small businesses. Just remember that it will take time to figure out which one is best for your situation and setting up the accounting procedures, so don't think your time is converted immediately.

So what have we learned from this? Get an accountant! Actually teaching you about the details of accounting could fill many books this size. And, having someone who understands all the information from the IRS can help keep you out of the bad place: an audit!

What about Handling All the Paperwork?

Well, there are two important things to remember: there is a lot of paperwork in business, and paperwork takes up a lot of time.

Having a simple filing system can help you with all your paperwork problems. Just get some bankers' boxes, some files, a marker, a stapler, a box of paperclips and away you go . . . wheee! The hardest part is keeping up with the massive amount of paperwork that will enter your life on a daily basis, but cherish it because it is a sign that your wonderful entrepreneurial spirit is soaring like an eagle to meet your greatest expectations. Furthermore, organization is critical. Losing legal or accounting documents is unacceptable and could be hazardous to the health of your business.

One more thing: clean up your paperwork about once a week. It will keep you organized and mentally attuned to how money is flowing in and out of your company to make your game a reality. It is recommended to keep the last five years of your business records in case you are audited. Sound advice, but understand that handling all this paperwork is a full-time job.

Receipts

There are so many receipts and in so many shapes and sizes it is almost impossible to keep track of them. We tried the "shove them in the pocket approach" for awhile, but one washing destroyed a whole fiscal quarter's worth of petty cash accounting. The simple solution is to take a box and sit it next to your desk like a trashcan (this just feels right). As you get your receipts, mark all of your receipts with information about the purchase, deposit, or payment. For smaller receipts staple them to a regular sheet of paper and write the date, cost, and reason for the expenditure on the paper. Then, put them in the box face down, and at the end of the week, you'll have a chronologically ordered record of your financial transactions.

Xerox® Sponsored Tip of the Day: Photocopy receipts that can fade. A friend, who operates her own business, clued us into this.

Allocation of Money

Tracking how money is spent is crucial to the survival of any company, and particularly important to fledgling game companies with little or no room for error. Your principal players in your company should have compensation details determined long before anyone starts working for your company. Cash flow may hinder what you can pay in any given pay period, but there should never be an argument over how much someone earned. Game employees, despite rumors to the contrary, do expect to be paid on occasion but are often flexible and committed enough to allow you to bend the rules on when and how much pay they receive. It is extremely important that owners and managers reward this flexibility with transparency, personal sacrifice, and communication so employees can take the necessary steps to adjust their lives for a delayed paycheck. And do not forget this: if you have a little extra money and your employees have been supportive through the bumpy financial times, reward them with bonuses or an increase in royalties.

It's really just common sense: food is a reward for crunching and cash is a reward for employees who eat into their savings to help the company's cash flow. Sometimes, it feels like every single penny counts, but at times like those, it is especially important to invest a bit of money to make people feel better about working with you.

Creating, Managing, and Eliminating Debt

It is important to have monetary flexibility during a period when you are trying to carve out a new product or service or changing niches altogether. As suggested earlier, controlling your spending is the single most important way you can stay out of debt. Make sure the person in charge is frugal and diligent in his quest to not spend the company's precious resources. When you do spend money through credit, make sure it is being spent on the most critical things you *must* have. If you are creating or pitching a demo, anything you buy should be able to be justified for that purpose. Also, documenting what you spend each month allows you to constantly reevaluate your budget priorities. Controlling spending and staying out of debt require that startups and development teams anticipate and communicate what their resource needs will be throughout the life of the project. "No surprises" is a good motto when dealing with money.

Sometimes, debt is a necessity. You may need to buy some big-ticket items, handle an emergency, help your cash flow, or upgrade some equipment. A good rule to follow (absent an emergency) is to save as much as you can in anticipation of the purchase. Any cash you can save is always good and allows you to pay a larger portion of the total, saving you potentially brutal interest rates. Always pay as much as you can over the minimum payment so you can keep you interest payments limited. You will thank yourself over the long term!

The Money Rules!

Well, money certainly does rule whether you have any or not. Here are some rules to keep in mind about how money works in a small business.

Rule 1: Cash Flow, Like Oxygen, Is Pretty Important

Cash flow is a simple enough concept to grasp. You have enough money on hand at any given time to operate effectively (that is, pay your bills). Technically, you can calculate your cash flow by adding noncash charges (such as depreciation) to the net income after taxes. But why? That is so boring and should be left strictly to your accountant who will no doubt thank you for the opportunity. Regardless of how you calculate it, cash flow is crucial to your company's survival and will change your perceptions about how and when you accept projects, bill for them, pay your employees, make investments, and pay your bills. So, make sure that no matter who is calculating and tracking it, that *you* understand how it works. Seriously, understand it. Love it. It is everything.

This reality really never hit us until we had to scramble to pay our $129.00 DSL bill to avoid having it turned off. Understand, we had about $27,000 in outstanding invoices from a deal we made with a French gaming company. The problem was, no one ever told us how long international money transfers took to complete—10 business days. Excuse me? That is not your money, Federal Bank of Chicago, why are you holding it from us? What do you possibly need to check that takes 10 days? You check the world's money on a daily basis and yet you do not work weekends? It makes us hot thinking about the grand picture of international financial transactions and how much money is made just by having it change hands so slowly.

Where were we? Oh yes, trying to collect $27,000 so we could pay a $129.00 bill. OK, 15 days later and many phone calls to our DSL provider to, "just please hold on for just one more day," we finally got it paid. And for the record, those 10 days do not include the five days working with our account rep trying to figure out why the wire transfer will not work in the first place (wrong last digit on the routing number). *sound of hand smacking head* Well, we finally got the money and paid for the DSL and we learned a nice lesson to boot. It takes a long time from completion of a project to when the money actually arrives and can be used for your business. This is true whether it is a simple contract or a six-figure milestone payment.

 Murphy's Stout Law: If anything can go wrong in delivering money to your company so payroll is threatened, it will occur and you will complain about it to the guy next to you at the pub.

Rule 2: Time Is Money. Money Is Time, but Time Is No Weekly World News

That sentence right there is worth $0.32 less without the commentary. The point is still true, however; time is money. Anytime you are not working to produce money, you have lost that opportunity. Time spent arguing with customer service about your bill is money. Time you spend correcting mistakes in documents is also money. Time you spend waiting in line is money. Time you spend talking people out of charging you late fees is more money. Not researching how to spend your money also costs money. It's all money, and that is why we are for eugenics. Oops, wrong book chapter.

Saving money and not spending money are both great habits to get into, and very hard tasks. First, make sure the person in charge of the money is tough on spending money and will spend his time wisely doing the business development. Someone who will ask pointed questions about the timing, need, cost, and overall importance of a purchase. Someone who understands contracts and can identify where resources should be allocated throughout the company.

 Socialist Tip of the Day: Do not skimp on the tools and training your employees need to do their job. Find a happy medium between what people need and your budget, and then incrementally upgrade your equipment, compensation, and facilities in a fair and inclusive way.

Rule 3: Money Is the Root of All Problems—Most of Them, Anyway

Money will always create tension, so mitigate that with transparency and fairness: make sure everyone benefits from how your money is spent and that all the owners can see the books. If you are actually bringing in more money than your monthly costs, try to build your savings. For Ninjaneering, our contract work was great money but never consistent. Three-month contract here, one month there, and the occasional six-month contract all added up to uncertainty and crazy cash flow. It required serious work on our part to create a good estimate of our future workload and ability to work on internal projects without starving a few months out of the year.

 Nine out of ten marriage counselors agree: Most relationships sour over money. Think you have problems balancing your checkbook at home? Wait until your business partners have troubles balancing all their checkbooks because cash flow is too low this month. It can put even the best of friends at each other's throats.

Rule 4: Short-Term Survival Is Crucial

Be ready to do just about any job for continued cash flow. Once Ninjaneering became a full-fledged MMO consulting house rather than a company trying to score a publisher, it became necessary to fill the space between contracts with work that may not be strictly inside the circle of business we call "games." Some of these contracts included network admin, Web site building, product identity packages, medical product animations, and some occasional working of the door at our local pub. Hey, some got paid in beer, and you really cannot argue with that!

The point is that all businesses need things, and most of the time they are not sure what they are, but when you show them you have skills, they will ask you to solve problems. For one company, network maintenance morphed into doing hardware purchasing and installation, copy writing, product identity creation, and a couple of stints as the receptionist. Do not be confused; all of these jobs required skills needed to succeed in the game industry and, more important, it kept the company alive to work on what we wanted. This may not sit well with your development team, but you do what you need to do to survive.

> "Pride only hurts, it never helps."
> —Marcellus Wallace, *Pulp Fiction* (1994)

To survive in the short term, it is important to know your burn rate. *Burn rate* is simply how long you can stay in business and depends on the answer to this equation: *cash + expected income – your costs*. Finding your costs in a small business is usually pretty easy; just go back and look at your checkbook and credit card statements. Some of the bills are normal monthly costs like paychecks, rent, utilities, Internet, games, and so forth. Some of your costs are less regular, like conferences, new hardware or software, and the always pleasant surprise, "I need a new transmission for my car." No matter what your expenses are, you should be able to get a solid idea of what your monthly outflow is along with a decent projection of what some of your "irregular expenses" might be over the coming year.

Yes, it is true that your expected income is not actual cash like you have in the bank, but you should include certain low-risk income sources into your burn rate calculation. For instance, unpaid invoices for completed work can reasonably be expected to be paid; however, *when* they actually get paid is a different question entirely, but it is reasonable to assume that they will be paid. Eventually. Income from a contract that is currently unsigned and still in negotiation is a much higher risk to include into a burn rate calculation. We suggest not doing that so your temptation to buy stuff with money you do not have is lessened. Emergency costs are just that, so squirreling away some savings for an emergency is never a bad idea. Then again, having health insurance is not a bad idea either.

The Daily Grind

The daily grind is a sample of the many things that will cross your business plate as you manage the business side of your game company. As said earlier, you and your friends are probably working some other jobs to help pay the bills as you develop your first game or game product. Do not feel bad; this is pretty typical and prepares you for the real world when you leave the game industry with your soul crushed. Now the following list is certainly not comprehensive, nor will the items appear every day, but it will give you a good idea of the on-going tasks and issues you will confront on any given day.

Get Out of Bed Early

No, really. If you are running a company, then getting up when banks, utilities, other businesses are open is a good idea. You may, of course, have your core hours for game development start and end later than this, but remember, this chapter is about understanding what it takes to start and run a business, and business is done early. This is especially true if you are consulting on a project or working for a publisher that resides in a later time zone, or, God forbid, Europe or Asia. They are going to want to talk at all kinds of ridiculous hours, so being available during the normal 9 to 5 schedule will help. Although, know your strengths. Occasionally, you will pull an all-night game design session, and it will align weariness into psychic synchronicity with your cell phone customer service representative as you finally get her to agree that five bars on her screen is actually *zero* on *your* phone and a solution to your problem would be nice.

Coffee and Email

First things first, right? Get to work, get a cup of coffee, and then start looking at your email. Once you delete all your spam and reply to a few friends, you are ready to *really* start working.

Paying Bills

Never, ever, pay bills first thing in the morning—it completely eliminates the morning buzz from caffeine and sugar. Yes, you should pay them and pay them on time. Schedule time for reviewing this daily or weekly.

Industry Research

It's 9:45 AM, the coffee and email are done, so now you can start looking at what the industry is doing, and that means playing games. Call it an occupational hazard. OK, now it is 12:30; time to get lunch, some more coffee, and back to what normal, boring people call "work."

Employee Relations

Often, you will find that your employees, contractors, or partners have a need that only you can address while playing the role of "the man." This could be anything from a clarification of an obscure health insurance clause to a request for more pens or printer paper. Whatever the request is, it will take time, and, as we now are fully aware, time costs money. Now it is almost 2:00 PM and you have answered your employee questions, but what about your contractors?

Contractor Relations

So, you have a few contracts going, a little programming and some Web site art, for example. Things are looking pretty good and you have hired a contract artist, but he has some questions about taxes, the deliverables, when you cut checks, or something or other that you do not care too much about because you finally have time to work on your game. So, how do you deal with that person? There are two schools of thought about this issue. One side suggests that contractors are no different from your employees so you should treat them with respect, listen to their questions and concerns like they are part of the company, trust their judgment, and finally provide the tools they need to succeed in a timely fashion. The other school of thought suggests that they are opportunistic weasels and, like ambulance chasers, they follow small companies that bite off projects they cannot handle and prey upon you with stiff rates and missed deadlines. You should crush their soul by using their desire to be in the game industry to get their rate to rock bottom and make them work overtime without pay. In no time, you will become the new EA and you will be driving a train of contractors (and regular employees) to their deaths.

Wait, *contractors are not animals!* This is a completely true story except for that last part and the stuff before it. Please treat your contractors with the respect and dignity they deserve.

Paying Bills

Never, ever, pay bills after dealing with your contractors; it completely ruins your power high from totally controlling someone else. Sometimes, it is fun to be petty like that.

Another task completed (deciding not to do something is a legitimate task!) and it's only 2:00 PM. You are really moving along now, but . . . what the hell is that noise coming from the printer?

Office Equipment Maintenance

There is nothing like the feeling of the deep psychic pain that comes with a request to fax your extended warranty receipt for your broken printer when your fax is broken as well. Office equipment's sole purpose is to be destroyed in a devilishly clever montage highlighted by angry rap lyrics about "the man." (Not you! Someone else, of course.) But until that happens, you will need to understand that some days are all about "un-jamming, downloading drivers, updating software, refilling ink, replacing cables, testing some hardware, and buying paper" rather than actually making your game or taking care of your clients. That is just the way it is, so get out your NWA and start the day swinging, but in your mind.

Wow, you fixed your printer with your pen and you have no idea how! Good work, and it is only 2:10 so you have time to go to the bank.

Financial Institutions

OK, hopefully we told you to get a checking and savings account that has your company name on it. If not, you should. Investors would probably prefer not to find out you keep all their money in cash stored in some dusty X-wing fighter swinging from the corner of the ceiling. Going to the bank is awesome when you are depositing a check; otherwise, it is a scary and lonely place not unlike the line to pay your bills on a Saturday morning at the local supermarket.

Maybe it is time for you to learn a bit about these creatures we call "banks."

So, How Do You Choose the Right Bank?

First, do not go to your parent's bank at any cost if they "just love them." Oh man, you will get screwed with the "age gap/fiscal responsibility" combo of death. Honestly, you could die. Game companies do not start out of a desire to be "fiscally responsible." Throwing your money away starting a business to develop games is one of the least fiscally responsible things anyone can ever do. Plus, old people do not play games, so how are they ever going to understand? We prefer local credit unions. We have no idea what "credit union" means, but we suspect that *credit* means "give us credit for being in banking when we are this small," and *union* means they "gouge for the masses." Since we are the masses—we're in! Also, they have cooler people than real banks—it's a union. They are set, so what do they have to be agitated about?

Or, if you want *good* advice, ask your lawyer or accountant for a good recommendation. For the most part, you don't need anything fancy. You'll want to write checks, perhaps have a check card for Internet payments, and be able to do wire transfers if you expect to make large purchases or receive milestone payments. Another nice benefit is being able to make federal payroll tax deposits at the bank if you choose to do your payroll yourself.

How Do I Navigate the Banking System?

You really are a game developer. All you really need to do is make a friend at the bank and explain how cool you are. Try to meet some of the account executives or managers and strike up conversations with them. Try to refrain from discussing the inner workings of whatever zombie head explosion you are developing in your particle system. Start small with the weather, or why they have a 10-day hold on your checks. By being seen and talking to people at the credit union, they will get to know you and inevitably want to do things for you because they cannot believe you would spend so much time in a "bank." They also have good coffee. Just do not hang around and not say anything because then you are "casing the joint," and that is considered rather unfriendly by the people there.

What Can the Credit Union (. . . and Banks) Do for Me?

They can do many things, so make sure you ask about the services they offer. You can get short-term loans to help with cash flow or to buy equipment, emergency waiving of check holds, help with marketing, better ATM rates, better credit card offers, and even better car and health insurance options. At a minimum, you can get a steady supply of cheap pens.

A Word about Electronic Bill Paying

Electronic bill paying is convenient, for sure. Who really hates the automation of their boring accounting system? However, if you are starting up a new business, then doing the bill paying by hand can be a better option. First, experiencing your cash flow and spending before turning it on "auto" is always a good plan. Remember, you can ease into auto pay one bill at a time, so start with the ones you can pay for sure every month. Second, if your cash flow is spotty, you risk spending more time working with the bank on delaying payment until you have money, which really defeats the purpose of having automatic payments. As your cash flow becomes more consistent and you become more confident with your accounting you can begin to link your accounting software and bank accounts to help automate your money management.

All right, now you are back from the bank and ready for the 3:00 PM caffeine break with 72 ounces of Mountain Dew.

Vendor Relations

There is no way around it. At some point, you are going to have to mow down the waves of bureaucratic minions thrown in your way as you try to achieve some sort of efficient process for getting vital products and services to your development team. You will be on the phone, email, and chat as you try to get service turned on, off, restored, and transferred for your cell phones, Internet service, and electricity. This is no easy task, as all customer service is designed to put you into the endless loop of centralized phone bank hell. Let us run through a typical scenario.

Your phone bill is way over your normal month's average so you call your local provider (who is only local in the same way that the Earth is local to our universe) to find out why the DSL has been turned off! The first person you will talk with always beams "friendly customer service rays of love." Understand that all of these people have been through years of training to learn to lie, stall, and generally frustrate you into giving up. Here is a customer service scenario we like to call, "Sir, your problem is easily fixable."

This is a classic scenario designed to create an expectation that your problem is a minor fix and will only take a few minutes to solve. After 30 minutes of answering questions about your customer file, mother's maiden name, and turning down numerous "optional" upsale opportunities to add new features to your service that is not at present working, you realize that this person in no way is going to "easily fix" your problem. You rightly ask to talk to a manager, but for some reason this is impossible for the following reasons: (1) the manager is away, (2) the person can honestly solve your problem if you just explain it again, or (3) the manager will take the time to call *you* back if you just leave a message. Inevitably, you either persist through this maze of unknown management tiers to get your problem fixed or you give up. Most people give up; this is by design. How many times have you been switched to a manager and it sends you back to the call center where you have to start over from scratch? Exactly! Everyone has been through that because it is by design. You see, for large vendors like the phone company, it is cheaper to pay people to stall and discourage than to actually fix the problem. Now, they are not all evil . . . well, yes they are. Anyway, here are a couple of lines to use to get past the first wave of minions to talk with a manager.

First, at the first sign of subterfuge or incompetence, scream into the phone, "Do you know who I am!?" When they answer "no" because you rattled the hell out of them, tell them, "What are you, stupid? My account is right in front of you, how can you possibly help me if you cannot read my file?! <quickly and with compassionate force you belt out> GET ME YOUR MANAGER!"

Second, before you say anything to them about your problem, ask if they are "authorized to give you cash." Be polite and repeat it as often as you need to until they wake from their stupor of rehearsed lines and say "Ummm . . . No?" Then ask for a manager. This one works a lot just because of the confusion factor. They simply cannot fathom why someone is calling and asking the phone company for cash, so they think you know something they do not about policy. Or they think you are crazy. Either way, you are getting passed on up to management.

Third, announce that you believe that the CS person is incredibly intelligent and thus is not only aware, but complicit, in the evil doings of the corporate mothership and thusly you will immediately come out cursing and screaming unless the CSR gets you to the right alien to solve your problem. Be extremely polite, even flattering during your explanation, and then start counting down from 10 very slowly. You should soon hear, "please hold for a manager." Look, they are not paid enough to be yelled at by insane people—that is what managers are for. Show them you have the "crazy eye" and "nukes" and everyone wants to talk friendly. It works for North Korea.

Finally, tell them that you are part of an Attorney General Fraud Monitoring study and that, "this call *might* be monitored for fraudulent CS tactics." The confusion alone should allow you to get some good digs in before they recover, thus reducing the chance of their save roll on any of the aforementioned techniques.

Last, try being friendly and understanding. Few people really use this technique, but some people have expressed success. Their logic goes like this: sometimes, people can actually help you if you give them a minute. Be clear and informative with them, and most importantly, if they do a great job, reward them by following up with their manager with a quality shout out. Also, get a direct way to contact them in the future. Remember, not everybody in the call center is evil; some are still in training and are ripe to be turned away from the dark side by you.

Additionally, anytime you are on the phone with vendors, make sure you keep a written record of who you talked to, at what time, and what was said to you. This might seem daunting as you go through the many levels of *Diablo 2*–style hell battles, but it is invaluable to impress upon them that you are watching what they do and reporting it as you go higher up in the chain of command to the boss man. Also, make sure you articulate exactly what you need done and in what order. "I need my DSL turned on, my account status changed, and the credits applied to my next bill," is a good example of giving a specific plan of action for them to follow. Lastly, and most importantly, get the manager's direct contact information and follow up to make sure you are getting what you want. Working with your vendor's customer service people can be tedious and painful, but it sure is cool when the Internet comes back on.

Personal Anecdote: Prior to working in the game industry, I took a prominent regional phone company to task regarding the incompetence of their DSL installation. After weeks of lies and misdirection, I decided that my life would now be devoted to crushing the will of this lobbyist-money created fossil of a communications company that thought cheating and stealing through monopoly practices was "good business." Screw the installation! That point did not matter; it was time to go all De Niro on them for crimes against customer service and humanity.

Using the simple advice given earlier, I managed, in just a few weeks, to (a) receive the direct contact information for a personal CS representative who to this day regrets giving me her home phone number, and (b) getting said representative to willfully except and acknowledge (in writing) that for every minute I spent solving this problem was time that should be paid for by someone other than me. Sure, any veteran can see my next move, but why kill a rookie when you could turn her to the light instead? I mean, sure, I billed them for my time (.75 the normal rate) and thoroughly itemized the invoice with discussion notes, but I never pursued it further once the greatest thing in the world happened. See, my clearly crushed "personal" CS person, after about four months of constant shelling from my "detailed notepad of corporate lies" decided to slide me a phone number via email with the very quick note . . . "I will be on vacation for the next six weeks". Six weeks.

I forced her into to rehab!

Victory enough?

For some maybe, but I pressed forward and made the call to the nameless number. It was picked up on the first ring. "This is Robert," said the voice. Well, that was enough for me. In less than 40 seconds, I had given a clear synopsis of my predicament, indictment, and request for just compensation.

Pause . . .

"Why am I getting this call?" Robert said.

"Because they told me only you could solve my problem," I said.

"Who are you?"

"Spencer."

"OK."

It was about two weeks later when I received our first DSL bill with a $430.00 credit and, get this, a phone call to ask if things were OK with the service. I smiled knowing that amount was the $160 we owed on the DSL that I refused to pay until this ordeal was resolved plus the amount straight off my invoice to them for my time . . . BOOOHYAH! Pwned!

The point is simple (no, really): getting good service can be a full-time job itself. Make sure you are prepared to go the extra mile by documenting and following up. Oh yeah, I never heard from the CS woman again and to this day I always hear two clicks anytime I talk on the phone, but the service has been great!

Game Making: Finally

So, now it is 4:15 PM and you have taken care of your daily business, so go put another pot of coffee on and get to the game making. First, see what your team is doing and put in a good six more hours being creative. Oh, wait, wait, wait. We forgot to add all the other stuff you might need to do to keep your business happening. The assumption has been that you *do not* have a publishing deal, normal jobs or contracting are your means to support your game development, and that means you have to do more business work. And you thought you were ready to work on the game. Damn!

Be prepared for this type of disappointment on a regular basis.

More Tasty Business Tasks!

Building your Rolodex™

The industry might seem like a tight circle of people and companies, but in reality, game development is affecting the entertainment industry, academia, the military, interactive media, advertising and marketing, and the training and professional development industries. This means that if you go to conferences and post in forums you are going to meet a variety of people who may not seem relevant at the time, but who might be doing something that crosses paths with the game industry in future. So get their contact information and start your Rolodex. Or, for you kids out there who have never seen a Rolodex, you should "add them to your friends list."

There are all kinds of ways to keep this information. You can use a simple spreadsheet, an actual Rolodex, online business and social networking services like LinkedIn (*http://www.linkedin.com/*), or enter their information into the "contacts" section of your email client. Personally, we use an online database that is hooked to our registration application on the GameCamp! Web site. However you do it is fine as long as you keep it updated.

Doing all your networking online is possible given the large number of Web sites, blogs, and forums about the game industry. Keeping networked in this way is important and should be a regular part of your routine, and talking to people regularly to see what they are working on is very important.

However, getting off your computer and meeting people in person is very important as well. Often face-to-face meetings are needed before you can form the short- and long-term alliances needed to succeed in the game industry. Sometimes, just by digging deeper in a conversation that has nothing to do with games, you will find people who can assist your business in ways you never thought about. You never know whom you might meet, and almost everyone loves to hear that you are in the game industry.

You can meet all sorts of people through local community organizations, events, associations, game clubs, schools, or at the coffee shop. Interestingly, some of the best things can come from relationships with people who have no connection with the game industry. Seriously, finding like-minded people in business and meeting them face to face helps build trust and often creates mutually beneficial relationships in areas like marketing, meeting investors, contract work, and finding staff.

Consulting Work

Survival in the game business is hard enough without a publisher or investor funding you. So, how can you supplement your company income while still finding time to work on your game? Great question, and there is no set answer. Our opinion is that there are two approaches you can take. First, look for contract work in the game industry that jibes with your company's skill sets. For us, we had people with networking, server, and graphics skills, so when we were light on cash we would do jobs on the fringe of the game industry. Whether it was building network charity casino machines or Web sites, we did whatever it took to make the monthly budget work.

Second, get known in your city. We had several clients who are engineering companies and needed help with everyday things like hardware purchases, network security, and email configuration. It may not be games, but it pays your bills and keeps your computer skills at a high level. We also found that the broader our marketing circle, the more we were introduced to people who had small game projects they were interested in funding but had no contact to the industry. Sometimes, working together can help get multiple dreams a little closer to reality.

Keys to Living through the Daily Grind: Communication

Starting and running your own business is never easy. Doing it in the game industry adds a new level of problems you must navigate. For your sanity, make sure that no matter what, you take the time to communicate with your team, document what you are doing, and follow up. The greatest game design in the world is irrelevant if you do not have a stable process to get the game made.

Everyone Is in the Marketing Department.

Everyone is in the marketing department. OK, you need more than that? First, get a marketing "strategery." Second, create a message. Third, make sure everyone can repeat it. Fourth, make sure everyone sends potential clients to the business development people for final sales. Fifth, read Chapter 5, "Marketing Is a Game, Too." Repeat: everyone is in the marketing department.

 Comedy Note: "Strategery" is from a classic SNL skit where Will Ferrell as George W. Bush gives his one-word summation of his campaign at the end of a presidential debate (aired October 7, 2000). If you do not know this, then you need to spend more time having fun and not so much time being a gamaworkaholic.

Government: The Horror and Insanity

So, you still want to start a game business? You will need to be a hardy breed. But, let us be clear, you are immediately inviting the state and federal government to participate in your new life just by forming a company. And face it, the government is not always the best partner to have. Which government you ask? Pick one; they all have their individual problems. Most have no concept of adjusting to a rapidly changing market nor do they know anything about games, they are improperly trained and underpaid, they have a very hard time coordinating data between their agencies and departments, they regulate you for no apparent reason, they tax you to death, and rarely do they give you money without jumping through these delightful "flaming-poison-acid-hoops of bureaucracy." Interestingly, some of our clients have this same description, but that is another story.

Getting an Employer Identification Number (EIN)

Getting an EIN is relatively painless and can be done online via the government's small business and tax Web portals. This number uniquely identifies your company with the federal and state government. Sole proprietorships use their Social Security number.

Tax Information

Taxes. We *hate* taxes. Mostly because it is math-based, but also because it never seems to come back and help our business. What good is paying taxes unless something tangible happens for us? For example, "the man" requires that your company withhold certain wages from employees. These withholdings include federal and state income taxes and Social Security insurance or FICA. Now how does that benefit us, again? Anyway, just know that you will have to pay these taxes no matter what entity you choose. Just take the time to find the proper information for taxation that is relevant to your company. This is really the best advice for any new business owner. Just bite the bullet and go to the Internal Revenue Service and your State Tax Collector Web sites and *thoroughly investigate* what your company is liable for regarding taxes. The IRS has a business tax kit they can send you, and most states have tax assistance available as well. The Social Security Administration should be able to assist you with the regulations regarding employee information and Social Security forms. If you have funding for your game company, then you need to hire an accountant who is familiar with your corporate structure and its implications on your tax liability. Once again, pay special attention to Chapter 11 in this book to learn about all this fun stuff.

Business and Employment Regulations

To run your business legitimately, there are going to be a host of licenses and taxes you'll have to pay. Also, all businesses with employees must meet state and federal regulations related to the protection of employees. For our companies, Texas law required that we be registered with the state for purposes of regulating our entity and determining our franchise tax burden. These requirements will be different in every state, so visit your federal, state, and city Web sites for information on licensing requirements and taxes.

Employment Eligibility

If you have employees, they need to complete an "Employment Eligibility Verification Form," also called the I-9. For businesses with funding, this is more applicable because you have employees. If you do not have funding, then see "Minimum Wage" because that is what *you* will be making. No really, you will be poor. Also, you may contract your developers so you should become familiar with the IRS Form 1099, which must be submitted to the contractor and the IRS if that contractor earns more than $600.00 any fiscal year.

Obtain more information from your Secretary of State or Comptroller regarding minimum wage requirements, overtime regulations, child labor information, and any miscellaneous laws that may have been added since this chapter was written.

Managing the Bureaucracy

Your relationship with your local, state, federal, and multinational lawmakers is a set of unique problems that only your company will experience. It will be a complex and confusing process. It will completely try your patience through endless filing of forms, contradictory policies, inaccurate instructions, misinterpretations, and delays. It is life-long learning at its finest. The truth is, you should:

- Stay fully documented by recording and filing everything you do with the government. Do this until you can pay a professional to take it off your plate. Make sure that the professional documents everything and updates you at least quarterly.
- Understand that it takes a lot of time for problems to get resolved. Make sure you follow up to check the status of your issue. Knowing the agencies' policies and procedures as stated on their Web sites will help you navigate the process more effectively.
- Try to make a friend. Anyone who can help to navigate you to the right people or information regarding your problem. This probably requires that you be nice. (Oh the humanity!)
- Talk to similar businesses about how they handled problems with the IRS or State Comptroller. In these conversations, you are looking for a contact (friend), source for information, or process that may work for your situation. It also never hurts to know that other businesses have been through similar craziness and it is not some elaborate conspiracy to stop you from making your great game.

Human Resources

The Birth of the "HR Person"

Human resource jobs only exist as a product of having to report to a regulatory agency of some sort. Seriously, if business were an unregulated free-for-all, would there be a single human resource person in your company? They are nice people and all, but really?

No one really knows when it started, except maybe for the rarely seen human resourceologists that scour the pre-post-industrial wasteland of contemporary business practices. One theory is that in the beginning, there were huge competing economic views prowling our now "globalized" world.

On one side, there is the "Capitalist Stallion of Death" philosophy, which allows larger companies and their government "friends" to stampede your company in the name of "competition." They specialize in stomping on all your potential resources (markets, employees, intellectual property, and clients) until you are dead (or significantly weakened right before entering a contract negotiation or dispute resolution). Their special emphasis is on small and medium-sized business eating. "Mmmm . . . what delicious IP," you might overhear them say on occasion.

On the other side is the "State" philosophy, to be viewed as a thick, sticky pool of oil. Their sole desire is to stop the Stallions by sucking them into their black abyss of oily forms, archaic regulations, miscommunications, plea bargains, and the occasional sweet, sweet "fines and/or imprisonment."

This war has gone on for eons. Years later, you started a game company and learned that at some point these galactic warriors had compromised and created an intricate system of laws, fees, taxes, forms, hearings, exemptions, loopholes, and judicial oversight that required an organizational interface now known as, you got it, the *Human Resource Person*.

What Does a Human Resources Person Do?

Simply put, human resource people are the backbone of every company. They handle all the things that no self-respecting gamer would ever be caught dead doing, like filing paperwork. They support the company by making sure that all of the internal, nonproject related issues companies must consider are handled in an organized and efficient way.

A few activities in the daily life of a human resource person might include organizing and articulating company policies, creating and updating personnel files, implementing professional development and staff training, recommending and implementing employee benefits like insurance and 401(k)s, or any of the things that go into complying with federal, state, and local laws concerning payroll, taxes, workers compensation, worker safety, privacy issues, workplace rights, and hiring and firing.

Any one of these issues has the potential to overwhelm any single individual. Take insurance, for example. There are mandated benefits like Social Security, workers' compensation, and unemployment insurance, all with their corresponding rules, regulations, and paperwork written especially for you in "bureaucracy-speak." Then there are benefits that your company wants to have like health insurance, life insurance, revenue sharing, retirement, and so forth. Again, all of these benefits could easily be singular areas of specialization, making handling all of these issues quite a daunting task. Luckily, your HR person is all over it and you can keep coding!!

We Can't Afford a Human Resources Person

OK, stop coding. If you are just starting out, you want to focus your "HR time" on compliance with your federal and state laws and regulations. The IRS and your State Comptroller's Web sites can provide you with all the necessary requirements and forms.

Take the time to understand them, and even go to your local state comptroller representative and walk through the requirements and forms with him or her. Once that is handled, revise your corporate agreements that you have made with your key business people and codify them into an office manual. You will also want to get your personnel files together by collecting all the relevant information about your employees. In this file will be all the required tax forms, compensation records, evaluations, and contact information. Include their legal name, Social Security number, current residence, resume, and contact information.

Your second set of priorities will depend on your direction and resource (money) availability. Health insurance is never a bad idea, but may still be out of reach at your present income level. If you can afford it, have your HR person do the research on the various policies that are out there. The psychic burden of not having health insurance gets heavier over time as you constantly try to avoid little kids, drugs, risky sex, and traveling to Darfur. At some point, you will get sick and you know it, so having even minimal coverage for catastrophic care is a good idea.

Your next set of priorities may include developing more formal files for potential contractors (much the same as employee files), creating an employee evaluation program, implementing management reporting systems, and often in a small company, taking on other responsibilities in accounting, marketing, business development and, wait for it, game development. Now how did that happen?

A Word about Health and the "Other" Insurances

Insurance is pretty darn important for game developers given the long hours, poor diet, lack of exercise, general frustration with not playing enough games, and lack of Vitamin D from coding in a sub-basement. Health insurance, in particular, is a very good thing and is usually the primary if not the only insurance concern that startups consider. Here are some things to consider about health insurance:

- Finding and comparing health policies is time consuming, but necessary.
- Customization and freedom in your health insurance policy cost more money.
- Everything is a trade-off. Do you want preventive care, dental, low-cost drugs, access to specialists, low deductible, mental health coverage (advised), long-term care, or any of dozens of other options? Make sure you know your staff priorities and that your health insurance policy reflects those priorities.
- Consult your accountant on ways to recoup your medical expenditures, especially if you are considered self-employed by the government.

Home Insurance Adjustments

Many game startups occur in someone's home. If this is the case, make sure you adjust your home insurance accordingly to cover your business possessions. You should also consult your accountant regarding tax benefits and liabilities.

Other insurance is available as well and may become appropriate for your company as your revenue and cash flow increases. As a matter of fact, just from the following list it seems like the insurance business is the one to be in, not the game industry. Who knew so many things could go wrong?!?

Some other insurance options include:

- Supplemental Health; one word, AFLAC
- Errors and Omissions
- Key Person
- Workers' Compensation
- Business Insurance
- Sexual Harassment
- Product Liability Insurance
- Business Interruption

Change: The Real End Game

Starting your own game company is hard work, like being president. Maintaining it is even harder, however. From when we started at Ninjaneering until this author left five years later, the MMO market lost some of its Wild West investment luster and began to move toward a more conservative approach to product development, marketing, and distribution. Most of the big publishers, once they had a few games in production, were really looking at games that hit the known formula for familiar gameplay, retention, and limited technological risks.

For Ninjaneering, this meant that our unique MMO called *Hollyworld* would be quite difficult to sell since it was not a franchise, was nonviolent, and turned the notion of grinding on its head by allowing player-created movie content to be continually viewed, edited, remixed, and marketed. Everyone loved the idea, but had a really hard time putting the square game into the round business model and finding investment. At the same time, "serious games" for business and education were gaining pop-ularity and business opportunities began to grow in those areas. So what did we do? We went with where the money was to survive. Pay attention! It is all about the *cash flow*! Well, anyway, we changed with the times and highlighted our skills as game con-sultants for MMOs and serious games.

One of the advantages to building your own self-funded company is that you are not subject to the whims of someone else's view of the market. You can control your destiny in relation to the niches and opportunities you deem to have potential.

Marketing Yourself

Marketing in its simplest form is the communication from one party to another regarding the opportunity for products and/or services to be exchanged (hopefully for money). Marketing may or may not be necessary at your current level of development, but if you are consulting to fund your game, then it is very important to consistently reach the people who have potential work for your team. So how do you do that?

Research

You have to stay on top of what is going on in the game industry and how the indus-try is changing and merging with other industries. It was always great to get a solid game-consulting gig that matched our skill sets—your skills stay sharp and it's good money. We also found great opportunities to work with companies using our exper-tise in design, networking, and 3D graphics for "serious games" and products that used "game-like" features. Additionally, we developed relationships with universities that needed assistance in developing materials for game development curriculums.

Local Networking

Spend the time to meet and work with people outside of the game industry. Start with local companies in and around the game industry and then branch out. Think of it as building your home field advantage. Everyone in your city wants a local game com-pany to make it and they will do what they can to help, even if it is just word of mouth that your city now has a new game company. Business people understand that markets change and they respect people who have the guts to be proactive about their direction. Make connections with other local game developers, game clubs and asso-ciations, and game stores. Often, someone you meet knows a friend or relative who is working on an independent project and needs some help. Build your alliances locally and then expand to universal domination.

Generating Marketing Materials

You don't need a slick TV or radio commercial, but you should have at least a one-page introduction to your company. This simple marketing piece should contain your company branding, contact information, list of services and prices, and other relevant information to selling your company.

Company Web Sites

A Web site is also a must and should be built from a template of product identity materials that are consistent across all your marketing materials. In today's world, it is much easier to build and host your own Web site. Just make sure you have the skills to maintain and troubleshoot it before you choose to do it all in-house. If you are not a webmaster or system administrator, then getting a good Web developer and hosting service may move farther up the "to-do" list.

The Consulting Trap

A word of caution about consulting to help pay the bills: it takes a lot of work to keep a company afloat with consulting money. Taking on a number of little projects can be great for your cash flow, but murder on your time for both your developers and your managers. Each new client brings issues and problems to the table and, unlike working on your game, you are not in charge of the design or schedule. It also means a whole new set of contracts and accounting processes, which, of course, mean more money and time.

Just like most things in life, the key is balance. Remember to make time for your game and to use your money earned through consulting to make it *easier* to build your game, not to put it on the back burner. One way to do this is to go out and get a couple of hired guns to help with the contracts. This of course lessens your cut of the contract, but it does allow you some flexibility in your schedule to meet your own internal milestones for your game. You may have to cut down some of your more optimistic development plans and stick to prototyping, documentation, and creating a solid pitch for the publishers, but that is all good as long as you are continuing to make progress.

Losing Key People

Losing members of your development team, including owners/partners, is inevitable. Whether they lose interest in the direction or get a better job offer, expect that the people you start with will not all be there at the end. Conversely, you will probably add new people over time as you realize that some skills are needed to get past certain chokepoints that arise in your development schedule. This turnover issue is best managed by maintaining a strong network of developers who can be plugged into consulting jobs or internal positions that arise. And, don't forget to get those founders agreements in place to establish the messy details when your key people leave.

Conclusion

Starting a successful company is extremely hard. It requires a tremendous amount of time and money, passion, teamwork, resilience, and sacrifice. The best approach is to be organized from the beginning, taking each step seriously, from incorporation to selling your first game. It is important to understand that each new day will bring unique problems that have nothing to do with the game you are making. To overcome these obstacles, you must be realistic about your team, goals, and money. You must constantly be aware of your market opportunities and use your flexibility to exploit niches. Most importantly, you need to communicate so that your team is aware of any changes in direction for the company or the game project.

So, the next step is simple. Read the rest of this book and then become an insurance broker! Just kidding, people. Stay true to your vision, work hard, and take some risks. That is what life as a game developer is all about.

Checklist for Starting a Business

- Diligently question your reasons for starting a game company. If you are partnering with other people, make sure everyone is in agreement on the goals and strategy.
- Research and articulate the pros and cons of starting your own game company. Evaluate your potential risks and gains with someone you trust who is not part of the business.
- Create a business model and development plan that includes an exit agreement. If partnering, make sure everyone agrees on the authority structure, management philosophies, financial strategy, and development process being implemented. Most importantly, everyone should understand and agree to his or her role.
- Choose a name and business entity that fits your goals.
- Consult a lawyer to draw up and file the necessary documents to make your company and/or partnership legal. This should include assistance in drawing up bylaws, company manual creation, and contracts.
- Consult an accountant to set up a basic accounting system.
- Open a checking and savings account.
- Create your personnel and record-keeping files.
- Start the game development and do not forget to have some fun!

CHAPTER 3

Business Operations

Matthew B. Doyle

matthewbriandoyle@gmail.com

The business of game development is at its worst a beast that is often horrific to behold in its size and difficult to control; however, at its best, it is a wild ride that can make legends of those who learn to master it. I have often heard from those far wiser than myself, when I posed the question as to whether one should want to run his own studio, the simple reply: "don't." Yet they still do it. Like any business, there is a strong possibility that you will fail many times before you succeed. The key is to always be learning and to never give up. Knowledge is indeed power and persistence does in fact pay off. With those things in mind, and knowing that you have most likely picked up this book because you are one of the bold few who desires to tame the beast, this particular chapter will hopefully give you a good broad understanding of what it takes to run a game studio. You should walk away from reading this with a solid understanding of the day-to-day operations of a game company.

Covered in this chapter are topics such as:

- Employee management
- Hiring and firing
- Pay rates and benefits
- Keeping morale up
- Budgeting and planning
- Seeking out opportunities and expanding

Employee Management

No company would function without employees, and any company is only as good as the people who work there. In general, most of your operating costs are employee related, including salaries, benefits, payroll taxes, and other such expenses. This expenditure has been estimated as high as 90% of the total budget for a game company.

Employees come in all shapes and flavors. Some are brilliant, some are diligent, and some are self-starters. Others require constant person-to-person contact, need to be told what to do, become easily bored, and goof off all day. Most of the time, you'll get a mix: brilliant employees who need to be told what to do, or diligent, hard workers who can get any assigned task done ahead of schedule but tend to lack that spark of imagination in their work.

Regardless of who your employees are, you are going to need managers to focus their energy properly, and good management starts with good managers. It may seem like common sense, after all the two words share the same root.

But, let's look at the Latin root: *manus*, meaning hand. A manager is someone who has a hand in the daily goings on of a business. A good manager is someone who has a "hands on" relationship with your employees. To employ an analogy, think of the studio head as the captain of the ship. While the captain usually does not get much one-on-one time with the crew (or employees in the case of our game studio), the First Mate (producers, leads, etc. at your studio) is in constant contact with those he manages, ensuring the smooth daily operation of the ship. Just like the crew of a ship, there are many kinds of managers and many levels of management. In larger studios, there may be several layers of management between the studio head and the employees who are responsible for the individual tasks of development.

What Makes a Good Manager?

The Ideal Manager
- 8 ounces interpersonal skills
- 16 ounces patience
- 8 ounces time management skills
- 3 cups relevant department knowledge
- A dash of humor
- Blend until smooth; serve warm

Anyone who has had the privilege of managing others can tell you it is a difficult task at best. In simple terms, a good manager must be able to keep his team on schedule, motivated, and happy. And if any of these conditions are not being met, a good manager needs to be able to figure out why things are off track and fix them. This is accomplished primarily by good communication.

Typically, you want development managers who are familiar with games, particularly the type of games you are producing. A manager who has no understanding of game development, in particular the role of his team in producing the game, will have a difficult time knowing what is wrong when there are problems. Someone who is at least familiar with the area of game development will have a better chance of seeing those problems before they arise, and the greater his knowledge of that area, the greater his ability in rooting out those problems before they are upgraded to full-blown disasters.

In addition to managing people, being able to keep the team on schedule is immensely important to the bottom line of the company. This can be quite difficult when you have multiple departments working in tandem, as there can be many inter-dependencies between these departments. Art cannot begin building a level until the tools have been provided by the tool programmers. Engineering cannot decide what code requests are doable until design has made a code request list and prioritized those requests. Then, once engineering decides what code requests they can do in the time they have, design must make revisions based on the feedback from engineering. This may also have a large impact on the artists who must now determine what assets need to be built based on these code requests. As you can see, scheduling in a situation like this can become a nightmare. Of course, the producer's job is to handle the big picture schedule, but it is up to each department head to handle the individual task scheduling for his own section, ensuring that those tasks are completed on time. They may use a spreadsheet or project file to keep track of all tasks, and update this daily.

Regardless of work-related knowledge or the ability to manage time well, not everyone makes a good manager. You may have a management candidate who knows every aspect of game development like the back of his hand. Maybe he could make his own game in his garage at night, working in the dark and telling jokes to himself as he laughs maniacally. However, when he talks to people, he looks the other way, is afraid to make eye contact, or is easily offended. This may not be someone who will be a good manager.

Good managers have to be good with people. These are people who make eye contact throughout the entire conversation; people who know when to tell a joke and when to be serious; people who are not afraid to speak their mind, but have the tact to do it without offending the other person. A good manager must also know how to set expectations effectively and, if those expectations are not met, when and how to take disciplinary action toward an employee. They do not use their position as a way to trump the team's ideas and they never speak negatively to anyone on the team. Good managers should have an excellent sense of humor. These are the people whom others think is a "swell guy or gal." The ideal manager is someone who is an easygoing person who makes an effort to be friendly with everyone. However, when it comes to business, a good manager never lets his friendship with others cause problems. Instead, he uses that friendship to elicit a better response from his team when trouble arises.

Organize Your Managers Well

Someone very wise once said that too much of a good thing can be bad. Too many levels of management can have a negative impact on your company; it can have the opposite effect of what you might expect. If you have just as many managers as you have employees, there is a good chance you will have a difficult time meeting your deadlines. The direness of the situation is compounded if your management structure is set up in such a way that you have an excessively multitiered management structure (managers who are in charge of other managers who are in charge of other managers, ad nauseam). Every manager has his own way of doing things, and every manager will have a strong desire to impose that way upon production. If you have a situation in which too many department heads are all vying for control of the project by doing things their way, the entire schedule can suddenly feel like it is moving backward. If you must have a multitiered management structure, a good solution for this phenomenon would be to ensure that there is a clearly defined chain of authority, ultimately ending at someone who has final authority such as the Creative Director.

Put together an organization chart using a flow-charting program or MS Word. This chart should show clear paths of management and what area each manager has direct authority over. Avoid organization charts in which many managers are at the same level.

I once worked at a well-known studio that had this very problem. In my position as a team lead, I had no less than five levels of management between the executive producer and me. And technically, as a team lead, I was considered a manager as well. After the producer, there were three more levels of management: the project lead or creative director, the vice president, and finally the president of the company. That was eight levels of management on the design side alone, each of these managers having a say in how things should be done, and each sometimes having a completely different opinion. It caused havoc with the schedule, as tasks constantly had to be redone to suit the manager who most recently stopped by to get a status report. In the end, the project lost many good team members due to over-management. When team members lose confidence in their management, you will quickly find their productivity dropping off, or even worse, they may migrate to other companies.

The best policy in situations like this is to cut out as many middle managers as possible. Keep your management structure simple and have clearly defined duties and powers for each manager. Avoid situations in which multiple managers can have equal say over the same tasks and teams. Give the proper managers the power they need to make a final decision that cannot be easily circumvented by another manager, even you!

Core Hours

Every business needs to have regular operating hours during the day. Team members are going to need to communicate with each other on a regular basis to get things done, whether they come in to the office or work over a VPN. The standard hours of operation throughout the industry range from a starting time ranging from 8:30 AM to 10:00 AM with a close of business time being anywhere from 5:30 PM to 7:00 PM. If you work for one of the larger companies, these times may be more strictly enforced (this type of company is rarely run by creative people). However, if you are going to run your own studio, avoid feeling like you need to stick to the paradigm of the 9 to 5/40-hour work week. The fact is, creative people do not always work well in overly structured environments. Some work better late at night, while others tend to work in bursts where they accomplish much and then require a few days to recharge. That being said, it is not possible to run a business in a chaotic environment in which everyone is coming and going at his leisure and expect to get anything done.

This is where core hours come into play. In a small studio full of dedicated employees who believe in the project and company, remember that many of these individuals will end up working beyond a 40-hour week simply because they love what they are doing. Therefore, it is to your company's benefit that you cut them a little slack in regard to their working hours. If someone shows up at noon and works until midnight, does it really matter that he showed up at noon? If someone is working 50 to 60 hours a week, does it really matter that he tends to show up 30 minutes late or an hour late? Of course not, as long as he accomplishes his work. Just make sure that all employees have up-to-date contact information where they may be reached in case they are needed. Ask that they let their immediate supervisor know if they expect to be late.

The importance of setting core hours has little to do with total amount of work time in a week. Everyone knows the minimum hours he should work, especially passionate teams. Setting core hours is, however, a good way to make sure everyone is available for meetings and discussion when things come up. Some studios have been known to set core hours somewhere along the lines of noon to 6 PM. As a result, most meetings should only be scheduled to fit within these core hours to make sure everyone is present. Having flexible hours allows people to feel like they are not working a boring 9-to-5 office job, but are still available for discussions that are necessary to make a game happen.

If someone is showing up late and going home early all the time, there is something more going on than someone who does not know when core hours are. There is a good chance this person is unhappy with the job. Take the time to talk with him before things go any further and find out what you can do to get him back on track. Be sure to gently remind him when core hours are and why he is important as a lead in to finding out what might be bothering him.

The Dreaded Crunch

Crunch time has become an all too depressing fact of life in the industry. It has been the downfall of many good developers and is part of the reason why burnout and divorce rates are so high in this industry. It seems that the more ambitious projects become, the more prevalent this phenomenon becomes. Poor planning is chief among the culprits for crunch time, as is a small selection of industry myths that have been perpetuated by managers who do not seem to be in touch with their employees.

What is crunch time? First, crunch time is not the same phenomenon that occurs in a small startup studio eager to make its mark in the industry. In these types of studios, the dedicated few will often work without sleeping for days, existing on cases of soft drinks and bags of potato chips while they pour out their hearts into the code, art, and design that will make them megastars among their peers and the fans of their game. No, the term *crunch time* for the purposes of this writing has an entirely different definition.

It is a period toward the end of a project being produced by an established studio in which the team is "asked" to stay late and work long hours, often through the weekend, to meet a milestone or other project goal. Sometimes, crunch time can last for months on a poorly planned and executed project. Studios are being pushed harder and harder to produce bigger and better products than ever before, without additional budget, time, or employees. The situation is exacerbated by publishers and studio heads willing to exploit employee enthusiasm for their work, and who seem to have forgotten that the department of labor instituted the 40-hour work week for a reason.

The Myths of Crunch Time—Crunched!

Myth #1: The more hours someone works in any given week, the more work he will get done.
This is a half-truth. Studies indicate that up to a certain point and for a limited duration, this is certainly true; however, once a person begins to work significantly past 40 hours, his efficiency begins to degrade exponentially. Working long hours over an extended period of time causes mistakes brought on by fatigue, and a project ends up losing time, rather than making it up. So an employee who works 60 hours a week for two weeks might actually only end up producing 60 hours of good work overall due to mistakes that must be corrected in the following week. This phenomenon is often called "negative productivity" or "anti-time." The more time an employee puts in beyond the standard 40-hour week, the more anti-time rears its ugly head. So, instead of gaining 20 extra hours of work, you have a net loss of 20 hours of work the next week.

Another thing to keep in mind is that you are dealing with creative types. Drawing fantastic concepts, designing masterful game systems, and writing elegant code is nothing like doing predictable, mechanical work such as one might perform on an assembly line. These things take a huge amount of mental effort to achieve and tend to leave a person drained at the end of the day. Pushing a person past the normal 40-hour week will many times result in creative works that are below the employee's normal level of ability.

Myth #2: Your employees won't mind some crunch time.
Your employees may not complain when you ask them to work longer hours. However, this initial enthusiasm may not last. Again, you have to realize that people can only do so much in a day or week before they become so fatigued that they just do not want to and cannot work anymore. Pushing your employees too hard will end up turning them all into the least pleasant of the seven dwarves. Even people with the best attitudes turn into grumpy, angry people when asked to work more than 40 hours a week. Not to mention sleepy ones! And grumpy, sleepy people are not going to get much done. The best-case scenario will be that the work needed is completed, but there is a good chance that the work will be subpar and your employees will be one notch closer to looking for another job. And that is going to cost you more lost time and money finding a replacement.

Myth #3: Crunch time is unavoidable.

Even if this were true, it does not make it right to insist that your employees work extra hours to make up for management's error in scheduling the project properly. It is the responsibility of the management team to come up with a realistic schedule that an appropriately large enough team can execute in the allotted time frame. Problems should be expected and scheduled for, as should the occasional employee migration, which can have a large impact on completing tasks on time. In other industries, working over 40 hours per week at the boss' request is referred to as "overtime." If you plan to ask your team to put in some crunch time, pay them the respect they deserve and inform them that anyone who puts in the time will be properly compensated. The small amount of extra money you must invest into their paycheck is not going to break your company, but it will have a very positive effect on their outlook. (If it does have a large impact on your bottom line, then you are not planning well enough.)

Myth #4: My employees will work long hours anyway.

This is not so much a myth as it is a bad point of view to have. It is true that many game developers work long hours for the joy of what they do; however, no one likes to be forced to do something, even if it is something he would do anyway. It is or should be common sense that people like to be asked if they are interested in doing something rather than being told they must do it. Remember, you are not the only game in town. If your employees feel you are taking advantage of their dedication, many other studios out there would be more than happy to take that dedication and refocus it onto their projects.

Avoiding the Crunch

So, what view of crunch time should we as studio heads take? The short answer is to avoid it like the plague. Simply put, working long hours is not a good solution for a project running behind schedule. How can a good manager avoid it?

The first step is good planning, beginning with preproduction. Every step of development should be written out and hours required for each step should be calculated. A good program for writing out and keeping track of the project time line is Microsoft® Project, but all that really matters is that you have every step of the project properly planned and that you allow some extra time in the schedule for unanticipated problems that may and certainly will arise. In fact, this plan should be written before you get funding for the project. Without this plan, you will not be able to accurately inform your investors of the total cost of the project and how long it will take to complete. The important thing is that your plan, if done well, should help keep crunch time to a minimum, if not eliminate it completely.

The Problems of Feature Creep and Unnecessary Redesign

Two secondary culprits responsible for unforeseen crunch time, even with a solidly laid-out plan, are feature creep and what we like to call the "Wouldn't it be better if . . ." or unnecessary redesign syndrome. Feature creep is a simple enough concept: as the project moves along, inevitably people will have brilliant new ideas to put into the game. (Well, sometimes the ideas are brilliant—a studio head once wanted to add blinking in his first person shooter because it was "realistic.") The problem with all these wonderful new ideas is that your well thought-out plan probably does not account for the time it will take to add all of them to your game design, or figure the impact of these changes on the game as a whole.

Okay, so this particular new idea is just too good not to add. It will help tie everything together and make the game 10 times more fun than without it. In that case, you are probably wishing you had accounted for a reasonable amount of flexibility in your schedule. If you were smart, you did. Otherwise, you need to try to keep feature creep to an absolute minimum. It can ruin a well-planned schedule quickly and end up causing crunch time. Don't worry; you can save that great new idea for the sequel!

Unnecessary redesign happens when the project has lost its vision, or worse yet, you have a project with several different visions fighting for control; this can happen if you have too many managers, as described previously. In this industry, there are many perfectionists, and many of us are just never happy with anything we do. The game could always be better if we just worked on it a little more. As artists, designers, and engineers we all have to stop at some point and say, "it is good enough!" At some point, you have to realize that if you keep redesigning that combat system, or you keep rewriting that AI subroutine, or keep redrawing that zombie concept, you'll never finish the game. This goes for studio heads, producers, and department heads as well.

As for lost or conflicting vision, that is a much larger problem that must be remedied as quickly as possible before it brings the entire project to a screeching halt. The best schedules and plans will end up falling apart if a project has lost its primary vision. And there will be plenty of crunch time required to get the project back on track and delivered within schedule.

Crunch Time Still Happens

Sometimes, no matter what you do, or because of what you do not do properly, crunch time will be required. If it is, there are a few important things to keep in mind. First and foremost among those things is that you must remember that your employees are people, too. They have lives outside of work that keep them healthy and well adjusted. Many of them have spouses or even children. Perish the thought that you be indirectly responsible for causing your employees to have family problems.

A few things you can do to ease crunch time include buying everyone dinner, letting them go home for a few hours to relax each night, renting movies for them, and letting their families come visit them. Make the crunch time as comfortable as possible. These people are working above and beyond what most employees would do for any other type of company, so show them the gratitude they deserve. Try instituting a revolving watch system in which employees choose which shift they want to work during crunch time. If your insurance will allow it, let them bring in a few alcoholic beverages to help the night go more smoothly. A six-pack in the refrigerator goes a long way toward helping someone feel relaxed, and being relaxed goes a long way toward helping creative people be creative.

And managers better be prepared to stay late as well. A good commander never orders his soldiers to do anything he would not do himself. Nothing kills morale faster than a manager appearing to not be doing his part.

Rewards for Extended Crunch Time

Once the smoke clears and the body counts have come in, it is time to dole out some of that gratitude we mentioned earlier in concrete form. There are a number of ways you can show your gratitude, but the best would be monetary compensation, extra time off, and a good solid public pat on the back. Monetary compensation could come in the form of a bonus on their next check; a bonus of 10% or more depending on the situation is a good guideline. It could also take the form of an extra 2 or 3% pay raise when review time comes around, or perhaps an early performance review while things are calming down. Time off is an easy reward as well. When crunch time is over, let your employees take a few days off in small groups. Give them an extra week of vacation time for the year. Encourage them to take time off to enjoy themselves and spend time with their family. What little time off or money they get is nothing compared to the sheer amount of work they have had to endure to get through the crunch time. And a good budget should already have accounted for these extra gratuities.

Finally, be sure to get them all together with the entire company in a nice big room and thank them for their dedication. Assure them that next time you will make sure there is even more beer in the refrigerator and even less crunch time to endure. Or, for a lasting impression, rent a hotel meeting hall and invite them all out for an evening of catered food and drinks, starting the evening off with a big thank-you!

In the end, just remember what early workers had to go through to get us the wonderful and sane 40-hour work week we take for granted today. Until the last 100 years, employers in the United States could work their employees as much as they liked and pay them as little as they liked. Those days are long gone, yet many in the game industry seem to think we are still living in those times. We can, and should, do better.

Who Does What?

Like a ship, a studio consists of many crewmembers working together toward a final goal, in this case a published game. Most of the crewmembers will have different skill sets and talents, while some will have similar duties. The range of positions in a studio will vary from game to game and genre to genre. For instance, MMOGs (massively multiplayer online games) may have quest developers, encounter developers, and world designers, whereas a smaller studio working on an adventure game may only have a level designer who essentially fills the role of all three. The following is by no means a complete list of roles to be found throughout the industry. Also keep in mind that different companies may use different titles for similar job descriptions. The list does, however, contain a good sampling of the types of positions you can expect to find in a typical studio and brief descriptions of what the expectations are for each position.

Upper Management

The *studio head* is traditionally the founder of the company. In the "good old days" of game development, the studio head was able to play a large role in the development process and was often an engineer and/or designer. Today, with games taking increasing numbers of employees and requiring tens of millions of dollars to make, the studio head rarely gets to take such an active role in development. They find themselves finding and dealing with investors, pitching game ideas to publishers, signing contracts, seeking out new technologies, working with the producers to ensure the development time line is on track, and other vital tasks to keep the company running and making money.

If you start your own company, be prepared to turn over all the fun stuff to your employees. As a studio head, you just won't have the time to be involved, unless you have no family and need only two hours of sleep each night. That being said, as studio head you have a tremendous amount of power, and it is ultimately your game that is being made; however, it is often best to trust your team to do their jobs well. An overzealous and micromanaging studio head can often cause more harm than good.

The *producer* is often not very well defined in game companies. Many times, much like the movie industry counterpart, a game producer is responsible for ensuring that a project is on track. The producer creates and maintains the overall schedule and sometimes the budget, and works closely with the various department heads to ensure the project is moving forward. In some companies, the producer also ensures that the vision of the project is being followed. The producer also tends to be the frontline when dealing with the project's publisher and reporting on milestones. The producer typically receives a majority of the praise or blame for how a project comes out. They can come in all shapes and sizes and will, in larger companies, often be followed around by many associate producers to lighten their load. The associate producers are often affectionately referred to as "ass prods," as their job is to work as an intermediary between the producer and the studio heads. Associate producers will often be the "go to" person for miscellaneous tasks around the office as well.

Producers are often game developers with a great deal of experience in many aspects of the process, but are more often than not former game designers themselves.

The *creative director* is responsible for the design aspects of the project and ensuring that the overall vision of the game is true to its design throughout the development process. They are often a big part of determining what that vision is and work closely with the studio head, producer, and department heads in keeping that project within the boundaries of that vision. Not every studio has a creative director, particularly smaller ones do not; however, when there is no one person in charge of the overall vision of the game, the cohesiveness of the various aspects of the game can fall apart, resulting in a mishmash of ideas.

Creative directors in larger companies often serve the role of the "idea man." They may come up with new game ideas every day and are required to pitch them to the upper echelons of management. They are also often responsible for hearing game pitches from third-party studios. A good creative director should know a great deal about every aspect of the industry, from engineering to art to design and even the business and legal side.

The *art director* determines visual aspects, including the look and feel, of the game. This is a person with a strong background in many areas of traditional art, and a great deal of experience in game art. The art director decides the game's visual style, from the characters to the environments, and ensures this style is followed by all the artists who will be creating art and building the game world. In a large studio, the art director rarely does any hands-on work; instead, he spends his time going over the latest art assets; having meetings with the art team, creative director, other department heads, and the producer; working out scheduling issues; and so forth.

The *director of engineering* handles the scheduling and disbursement of code tasks for the engineering team. In a smaller studio, he may also play a large role in actually writing code. It is the director of engineering's responsibility to establish the technical requirements, and ensure the code for the game is bug free and includes all the requested functionality of the design and art teams. He is responsible for writing many of the technical design documents and may take an active role in determining the best route to solve design issues in the code.

The *lead designer* is responsible for managing the design team. In larger studios, the lead designer may not have a hands-on role in designing the game; instead, he may find himself reviewing the design work of his team and approving or rejecting different recommendations. In smaller studios, the lead designer may be more engaged in the daily work of designing, and running the team. The lead designer is ultimately responsible for how much fun the game is to play. No pressure here! It is his job to ensure that all the game's systems, levels, characters, and so forth mesh into a single fun experience for the player. He must also handle scheduling of design tasks for his team. The lead designer is also usually the person who comes up with the original game idea in smaller studios. He is considered the highest level designer and is sometimes referred to as the design director.

The Holy Trinity: Engineers, Artists, and Designers

The three major positions in game development are engineers, artists, and designers. Each of these areas is vital to the development of the game, and each area is dependent on each other area. You need to have quality people in each of these areas to create a great game.

Engineers are the lifeblood of game development. They write the code necessary for the game to work, and develop the engines that handle AI, graphics, and physics.

Without engineers, you cannot create a computer or console game. Some of the job roles you will find in a studio include tools programmers, AI programmers, physics programmers, graphics programmers, server-side programmers, network programmers, client programmers, and so on. Engineers tend to be among the highest paid game developers, especially in the veteran range. Good, experienced engineers are hard to come by, particularly those who are experts on console development.

Artists make art. There was a time when engineers did their own art. Alas, those 16-color 2D sprite days are long gone as games have moved into the realms of modern pixel shader technology, high poly-count 3D worlds, and high-resolution 32-bit texture maps requiring specialized people to make these works. The art team is often made up of team members of varying degrees of skill and expertise in larger studios. Without artists, the wonderful ideas your designers come up with will have no visual representation in the game world. The job roles of artists on a game include concept artists, 3D character artists/animators, environment artists, texture artists, UI artists, and so forth. Sometimes, more often than not, artists are skilled at any number of positions and find themselves doing a variety of jobs during a project's life.

The role of the artist becomes increasingly important as game technology advances; as a result, they are being paid more as the job requirements increase.

Designers design the game, determining the details of how the game will play. Without designers, there would not be a game concept for engineers and artists to work on. These are the guys who come up with the ideas, from story to gameplay mechanics. Most of the time, designers do the front-end preproduction work, and end up doing the implementation—including level design, content development, scripting, and so on.

Designers come in many shapes and sizes with a varying list of titles, including world/level designers, systems designers, character/encounter designers, quest designers, and so on. Sometimes, in smaller studios, a designer is simply "a designer," responsible for coming up with all aspects of the game's design. These guys write pages upon pages of documents—requiring strong creative and technical writing skills—and some of the more artistic designers will do sketches and draw maps. Some designers, particularly those who do systems design, will have strong math skills. Others may focus on purely creative thinking. Without good designers, your game will be critically flawed from the beginning.

Hybrid developers are often found in some companies, particularly smaller companies that cannot afford many employees. These people combine disciplines from multiple areas, often acting as a bridge between different areas. Examples include technical artist (an artist/programmer who often helps develop art tools), scripter (a designer/programmer who works in a scripting language to implement gameplay behavior), and so forth. Unfortunately, many large companies have organizations that are too rigid to take advantage of people with these types of skills. However, someone with these skills will often find a warm welcome in smaller companies.

Figure 3.1 is a typical development team hierarchy diagram.

Video Game Production Hierarchy

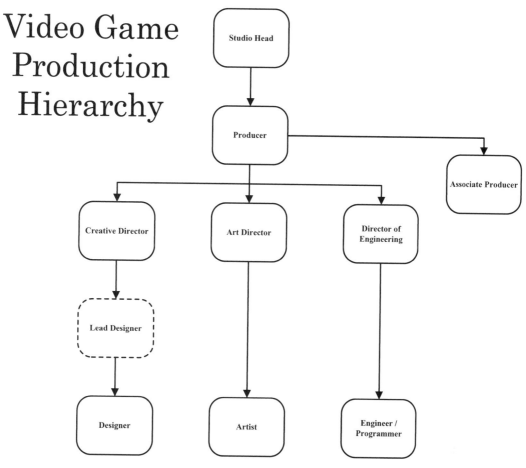

FIGURE 3.1   A typical hierarchy chart for a game development team.

The Rest (Not Necessarily the Least)

Quality assurance testers are responsible for testing and bug reporting. Quality Assurance (QA) is an extremely important part of game development that is often overlooked. These days, even small studios have their own internal quality assurance departments. Without testers, you are likely to miss important external milestones with your publisher due to bugs not being caught in time to be fixed. Even a small team of part-time testers can go a long way toward ensuring you meet those milestones.

It is a poorly kept secret in the game industry that QA is a good backdoor way into game development, the front door often being locked and requiring one to jump through impossible hoops to get into. Sometimes, you will find gems among these guys who you will want to promote to the art, design, or engineering departments.

Unfortunately, QA tends to be one of the least respected groups in the company. There is often some antagonism between the developers and QA; the developers feel that QA is being malicious in their bugs or spending too much time trying to suggest features instead of finding bugs. As a result, the QA department is often unappreciated. Be careful not to make this mistake! Remember that all the teams should be working on the common goal of developing and shipping the game.

Information Technology (IT) employees keep your technology running. They do tasks like fixing hardware, setting up networks, and establishing and backing up servers to store important information. With the rise of computer crime, it is important to have a security expert or two on your team to protect the company. Small studios may only need one or two IT people, but larger companies may have a whole department.

The *Operations* department is important for doing the everyday business stuff that needs to get done. Every good office needs someone to answer the phones. Your Operations department should include employees to handle payroll, phones, accounting, filing, maintaining the building, and so on. Depending on the size of the studio, this might be one person or could be many.

Marketing and Public Relations (PR) are perhaps the least loved areas in the company, especially by developers. The truth is that games often live and die based on their marketing. And, despite the old adage, not all attention is good attention, and it can be very important to have one or two marketing and PR gurus on your payroll. Say the wrong thing or say the right thing too soon, and your project could find itself in trouble. It is the job of these departments to make sure that only good things are said and only in due time. These people should be industry vets with lots of contacts in the traditional media and among the online sites. They decide what to release to the press and when to release it.

In addition to getting attention to your game, Marketing and PR can also help draw attention to your company. If your studio is developing a game under a traditional publishing agreement, the publisher has no incentive to give you any press. The marketing they will produce will talk about the game and their role as publisher. Therefore, it is important for your company to work on promoting the game and promoting your company. Having name recognition with gamers will give you more leverage when it comes time to negotiate the next contract. This is one of the biggest secrets of the success of development studios like BioWare®.

Often, developers do not like the Marketing department, often associating them with the downfall of original thinking, but the fact is we need them to get the word out about our products and our companies. And, they are often gaming enthusiasts just like the rest of us. A good studio head, or employee for that matter, knows that a good Marketing and PR strategy can be just what the project and company need to be successful.

The Prospective Employee

The hiring process is long and often expensive. However, taking your time and being thorough can save you problems in the future. It is imperative that all prospective employees are screened for talent, experience, attitude, and references. It may sound paranoid and untrusting, but a great resume is easy to fake and the temptation is always there to embellish a bit to break into the notoriously hard-to-enter industry. However, if employers are diligent and patient, they can get the facts they need to make an informed decision. That being said, the process should not take too long. A highly skilled and experienced candidate is quite likely interviewing with many companies and will not be on the market for long.

Finding the Perfect Employee

Online job sites, while not specialized to the game industry, are a good place to find qualified candidates. While finding a game industry veteran's resume on a site like this is rare, you will find many resumes for entry-level candidates who have a great deal of relevant talent and skills but lack experience in the industry. This is particularly true among programmers and artists. Specialist sites, such as Gamasutra, which cover game industry jobs, are great places to begin your search for experienced talent and entry-level candidates.

Recruiters are gaining popularity as the game industry matures. They function much like an agent in Hollywood, actively seeking job opportunities for their talented clients. The one drawback of using a recruiter is that you end up paying the recruiter roughly 10 to 20% of the new employee's yearly salary for the find. This 10 to 20%, however, is sometimes deducted from what you pay the new employee in his first year. The fact that you do not have to find the potential employees is certainly a plus; the recruiter practically drops them at your door.

The ideal way to find employees, however, is through referrals by current employees and industry peers. The game business is one big family. Many of us know each other and have worked together on more than one occasion at different companies.

Phone Interviewing

A phone interview is the first step after reviewing a resume. The goal is to get to know more about candidates, and find out what they are like in a more spontaneous medium. The candidates should also learn more about the company and the job they are applying for. The phone interview is a way to share information without the cost or hassle of a visit.

When first preparing to interview potential employees, be sure to write down all the questions you want to ask them and have their resumes in front of you. If possible, check their references before beginning the phone interview process. This includes calling previous studios candidates have listed on their resumes and making sure they did, in fact, work there and were good employees. Do not expect those studios to say much about the employees if they were unhappy with their work. It can create legal problems for them to do so; however, it will be obvious to you if the employees were well liked and good workers because they will have much to say. As mothers often say, "if you don't have anything good to say, don't say anything at all."

It's a good idea to do more than one phone interview, so be sure to get everyone the candidate would be working for involved in at least one phone interview. For instance, an art candidate should be interviewed by the art lead and art director, and possibly by the producer and/or creative director.

During the phone interview, be as thorough as possible. Try to ask questions related to the type of work the candidate has done in the past and why he left previous positions, why he wants to leave the current position, why he wants to work for your company, and other such important questions. Try to get an idea of how skilled he is by asking what processes he uses in his job. Be prepared to respond to any questions candidates might have for you, as well. What they ask and how much they know about you can tell you a lot about how much they are interested in the position.

If the phone interviews go well, some studios issue a test. For designers, this test could be a sample of their work level design, writing, and so forth. For artists, the test might include asking them to do a concept or quick 3D model according to specifications. And for engineers, it might be a few puzzles to solve with code and some questions about the primary language they will use.

The In-Person Visit

Once a candidate has passed the initial reference checks, phone interviews and tests, it is time to meet him face to face and find out how he is in person. If a candidate is from out of town (and many of them most likely will be), it is typical for a studio to fly him in. Make arrangements as early as possible, and share details with the candidate. Set up interview times and events, such as lunch or dinner, before the interview to make the most efficient use of time.

The first thing you will need to do before a visit is determine when a candidate is available. He may still be working with another studio, and so will most likely want to come in on a Friday or Monday and have some of the visit on the weekend. Once you have picked a mutually available date to interview on, you will need to purchase three things: two-way airline fare, a motel room, and a car to take the candidate between the motel and airport. Depending on the level of industry experience and "fame" the candidate has, you may want to spend a little more on a nicer room and town car, or maybe even a limo if the candidate has a high enough profile. Treat him like a rockstar, he'll love it. Remember, you are most likely not the only employer interested in hiring him, especially if he has significant experience.

It is best for the candidate's flight to arrive in the evening. The rental car or hired car should be available at the airport. It is typical to have someone from the office pick the candidate up at the motel if he does not have a rental car; this person should have something to do with the hiring process. If you are serious about hiring this person already, you might want to schedule the departure flight for the following Monday (if the interview was on a Friday). Give the candidate time to drive around the area over the weekend to get to know the area. Arrange someone to "hang out" with him over the weekend if possible.

When the candidate gets to the office, put the candidate at ease by showing him around and introducing everyone. It is a small industry, and you never know when the candidate might already know another of your employees. Have interviews with any people who will be working directly over the employee, including, but not limited to, the lead, the director of the department, the producer, and other related managers. Most studios will even have time for the candidate to interact with the rest of the team in his department just to measure chemistry. At this stage in the process, you are impressed with the candidate's qualifications and are trying to find out if this person is someone the team can work with. Make sure you give the candidate a chance to ask questions. He will certainly want to know about working conditions, benefits, and so forth. Finally, be sure to take him out to a nice meal with a few key individuals. If you have planned it right, the candidate's return flight should be at least a few hours after the last meetings, giving him enough time to get to the airport comfortably, unless you have scheduled a full weekend for their visit.

Closing the Deal

Once you have decided to hire the person, it is time to make an offer. You should already have a good idea of what you want to pay and possibly a good idea of what the person expects as compensation. Treat this like any negotiation; start a little lower than you have planned. The person will likely start high. Hopefully, you will both be satisfied with the final agreed salary. You may want to include a signing bonus if the candidate is sufficiently qualified and in high demand. This signing bonus is traditionally around 75% of one month's salary, but may be higher or lower depending on the candidate. Once you have that number, it is time to write the offer letter. Do this on company letterhead and include the agreed upon salary, the position offered, the direct manager's name, a projected start date (based on discussion with the candidate), and any other important details. Mail a copy to the candidate and ask that he sign it as soon as possible and return it. A good time limit on an offer letter is around a week, but some situations may require more time.

From here, you will want to begin helping the new employee get to his new job. While you do not have to, it is always nice to help him find housing, even temporary lodging if needed. Many companies will pay for all moving expenses up to a certain maximum, which is usually around 10% of the yearly salary. These expenses typically include moving van, gas, airline tickets, motel stays, storage, and so forth. They rarely include food expenses or rent/deposits due to federal tax restrictions. Some companies will even pay realtor costs to help a new employee sell his home, and early lease termination fees to apartment complexes.

Finally, consider hiring all employees as "at will." This allows you to let them go without cause. While this may sound callous, it is the best practice if you want to protect yourself from wrongful termination lawsuits. But remember, even this is not enough if you do terminate an employee without proper justification. The next section on disciplinary action goes into greater detail on protecting yourself if you ever need to let someone go.

New Hire Paperwork

The following paperwork is the bare minimum you should have all new employees fill out. This paperwork should be put on file for each employee.

The NDA: All interviewing employees should sign a nondisclosure agreement if they will see sensitive or copyrighted materials during the interviewing process. New hires should also sign NDAs. The NDA prohibits them from revealing company trade secrets to anyone outside the company.

The Non-Compete: This document prohibits the employee from working on other projects that would compete with your company while he is employed there. Some non-competes go so far as to prohibit an employee from working on any other competing projects for as long as a year to five years prior to termination of his employment with your company.

Assignment of Inventions: This document indicates that all work created by an employee during his term of employment belongs entirely to the company. The employee assigns all rights of those works to the company. The document should also include a page for the employee to list any works he created prior to his employment to which the company does not have rights.

Tax and Worker Eligibility Forms: These are the standard tax and eligibility forms that all companies provide new hires upon employment. In the United States, these include forms I-9 and W-4. You will also need to get a copy of the new employee's driver's license and social security card or other acceptable forms of identification to fill out the proper forms.

Application: Not all companies use applications, but it is a good way to get important background information such as references.

Background Check: Again, not all companies use background checks, but this is essentially a document that allows the company to perform a criminal record check on employees before hiring them.

What to Pay

A well-compensated employee is a happy employee. Never underpay your employees; if you are not willing to pay people what they are worth, there is another company out there who probably will. If an employee feels like he is not being paid fairly, he will call a recruiter and, before you know it, he's gone. You will be short a skilled worker and potentially valuable team member, forcing you to either miss a deadline or make the other employees crunch to pick up the slack. Putting more stress on the remaining workers causes even more employees to feel unhappy, and runs the risk of causing more of them to leave. It becomes a vicious cycle!

Expected Pay Rates for 2007

According to a survey in the Fall 2005 *Game Developer Magazine*, the average salaries in the United States ranged from $64,000 in Texas to $76,000 in California. Bearing in mind that the following salaries are an average, Table 3.1 indicates what you can expect to pay each type of employee in the year 2007. These salaries, taken from the aforementioned 2005 survey, have been rounded to the nearest thousand dollars and adjusted for an average of 4% yearly pay raise in 2006 and 2007 (8% total) to get the result.

As you can see, engineers and producers are among the highest paid employees in the industry, while designers and artists are fairly close.

TABLE 3.1 Projected Salaries for 2007

	Entry Level	Veteran (6 years+)
Programming		
Engineer	$58,000	$92,000
Lead Engineer	$62,000	$100,000
Technical Director	$68,000	$124,000
Art		
Artist	$45,000	$69,000
Animator	$47,000	$78,000
Lead Artist	$69,000	$84,000
Design		
Game Designer	$47,000	$72,000
Lead Designer	$46,000	$84,000
Production		
Producer	$64,000	$88,000
Executive Producer	$56,000	$127,000
QA		
Tester	$35,000	$51,000
Lead Tester	$46,000	$64,000

Remember, these figures are an average of many employees throughout the whole of the United States. When deciding what to pay an employee, keep in mind cost of living and state taxes. It can cost as much as $10K to $20K more per year to live in most parts of California as it does in another state, so a salary of $50K in Texas would be similar to a salary of $60K to $70K in California. Online salary calculators can help you translate salaries from one part of the country to another.

Performance Reviews and Raises

The department heads should review the performance of employees that report to them on a regular basis, usually annually and toward the end of the year. Likewise, the producer should review the department heads. These reviews will be used to determine what, if any, pay raise an employee is eligible for. Typical yearly pay raises range anywhere from 2 to 10%, with the average being closer to 4% at many studios. The biggest factors in determining raise amounts are the employees' work performance and cost of living increases in the area. How hard did they work? How often were they at work? Did they work well with others? How creative were they? How enthusiastic? Did they make their milestones? Raises are an important tool for keeping employees satisfied, and should be included in the budget.

Independent Contractors

Independent contractors can be a blessing or a curse depending on the dictates of your project. A positive point that certainly stands out regarding contractors is that you only have to pay them while you need them. Traditional employees require pay and benefits even while they pace back and forth, waiting for the next project to come down the pipe. The best thing about independent contractors is that you can get all the work you need at the level of skill you expect without having to provide benefits, Social Security, or pay unemployment tax, among other things.

Independent contractors make their own hours, which can be a bit frustrating for a studio with set hours. You may not be able to discuss what you want with the contractor when you want to. Although they do adhere to deadlines, they can work when and where they want between accepting the project and turning it in. That point alone could turn some studios off the idea of working with a contractor. Another problem is that not every contractor uses the same technology as your studio. In fact, the likelihood of the contractor knowing your technology is slim, so instead of just handing over a project, and having it started immediately, there is a space of time where you are paying the contractor to learn your technology for the work to get done. This can be an expensive proposal, not to mention one that could cause you to miss your own deadlines.

Finally, there are many laws and regulations concerning independent contractors. See Chapter 11, "Taxation," for more information about the differences between employees and independent contractors.

Bonuses

Bonuses have become a standard way of showing appreciation for a job particularly well done. They come in many forms, the most common of which are milestone based. Milestone bonuses work on a simple formula: if an employee or department meets their milestone, that employee or department receives a bonus check on the next payday. Milestones are often quarterly, so you may ultimately end up paying out four of these bonuses per employee who met his milestone per year.

A merit bonus is similar to a milestone bonus, except that it is often awarded to specific employees for hard work and dedication beyond expectations. Keep in mind that not all studios offer such bonuses, and studios that offer milestone bonuses usually do not offer merit bonuses. If an employee who has gone above and beyond the call of duty, and you want to show him your appreciation, offer him a merit bonus privately in addition to more public recognition. As with other forms of praise or rewards, excessive attention can cause problems and jealousy, so tread carefully here.

The holiday or Christmas bonus is typical throughout many industries, including the game industry. Each employer is different and therefore the amount of this bonus varies. While every project is different and some have more financial backing than others do, a good starting point for any kind of bonus is somewhere around 2.5% of the employee's yearly salary per bonus. Other bonuses may include company gifts or even additional time off. Some places will give everyone the week between Christmas Day and New Year's Day off in appreciation for the work done over the previous months. This time does not count toward used vacation days.

Benefits

The following is a brief list of benefits a studio should consider offering its employees. Explaining how each one of these benefits works is an involved task and beyond the scope of this chapter. There are, however, many good sources to look for more detailed information on each subject, most available through a simple Internet search.

Stock

Stock is a way for a company to make an employee feel more like a partner and less like an employee. When an employee has stock in a company, he is more concerned with how well that company will do. The stock of a company that has already gone public can be more secure than one that has not; stock from a company that is already public can be traded, whereas the stock of a company that is still privately owned has no real value other than the sometimes arbitrary value assigned to it by the company itself for financial reasons, and cannot be traded yet. If an employee leaves a privately held company, that employee's stock is typically reabsorbed into the company's stock pool or redistributed among the remaining employees. On the other hand, if an employee leaves a publicly traded company, the stock he owns remains his until he sells it.

However, the stock from a company before it goes public can be especially appealing. After the initial public offering, the value of that stock can increase significantly. The tales of overnight millionaires still fill some people's heads despite the dot-com crash. Unfortunately, few game development companies go public, so this dream is not fulfilled often. However, this may change in the future.

The most common way to distribute stock is through stock options. This motivates the employee to stick with your company and make it successful so he can purchase stock in the future when his options vest. Think of it as a reverse bonus. Another way is through an Employee Stock Purchase Plan (ESPP), which allows employees to use a little bit of each paycheck to purchase stock at a usually discounted price.

Just be sure to consult your accountant before you start handing out stock or options, as there are different types of stock: those that qualify for tax breaks and those that do not. There may also be issues in tax law regarding issuing of your company's stock to your employees.

Profit Sharing

Profit sharing is the payment of royalties to an employee, and it is a way to keep those highly valued employees on staff. The company agrees to offer an employee a percentage of all the company's profits once the company is profitable. This percentage varies from employee to employee and should always be based on the length of time an employee has been with the company and that employee's overall contribution to the success of the project. Inform your employees that this information should be kept in strict confidentiality, as should the payout of other benefits such as stock options. It is easy for jealousy to arise as many employees may feel their contribution is greater than others.

Profit sharing can be an incredible retention tool for a successful studio. Employees who have worked on multiple projects can have profit sharing for many projects coming in simultaneously. This means the employee would have to make significantly more money at another job to match the total income from the current position.

401(k)

The 401(k) account, named after a section of the Internal Revenue Code covering this type of account, is an investment plan offered by many companies to their employees. The account must be set up by an employer and allows the employee to defer all taxes on the investment until withdrawal. Typically, an employee is allowed to choose to invest money in an assortment of mutual funds, which are a diversified investment. Money is taken directly from the employee's check each pay period and deposited into the 401(k) account.

This account is a benefit that helps your employees prepare for retirement, replacing the pensions paid by some companies in the past. Some companies, typically larger ones, will match whatever dollar amount an employee elects to put into his 401(k) each pay period up to a limit, or may contribute profit sharing into the 401(k). The great thing about a 401(k) is that it can follow an employee from job to job as long as the new job offers a 401(k), and the 401(k) may also be rolled over into an IRA account.

There are companies that specialize in setting up employee benefits such as 401(k) plans. Consult with your accountant for advice if you wish to offer such a benefit.

Insurance

Medical and dental insurance are almost a required employee benefit in any company. If your employees do not maintain their health, they will miss work and cost you money. There are many insurance providers and many plans such as PPOs and HMOs, and you will need to consult with providers to get all the facts. A good basic plan, though, will provide your employee with full coverage for his immediate family and low deductibles, and the option to choose either an HMO or PPO at the bare minimum. Some companies pay fully, while others expect the employee to cover some of the burden, although this is usually a very small percentage.

Other benefits may include vision or chiropractic insurance plans. You may want to consider offering a Cafeteria plan. This plan allows your employees to pick and choose the benefits they desire, much like they would pick the food they wish to eat at a cafeteria.

Company Culture

It's very important for your team to feel like a family, as these people will be working very closely for several years even on a single project. This is where company culture comes in. To foster good communication and keep your team happy, you should create attitudes and behaviors that foster a positive company culture.

For example, a game development team needs time to play and enjoy themselves. Regular outings could be paid for by the company, such as going to the movies and having company picnics. Try to do these things at least once a month to keep people happy together. Of course, you can play in the office just as easily as you can outside of it. If it is possible, providing a company game room or making the latest games available is always nice to help people enjoy themselves as a team. The key thing to realize here is that working for a game company is a different beast from a traditional 9-to-5 job. Pressures are extremely high and burnout rate is just as high. Make it your business to ensure that everyone is having a good time. Work hard, play hard. If people on your team are not taking time to enjoy themselves, encourage them to do so. Remind them that they work at a game company. They should not come to work feeling like they have to be chained to their desk, trudging away at all times. Obviously, you will want to do this in a friendly way.

Do not allow company divisions to form! There are many prima donnas out there, and it is the natural tendency for people to form social cliques. This type of behavior is bad for the studio. Everyone should make an effort to get to know each other and work well together. There is no room for arrogant developers who have a way of looking down their noses at the "lesser" employees. If you think someone is acting this way, remind him that game development is a team effort and that no one person can take all the credit, no matter how long he has been in the industry. If you sense that some of your developers are having a hard time fitting in, try to help them by inviting them out to lunch with you and some of the other teammates. Find ways to interject them into important conversations. You will be surprised at how much a little attention can brighten up an employee's day.

Another small, but appreciated, benefit is to keep the break room refrigerator stocked with soft drinks and bottled water. Some companies just have vending machines, but if you can, it is better to have a delivery service bring these items every week or so on the company budget as an additional bonus to your employees.

Rewards and Punishment

Giving Praise

Praise for a job well done never falls on deaf ears. People love the warm feeling they get when someone tells them they are doing a great job or that they are an integral part of the team. Some examples of good praise include a discreet pat on the back and a few words of kindness at their desk, a small announcement of how well someone did to those in his department during one of their regular meetings, a lunch paid for by the company, and ultimately monetary compensation in the form of merit bonuses.

Most of the time, praise should be given without grand fanfare. The last thing you want to do is make your other employees feel like they are not doing a good job, and publicly praising an individual too often may have the effect of isolating him from their peers as the teacher's pet. However, sometimes a good public praising is just what the doctor ordered, especially if it is for more than one person such as a department or entire team. When offering public praise, try to remember the rest of the team. Always add a little side note that "everyone is doing a great job" as well. And of course, they are!

Giving Discipline

Discipline is defined as, "training to produce a specific character or pattern of behavior, especially training that produces improvement." Many times, discipline either has a negative connotation or is the result of negative behavior. When an employee has stepped across the line in some way, such as missing work too often, missing deadlines, or other serious offenses, it becomes necessary to discipline him. These times require a firm hand with a delicate touch. Discipline should aim at helping an employee get back on track.

In most cases, discipline should be given privately. There is no need to humiliate an employee in front of his peers, and doing so is considered a breach of ethics. That being said, it is often a good idea to bring a second manager, preferably one who is over the employee either directly or indirectly, into the room when the discipline is being given. Doing so will help mitigate any future litigation problems that may arise. Having a witness to disciplinary action and keeping good records are steps toward ensuring you will not be sued for wrongful termination. Document all action taken, the cause of said action, and have the employee sign the document.

The Disciplinary Process

Typically, there are four levels of disciplinary action, taken in order of increasing severity: verbal warnings, write-ups, probation, and, failing those, termination. One might argue that termination is the failure of discipline; however, even termination can teach someone a valuable lesson.

Verbal warnings are the first step to any breaches of conduct by an employee. The employee should be called into his supervisor's office discreetly, at which time he should be informed politely and professionally that his inappropriate actions have been observed and what steps can be taken to rectify the situation. If appropriate, the employee should be asked if there is another problem causing his breach of conduct and if the company can help improve the situation. This initial warning should be as brief as possible while still providing the necessary information; nobody likes to sit in the hot seat for long. If the breach of conduct is severe enough, this step may be skipped all together.

Write-ups occur when the verbal warning was insufficient. A write-up is generally executed by the direct manager of the employee and usually only after several verbal warnings have been made, at the manager's discretion. Some severe problems, such as sexual harassment, might require a write-up on the first offense. The write-up is an official record of repeated breaches of conduct and a serious step in the disciplinary process. These write-ups will affect the employee's performance reviews. Again, the employee should be called into his supervisor's office, and the write-up should be explained in a calm and polite manner. Keep the meeting short and inform the employee of the seriousness of the write-up and the consequences of continued violations.

Probation may or may not be part of the write-up process. Some companies put an employee on immediate probation when the employee has been written up even once. The point of probation is to tell an employee that his conduct has become a problem and that the company is considering terminating his employment. The employee should be informed of the length of the probation—three to six months is a good guide—and told that he will be observed closely during this time. At the end of the period, the company will decide whether the employee improved enough to be allowed to stay with the company. Continued infractions during the probationary period may result in moving to more severe disciplinary actions even before the employee's probation has ended.

Termination is the final step in the disciplinary chain of events, when all attempts at improving an employee's conduct have failed. This is always a hard step for both management and employees alike. There are many well-written essays on the best way to accomplish termination of an employee, but the basics are that you should be as professional as possible and everything should be well documented. When terminating an employee, be sure you do so as discreetly as possible—both for his benefit and yours. The last thing you need is a big scene to cause disruptions among the rest of your employees, nor do you want to cause the employee being terminated any unnecessary embarrassment in front of former coworkers.

Termination of an employee can have huge consequences for the company in any number of ways, including possible litigation for wrongful termination, missed deadlines, morale problems, and other show-stopping events. Avoid termination of employees unless necessary, and then, do everything in your power to ensure the company has done its due diligence prior to termination to mitigate these problems. Also be mindful of the impact the termination can have on the rest of the team and be considerate of their needs during this time.

Staying in the Black

The game business is not regarded as a service industry (with the exception of MMO subscriptions). This means that a game company does not begin to make money until it has shipped a product (title), especially if it is a new studio being considered. Even then, the studio will not make any money until the game has sold enough units to pay back the original cost to produce, market, package, and ship the game. Regardless of all this, running a game business is no different from running any other business: you must have more income than you have expenses, or "stay in the black" in accounting terms. The key to staying in the black is planning.

Write a Business Plan

The first step in any good business, games included, is a business plan. A good business plan lays out your entire strategy to potential investors, your managers, and yourself. You do not need a lawyer or business major to write one of these; just do a little research at your local library and online and you will find all you need to write an effective business plan. The plan should obviously be customized to your studio's individual goals, and should include items such as risk analysis, which tells everyone what risks are associated with your studio's goals, and how you plan to overcome those risks. Some other topics your plan should, at a minimum, include are discussed next.

The Market
- Who is your audience and how will you reach them?
- What is the state of the industry and how will you fit in?
- Where is all the money going?

The Competition
- What other projects are possible competitors?
- How is your project unique?

The Bottom Line
- What are your company's expected revenues and when can you expect them?
- How much is the project going to cost?
- Include a current and pro forma balance sheet, income statement, and cash flow analysis.

The Product
- What are your company's goals, both long and short term?
- What is your exit strategy?

The Team
- Who is your core team?
- What have they worked on in the past?
- What has your team worked on together?

A good business plan is mandatory when starting any kind of business because it presents all the information necessary to evaluate the company, even internally. The importance of one of these cannot be stressed enough.

Get a Good Accountant and a Good Lawyer

Whether you have one on staff or simply consult one regularly, find a good and trustworthy accountant. When you are dealing with large amounts of money, such as is the case in funding a video game of even moderate size and quality, you need someone to keep track of the books. Your accountant will make sure to keep track of all income and expenditures, and keep you up to date so you avoid going over your budget. He will also alert you to any problems he may see over the horizon. An accountant will also help protect you from the ire of the IRS. More information can be found in Chapter 11.

That being said, do not let your accountant go very long, maybe not even one week, without seeing you. Have regular meetings to go over the numbers. Make sure there is a paper trail for all transactions on file. The last thing you need is for your accountant to make some huge mistake that sends your budget tumbling out of control. And believe it or not, there are some dishonest people out there, accountants included, who will rob you blind if you do not pay constant attention to your money.

A lawyer is the person to protect you from everyone else. Counseling is a lot cheaper than litigation, and having a lawyer on retainer is not as expensive as you might think. Try to find a lawyer with game industry experience, particularly one with contract negotiation skills and experience with intellectual property (IP) rights. You can usually find one or someone who knows one by asking around at game conventions, or by looking at contributors to this book.

Budget with a Capital B

If there is one thing that will help you stay in the black, it is a well-tracked budget. A company that does not have a budget will be bad with money. Your accountant will keep track of the budget, probably using Excel, QuickBooks, or similar applications, but make sure as studio head that you understand and keep a sharp eye on the budget.

There are two different budgets we are most concerned with: the proposed budget of the project and the running budget. The proposed budget is more of a plan and is used to show investors and publishers what it will cost them for you to produce a game. It should include every dollar amount your business plans to spend on each project, from money spent on soft drinks to employee salaries to software licenses and so on. If it is not in the budget, you will not be able to get it later without finding a way to raise more money or take money from another area. Be sure to include yearly employee raises and bonuses in the budget too; it is surprising how many studios overlook these types of items and do not plan appropriately.

You will probably want to have two versions of this budget: one for yourself, which includes all the details, and one for investors and publishers that only breaks the budget down into primary categories (salary, software, office expenses, etc.). If a publisher would like to see more detail, offer them your version. Bear in mind one simple truth when writing your proposed budget: investors do not appreciate being asked for more money because the original investment was not enough. This shows lack of planning on your part and can spell doom for their investment. If you do ask for more money, they will often negotiate much harder and require more concessions when providing additional investment money. So, put a great deal of thought into the budget and make sure you do not have to ask for more money later.

What is a good budget for a startup? It depends on your strategy, but bear in mind that most investors are looking for companies that have long-term plans. In the game industry, this means plans to do more than one title. A new studio often does not make money until it has released a few games. It takes time for gamers to learn about a new studio and its titles. Therefore, unless you plan to be a one-hit wonder, it is sound advice to budget for more than one title. Doing so will also help ensure your employees that you will be able to keep them fed and sheltered for more than a few years. Finally, once you have your budget planned, increase it by as much as 1.5 times the amount you think you need. Chances are you will need that extra cushion.

The running budget is where you keep track of expenditures as your business operates. Spent $1,000 to fly in a new candidate for interviews? Took the company out to a movie? Bought a dozen 3ds Max™ licenses? Record all these costs in the running budget, or at least give your accountant the receipts to do so. The running budget allows you to see where you stand in relation to the initial project budget. It helps you ensure you don't go over budget and helps you spot possible problems before they hit.

If It Can Go Wrong, It Will

There are, of course, a few other considerations to keep in mind that will help you maintain "positive cash flow." First, do not make your budget so tight it squeaks. Give yourself some cushion, as mentioned previously. Investors will understand because they know that things do not always go as expected, and regardless of the best-laid plans, we always forget something. This leads us into the next nugget of wisdom. Plan for everything to go wrong! If it can happen, it will. If you do not plan for problems in your budget, you will never be able to cope with them when they inevitably arise. Employees quit. People have personal problems. Service providers go out of business. People try to sue you for violating their IP. The list of possible problems goes on and on. Ideally, you should address these types of risks in your business plan and provide for them in your budget. However, that is not always possible. You cannot hope to cover everything, but investors want to know that you are at least thinking ahead. Doing so will show them that you are serious about ensuring them a return on their investment.

Measuring Your Success

A great plan only works if you follow it. This means you need to have regular meetings with your management team to review your efforts in the context of the plan. But how will you know if you are on track? The answer is metrics. Metrics are milestones placed at key points on the development time line and in the business plan that you can use to track your progress.

Some examples of metrics include:

- Have full staff hired by 2nd quarter of operation after initial investment.
- Complete preproduction by 3rd quarter of operation after initial investment.
- Complete 1st level (art, encounters, code) by September 25, 2007.
- Have playable demo of game by a major conference 2008.
- Complete Project X by the end of 3rd quarter, 2008.

The preceding line items are just examples, and your metrics will be relative to your project. Metrics such as these will be an invaluable tool to ensure your project and company are on track. These metrics can be as detailed and drilled down as you need them and should cover every aspect of the development pipeline. For your business plan, metrics will most likely be broad and cover only top-level events such as hiring staff, completing projects, and so forth. For a project's plan, the metrics will be much more detailed and should include everything from concept art deadlines to level design deadlines, code, and so on.

Beware of Pitfalls!

A few things can destroy the best efforts of a good plan. Beware feature creep! And do not be afraid to cut features if it looks like you have been too optimistic in your design (and you almost certainly have been). Finally, keep in mind the myth of the man-month as described by Fred Brooks. People can only work so much in a year before falling to pieces, and throwing more manpower at a project that is already behind may actually make it worse.

How to Save Money

...on Employees

Salaries and benefits will probably be your biggest expenses. You may be able to find some young people fresh out of college, but highly skilled game developers demand and deserve good wages. But that does not mean you cannot find ways to save a little money on your needs. The best way to do this is to tap the resources of your company's fans and, even better, your local college.

Enthusiastic fans are usually willing to work for free if they can somehow get their name associated with your company and project. Be clear: we are not talking about exploitation in the negative, and potentially illegal, sense of the word. What we are talking about is offering some of your more talented fans a chance to help make their favorite future game a reality. Obviously, there is only so much this type of resource can give, but every little bit helps when you are trying to stay afloat. Keep in mind that many people do not really understand game development, and they might be disappointed when they learn the job is not as glamorous as they had first hoped.

Interns from local schools are the next, and often best, method of saving money on employees. Many schools today offer game development courses, and even the ones that do not often have students in computer graphics and programming courses who aspire to get into the game industry. All you need to do to tap into this powerful resource is to head over to those schools and talk with the internship department. You will find that the people there are usually more than happy to get your company involved with their school. Before you know it, they will be asking you to come down and give talks to their bright-eyed students. While interns usually cannot provide you with the skill set of an industry veteran, they are certainly eager to do as much as they can for you in the interest of gaining valuable industry experience—something they all need to land that first job.

...on Marketing and PR

Marketing is a tricky beast, but one you will want to master, especially if you are operating on limited funding and cannot afford a full Marketing and PR department. For a small upstart, proper PR can open doors like you would not believe. Assuming your company has very little funding, there are some types of marketing that can keep your studio in the limelight long enough to land those investor dollars that will turn your B title into a triple-A blockbuster.

Word of mouth is probably the best marketing for your investment. The idea is simple: you tell people about your game, they tell others, and those others tell more. This is where traveling to conventions and handing out business cards and one-sheets about your company can help. Do not just dump them on the conference floors, though; be sure to hand them out to people who really show some interest. Always be ready to talk about your company to people. You will find yourself saying the same thing over and over in your dreams, but your efforts here will multiply in a magical way. Better yet, find one or two of those enthusiastic fans and let them spread the gospel of your company. You probably will not even have to ask them to do so.

Having a quality *Web site* these days is a must. Every day, more people sign on to the Internet as a primary way to find things such as news, weather, driving directions, and entertainment. Invest a good deal of time and/or money into a top-notch Web site. Set up a forum for your returning visitors to gossip about your game, and make a habit of responding to them. Put as much information about your game and company on the site as you can without giving too much away too soon. Unless they have already spotted you on the radar, send out emails to all the major gaming Web sites to inform them of your Web presence. You may also want to invest a little money into having a Web site company that specializes in getting your site ranked high on search engines.

Getting good PR on a *game Web site* can also be a great way to get some notice. Game Web sites love a scrappy little developer, and you can often get interviewed to talk about your company and project with very little prodding. Having your key developers create content for fans and news sites can keep you being talked about. Other resources, such as developer diaries, can give you good visibility as well.

...on Tech

If you are not one of those companies that can afford to license the latest version of the Unreal or Quake engines, there are dozens of free and cheap game engines out there. You will find open source engines for just about every aspect of game development: physics engines, pathing engines, AI, graphics, and so forth. You can also find engines out there that are extremely cheap, such as Torque from GarageGames.com, which runs a very affordable $100 per seat for the basic engine. And don't let the price fool you, this engine (and others like it) is highly adaptable and comes with modern pixel shader support among other things, and a vibrant community and great support. See *http://www.GarageGames.com/* for more detailed information on licensing Torque.

Seeking Out Opportunities

Unfortunately, you probably cannot sit back and expect opportunities to come to you unless you have an incredibly impressive background. For the rest of us, company managers have to find opportunities or make them themselves if they want the company to grow and succeed. The good news is that once you start finding and successfully engaging opportunities, they will begin to multiply. The real trick in the beginning is finding those opportunities. The game industry is smaller than you might think, and if you stick with it long enough, someone you have met or worked with is bound to show up again later, and you never know what he or she will be doing. This is where good networking will help you land those opportunities, both personal ones and opportunities for your company.

Networking—How and Where

Take every opportunity you can to meet new people in the business. The easiest way to meet new other developers is to walk right up to them and introduce yourself as a fellow developer. Ask them if they have any advice to offer someone who is starting/ running his own studio. If it is in a casual setting, offer to buy them a drink. And be sure to keep quiet and really listen to everything they have to say. Show a genuine interest in them and try to find out about them and what they do. Be humble; do not brag about your plans to take over the world. Nobody likes an ego, even if your company is destined to be the next biggest thing in the industry. Honestly, they have probably heard it many times before from other inexperienced people.

The next thing you know, they will be introducing you to others they know. Every once in a while, you will make that magic contact that starts introducing you to people all over the country and throwing great opportunities your way. Soon, you will be wheeling and dealing with people who have been doing this since the days of the Commodore 64, being offered to take on small projects, and writing books about the game business.

So where do you find these people to network with? Great places to start are game conventions. It can be expensive to fly all over the country to attend them, but doing so can have great return on your investment. You will find game industry veterans from all over at these conventions and most of them are more than willing to offer some free advice to newcomers, even if it is only one nugget of wisdom. Do not be surprised, though, to find yourself in an hour-long conversation filled with 24-karat chunks of pure game business gold. Be sure to attend Game Developer's Conference (GDC) if you have not before. For online game developers, the Austin Game Conference is another great opportunity. Conferences like these offer great networking opportunities both during the conference and after hours. At GDC, you will find a lot of "famous" developers hanging out afterward in the bar or hotel lobby.

You should also try to attend your local IGDA (Independent Game Developer's Association—*www.igda.org*) meetings if there are any in your city. These meetings are usually held in a restaurant or bar and you never know who is going to show up. Do not just try to schmooze with the old timers, and be sure to talk with other newcomers such as yourself. For all you know, you might be talking to the next Will Wright or Warren Spector, or someone who shares your vision and would love to work with you. The game business is heavily family oriented, meaning that we help each other as much as we can. Do not just network for your own selfish reasons; find people newer than yourself and offer them advice to get where you are. Once you start making those contacts, be sure you let everyone know what your studio specializes in and that your people are ready and able for any opportunities that might come your way.

Smaller opportunities can easily begin to multiply so fast that you may find you need to hire more staff. And smaller opportunities can begin to lead to larger ones once your studio has proven itself. Just remember your manpower limits when taking on opportunities. The last thing you want to do is commit to something you cannot make happen due to resource limitations. You will quickly develop a reputation for biting off more than you can chew throughout the industry.

Maintaining Your Company's Independence

One of the goals most people starting game companies have is to remain independent. In this age of dominant large publishers, huge game development companies, and large mergers, it can be hard to stay independent. Here are a few tips to help you stay independent despite the odds.

Keep Your IP Rights (and Other Fairy Tales)

Sadly, it is rarely possible in a traditional publishing deal for a game development company to be able to keep some Intellectual Property (IP) like copyright to code and some control over licensing and advertising/marketing approval. It does happen on occasion, however.

To cover yourself on the off chance that your funding is pulled, consider having IP re-purchase options built into contracts from the beginning and, if you are really serious about keeping your IP, consider alternative financing means, such as venture capital firms or angel investors. Just make sure you are prepared for large portions of your company's profits to go to the investors and to fight for marketing, as publishers tend to spend less marketing dollars on a project in which they are not fully invested.

Chapter 7, "Intellectual Property" can provide you with more information on the details of IP and how to protect it.

Do Not Sign a Contract If You Do Not Like the Terms

Do not let contract negotiations intimidate you. Negotiations are standard practice, and you will soon find that everyone negotiates. There is no such thing as a "standard" contract given the wide variety of situations in the game industry.

In the end, however, there are only so many concessions a publisher will offer. Unless you are self-funded, you will most likely not be able to keep your IP, and most publisher deals will not begin to assign royalties to you until they have recouped the costs to market and produce the game. Do not expect to get a better deal here, especially if this is your first major project.

Have your lawyer look over the contract before signing anything, and be prepared to negotiate your contracts for months or even years in the worst cases. It surprises many people to learn that business moves incredibly slow. However, it is worth taking the time to ensure you are getting the best deal you can get. Ask for advice on the contract from other industry veterans who have dealt with publisher contracts before. They can help you determine if you're getting the best deal you can.

You will find more in-depth information on contracts and contract law in Chapter 4, "Contracts—A Brief Overview."

Knowing When to Expand

It is the dream of all business owners for their business to expand and grow, taking on more projects and more responsibilities. It can be very exciting to realize that your company has grown from a few friends in a garage to occupying most of the floor in an office building. However, it is important to grow at the right pace.

Do Not Grow Too Fast

Expansion is not always necessary for continued success. If you are still working on your first project as a company, chances are you are not ready to expand until you have released the first title, also known as "Going Gold." Even then, you may have to dedicate some resources to supporting the title after launch if there are patches to be made. It is important not to outgrow your resources, particularly your income.

Is expansion in your business plan? If not, then stay where you are until you can reevaluate your plan. If you are comfortable where you are, there may be no need to expand. Whichever you decide, to expand or not, be sure that your business plan reflects your decision. It may need to be rewritten, and a new round of funding may be needed to facilitate expansion.

When to Expand

You may find that you do not have enough personnel to finish a project. This should not necessarily be seen as a sign that expansion is needed, but is rather a symptom of poor planning. Your best course of action in this situation is to begin cutting features to fit the workforce you do have.

It is very easy to bite off more than you can chew when you begin the long road to expansion. Make sure funding is in place for the second project before you seek funding for the expansion itself and, remember, running one project is seemingly easy, but the management difficulty of each new project you take on grows significantly.

Conclusion

You have the knowledge necessary to run your business on a day-to-day basis. Handling employees will consume most of your time, but it can be very rewarding to build a good team that creates quality products. Knowing how to attract and hire quality employees, how to treat employees right, and knowing how to handle problem employees can help you along to this goal. Having great management to lead your employees is the final ingredient for your success.

Budgeting and planning for your business are also vital for keeping your company in operation. Attracting investment, spending within your means, and keeping on schedule without resorting to crunch time are vital steps in accomplishing your goals. You also need to network, seek out opportunities, and know when to expand.

Now is the time to go apply this knowledge. Start planning your company and take the steps necessary to succeed.

CHAPTER 4

Contracts—A Brief Overview

Matthew Hector

matthector@comcast.net

Contracts may not be the most fascinating subject to the lay public, and many people probably dismiss contracts as legal mumbo-jumbo that lawyers write to be as confusing as possible. However, the truth of the matter is that contracts touch our daily lives more than one might expect. They are, in fact, everywhere.

Contracts Basics

Look at your average day and you will be surprised at how many contracts affect your life on a daily basis. If you take public transit to work, the fine print that explains transfers on your transit ticket may be a contract. If you drive to work, your choices as a driver may affect your insurance policy, which is also a contract. If you buy a cup of coffee, you are entering into a contract with the seller of the coffee. If you tell the kid down the street that you will pay him $10.00 to mow your lawn, you have, again, just entered into a contract. Every time you use your credit card or debit card, you are subject to a contract.

Since the lion's share of the information in this chapter is based on U.S. law, readers located outside the United States would be wise to consult an attorney or solicitor in their home jurisdictions. This is especially important because contract law is, on a narrower scale, *state* law. Patent law is federal law so it is the same in every state. The rules for consideration and many other concepts concerning contract law throughout this chapter are expressed as general rules and they are often true, but can vary between states. Keep this in mind when working with your attorneys and with parties in other states. With so many different versions of contract law, it is good that people can pick which state's law will control the interpretation of a contract. This "choosing" of state law is important and is discussed in detail later.

What Is a Contract?

Most contracts are rather mundane compared to the types of contracts used in the video game industry. For example, the contract formed between a customer buying coffee and the Starbucks franchise is rather simple. By purchasing an extra hot, half caff, half skim, half soy latte, you have accepted an offer to enter into a contract (and likely annoyed the barista). You buy it; they'll make it. Included in the unwritten contract is the warranty that the coffee is fit for human consumption. This implied warranty does not normally matter to the average consumer. If it turns out the coffee is defective and harms the customer, that warranty becomes very important. Certainly, if you find a stray appendage in your latte, you will want to be reimbursed for your hassle.

The reason why most people do not realize that their coffee purchases are indeed contracts is that there is no meaningful bargaining taking place. In the first day of contracts class, aspiring attorneys are taught that a contract is a bargained-for exchange. In the coffee example, there really is no room to haggle. If you try to convince the coffee shop employee to give you a cheaper rate on your latte, odds are that you will not be successful. In many contract situations, you have little to no bargaining power. Unfortunately, game development contracts often fall into this category. For most retail sales, this is also the case. The consumer's bargaining power involves voting with his or her wallet. The same is true with many service contracts, and in the case of utilities, you may have no bargaining power, and therefore, no choice whatsoever.

When both parties to a contract have bargaining power, it is important to know how contracts are formed. As noted previously, a contract is a bargained-for exchange. What this means is that there is both an offer to enter into a contract and an acceptance of that offer. Sometimes, the path to agreement is longer than that, with parties exchanging offers and counteroffers. Certain exceptions may apply, depending on whether the contract is governed by statutory or common law. At the end of the day, a valid contract has an accepted offer and consideration.

What Is Consideration?

Consideration, quite simply, is an exchange of value between the parties. This is not to say that anything a person can claim as valuable is consideration. While one may feel that things like "love and affection" and "goodwill" are valuable, they are not consideration because they are not things for which one can normally bargain. A homeowner may pay a painter in U.S. dollars in exchange for the painter's labor and material costs. If both parties agreed, the homeowner could give the painter an antique car for the work. However, the homeowner's promise of love and affection in exchange for the painter's work, in addition to being potentially socially awkward, is probably not qualified as consideration in terms of contract law. In the games industry, people are generally paid cash for their efforts; for all practical purposes, consideration or the lack of consideration rarely comes into play.

When Is a Contract Formed?

To form a legally binding contract, it is not always necessary that the terms be in writing. With a few exceptions, almost any contract is binding, whether it is oral or written. Telling a friend, "I'd sell my car for a beer," could be the first step to creating a contract. The friend must simply accept the offer and hand over a beer. At that point, the thirsty party is most likely obligated to give up the car. Unfortunately for the friend, it is unlikely that a court would force the speaker to perform without more evidence than the friend's own testimony. Oral contracts are, admittedly, rather difficult to prove. However, an oral contract with subsequent conduct could indicate parties' intentions to enter into a bargained-for exchange. To put it simply, actions may speak louder than words.

In practice, every contract regarding a game development project should be in writing. If those contracts are poorly drafted, the conduct of the parties may be used to decide what should fill in the gaps. It is always wise to be as comprehensive and thorough as possible in the written agreement at the start of a project; this approach will save time and confusion should any conflict arise down the road. For example, a contract between a studio and an artist may not specify how both parties are to communicate with each other. If, historically, all communications were done either face to face or via email, and the artist decides to communicate with the studio via smoke signal, then the studio does not have reason to accept or expect that form of communication. Sometimes, the common actions of others in the industry are used to interpret vague clauses. Careful drafting can help all parties avoid future hassle. Careful reading can help catch errors before contracts are signed. Careful attention to detail by the parties and drafting attorneys is critical.

Unfortunately, most contracts are drafted in such a way that prevents most people from reading them. While some attorneys and legal writing professors advocate a move toward plain language in legal documents, certain legal terms of art- and industry-specific terms will always be necessary. Moreover, most contracts are not drafted in plain language. A good attorney should be able to interpret even the most Byzantine contract, but it is helpful to know contract law basics to help communicate your preferences more effectively. Knowing the key legal terms in this chapter helps demystify these long, tedious documents.

Reading and understanding contracts is especially important because you need to know how to properly describe what you want. A contract cannot truly embody the terms of the agreement and limit later confusion unless you understand it. Understanding some contracts may allow you to make strategic decisions; for example, it may be wiser to breach a contract and pay a pre-determined penalty than remain in that contract and suffer a greater harm from undesirable external circumstances. Similarly, if you fail to complete one of your contractual obligations on time, the contract may provide you a grace period to bring your performance into compliance. Being able to refer back to an old contract and find the proper clause yourself could save the expense of having to refer to your attorney. However, after finding this clause, you should send it to your attorney as a sample of what you want when creating a contract. It is never advisable to practice law yourself, because saving several hundred dollars in attorney's fees on this end of the contract often costs thousands or hundreds of thousands later. Would you take out your own appendix, even if you had a book telling you exactly how to do it? Drafting contracts is similar, even though many people in the game industry pretend otherwise.

Basic contract knowledge is especially important in the games industry, because the vast majority of the industry's transactions are handled by contracts. In addition to the agreement or agreements between a development studio and a publisher, there are privacy policies—End User License Agreements (EULA), Terms of Service (TOS), and intellectual property (IP) licenses, to name a few. There is a staggering number of "back end" contracts that get business done, such as independent contractor agreements, employment contracts, pre-incorporation agreements, non-disclosure agreements (NDAs), and service contracts with telecommunications companies. Getting business done requires a lot of paperwork.

To make matters worse, the games industry is young enough that there are few established practices, so interpreting poorly drafted contracts may be trickier than normal. Some agreements may contain page upon page of stock, or "boilerplate" language. Others may vary depending on the relative bargaining power of a specific party. The contract between an unproven development studio and an A-list publisher will look very different from that between a team made up of the latest wunderkinds and the same publisher. While it is always important to have an attorney review contracts and help negotiate modifications, a good understanding of contracts and how they impact the games industry can provide anyone with a definite competitive advantage.

Overview of Common Contract Terms

Some contracts are just simply ugly. They can be hard to read, have sections in ALL CAPS, use plenty of jargon, and seem to play hide the ball. Being able to recognize single words or phrases and extrapolate a general meaning from them will make contract reading easier. Attention to detail is also important, since some commonly used terms look similar but serve different legal functions. This fact is especially true when dealing with boilerplate contracts, where parties are defined via generic terms.

When a form, or boilerplate, contract is used, parties are often designated by a common root word ending in either –ee or –or, depending on the role of the party. For example, in a licensing agreement, the licensor is the person or entity that is giving the license. The licensee is the person who is obtaining the license for use in a game or other project. In general, the party with the –or suffix owns something or possesses rights of which the party with the –ee suffix wishes to make beneficial use. Unfortunately, this is not always the case. For instance, if your development company were to buy property and obtain a mortgage to pay for the land, it would be the mortgagor, with the bank as mortgagee. If you are ever in doubt, there are legal dictionaries available for free online use to help clarify terms.

Advances

Another tricky set of terms is generally used in reference to advances. An advance is simply money paid from publisher to developer before the product is complete. However, the type of advance makes a world of difference for the developer. A recoupable advance is one where the publisher is paid back by taking a certain portion of the developer's royalties. It is not unusual to see little to no royalties paid to a developer until the entirety of the recoupable advance is paid off, but it ultimately depends on the bargaining power of the developer and the publisher. It may be possible to negotiate an escalating royalty that allows the publisher to recoup costs early, but still provide a modest cash flow to the developer. As the publisher sells more units, the cash to the developer increases as the publisher recoups development costs until the maximum royalty rate is achieved after the publisher completely recoups its costs. This recoupment mechanism takes longer to pay off the publisher, but is often desirable for developers who want to avoid a period completely without cash flow.

Do not confuse recoupable advances with repayable or recoverable advances. At first glance, the terms do not seem that different. Both imply that the *advancer* can recover funds from the *advancee* at some point. However, the way the advance is recovered varies significantly. With repayable and recoverable advances, the publisher is entitled to recover the entire amount of the advance, even if the publisher never sells a single copy of the product. Essentially, the advancee is on the hook for the entire amount of the advance, even if that means paying it back out of pocket. If possible, avoid recoverable/repayable advances at all costs. This type of advance is rare in the games industry. Similar to the term "cross-collateralization" discussed next, this onerous term is in some development contracts.

Cross-Collateralization

A careful reader will also pay attention to language that hints at cross-collateralization. Quite simply, cross-collateralization allows a publisher to recoup, recover, or repay the advance for one project from the royalties from another project. Publishers often want cross-collateralization because it provides the large financial benefit of distributing investment risk over multiple projects. This concept originated in the record industry and is still seen occasionally in the games industry. Be careful; this will generally appear in the contract language that discusses advances. The actual word, "cross-collateralization," may not appear in the text of the contract, but the language will refer to advances being paid back in connection with other projects.

Publishers commonly seek cross-collateralization when the same game is being developed for simultaneous release on multiple platforms. Assume that Hypothetical Developer, LLC is making a game for Big Publisher, Inc., which is to be released for the PC and two competing consoles. Each ported version of the title will be sold and tallied separately. Cross-collateralization allows the publisher to essentially treat each version as the same, paying off advances from the profits of whichever title it can. Other, less developer-friendly uses of cross-collateralization also exist, and are discussed later.

Gross and Net

Contracts also contain other financial provisions, and there are many ways of structuring payment. First, it is handy to know the difference between "gross" and "net." When tabulating sales, profit and the like, the difference between these two terms is usually rather large. For example, gross receipts do not represent the actual money received by the publisher. Gross receipts (or sales, or profits) could be the sum total of every register receipt for each unit of product sold. Net receipts or net sales are the amount of gross receipts less several costs. Some costs, such as taxes, manufacturing, shipping, licensing, and returns are standard. However, other costs, such as marketing and advertising, third-party license fees, and the maximum manufacturing cost may be negotiable. With enough bargaining power, some of the "standard" costs are themselves negotiable. Suffice it to say that net receipts and net sales are represented by a smaller number than the one used for gross. This definition and the calculation of any royalty numbers that depend on it is probably the single most critical area of negotiation for any game development contract.

Assignments and Sublicenses

Understanding the difference between an assignment and a sublicense is also helpful when reading or negotiating contracts. In legal parlance, an assignment is a complete transfer of contractual rights or duties to a third party. The assignor is removed from the equation entirely, putting the assignee in his shoes. A sublicense transfers specific contractual rights or duties to a third party. The sublicensor still plays a role in the overall deal, bearing final responsibility to the other principal party. In development contracts, publishers do not want developers to go around assigning or sublicensing things without approval, and the contract will reflect that. Publishers will often keep their options open for sublicenses, especially when distribution of a title takes place worldwide. In fact, it is necessary for publishers to sublicense for international distribution (see Chapter 10, "Selling Internationally"). A publisher launching an MMO title will probably have different companies handling the release in the United States, Europe, and Asia. In such a situation, the developer or publisher may even have the limited right to sublicense the translation work associated with various localizations of the game.

Termination and Breach of Contract

Most development contracts also discuss two types of termination—for either cause or convenience. The effect of these clauses is to determine what happens when a party terminates the contract before it is completed. A termination for convenience is when one party seeks to break the contract solely for "personal reasons." This breach could be a chance to capitalize on a better deal or more interesting project. Termination for cause occurs when the other party breaches the contract or fails to meet its obligations. The basic idea behind these termination clauses is to restore the nonacting party to its original position. For example, if a publisher terminates a contract for convenience, one should not expect to see the developer losing money. If the publisher terminates for cause, do not expect to see the developer get off the hook cheaply. Sometimes, it may make sense to terminate a contract. These clauses will tell you what happens if you decide to go that route.

Failure to perform any obligation within a contract, unless the party is legally excused from performance of it, is called a "breach." As mentioned previously, terminating a contract "for cause" usually refers to the decision to terminate a contract based on another party's breach. There are two types of breach, "material" and "immaterial." Material breach is generally a cause for termination of the contract, while immaterial breach is not. Material breaches involve elements of the contract that are essential to performing the duties described in the contract itself. Immaterial breaches still violate a term of the contract, but are usually curable and do not prevent the contract from going forward. Knowing whether a party's breach is material or immaterial is essential to making the decision to terminate a contract.

For example, if Sam and Dave agree that Sam will paint Dave's house blue, and then Sam paints it red, Sam has breached the contract. In this situation, Dave could sue Sam for damages associated with his house being painted the wrong color. This type of breach, without more, generally does not trigger a "for cause" termination.

Generally speaking, material breach is an entirely different beast. Much like all squares are rectangles, but not all rectangles are squares, all material breaches are breaches, but not all breaches are material. A material breach is so severe that it involves an essential element of the contract. For instance, missing a milestone by one day may not be a material breach. Agreeing to make a game in a high-fantasy setting, but instead, delivering a science fiction title, is a material breach. Breaches that can or do cause substantial harm or that can or do deprive the other party of a substantial benefit of the contract are also material. If a development studio uses IP that it does not own and has not licensed without informing the publisher, that action is most likely a material breach of the contract. Finally, material breach can be anything the parties define in the contract as material. If the contract states, "Failing to use the Times New Roman font in design documents will be considered a material breach," the parties have then bound themselves to that standard. Even though being one minute late is most likely immaterial, if the contract itself defines that type of breach as material, then it is a material breach. To this extent, be careful when drafting and negotiating contracts. Defining a relatively minor breach as material may come back to haunt you.

In the case of material breach, the nonbreaching party is entitled to damages, and may also cease performance of its duties and consider the contract terminated. In addition to termination clauses, contracts often allow for a notice and cure period to ease the blow of material breaches. Typically, the nonbreaching party will provide the breaching party with notice of the material breach. The breaching party then has a set amount of time to "cure" the breach by meeting the contract's terms. Notice and cure language is important, because it is generally easier to allow the breaching party to fix its mistake than it is to terminate the contract and find a new party to finish the deal. It also allows the breaching party a chance to fix problems and maintain the contract.

Indemnification

Some mistakes cannot be fixed, and some can expose a company party to lawsuits. For those situations, there is indemnification. Indemnification is essentially a promise to step into the shoes of the party being sued. When a developer provides its own game engine for a publisher's project, part of the IP license contains assurances that the developer is the rightful owner of the game engine. In addition to that promise, the developer usually agrees to indemnify the publisher against any claims arising from the use of the engine. If a copyright claim were filed against the publisher, the developer would take the publisher's place in the litigation, hire attorneys, and defend the claim. Sometimes, these clauses also stipulate various conditions wherein a settlement must be accepted, or else the indemnifying party is off the hook.

Indemnification language is present in every development contract. It is often one-sided and there is a good reason for this. Consider the basic structure of the game development deal. The developer creates the game, including all of the IP associated with the game, and the publisher provides money, advertising, and distribution.

Consider what each party brings to the table when determining liability, which is the whole reason for indemnification. Money from the publisher is never found infringing of anything or liable for anything. However, the developer provides the game itself and all the associated IP. Here is where the risk lies: improperly licensed open source code, stolen code, characters, story, or music can all lead to liability.

Indemnification language is often coupled with representations and warranties. Representations and warranties are a set of disclosures and promises on the part of both parties, most importantly, the developer. For instance, a development contract may include a representation of what third-party technology the developer is using, along with a warranty that all third-party technology is owned by, licensed, or assigned to the developer. If the developer provides its own game engine, there may be warranties that the engine itself is wholly the developer's own creation. If a publisher hires a developer to design a game based on a specific license, the publisher may provide a warranty that it is allowed to sublicense or assign its development duties pursuant to the license to the developer. Make sure you are not making promises you cannot keep. These clauses seem standard, but they are important.

Choice of Law, Arbitration, and Equitable Relief Clauses

Tucked away at the end of most contracts are a handful of clauses that many people gloss over, but they certainly merit discussion. Choice of law clauses state which state or country's laws apply to govern any dispute arising under the contract. Choice of venue clauses dictate which specific jurisdiction within a state is the proper venue for filing a lawsuit. For instance, Southern California–based publishers may push for a choice of law clause where California law governs the contract, and a choice of venue clause that makes the state and federal courts in Los Angeles the proper venue. These clauses are used to avoid jurisdiction and venue-based issues at trial. It is important to note that these clauses usually choose a state and venue jurisdiction that has some rational relationship to the parties of the contract. If the developer is based in Illinois and the publisher is based in California, choosing Massachusetts as the forum state may be improper. In this case, look to the home states of the parties for valid forum state candidates. Choice of venue clauses should be drafted given similar consideration.

Finally, keep an eye out for arbitration and equitable relief clauses. Arbitration clauses are generally enforceable, as long as they are not patently unfair to either party. The Federal Arbitration Act adds strength to most arbitration clauses, making the decisions of arbitration panels enforceable by court order. Arbitration is steadily gaining popularity, especially in the entertainment industry. It save the costs of expensive and lengthy litigation, and can often resolve disputes without engendering the bad feelings sometimes caused by a full-blown trial. Moreover, work does not have to come to a halt while the dispute is litigated. Arbitration often allows development to continue while the issues are hammered out by the arbitration panel. The American Arbitration Association website has sample rules and guidelines that its panels use. However, parties can agree to different rules if they wish. This flexibility is another factor that makes arbitration popular.

Another remedy discussed in some contracts is equitable relief. In addition to, or instead of, money damages, a party can ask the court to force the opposing party to do or stop doing a specific activity. Generally, clauses that can invoke this type of action bear a heading that reads, "equitable relief" or "injunctive relief." These clauses frequently appear in NDAs, noncompetition agreements, and other contracts that deal with secrets. Equitable relief is essentially obtaining a "court order." A common example is a restraining order. When the court orders Sam to stay at least 500 feet away from Dave at all times, that is a form of equitable relief. When a court orders a publisher to stop selling a particular game due to misappropriated IP, that is also a form of equitable relief. Equitable relief is used when monetary damages are impossible to calculate, or could not possibly make a party whole again. The most common type of equitable relief in the games industry is called an "injunction." The term for a party that has an injunction against it is an "enjoined" party. An injunction prevents a party from doing a certain act such as selling a game. Clearly, an injunction is a powerful litigation tool, and any clauses that implicate an injunction should be thoroughly considered.

In addition to development contracts, NDAs often have equitable relief clauses. If Hypothetical Developer, LLC has a revolutionary new game engine and wants to show it to Big Publisher, Inc., it may use an NDA to keep its new engine under wraps. Closely guarded trade secrets are worthless if they are exposed to the public at large. The harm created by their exposure is irreparable. To better protect secrets, contracts can include equitable relief language. The party being told the secret agrees that, if it was to breach the contract, equitable relief is the only appropriate remedy. Since it is entirely possible to relinquish elements of one's legal rights via contract, these clauses often amount to an agreement to be enjoined without arguing the merits in court.

While the preceding section is not exhaustive, it covers the majority of common terms and concepts you'll encounter in the contract negotiation process. Keep in mind that a good attorney will be invaluable for helping you understand particularly tedious clauses. Knowing some of the basics gives you a starting point for early negotiations, which may be more easily (and inexpensively!) done between the parties.

Controlling Legal Fees Associated with Contracts

Attorneys are also often asked how much a certain contract will cost. That depends greatly on three items: first, the complexity of the deal; second, the amount of value involved in the transaction; and third, the negotiation/drafting mechanism employed. Some of these factors are more easily controlled than others. The third factor often adds the most cost, but fortunately, it is also the most easily controlled.

The complexity of the deal and the amount of value involved in the transaction should be considered together because they often depend on each other. A $3,000 work-for-hire agreement with a contract artist is handled differently than a $40,000,000 MMO development deal with parties on three continents. In terms of the contract, value could include stock, potential royalty streams, IP rights, and other less tangible elements that all come into the picture when deal value is considered. In short, it should be intuitive that as value, number of parties, deal terms, countries, currencies, and the like increase, the cost of negotiating and drafting the contract goes up.

The third factor in contract cost is negotiating and drafting structure. This is probably the most important factor in adding cost to any deal. Drafting and negotiating structure means knowing what you as a party want from the deal knowing exactly how negotiation with the other party will be done and how the drafting of the documents will be done.

As the name implies, the drafting and negotiating structure has two responsibilities: drafting and negotiating. As a party, decide early who has the authority to draft and who has the authority to negotiate a deal. It is possible to convey the most critical deal points to attorneys and have them draft and negotiate the entire deal. The attorneys communicate with the primary parties when critical or unexpected issues are raised. This is often done and can be very efficient, particularly if the party has a long relationship with the attorney with a mutual understanding of what is important to each other.

Another efficient mechanism is to have business representatives from the primary parties negotiate the deal points thoroughly and then hand these off to attorneys to draft. If the businesspeople have thoroughly negotiated the deal, the points will be firm and very little will be left to interpretation or negotiation. A related method used for repetitive small value deals is to use a prior agreement edited in-house and reviewed by an attorney. This variant of the previous mechanism is efficient for common, low-value transactions.

Unfortunately, the following method is the most common and expensive method for negotiating a contract. The business parties either deliberately or mistakenly leave large elements of the deal unnegotiated. This is a critical mistake, because the drafting is then rendered much more difficult. For example, dollar amounts are negotiated, but payment structure is left out. Often, after following up, the parties are not able to agree on the unnegotiated terms and attorneys are forced to guess, or insert standard contract language into the agreement. After several rounds of negotiation and drafting, to help clean up the deal, the documents are then edited in-house just to polish them to save on the escalating legal cost. This last-minute editing and passing between the parties who are usually not well informed about the negotiation history, leading to errors getting into the agreement concerning ground previously covered.

Even though this is so common, it does not have to work this way. Saving money by editing the final drafts in-house can be very costly down the road. If the agreement is to be negotiated in-house, do that from the beginning. If outside counsel are trusted to negotiate the deal from the beginning, allow them to finish the negotiation. Keep in mind that the only binding document is the last one everyone signs. Saving a few percent on the last few drafts by changing the negotiating mechanism, but allowing the other party to manipulate critical deal terms is not worth it. Does it make sense to have your attorney read the first 25 drafts, but not the last one?

Following is a summary of three critical points about drafting and negotiating structure to prevent your company from making the mistakes just discussed.

Know what you want as a party to a contract. Know what is not as important to you and what you are willing to give up. It is never as simple as X dollars. Is the venue clause important to you, or warranties, indemnification, escalating royalty structure, New York Law versus California Law, on being paid in U.S. dollars versus yen? These are just a few of the parts of a contract that can become more important than just the monetary payout. What elements of the deal, including and beyond money, are important enough to negotiate for?

Know who has authority to make decisions. Avoid internal disputes by working this out in advance. It is embarrassing, and yet it happens often, that people must backpedal or re-open issues after they have been over-ruled internally. It damages credibility and leads to re-drafting, which increases cost.

Be consistent in the drafting and negotiating structure. Changing the process mid-stream almost always results in a weaker deal for the party that changes the mechanism. Do not have attorneys draft the first 25 versions of a $40,000,000 deal and then take the documents in-house for the last three drafts to just polish up the document based on the last few rounds of negotiation. Do not switch negotiators or authority figures halfway through the deal for the same reasons. You lose consistency and credibility. Tremendous mistakes can be made in the name of economy or perceived urgency.

Non-Disclosure Agreements

A non-disclosure agreement (NDA) is used to protect trade secrets and to generally keep people from sharing information about specific subjects. Some gamers may be familiar with NDAs in the context of the beta test. These NDAs are somewhat effective in preventing early release of information about the nascent game system. These agreements are also useful when someone wants to protect business-related information presented to a third party.

Sam runs a small development studio with a secret new game engine that includes revolutionary character AI. In the course of developing a game for Dave, the publisher, Sam realizes that he needs to create a few localizations of the game. Sam does not have any staff capable of doing the necessary translation work, so he hires Wilson to assist him. Sam does not want Wilson discussing the finer points of the game engine with anyone outside his studio, so he has Wilson sign an NDA. If Wilson were to violate the NDA, Sam would be able to use equitable relief, as discussed previously, to enjoin him from discussing it with anyone else and probably punish him in other ways as well, including fines that both parties agreed on in the contract.

Sometimes, it is necessary to keep your employees from divulging your company's secrets, even after they leave your employ. NDAs can extend beyond the period of employment, and while it is possible to contract for any time period, only the most durable secrets should be protected forever. Many software-based secrets may be obsolete in a matter of months. Others, like the secret formula for a popular soft drink, may always be valuable as long as they remain secret. When drafting NDAs, keep the nature of the secret in mind. A court is more likely to enforce an agreement where the duration reasonably fits the type of secret. In the previous example of Sam, Dave, and Wilson, Sam's revolutionary new character AI will be valuable until similar technology is developed separately by a competitor. A duration of two to three years is probably sufficient in a case like this.

In addition to keeping others from divulging corporate secrets, NDAs also help companies control copies of their work product. Most NDAs have provisions that require the recipient of materials to return them on demand, or to destroy them if asked. Failure to do so would constitute a breach of the agreement, triggering the remedies clauses. One equitable remedy that would be appropriate in such a situation is specific performance. Specific performance is much like it sounds; the court simply orders someone to do a specific thing. Since it is easy to monitor the return or destruction of property, it is likely that a court would issue such an order.

NDAs are almost universally enforced via equitable remedies as defined previously. This is because the secrets protected by NDAs only have value if they remain secret. It is difficult, if not impossible, to determine what monetary damages would compensate for a revealed trade secret. Similarly, it would be nigh impossible to determine the monetary impact of negative word of mouth from early beta reports based on incomplete information. In these situations, it may ultimately be necessary to seek an injunction. Although it may seem excessive to seek an injunction against a loose-lipped beta tester, if that tester also writes for a media outlet, simply revoking beta access may not be enough.

The following is a sample non-disclosure agreement:

Confidentiality and Non-Disclosure Agreement

This agreement is entered into by Disclosing Party (Secrets McGee) and
_____ (Receiving Party) on this ___ day of _____, 20___.

1. Confidential Information

Confidential information includes, but is not limited to, any and all proprietary information, source code, writings, verbal statements and disclosures, computer programs, manuals, computer displays or screen captures of displays, any and all marketing or business plans, lists of actual or potential suppliers, distributors, or customers, and any other information that Secrets McGee has taken all reasonable efforts under the circumstances to maintain its secrecy or confidentiality.

2. Disclosure

Secrets McGee has invested significant time and money to develop all disclosed information and has treated the information as confidential and wishes that said information remains confidential. Receiving Party may not disclose any information provided to it by Secrets McGee to any third parties under any circumstances. If information must be disclosed to a third party to facilitate Receiving Party's duties and obligations to Secrets McGee, Secrets McGee will disclose the information to the third party for the Receiving Party.

3. Rights in Disclosed Information

Secrets McGee retains all rights to any information disclosed to Receiving Party. Receiving Party will not use any information disclosed by Secrets McGee to its own benefit or for the benefit of others. The Receiving Party acknowledges that it will take every reasonable step to keep disclosed information confidential. Receiving Party will not copy or reproduce any disclosed information in any fashion, except for those copies that are necessary for Receiving Party to perform its duties toward Secrets McGee (for example, installing software on Receiving Party's computers).

4. Duty to Preserve Confidentiality

Receiving Party agrees to exercise utmost care to protect the secrecy of all information disclosed by Secrets McGee. Receiving Party shall not disclose any confidential information to any third parties for any reason. Receiving Party agrees that any employees or agents who receive confidential information will sign non-disclosure agreements that provide Receiving Party the power to enforce this agreement.

Receiving Party shall return all disclosed confidential information and any copies to Secrets McGee within thirty (30) days of receipt of a written request by Secrets McGee. All copies of any nature, in any media, must be returned to Secrets McGee.

→

5. Duration, Termination

Receiving Party will not disclose any confidential information for a period of two (2) years from the date of disclosure to Receiving Party. Even if Receiving Party and Secrets McGee terminate their other relationships prior to the two (2) year period's end, this agreement remains in full force and effect. This Agreement cannot be terminated, except in writing by Secrets McGee.

6. Equitable Relief, Choice of Law

Receiving Party agrees that any breach of Confidentiality would result in irreparable harm to Secrets McGee, providing Secrets McGee without an adequate remedy at law. Receiving Party further agrees that it waives any bond, cash or other, that a court of equity may wish to impose if Secrets McGee seeks injunctive relief against Receiving Party for any breach of this agreement. Receiving Party also agrees that preliminary injunction or other equitable relief is proper for any breach of this agreement.

This Agreement shall be governed by the laws of the State of California. Receiving Party and Secrets McGee agree that the exclusive jurisdiction and venue for any action, suit, or proceeding based on any matter, claim, or controversy arising hereunder or relating hereto shall be in the state or federal courts located in the State of California and County of Los Angeles.

Aside from signature lines at the bottom, this is what a non-disclosure agreement would look like. This sample is a bit "boilerplate," but it is drafted in as much plain language as possible. The definition of what is confidential information is broad, partially so that this would be a reusable agreement for most of Secret McGee's needs. It is also broad to keep the Receiving Party from having too much wiggle room. Although most people think of NDAs as simply limiting someone's ability to talk about a subject, the next few clauses of the sample indicate just the opposite. In addition to not disclosing any information, the Receiving Party cannot make copies of the information, and has a duty to bind its employees and associates to similar agreements. This means that if an employee of the Receiving Party violates the agreement, the Receiving Party is the one legally responsible for the disclosure.

This agreement's equitable relief clause is clearly marked. Sometimes, one may encounter the same language in a section similar to number four, "Duty to Preserve Confidentiality." The choice of law clause may also be a bit hidden in other agreements. In some agreements, a section with the heading, "Miscellaneous," can contain several sub-clauses that have widely varying legal effects. Every part of the contract is important; do not skim simply because the title is dismissive!

Employment Contracts

Unless you are a one-person studio, odds are that you will eventually need to hire some people to help do the heavy lifting. If things go well, you might even need support staff! You will be elated to discover that contracts play a big part in this segment of the industry as well. In addition to independent contractor agreements, sometimes regular employees have contracts as well. In some extreme cases, employees may even argue that an employment contract existed where you never intended for one to exist! Since employees and independent contractors are treated differently for tax purposes, the distinction between the two is important. More information about tax can be found in Chapter 11, "Taxation." Moreover, the differences between employees and independent contractors create specific advantages and disadvantages for employers. For instance, when employees are hired to create software, the software they create as employees is considered a "work for hire." This means that, in the eyes of the law, the employer is the creator of the software. The convenience this creates cannot be understated. If an employee is terminated, there are no concerns about the company retaining the rights to work created by that employee. Since all employee work is owned and "created" by the employer, employees are not entitled to royalties or other compensation beyond their paychecks and benefits.

Independent Contractors

Although employees have distinct advantages, sometimes it is cost-effective to hire independent contractors. Employers do not have to pay withholding taxes for independent contractors, making paying them much simpler. Additionally, independent contractors generally provide their own tools, reducing the need for office infrastructure.

Since they are bound by contract, the conditions for terminating independent contractors are solely up to the parties. On the other side of the coin, employers have much less control over how an independent contractor does his job. In fact, exerting too much control over an independent contractor may create an employer-employee relationship.

When drafting an independent contractor agreement, be sure to keep the fine line between employee and independent contractor very clear. For instance, it is smart to include a section that outlines the relationship between the parties. This section includes an explicit statement that any relationship between the parties is not an offer of employment and that the contractor is not entitled to health care or other benefits. Moreover, it is wise to describe exactly how much control the employer may exert over the contractor. If you want your independent contractors to attend weekly meetings at your offices, it would be wise to add in language reflecting that. It is important that you make clear that while you will not direct the contractor in the performance of his duties, it is reasonable for you to dictate what the contractor creates. If you contract with an artist to design several handcrafted game areas, it is entirely reasonable that you dictate what genre of game those areas must fit. However, you generally cannot dictate what hours the contractor must work or assign new duties to the contractor without additional agreements.

Another concern about independent contractors is that the work they do may not be a "work for hire" because they are not employees, and because the types of works that may be commissioned as "for hire" are very limited. For this reason, some independent contractor agreements are incredibly complex and lengthy, with clauses assigning IP rights in all work created by the contractor, providing warranties that all work is original, and promising to indemnify the employer in the event of a lawsuit. Although authorship does not vest in the employer, this relationship has a distinct advantage to the employer-employee relationship. When an employee steals IP in the course of his or her employment, the employer is most likely liable for the employee's action. This is not the case with an independent contractor who agrees to indemnify the employer.

When drafting independent contractor agreements for content creators, it is essential that those contractors indemnify you for any IP theft, defamation, or other legal issues that may arise as a result of the work done. It is also important to acquire any rights in work created by the contractor. Ideally, you want a wholesale transfer of any and all rights in the content. This way, you are free to exploit the work in whatever way you choose while minimizing the risk of the contractor challenging ownership or requiring additional compensation.

It may turn out that some positions are better filled by employees, and that others are best served by independent contractors. Support staff, coders, and other content creators could be employees, with testers/QA staff as independent contractors in a typical development company. Translators hired to do localizations make perfect independent contractors since they are only needed for a short period of time. If you elect to hire short-term employees, it may be useful to have an employment contract.

"At Will" Employees

In many states, employees without an employment contract are considered "at will" employees. These employees are free to quit whenever they choose and employers are free to terminate employees for any reason. However, sometimes it is advantageous to have employees who work pursuant to an employment contract. Such a contract would establish duties, salary, confidentiality requirements, non-competition, and conditions for termination. When an employee has an enumerated list of actions that will result in termination, that employee can only be terminated "for cause." Odds are that you will keep support staff, like receptionists, on an "at will" basis. Upper-level employees may be better candidates for employment contracts. In addition to their exposure to sensitive corporate information, losing them to a competitor is generally more damaging.

For example, Celebrity McGameDesigner leaves his current employer and founds his own studio. He quickly assembles a development team and begins work on a new game. Development progresses rapidly and the new company launches the game shortly after Celebrity McGameDesigner's former employer launched a very similar game. Because the newer game is associated with Celebrity McGameDesigner's name, it sells well, most likely diluting the sales for his former employer. Situations like this are why employers should consider using non-competition agreements in their employee contracts.

Non-competition Agreements

Non-competition agreements are tricky contracts because they must be drafted very carefully and with great precision. In some states, they are nearly unenforceable. Public policy weighs heavily against hampering someone's ability to earn a living. As a result, some professionals cannot be bound by non-competition agreements. Game designers, programmers, and artists are not part of this group. Although most employees a game company retains can be bound by a non-competition agreement, the agreement itself must be reasonable. In general, courts look at the geographic and temporal scope of the agreement to determine whether it is enforceable. Keep in mind that many potential employees may not want to sign a non-competition agreement. Unless you are working with high-visibility "celebrity" designers and the like, it is probably not necessary to waste resources drafting non-competition agreements for every single employee.

All employment contracts require a large amount of detail work that is beyond the scope of this chapter. Whether hiring an independent contractor or an employee with a contract, it is important to consult an attorney for assistance in drafting agreements that comply with the laws in your state. Much of employment law, like general contract law, is state law. Therefore, the rules regarding employment contracts can vary from state to state. This issue makes the sample contracts available on the Internet a potentially unsafe proposition. While hiring an attorney to draft the agreements for you may cost money, it also is money well spent if it can help prevent later legal problems.

Intellectual Property Licensing and Assignments

Your company can make additional money on the strength of your licensing contracts. Licensing IP from a publisher or third party, licensing your technology to other companies, and similar agreements can be very profitable for the company. Read Chapter 7, "Intellectual Property," for more information about IP with detailed definitions and explanations. Also note Chapter 8, "Licensing Intellectual Property," with details on licensing IP from third parties and licensing your IP to other parties. This section will deal with the aspects of licensing important in considering contracts.

Licensing versus Assignment

Although some people tend to lump them together, licenses and assignments are functionally different. Although they were discussed in a different context earlier, IP licensing and assignments work similarly. A license generally conveys the right to use someone's IP, but does not completely transfer that right from the IP owner to the licensee. An assignment, on the other hand, seeks to convey the entire interest in someone's IP to another person.

Certainly, having someone assign his IP to you is a great deal. However, an assignment should carry a hefty price tag to reflect the nature of the transaction. On the other hand, a license may not cost as much, if anything, besides a cut of royalties. If you are the one assigning or licensing your own IP, it usually makes more sense to license it so you can still retain some level of control. Moreover, the owners of valuable IP may be unwilling to fully assign their ownership to someone else. Keep in mind that licenses are flexible. They can be "non-exclusive" or "exclusive," meaning that the person licensing the property to a company may or may not be able to license it to another company. Licenses can also come with a large variety of control, rendering some strong licenses very similar to assignments and some weak licenses similar to no property right at all.

One important thing to keep in mind when reviewing contracts is that language that assigns or transfers IP can be present in contracts that may not normally contain such language. One example would be independent contractor agreements—not every agreement has IP language, but some do. Moreover, IP licenses are not just used to create games based on film, television, and literary franchises. IP licensing also deals with technology from game engines to source code and development kits. If a development studio is making games for a specific game console, odds are that studio also has some kind of licensing agreement with the console manufacturer.

End User License Agreements

End User License Agreements (EULAs) are licenses between the maker of a game and its users. Since loading a game on your computer or game console creates a copy of the software, these licenses exist to keep players from running afoul of the law. Some of these agreements also claim IP rights in content created by players. This claim takes the form of an assignment of IP rights from the player to the licensor.

EULAs are generally revocable at any time for any reason, and have been widely upheld by courts as valid. In the case of *ProCD, Inc. v. Zeidenberg*[1], the U.S. Court of Appeals for the Seventh Circuit held that "shrinkwrap" licenses were valid and enforceable. The court found that since purchasers had notice of the license on the outside of the package, and an opportunity to return the product after purchase, the contract itself was enforceable. It also pointed out that software purchases are not the only type of transaction where the detailed contract terms are not communicated before purchase, listing other examples such as insurance purchases, concert tickets, and movie tickets. Shrinkwrap licenses are essentially the same as the EULAs that most games currently use. In a game-specific case, *Davidson & Associates v. Internet Gateway*[2], the U.S. District Court for the Eastern District of Missouri held that EULAs and Terms of Use (TOUs) were both enforceable. In its analysis, the court indicated that EULAs might be more enforceable than their shrinkwrap counterparts because they require some amount of interaction with the consumer. Clicking on the "I Agree" button is an affirmative action that indicates agreement. On appeal, the *Davidson* case did not revisit whether EULAs and TOUs are enforceable. To this extent, it seems that, barring a unique situation, these agreements are generally valid. Courts will consider EULAs and TOUs on an individual basis. If a specific agreement is unenforceable for a particular reason, it does not mean they are generally unenforceable.

Other license agreements that deserve mention are fan site license agreements and game modification ("mod") license agreements. Player communities help drive sales, and sales are key to eventually collecting royalties. To this extent, it is important to provide your fan base with tools to create websites dedicated to the game (fan sites) that may use some of your logos and other content that may be protected by copyright or trademark.

Trademarks are especially important to protect, because failing to enforce your trademark rights can lead to your trademark being revoked. For example, Xerox periodically runs ads asking people to call the act of using one of their machines "photocopying" instead of "Xeroxing." If "Xeroxing" became a verb in common usage, the company's trademarked name would become a generic term and no longer enjoy protection as a trademark.

Game mod license agreements are another way to help build community around your games. Moreover, some popular game mods like Counter-Strike™, a modification of the game Half-Life®, have become their own games. These agreements are designed to provide players with the tools needed to create their own maps, items, and rules for the modified games. Since a developer or publisher wants to retain your rights in the game itself, these licenses convey a very small amount of rights. Some may claim that all mods created are owned by the game developer/publisher, or that the developer/publisher has a right to use the mod for purposes of promoting the game. Like most licenses, it is important to draft these licenses with care.

Publishing and Developer Contracts

The contracts most people think about in relationship to the games industry are publishing and developer contracts. Without these contracts, games would not be made or distributed. As this section demonstrates, publishers tend to have the upper hand in negotiating these agreements. Knowing what bargaining points are "must haves" and which are less important can help you focus on fighting only the most important battles. Keep in mind that there are plenty of developers looking for publishers, so if your negotiation tactics short-circuit the process, you may lose the deal entirely.

As a developer, a perfect deal may be very difficult to get. Although you bring talent and expertise to the table, publishers are the ones risking a cash investment, and they consider that more important. However, the publisher's monetary concerns do not mean a developer should not try to get the best deal possible. Some bargaining points may be impossible to win on, but it is important to decide what factors are the most crucial for your company.

Payments and Royalties

Since a studio cannot exist without money to pay the bills, it is only natural that two very crucial factors in negotiating an agreement involve calculating payments of royalties. As discussed previously, cross-collateralization may be a factor in royalty calculation. Ideally, for the developer, nothing will be cross-collateralized because it makes it more difficult to pay off an advance and receive royalties on your game. This is especially true when the cross-collateralized titles are not at all related. For instance, if you are developing a fantasy role-playing game and an auto racing game for the same publisher, royalties might take longer to accrue, or you might never see royalties. Since cross-collateralization allows the publisher to retain a revenue stream to pay off advances, if one title sells well, and one does not, the more popular title may end up simply paying back the development costs for the less popular game. Publishers will want to use cross-collateralization to protect their investments made with a single developer.

Recoupable, Repayable, and Recoverable Advances

Another crucial bargaining point is whether advances are recoupable or repayable/recoverable. Repayable/recoverable advances are due to the publisher regardless of whether the game is a hit or a flop. This is essentially a no-brainer for a developer since repayable advances are a significant financial risk for any developer, especially for small studios that are just starting out. A failed game could lead to significant out-of-pocket expenses that can sink a small studio without much reserve cash. Moreover, these types of advances give the publisher little incentive to fully support the game, since its money can be recovered regardless of whether the game is profitable. Some publishers may insist on this clause to protect their investment. Recoupable advances, paid from royalties received, are ultimately the fairest to the developer. A recoupable advance is not due to the publisher if the game flops. The only way for a publisher to get its money back is to actually sell your game. In most cases, a developer should try to get a recoupable advance, not one that is repayable or recoverable.

Receipts and Deductible Expenses

Another significant financial consideration for negotiating development and publishing agreements is how the receipts are calculated. As you may recall from the previous discussion of the difference between gross and net receipts, net receipts are the amount of money remaining after various expenses are paid from the gross receipts. Royalties cannot be calculated until these deductions are made. The key is to understand what determines the net income and the percentage paid on that amount.

The negotiations for payment hinge on what expenses are deducted from the gross receipts. For instance, the costs of taxes and distribution are reasonable deductions. These costs are the cost of doing business, and demanding they not be deducted can easily kill a deal. Another reasonable deduction is for returned merchandise. Since returned merchandise does not generate profit, it is difficult to argue against this deduction. Be careful with returned merchandise deductions, however. Some publishers may want to hold a percentage of receipts in reserve to cover unexpected returns. While it may be impossible to prevent this, a reserve fund for returned games may not be necessary after the first six months of a game's life cycle. Hopefully, the game will have the rare opportunity to have a life cycle longer than six months. Moreover, the percentage of receipts held back usually does not exceed 25%. Some publishers may require a higher percentage closer to retail launch, and may then be willing to decrease the percentage on a quarterly basis.

Other categories of expenses deducted from gross receipts may include manufacturing costs, marketing costs, and license fees. License fees are a fair deduction when the publisher has to pay a third party such as a console manufacturer. If the publisher also owns the console manufacturer, this deduction may be unfair and there may be negotiating room here. Keep in mind that the console manufacturer and the publisher may be owned by the same parent company, but they are *not* the same company. The console manufacturer sends a bill to the publisher just like any other client, and the publisher has to pay the bill. Hopefully, this is a discounted invoice and the publisher may be able to pass these costs savings on to the developer. Manufacturing costs cover the cost of packaging and media. It is not unusual for this deduction to be present, but try to get a hard cap per unit—special packaging for various "editions" of a game can often be more expensive than you think. For the most part, however, manufacturing costs are fair deductions.

Marketing costs, on the other hand, are not something most developers want to pay. Marketing costs are arguably one of the most expensive costs associated with releasing a game, as large amounts of money are spent on print and television ads. Deducting these costs from the gross receipts severely cuts into the royalties a developer can earn, and can push the point where developers receive royalties into the distant future. If forced to deduct marketing costs, a developer should at least try to limit the costs to a few items within the heading, as opposed to the entire sum. Some argue that marketing costs should be borne by the publisher completely. The key here is to make sure that however this aspect of the negotiation comes out, the chances of success for the game are not harmed. A minimal marketing budget can kill a potentially great game as fast or faster than development problems.

Another bargaining point in determining gross and net receipts is what number is initially used for the gross receipts. Generally, publishers push for actual cash received. A developer ideally wants net receipts to be calculated based on accrual—cash expected based on units shipped. Publishers generally win this fight, since the developer is essentially asking for gross receipts to be calculated from money that has not yet been received.

Milestones

Another exceptionally important bargaining point is the way the development or publisher contract handles milestones. Milestones are future dates when a specific stage of game development must be completed to the satisfaction of the publisher. They also determine when advance payments are issued and sometimes determine whether the contract goes forward or is terminated. When setting the dates for milestones, developers should attempt to calculate some room for error. You never know when an unexpected disaster or changed requirements result in missing a crucial milestone.

Milestones should involve a process in which the developer submits the deliverable, and the publisher has a specified amount of time to review it and submit changes. In a developer-friendly contract, if the publisher does not respond to the milestone deliverable submission with changes within the time allowed, the next milestone payment is due, but the publisher can still request changes. If the publisher requests changes, the developer usually has a specific amount of time to make the changes and resubmit the deliverable. Depending on the terms of the contract, this time period may be the only chance the developer has to fix the problem before the contract is terminated. The more bargaining power a developer has, the more attempts it can demand.

It is also important that the particular requirements of the deliverables be sufficiently and specifically defined to avoid the need for multiple fixes. Since failure to properly deliver a milestone can result in termination, it is in the interest of the developer and the publisher that the requirements for each deliverable are clear. Although the publisher may not lose money by terminating the contract with the developer, it will lose time trying to find a new developer to either restart or continue with the project. Well-defined milestones can help prevent this.

In addition to well-defined milestones, there should also be a well-defined milestone approval process. Both parties should know the following items with complete clarity:

When are milestones submitted? Simply put, when do these come to the publisher, and is that date a date for mailing or a date for receipt?

What do those milestones consist of exactly? As mentioned previously, the publisher should be completely clear about what the developer is producing.

How will those milestones be tested for compliance? To the extent possible, milestones should consist of objectively testable attributes. This will save many headaches over artistic differences later.

How long does the publisher have to approve or deny a milestone? This keeps publishers from sitting on milestones for months while they get around to evaluating it.

What happens if a publisher takes too long to approve or deny a milestone? If the publisher takes too long, they should pay at least a part of the upcoming milestone payment so the developer can keep moving ahead and meet payroll.

How much time is allowed for, and what is the general process to correct a milestone? What happens on the publisher's end when a milestone is submitted? What is the process and where are the potential hold-ups? If the publisher is evaluating the developer's work, it is only fair for the developer to know what the tests and processes are.

Who is responsible at the publisher for approving or denying the milestone? Is one person ultimately responsible for giving the go-ahead to cut the milestone check? Does the milestone need to go through a committee or group? No matter what, some person or "named position" within the publisher should be responsible for the milestone payment. In short, this is the person the developer calls to discuss the process if there are any problems or questions.

How long after approval is a milestone paid? If the milestone is approved, but it takes 120 days to make the payment, the developer can still go out of business.

The Realities of Negotiation

It is important to understand that the negotiation process will never go 100% in favor of any developer. The nature of the games industry dictates that some concessions have to be made to the publisher since they hold a majority of the bargaining power. To this extent, it is necessary to consider your track record as a developer. If your studio is new and unproven, it does not have much bargaining power. Studios that have produced a few titles bargain better than unproven studios; those that have produced blockbuster titles can probably afford to make some demands beyond the standard agreements. However, small victories such as managing to get a recoupable advance as opposed to a recoverable or repayable one may be a major victory for a startup game studio.

Here it is appropriate to address a special case that is common in the industry. Four guys leave old game company after just finishing "Biggest Hit Game Ever." Do not delude yourself into believing that these four guys from "Biggest Hit Game Ever" are going to be treated as if they were still in the old company. The previous company made "Biggest Hit Game Ever" and those guys helped, but that is not the same thing as the new company, even if one of the people starting the new game company carried the title of "lead designer" at the old company. The editors and authors of this chapter have actually seen situations exactly like this, where a few people from "Biggest Hit Game Ever" put in a half-page game design document and requested six-figure signing bonuses as part of the initial funding of their company and new game project. It may take some shaking and slapping to persuade a person with a swollen ego of the reality of the situation, but it is true that many elements are actually working against these people starting a new game company. Perhaps as many as 20 to 60 other people helped make that game, too. There may have been brand loyalty and a license involved. Moreover, the old company might get jealous of new-found success and bring a case against the new company for breaching an NDA, employment agreement, or stealing trade secrets. This type of conflict is even more likely if the new game company's game is successful and perhaps in a similar market as "Biggest Hit Game Ever." There are many risks in starting a new game company and for a publisher picking employees that left the company that made "Biggest Hit Game Ever." Do not fall into the trap of believing the emigrant developers deserve a sweetheart deal right off the bat. Yes, the new studio is better than a studio with no track record at all, but the new studio has special legal and financial risks as well.

Finally, keep in mind that although a developer may not get the best terms, it is important to take a serious look at the contract to keep it realistic. Having a contract that does not meet the needs of a developer will not do anyone any good. For example, if the milestone payments do not meet basic expenses for developing the game, the developer will almost certainly have troubles before the game is finished. If the contract does not make sense for the development company, it is better to walk away from the deal rather than wasting everyone's time and money on a contract you simply cannot fulfill. Always be aware of practical limitations while negotiating. No matter how hard it is to negotiate the contract the first time, it will always be worse to re-negotiate later when the company desperately needs money to make payroll. Do not get caught up in the excitement of landing a contract, because it could potentially ruin the company with a bad deal.

Figure 4.1 is a summary of the process of negotiating a contract.

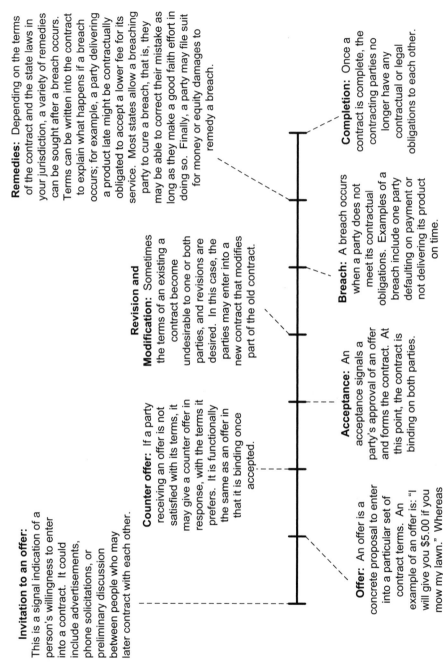

Invitation to an offer:
This is a signal indication of a person's willingness to enter into a contract. It could include advertisements, phone solicitations, or preliminary discussion between people who may later contract with each other.

Offer: An offer is a concrete proposal to enter into a particular set of contract terms. An example of an offer is: "I will give you $5.00 if you mow my lawn." Whereas an invitation to an offer might just be throwing ideas around, an actual offer is expected to be binding and contract-forming once the other party accepts it.

Counter offer: If a party receiving an offer is not satisfied with its terms, it may give a counter offer in response, with the terms it prefers. It is functionally the same as an offer in that it is binding once accepted.

Acceptance: An acceptance signals a party's approval of an offer and forms the contract. At this point, the contract is binding on both parties.

Revision and Modification: Sometimes the terms of an existing a contract become undesirable to one or both parties, and revisions are desired. In this case, the parties may enter into a new contract that modifies part of the old contract.

Breach: A breach occurs when a party does not meet its contractual obligations. Examples of a breach include one party defaulting on payment or not delivering its product on time.

Remedies: Depending on the terms of the contract and the state laws in your jurisdiction, a variety of remedies can be sought after a breach occurs. Terms can be written into the contract to explain what happens if a breach occurs; for example, a party delivering a product late might be contractually obligated to accept a lower fee for its service. Most states allow a breaching party to cure a breach, that is, they may be able to correct their mistake as long as they make a good faith effort in doing so. Finally, a party may file suit for money or equity damages to remedy a breach.

Completion: Once a contract is complete, the contracting parties no longer have any contractual or legal obligations to each other.

FIGURE 4.1   The chronology of a contract negotiation.

Conclusion

Although the games industry has seen tremendous growth in the past decade and shows no signs of slowing down, publishers are not throwing money at every half-baked idea that comes along. It takes more than thinking that you can make a game better than the developer who made that game you hated. Even if you have a few friends who worked for a major publisher or developer willing to get on board, you will not have the bargaining power to demand much. It is very important to pick and choose your battles, keeping in mind what you can do as a developer. Committing to advances and milestones that are unrealistic for your operating costs and your team's size may lead to many problems later down the line when you cannot pay your bills or when you miss a crucial milestone. Sometimes, it may be in your best interest to pass on a deal and look for something better.

To know what the best deal is for you, be sure to read contracts carefully. Additionally, if you don't understand the language of the deal, either ask for the contract to be drafted in a better way, or ask your attorney to explain it for you. Most importantly, make sure your obligations are well defined in language you can understand. Doing something wrong because you didn't understand what was asked is a terrible way to lose a development deal.

Be sure to be aware of other contracts that may have an effect on your business. In addition to contracts that bind you, contracts that bind others who work with or for you can impact your studio. If you hire some programmers from a large company that has just released a major title, be sure they are not bound by non-competition agreements. Similarly, be sure that nobody is using proprietary code to which you do not have the rights. The last thing a new studio needs is an injunction against it or its employees.

Not surprisingly, the games industry requires that you pay your proverbial dues before you really "make it big." Being familiar with contract language and terms will hopefully help you make better deals with publishers. This, in turn, should give you the foundation to build up to the truly great deals. In whatever you do, you will find yourself surrounded by contracts. No matter what, be sure to read everything and ask questions before signing any contract. Although contract language may sometimes seem complex, it is nothing that some slow reading and careful questioning cannot decipher.

Endnotes

1. 86 F.3d 1447 (7th Cir. 1996)
2. 334 F. Supp. 2d 1164 (E.D. Mo. 2004)

CHAPTER 5

Marketing Is a Game, Too

Roxanne Christ

Roxanne.Christ@lw.com*

You might be pleased to know that you have already made it halfway to a successful marketing campaign: you are creating a great game that people will want to play. Now all you have to do is get the word out. How do you do that? This chapter explores the various media of marketing, marketing strategies and mistakes, and methods to measure the success of your marketing campaign. You will learn about the importance of market research identifying your target audience, and the best ways to reach your potential customers.

Independent developers, especially those just starting out, may face more challenges in marketing their games than large, established publishers. Because much of the following information is geared toward developers who need help overcoming these challenges, the term "developer" is used throughout the chapter. However, many of the do's and don'ts of video game marketing apply to publishers and developers of all sizes, so the information you are about to read will be helpful regardless of your role in the industry.

Marketing versus PR

Marketing has many different definitions. Some define marketing as any process aimed at persuading a consumer to purchase a company's products.[1] The American Marketing Association's definition includes managing customer relations in ways that benefit the organization.[2] However, the most widely accepted definition comes from the Chartered Institute of Marketing, the largest marketing body in the world in terms of membership: "Marketing is the management process of anticipating, identifying, and satisfying customer requirements profitably."[3]

Marketing differs from public relations, which focuses on activities used to create public interest in a person, company, or product. While the aim of public relations is to generate interest, the purpose of marketing is more closely tied to sales. Marketers want to satisfy customers, not necessarily the public at large, and they want to do so profitably. To this end, market researchers and market strategists attempt to assess what customers want, and then they find the best ways for companies to meet those wants.

Marketing Your Game versus Marketing Your Company

Keep in mind when planning your marketing campaign that marketing your game and marketing your company, while obviously linked, are two very different things. The first and foremost object of your campaign is to sell your game, or, if you are providing the game for free, to expose it to a broad audience. Your initial marketing efforts should be focused on informing the public that your game exists; as time goes on, you can begin to inform customers about the specifics of the game, and give them a reason to purchase your game over others.

Once you have succeeded in getting the word out about your game, consider marketing tactics aimed at introducing your customers to you as a developer. Developers that have had hit games are sure to include their successes in subsequent ad campaigns, and if you have such a success under your belt, so much the better. But new developers should also take advantage of this marketing strategy. This game may be your first, but it is never too early to start introducing the public to the developer in you. Brand marketing is an especially cost-effective strategy because it enables you to promote all your games at once, while inspiring consumers to anticipate your next release. When you make your next game, marketing it will be that much easier because you have already built up an interest for your work in general.

Ad Dollars

The current trend in video game advertising has companies allocating larger portions of their ad budgets to online outlets. MySpace®, viral marketing, and in-game advertisements offer lucrative opportunities for developers to market their games in the places most frequented by gamers. This shift reflects the current attitude of other industries, which are also moving a larger percentage of their advertising dollars into various types of Internet marketing.[4]

Developing Your Marketing Strategy

The starting point of a marketing strategy: Defining your goals.
Product: Perfecting your video game.
Price: Deciding whether more is less, less is more, or more is more.
Place: The media of video games.
Promotion: PR plus advertising equals sales.
Going through the motions: Pre-release, release, and post-release marketing.

Marketing Basics: the Four Ps

A marketing strategy is necessary for any successful business.[5] The first and most important step in creating a marketing strategy is to define your goals. What do you hope to achieve? You cannot map out a course until you know your destination. Once you know what your goals are, you can make the appropriate decisions for each step in creating your marketing strategy. In addition, your goals should have a time line. For example, your initial goal for the next six months might be to achieve a certain amount of sales, but your longer-term goal might be to create a sequel by the end of the year.

There are four main areas to address when planning a marketing strategy for a video game. These are known in marketing as the "marketing mix four Ps": **P**roduct, **P**rice, **P**lace, and **P**romotion.[6] Each element does not necessarily carry the same weight, but all four are necessary considerations in creating your marketing strategy.

Product

The product is the most important piece of the puzzle.[7] A great game is clearly much easier to market than a bad one.[8] With so many different types of games on the market, your game should offer players something new. Your game does not necessarily need to be unique to the video game world, but there should be something appealing or distinctive that your game brings to the table. In the early stages, you should identify a potential market for your game and determine what people are looking for in that market, or at least determine whether game players would be interested in what your game has to offer.

First, people should want to play your game. People initially will buy your game because something about it appeals to them; for example, a particular theme, genre, or feature may entice a player to purchase your game. However, a gamer will only continue to play your game if he or she enjoys it. A little bit of market research will tell you what appeals to consumers and what types of games people enjoy.

Second, your game should work. Even the best-engineered games may have a bug here or there, but do your best to keep bugs to a minimum. Sophisticated gamers have a short fuse for technology foul-ups, and one quick way to lose a customer is to market a game that frustrates players.

Third, your product should speak for itself; gameplay should feel comfortable to the player. Your player should not have to read a dissertation to learn how to play.[9] Obviously, some of the more interactive and complicated games involve a decent amount of "how to," but those in your target market should be capable of figuring it out relatively quickly. Whether this means you have to tailor your game to the age group, maturity level, or technological IQ of your target audience, those whom you want to play your game should not find it frustrating to do so.

Price

Pricing can be a complicated issue, and largely depends on how you plan to make money. Will it be from selling game units at retail or from subscriptions? Or will it be from ancillary advertising? Or from some other model? Let us assume for simplicity's sake that you plan to make money by selling game units. You do not want to price too low because you will not make enough money from the game. However, you cannot price your game too high or consumers will choose a competitor's less expensive but otherwise comparable product instead.

Also, keep in mind that your game's price conveys an image, so when it comes to price you will have an important decision to make: should you price your game low and hope to sell more, or should you price it high and resign yourself to selling fewer units? Both options present the opportunity to make a similar profit. An established game developer can get away with charging a higher price because it has a loyal customer base. However, a novice might want to consider pricing its game a bit lower to gain a larger audience and attract a following.[10] Keep in mind that you can adjust your price over time. If you find that people are not willing to pay $29.99, try selling your game for $24.99 or $19.99. Conversely, if the game is selling very well at $9.99, you may want to consider selling it at $14.99.

You should also consider your target market. Everyone has a maximum price point, and it is imperative to ensure that a majority of the customers who are interested in your game can and will buy it. If your game caters to younger teens and pre-teens, you may want to consider lowering your price. If your game is geared toward older teens and adults, you might have leeway to charge a higher price.

Depending on how you plan to distribute your game, you may have to set up two different pricing schemes. First, you will need to set a price at which to sell to your direct consumer. If you sell the product yourself and not through a retailer, this price will be the only one you need to set. Second, you need to set the price at which you will sell your game to retailers, which will be lower than your estimated price to the consumer because most retailers seek a certain percentage of profits from the products they sell. You should research the retailer you plan to work with to determine what an appropriate price would be.

If you decide to work with a retailer, you may want to provide a suggested retail price; this is the price at which you think the product should be sold. Larger retailers and outlets often sell products below the suggested retail price to attract more customers. Another term you should be aware of is the minimum advertised price, or MAP. Generally, a large manufacturer will subsidize the cost of advertising its product at a given retail outlet, but in exchange, it will prohibit retailers from advertising the product below a given price: the MAP. Many retailers rely on the advertising subsidy, and therefore adhere to the minimum price request of the manufacturer. The Federal Trade Commission (FTC) keeps a close eye on these types of agreements because setting a "floor price" for large retailers can create a form of price-fixing. A large-scale game developer should be aware of the legal issues arising from the use of a MAP, since the FTC believes there is a fine line between acceptable MAPs and unacceptable price-fixing. Smaller game developers should at least be aware that they cannot force a retailer to sell above a minimum price. However, the government does not control who game developers do business with, so if you do not like the price a retailer sets for your game, you may have to stop doing business with that retailer.

When formulating pricing, you should go back and review what your goals are. For instance, if you want to reach out to a broad audience of people to get them interested in your company's games, then a lower price might be more appropriate. If your goal is to achieve a certain amount of revenue, you should market your game at a price that will result in the corresponding amount of sales.

Place

Place of distribution refers to the medium through which consumers can find your game to try it or buy it.[11] Your "place" will depend on several factors, including your budget, company size, and, of course, your goals. Video game developers have several options, including download, game portals, CDs, or retail.[12] The best way to sell your game directly is via downloads or CDs from your own Web site. Selling your product on your own can be beneficial in many ways; the most important benefit is that you will not have to share a percentage of the profits. However, you will need to attract customers to your Web site, which will mean beefing up your PR efforts to get your name out. Do not assume that one game medium is preferred over another. Some gamers prefer a CD, while others prefer to download their games. You should offer both if you can.

Downloads and CDs are the preferred means of commercial distribution, and are also the preferred means of pirated distribution. In recent news, much has been made of music and movie piracy, but piracy is a major problem in the gaming world as well. In February 2005, Macrovision® announced the results of a study on video game piracy.[13] The study revealed that 21% of PlayStation® 2 and Xbox® gamers play pirated games, and two-thirds of these gamers would have purchased the game within a month had the free version not become available.[14] In 1998, the Interactive Digital Software Association reported that piracy cost the industry approximately $3.2 billion, or about 20% of the $16 billion in sales projected for that year.[15] With the rise of broadband Internet, these numbers have likely increased since the 1998 report.

There are two general means of pirating a video game. First, a gamer can download a ROM—a copy of an original Read Only Memory file. A gamer can play a ROM on his or her computer with software that emulates the operating system of a particular game console. Emulation software is generally not considered illegal, although there is a push by the industry to either make it illegal or at least regulate its use.

Second, a gamer can also modify his or her game system with a mod-chip. A mod-chip enables gamers to play copies of games burned to standard CD-R media. Mod-chips are generally used when a person wants to play a foreign game on his or her U.S. game system; however, these chips are increasingly used to play illegally copied games. Whether mod-chips themselves are illegal is still unclear.

Downloads and CDs are not the only outlets available for distributing your video game. If you have a simple casual game, you may want to consider game portals such as the AOL® Games Channel, Yahoo!® Games, or Bigfish. Game portals can drive an increased amount of traffic to your game, but you will have to share revenue with big-name Web sites. Before you decide whether to work with a game portal, you should research what types of games are popular on each site to determine where your game will best fit in. You also need to research whether the game portal caters to your target market. Your target audience should coincide with that of the game portal you select. Furthermore, before you decide to work with a particular portal, make sure your game is compatible with what they are looking for, because many game portals have specific guidelines for developers to follow.[16] Always keep your goals in mind; if you are looking for company exposure, game portals may not be for you because most game portals do not advertise the name of a game's developer. On the other hand, if you are focused on exposing your game to a wide audience, the high volume of traffic on a portal could help.

Another way to reach a mass market is to sell your game in hard copy at a retail store. If your budget permits, attempt to place your game in a large retail store that does not exclusively cater to gamers. This strategy is particularly appropriate if your game is intended for mass consumption. However, getting your game on the shelves of a large retail outlet is expensive[17] because of the capital costs of producing enough inventory to meet a major retailer's stock requirements and their insistence that you let them return any unsold units. Getting into large retailers is also difficult because such retailers often prefer dealing with a limited number of vendors. Realistically, smaller retail stores are a more feasible option for independent game developers.

Before signing with any retailer, you should carefully review the contract—you may even want to contact an attorney. Make sure, at the very least, that you lay out: 1) what you are getting paid, 2) when you are getting paid, and 3) what your obligation to take product returns or issue credits is. One option is to have the retail store pay for the games upfront; then, if the game does not sell you can buy back the stock, either at the same price the store paid or at another negotiated price. Alternatively, you may agree to be paid as the game sells. Before negotiating the terms of the contract, determine what your deal breakers are and practice your bargaining techniques.

Promotion

Promotion entails creating a buzz for your product. There are numerous ways to get the word out about your game, and your market research should identify the best ways to reach *your* target audience. Do not assume that the costly strategy of blanketing the Internet with ads will be your best choice, because different types of gamers find information in different places. For example, PC gamers typically get most of their information from the Internet, while console gamers get their information through television. Hardcore gamers are more likely to buy gaming magazines, but casual gamers are better targeted through strategically placed Web ads.

Once you know where to find your audience, you need to give them enough information to make them interested in your game. Your ads should be uncluttered but informative enough to draw readers to your Web site or into the store. Do not underestimate the power of the Internet, but do not overestimate it either. Diversify your marketing media to reach as much of your target audience as possible.

One of the most powerful tools in your marketing toolbox is your Web site. This is where people will learn about your game and find out how to buy it. Be creative! The tone of your Web site should reflect the tone of your game. Your Web page should be eye-catching without visual over-stimulation. Place information about how to buy your game in a prominent location. Also, make sure the Web page is easy for Internet users to search for and navigate.

If you decide to market your game through a Web site, it is essential to clearly and succinctly articulate your privacy policy in compliance with federal law. Your privacy policy should include, at a minimum, an explanation of:

- How you treat personal information collected and received through your Web site
- How the information is collected and why
- How the information will be used
- Whether the information will be shared with other affiliates
- The users' ability to edit and delete their personal information and preferences
- The accessibility of personal information by authorized personnel

Especially noteworthy in the video game online sale context is the Children's Online Privacy Protection Act (COPPA), which is applicable to data collected from children younger than 13 years of age. COPPA outlines what your Web site must include in terms of privacy policy, when and how to obtain verifiable parental consent, and your responsibilities for protecting child privacy and online safety.[18]

A clear articulation on your Web site of the "terms of use" is essential to protect your game from inappropriate exploitation. Your terms of use set forth the acceptable means of using your game, the obligations of the user, your proprietary rights, and limitations on liability. Obtaining consent from the user, before granting access to your game, will provide better protection than simply listing them. You may also want to post a separate disclaimer that spells out your intellectual property ownership rights. Further legal advice should be sought on how best to construct your terms of use to fit your game.

Three Phases of Marketing Your Developed Game

Technically, there are four, not three, phases of marketing. The marketing research conducted before you even develop a game is really the first step of your marketing scheme. Pre-development research includes all of the market studies that tell you what the gaming world already has, what it is looking for, and what it does not want. Creating a game and then discovering that there are 10 games just like it is frustrating, and a waste of time and resources. Good market research can help you avoid this. The three post-development phases of video game marketing are 1) pre-release, 2) the big release, and 3) post-release.

Pre-Release
- Perfect your game
  - Make sure you work out all the bugs and everything is running smoothly.
  - Test your game with players from your target audience.
  - Make improvements based on players' comments and real-time feedback.
- Web site
  - Get your Web site up and running.
  - Make sure the Web site contains all the necessary information about your game and all prudent and required legal statements.
  - Make sure your Web site is quickly and easily accessible through search engines.
- Public relations
  - Prepare a press kit, complete with a press release and other relevant information. Distribute this material to appropriate media outlets and have extras on hand to meet additional requests.
  - Develop a demo.
  - Let members of the press, or key players in the gaming community, preview your game.
  - Begin promotion efforts to generate hype about your game. Get people talking.
- Price
  - Conduct market research on pricing. Develop a price point for consumers and retailers.

The Big Release
- Sell, sell, sell
  - Make sure your game is ready to download, ship, or otherwise distribute.
- Measure sales
  - Start gathering sales data, including data about the demographics of your customers.
  - Make any necessary adjustments to price.
  - Talk to players and get some initial feedback.
- Put your PR into overdrive
  - Advertise and get your game's name out there.
  - Send out updated press kits throughout the marketing process.
  - Pitch stories to journalists to encourage them to write about your game.
  - Set up interviews with journalists, bloggers, etc.
  - Sign on to blogs and introduce your game.

Post-Release
- Do not stop promoting!
  - Even though your game has been out in the world for a while, continue to update your marketing strategy.

- Measure sales
  - Make sure you are getting the return and percentages you are aiming for.
  - Review sales data and demographics. Look for surprises or inconsistencies.
  - Evaluate your advertising. Make sure you have been reaching your target audience.
- Game adjustments
  - Get customer feedback and make adjustments if necessary. Many gamers do not take the time to fill out evaluations. A better way to find out what people think about your game is to read what they are saying about it in blogs and chat rooms.
- Explore your options
  - Consider working with a distributor. On your own, you will only generate a certain amount of direct sales. If you have not already done so, explore the world of third-party promotion.
  - Consider in-game advertising. If your game is popular enough, there may be someone out there who wants to place an ad in it. Remember to consider whether ads will disrupt gameplay or annoy players. In-game advertising is discussed in more detail later in this chapter.
  - Consider a second version of your game.

Knowing Your Audience

Do your research: The more you know, the better your marketing plan.

Not just for kids: New gamers are older, and women and Hispanics are a larger part of the market, especially among casual gamers.

Market segmentation: Define your target subgroup.

User types: Who is your game intended for?

You probably already know that you have to market to the masses, but what comes next? First, who are the masses? In other words, to whom are you marketing? You might have the snappiest ad campaign imaginable and the most innovative game on the market, but it will not attract a single new customer if you do not aim your marketing in the right direction. In the marketing industry, this process is called finding your target audience. A target audience is the primary group of people that a marketing campaign is aimed at attracting. This audience may be composed of a certain age group, gender, marital status, or other defined subgroup. A certain combination of these subgroups will be your target audience. While men ages 18 to 34 are often cited as the ideal target audience in the video game industry, target audiences are broadening as casual gaming grows in popularity. The importance of knowing to whom you are marketing cannot be overstated and can make the difference between a smash hit and a complete flop.

Market Research

The easiest way to find your target audience is through simple market research, which can provide you with a solid foundation on which to base your ultimate marketing plan. Research can be complicated (percentage of female gamers over 18 who play online chess) or straightforward (percentage of the market held by men). There are studies available for free online that contain basic market and demographic information. For example, the U.S. Census Web site at *http://www.census.gov/* offers general demographic information, as does *http://www.freedemographics.com/*. Also, the Entertainment Software Association, a video game trade group, devotes the "Facts and Research" section of its Web site, at *http://www.theesa.com/*, to statistical information about video games. In addition, an education-focused site, *http://www.medialiteracy.com/*, features statistical information and research reports related to video game use by American youth. Customized research is, of course, more specific but can be costly.

There are presently two custom market research options available to game developers: 1) you can pay a market research company to conduct a survey among gamers; or 2) you can conduct the survey yourself. Paying a market research company to conduct a survey allows you to gather more tailored information, with your budget and time frame as the main limitations. Conducting a survey yourself may be as simple as posting a "question of the day" on your Web site. Request that visitors fill out a form telling you a little bit about themselves when answering this question. Visitors who frequent the Web site will provide you with information on your target demographic with relatively little work required on your part. Hopefully, within a few months you will have sufficient information to understand your target audience and you can incorporate this new understanding into your marketing campaign. A third possibility is to license relevant data from another similar Web site or third-party provider. The key here is to know the data is relevant and can be shared. In all cases, care must be taken to comply with applicable privacy laws and policies.

Recognizing Demographic Trends

The U.S. video game marketplace is still evolving and maturing; it is important to recognize demographic trends and business developments early on. A game developer who recognizes a trend early on can gain a significant edge on the market. Again, market research can help reveal shifts and unmet needs within the marketplace. Fortunately, as gaming matures and the gaming community grows, trends appear more mainstream because gamers now span nearly every generation and nationality, and are no longer male-dominated.

You probably know that video games are no longer just for kids. While many developers still cater to the 18–35 male demographic, more and more developers are catering to an older crowd. According to a 2004 Entertainment Software Association study, the average age of gamers was then 29, and the average age of game buyers was

36.[19] A 2006 Entertainment Software Association survey revealed that the average age of video game players has risen to 33, and over one quarter of all gamers are now 50 or older.[20] Gamers who cut their teeth on Atari, Nintendo®, and the Commodore 64 are evidently still playing games, not just on later-generation game consoles and high-powered game-centric PCs, but even on their cell phones and PDAs. The average adult gamer has been playing video games for 12 years.[21]

Moreover, games are no longer mainly for men and boys. Females 18 and older make up a significantly larger share of the game-playing population (30%) than males 17 and younger (23%). This shift coincides with the increased popularity of casual games. Casual games are free online or pre-installed games that allow the user to play for a few minutes at a time. Web sites like zone.msn.com, Pogo.com, and RealArcade feature hundreds of free online games and have millions of subscribers. Popular casual games include online puzzle games like *Zuma*, *Snood*, and *Bejeweled*, among countless others found all over the Internet. Casual games also include pre-installed PC games like *Minesweeper* and *Solitaire*. A recent AOL study found that 64% of casual gamers were females 30 and over.[22] Zone.msn.com and RealArcade both report that their audiences are over 60% female as well. Beyond Web-based games, women's presence in the video game market is strong and growing. In 1987, females accounted for just over 14% of the general entertainment software market, which includes all video games: console, PC, online, handheld, and mobile.[23] As of 2005, females accounted for 38% of this market.[24] Moreover, as many as one-third of Nintendo GameCube and Nintendo Game Boy Advance players are female.

Another audience yet to be fully appreciated is the ever-growing Hispanic population. According to the 1990 United States Census, the Hispanic population was just over 22 million people, or 9% of the total U.S. population. In 2005, an informal Census Bureau study found that the Hispanic community had grown to an estimated 42 million people, or 14% of the total population.[25] Hispanics represent the largest minority group, and spend an estimated $650 billion annually. Experts say console gaming is more popular with the Hispanic population than with any other ethnic group: one out of every four Hispanics is a console gamer.[26] The Hispanic population represents incredible potential for growth within the gaming industry in the coming years.

The cell phone market also offers valuable opportunities for game developers. Over 140 million cell phones were sold in the United States in 2005, with just over half having game-playing capabilities. Mobile games are a quick fix for gamers while they are away from their consoles and PCs.[27] Further, consumers who play games on other devices are twice as likely to play on their cell phones. Interestingly enough, the United States as a whole is significantly behind the rest of the world when it comes to mobile gaming. China, South Korea, and Europe all have significantly more mobile gamers than the United States. Additionally, it is worth noting that a disproportionate number of mobile gamers are members of minority groups.

Segmenting the Video Game Market

Most successful businesses have a well-defined idea of the customers they are seeking to attract. In the video game industry, it is not as simple as looking at the age, gender, or nationality of the average gamer. To properly reach your target audience, you must dissect the audience for your game type. Within the marketing industry, this process is often referred to as segmenting the consumer market. Market segmentation is the process of grouping a market into smaller subgroups. The four most common marketing segmentation variable types are geographic (most likely world, region, or country), demographic (age, gender, education, etc.), psychographic (social class, lifestyle, personality), and behavioral (casual to heavy gamers, genre, favorite games). The gamers' technical capabilities (speed of Internet connection, age of computer) could also be included in the segmentation.[28] While the geographic, demographic, and psychographic subgroups are somewhat self-explanatory, the behavioral segment merits more attention; in particular, user type can be quite complicated.

Generally, there are four different types of users: hardcore gamers, casual gamers, niche gamers, and interstitial gamers. Hardcore gamers are those who purchase a game and play it for several hours a day. Casual gamers play free online games (Minesweeper, chess, puzzle games) and might only play for a few minutes at a time. Niche gamers play niche genres like turn-based historical strategy war games or flight simulators. Interstitial gamers are ex-hardcore gamers who no longer have several hours a day to devote to a particular game, but might still play several hours a week.[29]

Each user type is made up of certain demographics. For instance, females 18 and older comprise 60% of the casual gaming market. Niche gamers, on the other hand, are more likely to be 18- to 34-year-old males. Hardcore gamers are generally teenagers and college-aged men who have significant amounts of free time to devote to video games. Interstitial gamers include old and young gamers alike; their common characteristic is that they are all too busy with work, school, family, or other responsibilities to devote the kind of time hardcore gamers spend playing. In marketing your game, you should consider what type of user you are trying to attract before breaking your target audience down into tighter demographic groups. This will help you keep your marketing focused and efficient.

Live Advertising: Trade Shows

- Trade shows are the forum of choice for big announcements by industry leaders.
- Gamers talk; reviews from trade shows disseminate quickly, so a good showing goes a long way.

Like most industries, the video game industry has a series of trade shows that serve as showcases for the industry's products and achievements. Such trade shows include the Tokyo Game Show, SpaceWorld, the Consumer Electronics Show, and the Game Developers Conference.[30] By far, the biggest live event in the video game industry was the Electronic Entertainment Expo, known as E3.[31]

E3 was traditionally held each May at the Los Angeles Convention Center. Aimed mostly at the press and retailers, E3 provided a forum for game designers to preview their newest games and consoles. The physical layout of E3 follows the traditional convention-style format: companies bought booth space well in advance and spent millions of dollars on extravagant displays and structures for their bigger titles. Most booths contained playable demos of the games being promoted. More elaborate booths also sometimes featured giveaways and prizes. Recently, it was announced that the show was going to be replaced by a much smaller show focused on giving extensive press coverage to larger publishers and developers. There is some speculation as to whether another trade show will replace the traditional E3 experience in the future (Figure 5.1).

FIGURE 5.1   The Konami booth at E3 2005. This photo comes from *http://en.wikipedia.org/wiki/ Image:Konami_at_e3_2005.jpg* and is copyrighted. The copyright holder, Cian Ginty, states on the Wikipedia Web page that the photo may be used for any purpose as long as the copyright holder is given credit.

A game's showing at a large trade show, such as E3, can have a significant impact on its success. Serious gamers are usually the first to purchase newly released products, and their opinions influence casual gamers and other hardcore gamers alike.[32] Retailers' and journalists' impressions from these large trade shows are quickly disseminated to the rest of the gaming world via the Internet and gaming magazines. For example, the July 2006 issue of *Electronic Gaming Monthly* contains an "Opinionated Preview Guide" to 80 games the authors played at the 2006 E3. Each of the games featured in the article received one of four labels: "Awesome," "Good," "So-So," and "Terrible."[33] Receiving the label "Terrible" (as seven games do in this article) from *Electronic Gaming Monthly* can doom a game before it has even been launched.

Print Marketing

Creativity required: Print ads cannot display video, so you must persuade customers to buy your game through other means.

Gamers are suspicious of ads: Back up the claims you make about your game with industry awards and quotations from reviewers.

Ads that generate awareness: Consider using print ads to demonstrate the availability of your game while encouraging customers to seek further information in a more interactive medium.

Develop yourself as a brand: Publicizing your image will help you market your next game.

Limitations of Print Advertising

Print ads for video games suffer from a crucial limitation: they cannot provide the consumer with moving pictures. On the other hand, media that allow the consumer to watch the game being played, like television ads and some Internet ads, provide the consumer with an experience that is only once removed from the pure gaming experience. With a print ad, the consumer does not get to see the game being played at all—at best, he or she sees a few screenshots from the game.

The further removed an advertising medium is from a pure gaming experience, the more opportunity there is for skillful advertising to influence consumer perceptions of the game. But beware, this could be more of a challenge than an opportunity. Gamers—particularly the hardcore, early-adopter gamers—can be extremely suspicious of advertising. Most gamers have purchased a game on impulse at some point, based on the exciting description and phenomenal screenshots on the box, only to find that the game itself is not at all what they expected. This is an experience gamers will not want to repeat. Moreover, in a world in which unbiased reviews of just about any video game are a Google™ search away, most gamers are hesitant to make their buying decisions based solely on what they may perceive to be biased advertising.

How to Mitigate Those Limitations

Despite the obstacles discussed earlier, print ads can be effective if they are designed strategically. Traditional print ads tend to feature the same elements: the game's title, screenshots or an artist's rendering that is evocative of the game's genre and gameplay, listings of industry awards, and quotations from reviews of the game. These ads are intended to promote the game and provide the customer with important information about why and how to buy it.

One of the most important features of these ads is the testimonials. Although gamers are suspicious of advertising they believe to be biased, they may find quotations from respected independent reviewers persuasive. Feature articles, reviews, and previews of a game by a magazine or Web site are among the best print promotion a developer can get, so be sure to maintain an updated press kit, and stay in contact with the print media throughout your game's marketing cycle. Getting a journalist to write a feature about you or your game is great, but even a short review can provide you with quotations to use in your own print ads. Capitalize on any contacts you have in the media, and never stop trying to publicize your name and your game.

Some developers choose a different approach—using ads to generate awareness about their games, but encouraging potential customers to seek out information in other, more interactive media. These ads often do not have screenshots, testimonials, or descriptions beyond what is obvious from the photo and game title. Instead, such ads direct customers to the game's Web site, which features more screenshots and testimonials than would fit in a typical print ad. If you have a demo of your game, this strategy is particularly effective; the two-pronged approach of the print ad and Web site is more likely to attract attention than a strategy that employs only one of these methods.

A third approach for print ads is to focus on the developer, in addition to the game. This approach may be particularly useful for games where testimonial ads are not possible because you do not yet have a playable demo for reviewers and potential customers. A recent ad by Electronic Arts for its *NCAA Football 07* game focused only indirectly on the game and instead highlighted the game developers' efforts. For example, the ad describes how a team of designers from Tiburon Studios watched over 500 football games to reverse-engineer the playbooks of all 119 NCAA Division 1-A teams[34] (Figure 5.2).

In much the same way that consumers equate Steven Spielberg with quality movies, gamers equate certain developers with great games. In this way, those who have had a hit game can leverage their success to generate strong brand recognition. Developers like Rockstar Games (creator of the wildly successful *Grand Theft Auto* series) and Will Wright (creator of *The Sims*™, the best-selling PC game of all time) enjoy such recognition, and ad campaigns for their games are sure to pinpoint the association. For EA, relating the attractive aspects of the game through anecdotes about the development team markets *NCAA Football 07*, and the Tiburon developers themselves. If this marketing strategy proves successful, it will allow EA to give future products more credibility simply by being associated with Tiburon Studios.

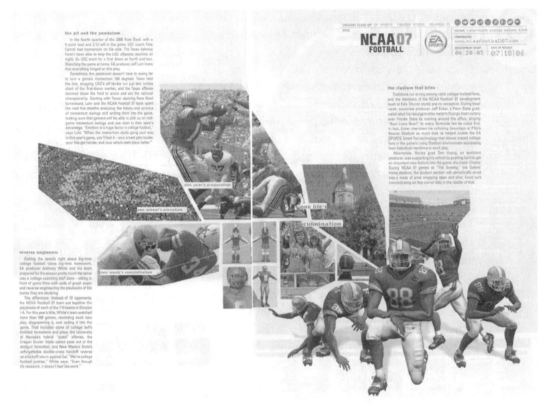

FIGURE 5.2 NCAA® Football 07 image. © 2006 Electronic Arts Inc. EA, EA SPORTS and the EA SPORTS logo are trademarks or registered trademarks of Electronic Arts Inc. in the U.S. and/or other countries. All Rights Reserved. All names, logos, team icons, and mascots associated with the NCAA, universities, bowls and conferences are the exlusive properties of the respective institutions. NCAA is a registered trademark of National Collegiate Athletic Association. Used with permission.

Traditional Television, Radio, and Movie Marketing

- Capitalize on audiences already interested in games to maximize the response to your marketing.
- Associate your game with the larger world of entertainment: celebrity interest is a big boost.
- Make sure you have contracts that give you the right to use celebrity testimonials.

Commercials on television and the radio are traditional marketing methods that should not be overlooked. While new marketing avenues are appealing and can be successful, developers can still use television and radio to expose their products to a wider audience. However, commercials are not cheap, so first consider the types of programs your target audience is likely to be listening to or watching. Your marketing dollars are put to the best use when you can generate interest among people who are already video game consumers. You will not need to convince them that they want to play games—only that your game is worth playing. While you should pay attention to established gamers, keep in mind that a much wider audience can be reached through mass media. If your marketing is effective, you may be able to turn some consumers into gamers—consumers who will want to buy your game.

Product placement in TV shows and movies can also help generate interest in the game, so consider what types of entertainment your target audience is likely to watch, and see if you can work out a deal to feature your product in that show or movie. Any association with the larger world of entertainment will expose a wider audience to the game, so creating buzz is in your best interest, and things like celebrity attention can provide a major marketing boost. Julia Roberts is reportedly a fan of *Halo*™, while Busta Rhymes is said to have multiple PS2s throughout his house.[35] EA Sports sponsors the Madden Bowl, where professional football players compete to win a video game tournament, televised on ESPN.[36] Countless episodes of MTV's *Cribs* have publicized the massive entertainment and video game systems of the rich and famous, and celebrities like 50 Cent and Tony Hawk even have games based on their personalities.[37] In a time when many people are nearly obsessed with celebrities, a celebrity's interest in a game can be an important asset to a developer. Some developers may provide free copies of their games to celebrities in the hope that one of them will become a personal favorite, and that the celebrity's interest can then be used to further market the game.

To avoid any legal troubles in using celebrity names or likenesses in your game ads, it is essential to acquire a license. A license is an agreement giving permission to the advertiser to use the celebrity's name or likeness with the objective of achieving commercial gain. An in-depth discussion on licensing is beyond the scope of this chapter, but be sure to obtain professional legal advice before attempting to draft such an agreement.

In-Game Advertising (Product Placement)

In-game advertising and advergames: Create a marketing partnership with a product sponsor to share costs and exposure.

Pros and cons: Consider the different types of in-game ads and how much post-release maintenance will be required.

Do not forget about the player: Only include in-game ads if they do not detract from the gaming experience.

Beware of legal challenges: Make sure your rights to use others' intellectual property ownership rights are spelled out in a contract.

Picture this: you are at a baseball game, and as the star hitter knocks one out of the park, the ball flies over a well-placed ad for Coca-Cola®. The same thing can happen in a video game: the digital ball can fly over a billboard programmed to display a Coca-Cola ad instead of an ad for a company made up by the game developer.

Over the years, consumers have become accustomed to seeing ads for products on television and in movies. However, the new product placement trend is to incorporate products into video games, creating a mutually beneficial marketing partnership between the game developers on the one hand, and advertisers on the other. Game developers receive financial support from advertisers who pay to place their ads in games, advertisers receive increased exposure of their products, and the two can work together to enhance the marketing of both the game and the product.

In-game ads are increasingly important in a media savvy world where people are spending more time gaming and less time using other media. A recent survey showed that 32% of people who increased their game-playing time did so at the expense of television time.[38] Because television audiences now own machines like DVRs and TiVo®s that enable them to fast-forward through commercials, and because online gamers have found ways to avoid pop-up ads, banners, and spam, placing ads in games is one of the few ways to guarantee that a large audience of gamers will see the ad. According to a recent report by the research firm The Yankee Group, the number of games with in-game advertising is expected to double next year, and market value will reach over $700 million by 2010.[39] Some of the world's biggest and wealthiest companies are placing their products in games, and Microsoft's recent purchase of Massive, Inc., a company that provides networking for in-game ads, indicates that the industry is expected to continue to grow rapidly for the next few years.[40]

Product placement can be interactive or noninteractive, and current games show varying degrees of incorporation. In-game advertisements appear in all forms of games: PC-based games, console games, online games, and mobile games. For example, *Madden NFL 06* displays noninteractive scoreboard ads for companies such as Reebok and Heinz.[41] Others allow players to use the products as an interactive part of the game: characters in *The Sims* can use Intel Centrino laptops or own a McDonald's franchise.[42] Some games even take this approach one step further, providing products not to game characters but to the players themselves. For example, in 2005, Pizza Hut and Sony teamed up to offer *EverQuest® II* players the ability to order a pizza, simply by typing a command that would bring up an order form, without ever leaving the game.[43] The most interactive and arguably effective ads are those that are integrated directly into the game's storyline; for example, the *CSI3* game included Visa's identity theft protection as part of its plot.[44]

Developers, and advertisers, should consider the pros and cons of each of these product placement strategies. Noninteractive ads are easier to create and simpler to maintain, while interactive ads are more costly to create and operate. On the other hand, interactive ads increase product exposure, and players likely identify more with products they actually use during gameplay than those they simply see in the background. Highly interactive product placement, like intertwining the Visa brand in the *CSI3* storyline, affords the greatest amount of exposure, but there are fewer interactive placement applications. Otherwise, a game could overwhelm players with entirely ad-driven plots.

In-game ads can be created in two ways. Some games, usually console games, have static ads programmed into them. Once the game is completed and distributed, the ads remain the same. Dynamic ads in games played through the Internet, like Xbox 360 live games, can be updated through an always-on network. In these situations, a space is created for the ad within the game, but the information placed in that space can be changed as the game developer or operator chooses. If your game is capable of maintaining either static or dynamic ads, carefully consider which type you want to use. Static ads are easier to create and require no maintenance once development is completed. Dynamic ads are more complicated and have higher maintenance costs, but also allow for product rotation. Developers may appreciate dynamic ads because they can generate revenue from more product sponsors, while sponsors appreciate dynamic ads because they can be updated as the sponsors' marketing strategy changes.

Developers and advertisers must always consider the player when designing in-game ads. Surveys indicate that many players do not object to in-game ads as long as they do not interfere with gameplay, and some even find that the ads make the game more realistic.[45] In-game ads are better suited to certain kinds of games: sports and urban games provide opportunities for ads in environments where players are used to seeing ads, while games that take place in fantasy worlds like *EverQuest* or *World of Warcraft* present more of a challenge for seamless incorporation. Pay attention to how the ads are presented, and be certain there are no bugs associated with the ads that will cause problems that frustrate players. Developers might also consider reducing the price of games that include ads and making sure the player knows he or she is getting a discount offset by advertising revenue generated from within the game.

Legal Issues

In-game advertisements, while potentially very lucrative, raise legal issues. License agreements that address ownership rights of intellectual property are essential to an effective marketing relationship. Two types of intellectual property are at issue when a game developer works with a product sponsor to create an in-game ad: the sponsor's trademark or logo and the developer's copyrighted code.

The way the product sponsor normally uses its trademark might not fit the appearance or plot of the game, so the developer might have to manipulate it in some way. Such manipulation may raise questions of ownership. Does the newly created in-game image belong to the product sponsor that licensed its trademark for use, or to the developer who changed an image into code and may have changed the appearance of the mark as well? This issue has not yet been addressed by the courts, so is not clear which party would prevail if a licensing agreement between the parties did not address these issues. The product sponsor has a strong argument that the in-game image is based off its trademark. If consumers identify the trademark with the sponsoring company and its products, which is one of the goals of trademark law, then the trademark owner has an even better argument. However, the game developer has created the in-game image, and may be able to demonstrate that the sponsoring company only provided the original image, while the developer created the actual computer code.

Copyrights are also at issue in product placement situations (whether those copyrights are owned by the developer or the publisher of the game). The developer's rendering of the trademark may be based on the original mark but presented in a new and different way. Perhaps the mark has been animated so it catches the eye when a certain game event occurs—like making the Coca-Cola mark on the baseball billboard dance when the home run passes over it. Or perhaps the trademark has been turned into a character that players can interact with during gameplay. It is possible that the developer may hold a copyright on these new images, and such a determination is likely to be based on whether the new image has been assembled from the old or transformed. Assembly occurs when the only modifications to the image are those required to change it into code. If the new image is merely assembled from the original graphic, then the trademark owner can probably reuse it without the risk of copyright infringement litigation. Transformation occurs when creative changes are made to the image. In this case, the company might be unable to reproduce the new image without obtaining permission from the developer.

The best solution to these intellectual property issues is to work them out in advance through a properly crafted licensing agreement. The agreement should spell out whether the developer or the product sponsor has ownership rights in the various trademark and copyright material that appears in the game. The agreement should also lay out what level of creativity the developer is allowed in integrating the trademark into the game, and how disputes about the appearance of the in-game ads will be resolved.

Advergaming

Advergaming occurs when a company designs, or hires a developer to design, a game specifically intended to promote the company or its products.[46] One of the best-known and most successful examples is Wrigley's Candystand.com, which contains over 60 specially created games that feature brands like Lifesavers® candy and Juicy Fruit® gum. At one point, Candystand.com had 2.5 million visitors per month.[47] Advergaming can also be used to promote entertainment: Fox created an online game to promote a new season of the popular show 24, and doubled the bang for its buck by including LG phones for players to use.[48] In a "serious game" example, *America's Army*, designed by the United States Army to encourage enlistment and to educate people about the military, has over 6 million registered users, and is ranked among the top five PC online action games.[49] Army enlistment increased during the two-year period after the game's initial release.[50]

Advergames are almost always free. They can be accessed through the product sponsor's Web site. Providing a link, however, is only the start of a successful marketing strategy. The purpose of an advergame is primarily to promote the product or company sponsoring it. So, much of the marketing should link the game and the product. Game developers and product sponsors can work together to create a marketing strategy that achieves these joint goals. While advergames can also stand on their own as advertisements, they still need to be marketed as games. People play games first and foremost because they are fun, not to research a particular product. Attract interest for an advergame with any of the marketing strategies that are successful for regular games, and interest in the product will follow. Finally, a developer should always endeavor to be credited for creating the game, ensuring additional publicity and perhaps beginning a fan base among those who like the game.

From a legal standpoint, there is one more thing to take care of when releasing an advergame: be sure to disclose that the game's purpose is for advertising.

Other Internet Options

Gamers use the Internet: Advertise through popups, MySpace, viral marketing, demos, and game portals.

Gamers first: Attract the attention of dedicated players first, and the general public second.

Do not forget about access: Create an informative Web site and make sure all your ads encourage potential customers to go there.

The most general form of Internet marketing is through pop-up ads or click ads. While such ads can appear when an Internet user visits any Web page, a more effective marketing strategy is to link these ads directly to sites that appeal to your target audience. Widespread marketing on various sites may reach a larger audience, but concentrated marketing that appears on sites dedicated to gaming will attract the attention of those most likely to purchase your game.

With the increased popularity of sites like MySpace, Friendster, and Facebook, game developers have new ways of reaching gamers. Each of these sites is a network that links people around the world, sometimes by the schools they have attended or shared interests. Ads on these sites tend to be cheaper than other Internet ads. For instance, as of July 2006 a registered user on Facebook can display a flyer 10,000 times for only $5.00.[51] Again, general ads can appear all over the pages on these sites, but developers fare better by seeking out groups that are interested in video games. Ads should be directed at the appropriate interest groups and age levels first, and then presented to a wider audience if finances permit. Blogs present similar opportunities and should be addressed analogously. Developers can start their own blogs, or post on already existing blogs frequented by gamers.

Viral marketing, sometimes referred to as word-of-mouth marketing, is also an increasingly effective way to market a game. When a group of people receives an email providing them with access to a game, a certain percentage will forward it to their friends. If the percentage is large enough, the number of people who play the game can snowball quickly, and your game might reap widespread exposure from just a small initial effort. The activist game *Darfur is Dying*, available at *mtvU.com*, was played by over 700,000 people in two months. Its fast popularity was attributed to a successful viral marketing campaign. The advice for viral marketing is the same as for any other type of marketing: make a great game! If people enjoy playing your game, they will forward it to their friends. Good gameplay, entertaining graphics, and a strong message are key to this type of campaign.

With any form of Internet marketing, make sure to include all the pertinent information about your game, and above all else, provide a Web site where interested players can go to learn more and access the game. Make sure your Web site is easily accessed through search engines, and think carefully about tailoring your keywords to accurately reflect your game and attract the attention of your target audience. Provide mailing list subscriptions and message boards with access through your Web site, so your soon-to-be fan base has a place to go to discuss the game.

One of the newest trends in game marketing is through the games themselves. *Second Life*®, a massively multiplayer online game that allows players to create everything in their virtual world, is the newest marketplace where developers have found success in publicizing and selling their games. Nathan Keir, 31-year-old programmer, created a mix of bingo and Tetris called *Tringo*. He has sold 226 copies to other players for approximately $50 each. The game became so popular within *Second Life* that a real-world company licensed the game for a fee in the low five figures, and it will soon appear on Game Boy Advance and cell phones.[52]

Moreover, free downloadable demos are an excellent way to market your game, especially for smaller developers with original titles. EA may not need to provide demos of each year's new *Madden* game, but original games do not share the same established player base. Demos introduce prospective customers to the game, and have the potential, if enough effort is made, to engage players who eagerly await the game's release. Linking these demos with Web sites associated with gaming will attract interest and generate buzz, and can help the developer work out bugs based on player feedback. Even games with well-known titles, such as *King Kong* and *X-Men Legends*™, offer free downloadable demos.[53] The attention of potential customers is well worth the substantial effort required to create a properly working demo with the same quality as the finished game.

Finally, consider promoting your game through portals like Yahoo! Games, the AOL Games Channel, or AddictingGames.com. These sites maintain a vast database of games that players can access for free, and each site attracts millions of users looking for casual games. AddictingGames promotes 12 new games per week, so opportunities abound for developers willing to offer free access to their games in exchange for exposure. Games on these sites are short and often cost under $5,000 to develop, but popular games enjoy a great deal of exposure to the large number of people who visit these sites. However, do not assume you can sacrifice quality just because you will not be receiving profits from the game; players are looking for good games and interesting ideas, and a half-hearted effort will neither gain you customers nor help you build your brand.

False Advertising

Irrespective of whether you choose print, television, or the Internet as your advertising medium, beware of false advertising claims. For example, the use of screenshots that depict full-motion video-cut scenes rather than actual gameplay may give rise to false advertising claims. Cut scenes are often more visually stunning than actual gameplay, but can result in legal complications when they are not representative of the total gaming experience. While this tactic has not typically led to false advertising lawsuits, consumers who purchase a game based on these screenshots may feel duped when they discover that the screenshots are not representative of actual gameplay. The resulting loss of goodwill is likely not worth the additional sales such a strategy might produce. Moreover, given the litigious society we live in, this strategy may be an invitation to a false advertising suit.

When Activision implemented this strategy, it was forced to pull its ads for *Call of Duty® 2* and *Call of Duty 2: Big Red One*, by the United Kingdom's Advertising Standards Authority. The ads used pre-rendered footage that did not appear in the actual video game. Despite Activision's argument that the use of such pre-rendered footage in advertisements was common industry practice, the Advertising Standards Authority ordered the ads to be removed.[54] While there is an obvious distinction between using footage from a cut scene that appears in the game and using footage that does not actually appear in the game, the principle remains the same—consumers are buying the video game based on footage that does not accurately reflect the actual gameplay.

Developers should also be wary of what they include in the game itself. Take-Two Interactive Software, Inc. and its subsidiary Rockstar Games, makers of the *Grand Theft Auto* series, faced a panoply of legal problems for their inclusion of a sex scene in *Grand Theft Auto: San Andreas*. The scene was only viewable if the player downloaded a software modification from the Internet. After news of the sex scene broke, the game's rating was changed from M for mature to AO for adults only. The FTC instituted an inquiry into Take-Two's advertising practices,[55] the Los Angeles City Attorney filed a civil lawsuit,[56] and an 85-year-old grandmother who had bought the game for her 14-year-old grandson instituted a class action lawsuit after learning of the sex scene.[57]

While it remains to be seen how these lawsuits will unfold, it is clear that developers must be careful in the current regulatory environment. Video games are an easy scapegoat for politicians and family groups, and pressure has long been building for increased regulation of the video game industry. Any misstep by the industry will receive close scrutiny from Congress, the FTC, courts, and various interest groups. The FTC investigation of *Grand Theft Auto: San Andreas*, for example, came at the behest of the House of Representatives, who voted 355 to 21 in favor of asking the FTC to investigate Take-Two Interactive.[58] The video game industry is under intense scrutiny as is; developers should therefore be wary of providing its opponents with additional ammunition.

Measuring Marketing Success

Market measurements: Understand the size of the video game industry.
Why measure your marketing: Do not waste time and money.
More than just yardsticks: Use conversion rates, focus groups, and surveys.

In 2004, Microsoft Game Studios released *Halo 2*, the sequel to one of Xbox's most successful games to date. In its first 24 hours on the shelves, almost 2.4 million copies were sold, generating approximately $125 million. By comparison, the then-highest one-day box office hit—Spiderman® 2—grossed only $116 million. Even more staggering is the fact that the video game industry recorded over $10 billion in software, hardware, and accessories sales in 2005.[59] With such a huge marketplace, it may be easy to lose sight of your own personal successes.

While it is unlikely that an independently developed game will break records any time soon, it is important to set reasonable goals for your game and to measure the success of your marketing campaign in relation to those goals. By measuring your marketing campaign's effectiveness, you can ensure that dollars are not being wasted on advertisements that are simply not working. It is not easy to measure marketing success with a limited budget, but there are several ways to do so without breaking the bank.

Set a Marketing Goal: Conversion Rates

One way to gauge the effectiveness of your marketing efforts is to measure conversion rates. A conversion rate is the number of customers who *purchase* your game after downloading a trial version or demo, divided by the total number of people who downloaded the trial version or demo. For example, if 1 out of every 100 people purchases your game, the conversion rate would be 1%. This percentage indicates both the desirability of your game in general and the effectiveness of the trial or demo. Prior to putting your game on the market, it is helpful to set a goal for your conversion rate and a monthly or quarterly monitoring system to gauge whether your game is meeting that goal. If you are not meeting your goals, try lowering the price or offering a longer trial period. You should also set a corresponding monetary goal on the same monthly or quarterly timeline. To make $5,000 in the first quarter selling the game at $10 per unit, with a 1% conversion rate you would need to have at least 50,000 downloads (with 500 people actually purchasing the game) to meet that goal. As a gauge, 5% is considered a good conversion rate by most video game developers.

Another reason to keep track of your conversion rate and related sales data is that access to this information is often key when negotiating contract terms with in-game advertisers. Companies who place ads within your game will want to know that players are seeing those ads and getting their money's worth. This data demonstrates how many players view each ad within a given period of time; your ability to provide access to this data can make or break an advertising deal. Likewise, when contracting with third-party advertising brokers, like Massive, Inc. or Double Fusion, be sure to include terms guaranteeing that all parties have access to such data so that you, and the advertisers, can monitor the success of each advertising strategy.

Focus Groups

A presale method of measuring marketing success is to use a traditional focus group. A focus group is a form of qualitative research (which gauges the opinions of a small number of customers, but does not result in statistically significant results) in which a group of people are asked about their attitude toward a product, concept, advertisement, idea, or packaging. A professional moderator asks questions in an interactive group setting where participants are encouraged to exchange opinions with other group members. In the world of marketing, focus groups are an important tool for acquiring feedback about new products and marketing campaigns. In particular, focus groups allow companies looking to develop, package, name, or test a new product to do so before the product is made available to the public. Focus groups can provide invaluable information about the potential market acceptance of the product, the best way to position the product in the market, and which segments of the market will be most receptive to the product. If your budget does not allow for hiring a professional moderator or conducting a lengthy series of formal sessions, an informal conversation with a few gamers you know can be a good substitute. Keep in mind that your game's identifying information should be withheld from the group to ensure unbiased feedback.

From a marketing perspective, focus groups can evaluate the effectiveness of marketing campaigns. The respondents participating in the session should be pre-screened to ensure the group is representative of your target market segment and that none of the respondents is so deeply involved in the video game industry that he or she cannot present objective views. A simple approach is to gather between four and eight typical customers with a moderator and have them look at several different Web sites featuring advertising for your game and other games. The moderator should engage the group in a discussion about the ads and how they compare to one another. Focus groups provide particularly useful insights into the mindset of your customers because the moderator can probe respondents for the reasons behind their opinions. What about the advertising design attracts them to the game? Why do certain words, fonts, or features appeal to them more than others do? What aspects of the marketing effort would discourage them from purchasing the product? To enhance the results, it is helpful to repeat this process multiple times, tweaking the ads based on the feedback of each group.

Surveys

An inexpensive, practical way to get feedback is to solicit gamers to fill out surveys. A survey is an efficient way of collecting information from a large number of respondents and is typically easy to administer. Quantitative research, such as that collected through a survey, is especially useful for a game developer who is looking for statistical information and predictive responses on a large scale. Online surveys are particularly effective, as there is little effort required of the respondent, and the game developer can easily modify the survey based on changes in the marketplace or preliminary results. Also, because gamers and developers alike are comfortable in front of the computer screen, online surveys may be more likely than paper surveys to elicit truthful responses from gaming customers. However, it can be harder to ensure that you are getting unique responses from different individuals online.

Depending on your objectives, you will want to survey different people at different times. If you are interested in understanding why people have decided to try your game, you may want to gather survey responses at the expiration of the game's trial period or at the end of the demo. To collect information from customers who have already purchased your game, use the contact information customers provided when they bought or registered your game. If you wish to survey customers who have not yet expressed an interest in your game, post a survey solicitation on a discussion board or send a solicitation email to a gamer listserve. If gamers fail to respond to such requests, persuade them to participate by offering incentives, such as extended trial periods or product discounts. If offering discounts to all respondents is too expensive, a lottery incentive may be preferable: offer a fantastic prize to one lucky randomly selected respondent. Incentives may also improve the quality of your results, because compensated respondents are more likely to provide honest and thorough feedback than respondents who fill out the survey for free.

A well-crafted survey can provide information about your target audience and the effectiveness of your marketing efforts. Surveys should always begin with questions about respondents' demographic information and background. Answers to such questions enable the game developer to analyze his or her customer base and to exclude answers from atypical respondents. More substantive questions might ask where respondents learned of the game and whether advertising on certain Web sites played any significant part in piquing their interest. The survey could also include a space for suggestions on how to improve the marketing campaign or even the game itself. Analyzing this data at an aggregate level can illuminate the strengths and weaknesses of your marketing campaign. In addition, results that are segmented by demographic information or responses to particular questions can provide insights into the best ways to market to particular subsets of customers. For example, adults may respond differently to advertisements than younger gamers, and males may respond differently than females.

In any market research project, cover your legal bases. Focus groups and surveys are a prime opportunity for competitors to gain inside information about your product. Require all participants to sign nondisclosure agreements (NDAs) before allowing them to participate. To protect your trade secrets, only convey information that is necessary to answer the survey questions. After working so hard to develop and market your game, the last thing you want is for someone to steal your ideas.

Marketing Mistakes and How to Avoid Them

Lack of a vision: Do not forget to develop a marketing plan.
Inadequate research: Get to know your target audience.
Design duds: Be creative with your image.
Thinking too small: Do not assume that you need big bucks to market effectively.
Not knowing when to stop: Avoid over-marketing.

In the process of creating and executing your marketing campaign, keep in mind the marketing pitfalls that can plague a developer. Even the best games can fail in the marketplace if developers make the kinds of mistakes that are common to small businesses.

Failure to Create a Marketing Plan

One huge mistake a developer can make in its marketing efforts is to underestimate the importance of a marketing plan that identifies target customers and outlines a strategy to attract and retain those customers.[60] A marketing plan should accomplish four objectives:

- Determining customer needs and wants through market research.
- Pinpointing the specific target market to be served.
- Analyzing the company's competitive advantages and building a market strategy around them.
- Developing a mix of games that meets the needs and wants of different customers.[61]

A well-considered marketing plan will ensure that you convey a consistent, persuasive message to your target audience. As you develop your marketing plan, be sure to keep in mind the unique qualities of your customers and your game.[62]

A key step in any marketing plan is to conduct a situation analysis that identifies the factors, behaviors, and trends that may have a direct bearing on your marketing plan.[63] This process should include extensive research into potential customers. Essential questions to ask, and more importantly to accurately answer, are:

- Who is the customer?
- What does the customer desire from the product?
- Where will the customer purchase the product?
- Why does the customer buy the product?
- When does the customer purchase the product?
- How does the customer seek satisfaction in the market?[64]

Use the market research tools described throughout this chapter to analyze the answers to these questions.

Tailor your marketing plan according to the results of your research. Every product must be marketed differently; pay attention to what your customers are telling you about the best ways to reach them. Your marketing plan should spell out your overall strategy and the tactics you will use to achieve your particular business objectives. "Any marketing program has a better chance of being productive if it is timed, designed, and written to solve a problem for potential customers and is carried out in a way that the customer understands and trusts."[65]

Inadequate Research on Your Target Market

A failure to identify and understand your target market is detrimental to the success of marketing your game: if you do not know who will buy your product, chances are they will not know to buy your product either. Such a failure will make it impossible to position your product in a way that catches your target customers' attention.

Effective market research "uncovers unmet needs in the market that [game developers] can take advantage of."[66] Small companies, such as independent game developers, that identify unique demographic trends and act early on such trends can gain a competitive advantage in the marketplace.[67] Targeting the correct group of potential buyers requires accepting the reality that your game may not be needed or wanted by everyone in the market.[68]

Avoid the fatal marketing mistake of misidentifying or not understanding your target market by using the results of your market research. Pay special attention to potential buyers' age, gender, personality, and lifestyle.[69] Also, try to gain a comprehensive understanding of the consumers' purchase approach (the method of acquisition of the product) and choice criteria (why the consumer is selecting the product).[70] This will enable you to develop a meaningful and effective marketing strategy.

Lack of Creative Design and Image

Never forget that your game is a unique bundle of features and characteristics, distinct from any other product on the market. Managing this bundle of characteristics includes making creative marketing decisions about packaging and title.[71] By emphasizing the unique features of your game in your marketing efforts, you will "create an appealing, visually attractive and distinctive need satisfier" for the customer.[72]

One way to highlight the unique aspects of your game is to creatively design the game's packaging. A failure to distinguish your game through its packaging may undermine the success of your business. You may have a great game, but consumers will not know that unless the package succeeds at getting their attention and conveying the desirability of your product. Without a demonstration, the package is all you have to attract your customers' attention and give them a feel of what your product is all about. When designing your packaging, use the same creativity that went into developing your game.[73] Choosing color, trademark location, title placement, and overall appearance are all important decisions. Of course, you should also be careful to avoid the error of choosing packaging that does not adequately protect the technology you have worked so hard to develop.

A bad title can be as fatal a flaw as poor packaging. Select a title that is simple, specific, and special. Your title should be catchy and easy to remember. At the same time, it should highlight the unique selling points of your game. Also, be sure to choose a title that sets your product apart from other games on the market.[74] What independent game developers lack in capital and liquid assets should be compensated for with ingenuity and creativity.

Fabulous Marketing Does Not Require a Fabulously Large Budget

Small game developers often make the mistake of assuming that they simply cannot afford to effectively market their products. Although small independent game developers may not have the resources of their larger rivals, they can harness their creativity to approach marketing in a fresh and innovative manner.[75] Marketers have come up with a strategy that is especially appropriate for small businesses in exactly this situation: guerilla marketing.[76] Guerilla marketing signifies "unconventional, low-cost, creative techniques [where] small companies can wring as much or more 'bang' from their marketing bucks."[77] Examples of guerilla marketing include giveaways, seminars, word of mouth campaigns, classified ads, and even personal letters.[78] Things to keep in mind when developing a creative approach are:

- Keep it simple and avoid confusing the audience.
- Have one basic idea and focus on that benefit.
- Make your point clear.
- Identify your product and company clearly and often.[79]

By applying this strategy to the marketing media discussed throughout this chapter, you will be able to get your message to your target audience even if you do not have millions (or even thousands) of dollars to spend.

Enough Is Enough: The Problem of Over-Marketing

Some game developers become so obsessed with the notion of marketing their product that they actually spend *too* much time and effort on the marketing process. Unfortunately, "most small businesses follow a 'shotgun approach' to marketing, firing marketing blasts at every customer they see, hoping to capture just some of them."[80] Such over-marketing can be especially tragic for small businesses whose economic resources are limited. Small businesses should recognize that they probably cannot compete with their larger rivals, at least not yet.[81] Many small businesses "attempt to reach everyone and end up reaching no one; they spend precious resources trying to reach customer[s] who are not the most profitable."[82] To avoid this problem, keep the customer in the forefront of your mind at all times, creatively tailoring a marketing approach that best serves the well-defined target market.

Conclusion

Now that you understand the basics of marketing your video game, it is time to take action. The first and most important step in creating your marketing plan is to assess your game and your goals. What are your strengths and weaknesses? What results are you looking for in the next six months? The next year or five years? Identifying and setting goals for yourself will help keep your marketing plan on track. Remember to be honest with yourself; do not have unrealistic expectations. It is better to run a small marketing campaign effectively than to blitz the public with too much information.

Do market research, and identify your target audience early on. Consider the different media in which you can place your ads, and ask yourself which will best enable you to reach your target customers. Diversify if you can, but concentrate first on areas frequented by gamers. Most of your business is likely to come from dedicated gamers, so sell them on the merits of your game before you move on to wider audiences. Continually assess your marketing campaign as you go. Customer feedback is one of the most important assets you have; *listen* to what your customers are telling you and respond to it. As you now know, marketing is about satisfying consumer needs and wants, and consumers are the best people to tell you how to do so. Treat marketing like a game, with sales and exposure as the final prize.

Endnotes

*The author would like to thank Farnaz Alemi, Monica Awadalla, Jennifer Heger, Kyle Johnson, Blair Kaminsky, Michael Scalera, Lyndsay Speece, and Michelle Velasquez for their enormous contributions to this chapter.

1. *http://www.briannorris.com/whatismarketing.html*
2. *http://www.marketingpower.com/mg-dictionary-view1862.php*
3. *http://www.cim.co.uk/cim/ser/html/infQuiGlo.cfm?letter=M*
4. *http://news.com.com/Internet+ad+revenue+climbs+26+percent/2100-1024_3-5882670.html*
5. Norman M. Scarborough and Thomas W. Zimmer, *Effective Small Business Management*, Upper Saddle River, NJ: Prentice-Hall (6th ed. 2000), p. 173.
6. *Marketing: The 4Ps* by Joseph Lieberman—available at *http://www.vgsmart.com/tips.html* (last visited June 22, 2006).
7. *Id.*
8. *Id.*
9. *Id.*
10. *Id.*
11. *Id.*
12. *http://www.gamasutra.com/features/20060519/jusso_01.shtml*
13. See *http://www.macrovision.com/company/news/press/newsdetail.jsp?id=Mon%20Mar%2014% 2006:50:17%20PST%202005.*
14. *Id.*
15. *http://news.zdnet.com/2100-9595_22-515372.html*
16. *Id.*

17. *Marketing: The 4Ps* by Joseph Lieberman—available at *http://www.vgsmart.com/tips.html* (last visited June 22, 2006).

18. A detailed discussion of the intricacies and requirements of COPPA is beyond the scope of this chapter. COPPA guidelines are codified at 15 U.S.C. § 6501–6506 and further information is available at *http://www.ftc.gov/bcp/conline/pubs/buspubs/coppa.htm.*

19. *http://www.usatoday.com/tech/news/2004-05-12-gamer-demographics_x.htm*

20. *http://www.theesa.com/archives/files/Essential%20Facts%202006.pdf*, page 2

21. *Id.*

22. Screen Digest Study

23. Peter J. Coughlan, *Note on Home Video Game Technology and Industry Structure*, Harvard Business School, 9-700-107, Rev. June 13, 2001, at 9.

24. *http://www.theesa.com/archives/files/Essential%20Facts%202006.pdf*, page 5

25. *http://www.census.gov/*

26. *http://www.hispaniconline.com/magazine/2004/dec/Features/gifts.html*

27. *http://retailindustry.about.com/od/seg_toys/a/mobile_games.htm*

28. *http://www.gamasutra.com/features/20060519/jusso_02.shtml*

29. *http://www.gamasutra.com/features/20050809/eilers_01.shtml*

30. *E3*, available at *http://en.wikipedia.org/wiki/E%C2%B3.*

31. *Id.*

32. Dawn C. Chmielewski, *Sony Set to Unveil PS3* Los Angeles Times (LATWP News Service), May 7, 2006.

33. *EGM's Opinionated Preview Guide*, Electronic Gaming Monthly, July 2006, at 56–77.

34. Advertisement for *NCAA Football 07*, in Electronic Gaming Monthly, July 2006, at 8–9.

35. *http://www.pbs.org/cgi-registry/generic/trivia.cgi*

36. *http://www.gamespot.com/ps2/sports/maddennfl2006/news.html?sid=6147928*

37. *http://abcnews.go.com/Technology/story?id=1981149&page=1*

38. *http://www.usatoday.com/tech/news/2004-05-12-gamer-demographics_x.htm*

39. *http://www.yankeegroup.com/public/news_releases/news_release_detail.jsp?ID= PressReleases/ news_4172006_InGameAdvertising.htm*

40. *http://www.clickz.com/news/article.php/3604001*

41. *http://www.neoseeker.com/Games/Products/PS2/madden_nfl_2006/screens.html*

42. *http://news.zdnet.com/2100-9595_22-958098.html*

43. *http://news.com.com/EverQuest+gets+pizza+partner/2061-1043_3-5582977.html*

44. *http://www.crm-daily.com/story.xhtml?story_id=112008C5BVR4*

45. *http://www.businessweek.com/innovate/content/mar2006/id20060324_990680.htm? chan= innovation_game+room_game+developers+conference*

46. *http://www.ebusinessforum.com/index.asp?layout=rich_story&doc_id=7282&   categoryid= &channelid=&search=video+games*

47. *http://www.imediaconnection.com/content/1060.asp*

48. *http://www.fox.com/24/game/index.htm*

49. *http://www.americasarmy.com/*

50. *http://www.sourcewatch.org/index.php?title=America's_Army*

51. *http://www.facebook.com/flyers.php*

52. *http://www.businessweek.com/magazine/content/06_18/b3982001.htm*

53. *http://www.kidzworld.com/site/p6415.htm*

54. Call of Duty Ads Pulled from UK TV, *http://www.joystiq.com/2006/02/22/call-of-duty-ads-pulled-from-uk-tv/* (Feb. 22, 2006, 13:00 EST).

55. Curt Feldman & Tor Thorson, *Take-Two sued, confirms FTC investigation*, July 27, 2005, at *http://www.videogames.yahoo.com/newsarticle?eid=385620&page=0*.

56. Hilary Potkewitz, *It's Take Two on Suit Over Hot Tub Scene in 'Grand Theft Auto'*, Jan. 30, 2006, available at *http://www.allbusiness.com/periodicals/article/871439-1.html*.

57. Associated Press, *Grandmother Sues 'Grand Theft Auto' Maker*, July 27, 2005, at *http://www.msnbc.msn.com/id/8728577/*.

58. *Id.*

59. *http://www.npd.com/dynamic/releases/press_060117.html*

60. Scarborough & Zimmer, *supra* note 5, at 172.

61. Scarborough & Zimmer, *supra* note 5, at 173.

62. Burnett, *supra* note 1, at 18–19.

63. Burnett, *supra* note 1, at 19.

64. *Id.* at 55.

65. Managing a Small Business, *http://www.bizmove.com/marketing* (last visited June 13, 2006).

66. *Id.* at 175.

67. *Id.* at 174.

68. Burnett, *supra* note 1, at 31.

69. *Id.* at 36.

70. *Id.*

71. *Id.* at 162.

72. Burnett, *supra* note 1, at 162

73. *Id.* at 163.

74. *Id.*

75. Scarborough & Zimmer, *supra* note 5, at 172.

76. *Id.*

77. *Id.*

78. *http://en.wikipedia.org/wiki/Guerilla_marketing*

79. *Id.* at 350.

80. *Id.* at 181.

81. *Id.*

82. Scaborough & Zimmer, *supra* note 5, at 181.

CHAPTER 6

PR Plans and Programs for the Game Developer

Ted Brockwood

ted@calico-media.com

Public relations (PR) is one of the more misunderstood pieces of the product development and publishing puzzle. It is often confused (or even lumped in) with marketing, but the two are different disciplines. Ignoring either element is a sure way to marginalize your game, since both are needed to build buzz around the game and your company.

The Question Everybody Asks: What Is PR?

When you look at them under the microscope, marketing is about *getting consumers interested in your game*, while PR is about *getting editors and journalists interested in your game*. While the ultimate goal of getting media interest in your game is to get information to your potential audience, you must take a slightly different approach.

Getting editors talking about your game is extremely important. Without editorial coverage, both in print publications and online, your game will lack the buzz at the start of development that gets people interested and the ongoing buzz that keeps them interested. As you make your way through this chapter, you will learn how a well-coordinated PR effort, even one with zero dollars behind it, can boost a game's image within the industry. Getting editors and industry insiders talking will then boost the efforts of your marketing programs. If you are a developer without a publisher, a good public relations campaign can help get your game in front of those elusive publishers once they see what kind of buzz your game is getting.

"What is buzz?" you ask? Buzz is excitement, interest, and anticipation for a product. Buzz is what gets publishers to look at your game, gets retailers to think about stocking your game, and gets consumers prepared to buy your game. Buzz will not guarantee sales, but it will let people know more about your game, which can drive more sales. Where does buzz get built? Buzz gets built in forums, blogs, magazines, on TV and radio, on Web sites, and in newspapers. Every comment about your game is a bit of buzz, for better or worse, and it is up to you to use every opportunity available to you to build buzz. Even negative buzz can be an opportunity, as long as you have planned for it and understand how to respond.

Do It Yourself versus Hiring Someone

PR is something you can do yourself, or you can bring in the help of contractors or big agencies. As with other industries, there are PR firms that specialize in electronic entertainment and plenty of individual contractors. So the first question to ask yourself when you are ready to start PR for your game is, "do it yourself, or hire out?"

The advantage of doing it yourself (DIY) is twofold: first, it is economical, since all the work is handled by you. DIY PR, however, means a lot of legwork as you will need to create press lists, get on editors' radars, and learn to put together and distribute press kits, assets (screenshots, trailers, and documentation), and preview/review mailings. PR agencies and contractors, on the other hand, typically offer experienced staff who are already knowledgeable about working with the media, have extensive contact lists, and are skilled at developing PR plans. The downside to hiring someone to do your PR is cost; most agencies and even individuals command an hourly rate that a DIY developer might not be able to bear, especially if it is your first title. Even if you decide to use an outside agency or individual, it is important to understand the elements required to maximize the effect of your PR. What follows is the "Guide to Getting Buzz Going on Your Game."

PR Planning

First and foremost, you need a PR plan. A PR plan consists of a schedule of assets you want to make available, press releases you want to issue, and a preview/review schedule. You can put your plan together in any format you like, such as Excel, Word, or another program. Make sure it is something you are comfortable using because you will need to refer to it frequently. There are also online project management tools such as basecamp™ (*www.basecamphq.com*) that will allow you to create a project plan and invite others to contribute to the plan.

Planning Assets

Assets are items you plan to distribute to the media to show off your game. Example assets you might schedule in your plan include:

- Screenshots
- Video trailers
- Developer diaries
- Interviews/Q&As
- A fact sheet

These five items are what most professionals would consider a minimum for asset planning. There are no hard and fast rules for how many of each asset you should make available, but it should be enough to keep your game in front of the media from the time your PR efforts launch to at least a month after your game ships for a typical single-player game. Games with primarily online components, such as MMOs, will need a more sustained PR plan.

Planning a Schedule

When should your start your PR efforts? That is one question with no absolute answer, but a good rule of thumb is to start between one year and six months before you expect to ship the finished version of your game. If you start PR only a few months before your ship date, there is no chance for your buzz to build up. If you start more than a year out, you will dilute the interest in your game, as editors and readers think, "ho hum, another set of screens for Ultra Pinball XWar, but is it ever going to ship?"

Along with planning asset distribution, you need to plan for press releases, which are used to announce the various stages of your game's development. Plan to have a press release to announce your game is in development, then plan for another to announce that it has "Gone Gold" (development is completed and it is getting packaged for retail or download), and one for when your game has "Shipped" (is available to consumers). Other items you should announce to the media, but do not require a full-blown press release include:

- Launching an official website for your game
- Releasing PR assets
- Releasing a demo

The preceding items do not warrant a press release; they typically are announced through a more informal email to editors, either a simple "Hi, we released this item today" type of email, or if you are feeling formal, a Media/News Alert. News Alerts (also called Media Alerts) contain most of the elements of a press release but are less involved. Large publishers tend to use alerts when they want to announce something related to their product, but do not want to deal with the legal issues involved in a press release; press releases have to be kept on file and checked by lawyers when issued by a publicly traded company.

Planning the Campaign

Scheduling a PR campaign is not as tricky as it might initially sound. First, put together the list of assets you hope to make available, along with your ideas for press releases and media alerts. Then, try to spread out your asset distribution. For example, if you know you can put together 30 high-quality screens of your game over the next six months of the plan, try to plan to release five per month. Try not to overdo it; if you blast out ten to twenty screens a month and they are not all that different from month to month, you are going to bore editors and readers alike. So, be honest with how many top-quality screens you think you can produce, and split them out over the schedule.

Videos should be huge affairs and huge files, so you will probably only send out two or three during your PR plan. Launching one with your game announcement as a sort of "preview" of the game, then sending out another two to three months later, and finally releasing one just before shipping should be more than enough. These videos should show off your game in action, demonstrating gameplay and any spectacular effects that may not be properly captured by static screenshots.

Demos typically do well when released just before the game ships, using final code whenever possible. The demo should give your potential customers a good taste of the game that leaves them wanting more. A bad demo, released months before a game ships, can do harm and kill buzz quickly. More details on these issues are discussed in the section "Asset Planning."

Crafting a Press Release

Before you begin working on your first press release, ask yourself what kind of writer you are. If you received horrible grades in school for your writing skills, then see if a friend can help with your release. If you cannot write, do not pretend you can. Like it or not, a poorly written release reflects on the quality of your product, so do not botch this chance to make a good first impression. Just because you can write spotless code does not mean you have perfect English grammar. But if you do, let us get to work.

A press release has the following base components:

- Descriptive but short subject line
- Intro paragraph
- Product "boilerplate"
- Developer "boilerplate"
- Any additional "boilerplates"

What are "boilerplates?" In this context, they refer to a block of standard text included in your press releases and other documentation. For example, the "developer boilerplate" is text added to every press release issued by your development company explaining who the developer is. The different types of boilerplates are described here.

To break down a press release, start with the subject line. This is incredibly important and will determine if your release is read by an editor or sent to the email trash bin. It is fine to be clever and creative, but you must always be sure that the subject line conveys what the release is about. For example, let us say your development company, DeveloperXYZ, is announcing the game "Galaxy Dynamo" for Windows. There are a couple of ways to approach the subject. First, is the straightforward approach:

DeveloperXYZ Announces Galaxy Dynamo for Windows

It may not be creative, but it gets the point across. However, it could use a bit more info, such as:

DeveloperXYZ Announces New 4X Space Sim—Galaxy Dynamo for Windows

This subject adds more meat, but still maintains a good length. Remember, many email readers (especially Web-based email) cut off long subject lines, so try to keep it under control. This is more a "feel" decision, but when was the last time you read an email with a subject like this:

DeveloperXYZ Announces Groundbreaking New 4X Space Sim—Galaxy Dynamo for Windows with Mac and Linux Client to come

That is simply too long and will probably make its way into the trash bin. Moreover, the part about the Mac and Linux Clients is something you can include in the release as a sub-headline.

Working with the second subject line, you can get a little creative.

DeveloperXYZ Launches Galactic Conquest Plans with Galaxy Dynamo—a 4X Space Sim

This is a bit longer than before, but not so long that it will be cut off in an email reader. In addition, it has a more "fun" element to it (". . . Galactic Conquest Plans . . ."), which for some editors is a nice change from the daily deluge of "XYZ Announced Today" releases they receive. Creative headlines do not guarantee your release will be read, but if it is read, the editors may associate your game with a more fun/creative feeling.

Once you have a subject line, it is time to develop the introductory paragraph. This should simply announce your game and give some basic information about it. Do not go into too much detail; we are just trying to get the recipient to start reading, and flooding them with details from the start is a sure way to turn them off. In the example of Galaxy Dynamo, this could be the introductory paragraph:

> March 11, 2007—DeveloperXYZ has today announced the development of Galaxy Dynamo, an exciting 4X space simulation for Windows. Galaxy Dynamo will set gamers in the middle of a galactic war, where each decision can mean a stunning victory or horrible defeat at the hands of a variety of alien races. With a powerful game engine, players will be challenged to act as diplomats, military leaders, and ship designers. For more information, please visit (your game's homepage).

The preceding paragraph accomplishes a few basic goals:

- It gets the reader's interest by announcing the game.
- It tells the reader the basic concept of the game.
- It teases with some details about game elements.

The next paragraph should be your product boilerplate, a description of the game that fleshes out all the details. Once you have settled on a boilerplate, you should continue to use it in every release and announcement unless you add or remove features. If your feature list changes, you should update the product boilerplate as well. The following is a sample product boilerplate for Galaxy Dynamo:

> In development by DeveloperXYZ, Galaxy Dynamo is a 4X space-sim on an epic scale. Setting players in a universe populated by eight distinct alien races spread across 20 planets, the game's single- and multiplayer gameplay will offer dozens of hours of replay value. With more than fifteen styles of spacecraft and two hundred customization options for each, including special weapons, wing designs, hull layouts, and battle computers, no two ships will ever look or play the same. The goal of Galaxy Dynamo is complete dominance of the known galaxy—which players can achieve through a skillful combination of diplomacy, trade, and military might. A customized 3D graphics engine will render everything in beautiful detail—from the insignia on uniforms to the battered hull of a ship that has passed through an asteroid field.

Notice how much information has been put into just one paragraph? Notice how it has been done in a way as to not seem forced? Sentences flow into one another and keep the readers interested as they learn more about the specific details of the game.

Once the game ships, it is important to change the tense of the boilerplate. During development, you use the future tense. Once the game ships, you should edit your product boilerplate to read in a mix of present and past tense. For example, the first two sentences in the preceding example would be reworked as:

> Designed and developed by DeveloperXYZ, Galaxy Dynamo is a 4X space-sim on an epic scale. Setting players in a universe populated by eight distinct alien races spread across 20 planets, the game's single- and multiplayer gameplay offers dozens of hours of replay value.

Tense may seem to be a nitpicky detail, but remember that every press release you issue reflects your writing skills, your product, and your company. You must always make the best impression possible. Sloppy releases will not help your image.

Following the product boilerplate is your company boilerplate. This is a description of your company that should be included with every press release you issue. Try to keep it short and simple; just cover some basics about your company, past titles you have worked on, and future titles you have in process. For example:

> DeveloperXYZ, an independent game-design company based in Austin, Texas, is dedicated to creating top-tier shareware games. Joe Smith, the company chairman and lead developer, is experienced in development for Windows, Linux, and Macintosh platforms. Past titles developed by Mr. Smith and DeveloperXYZ include, Friday Funk, Siver Shadowdown, and Racing Marmots. More information about DeveloperXYZ can be found at (your company website).

Additional boilerplates may sometimes be required; usually, if you are working with a publisher, another developer, or any other company, you want to give credit where it is due. If you are going to include additional boilerplates, ask the parties involved for one they have put together, and as a courtesy, let them see the final press release before you send it out.

Lastly, be sure to include relevant contact information. There should always be a URL for your company included (do not point to personal websites—have one made for your company), along with email and telephone contact information. Editors need a way to quickly contact you and/or receive more information about you and your game, and providing this is the most convenient (and appreciated) way to do so. If you do not include this information, editors will not contact you and your PR will not be as efficient as it could be.

Now that your press release is written and spell-checked, pass it along to a few friends to have them check it for readability, grammar, and content. It helps if you have an editor friend or two take a look, as they see hundreds of releases a week and can tell you what catches their interest and what enters their virtual circular file. If you do not have any editor friends, *make some*. This is the best way to start getting good PR.

After you have finalized your press release, you need to distribute it. There are several ways to do this: you can use a service like PRWeb, pay for a game industry-specific service, or create your own mailing list and send it yourself. Determining how to send out your release is a matter of budget and time. For example, services like PRWeb are inexpensive, but do not directly target some of the editors you might wish to reach, unless you pay extra. Game industry–specific release services will ensure you hit the right editors, but can also be expensive, some up to $500 or more to send one release. Lastly, there is the DIY method, which is easy on the wallet, but can require some time investment. Doing it yourself means you will know exactly what editors are on your mailing lists and you can send releases whenever you want, but it also means spending plenty of time putting together your contact lists.

When it comes to DIY contact lists, the Web is your best friend. First, you need to visit the sites you hope to get coverage on, such as GameSpot, GameSpy, and IGN. Look around at past stories and news items, and put together a list of the writers' names (keep this in a spreadsheet for easy access and usage) and their contact information. Some sites mask editor contact information with a generic address, such as *mailbag@xyz.com*. This will sometimes work for you, but it is best to find the direct email for news editors. To do this, you can ask around with other developers and editors, or start doing Web searches. Sites such as Google, when searched properly, can yield volumes of contact information. Failing that, the next step is to send an email to a publication/site's generic address saying who you are, and that you would like the news editor's contact information so you can send him your releases.

One more thing: to get editors interested in your game, it helps to make available a few screenshots with your press release. That said, do not include multi-megabyte attachments with the release. Instead, grab five or six great screens from your game, zip them, and post them on your FTP server. Then, include the URL to the screens in your release. Even if the screens show an early version of the interface, characters, or other elements, editors will post them and understand they are early screenshots. If you are concerned about the treatment your screens may get, you could include a note such as, *"Note to Editors: Screenshots from our current Alpha (Beta, demo) build are available at: URL."* This lets the editor know you have screens, and sets expectations as to the screens' quality.

With your mailing list in hand, it is time to distribute your press release. There are no hard and fast rules on the best time and days to send them out, although some email distribution services that are paid to process, distribute, and track email campaigns have reported that Friday is the best day to send news and releases. You should experiment and see what gets the best response. It is important to keep holidays in mind, as some online publications close for several days around major U.S. holidays. If you send your release during a holiday, it may fall on deaf (or vacationing) ears. It is best to try to avoid sending a release the day of, before, or after a holiday. For Christmas, you should plan to get your release out at least three days beforehand or three days after the New Year's holiday.

Follow-up is something you should not ignore. A day after sending a release, if you have noticed it did not make it on a major site you were targeting, try to give the editor a call or send an email. Do not send emails like "did you get my press release?" Frankly, that is just annoying. Instead, drop the editor another email mentioning you sent a release, but noticed he did not post it. Say that you were hoping he could help you understand why so you can get his interest in the future. If you can call the editor, do not whine or complain about not getting your release published—just ask if he can help you better understand how you can interest him in your game. Contact with editors is crucial, and if you develop an early rapport with specific editors, it becomes much easier to receive continued editorial coverage of your game and pitch those same editors on special features, such as developer diaries or question and answer sessions.

Fact Sheet Development

A key part of your PR plan and press kit is your fact sheet. A fact sheet is a basic overview of the game and, as with your other assets, it is targeted toward editors instead of consumers. Since it is designed for editors' eyes, you need to keep the flowery language to a minimum—the fact sheet is there to spell out in bullet points what your game is about and what its features are. A fact sheet is something you will always need handy when the press asks for more information about your game. It also gives you a handy reference to those features you might forget about when you are in the middle of a question and answer session with a reporter. Finally, some editors, especially at smaller publications, will use your fact sheet to build an early preview of your game. Be sure you have a quality fact sheet ready when you announce your game.

The typical fact sheet consists of:

- Your game's logo (if you do not have one, get one made immediately)
- An introductory paragraph
- Five to six bullet points that detail key features
- Your company's boilerplate

The introductory paragraph is simple to put together if you have already completed your first press release; just re-use the game boilerplate you created. It is OK to recycle your content.

The bullet points are key. Take the major features of your game and boil them down into quick, digestible bits. Do not get wordy with bullet points; they are called "bullets", because they are quick and effective. These bullet points are your 30-second shot at describing your game and grabbing the interest of editors.

What sort of features should you focus on? You need to first decide what makes your game unique compared to others in the genre. Is it the first 3D title in the genre? Maybe it has more races (in the case of Galaxy Dynamo) than any other game. Pick at least one or two unique features to include, and then include other special features in your game.

Remember, however, that no matter how great your features are, each should be described as succinctly as possible, with a minimum of qualitative descriptions. A quick way to develop your list is to look at the boilerplate for your game, and then distill those features into your bullet points. Some examples of bullet points for Galaxy Dynamo:

- "From the cockpit" action-oriented gameplay: Galaxy Dynamo is the first 4X space simulation to offer the player direct control of units from an "in cockpit" perspective.
- A dynamic universe featuring eight unique races competing for control of 20 planets.
- Single- and multiplayer play via LAN or over the Internet featuring a persistent "capture the galaxy" mode in online play. Players can check the status of their race's conquests at *http://www.galaxydynamo.com/*.
- A powerful 3D engine dynamically renders spacecraft, aliens, and planets in real time.
- A deep single-player campaign storyline written by renowned comic-book writer Haggis McWritt.

There you have it, five bullet points with one unique feature listed right at the start to grab the reader's attention. A completed fact sheet can look like:

Developer XYZ

Galaxy Dynamo

Fact Sheet

Galaxy Dynamo is a 4X space-sim on an epic scale. Setting players in a universe populated by eight distinct alien races spread across 20 planets, the game's single- and multiplayer gameplay offers dozens of hours of replay value. With more than 15 styles of spacecraft and 200 customization options for each, including special weapons, wing designs, hull layouts, and battle computers, no two ships will ever look or play the same. The goal of Galaxy Dynamo is complete dominance of the known galaxy, which players can achieve through a skillful combination of diplomacy, trade, and military might. A customized 3D graphics engine will render everything in beautiful detail—from the insignia on uniforms to the scratches on the hull of a ship that has passed through an asteroid field.

- "From the cockpit" action-oriented gameplay: Galaxy Dynamo is the first 4X space simulation to offer the player direct control of units from an "in cockpit" perspective.
- A dynamic universe featuring eight unique races competing for control of 20 planets.
- Single- and multiplayer play via LAN or over the Internet featuring a persistent "capture the galaxy" mode in online play. Players can check the status of their race's conquests at *www.galaxydynamo.com*.
- A powerful 3D engine dynamically renders spacecraft, aliens, and planets in real time.
- A deep single-player campaign storyline written by renowned comic-book writer Haggis McWritt.

DeveloperXYZ, an independent game-design company based in Austin, Texas, is dedicated to creating top-tier shareware games. Joe Smith, the company chairman and lead developer, is experienced in development for Windows, Linux, and Macintosh platforms. Past titles developed by Mr. Smith and DeveloperXYZ include Friday Funk, Siver Shadowdown, and Racing Marmots. More information about DeveloperXYZ can be found at *http://www.developer-xyz.com/*.

Contact: John Xavius, *john@developer-xyz.com*, ph. 555.555.5555

Asset Development

As already mentioned, you need to develop a plan to distribute assets such as screenshots, video trailers, and demos. Scheduling development of these assets keeps you on track. Without a plan, you will quickly find yourself scrambling to collect and distribute assets after realizing, "there is nothing out there about my game!" We have already discussed putting a plan together; now it is time to create those assets. It does not do your game any good to snap a few random screens, compress them heavily so you can fit them in an email, and send them off. It will do you, your sanity, and your game much better to develop quality assets to start with.

Developing Screenshots

An excellent set of screenshots is the first thing you should put together for your game. Plan to release packs of five to ten of them on a regular basis during your PR plan. If you are executing a six-month PR plan, then one pack per month should be more than enough, or even one pack every two months. It is perfectly acceptable for your screenshot quality to get better during the development and PR process—readers and editors understand that game visuals evolve during production, but you should not release anything you feel is sub-standard. You do not ever want someone to see a bad image of your game and form a poor opinion.

First and foremost, you have to decide what tool you will use to capture images from your game. You can write your own, or save some time (if you are writing a game for Windows) and use Fraps (*http://www.fraps.com/*), a popular tool that allows you to set capture quality for screenshots and video alike. While jpegs are a good format for keeping file size down, you should not rely on them for high-quality images, especially if you will be working with editors from print publications. Instead, try to capture screens in tiff or bitmap format, as they use minimal compression. This will lead to huge file sizes, but you will be posting the images in zip format on your own server for download rather than attaching them to an email (which is a major *faux pas*), so large file sizes are fine in this case. Alternatively, you could have your screenshots in multiple formats so small website operators can download the screenshots and put them up with little effort.

Choosing what parts of your game to feature in a pack of screenshots is up to you. One good starting point is to focus on important features. The first pack, for example, could contain images that show a few units in hi-resolution detail, combat taking place, and a strategic map. Another idea is to develop packs of theme-based images. For example, in the case of Galaxy Dynamo, you could release a pack of screenshots for each race in the game, a pack featuring a variety of ships, and so forth. Whatever you choose, you can always change it, but it is good to have some sort of guiding principle behind your screenshot releases.

Developing Videos

Videos are another key asset you should plan to release regularly. However, they are time-consuming to create, so do not overextend yourself or your team by trying to create too many. In a six-month span, two to three videos will be more than enough to show off your game.

Videos should be of the highest quality possible. You can create some in-game footage using Fraps again, if your game is on Windows. Each video can be a mix of gameplay scenes and cut scenes, demonstrating the feel and flavor of your game. A supporting musical track helps set the pace for the video trailer, but be sure you do not use a copyrighted work without permission.

Developing a Q&A

Along with videos and screenshots, it can also help to create a general Q&A. The general Q&A is something that helps you maintain a specific message about your game whenever someone interviews you. To develop a general Q&A, simply sit down and write down ten to twenty questions you think the media would ask about your game. Then, answer each as if you were being interviewed, sounding as professional as possible but also maintaining your own personal style. The reason you need this is so you stay on track when handling interviews. There is nothing worse than realizing you gave a completely different answer to the same question asked by multiple reporters and then seeing your different answers pop up online or in print. Or worse, giving contradictory answers to similar questions, confusing readers and editors alike. It is important to note that you should also anticipate any rude or negative questions and have answers ready for them. It might be hard to think that someone might attack your pride and joy, but it can happen. Questions might be especially tough if your game contains any elements that might be hot-button issues in the media.

Developing a Walkthrough and Strategy Guide

A walkthrough is helpful when you are sending preview and review builds of your game to the media. These should contain a quick walkthrough of the first few levels of the game, even if your game already contains a tutorial. This helps an editor jump into the game immediately and helps you point out some of the more important aspects of your game that could be overlooked. For example, Galaxy Dynamo might have a first mission that features multiple alien races, an opportunity for the players to design their own ship, and some great interactions with AI-controlled characters. Unless your game is linear, which many editors dislike these days, the preview writer may miss some of these elements as he explores the level. A walkthrough that follows the format of "go here and meet this alien, then go here and talk to this character, finally getting permission to enter the docking bay to enter ship-building mode" gives editors a chance to go straight to your important elements immediately. They will not see this as reflecting on whether your game is linear in nature; rather, they will look at it as a time saver so they can learn more about those bullet points from your fact sheet. Do not kill yourself making a walkthrough, just look at the first few levels and pick out key elements you believe are important for everyone looking at your game to notice. Then, find a way to string them together in an interesting path and write it all up. Include screenshots for any time you expect there to be a lot of interaction with the game's interface. Your well-designed and intuitive interface may not seem that way to an editor who has never seen your game before and has limited time to grasp it.

Strategy guides are optional, but can help increase coverage of your game. A strategy guide is different from a walkthrough in that you should use it to cover helpful tips for enjoying the game, not walking the player through the game. For example, in Galaxy Dynamo, rather than saying, "always have 400 kilotons of Ore, 100 of fuel and 10 of water," you could say, "Ore is the most important thing in Galaxy Dynamo, followed by fuel and water, so if you have limited credits, it is best to use them to build ore refineries first when you start a mission." You want to give tips, not a direct path through each mission in your game. Strategy guides are typically something online editors will happily post for you, as long as they are well written. Remember to have a friend fact-check the guide and check your grammar. If you find that nobody is interested in your strategy guide, you can always convert it to a PDF and post it to your game's official site and include it with copies of your game.

Developing Descriptive Text

Last, but certainly not least, you should put together some descriptive text for key elements of your game. For example, Galaxy Dynamo has eight races and 20 planets in its universe, so you should have a description of each race and each planet available. Often, these descriptions might be found within the game itself.

You can pitch these descriptions to editors for features such as "The Races of Galaxy Dynamo" and "Exploring the Universe of Galaxy Dynamo." Look for other feature ideas based on elements of your game. Another example from Galaxy Dynamo would be, "Ships of the Line—From Freighters to Cruisers," which you could pitch to an editor as an idea and provide him with the descriptive text for all the ships in the game.

The Story Pitching Process

Now that you have plenty of assets, an introductory press release, a PR plan, and some story ideas, it is time to reach out to the media, or "pitch" them, as the PR pros like to say. Pitching is not a complex science; it is simply picking up the phone or sending an email to contact an editor with a story idea. It is a bit tricky at first, since you have probably had no contact with these editors before, but as long as you have a good pitch and a good game, you will stand a good chance of grabbing their interest.

Story ideas are basic frameworks for features you are hoping editors will put together about your game. For example, if you are working on an RPG, you might come up with a story idea related to the skill-tree in the game. Along with that, you might pitch a story idea related to the weapons, NPCs, and other elements of the game. A good story idea should focus on unique elements from within your game. Popular features often include developer diaries, general stories about how a game was conceived, and, as already mentioned, core elements of the game.

Obviously, you first need a list of PR contacts. Again, to develop your contact list, look at the sites and magazines you are hoping to get talking about your game. Do not limit yourself to just three or four of the big hitters, either. Take a good look around and see who you think might cover your game—from independent game developer sites to consumer and entertainment publications, it is all fair game as long as you can find an angle that gets them interested in your story. A good example: Galaxy Dynamo has what the developer considers some incredibly well crafted cinematics and a powerful graphics engine to support players making their own cut scenes. In this case, you would be wise to expand your pitching targets to sites and publications that cover animation, computer animation, digital art, and machinima. It bears mention that online sites are probably your best chance to be noticed at first, building up buzz to attract the more limited attention of print magazines. TV and radio are still tough nuts to crack for games, unless you have an amazingly unique story, such as hundreds of people lining up outside your development offices (or house, as the case may be) to get a sneak peek at your game.

Getting contact information so you can call or email the editor can be a challenge. It is harder dealing with print publications, and much harder for TV and radio, should you be interested in trying those venues, since they typically do not list their direct contact information in print. If you dig around most magazines, however, you can find a central phone number and editor's name in the masthead, and once you call that, you can ask directly for the editor and hope to be put through. For online editors, it is typically much easier, since they post their own email addresses or at least a central email address. If it is just a general mailbox, such as mailbox@ultragamingwebsite.com, then send an email to that address—but do not pitch your story to it. Instead, ask for contact information for the editor, and when you get that, send the story pitch directly to the editor.

Once you have your targets sighted, it is time to get down to creating story ideas. Remember in the asset plan for Galaxy Dynamo where we created a list of alien races and fleshed out their unique characteristics? This is a perfect story to pitch to a game editor, or even to the editor of a science-fiction publication. So it is time to get on the phone or put together a compelling email.

A story pitch should be simple and to the point, but be sure to open it by simply introducing yourself and your part on the development team. Always remember that these editors receive dozens, if not sometimes hundreds, of emails a day, so keep your introduction and pitch short and to the point, offering links to your website for more information and, of course, plenty of contact information. Make yourself as available as possible, offering phone, cell phone, and email information. If editors are interested, but cannot get in touch with you, there goes your story, as they will quickly move on to something else. Make yourself accessible when pitching stories.

Checking back after contacting an editor is important, but you should not make a nuisance of yourself. If you have not heard back from the editor after two or three days, feel free to check in again, but keep your call or email short and to the point. If you have been relying solely on email to open a dialog with an editor, it is worth giving a call after a few days, as sometimes that person might be just too busy to answer every email. A polite nudge via the telephone can often mean the difference between never hearing back and getting a great front-page feature.

The last part of the pitching process, follow-up, is incredibly important. You cannot drop the ball at any time. You should be ready to answer an editor's questions at all times. This may mean you have to take an hour break from writing code, putting together a website, or working on marketing materials. If you do not follow up on requests for information, it will send a very negative message to those editors who are actually excited about your project.

In the end, the story pitching process is straightforward—you come up with some interesting story angles for your game (developer diaries, character biographies, etc.), pick some sites and magazines to pitch, and then start calling and emailing.

The Demo Process

Demos are incredibly important to the PR process for your game. A demo is a potential customer's first taste of your game, and it can make or break potential sales. Along with the consumer interest a demo generates, demos also boost editors' interest, as a good demo shows you are serious about your game. The demo will get editors to take you more seriously. On top of that, websites love to be the first to post a demo for a new game, so a good demo can help build PR coverage as you offer important sites first opportunity on hosting the demo. Often, a site will feature a demo on their front page for several days, giving it a huge PR and marketing boost. However, no amount of front-page coverage can save a game if the demo is bad, so you need to know what makes a good demo.

First, a good demo contains a strong sampling of what is in your game without giving the entire game away. If you are creating a first-person shooter (FPS), it is good to include a variety of levels. If an FPS you are working on features battles in a wide variety of military environments, then try to use that variety to your advantage. Have one demo level take place indoors at a base, another on the deck of a ship, and perhaps the last level inside a secret aquatic base, to show that your game is more than just running around indoors. Galaxy Dynamo's demo, for example, might have one mission where the player takes on the role of one alien race, then another mission as another race with completely different ships and resources to show off the variety of alien races.

The length of the demo is up to you, but one-level demos are rarely well received by gamers or editors, unless they feature a good mix of gameplay features and are more than just a few minutes long. More than one developer has released a one-level demo that only lasted 10 minutes and left gamers and writers scratching their heads wondering, "Why even bother with this?" You do not ever want anyone asking that question; you want them begging for more and excited about the final product. Look at your game as a whole, pick out elements you think will be exciting for players to see, and try to build a demo around that. Also, do not make the mistake of creating a demo that is the full game with some levels simply locked out through programming. It is lazy and will make more than one person unhappy to download a large amount of data to only play three levels. It will make game pirates very happy, as they will surely find a way to crack your protection scheme and unlock the rest of the game without paying you anything.

Once you have a demo ready, be sure to have friends and fellow developers play test it for balance and bugs. You do not want to release a demo in which pistols are 10 times more powerful than rockets, or a demo where the sound cuts out halfway into the first mission. Bugs in the demo will make potential customers expect huge bugs in your final product, which will not help sales.

Finally, when you release the demo, be sure to announce it wherever possible. If it is not exclusive to one site, dig around and find all the popular download sites, such as 3D Gamers, File Planet, File Front, and so forth, and get a copy of it to each. Generally, these sites are happy for the content, and if you get the demo to them two or three days before you want to officially announce it, you can often convince them to produce some sort of promotional graphics for it that they will feature on their front page. This is where it pays to have renders and screenshots available at all times, since the editors at the download sites can quickly use them to put together promotional materials.

Online Communities

Forums, blogs, and fan sites are other editorial opportunities for your game. While these sites do not follow the standard editorial conventions of most print publications, many have very loyal followings and should not be overlooked. However, they do require more legwork on your part and should be treated with special care at all times.

Posting in Online Forums

If you have never spent time on a game or entertainment forum, there is no time like the present to get started. They provide a rich library of feedback from your game's potential purchasers. Pick some of the major forums, such as those at IGN.com, GameSpot.com, and 1Up.com, and spend a few hours each week reading them and looking for discussion topics that could be related to your game. Look for discussions about related genres, developers, and competing games. You will find more information than you will know what to do with.

If you are a long-standing member of an online forum, you could post a few tidbits of information about your game. You should be careful to never market your game in a forum, however, as that is considered a breach of etiquette. Be especially careful about posting on forums where you have not been a long-standing member, because your posts will be flamed and ridiculed as unwelcome spam. At most, a post about your own product should be limited to two or three sentences about the overall concept, a sentence about your company (or, if going it alone, your history in games), and a link for more infomation.

Do not flood forums with useless messages by posting simple marketing messages or subjective messages such as, "Galaxy Dynamo is really going to be fantastic! Check it out!" You should be professional and only post to a limited number of sites where you are already a member in good standing. Again, do not post simple advertisements; just tell your fellow forum members what you are working on, what a few features are, and give them a link so they can decide if they are interested in more information. Some companies have no qualms about spamming forums with "product XYZ will be the best ever!!!!" These types of messages tend to provoke gamers to retaliate with negative commentary and the whole process creates very negative feelings toward the company and the product.

Finally, treat forums very carefully. Reading a popular forum is not a replacement for market research, since only the most dedicated and hardcore players tend to post on these types of forums. You will see extreme behavior and attitudes, and it can be easy to get into a heated discussion about a topic and upset some of the posters or lurking readers of the forum. Always project the right image when you post on the forums to support your game. Follow the established etiquette of the forum. The people on these forums can be great for spreading the word about your game to their friends, but they can just as easily spread negative word of mouth if you upset them.

Getting Blog Coverage

Blogs have been getting more attention recently, and many have become almost as respectable as more traditional media. Bloggers tend to be more honest, so working with bloggers is something that requires a different tack than working with traditional editors. Bloggers tend to be looking for less "fluff" and more meat about a game. They will have no qualms calling out a bad game or championing an under appreciated underdog. Many consider the issuing of screenshots fluff, as they would much rather get their hands on the game than see what it is supposed to look like. Remember that most are not paid to blog; they are doing it out of a love of their subject material. You want to respect that and not take up too much of their time, or pitch them on a game that is too early for a hands-on demo or that has nothing to do with the type of games they like to cover. The best tip for working with bloggers is to simply read as many game blogs as you can find time for, get a feel for their style and what they focus on, and then pitch them an appropriate story or send them assets. Do not blindly blanket them with screenshots and hope they post a few—bloggers prefer a more personal touch on every level. Before you start inundating them with assets, be sure to introduce yourself and tell them your story and the story of your game, from how you started in the industry to what you are hoping to accomplish with your game.

Working with Fan Sites

Fan sites are another special editorial outlet that requires specific care and feeding in your PR plan. A fan site, as the name implies, is a site built by someone who loves your game, its genre, or even a competing title. They are built and maintained by passionate people who may not be professional writers, but have a deep knowledge of their subject matter. When you are "PRing" your game, you should search for fan sites related to your game, usually specific genre sites, such as RTS, FPS, and so forth, or even older competing titles. Although some sites are dedicated to your competitors, the editors of fan sites often enjoy discussing all related titles, so do not ignore these competing sites. Offer the editors of fan sites as much information as you would offer editors of large game sites—screenshots, Q&As, videos, and so forth. These sites serve a very targeted audience that may not be large, but is typically ravenous for information about related titles. Do not be afraid to work out special features with them. It can certainly help to hold onto a batch of screenshots that you can divvy up as exclusives to fan sites. They will appreciate you for it and work hard to give you as much coverage as they can. Editors on general or competing sites may even build out a special new site, or subsection of their main site, dedicated specifically to your game, and this is where the Fan Site Kit comes into play.

A Fan Site Kit, or FSK for short, is a collection of screens, videos, banners, logos, and other game info you package into one file and post freely for gamers to use to build a fan site for your game. Since you have provided specific assets, it ensures that any fan sites related to your game have a good starting point that shows your game in its best light. Sometimes, especially with lesser-known games, it takes a special nudge to get fan sites started. One of the best ways to nudge people is to offer a "best fan site contest." It is simple enough—you release the basic FSK, and in the news alert that announces the availability of the kit you mention a contest being held for "best fan site." The rules are up to you, but be sure to talk to some people in the know about the legalities of holding contests in your country. Prizes are likewise up to your discretion—you might make the winner the "new official site" for your game, or give the best three sites free copies of your game when it ships. It is all up to you.

Once you have a fan site or two to work with, do not forget to help the editors/webmasters maintain them by providing a continual stream of new and updated assets. There is nothing worse than a fan site that has out-of-date information about a game that is supposed to be their key focus. Offer the fan site webmaster exclusive screens, a Q&A with you and your team, or an exclusive video. You need to treat these sites as something special—which they are—as someone spending the time, effort, and money to make a site about a game they will not share in the profit from. Make them feel like part of the process and they will become fantastic allies in promoting your game. There are plenty of older games out there, such as *Quake* and *Half-Life*, which to this day still have thriving fan communities that keep people buying those titles years after they have launched and eagerly following the sequels.

Press Tours

While sending out preview and review builds helps get your game in front of editors, there is nothing like a face-to-face meeting to really sell your game to them. This is where the press tour comes in. Take the latest and greatest version of your game and head to San Francisco, the world headquarters of most of the game industry's media powerhouses GameSpot, IGN, PC Gamer, Computer Gaming World, and so forth—

they are all there, and showing up on their doorsteps with game in hand will do a lot for getting you coverage and building a strong rapport with them.

Unless you live in the San Francisco area, a press tour will probably be costly since you will need one or two days to cover most of the major publications. However, if you can gather the money needed, it is worth visiting for a preview tour and a final review tour. If, however, you can only afford one trip and this is your first game, it is probably best to set up a preview tour. This way, you get on editors' radars early on, and you will have a relationship in place before you ship review builds. Remember, the press tour is not just about showing your game, it is also about making contacts, starting up a conversation with key media, and showing you are serious about your game.

Putting together a press tour starts with having a good build to show. Do not expect to get very good results from a tour if you show up with a build of one level that crashes every five minutes. The build, just like that demo you are planning to release, should give editors a good taste of key elements of the game along with a basic sense of the graphics, sound, and interface elements. The build does not have to be a near-complete copy of the game—editors understand when they are being shown early product—but there needs to be some substance to what you are going to show them. In addition, you should plan to leave behind a copy of your game build with each editor you meet. Builds should be clearly labeled (especially if they span multiple disks), and you should include contact information and a fact sheet. A CD or DVD of new assets, such as screenshots and videos, are always welcomed by editors.

Next comes the preparation of your demo script. While you would certainly love to be able to spend two hours showing your game to all the editors, they rarely have that much time available. Thus, you need to put together a walkthrough that you can use to take the editor through about 45 minutes of gameplay. The other 15 minutes you will want to leave free for question and answer time.

The script needs to be concise and direct, and you need to write it down and rehearse it. The need to rehearse cannot be stressed enough, because if you start fumbling through your demo, it is going to go downhill quickly and you will lose valuable time trying to get back on track. Sit down with your demo and walk through it, taking notes and creating a path of "do this, then this, then this" with pauses for you to explain key elements. Even though your demo is scripted, expect some random questions and have your Q&A memorized beforehand.

Some developers prefer to open a demo with a slideshow presentation of screen-shots and bullet points illustrating key elements of the game. When done properly, this can be a useful lead-in, as it gives editors a quick overview of what they are about to see and allows them to mentally prepare a few questions before you start. If you go this route, however, your slideshow needs to be short, as the actual demo is where you will get into more detail. Do not go longer than five minutes with your slide presentation. Editors want to see the game, not just a presentation about it. Keep that presentation handy, as it may be valuable to show your game to potential publishers.

After choosing your build and planning your demo script, you will next need to plan the tour. Pick a date to arrive in San Francisco and plan to spend two full days there. Before you leave, put together a list of time slots you hope to book, understanding that it is best not to show up at a publication's office before 10:00 AM, and you should not have any appointments that run past 5:00 PM. If you already get along well with a particular editor, you might be able to make some dinner appointments, but do not count on this your first time around.

When it comes to booking time with editors, the phone is your best friend. While email is easy, you stand a better chance of getting immediate responses by picking up the phone. If you do not have the direct phone number of an editor, you can usually search the San Francisco phonebook online to get the publication office's main number. From there, it is as simple as calling and asking for the specific editor. Introduce yourself, tell him or her you are coming to town and would like to show your game, and suggest a time slot you have available. While you may not get to meet with the specific editor you have targeted, most will try to find a time for someone on staff to meet with you.

Once your schedule is set, all that is left is to fly out and make your meetings. Do not kill yourself if you fall behind; editors are generally flexible with their schedules. If one meeting runs long, just call ahead to the next and let them know you will be late. It may mean cutting down the length of your demo or scheduling it for another time, but they will most likely still meet with you.

After the press tour, make sure you follow up with all the editors to thank them for meeting with you, and offer any additional assets they may need. The follow-up is a courtesy that is very much appreciated.

On a related note, there is a constant argument in PR as to whether little trinkets, called swag or tchotchkes, help when an editor is deciding to write about your game. While swag is sometimes cute and fun, it is not really going to affect how an editor views your game. At most, it might be a helpful reminder that the game is sitting on their desk waiting to be written about, but that is all. No matter how cool that custom-made T-shirt is, it is not going to get you better coverage, but feel free to give some out as a friendly gesture. Everyone loves a good t-shirt, coffee cup, or plush toy. However, if you are going to leave behind a tchotchke, do not be cheap about it. People never forget, and rarely forgive, cheapness.

Industry Events

The game industry is a serious business and there are plenty of events related to the trade. While there are several big name conferences, such as E3 and the Game Developers Conference (GDC), those might be outside the range of your budget. If so, try to think small, but accessible. The Indie Games Con (*http://www.indiegamescon.com/*), for example, is a yearly show-and-tell session combined with classes on development,

PR, marketing, and other important issues to the small developer. It is just one of the many events that are perfect for developers with limited budgets to use to get the word out. A little research should lead you to two or three conferences or conventions that meet your needs and budget.

If you decide to attend a conference and show your game, be sure it is in optimal shape to be on public display. That means you should have a playable demo handy—one that is fairly robust (read: does not crash constantly when played without supervision) and shows off the best aspects of your game. Some shows will have several PCs set up for developers to load their games onto, which means attendees will get plenty of free play. This means you may not always be there when your demo gets played, so be sure it is intuitive and stable enough to be played by just about anyone.

Before you head out for a big event, send out a brief news blurb to your press contacts letting them know you will be at the event and will have something playable to show. If this is the first time your game is being shown, you should definitely let the press know there will be a playable build available so they can be sure to have any attending editors check it out.

Lastly, should you win any awards at the event, do not forget to let the media know. This can suddenly pique the interest of editors who had not yet covered your game.

Viral Marketing

Viral marketing is a recent hot topic and something you can consider trying during the PR process for your game. Although it is referred to as "marketing," it is a function often handled by PR since it often includes media outreach.

Viral marketing is an attempt to create a campaign that spreads by word of mouth rather than through traditional direct PR and marketing efforts. Recent examples in the game industry include Microsoft's *Halo 2* "ilovebees" campaign, Sony's "Giantology" site, and SEGA's "Beta-7" blog. All of these were campaigns created by PR and marketing teams, but were spread primarily through consumer word of mouth rather than press releases and advertising. These types of campaigns can be very effective, even though they do not relate directly to the game. The ilovebees campaign, for example, was so popular that thousands of people have been digging for clues about the program, discussing it in forums, blogs, and even garnering mainstream media interest.

Viral campaigns do not have to be as involved as the PR campaigns previously mentioned. You could, for example, create a website based on characters from your game that seems to be produced by the characters themselves. By releasing a few unique trailers, which you could link to from appropriate online forums and submit to various blogs, you would build traffic to this site, and get people talking about your game. The one thing to be careful about when creating viral campaigns is you should not send out unsolicited emails, nor should you spam forums or blogs. Try to find appropriate outlets for your viral media; contact the webmaster or blogger, and ask if they will work with you on seeding your assets. It cannot be stressed enough—never randomly spam sites or blogs; it will almost instantly lead to negative feelings and negative word of mouth about you, your game, and anything or anyone related.

While we are on the topic of viral marketing, there are several viral outlets you should not ignore—Google Video and YouTube. Both offer free hosting of videos, and track the newest and most popular videos. Should your video be noticed, you may find thousands of people suddenly becoming interested in your game, including people who had never heard of it before. If you are going to "go viral," do not miss these opportunities to spread your video assets, perhaps even creating something extra-special for use on these sites to capture attention.

Contests

People love free stuff, and having a contest to give away a few copies of your game can often help boost its visibility with consumers. Contests are usually a part of a PR campaign, since you will work with publications, especially online sites, to announce and feature your contest. Having a major site actually run your contest saves you from many legal issues involved with giveaways, and generally eases the logistical load from your back.

What kind of contest to have is completely up to you. Using Galaxy Dynamo as an example, after releasing the fan site kit, you could hold a contest for the best fan site. The winner would receive several copies of the game when it ships, including a few spare copies to give to visitors. You obviously do not want to give away too many copies, but five or six to a larger site should do nicely. If you want to give more incentive to people to sign up for your contest, be sure to offer prizes such as T-shirts, stickers, game guides, and so forth for other places besides first place.

Other contest ideas for our hypothetical space sim could be:

- Name an alien race in the game and the name will be used in the final game.
- Have entrants create an alien hero based on their personality, submitting a short description and a drawing or photo. The winner becomes a character in the game.
- After the demo is released, hold a fan contest to create the best video trailer. The winning video becomes an "official" video distributed for the game and would be included in the final game.
- Design the game's packaging and get credit on the box for it.

All of these ideas get fans, or just people with a competitive streak and a lust for fame, to check out your game and help generate buzz (and assets) for you. Contests that bring entrants into the game development process become viral on their own, as everyone wants his or her 15 minutes of fame, even if it is something as simple as getting credited on a game box.

A Sample PR Program for Galaxy Dynamo

The easiest way to understand a PR plan/program is to see a completed plan. Therefore, what follows is a complete plan for Galaxy Dynamo, our example game of galactic conquest. You can design the plan as a word processing document, spreadsheet, or project management application. Whatever you use, be sure it is something you are comfortable with and can make changes on-the-fly, because PR plans are constantly in flux. A plan should be used as a guide, and you should expect it to be changed to adapt to everything from the press response to your game to changes in the market for games of your chosen genre.

What follows is a fairly simple plan, but can serve as a handy reference when you are not sure where to start. If you were to work with a PR contractor or agency, you could expect a much more detailed and formalized PR plan with dates assets are needed by versus dates they will be provided to the media, who is responsible for what asset, and so forth.

You will notice that the plan aims to provide some sort of asset or information about the game for each month from the start of the plan until the game ships. That is a good schedule to plan for if you can keep up with the resource needs.

Sample PR Program
_____

Title: Galaxy Dynamo
PR program launch date: June 1, 2007
Anticipated game ship date: December 31, 2007
Fact sheet

Press releases/news alerts
June 1, 2007—"Game in development" press release.
August 1, 2007—"Fan site kit" news alert.
September 1, 2007— "Design our box art contest" news alert.
November 15, 2007—"Single-player demo available" news alert.
November 30, 2007—"Multiplayer demo available" news alert.
December 15, 2007—"Galaxy Dynamo goes Gold" news alert.
December 31, 2007—"Galaxy Dynamo available in stores" press release.

Screenshot releases
June 1, 2007—Six mixed screens to include with press release.
August 1, 2007—Six mixed screens to include within the fan site kit.
September 15, 2007—Eight screens, one of each race in the game. Be sure to include text in the email saying that these screens illustrate the diverse alien races.

$\rightarrow$

October 15, 2007—Ten screens of various environments, landscapes, and structures available within the game. Include text describing the aspects of the game these screens illustrate.

November 20, 2007 (release between demos)—Six screens focusing on various ships in the game. Briefly describe each ship with one sentence in the included text.

December 15, 2007—Four screens to include with "Gone Gold" news alert.

December 31, 2007—Four screens to include with "Available in stores" press release.

Video releases

July 15, 2007—Teaser trailer (2–3 minutes long) providing a video preview of the overall theme of the game and key concepts.

October 20, 2007—Gameplay trailer (2–3 minutes long) providing snippets of in-game action.

January 3, 2007—In-game trailer focusing on elements of the game along with cut scenes to illustrate the quality of the final game. Releasing these after shipping the game helps spark additional interest in the title for consumers who may have missed the "game ships" announcement or may be on the fence about buying the game without a taste of the final product.

Demos

November 13, 2007—Embargoed release of single-player demo to major online sites, prohibiting release until the 15th. The embargo lets sites play the demo early, giving them time to prepare editorial and front-page feature graphics for when they post the demo.

November 28, 2007—Embargoed release of multiplayer demo. As with single-player demo, releasing to major sites early allows them time to evaluate the demo and prepare editorial coverage before the actual release of the demo.

Fan site kit

August 1, 2007—Needs for the fan site kit include:

Six screenshots (accounted for in screenshot releases section).

Video preview (re-use video from July 15).

Banners and logos for Galaxy Dynamo in multiple formats (jpeg, layered psd files, tiff files).

Small forum avatars (80 × 80 pixel headshot icons) for each alien race.

Miscellaneous

June 1, 2007—Fact sheet and general question and answer page. A link to the fact sheet should be provided in the "game announcement" press release.

Feature pitches

September 1, 2007—Race profiles: Story focusing on the eight races in the game, their biases, and how they react to one another.

October 1, 2007—Ships of Galaxy Dynamo: Story focusing on various ship types in the game as used by the various races.

December 1, 2007—The Galaxy Dynamo Universe: A feature combining major aspects of gameplay: shipbuilding, combat, strategy, diplomacy, and mission design.

$\rightarrow$

Contest/Viral program

September 1, 2007—"Design our box art" contest. In cooperation with a major online publication, launch a contest where entrants use elements of the fan site kit and available screenshots to design the front-cover box art for Galaxy Dynamo. Judging of the top three entries to be done by the public, with the final choice being made by the developer. Final design becomes property of the developer, which could be used for the actual box art. Winner will receive credit on the box and in the game's credits if design is used, along with several copies of the game.

Create a Web site dedicated to the contest where entries are posted publicly. Visitors can vote for up to three designs, and click on a link to send a design to a friend via email for voting. Voters can sign up for a mailing list, so as new designs become available, an email is sent to voters giving them the opportunity to change their vote and provides them with a reminder about the game.

Events

Date TBD—Secure a booth at "Sci-Fi Fest." Set up several PCs with Galaxy Demo playing throughout the event, and offer guided demos and self-directed play sessions.

Preview/Review program

October 1, 2007—Provide 50 preview copies to key online and print editors. Provide game saves, and cheat codes to allow previewers to sample a variety of missions and gameplay modes.

December 15, 2007—Provide 50 pre-release review copies (gold masters) to top-tier print and online media. Embargo reviews until December 31 (the day Galaxy Dynamo ships to retail) and offer saves, cheat codes, and additional assets to help editors sample the game in its entirety.

Post launch

After the game ships, reach out to various LAN party organizations to offer copies of the game for use at events and as prizes.

Follow up with editors who have not yet posted reviews, offering additional assets such as screenshots and a Q&A to help with their final reviews.

There you have it, a basic PR plan and asset schedule for Galaxy Dynamo. Not every developer will have a budget for things like the "Sci-Fi Fest" booth, but everyone should be able to provide plenty of assets while writing and distributing their own press releases and news alerts.

Contingency Planning

One thing that has not been discussed so far is contingency planning, which is an important part of the PR process. Whether you are working with a big publisher or doing it yourself, you need to plan for the "oh no!" moments that happen anytime during the game development process. There is nothing worse for your mental stability or your game development time line than having to stop everything to handle some horrible news about your game.

A good example of planning for a contingency comes when dealing with demos. On the PC platform, it is not uncommon for a demo to have issues with various types of hardware. This is acceptable to most hardcore gamers if the problem comes from cheap or generic hardware—but let us assume your game fails miserably on one of the more recent video cards. You have three options:

- Own up to the problem and set about creating a fix.
- Admit the problem, but offer no fix.
- Cover your head and hide (or blame the hardware maker for creating poor drivers).

Option 1, in the minds of most developers and PR people, is your best bet. It shows you are serious about your game and willing to do what it takes to keep consumers happy, even though this is a free demo and not the final code.

Option 2 is less desirable, but at least you are being honest about the problem. You will not make any friends with those who use the offending hardware, but by admitting you just do not have the resources to fix the problem in a demo and that you are working on resolving the issue for the final game, you will still earn a few honesty points with consumers. Just dedicate the resources to be sure the problem is fixed in the final game.

Option 3 is such a bad idea, it should not even be listed as an option at all. It is listed here because, in all honesty, it has been used and abused by more than one publisher or developer. While this passing of the buck may take the heat off you temporarily, in the long run, it is going to come back to bite you. In the age of the Internet, lies do not last long. As sure as the sun rises every day, there will be a contingent of gamers who will prove you wrong while making you out to be the worst developer in the history of the industry.

The lesson here is that you have to plan for contingencies and how you would respond. As you develop your PR plan, keep asking yourself, "what if this went wrong?" or "what if that went right?" Wait . . . plan for something going right? Yes, you need to plan for the good and the bad. For example, what if your demo is such a huge hit that people want to start pre-ordering and you do not have a pre-order system in place? How are you going to fix that issue and let the world know how you have fixed it? In general, remember that it is always best to be honest and up front in the case of bad news. Own up to it and announce a plan to fix the problem(s) as soon as you can.

Conclusion

A good PR program can help boost the visibility of a game among editors and journalists, which in turn helps get the game in front of consumers. It is very important to design a PR plan right from the start, setting realistic goals and deadlines for the program while maintaining some flexibility to deal with those "oh no" moments and those glorious "we want to write about your game, but need…" calls from editors.

In the end, remember that most editors are not ogres looking for a new game to trash. For the most part, they are genuinely good people and avid gamers who can become as excited about your game as you are—you just need to give them a reason to get excited.

CHAPTER 7

Intellectual Property

S. Gregory Boyd

GBoyd@kenyon.com

Intellectual property, almost always abbreviated as IP, is arguably the most important branch of law for game developers and publishers to understand. IP is a vital topic of game development contracts, employment agreements, and nearly every license in the game industry. Games are made from works in other media, such as film, through an exchange of IP. Furthermore, as houses are made from wood and stone, games are made almost exclusively from IP.

A thousand years ago, it was easy to protect the most valuable types of property. A person might have a plot of land or a gold mine and would put a fence up, perhaps with some guards, and the property was protected. People might have tried to come and take the property, but the barriers built would work to keep them out. Times have changed, and now the most valuable assets in the world, particularly in the world of game development, are not merely physical. The most valuable asset in the world of ideas is your intellectual property. No guards or fences will protect a game once its source code is leaked and placed on servers throughout the world.

The Importance of IP

Why is IP important for a game company? Because these laws are about protecting you and your creative work. It protects you, the developer, from consumers who want to take your work and use it without paying you. It protects you from some publishers who might be tempted to use your hard work without actually paying anything. It protects you from unscrupulous competitors who would love to steal your confidential information and use it for themselves.

So, yes, it is important. But, does IP really cover so much of game development? Consider this: what does someone buy when buying a game? In the old days before digital distribution, there were retail computer and video game stores. People would actually drive or walk down to a physical building called a video game store. They bought a box with a manual and a CD made from less than $5.00 of material. How then, could people be persuaded to pay $50.00 or $60.00 for this product we call a "game?" People are persuaded, even eager, because they are really buying the IP. Actually buying a limited license to the IP, so this topic is important even in the sale. The game code, manual text, box art, game art, music, story, world, and graphics engine are all IP. Behind the final physical product is the game company's IP. As a member of the game industry, you should understand the legal nature of your creation.

As we venture into the next generation of game consoles, more money than ever is put into game development. This trend will continue into successive console, handheld, and PC generations. As a result, protecting that ever-growing capital investment from competitors and pirates is becoming increasingly important. Of equal importance is harnessing the IP in a game for maximum value to recoup costs. As simplistic as these statements are, the questions and strategies generated by them are immediately more complex.

It is appropriate to address right at the front of this chapter that IP is an emotionally charged issue in the software community generally and the game development community in particular. Many people are in favor of open source initiatives and are against software patents, patents in general, or even intellectual property in general. Many intelligent and insightful people follow this movement. These points of view are clearly influential and hotly debated at the highest public policy and legislative levels throughout the world. But, it is not the purpose of this book to take sides on this or any other public policy issue. As an educational and reference tool, this chapter and this book as a whole should serve as a guide to what the legal issues currently *are*, not how they might eventually evolve, or how they *should* be. To be clear, the author and editors are not taking any side on this debate. Our goal is to objectively convey important concepts as they currently exist in IP law.

Putting all disputes aside, everyone agrees that there is room for improvement in the IP system and that the system is evolving. In addition, the current system is complex. Competitors are sophisticated and will try to use the IP system against your company. For this reason alone, it is important to understand the current IP legal framework.

Intellectual property can be daunting from a distance. Donald Chisum, one of the most famous modern commentators on IP, admits that IP has been called a "pretentious concept."[1] More than 165 years ago, judges were calling intellectual property, the "metaphysics of law . . . where the distinctions are, or at least may be, very subtle and refined, and, sometimes, almost evanescent."[2] It has not gotten easier as we enter the 21st century with digital distribution, virtual item trade, and pirate servers across the globe. In spite of this complexity, it is the primary goal of this chapter to summarize some of the most important IP concepts as they relate to game development and show how to use those concepts to protect the products of game development.

In an effort to get started summarizing these concepts and as a preview for the remainder of the chapter, Table 7.1 lists examples from a game project and the type of IP law used to protect each component.

TABLE 7.1   Game Projects and IP Law

Copyright	Trade Secret	Trademark	Patent
Music	Customer mailing lists	Company name	Inventive gameplay or game design elements
Story	Publisher contacts	Company logo	
Characters	Middleware contacts	Game title	Technical innovations such as elements in software, networking, or database design
Art	Developer contacts	Game subtitle	
Box design	In-house development tools	Identifiable "catch phrases" associated with the game or company	Hardware technical innovations
Web site design	Deal terms		

Copyright

Copyright is arguably the most important IP protection for most small and mid-sized game companies. In the area of game industry IP, copyright easily qualifies as the best tool for protecting game property because of its ease of use, power, and versatility.

Similar to patents, copyright is an area of law that also has its roots in the United States through the Constitution. In fact, we derive copyright law from the same section that is used to derive patent rights. Article I, Section 8, Clause 8 provides that Congress shall have the power: "To promote the progress of science and the useful arts, by securing for limited times to authors and inventors the exclusive right to their respective writings and discoveries." The "writings" language is the focus to derive the power of Congress to make laws for copyright. Copyright is meant to protect these writings for a limited time.

What Can Be Protected by Copyright?

In the United States, eight categories are eligible for copyright protection. These are listed in the statute 17 U.S.C. § 102(a). They are:

- Literary works
- Musical works, including any accompanying words
- Dramatic works, including any accompanying music
- Pantomimes and choreographic works
- Pictorial, graphic, and sculptural works
- Motion pictures and other audiovisual works
- Sound recordings
- Architectural works

Interactive entertainment is protected as either an "other audiovisual work" or, perhaps surprisingly to some, as a "literary work." It is common for some endeavors to fall into more than one category. The only time this is important is for the registration of copyright. Registration under the literary work category may seem strange for a computer program, but literary works are defined in Section 101 of that statute to include works expressed in "words, numbers or other verbal or numerical symbols or indicia, regardless of the nature of the material objects such as books, periodicals, manuscripts, phonorecords, film, tapes, disks, or cards, in which they are embodied." Clearly, the source code is a collection of words, numbers, and symbols, stored on some media.

The Copyright Office maintains a useful Web site at *http://www.copyright.gov/* to help people through the process of copyright registration and has informational documents called Circulars. These Circulars, written in nontechnical English, explain copyright registration and other topics for creative works. At the time of this writing, the *Copyright Office Circular 61*, freely available on the Web site, gives detailed information about the copyright registration of computer and video games.

Generally speaking, Table 7.1 shows that copyright protects the fixed expression of ideas. As far as games are concerned, copyright covers stories, characters, places, music, graphics, and the software source code. Moreover, it also protects the entire game as registered under the category of audiovisual or literary work. A critical but often misunderstood aspect is that copyright protects the *expression* of ideas, not the *ideas* themselves. This leads to two consequences. First, no game ideas are protected by copyright until they are fixed into some expressive medium (like code or print or a saved art file). Second, similar ideas expressed in different ways are allowable with copyright. Determining infringement in copyright requires comparing the fixed expression in the copyrighted game to the fixed expression of the accused infringer.

What Rights Are Conferred by Copyright?

Copyright is a negative right in that it does not grant the holder the right to reproduce a work, but rather grants the holder the right to prevent others from reproducing a work. The list of rights specifically listed in the U.S. statute includes the rights to make copies, make derivative works, distribute, public performance, and public display.

Copyright is also easy to invoke. Copyright comes into being as soon as an original work is fixed in a tangible medium. In contrast, patents and trademarks have important and complex application processes with registration fees and trade secrets, require that certain steps be followed within the company, and need constant vigilance to protect the secrets. Even though registration is not necessary, it is still a good idea.

Some Examples of Copyrights

One key element of copyright is that the definition of art is surprisingly broad beyond the minimal standards of original expression. From Botticelli to *Breakout*, all fixed original creations can be protected by copyright.

The game *Breakout* is an interesting example because it was the subject of a series of cases surrounding the minimal level of creativity necessary for copyright. Atari tried at least twice to register the game for copyright, but registration was initially rejected because of the simplicity in the artistic display in the game. *Breakout* was merely a rectangular object moving in one plane that reflected a small ball into a multicolored wall of rectangles. The ball eliminated a portion of the wall of rectangles and rebounded toward the bottom of the screen, where the player attempted to move the lower rectangle to redirect the ball back toward the wall of rectangles. Atari had to fight a series of cases over the application rejection from 1989 to 1992, eventually winning the fight. This series of cases is important, not only to game IP, but to copyright in general. Those cases stand for the proposition that courts or the Register of Copyright will not judge the creativity or artistic quality in copyright. Any original fixed work in a tangible medium is protected.

Copyright Information

Although any work is copyrighted as soon as it comes into existence, you can also register the copyright for additional rights. Copyright registration is mandatory to litigate over copyright infringement. Consequently, it is also prudent to register copyright before even writing a "cease and desist" letter to potential infringers. Balancing all the factors, the registration is so cheap, easy, and necessary for real legal teeth that the cost and effort necessary for the federal registration are easily worth it.

Process and Cost

The form required to register a copyright is only a few pages long and the cost is approximately $30.00. The Copyright Office has detailed instructions and information on completing the forms and contact information for questions. Of the forms of IP that benefit from registration, this is the easiest and cheapest process.

Length of Copyright Protection

The length of copyright is another element that makes it attractive for game developers. Copyright is long, not immortal like trademark, but long enough to outlive creators. At different times, copyright has varied in length, and the history of copyright contains enough different lengths for such protection to make it seem comical. Luckily for computer games, the length of copyright for works created after 1978 can easily be remembered as 95 years after publication or 120 years after creation. This means that no one can copy the original *Pac-Man* until about 2100. This also means that derivative works require a license until that time expires as well. For Pac-Man, this means no cartoons, board games, clothing, or re-creating that yummy Pac-Man cereal is allowed without the appropriate legal permissions. Around 2100, people can go wild and cover the planet with copies and derivative works after the original game falls into the public domain.

Consider how length affects what is possible for copyright. The length of protection is intimately tied to potential revenue generation. Game developers can use copyright to protect their ideas, build new games, and sell related products for a century. Copyright in a property can literally be developed and exploited over generations. Mickey Mouse, Star Wars, and Superman are excellent examples of this. These IP examples have existed for decades and have been exploited across multiple media, including games.

Protecting Copyright

The most basic step in dealing with copyright infringement is to send out a "cease and desist" letter. This letter simply explains that you own the copyrighted material, the material is registered, and that the other party is using the material without a license. The letter usually goes on to explain the penalties for infringement and demands the other party "cease and desist" from using the material. If the infringement is online, a similar letter or DMCA takedown notice can be sent to the other party's ISP. Most ISPs do not want the potential liability for hosting copyright infringing material. This letter to the infringer and/or his ISP is often enough to stop an infringer. In any event, this process should be managed by and the letters should come from your attorney.

Penalties for Infringement

Heavy potential punishment is a necessary part of any substantial IP protection, and copyright has it. Punishment for copyright infringement allows game developers to prevent infringing parties from selling works that include the developer's copyrighted work. Developers can also sue for damages and profits equal to the profits the infringing parties made from selling the illegal works. Furthermore, willful copyright infringement carries a statutory penalty of up to $150,000 per work infringed.

In a typical copyright lawsuit filed in June 2004, Midway brought a case against Sony Ericsson for violating its copyright on the game *Defender* from 1980. Midway claimed that Ericsson was using the game on its mobile phones without permission. Midway requested that the court award damages, reimbursement of its legal fees, and require Sony Ericsson to turn over all mobile phones, software, and other materials in its possession related to the alleged copyright violation. The case was settled out of court and dismissed a few months later, but still serves as an excellent example of what remedies can be requested in copyright cases.

There are also potential criminal penalties that can result in prison time, when people are caught violating copyright by selling or distributing games over the Internet, under 17 U.S.C. § 506(a) and 18 U.S.C. § 2319. An instance of this came to light in February 2004 when Sean Michael Breen, leader of the Razor1911 warez group, received a four-year prison sentence and was ordered to pay nearly $700,000 in damages for copyright infringement. He was one of 40 people arrested in a sting operation by the U.S. Customs Service "Operation Buccaneer." An even more amusing example surfaced in early 2006 when Yonatan Cohen was convicted of criminal copyright infringement in Minnesota for making a game console that included unlicensed Nintendo games. He was sentenced to five years in prison, lost hundreds of thousands of dollars in cash and property, and was deported to Israel. Worse, his punishment included using his own resources to pay for advertisements in game magazines warning about the penalties for copyright violation. The advertisements had his picture in the center, a picture of his copyright violating device, a description of his punishment, and a caption that read: "This ad was paid for by Yonatan Cohen as part of his restitution to warn others about the dangers and penalties associated with violating the copyrights laws."

Derivative Works

The idea of a "derivative work" is critically important in the way copyright is used in the game industry. It is a new work derived from an existing copyrighted work. The language of the statute defines a derivative work as a work that "is based upon one or more preexisting works, such as a translation, musical arrangement, dramatization, fictionalization, motion picture version, sound recording, art reproduction, abridgement, condensation, or any other form in which a work may be recast, transformed, or adapted."

What does it mean when you read that a company has acquired "the rights" to make a game based on a film? In the copyright sense, this means that a game company has acquired the right to make a derivative work of the film. This is how films are made from games as well. *Doom* the movie was a derivative work created from *Doom*™ the game. The same concept works in reverse as well. *Shrek*® was first a film and then a derivative work was created turning the copyrighted material in the film into a game. Now, it is easy to imagine that this process gets complex quickly. Consider *The Lord of the Rings*, a world described in a series of books by J. R. R. Tolkien. The entity that controls the copyright to this world has granted a copyright license to make derivative works for board games, computer games, films, and replica weapons; all of those products are derivative works that also have their own copyright. Any material in a derivative work that is not contained in the underlying work is copyrightable as a new work. Furthermore, this new material may even be licensable itself!

Continuing with *The Lord of the Rings* example, this property offers a fascinating derivative works case study in the game industry. Starting in 2001, Electronic Arts had developed games including the first *Battle for Middle Earth*™ game based on a license from the Peter Jackson films. This meant that the games from EA could only produce game content, or derivative work, that came from the Jackson films. In 2005 while creating the *Battle for Middle Earth* sequel and other *Rings* games, EA acquired a license to produce games based on the entire world of fiction as described in the Tolkien books. This license to make derivative works based on the books opened up a great deal of new territory for creativity. Here, EA was licensing a subset of material from one derivative work and later acquired a license for the entire base of material.

The Public Domain

What happens to copyrighted works after the protection expires, and how does that affect game copyrights specifically? The short answer is that formerly protected work that loses its IP protection passes into the public domain. This is a particularly exciting idea because anyone, even game developers, can use material in the public domain to create new works. As a rule of thumb, the older a work is, the more likely it is to safely be in the public domain. Table 7.2 shows a greatly simplified set of rules for determining when a work passes into the public domain. Law professor Laura Gasaway has produced a much better chart, which is one of the most cited tables for determining the expiration of copyright. The Gasaway chart and another one from Cornell are referenced in Table 7.2.

TABLE 7.2 Rules for Public Domain

Is the Work in the Public Domain?	
Before 1923	Public domain
1923–March 1989	Depends if the work was published with a notice of copyright registration and if the registration was renewed.
After March 1989	Under copyright for 70 years after death of author, or if work of corporate authorship, the shorter of 95 years from publication, or 120 years from creation.

For U.S. works only. More thorough charts can be found through UNC-Chapel Hill or Cornell.

http://www.copyright.cornell.edu/training/Hirtle_Public_Domain.htm

http://www.unc.edu/~unclng/public-d.htm

Before making any final decision, it is prudent to check with IP counsel before using works assumed to be in the public domain. Particular caution should be used for works created outside the United States or works created in the United States between 1923 and 1989. There may also be special circumstances surrounding a particular work that limit its use in a game. A common example of these special circumstances is when public domain works have been previously used to create new works. As discussed earlier, these new works are derivative works. They have their own new IP protection for the new elements contained within them, but the underlying public domain works remain in the public domain.

The story of Robin Hood is an excellent example of a special public domain situation, because the story is so old it is practically a fairy tale; there may have been someone who performed similar feats in medieval England, but the myriad of stories do appear a wee bit exaggerated. It is also true that there have been countless books and movies using the Robin Hood story. There have also been several videogames based on Robin Hood, his merry men, the Sheriff of Nottingham, and Maid Marian. The main point here is that the underlying story and characters are part of the public domain, but when creating new stories using this inspiration, developers should be careful not to infringe on modern works that still have copyright protection. The license-hungry game developer should be encouraged by a secondary point implicit here: there are many popular stories and characters now available for free game development, including much of the great art and literature from the 19th century and earlier.

Another important example of the public domain comes in the form of myths, history, and cultural lore. Anyone can use these as familiar settings to build games because they are so old and their authorship is collective and forgotten. However, place names, especially story-critical place names, are considered important story elements and may be protected with copyright as story elements. Specifically, using place names in a way that evokes associations with a previous story may or may not contribute to copyright infringement, depending on the several infringement factors discussed here. Note that some place names may also be subject to trademark.

Before the trademark dispute and subsequent cancellation of the Microsoft project *Mythica*, the game was going to use the place name Muspellheim. *Dark Age of Camelot*® also uses the name Muspellheim. They can both do this because Muspellheim is a place from Norse mythology that both used as a setting for their games. That story is not under copyright protection because the author or authors of those myths have been dead for centuries. This is similar to using "Mount Olympus" or "Hell" as a setting in a game. On the other hand, using "The Death Star" or "Tatooine" for game development names would be an entirely different case because these places, as story elements, are the intellectual property of the *Star Wars*® universe. These names were created recently by an author and are protected by copyright as story elements. Even though they are such a pervasive part of our cultural consciousness and even better known than Muspellheim, they cannot be used in games without permission because the stories they are part of are still protected by copyright. Any use of these names in new and similar stories would contribute to a finding of copyright infringement.

Historical events are also not subject to copyright, but the stories created out of them are. An example is World War II, a fertile area for game development in the last five years. No one can copyright the specific events of that or any time period. *Battlefield 1942*™ and *Medal of Honor*™ can both use tanks, weapons, and uniforms that are historically accurate. Furthermore, they are not infringing each other's copyright because the games are merely representing historical facts.

It is important to remember that copying a story inspired by historical facts is still copyright infringement, but merely copying the historical facts is not. For instance, a developer cannot make a game based on the movie *Saving Private Ryan* without the appropriate license. A developer can however, make a game about Pearl Harbor as long as she or he is creating the game around the historical event and not the movie of the same name.

Scenes a Fair Doctrine

The Scenes a Fair Doctrine is similar to public domain property. This doctrine recognizes that some expressions of ideas are so often used that they cannot be copyrighted by themselves. An example of this is the fairy tale beginning, "Once upon a time . . . ." So many fairy tales begin that way that a fairy tale–based game could certainly begin that way, too. Other Scenes a Fair Doctrine examples would be the generic elements of a fantasy story such as wizards or dragons. These races and their general stereotypes are not copyrighted, but specific instances of these races that are clear characters such as Gandalf or Drizzt would be.

Fair Use

The concept of "fair use" is commonly discussed and misunderstood in copyright law. As a general notion, fair use is the idea that one party may use a portion of a copyrighted work for a limited purpose without paying the copyright holder for a license. This concept is derived from a U.S. statute that states four conditions must be met (Table 7.3).

TABLE 7.3 Four Factors in "Fair Use"

The purpose and character of your use	Educational uses and uses in parody are more often protected than strict commercial copying.
The nature of the copyrighted work	Using sections of a commercial work is more likely to result in a finding of infringement. Copying creative fictional works are more likely to result in a finding of infringement than copying factual compilations.
The amount and substantiality of the portion taken	Taking a large portion from a work is more likely to result in a finding of infringement than taking a small portion.
The effect of the use on the potential market	Demonstrably weakening the market for the copyrighted work is more likely to result in a finding of infringement.

As one might imagine, fair use can be a muddy issue at times. It is commonly brought up by parties opposing copyright infringement, but it is not a perfect defense.

There are two common pitfalls relating to fair use to keep in mind. First, fair use is a U.S. concept. Most other countries do not contain provisions allowing copyrighted material to be used without a license. This means that a game company hoping to incorporate some copyrighted material into a game as a "parody" or other traditionally shielded type of fair use may run into problems selling their game in other countries. A small clip intended as a humorous interlude may lead to the company in litigation or forgoing sales outside the United States.

The second issue to remember about fair use is that fair use is a *defense* to a claim of copyright infringement. This means that a copyright holder in the United States can certainly sue the company that included the clip for using a copyrighted work or a derivative of that work without a license. After the case is brought, the law now grants the offending company the opportunity to argue the merits of fair use. This means that a company plainly operating in the traditional boundaries of fair use is still open to litigation and therefore open to the associated costs and bad publicity associated with a copyright litigation. In short, the decision to use copyrighted material in a game under the protection of fair use poses a risk and should be weighed heavily.

Common Questions about Copyright

Is producing code to an attorney a copyright violation?

Copyright is broad, but the protection does have its limits. For instance, a person can sing a copyrighted song in the shower without violating copyright. Similarly, developers and publishers can give their own copyrighted code to attorneys for the purposes of litigation without violating copyright. Remember that copyright prevents copying, public performance, and the other items described in this chapter. There is no prohibition against making copies of copyrighted material for use in judicial processes. In this author's career as an attorney in the game industry, this issue comes up constantly. Even after substantial explaining, people are very reluctant to hand over archived code because they fear copyright violation.

To be absolutely clear, there has never been a case of copyright infringement brought for producing code to an attorney for the purposes of a litigation, patent analysis, or similar proceeding. There are reasons for not wanting to produce material for legal proceedings, but copyright infringement is not one of them. Lastly, it is possible to be judicially "forced" to produce code through a document subpoena in a litigation setting. In short, a developer refusing to turn over code because they believe the code is protected by copyright is acting on a wrong assumption, and likely to lead to a subpoena forcing production of the code.

Is mailing a sealed envelope proof of copyright?

Mailing a sealed envelope to a person with a copy of the company's newest game is not remotely the same as registering the copyright for the game. Sometimes called "the poor man's copyright," this procedure has no legal effect. At best, it may prove that the material was in a certain form on a certain date, but that evidence is open to challenge since an individual can mail an unsealed envelope to himself. Actual copyright registration is easy and inexpensive, so there is little reason to resort to this when mailing a form and payment to the Copyright Office is nearly as easy.

Is a copyright holder entitled to $150,000 in damages per instance of infringement?

The statutory damages clause for copyright infringement is often misinterpreted. A copyright holder is entitled to *up to* $150,000 in damages per instance of copyright infringement. This is for *willful* infringement of a registered copyrighted work. Furthermore, it is not per copy of the registered work, it is per instance of infringement. Making 10,000 copies of a particular game or film does not multiply the damages by 10,000. The game or film is one copyrighted work and counts as one instance of infringement. The damage calculation may end up becoming more than $150,000 through other damage calculation mechanisms such as calculating ill-gotten profits or lost sales, but it is not the result of multiplying the number of copied units by

$150,000. The damages may also add up because most games actually contain many copyright works. The number of copies does not directly multiply the damages under the willful damages statutory section. The number of works, not the number of copies, is most significant.

Are personal assets at stake for copyright infringement?

The corporate form is an ingenious device that usually protects shareholders from liability. It is a way of maximizing personal profit, while minimizing personal risk. The risks associated with willful copyright infringement are not one of those risks a corporate form can reliably shield a person from. This law does vary by jurisdiction, but one factor that often weighs in the court's decision is controlling ownership interest in the company, management within the company, and ability to supervise the infringing activity. For instance, if a game developer who was also an officer and controlling shareholder in a studio purposefully steals music to put in a game, that person would be risking personal assets if the court found willful copyright infringement. The same is often true for willful infringement of other IP, such as trademarks. This rule makes sense from a policy perspective, because getting around IP infringement should not be as easy as setting up a corporation for the purposes of stealing IP.

Is Creative Commons or GPL replacing copyright?

The use of Creative Commons[3] has grown substantially since the nonprofit organization was founded in 2001. Many people in the game industry and elsewhere are interested in Creative Commons licenses and how these can be used to distribute content on the Web and other software content. The critical misunderstanding is that a Creative Commons license is a replacement for copyright. In truth, these are merely simplified licenses that work within the existing copyright law framework. These licenses describe what types of uses and duplication of the work are allowed, and what rights are reserved within the traditional copyright context. Certainly, the people who work for Creative Commons understand this and it is clearly described on their Web site and related literature. However, in spite of those efforts, a misunderstanding about the relationship of a Creative Commons license to copyright is prevalent in the game industry. The same holds true for copyleft, the GPL license, and many of the other parts of the open source movement. Generally speaking, there may be the deeper political agenda of changing copyright law, but these licenses work within the existing framework for their legal effect.

Trade Secret

Trade secret can be thought of as the oldest form of intellectual property. Even 2 million years ago, *Homo habilis* could keep his competitive advantage for a new stone tool through IP protection. He could keep the use and construction of that tool as a "trade secret." The mechanism then, as now, was merely to keep the idea a secret. The processes have grown more complex, but at its root, the idea is the same.

In modern times, a trade secret is loosely defined as some information that may be used for business advantage that a company keeps secret. This is the only form of IP that is not disclosed publicly; patents, copyrights, and trademarks all rely on some form of public disclosure. Trade secrets are company business secrets. The Uniform Trade Secrets Act defines a Trade Secret as:

> "Trade secret" means information, including a formula, pattern, compilation, program device, method, technique, or process, that: (i) derives independent economic value, actual or potential, from not being generally known to, and not being readily ascertainable by proper means by, other persons who can obtain economic value from its disclosure or use, and (ii) is the subject of efforts that are reasonable under the circumstances to maintain its secrecy.

What Can Be a Trade Secret?

Any idea can be a trade secret as long as it is an idea that confers some business advantage and can be kept secret. Trade secret rights can extend to virtually any concrete information that grants a business advantage such as formulae, data compilations, devices, processes, and customer lists. The most well-known example of a trade secret is the formula for Coca-Cola. The formula is known by some people at the company, but it is not known for certain anywhere else. The secret has been held by the company for more than 100 years. Although many public descriptions exist, none has been verified.[4] Furthermore, great steps are taken to prevent anyone from discovering the secret. Other examples of trade secrets include customer lists, notes on game development, business contacts, license terms, and other internal business items that are valuable to game development but not protected with the other IP tools.

Two advantages of trade secret are that they have no registration cost and can be protected quickly. Trademark requires using the mark, and patents require an application and a lengthy approval process. Both also require federal registration fees. While there is no registration fee for trade secrets, it would not be entirely fair to say that their protection is free. A company must make structured efforts to keep valuable business information a secret if that company wants to claim that information as a trade secret, as described later.

What Rights Are Conferred by Trade Secrets?

The rights given to a trade secret holder include the right to prevent others from using the trade secret unless the other party discovers the secret through legitimate research. Speaking in terms of the Uniform Trade Secrets Act, a company has the right to prevent others from "misappropriating" a trade secret. The Act describes misappropriation in this way:

"Misappropriation" means: (i) acquisition of a trade secret of another by a person who knows or has reason to know that the trade secret was acquired by improper means; or (ii) disclosure or use of a trade secret of another without express or implied consent by a person who (A) used improper means to acquire knowledge of the trade secret; or (B) at the time of disclosure or use knew or had reason to know that his knowledge of the trade secret was (I) derived from or through a person who has utilized improper means to acquire it; (II) acquired under circumstances giving rise to a duty to maintain its secrecy or limit its use; or (III) derived from or through a person who owed a duty to the person seeking relief to maintain its secrecy or limit its use; or (C) before a material change of his position, knew or had reason to know that it was a trade secret ad that knowledge of it had been acquired by accident or mistake.

Some Examples of Trade Secrets

As an example, consider mailing list data for subscribers of an MMO as a type of trade secret. These people have subscribed to Company A's MMO for years and have each paid literally hundreds of dollars to the publisher. If an employee steals the MMO contact list, this employee can now have easy access to people interested in playing an MMO and willing to pay for it in the long term. This information could be enormously valuable for a competitor.

Development tools could also be trade secrets. Consider a development tool that may populate a 3D level intelligently with environmental objects by pulling these objects from a specified directory. This software was written in-house for one development project, but could easily be modified to work with other projects, saving programmers and level designers many hours of work by placing a "skeleton" level down according to certain conditions. Now, this tool is certainly also covered by copyright, but if it is never sold, published, or patented, it could also be a trade secret. To be clear, like Coca-Cola, some elements of the tool could remain trade secrets even if the tool itself were sold. An employee leaving with the code for this design tool and taking it to a competitor is stealing a trade secret.

Details about licensing agreements can also be a trade secret. In fact, license agreements and other contract secrets are one of the most common trade secrets in the game industry. Often, both parties do not want deal details leaked to the public. This class of secrets covers obvious clauses such as how much is paid and when. It also covers less obvious, but equally important, information such as which employees are "key employees" for fulfilling a development agreement.

Trade Secret Information

Length of Protection

Trade secrets last as long as the owner of the information prevents it from becoming common knowledge. This, like trademark, is potentially immortal. The only limitation is the time the information can be kept "secret."

Process and Cost

Unlike patents, copyright, and trademarks, there are no formalities such as registration required to obtain trade secret rights.

It is often said that having a trade secret is "free." This is true to some extent. There are no registration or maintenance fees required. Yet, trade secrets require a process. They must be handled carefully and have some efforts made by the company to keep them secret as described later in this chapter.

Protecting Trade Secrets

Common protections include recording trade secrets and having employees sign documents stating they understand certain information is a trade secret and that information has special restrictions on dissemination. Controlled access is an important part of a trade secret. If the trade secrets are electronic files, allow only certain people to access those files and place special protections on modifying or copying the files.

Protection of trade secrets also includes not telling anyone unless that person needs to know the information, but it also can include other internal security measures to protect the information. Measures such as restricted access to the information internally, passwords, locked cabinets, and nondisclosure documents all help protect the company's trade secrets.

If you find that someone has leaked trade secrets, you should take specific actions. First, your company should do whatever is necessary to stop the leaked information. This may include further restricting access, changing passwords, and perhaps moving databases. This may also include sending ISP and/or webmaster notices if the trade secret information is being hosted online. The company usually also places the offender on notice that the offender is distributing a trade secret. This notice, similar to other such webmaster/ISP notices, will demand the offender "cease and desist" from distributing the secret. Finally, if this fails to remedy the harm caused by the leak of the trade secret, litigation may be in order. Similar to copyright and other types of IP enforcement, each of these steps should be done in concert with your attorney.

Penalties for Infringement

The Uniform Trade Secret Act allows damages for misappropriating trade secrets. These damages can be measured in three ways. First, the damages may be measured as the loss of profits by the party that originally held the secret. Second, the damages may be measured by the profit of the party that used or disclosed the misappropriated trade secret. Finally, if appropriate, the measurement could be as a reasonable royalty payment for the trade secret. In addition or as an alternative to damages, a party may be able to enjoin (or stop) the misappropriating party from using the trade secret. Legally, this is referred to as seeking an injunction against the misappropriating party.

Trade Secret Is State Law

Copyright, federally registered trademarks, and patents are all controlled almost exclusively by federal law. Trade secret, on the other hand, is controlled by the law of the individual states. Therefore, it can be more variable than other IP laws because it can differ from state to state. Throughout this chapter, information has come from general principles contained in state law or from the Uniform Trade Secrets Act. The Uniform Trade Secrets Act is a model that approximately 40 states have adopted or have used as a guide in creating their own law. There is no substitute for a qualified attorney familiar with state laws when it comes to trade secret matters. As a rule, most attorneys will be comfortable working with trade secret law in their home state, New York, and California.

Common Questions about Trade Secrets

Can trade secret help protect my IP from reverse engineering?

Unfortunately, trade secret cannot provide full protection from one of the biggest assaults against game IP: reverse engineering. A truly legal reverse engineering job is performed when hardware or software is inspected and ultimately re-created without misappropriating a blueprint, source code, or other related information. This process, while in no way easy, has been accomplished for some relatively secure gaming systems and software. However, trade secret can protect game developers from reverse engineering, since the difficulty of reverse engineering is sometimes well beyond the realm of human capability, and is only possible if some inside information (i.e., trade secret) is leaked to the public. Trade secret can help protect against this leak, and potentially cut off reverse engineering attempts before they become feasible.

At what stage should game companies use trade secret?

The best advice for a gaming company embarking on any new project is to maintain some planned secrecy at every stage. Try to keep key in-game calculations, customer lists, community information, and key business contacts a secret. As long as proper nondisclosure measures are followed along the way, it is possible to amass quite a bit of trade secret knowledge that should prevent your game ideas from being stolen or reproduced. The major reason why game companies lose trade secrets is the cost and trust issues associated with maintaining such secrets. Quite often, a small game company may be started with a group of friends who feel that such measures would be unnecessary because of a high level of trust between the founders. Although this may be the case, it is always better to ensure the protection of valuable resources with the proper measures before there are any problems.

Trademark

Where trade secret focuses on keeping information about a company behind closed doors, trademark focuses on pushing information out into the public. In fact, a successful trademark is one that allows consumers to instantly recognize the company and its products when they see the mark. The Xbox and PlayStation logos are immediately recognizable, and consumers have certain thoughts and feelings associated with those marks. That brand recognition and association with a particular company is the purpose of trademark.

Trademarks are arguably the second most important IP protection for game companies after copyright, since a good trademark can set a company and its games apart from others in the minds of consumers.

What Can Be Trademarked?

The most common trademarks are a word, name, symbol, graphic, or short phrase used in business to identify a specific company's products. More exotic trademarks can be smells, sounds, or colors, but these are rarely used. Trademarks come into being when they are used in business by a company to identify products or services. To identify a trademark for a game company, the company only has to use a superscript ™ after the mark, like this—mark™. Of all the types of IP, only copyright is easier to invoke because it only requires the fixation of a creative work. Simply placing the ™ designation after a word puts the world on notice of "common law" trademark rights. Common law trademark rights are derived from use of the mark in commerce. Through business use, trademarks become associated with a company and perhaps with a particular product or service within the company. Common law rights are also controlled by state law and the mark is not protected throughout the United States. The mark is only protected in the area it is in use.

Some Examples of Trademarks

The strongest trademarks are words that have only the meaning a company has given to them, like Xbox, Sony, or Nintendo. The words do not mean anything alone. In other words, the more imaginary the trademark is, the stronger it is.

Microsoft learned some lessons twice the hard way in the game context. The first time was just before the launch of the first Xbox. The Xbox trademark was in use by another software company when Microsoft started marketing the Xbox. Worse, the competing company was a publicly traded company that should have been easy to find in a standard trademark search. Clearly, this should have been found and negotiated much earlier in the launch cycle, or perhaps another name should have been chosen. This case was eventually settled out of court and probably cost Microsoft a substantial amount of money.

The second and most recent trademark lesson for Microsoft came in 2003 with the planned MMORPG *Mythica*. One of the most popular games in that market, *Dark Age of Camelot*, is made by Mythic Entertainment. This potential trademark conflict was so obvious it did not really require a search, and could have been uncovered simply by asking just about anyone familiar with the genre. In response to the clear "Mythica"/"Mythic" conflict, Mythic initiated a case against Microsoft for trademark infringement. Around the time of the case, Mark Jacobs was famously quoted as telling a Microsoft lead designer at E3 that Mythic was going to call its next game "Microsofta."[5] Whether causally related or not, Microsoft canceled the whole *Mythica* project after the dispute arose. Microsoft settled the suit with Mythic, agreeing not to use the term "Mythica" and to drop its U.S. applications to register "Mythica" as a trademark. As part of the settlement, Microsoft also assigned Mythic the rights to international trademark applications and registrations for "Mythica," and the associated domain names. The lesson here is that trademark searches should not be considered an additional frivolous cost for a game company. Instead, these searches are an essential part of the registration process, and mistakes have in the past and will in the future cost game companies literally millions of dollars and will potentially be involved in the failure of entire projects.

Trademark Information

Length of Protection
In the United States, trademarks can be immortal. If the mark is used continuously in commerce and the relevant fees are paid, the mark can exist forever. Some marks in the United States have been used for more than 100 years.

Process and Cost
A trademark may also be registered with the federal government for wider and stronger protection. The registration is more complex than the copyright registration process, but not as complex as the patent registration process. For this reason, it is usually done through a law firm with paralegals and attorneys who specialize in trademark registration. The process should begin with a trademark search that examines U.S. and perhaps international sources to try to discover if other companies have been using the mark. If other companies have been using the mark, then the search can try to determine if the mark is being used in a related field. After the company has the results of this search, the company can decide to move forward with the federal registration process or reconsider the mark. As routine as this initial search process is, sometimes the process fails in spectacular ways—even for very established companies.

After the trademark search, the federal registration process with the USPTO begins. This usually takes less than a year and costs approximately $3,000 to $4,000, including the earlier trademark search. After the mark has been federally registered, this registration and the litigations surrounding it are controlled by federal law. The registration is at this point, good throughout the entire United States.

The fees for renewing a trademark are currently lower than patent maintenance fees. The fees can vary based on how many trademark "classes" are covered by the trademark. A class can be thought of as a class of products. At the time of this writing, the cost for renewing a trademark in one class and filing the appropriate declaration of use is $500.

Protecting Trademarks

All trademarks should be noted with the appropriate symbols. Use the symbol ™ to indicate if the mark is being used in business. If the trademark registration is successful, the applicant can use the "®" symbol following the mark as an indication that the mark has been registered with the USPTO.

Policing trademark is similar to policing other types of IP. One important difference is that a trademark used by unauthorized companies can actually damage the value of the trademark. In the United States, if this unauthorized use becomes rampant, the mark runs the risk of "genericide," where the mark loses all value. This has happened in the United States to trademarks that were so often misused, they became household words such as aspirin and thermos. Both of these were trademarks at one time, but have died a death of misuse and over-popularity.

There are companies that specialize in searching for infringing uses of trademarks. These companies can perform searches on a regular schedule and send your game development company reports on potential infringers. As with most types of IP, one of the early steps in policing the IP is sending a "cease and desist" letter. Later steps can include litigation over the trademark.

Penalties for Infringement

The penalties for trademark infringement can be harsh and are similar to copyright infringement. These penalties can include the destruction of the infringing items if the items are considered counterfeit. An injunction, stopping the use of the infringing trademark, is also an option. Money damages based on loss of profits or ill-gotten gains are also possible. Similar to copyright, personal liability through the corporate shield is also possible. The specific damage calculation for each case is dependent on the circumstances surrounding the infringement.

Picking a Good Trademark

In the United States, trademarks are divided into five categories, broken down to reflect the relative strength of the mark. Mark strength is an indicator of strength of protection. That strength of protection should also contribute to IP value. The five categories of trademark strength are fanciful, arbitrary, suggestive, descriptive, and generic.

Fanciful marks are the strongest marks. They have no meaning other than the meaning a company associates with them. Examples of fanciful marks include Xbox, BioWare, NVIDIA, *Tetris*, and Eidos.

Arbitrary marks are also strong, but less so than fanciful marks. They are words, but are not associated with the particular product until the company associates them. An example of an arbitrary mark is "Apple" for computers or "id" for a development studio.

Suggestive marks can be a natural word that suggests the product it represents, but does not directly describe it. These are the weakest marks that companies can normally obtain protection for. Examples of suggestive marks are Electronic Arts for a maker of video games, PlayStation for a console game platform, Sonic the Hedgehog for a fast-moving hedgehog, *Space Invaders* for a game starring invaders from space, or *Centipede* for a game featuring a centipede.

Descriptive marks are extremely weak marks. They are essentially useless unless a company has used them so much that they have acquired something called "secondary meaning." Secondary meaning can only be acquired through extensive marketing and public exposure. Examples of descriptive marks include Vision Center for a store that specializes in glasses, or Computerland for a computer store.

Generic marks are things like video card, controller, or video game. The term "generic" is the polar opposite of trademark and a generic term can never be converted to a trademark in the United States. Table 7.4 lists the five categories of trademark strength.

TABLE 7.4   The Five Categories of Trademark Strength

Mark Category	Description	Example
Fanciful	Words that have no meaning beyond that given by the company.	Xbox
Arbitrary	Words previously unassociated with a type source.	Apple (for computers)
Suggestive	Words that suggest something about the source.	Electronic Arts
Descriptive	Words that merely describe the source.	Computerland
Generic	Generic descriptor; cannot be a trademark.	video game

It should be obvious that you should not name your next game and development company, *Game* by "Game Development Company." Those terms are too generic to become trademarks at all. Examples outside the game industry such as Exxon, Intervolve, and Kodak are great trademarks because they do not have any meaning besides the meaning the company generates in them. When naming a new company or product, it is worth it to try to create a fanciful or arbitrary mark. The increased strength legally afforded to creative marks is a fascinating example of how IP law respects and promotes creativity.

Notable International Variation

Although trademark law is respected in most countries, the realities of enforcing a trademark on foreign soil will be different from enforcing a trademark inside the United States. For example, some countries in Europe require use of the mark in commerce, whereas others give a grace period but still require use within several years. In addition, the registration of a mark in the United States does not mean that the mark is enforceable in another country; it merely means that should the foreign business with a similar trademark attempt to bring its product into the United States, you could then enforce your rights.

An interesting phenomenon to take note of in the foreign market is the Community Trade Mark (CTM) that one can apply for in Europe. This mark, if granted, can be used across many countries in Europe and may be a very cost-effective way of establishing trademark rights over a broad array of countries. However, there are complexities and alternatives to this type of trademark that are beyond the scope of this chapter. The most important alternative to discuss with your IP attorney is using the Madrid Protocol to obtain international protection. In short, this area becomes complicated very quickly, and if your company has the products and resources to consider international protection, the company should make sure it has appropriate counsel to arrange for such protection.

Common Questions about Trademarks

Do I have to use a trademark in commerce?

Actual use is always better for bolstering trademark rights, but in the United States, it is possible to establish such rights for a short time merely by establishing an intent-to-use. In 1988, trademark law changed when this intent-to-use provision was added. Prior to this addition, a mark needed to be used in commerce; since 1988, it has been possible to merely apply for a federal registration with the stipulation that there is a bona fide intent-to-use the mark in commerce.

Can I let fans use my trademark without a formal license?

This is commonly done in the game industry for both copyrighted material and trademarks. Game companies often create fan site packages that include material and conditions for using that material. The allowed uses are case specific and it is often not economically feasible to attack every Web site "infringer" that pops up. Game companies also recognize the advertising value in game-related communities. In short, make sure the fan sites know what uses your game company is comfortable with. Be as clear as possible about the rules and try to stress that appropriate attribution is important. For example, a fan Web site kit may include appropriate legal attribution for a trademark. The notice may say something similar to, "*Title* is a trademark of GameCompany" or "*Title* is a registered trademark of GameCompany." This situation becomes more complicated if there is a substantial commercial component for the Web site or if the Web site is spreading misinformation that is harmful for your game sales. In the case of a commercial component, the Web site may be making money using your game company's trademarks and perhaps copyrighted material. As mentioned earlier, the appropriate action, if any, is dependent on the individual circumstances. A negotiated license and/or a "cease and desist" letter may be in order to stop unwarranted uses.

Patents

The patent system in the United States is descended from the 1623 Statute of Monopolies in England, which sought to overturn earlier royal monopoly grants but preserved inventors' rights for 14 years with grants of "letters patents" for "new manufactures." In the United States, patents go all the way back to the Constitution. Article I, § 8 clause 8 grants Congress the power to "promote the progress of science and the useful arts, by securing for limited times to authors and inventors the exclusive right to their respective writings and discoveries." Since that time, patent law has undergone and continues to undergo revision, sometimes significant.

Although extremely important for some hardware, software, development tool, and other middleware companies, patents are not used as often in the game context. This may change as the industry matures, but for the time being, patents are not often used throughout the majority of the game industry.

What Can Be Patented?

The Patent Act defines potentially patentable subject matter as any "new and useful process, machine, manufacture, or composition of matter . . . ."[6] Examples include machines, pharmaceuticals, medical equipment, video cards, or a better mousetrap. Patents do not usually protect games themselves because they do not usually meet the statutory criteria. Yet, there is a growing number of game-related patents, usually in the areas of hardware or inventive gameplay.

What Rights Are Conferred by Patents?

A common misconception is that a patent grants the right to make an invention, but this is not true. Similar to copyright, patents grant a negative right, meaning they grant a right that prevents others from doing something. In other words, a patent confers the right to prevent other people from making, using, selling, or importing an invention. The patent owner is under no obligation to actually construct the patented invention, but can prevent others from practicing the invention.

Patent Information

Patents are perhaps the most complex form of IP protection. It is important to understand the details about this form of IP if you plan to use it in your business.

Length of Protection

Patents have a limited lifespan, which is relatively short compared to other forms of IP. Some people may think a patent expiration date would be printed on the front of a patent. Unfortunately, nothing could be further from the truth. Currently, patents that pay the required maintenance fees are valid for 20 years from the time they are filed. Before June 1995, this calculation was not so simple. For these older patents, the patents are valid for either 17 years from the patent issue date or 20 years from filing—whichever is longer. Just to make the calculation more complicated, it is not unusual for patents to be shortened or extended for some time through a variety of mechanisms. It is possible to *estimate* a patent term by looking at basic dates on the face of a patent, but a full review of the patent history and related documents is necessary to find an exact expiration date.

Process and Cost

Of all the types of IP registration, this is the longest and most complicated. The process takes two to three years and includes creating all of the written material for the patent application, including all relevant figures. The process also includes regularly corresponding with the patent office, complying with, or writing rebuttals to, patent office arguments. Although it is possible to go through this process without a patent attorney, that direction is strongly not recommended.

Two main sections make up a patent. The first section is called the specification and is the narrative description that makes up most of the written material in a patent. This section includes a background of the invention that goes through the state of the technology leading up to the invention. There is also a detailed description of the invention with figures and examples. In theory, a person reading this section can learn everything there is to know about how to make and use this invention. Remember that a patent is a deal with the government: in exchange for sharing complete knowledge of the invention with the world, the patent holder is granted a limited monopoly on that invention.

The second main section is the patent claims. These claims are numbered sentences found at the end of a patent. There has to be at least one claim, but there is no absolute upper limit on the number of claims. However, in the United States, every patent claim over 20 costs an additional amount of money, so high numbers of claims are economically discouraged. The average patent has about 3 to 15 claims. The patent claims are the most important section of the patent because this is the portion of the patent that describes exactly what the patent protects. In fact, material in the specification that is not included in the claims is given away to the public. Be very careful that patent claims adequately and completely describe your invention.

The cost of filing a patent application varies based on several factors: the complexity of the technology, the number of other patents in the field, and the amount of material your company can provide the patent attorney. If technology is complicated, there are many patents in the field, and you call your patent attorney with an idea written down on an index card, the cost is going to increase. A general price range for total cost of application can be between $10,000 and $30,000. This includes the costs to file an application and shepherd it through the patent office. The range also depends on the number of mailings, called "Office Actions," from the patent office and the time spent preparing answers to those Office Actions.

Beware of companies that offer to "file" a patent application for $2,000 or some other very small number. These companies are hiding costs in at least two areas. The first is that the USPTO fees are usually not included in these costs. Second, the low estimate is usually only for "filing" the patent application. The cost of answering Office Actions and doing the other work necessary to get the patent is not included in that estimate. This is similar to stating that skydiving costs $200, but the parachute is extra.

The good news is that patent costs tend to be spread out over the whole period of the application. There will be costs to prepare and file the application, but paying for the Office Action work is not necessary until many months later when the patent application has been acted on by the patent office. It is also possible, but unlikely, that an application can go straight through to become an issued patent.

There are also ongoing costs for patents in addition to filing costs. To keep a patent enforceable during its term, maintenance fees must be paid to the U.S. Patent and Trademark Office. These maintenance fees are due at 3.5, 7.5, and 11.5 years after issuance. The fee amounts change often and the best source of information regarding these fees is your IP attorney. If the fees are not paid, the patents will expire and it takes substantial effort to revive them, if it is possible at all. The difficulty reviving the patent is dependent on the length of time since the fees were due and the circumstances surrounding the failure to pay fees. Make certain your company plans for this and has someone designated to monitor that these payments are made.

Protecting Patents

If another company is violating your patent rights, the first step in policing this type of IP is to put the other company on notice by sending them the patent and a letter about the potential infringement. Hopefully, the parties can work out some suitable licensing settlement, but this is sometimes not the case. If the parties cannot come to an agreement, litigation may be in order.

Patent Litigation and Penalties for Infringing Patents

Litigation is discussed in detail in Chapter 9, "Intellectual Property Litigation." Generally speaking, patent litigation itself is punishment for both parties. Even the winner of the litigation often does so at substantial cost in time, money, and other resources. Patent litigation is complicated, ultra-niche litigation. It is not surprising that it is expensive, and costs often run well past $1,000,000 in legal fees. There is also no doubt that this will become substantially more expensive in the future.

Winning a patent litigation normally results in two remedies. First, the patent holder can win an injunction that stops the losing party from practicing the invention. Second, the infringing company may be forced to pay damages for past infringement and potentially a royalty on units sold going forward.

Patent Pending and Provisional Patent Applications

The use of "patent pending" is only appropriate when an application or provisional application has been filed with the USPTO. The marking is not mandatory, but can be important when proving notice and calculating potential damage for patent infringement. Some people also argue the notice adds value to the product in the eyes of investors and consumers and expresses a certain level of business sophistication.

In the United States, provisional patent applications are often an attractive option for small or mid-sized game companies with a patentable invention. These applications cost less than pursuing a standard patent application and preserve the priority date for the invention. These provisional applications resemble complete patent applications except that they will not be examined at the USPTO without further action on behalf of the inventor. The inventor has one year from filing a provisional application to file a standard patent application based on the provisional. If successful, the applicant will be able to use the date of the provisional application as the date of invention. Finally, the expiration date of the patent is still counted from the date the full application is filed so the company does not pay any time-related penalty for filing the provisional application.

It is common for an early stage game company to be cash poor, but perhaps they have an invention or several patentable inventions that are potentially worth a great deal. This is particularly true with middleware companies. The company may fear its competition stealing the invention, but still wants to market the product and raise money. This is potentially a great position for a provisional patent application. After the company files the application, it now has three issues covered. First, the invention is on file with the USPTO and the invention priority date is set. The company can market the invention without fear of losing it due to a statutory bar or competitor copying. Second, the company has spent a fraction of the full cost of a patent application. Finally, the company can point to the pending application for both product sales and as a valuable addition to the company for capital acquisition.

Patent Invalidity

There are two circumstances when patent invalidity is particularly important in the game industry. The first instance is when a game company is trying to get a patent issued through the USPTO. The second instance is when a game company is being sued by a patent holder for infringement. In the first instance, the company will want to show that its patent application represents a valid invention. In the second instance, the company will try to prove the patent holder's patent does not represent a valid invention. This area of patent law is enormously complex, and the ideas contained in the sections following should be considered minimal summaries.

Anticipation and Obviousness

Many mechanisms lead to patents being declared invalid. Two of the most often discussed are anticipation and obviousness. Anticipation is found when something in the prior art meets every element of a patent claim. An easy way to think about anticipation is using this idea—that which infringes if after would anticipate if before. In other words, a patent cannot be valid if there is something found in the prior art that would have infringed the patent. This means there must be something in the prior art that met each and every portion of the claim being invalidated.

The second common way patents are declared invalid is through obviousness. With obviousness, every patent claim portion does not have to be met by just one invention or publication. Instead, inventions and publications can be blended together with other knowledge that was present before the patent. The standard here is what would a person of ordinary skill in the relevant scientific discipline know and do with the information available to him. A simplified way to look at it involves three steps. First, were all of the pieces of an invention present? Second, was there a reason to put those pieces together? Third, could a person of ordinary skill put those pieces together to make the patented invention? If these steps are all met, the patent is invalid for obviousness.

"On Sale Bar" and "Public Use"

Game developers pursing patents should be aware of two important mistakes that can lead to invalidation of their patents later or prevent their patent from being issued. The statute 35 U.S.C. 102(b) writes that no invention can be patented in the United States if it has been "on sale" or in "public use" for more than a year before a patent application is filed. These two items are special forms of invalidity by anticipation as discussed earlier. Importantly for game development, "on sale" includes efforts to sell the invention and actual sales. Be aware that licensing inventive technology without the appropriate safeguards can also be considered public use or sale of the invention.

Some types of licensing and use are permitted. These include the "experimental use" negation of the 102(b) bar. This experimental use, simply stated, is that some types of use or sale are allowable if they are for experimental purposes. This is not a defense to rely on if the company can plan in advance—it is difficult to prove and often unsuccessful. Clearly, the best way for an inventor to treat these 102(b) bars to patenting is to do nothing that can appear to be a public use or sale. Inventors should guard their inventions with secrecy until the time of application. This includes no attempts to sell, license, loan out, or use the invention until the patent application is filed. Specifically for games, beware of beta tests, particularly open beta tests. The game company may be literally giving away patentable material in these situations.

Also, be careful of the one-year grace period in the United States. In many non-U.S. jurisdictions, this grace period does not exist and the inventor immediately forfeits his right to patent the invention. The safest way to proceed is to file all patents before publicly releasing or attempting to sell products.

As mentioned previously, there are other ways for patents to be found invalid beyond those discussed in this chapter. These include keeping information from the Patent Office, affirmatively lying to the Patent Office, and a variety of technical issues. As always, the best advice beyond understanding this simple summary is to consult your patent attorney and the more specialized sections of this text.

Common Questions

What can our company put "patent pending" on?

Writing "patent pending" can only be done in the United States if an actual patent application or provisional patent application has been filed with the USPTO. Putting this marking on a product that does not meet these criteria could result in liability.

While the mark of "patent pending" does not directly grant patent rights to the user, it serves to put potential future infringers on notice. Some companies hold the common misconception that they should always put patent pending on any invention. Yet, patent pending is not like trademark. This notice does not grant the common-law rights the symbol ™ does. In addition, if the patent is not granted, it is not proper to keep this marking on the unpatented item. As a final consideration, placing patent pending on a product when there is no patent application is a violation of 35 U.S.C. § 292. There are financial penalties for marking products incorrectly.

Patent agents and patent attorneys in the United States— what is the difference?

As you can see by all the information presented in this chapter, patent law is a complex legal specialty. It may not be surprising to learn that most attorneys practicing patent law have additional qualifications and specialized study. In the United Kingdom, becoming a patent attorney is a very different legal educational process from other attorneys. In the United States, law school is the same for all attorneys, and all practicing attorneys are required to take a state bar to practice law, but only patent law has an additional examination necessary to be a "registered patent attorney." This exam covers patent law and particularly the rules dealing with patent applications. The test is administered by the USPTO and may be taken by either attorneys or nonattorneys. One requirement for this exam is a college-level scientific or technical education. The exam is difficult and in some years, only about 50% of people pass it. An attorney who passes this exam is considered a "patent attorney." A nonattorney who passes the exam is a "patent agent." Patent agents can aid in writing patent applications and other matters before the USPTO, but their abilities are more limited than registered patent attorneys.

Rights of Publicity

Publicity rights, also known as rights of publicity, are sometimes considered an intellectual property right because they are intangible property rights. Furthermore, these rights are considered in any creative endeavor that may use someone's image. Generally speaking, publicity rights are a set of rights that allow a person to control the commercial distribution of his own name, image, likeness, voice, or other identifiable representation of personality. This right allows a celebrity to be paid to endorse a certain product and simultaneously allows that celebrity to prevent a business from faking an endorsement by that celebrity.

The rights of publicity are similar to trade secret rights in that they are governed by state law. There is no federal registration process or federal law for publicity rights. These rights come about through state law statutes, or some have come about merely through court cases with no statute behind them. Importantly, there are state law statutes in many states responsible for the bulk of game development in the United States, including California, New York, Texas, and Massachusetts. Also, keep in mind that some states allow publicity rights to pass through a person's estate so that person may still be protected for a period even after death.

Publicity rights exist for several policy reasons, including the idea that the right to one's identity is among the most fundamental human rights. There is an additional line of argument that rights of publicity prevent fraud and unfair business practices that could derive from a fake endorsement.

Publicity rights are important in the game context in a few instances. First, using a person in a game or to advertise a game usually requires that person's permission. The same is true for using a person's voice or other recognizable characteristic. Failing to obtain the person's permission could result in a court granting an injunction to halting sales of the game and/or ordering damages to the person whose image was used without consent.

IP Strategy 101

When looking at your bottom line, your IP is the lifeblood of your company. Following are some tips for how to best protect your IP in your day-to-day business.

Have a Relationship with Experienced IP Counsel

At the risk of sounding repetitive, this cannot be said enough. And you should ideally find an attorney with game industry experience if you can. This relationship is the beginning of educating the development team about IP rights surrounding the game project and building protections for those rights. This person can help developers of any size protect IP by drafting and reviewing documents and offering advice. Having this relationship ensures the developer has taken the appropriate steps in advance of pitching the game. This relationship also ensures the best possible case-by-case advice while interacting with publishers or investors.

Protect IP in Advance

Register trademarks, and from then on, use the appropriate symbol (™ or ®) when they are used in documents. Keep trade secrets, especially when pitching a game, and understand that sharing those secrets can jeopardize their protection. Publishers and other parties understand that developers cannot give away the farm. Answering that some delicate information is proprietary is expected. Developers can always describe processes in general without going into detail. For copyright protection and date confirmation, developers should always write critical game design ideas out in detail and save concept art and early screen shots. Before pitching ideas to publishers and investors, discuss patent registration possibilities with your attorney. Finally, and most importantly, keep good records to document the earliest possible ownership, development, and use of the idea for all types of IP.

Protecting IP While Pitching a Game to Publishers and Investors

Understand that publishers and investors want to limit their legal exposure, and many "standard" NDAs are essentially one-sided documents to protect the other party and not you or your business. The development team should have its own NDA and ask if the publisher or investor would consider signing it. This negotiation can take some time and should be done before the pitch day. It is impolite and unprofessional to wait until the last minute to produce this document. Advice of IP counsel in this area is critical in drafting an NDA to protect the developer's interests and in deciphering the other party's NDA.

The Process Is Complex, but Results Are Achievable

Since the process of protecting IP is often so complex and an attorney is a necessary part of it, why should a game developer even bother? First, a knowledgeable game developer can ask good questions when dealing with IP advisors, saving everyone time and money. Second, a game developer familiar with IP may recognize the warning signs of IP infringement in game development early, before money is wasted on creating an infringing character, story line, or feature. In addition, much of IP protection requires planning and structure within the development company. An educated consumer of IP advice is best situated to understand that advice and implement structure within the company that protects IP. Most importantly, all the contracts and licenses surrounding games deal with IP, from the work-for-hire contracts for employees to publishing deals, royalty structures, and movie rights. Even though the developer is working with attorneys, the developer makes the final decisions and should know that the ultimate responsibility for protecting and selling the game rests on him. Given everything discussed in this chapter, that burden requires an understanding of this extremely important topic.

Strategies for Small Companies and Individual Developers

Small companies and individual developers should concentrate on low-cost options to protect their IP. These companies do not usually have the staff or the resources necessary for elaborate IP strategy. Most of these companies will not even have a single employee tasked solely with developing and implementing an IP strategy.

The low-cost options for IP protection include simple copyright registration for commercially available products. The plan may also include federally registering the company's one or two most important marks to receive the ® designation. The company's most important mark is usually the name or name/logo combination of the company. Trade secret processes are also relatively inexpensive and easy to put in place for a small company.

Small companies and individuals will probably not be as interested in international protection, but this option should be considered carefully for a company distributing their games over the Internet. These companies will also be less interested in patent protection unless patent protection is involved in the core business model, such as hardware development.

Strategies for Large Developers and Publishers

Larger developers and publishers should implement everything in the lower-cost plan for small companies, but should also expand IP protection to include more resource-intensive protection. This includes federally registering the trademark for all major titles put out by the company. This may also include international registration and policing of the company's most important trademarks. Large publishers and developers should also consider filing separate copyright applications for music and other protectable components associated with game titles.

An upgraded IP program may include building a patent portfolio. Some game companies pay bonuses to employees in the company who submit patentable ideas and help complete the patent process. After a company has developed and/or purchased a patent portfolio, larger companies should consider monetizing this portfolio by seeking out licensing partners. These patents can be used as friendly negotiating tools with partners to add value to negotiated transactions, or to force competitors into paying licensing fees or designing their product around the patented invention.

Patents, even though they are legally a purely offensive instrument, also have a certain perceived defensive value. This value comes from the fact that litigants often find companies with large patent portfolios "menacing." A large patent portfolio is usually indicative of the company having significant legal resources and sophistication. Of course, there is also the idea that a company with a large patent portfolio may file a counter-claim for patent infringement in any litigation against the company.

Three Important Points

Before we conclude the chapter, let us take another look at all the different forms of IP and some of the important details (Table 7.5).

TABLE 7.5   The Different Forms of IP

IP in the Game Industry	Patents	Trademark	Trade Secret	Copyright
Length	20 Years	Immortal	Immortal	95/120 Years
Cost	High	Medium	Medium	Low
Ease of obtaining	Tough	Medium	Medium	Easy
Use	Rare	Often	Often	Often
Registration?	Yes	Recommended	No	Recommended
Coverage	Medium	Narrow	Large	Large

Even the largest game development and publishing companies can make trivial errors in IP protection that cost significant money or, worse, the rights to a whole game. These errors can sometimes be avoided with an introductory understanding of IP and a relationship with a competent, experienced attorney. Failing to take these steps is the metaphorical equivalent of leaving the city gates open and letting the Visigoths rush in.

Game developers can take three steps to avoid these potentially disastrous IP pitfalls. First, developers should have a basic understanding of IP protection and what it means to them, especially the areas that are most important to the creation of games. Sources of information include this chapter and the IGDA IP Rights White Paper. The IGDA White Paper was written by an international collection of attorneys and game developers with the goal of spreading IP information to the game development community. It is available for download for free from the IGDA Web site, *http://www.idga.org/*.

As a second step, developers should have an attorney with broad experience in IP, especially trademark and copyright. This attorney, who may or may not be the same attorney used for other business issues, can help set up the most efficient and protective internal structures to protect IP. As discussed throughout this chapter, this attorney can also aid in negotiating the myriad of game contracts that are literally filled with IP-related language.

Third, developers should ensure that their employees and contractors sign appropriate agreements assigning all the IP they produce to the company. These three steps are necessary to build solid legal defenses around valuable game property. It is not an understatement to say the life and future of your game depends on it.

Conclusion

Intellectual property law is a complex and important topic in game development. In the final analysis, intellectual property is the material games are made of. It is the author's sincere hope that this chapter contains the basic information necessary for any developer to work with an attorney to put together an IP strategy that best serves the developer's individual needs.

Sources of Further Information

United States Patent and Trademark Office (USPTO): *http://www.uspto.gov/*
Copyright Office: *http://www.copyright.gov/*
World Intellectual Property Organization (WIPO):
http://www.wipo.int/portal/index.html.en

Endnotes

1. Chisum, Donald S. and Michael A. Jacobs, *Understanding Intellectual Property Law,* Introduction 1–3 §1B (1992).
2. *Folsom v. Marsh*, 9 F. Cas. 342, 344 (C.C.D. Mass. 1841)(No. 4,901) New York: Matthew Bender.
3. More information can be found at *http://creativecommons.org/*.
4. With modern chemical analytic methods, discovering the composition of any food product borders on trivial, but this is a well-known example in the legal field.
5. December 22, 2003, RPG Vault Interview with Mark Jacobs.
6. 35 § U.S.C. 101.

CHAPTER 8

Licensing Intellectual Property

Gary S. Morris and Richard A. Beyman

gmorris@kenyon.com
rbeyman@fwrv.com

You receive a letter accusing you of violating the sender's patent, copyright, trademark, or other intangible rights and demanding that you stop immediately. Or, you have developed a groundbreaking technical solution to a long-standing problem in the industry and want to make sure it does not get ripped off by everybody else when you deploy it. Or, you want to understand what you can do when some of your software mysteriously appears in a competitor's product. You want to base your game on a best-selling novel, or use a piece of well-known music for marketing the game. All of these scenarios are based on the ideas of intellectual property (IP). This chapter is meant to give you a basic understanding of the basics of licensing intellectual property in context of computer games.

The Nature of Intellectual Property

All ownership of property carries with it the right to exclude others from certain uses and enjoyments. Personal property relates to movable objects, such as a piece of furniture. If you own the couch, you have absolute legal authority as to who may sit on it. Real property relates to immovable objects, such as buildings and land. Violations of the owner's right to exclude from real property fall under *trespass*. Intellectual property relates to products of the human mind, such as creative expression, technical innovations, reputation, and the commercial exploitation of an individual's persona. Just as for real and personal property, an owner of intellectual property rights can prevent others from using and enjoying his intellectual property.

In reality, intellectual property is often found mixed in with other forms of property. An iPod® is personal property that also embodies intellectual property in the form of the technology that runs it and the music it stores. A building is real property that embodies intellectual property in its architectural drawings and the materials and systems that make it up. A computer game implemented on servers (personal property) includes intellectual property in its software, its reputation (trademarks), and its technical innovations.

Intellectual property rights are widely enforced. Courts routinely order changes in behavior and monetary damages to remedy infringements. For example, a court may order an infringer to stop selling a product that embodies a particular technology or technique the infringer has no license or other right to sell. A court order to stop doing something is called an *injunction*. If the court does not issue an injunction, it may order the infringer to make ongoing royalty payments to the owner in exchange for permission to continue using the intellectual property. The court may also award money, also known as *damages*, to the owner in an amount equal to royalties the infringer would have paid in the past or profits lost by the owner because of the infringement.

Needless to say, these penalties can wreak havoc on a business model, not to mention the business itself. For example, in one case, a patentee was awarded tens of millions of dollars in past damages and over a one-percent ongoing royalty on the sale of game consoles that included certain technology. In the course of obtaining the verdict, the manufacturer was confronted with the possibility of an injunction that could have stopped all sales of the console.

In any event, the preceding examples make clear the importance of intellectual property to the modern developer and publisher. More information about this topic can be found in Chapter 7, "Intellectual Property."

Intellectual Property Rights

Intellectual property rights are best thought of as bundles of individual rights. Each right can be separately allocated (that is, licensed) or reserved. When all of the rights in a given bundle (e.g., patent rights) are sold or given by their owner to another, the rights are said to be *assigned*. When a subset of the rights held by the owner is allocated to another party, the rights are said to be *licensed*.

Copyright

Copyright includes the exclusive rights to reproduce (copy), distribute, import, export, publicly perform, and create derivative works based on an original work of authorship. Examples of works covered by copyright include software, graphics, videos, music, and the like. One need not register a work with the U.S. government to establish a copyright; this right arises as soon as a creative work is fixed in a tangible medium; for example, when original software is created and stored on a hard disk.

Copyright endures for a limited period of time that typically runs during the life of the author, plus 70 years. It is best to carefully secure the rights to property needed for a project under copyright at the project's inception. If such rights are not secured, the copyright owner can seek to stop the distribution of a product that incorporates infringing material and demand damages.

An assignment of copyright is a complete transfer of ownership of all of the copyright in a work to another. A license, on the other hand, is a transfer of a subset of rights. For example, a contractor can assign all of his copyright in software he develops under a development agreement to the party that hired him to do so. Or, a publisher (the *licensor*) can license the right to import and distribute a game to a foreign distributor (the *licensee*), while retaining the rest of the rights. In exchange for the licensed right, the foreign distributor might pay royalties to the licensor.

Licensed rights can generally be parceled out any way the parties desire. As in the example of a publisher licensing the game to a foreign distributor, a licensed right can have a territorial restriction. The distributor can be given a license to import copies of the game made by the licensor into the Czech Republic and distribute the copies only in that country and Slovakia. Licenses can also impose field-of-use restrictions; for example, a right to use copies of software only for noncommercial uses may be granted.

The author of the work is ordinarily the owner of the copyright. If an employee created the work as an activity within the scope of his employment, the work is a *work made for hire* and the employer is the owner. However, if the work was created by an independent contractor, the contractor will ordinarily own the rights unless an agreement is executed between the contractor and the hiring party. This can be a significant issue when an outside party is hired to develop software, images, or music for a game.

Under U.S. copyright law, all of the rights to a work that is created by a contractor can be transferred to the hiring party in two ways. First, if the work is specially ordered or commissioned for use in an audiovisual work such as a video game (or certain other works), a written agreement between the parties can designate the work as a "work made for hire" whose rights belong to the hiring party, not the contractor. The written agreement can also (or instead) state that the contractor assigns all rights in the work to be created to the hiring party. Naturally, it is generally much easier to reach such an agreement at the outset of a relationship and not wait until work has commenced or is complete. Once a relationship has been established and the development of the work is underway, the developer often sees an attempt to secure copyright by the hiring party as a change in expectations for which he may want additional compensation.

Registering the copyright in a work with the Library of Congress can confer several important legal advantages upon the copyright owner. It can make available to the owner statutory damages of up to $150,000 per act of infringement, plus attorney fees, from the infringer. This can relieve the owner of the burden of having to prove the existence and amount of such damages in order to collect them. Also, a court must presume that the copyright is valid and that the facts stated in the registration certificate are true. The burden of proof as to the veracity of these facts is thus shifted. Ordinarily, the owner would have to prove they are true, but with a registration in place, they are presumed true and it is up to the defendant to prove they are not true. This can make it easier for the owner to enforce his copyright.

Under section 106 of the Copyright Act, a copyright owner has the exclusive rights to produce copies or reproductions of the work and to sell those copies (including electronic copies); to import or export the work; to create derivative works (works that adapt the original work); to perform or display the work publicly; and to sell or assign these rights to others.

It is not uncommon that the developer wants to retain some rights to a work, even when ownership is properly addressed at the inception of a relationship. Again, the separable nature of the bundle of rights can come to the rescue. Both parties are usually able to reach mutual agreement based on the right allocation of rights to the satisfaction of each. If the hiring party owns the copyright, that ownership of the specific rights under copyright can be derogated as appropriate to satisfy the contractor. For example, a game developer hired by a publisher may wish to retain ownership of the copyright, but the publisher may insist on exclusive reproduction and distribution rights. The developer may ask for an exception to the reproduction right by demanding permission to produce copies for beta testing. The resulting license may give the developer ownership of the copyright, the publisher an exclusive distribution right and a nonexclusive reproduction right, and the developer the right to reproduce solely for the purpose of beta testing. This back-and-forth negotiation can produce licenses that properly satisfy the particular needs of the parties.

It can be helpful to create a chart showing copyright in a work and the parties among whom these rights are to be divided. For example, Table 8.1 reflects the terms of imaginary agreements between the parties across the top.

TABLE 8.1   Copyright Agreements Among Parties

Right	Developer	Publisher	Distributor	End User
Reproduce	Yes, but for Developer's own use only	Yes	Yes, within terms of Distribution Agreement	No
Distribute (sell)	No	Yes	Yes, within geographic territory designated in Distribution Agreement	No
Import	N/A	Yes	Yes, but only from Publisher	Yes, but only from authorized Distributor
Export	Yes, but only to Developer's and Publisher's offices in other countries	Yes	Yes, but only to geographic areas specified in Distribution Agreement	No
Publicly perform	No	No	No	No
Create derivative works	Yes, but only for ports and sequels as specified in Agreement with Publisher	No, this has been exclusively reserved to Developer	No	No

Trademark

A trademark is any word, name, symbol, or device (a *designation*) used to identify and distinguish the source of goods from those manufactured or sold by others and to indicate the source of the goods. Unlike copyright, which exists from the moment of the fixation of a work in a tangible medium, trademark rights in the United States arise from the use of a designation in association with a good or service such that the designation identifies the source. Trademark rights include the right to exclude others from using the same or a similar mark in association with the same or similar goods, if doing so is likely to cause confusion in the marketplace as to the source of the goods.

Trademark rights are territorial; that is, they extend to the borders of the countries in which they exist. Here, we focus on trademark law of the United States, where rights arise based on use of the mark in commerce. It is worth noting that outside the United States, trademark rights generally arise not as a result of use, but as the result of a registration of the trademark.

Like other forms of intellectual property, trademark rights can be licensed. However, to maintain his trademark rights, the owner must control the use of the mark. This extends to licensing a trademark to another. The owner must take measures to ensure that the quality of goods or services provided under the mark is at least as high as the quality provided by the owner. In this way, the owner controls the use of the mark by the licensee. It is very important to remember to include appropriate quality control provisions in a trademark license. Otherwise, the licensor could actually lose his rights in the mark altogether.

It should be noted that a distributor need not license the trademark of the product being distributed. For example, a Ford dealership does not license the FORD trademark from Ford Motor Company. This is because there is no possibility that a customer would confuse a dealership as being the manufacturer of a car sold there. It is understood that the dealership merely acts as a distributor. Likewise, the distributor or reseller of a game need not ordinarily execute a trademark license with the maker.

Indeed, the very idea of letting another entity use a mark in which you have created a reputation ("goodwill") seems contradictory to the overall goal of trademarks: to designate the source of a product. For example, what if Coca-Cola granted a license to Pepsi® Cola to sell its soda under the COKE trademark? Without quality control provisions imposed by Coca-Cola, the COKE mark could lose its ability to distinguish Coca-Cola from Pepsi Cola as the source of the soda. To prevent this, Coca-Cola would have to mandate that the soda produced by Pepsi Cola to be sold under the COKE mark would have to have a given sweetness, color, carbonation, and so forth, such that it meets or exceeds the quality of the soda sold by Coca-Cola itself under the COKE mark. In fact, such a license may even require Pepsi Cola to manufacture the soda to be sold under the COKE mark using Coca-Cola's own formula. The quality control provisions typically include the right to audit and test the licensed product by the licensor.

Just as trademark rights can be licensed, they can also be assigned. A company may sell a game or line of games to another company, which sale includes the right to use the name of the game. It is essential that the agreement assigning the trademark rights also transfer all of the goodwill associated with the marks. Here, *goodwill* is a legal term signifying reputation; goodwill is often not all "good." Absent a transfer of goodwill along with the marks, the trademark can be lost.

Patent

Patents relate to ideas. While a copyright for a software program may protect a particular source code expression of the ideas underlying the program, a patent could protect the ideas themselves. In this sense, a patent can have greater scope than a copyright. A person who implements the ideas underlying the program by independently writing his own version would not infringe the original creator's copyright. However, he may well infringe upon the creator's patents if they cover the same ideas.

A patent gives an inventor the right to exclude others from practicing his invention for a limited period of time, usually about 17 years. In exchange, the inventor agrees to disclose and teach how to make his invention, which he might otherwise have kept secret. To obtain a patent, an invention must be new, useful, and sufficiently inventive over what has come before (the *prior art*). Unlike copyright and trademark rights, patent rights arise from applications that must be submitted to and examined by the United States Patent and Trademark Office. If the Patent Office decides that the invention described in the application is sufficiently inventive and useful, it will issue a patent. Otherwise, the application can be rejected.

In the United States and certain other jurisdictions, software can be patented under the established system for patents. In Europe, patents that are explicitly directed to software can be rejected. However, applications for software inventions can often be written to satisfy European requirements for patentability.

Patent rights generally allow the patent owner, known as the *patentee*, the right to exclude others from making, using, and selling the patented invention. These rights can be allocated in a license as the licensor and licensee see fit. For example, a EULA may give the end user the right to use a patented program and to sell it once, provided he destroys his own copy. Such a license would not, of course, give the end user the right to make the program himself. Likewise, a license with a distributor may give the distributor the right to make and sell the program, but not to use it.

Elements of a License

Not every license has all of the elements discussed in this section; rather, this should serve as an overview of some of the possibilities available to parties to formulate a license that meets their needs.

Field of Use

Field of use limitations restrict the ways in which a licensed right may be used. For example, a right to use may be licensed only to end users for their private, noncommercial use. A licensed right to distribute may be restricted to retailers only, with no right to distribute to end users. A right to copy may be limited to a single backup copy. Field of use limitations can be useful for ensuring that different licensees do not conflict with each other commercially.

Duration

A license is an agreement, and like every agreement, the term should be specified, even if it is perpetual. If the license is for a finite time, provision should be made for what happens after the term ends. For example, a right can revert to the licensor or be transferred to a third party at the end of the license term. A licensor may wish to license the right to use a game to end users forever, while licensing the right to distribute the game to a publisher for a limited time. The agreement may specify that the license is automatically renewed at the end of the stated term unless either party provides notice otherwise to the other a certain amount of time before the expiration of the term.

Geographic

A license may be limited by geographic scope. The property may be licensed on a country-by-country basis, a region (e.g., regional encoding), and so forth. For example, a license may give a particular distributor the right to make copies and distribute those copies only in the States of the European Union, Canada, and so on. Geographic scope can also be defined by landmarks; for example, east of the Mississippi River in the United States.

Warranty and Indemnity

Every license should contain warranties and indemnities. A warranty is a promise proffered by the warrantor as consideration for entering into the agreement. For example, a party can warrant that none of the property being licensed violates the intellectual property rights of a third party. If a warranty is broken, the parties can consider the broken promise a material breach of the agreement, which can entitle the party to terminate the agreement and possibly seek damages. Other examples of warranties include warranting that the party has full legal title to the licensed property; that the party has the legal authority to enter into the license; and so forth.

An indemnity is a promise by one party to make the other party whole in the event the other party is damaged by the occurrence of specified events. These can often correspond to some of the warranties. For example, a warranty may promise that something will not happen, while the corresponding indemnity promises to make good to the other party if it does. For example, a warranty can promise that the product does not infringe the intellectual property rights of any third party. The corresponding indemnity can promise to legally defend the other party from any claim against the other party alleging that the product infringes the intellectual property rights of a third party and to pay any damages that may arise from such a claim.

At times, the indemnitor may wish to cap the maximum liability it indemnifies. Common caps include the total amount paid by the indemnitor to the indemnitee under the agreement and a specific amount of money, oftentimes whichever is greater. It is important to consider the financial capacity of an indemnitor when negotiating the agreement. A $10,000,000 indemnity from a small company with less than $1,000,000 in annual revenues may be impossible to collect. Insurance can remedy this situation in some cases.

Inevitably, the cost of the insurance to the indemnitor is priced into the deal, so the indemnitee often pays in some way for the added reliability.

Sublicensing

A license may give the licensee the right to *sublicense*, or in other words, to give the same or similar rights to a third party. For example, a license may grant the licensee the right to sublicense the right to make copies. This is common when a game is published by a licensee that does not have a global presence and is forced to rely on other distributors to sell copies of the game in some foreign markets. A sublicense right can be circumscribed with its own royalty and payment terms or field of use and geographic restrictions.

Cross-Licensing

Not all licenses are one-way affairs, with intellectual property rights going one way and money the other. Parties can *cross-license* their respective rights. For example, a publisher may grant certain rights in a game to a developer, while the developer may grant to the publisher technology rights in a development engine the publisher can share with other developers under certain circumstances.

Licensing for Rights in Literary Works

Whether a magazine article, novel, stage play, screenplay, or in some other form, an existing literary work offers the developer a host of elements from which to draw inspiration. These elements include the narrative, the themes, plots, characters, settings, title, and other material that can serve as the environment in which the game is set.

An analysis of the rights required to an underlying literary work is the necessary starting point. Where the work is one of fiction, unless the copyright has entered the public domain, rights to the underlying literary work must be acquired from the copyright holder. (See Chapter 7 for more information about the public domain.) Where the work is nonfiction, as, for example, an exposition of an historical event, the need to acquire underlying literary rights is less certain. It is well established that copyright cannot be claimed in historical facts. A game developer who wishes to recreate military battles is generally free to do so without the need to obtain rights from those who have written previously about the historical occurrence. The facts surrounding such events cannot be copyrighted and may be available from a number of different sources. However, the *expression* of facts is subject to copyright protection. Thus, the description of the historical event as uniquely told by the author, an original manner in which facts are organized (which would not include organization in merely chronological order), and other aspects of the fact-based writing are protected by copyright and not available for use by the game developer without permission. Other reasons to acquire rights from a nonfiction author may be to bargain for the author's cooperation, for access to the author's research, or for the right to market the game as a tie-in to the work on which it is based.

A critical question is what rights, if any, have been previously granted in the work and whether they are exclusive. Rights to a published novel, for example, will likely be subject to a publishing agreement under which the author has granted rights under copyright to the book publisher. If the book has been optioned or made into a motion picture or television program, rights will also have been granted for that purpose. The game developer must determine if any such previous grant will overlap with the rights the developer needs to exploit. For example, authors customarily grant to the book publisher the right to publish printed editions of the work, and to exploit certain ancillary and subsidiary rights. If the work has been more recently published, these may include audiovisual rights and rights of distribution by electronic means. While it may have been intended that this relates to means of promoting, selling, or delivering the book in ways that would not interfere with the rights needed by a game developer, the breadth of the language of the grant to the book publisher may conflict with or overlap with the rights sought by the developer. If the grant to the publisher is clearly limited to various means of exploitation of the text of the work by electronic means such as digital download, excluding audiovisual depictions, the game developer may have greater certainty that the rights it requires are available.

The developer may wish to have rights that will certainly overlap with the book publisher, such as print publication rights in the original work to advertise and promote the game or to incorporate written text into the game itself for on-screen presentation of narrative elements or dialogue. For a previously published work, the game developer reasonably can only expect to have these rights on a nonexclusive basis with limited scope. To avoid doubt, the game developer can require the author to obtain the publisher's acknowledgment that the publisher does not have conflicting rights to those being sought.

If rights to the literary work previously have been granted for audiovisual exploitation, the author of the work may no longer be in control of the rights for game development. Such rights may have been included as part of the bundle of ancillary rights included in the grant to a motion picture studio that has the right to make motion pictures, television programs, or other audiovisual adaptations of the work. An examination of the previous grant may lead to the conclusion that the developer will need to acquire rights from the prior grantee in lieu of, or in addition to, the author.

Assuming that a developer has determined that rights to an underlying literary work are necessary and available, an agreement for the rights acquisition or option to acquire such rights with the author must be made. This agreement will be the touchstone for development of the game.

Structure of Agreement

In structuring the agreement with the proprietor of rights to a literary work, the game developer may consider acquiring all rights at the outset, or in the alternative, structuring the agreement as an option to acquire the rights within a defined option period as is customary in the development of motion pictures. In the latter instance, a small amount of money may be paid for the grant of option as an advance against a larger purchase price paid if the option is exercised. The option period would allow the developer to engage in development activities before determining whether it wishes to pay the full purchase price. The full panoply of rights to the literary work customarily stays with the author until the option is exercised. This structure may be an advantage where the work is well known and the purchase price relatively high, and in situations where it is unclear whether a marketable game based on the property can be developed. A third structure would be to acquire all rights at the outset, but have them subject to a reversion if the developer does not publish a game within a set period.

Factors to Consider

The game developer will probably want the right to vary and change events, characters, and other elements of the literary work in any way the game requires, including the creation of new plots, characters, and settings. The grant of rights should specifically allow this. The developer will also want game rights to be exclusive, across existing platforms (Xbox, PlayStation, PC, handhelds, etc.) and any other platforms that may be devised in the future. The grant should make specific mention of existing technology for gameplay and delivery that is to be exploited, including remote delivery across the Internet from a central server. The license should also envision new technologies or methods of delivery that may be developed. Rights to create more than one version of the game and sequels or other future editions that may include different, additional, or changed plot elements are also highly desirable. The developer will want the term of all rights to run in perpetuity. The developer should also consider acquiring the right to adapt the game in other settings (e.g., a television series or motion picture that may originate from a successful video game), and for use in merchandising if such rights are available.

An important issue for negotiation is the degree to which the author reserves rights in the work. At minimum, an author of a previously published literary work will want to retain print publication rights. However, as noted earlier, the game developer will want to secure the use of text excerpts, synopses, and summaries in the game and in connection with promotion and advertising even where publishing rights are reserved by the author.

Other rights the author may seek to retain include the right to present the work on stage and the right to write and publish sequels to the work. A *sequel* is typically defined as a work using characters taken from the original property in a different plot. Ideally, the game developer would want to have the right to use sequels for subsequent games. Acquiring such rights is of particular value where the property is largely character driven or features a well-known title. If not included, the game developer will at least want to secure exclusivity in the characters by preventing the author from granting rights to a sequel to another developer. This can be done by having such rights frozen completely so the author may never grant them, or making them subject to a holdback. If the developer cannot get the author to agree to a perpetual prohibition, the holdback should at least continue until some period of time after the game and any permitted subsequent editions have been released. The game developer should also bargain either for the right to acquire sequels following the holdback period at a specified cost when and if the author wishes to exploit them, or have a *right of first negotiation* to acquire such rights, followed by a *right of last refusal* to match the offer of any third party for such rights if no agreement can be reached.

Most authors prefer to retain some creative involvement in the adaptation of their work. A well-crafted game will increase the value of the literary property and the rights reserved to the author, while a poorly executed game could have the opposite effect. As a result, the author may wish to place conditions and restrictions on the adaptation, including the right to approve certain aspects of the game such as depictions of characters, plot, setting, or other narrative or visual elements of the game. The ability to do so will reflect the relative bargaining position of the author and the game developer. The developer generally wants to avoid any such limitations and will prefer an agreement to consult with, rather than give approval to, the author on key creative issues with the developer having the final decision-making authority.

If rights of approval are given, the time line and process for submission will be of critical importance. It is in the interest of both parties to avoid later disputes by detailing exactly what is subject to approval, how the approval process will work, and what time restrictions exist on the process. A general right of approval that lacks such details can delay the development of the game. Even where it is agreed that approval will not be unreasonably withheld, it is essential that the developer feel confident that approval ultimately can be obtained or deemed given. This can be achieved by limiting the scope of approval, limiting the number of times the developer is required to submit the same matter for approval, and by requiring the author to identify specifically the changes necessary for approval to be granted. As an alternative to approval, the game developer might consider an agreement by which it agrees that it will not make certain changes or depictions such as having a character die or engaging in activity contrary to the image of the character.

Depending on negotiating leverage, an author may seek other more advantageous provisions in the rights agreement. For example, the author may want the underlying rights to revert if they are not exploited within a certain period of time or if future editions or sequels to the work are not created, produced, and released within specified periods of time following publication of the most recent game. If a reversion of rights to the author does occur, the developer should retain the right to continue to exploit any game that has been released; however, this right would be of questionable value unless updates or new software versions can be made. The author may also want permission from the game developer to use new characters or other elements originating in the game in connection with the author's own sequels. In addition, the author may also ask for the right to use artwork or depictions from the game as a tie-in to the exercise of the author's reserved rights.

A license will typically include representations and warranties by the author relating to the work. Most importantly, these include a warranty that the author or other grantor owns and controls the rights, that the work is original and not in the public domain, and that the work does not infringe upon the copyright or other rights of a third party. The indemnification provisions of the agreement should provide that the licensor is responsible for defense costs, damages, and liabilities arising from a breach, and possibly those that arise from the mere allegation of a breach. Nonetheless, preventing a problem is better than solving one that later arises. The game developer should seek verification of underlying rights to make certain the work has been properly registered for copyright and there are no conflicting claims or overlapping grant of rights. The author should provide documentation showing the chain of title of the underlying work and prior agreements, if any, with a publisher and/or other third-party grantees of rights. In addition, the game developer should require the author to commit to protect the copyright against any third-party infringements and, if needed, to confirm the rights granted to the developer by signing additional instruments evidencing the transfer of rights to the game developer.

Licensing for Rights in Musical Works

The point of departure for licensing rights in music is the recognition that audible music, as heard in a game or elsewhere, is protected by two distinct copyrights: the copyright in the underlying musical composition, and the separate and distinct copyright in the sound recording or master (denominated as a ℗). Users of music in a video game must ensure that rights to both copyrights have been obtained. Complexity may arise because these two copyrights are often owned or controlled by different parties. Note that a game that generates its own music through computer software would not involve licensing a preexisting sound recording.

The inherent difficulty in having to acquire rights from more than one party is an impetus for the tradition in game development to have original music composed and recorded for use as the complete underscore for a game. In such instances, the developer can commission the music, and both copyrights in audible music, as works made for hire under the Copyright Act and would own the copyrights. Even if ownership of either the copyright in the master recording or in the underlying music composition is to be retained by the composer, the developer can make certain that it has locked in exclusive rights for all conceivable uses relating to its game, including advertising, publicity, and exploitation in all media through the licensing agreement. In addition, the developer can include a restrictive covenant to ensure the owner does not license such music to any third party in a game that might be competitive with the game being developed. As a matter of best legal practice, however, contractual protections with the composer are never as good a protection for the developer as outright ownership by commissioning the music as a work made for hire.

Where a developer wishes to use well-known or recognizable music or the talents of established artists as performers for music in a game, the developer will need to license or acquire the necessary rights.

Master Recordings

Ordinarily, rights to a previously commercially released master recording will be owned by a single party and may be the easier of the two copyrights to license. If the song has been released to the public previously, the master will likely be owned or exclusively controlled by the record company that released it. Alternatively, the game developer may elect to have performers record music for it to own as a work for hire. In such instances, the developer will need to engage the performers directly. The advantages in doing so include the ability to acquire name, image, and likeness rights, and perhaps cooperation in publicity and promotion for the game directly from the artists. If any use of the artist's name or likenesses is contemplated other than a listing of credits for the licensed music, it is important to acquire personal publicity rights directly from the artist.

If the artist is signed to an exclusive recording agreement with a record label, consent of that label is likely also required even if the master owned by that label is not to be used. This requirement derives from the fact that an exclusive recording artist may have granted the record company the exclusive right to record and exploit performances of the artist on all forms of "records" during the term of the recording agreement, and to exploit the artist's name, image, and likeness in connection with any recorded music. Records as typically defined in a recording agreement will encompass audio-only formats such as compact discs, and any so-called sight and/or sound device created for distribution to the public, including distribution by electronic means. This would include videocassettes, DVDs, and games embodied on CD-ROMs or other physical media. Having to negotiate with both the artist and his or her record company may be cumbersome. Ultimately, the developer must hope that the record company will want to cooperate for the benefit of the exposure of their artist. Even then, the record label will not want to permit the release of products it views as competitive to its own exploitation. As a result, the record label may impose conditions on its consent, which may include restrictions on how the sound recording can be exploited, such as a prohibition on releasing the sound recording on an audio-only record. The label may also require or seek a license back from the game developer for it to exploit the sound recording on its records. The label may even go so far as to condition its consent on having ownership of the sound recording to be used in the game.

Where an existing previously produced master recording produced under union jurisdiction is to be used, reuse of the master in a video game may require payment to the musicians of additional session fees and/or residuals. The game developer should recognize that the owner of the master will undoubtedly want to make any such payment the obligation of the developer and should factor that into its decision making. Where the master is orchestral, for example, the required payment to the large number of musicians involved may make the use of the recording prohibitively costly.

Musical Compositions

Often, the more complex copyright to obtain in music licensing is the copyright in the underlying composition. The license for use of a musical composition in an audiovisual work like a video game is typically referred to as a *synchronization license* since the music accompanies and synchronizes with the moving images. In a modern game with many different potential uses of the music across multiple platforms and varying means of transmission, the license required by a game developer should provide for much more than a traditional synchronization license. The interactive nature of a game will require the license to permit music to be heard in a variety of situations. If the work is an original composition composed especially for the game developer, even in situations where the developer agrees that the publishing rights will be retained by the composer, the game developer should require that its license grant all uses of the composition in the context of the game and in all ancillary means of exploitation and in future versions or editions. If, however, the music is controlled by a third-party publisher (as may be the case even if a composer engaged by the developer to create the music, but that composer is signed to an exclusive songwriting agreement or if the song was previously written), then a license from such publisher is needed. Where more than one songwriter is involved, the copyright to the musical composition may be held in fractional shares and by more than one publisher. As a rule, the developer will want to obtain clearance of all of such interests.

Some argument can be made that, where the work is a joint work, a nonexclusive license from any copyright owner would enable the developer to exploit the composition. Because of the potential of having the other nonlicensed interests make a claim for payment, the best practice is to license all interests in the song. If multiple publishers are involved, the developer will want to license the song for a single fee to be allocated proportionately among the fractional interests.

A publisher licensing a preexisting composition will prefer to grant the most limited license it can in terms of the description of media and exploitation. Therefore, it is the convention in the music publishing industry for the publisher to describe the license granted in as narrow terms as possible so the publisher retains tight control over the copyright it administers. If the game is successful and becomes identified with certain music, the possibility of the developer wanting to use the music in subsequent editions of the game or by technological means not initially contemplated by the license creates opportunities for the publisher to negotiate for additional payment to permit further exploitation of the copyright. This will be unfavorable to the game developer who envisions a game being exploited across a variety of platforms, including standalone games and multiplayer applications where music used in the game may be stored on and originate from user computers, intermediary servers, or other remote locations.

The key to negotiating the adequate license is to identify the rights under copyright the developer's use of the music will exploit. This will involve an analysis of where and how many copies of the music a given application requires, whether music is to be publicly performed (e.g., by means of Internet stream or in advertising on television), and whether and to what extent there will be permanent or transient reproductions made of the music. For example, a game developer wishing to use music in a central location as a server copy from which streams or downloads to individual users is implicating a variety of rights that go beyond mere reproduction on CD-ROMs for distribution to end users. In licensing third-party music, the developer must seek a license that will encompass all anticipated means of exploitation, and those that may be developed in the future. A closer examination of these uses and the attendant fees that licensors require may lead the developer to determine that the complexity of adequately identifying all potential uses of the music and the cost of licensing them can outweigh the benefit of using well-known music; commissioning original music as a work for hire may be a better decision.

Licenses for Rights in Audiovisual Works

A motion picture or television program often is the basis for development of a video game. Indeed, it has become a staple of major motion picture releases to license a tie-in to a video game as one means of ancillary exploitation. The rights to an audiovisual work implicate the copyright in the film or audiovisual work itself, particularly if actual footage is to be used, and a host of other copyrights. These could include the underlying literary work on which such audiovisual work is based, third-party licensed materials appearing in the film such as soundtrack music, the use of actors' names and likenesses, or any other materials or elements that may have been embodied in the original audiovisual work and will be included in the game. A license for rights to audiovisual works thus implicates all or some of the factors described earlier for literary works, music, name and likeness rights to individuals, and possibly other elements.

The license for rights to an audiovisual work to the developer should include adequate representations and warranties from the licensor that it owns or controls all necessary rights to the audiovisual work and all component elements, and that the use of such work as permitted by the license will not infringe upon the rights of any third party. In addition to any such warranties, the developer may want to examine underlying rights agreements for these elements. This is especially true if the proprietor of the audiovisual work is unwilling to give full representations or warranties or will grant a license only on a quitclaim or "as is" basis. If any deficiencies are found, some action may be required to cure them by obtaining whatever rights are lacking. If enough rights need to be obtained, the game developer might consider avoiding use of the work altogether.

A particular area of concern is the computer-generated representation of characters appearing in the audiovisual work to be licensed. While actors may have agreed to grant rights in their name and likeness for use in a motion picture, the game developer will want to also have the right to create images of these characters engaging in actions that are not part of the original action, either using or recreating the voices or other physical characteristics of the actors who portrayed them. Direct consents from such actors for the use of their names and likenesses in the context of the game may be required. Where actors or other participants do not wish to participate, the game developer may need to change the portrayal of such character so the likeness of the character does not resemble the actor.

In constructing the game, the developer may insert the player as a new character within the environment of an existing audiovisual work to create new action with story and setting. The developer could include this character in recreations of memorable scenes or other recognizable aspects of the work. This recreation could require acquisition of the underlying rights, including the literary work on which the audiovisual work was based and possibly other unique elements incorporated into the film. For example, a scene taking place in front of a piece of artwork may require a license for copyright in the artwork for use separate from the film.

Other elements of an audiovisual work the game developer will want to acquire include artwork with which the audiovisual work is closely identified. This so-called *key artwork* may often be found in the one-sheet poster for a film, on packaging for DVDs of the film, or soundtrack packages. Indeed, the motion picture studio may require that such artwork be used and that credits be given to creative contributors to the film. As discussed before, music in a film may require obtaining separate rights from the owner of the master recording and the underlying publisher of musical compositions, whose grant may be restricted to the use in the original audiovisual work. Recreating a scene taken from a film by computer generation in which music is embodied may require separate and additional licenses of the musical composition and sound recordings.

An analysis for licensing rights to an audiovisual work requires consideration of all the elements and property rights that are embodied in such a work. Where all of these rights cannot be obtained from the proprietor of the audiovisual work in a manner that gives a level of comfort to the developer, the developer may determine that creating new elements is a less cumbersome and affordable approach.

Licensing for Rights to Name, Image, Likeness, and Indicia Rights of Individuals

In any context where an actual person, living or dead, is to be embodied in a game, the game developer must consider whether rights to that individual's name, image, and likeness must be obtained. Where the developer is going to computer-generate new images and actions of the character, obtaining name and likeness rights directly from the individuals depicted is likely warranted. While one may hope that such rights can be acquired from a third-party licensor of underlying materials on which the game is to be based, such as a motion picture studio granting rights in an audiovisual work in which the performance of the actors is embodied, that often is not the case. The actor may not have granted rights that enable computerized likenesses to perform new actions not in the original film; indeed, the original acting agreement may not have contemplated any such use. For example, in the *Godfather* game from Electronic Arts released in the spring of 2006, it is understood that name and likeness rights were obtained for principal characters, including Marlon Brando who provided some limited voiceover services prior to his death. The notable exception is Al Pacino, who is reported to have declined to participate. As a result, the character Michael Corleone from the film as portrayed in this game is not a depiction of Al Pacino.

Use of footage taken directly from an audiovisual work also may trigger additional payment to the actors for which the licensor will make the game developer responsible. In addition, developers may wish for the actor to provide voiceover work or other services to incorporate new material as part of the game.

The rules applying to the depiction of real persons in a game are generally no different from those applying to use of an individual's name or likeness in any other audiovisual work or other product or service. This need for permission arises from the personal privacy and publicity rights of the individual depicted.

Personal Privacy and Publicity Rights

Individual name, likeness, and indicia rights derive from the evolving law of privacy and publicity. A right of privacy is a personal right that embraces protection against intrusion into one's private affairs, disclosure of embarrassing facts, publicity by placing one in a false light in the public eye, and appropriation of name and likeness for commercial advantage.[1] This last element, a right to protect against appropriation for commercial advantage, is at the root of what has become known as a *right of publicity* meant to preserve an individual's exclusive right to the commercial value of his or her own identity. Protection against nonconsensual commercial exploitation extends to name and likeness, and to other aspects of identity such as voice, photograph, portrait, caricature, or other distinguishable indicia of persona. Obviously, it is the celebrity or otherwise well-known individual to whom rights of publicity will be most valuable and from whom such rights are most often sought to be licensed.

In various states, these rights are protected by statute, by precedent under common law, or both. States enacting statutes governing rights of publicity have, in many cases, recognized the value of personality as a form of property right the owner has the generally exclusive right to exploit and thus license. Many of these recognize that this right also survives the death of the individual and is descendible. The interlacing of these statutes and common law precedent leaves no doubt that, with limited exception, the game developer seeking to distribute and exploit a game in the United States will need to acquire the necessary rights from or on behalf of individuals recognizable in the game.

New York and California have had occasion to address these issues in the context of the entertainment industry. In New York, Section 51 of the Civil Rights Law prohibits the use of the name or likeness of any person "for advertising or for the purpose of trade" without written consent.[2] No comparable common law right exists in New York. In California, a common law right of publicity exists, but California also has two relevant statutes. California Civil Code Section 3344 proscribes the use of "another's name, voice, signature, photograph, or likeness, in any manner, on or in products, merchandise, goods or services" without such person's prior consent.[3] California Civil Code Section 3344.1 extends this protection to the use of a "deceased personality's name, voice, signature, photograph, or likeness, in any manner, on or in products, merchandise, or goods, or for purposes of advertising or selling, or soliciting purchases of, products, merchandise, goods or services," without the prior consent of the heirs of the deceased or other persons to whom such rights have been transferred.[4] Both of the California statutes provide exceptions that permit use in connection with any news, public affairs, sports broadcast or account, or any political campaign.[5] In the case of deceased personalities, an additional exception allows use in plays, books, magazines, newspapers, musical compositions, film, radio, or television programs other than as an advertisement.[6] Video games are notably absent from the categories specifically mentioned in these exceptions relating to the deceased. For living persons, there is no specific exception for film, radio, television, or other such categories.

As evident in the language of the California statute, protection also has been extended beyond the name and likeness of the celebrity to apply to the unauthorized use of *indicia* or other characteristics for which the celebrity is well known, such as voice and signature. California court decisions have even gone further to cover other aspects of identity. Thus, in California, claims have been upheld: by Bette Midler for use of a "sound alike" voice in an advertisement where her consent was not given,[7] by Vanna White for an unauthorized robotic replication of her attributes as a game show icon,[8] and by actors from the television series *Cheers* against unauthorized use of animatronic robotic figures in airport bars depicting characters they portrayed even though a license from the copyright owner of the series had been obtained.[9] These cases should have a particular resonance for the game developer who may be creating computer imagery meant to replicate or suggest well-known individuals.

Federal statute and constitutional concerns also factor into the analysis. The Lanham Act, for example, permits a civil action against the false designation of origin or any false or misleading description or representation of fact that causes or is likely to cause confusion as to the association or approval over goods or services. In the context of an individual, this can support a claim of false endorsement or association.[10] An example might be having software-generated characters with the attributes of well-known individuals, who are depicted as endorsing the product to the benefit of the developer. To the benefit of the developer, the First Amendment protection of free speech takes precedence in certain situations over the right of an individual to exclusively control any commercial exploitation of his or her name or likeness. Thus, where the subject matter is of public interest or concern, there may not be any right of privacy or publicity. This might apply, for example, in the context of a game depicting a historical event in which public figures are depicted in the context of the event.

Factors to Consider

Having determined that consent from a well-known individual is desirable, the game developer will need to consider where such a release can be obtained and what it should contain. In some cases, individual members of a union may have granted the right to engage in group licensing in certain contexts to their union. This is true for many professional sports. For example, the Major League Baseball Player's Association has a "Player's Choice Group Licensing Program." Through individual agreements with members of the union, the Player's Association has the right to grant rights for products and services involving baseball players where three or more players are featured. This enables a game developer wishing to create a baseball-related game to acquire rights for players in a single license without having to obtain consent from each individual player, which would undoubtedly be unwieldy and costly. Where certain players are featured, however, the individual likeness consent may be required. In addition, it may be that players can opt out of such a licensing arrangement and their individual consents will still be needed. Barry Bonds, for example, is reported to have become the first player to opt out of the union's group licensing program; game developers wishing to include him or his likeness in a game would need to obtain permission from him directly.

With respect to an individual's consent, there are a number of provisions in an agreement the game developer will want included. The agreement should contain permission to use the name and likeness and aspects of personality and indicia including, without limitation, voice, nicknames, biography, and personality traits. The grant should relate to embodiment in the game, and in all advertising, promotion, and publicity related to it, including, without limitation, packaging and key artwork to be used for marketing. The agreement should include the right for the game developer to make changes to an individual's characteristics as necessary for the game. Whether making such changes is the developer's intention, this provision will forestall any complaint that such characteristics are not accurately portrayed. The developer will want to strive to retain complete creative freedom to make a fun game. The release aspect of an agreement should include a covenant preventing any kind of legal action or complaint for violation of any right of publicity, right of privacy, or other personal right, including, without limitation, any claim of defamation or slander.

It can be expected that a well-known individual may request creative approvals, and the developer should anticipate accommodating such approvals to the extent practical without creating a situation that could prevent development or exploitation of the game. For example, where there are graphic likenesses to be used, the developer can submit proposed likenesses at early stages of development with the understanding that there will be a process by which comments are addressed and resubmitted for further review a finite number of times after which approval is deemed given.

Conclusion

The key to the effective acquisition of intellectual property rights is to identify the intellectual property rights that are sought, their availability, and the scope of the license needed. The goal is to craft a license that specifies the intellectual property, duration, use, and media the developer needs, and includes a grant of rights broad enough to include new game versions, platforms, or other methods of exploitation that may arise in the future. This will entail consideration of the rights that will be granted to the developer on an exclusive basis, which are granted nonexclusively, and any rights that will be reserved by the owner.

The developer will need to determine what particular copyrights are involved, and whether rights have previously been granted that might preclude the developer from fully exploiting the property. The sooner this determination is done, the better, so that acquisition can be accomplished before significant development funds are expended and alternatives can be considered if necessary. Where a game is to be developed using an existing literary work or motion picture, previous grants of rights may have included video game rights as a part of electronic publishing rights granted to a publisher, or as merchandising to a motion picture company as part of ancillary and subsidiary rights. The developer must also recognize that a licensed work, such as an audiovisual clip, may embody separately copyrighted elements for which a separate license may be required. For licensed materials that are less integral to the game, such as a piece of music that could be substituted, alternatives can be considered. The developer should also weigh the expense of licensing against the possibility of avoiding a license altogether by commissioning original music or recordings directly from composers or artists.

A related area to intellectual property is the property rights individuals have in their own names and likenesses. The game developer may envision developing a game using licensed materials in which names and likenesses of individuals are embodied. The developer must be mindful that individuals retain an interest in the use of their names and likenesses, particularly in commercial settings. The developer will need to determine if the rights to these individuals can be included in the grant of underlying property rights, or whether separate releases and consents will be required.

Appropriate planning and analysis for licensing underlying intellectual property rights is the necessary protocol to maximize efficiency in developing games and to avoid receiving claims from an existing intellectual property rights holder. Avoiding such pitfalls is a practical necessity that will have direct impact on the commercial viability of the video game.

Endnotes

1. These four areas of protection around which a right of privacy is often described are commonly attributed to William Prosser and his well-known law review article on the subject. Prosser, *Privacy,* 48 Calif. L. Rev (1960). *See* McCarthy, J. Thomas, *Rights of Publicity and Privacy,* (2nd Ed) (West, 2003).
2. New York Civil Rights Law §51
3. West's Ann. Cal Civ Code §3344
4. West's Ann. Cal Civ Code §3344.1 pertaining to deceased personalities covers use within 70 years of death.
5. West's Ann. Cal Civ Code §3344(d); West's Ann. Cal Civ Code §3344.1(j)
6. West's Ann. Cal Civ Code §3344.1(a)(2)
7. Bette Midler v. Ford Motor Co., 849 F.2d. 460 (9th Cir. 1988)
8. Vanna White v. Samsung, 917 F.2d 1395 (9th Cir. 1992)
9. Wendt v. Host International, Inc. 125 F.3d 806 (9th Cir. 1997), *rehearing denied,* 197 F.3d 1284 (9th Cir. 1999) (*en banc*).
10. 15 U.S.C. §1125(a)

CHAPTER 9

Intellectual Property Litigation (Avoiding It, But Winning If You Have to Fight)

John Flock

jflock@kenyon.com[1]

Not long ago, intellectual property (IP) litigation was nothing more than an obscure legal practice, overshadowed by the typical television portrayals of the heroic efforts of district attorneys or the popular news stories of scandalous civil trials. In mainstream media, there were virtually no news reports about lawsuits involving IP rights. But more recently, IP litigation has caught the attention of industry-savvy corporate executives and the mainstream media as patent infringement verdicts of hundreds of millions of dollars have become increasingly common.[2] Patent litigation news has become a front-page phenomenon as recently evidenced by stories of the threatened injunction against continued BlackBerry™ service and Internet auctions, while major cable news networks have aired vibrant discussions and in-depth commentaries of the latest IP lawsuits by legal and corporate experts.[3]

Together with this rise in media exposure, companies have come to better understand the importance of protecting—and capitalizing on—their IP rights. For some companies, IP litigation has moved from being a burdensome potential cost of doing business to a growing expense that, in some cases, threatens a company's very viability. For other companies, IP litigation has become a necessary licensing tool to fully realize the value of their intangible assets and thereby, drive up their stock price.

This chapter describes how litigation arises, what happens to a party involved in a case, and what that party can do to be well-prepared to win.

Litigation—Forced Dispute Resolution

Chapter 7, "Intellectual Property," offers an excellent summary of the principles of IP law. One of those principles is that if a company (or an individual) owns intellectual property rights—whether patent, trademark, copyright, or trade secret—that company has the right to stop others from using those intangible assets. In most cases, a patent owner chooses to license its IP rights in exchange for some type of compensation, typically a payment or cross license.

Ideally, the IP owner would negotiate with a party that wanted to use the IP, a value would be agreed upon, and a deal would be struck. Unfortunately, business dealings are never that simple. Parties often disagree over the most fundamental licensing issues, such as whether IP is being used at all and, if so, what is the value of that IP. As a result, the parties sometimes walk away, change their business models, or fight. For purposes of illustration, this chapter mainly uses examples from the most bitterly fought lawsuits in the IP field—patent infringement litigation—to demonstrate legal principles and litigation strategies.

While some companies are able to resolve patent disputes through resolution processes other than litigation (these alternatives are discussed later in this chapter), in certain instances, talking does not always lead to an agreement. One of the parties, typically the patent owner, may choose to force a resolution by filing a lawsuit. In litigation, the pattern of events includes the patent owner providing a notice of the complaint, the accused party answering, the parties exchanging information about the liability and financial issues in the case, and a judge or jury deciding the dispute after a trial. Given the confrontational nature of litigation, these ostensibly simple steps often turn out to be disruptive and costly to the companies involved. The complexity and difficulty of litigation is compounded by the fact that the ultimate decision (with far-reaching impacts such as compensatory money damages, potential enhanced damages, and possibly an injunction prohibiting further sales) is made by a judge or jury who typically do not have the level of technical and business understanding of the engineers and businesspersons whose futures are affected by the verdict. Given the uncertainties and risks, resolving a patent dispute through litigation should be a well-considered decision, and typically a last resort. However, if litigation is an unavoidable reality, the parties involved must be prepared to effectively litigate and win.

Before the Suit Begins

Before a party files a lawsuit to protect its IP rights, there are several factors worth considering: whether there has been sufficient investigation of the accused device and the patent; whether the opponent may file a declaratory judgment; and where are the most favorable jurisdictions in which to file.

Some of the following information references the *Federal Rules of Civil Procedure*. The Federal Rules of Civil Procedure (abbreviated as Fed. R. Civ. P.) are statutes that govern the conduct and procedures during litigation and trial in federal courts.

Pre-Filing Requirements

Before initiating a patent lawsuit, a party must conduct an investigation to show it has a reasonable basis for going forward. Rule 11 of the Federal Rules of Civil Procedure requires the party's attorney to certify that the attorney believes the case is warranted.

This is true for patent infringement cases and other civil cases. If the pre-filing investigation is found insufficient, legal sanctions may be imposed.

An example of insufficient investigation is shown in *View Engineering v. Robotic Visions Systems.*[4] View Engineering and Robotic Visions were competitors in the field of 3D vision technology, which was mainly used to scan computer chips to insure the leads were properly aligned. View Engineering filed a declaratory judgment action against Robotic Vision, seeking to have Robotic Vision's patent declared invalid or not infringed. Robotic Vision counterclaimed that View Engineering infringed eight of its patents. (A counterclaim is a claim for relief brought by a noninitiating party against an opposing party, usually the plaintiff, after the original cause of action has been filed. Rule 11 applies to counterclaims with equal force as to the claims in the original complaint.)

Robotic Vision's attorneys were required to perform an infringement analysis, including the interpretation of the patent claims (which is an analysis of the meaning of the patent claims as a practitioner of the technical field [one of "ordinary skill in the art"] would understand them) by the attorneys and a finding that the patent claims cover the accused devices.[5] Courts accord deference to the attorneys' pre-filing claim interpretations, as long as they follow the standard canons of claim construction, as discussed later in this chapter. In *View Engineering*, the Court of Appeals for the Federal Circuit (a specialized court that hears patent appeals from all over the country and usually referred to simply as the Federal Circuit) determined that Robotic Vision's investigations were insufficient to meet the requirements of Rule 11, because the attorneys neither performed any independent claim construction analysis nor conducted any infringement analysis. The Court found that the attorneys filed the counterclaims solely based on their client's knowledge of its patents and the client's knowledge of View Engineering's advertisements and statements to customers. The Federal Circuit did not empathize with Robotic Vision's argument that obtaining an accused View Engineering device was difficult, if not impossible. In fact, the Federal Circuit pointed out that the attorneys could have mitigated their circumstances by (1) filing immediately for a protective order that would allow initial discovery of the accused devices, (2) appointing an outside expert to review View Engineering's products, or (3) speaking with Robotic Vision's sales representatives to learn their knowledge of View Engineering's devices.

In sum, sanctions can be avoided by actions such as obtaining and testing a sample of the allegedly infringing product, attempting to reverse engineer an accused device, or seeking relevant technical and sales information from the opposing party.[6]

Declaratory Judgment Action

A company that has been threatened with patent infringement can initiate a lawsuit, instead of waiting to be sued, by filing a declaratory judgment action seeking a finding of noninfringement or invalidity of the patents.[7] This allows the threatened company to choose the place and timing of a case. For example, the plaintiff in *Lewis Galoob Toys,*

Inc. v. Nintendo of America, Inc.,[8] filed the original action in a U.S. district court for a declaratory judgment against Nintendo of America. The plaintiff was seeking a finding that its marketing, distribution, and sale of a videogame accessory, if used with Nintendo's video games and video game console to temporarily create new variations of the games, did not infringe Nintendo's copyright in the games. The appellate court affirmed the lower court's decision of noninfringement. Similarly, in *Team Play, Inc. v. Boyer*,[9] after receiving Boyer's letter alleging copyright infringement, the plaintiff brought a declaratory judgment action against Boyer in a U.S. district court seeking a finding that its development, marketing, and sale of a video game did not infringe Stephen Boyer's copyright in his videogames. The trial court granted summary judgment for noninfringement of one of Boyer's games.

To file the declaratory judgment action, the plaintiffs in *Lewis Galoob* and *Team Play* had to be able to show both that the threat of a lawsuit by patentee was real and the lawsuit was imminent. Specifically, declaratory judgment jurisdiction requires two proofs: (1) an explicit threat or other action by the patentee that creates a reasonable apprehension on the part of the plaintiff that it faces an infringement suit; and (2) present activity by the plaintiff that could constitute infringement, or concrete steps taken with the intent to conduct such activity.[10]

Where Does the Fight Occur?

Courts are not the same in all areas of the country. They may have different rules of procedure and evidence; the judges' experience with patent and technology cases may vary; and the jury pools may be vastly different.

Typically, a party can be sued in a state where the party has sufficient contacts related to the cause of action or other major contacts unrelated to the cause of action. For example, an individual or corporation that conducts business regularly in a state can be found to be generally "doing business" in the state, and therefore subject to the jurisdiction of that state regardless of whether the business is related to the lawsuit at hand. If an individual or corporation does not regularly conduct business in a state, jurisdiction can also be, and usually is, found if the company has engaged in the allegedly infringing behavior in the state. Consequently, an accused company that sells its products nationwide typically can be sued anywhere in the country. A company can sometimes be sued in a state even if its presence is only over the Internet.[11] This also applies to foreign corporations based on the theory that if they are selling products within the country, they should be prepared to accept the consequences of those sales.[12]

If a defendant finds itself properly in an unfavorable forum, a defendant can file a motion to transfer to another district based on factors that include the relative speed of resolution of the action in a given forum, the relative convenience of the plaintiff's choice of forum, and the familiarity of the requested court with any issues in the case.[13] The courts balance these factors with regard to the parties, while giving some extra deference to the plaintiff's choice of forum. However, in the vast majority of cases, a sued party is unable to change the location of the lawsuit.

In addition to choosing a state, the filer of a lawsuit can also sometimes choose whether to file in state or federal court. Many businesses would prefer to be in federal court because of the smaller volume of cases handled, the more limited number of judges, and the belief that there is a greater level of attention devoted to a case. Some IP cases can be brought in either federal or state court, assuming certain criteria can be met. These cases include employment matters, contracts, unfair competition, misappropriation, and theft of trade secrets. In most instances, there are threshold requirements that qualify a case for a particular court. Patent infringement cases, by statute,[14] must be brought in federal court (or follow an alternative procedural route in the International Trade Commission in Washington DC as discussed later in this chapter). The districts with the most intellectual property cases filed in calendar year 2005 were New York, Pennsylvania, Texas, and California.[15]

When the Lawsuit Is Filed

A lawsuit begins with a party's filing of a complaint, followed by the opposing party's answer, and by a conference between the judge and all the parties to discuss and resolve initial administrative matters.

The Notice

A case is initiated by the filing of the *complaint*, a document that puts the defendant on notice of the allegations of the case. The complaint generally need not be detailed in its allegations. For example, in a patent case, the complaint must name the asserted patent, but need not specify which claims are alleged to be infringed or how the alleged infringement was carried out. However, it must contain (1) a recitation of the causes of action, (2) a list of the parties, (3) a concise statement of the facts constituting the cause of action, and (4) a demand for the relief sought. Note that certain causes of action must be pled in detail, such as fraud (including inequitable conduct in a patent case).

When a company has been sued, it can counter-sue to assert its own rights; it can also try to bring other needed parties into the case, such as indemnitors who provide the accused device or service.

Setting the Schedule

Early in the litigation, the court schedules a meeting with all the parties to get an overview of the case, assess the issues of fact or law involved, and set a schedule for the discovery, pre-trial events, and the trial itself. Quite often, multiple pre-trial conferences are held while the suit is proceeding to assess progress and adjust scheduling. The Federal Rules of Civil Procedure, the local rules of the jurisdiction, and the judge's individual rules provide guidelines and requirements for the case deadlines.

Official implementation of a discovery schedule occurs at the Rule 26(f) scheduling conference; although changes may occur through the close of discovery. An effective strategy requires diligence on every aspect of discovery. Cases can be won or lost during the discovery period. Decisive judgments can be issued during this period and information that makes the difference between winning and losing can surface during this time. Issues that should be considered and incorporated into a discovery schedule include when to exchange expert reports and begin expert deposition, when to schedule the *Markman* hearing to interpret the claims,[16] whether dispositive motions can be filed early in the case, when to set the deadline by which the accused infringer must acknowledge reliance on an opinion of counsel, and when to begin depositions.

A mediation session may be suggested by the court or may be required by local rules. Typically, the trial judge is not involved in mediation, delegating the role to a magistrate judge or a court-appointed mediator. A court-ordered mediation or settlement conference can sometimes allow the parties to engage in discussions they otherwise would have been reluctant to initiate for fear of showing weakness.

The Quick Knockouts

To conserve cost and time, and to dispose of a litigation efficiently, parties may petition the court to issue a preliminary injunction or dispositive opinions early during the litigation.

Preliminary Injunctions

A court may issue a preliminary injunction—a court order directing a party to cease certain activity—if the court believes the restriction is necessary to prevent an injustice. To secure preliminary injunction, a patentee must prove (1) a reasonable likelihood of success on the merits of its case; (2) irreparable harm if an injunction is not granted; (3) a balance of hardships tipping in its favor; and (4) the injunction's favorable impact on the public interest.[17] How these factors are balanced is left to the court's judgment. Typically, a court balances the factors against each other and the form and magnitude of the relief requested; however, as a practical matter, the first two factors tend to have greater importance than the latter two.[18]

In a patent case, evaluation of the likelihood of success on the merits involves an evaluation of infringement, invalidity, and inequitable conduct. Irreparable harm typically requires proof that monetary damages after trial would be insufficient to fully compensate the patentee.[19] For example, in the case of competing companies, the patentee may claim that ongoing infringement will prevent it from obtaining the market share to which it is entitled, unless there is a preliminary injunction. If the patentee is able to make a clear showing of validity and infringement, the party is entitled to a presumption of irreparable harm.[20]

A preliminary injunction was sought in one of the earliest video game litigations that involved the IP rights associated with Pac-Man. Midway Manufacturing, which produced arcade video games, owned the rights to Pac-Man (having obtained them from Namco). Midway sued infringers and was able to make the showing required under the four criteria that entitled it to a preliminary injunction against the accused (the Pac-Man infringers).[21] In granting the preliminary injunction, the Court reasoned that plaintiff would suffer substantial harm without a preliminary injunction because of its substantial investment in development of the Pac-Man games and the short-lived commercial viability of video games. Further, the Court noted that it was in the public's interest to issue the injunction because such an order would encourage creativity by rewarding plaintiff's creative investment and fostering development of new and challenging audiovisual games.

A preliminary injunction decision may result in an early disposition of the case in its entirety. Whichever side loses may have to reassess the merits of its case since the decision may be based on the court's view of the first factor; in other words, the strength of merits. Also, in many cases, the parties take the issuance of a preliminary injunction as an opportunity to renew settlement discussions. An enjoined defendant may decide that royalty payments are the only possible route to continue its sales, that designing around a patent is a real option, or that it must get out of the business altogether.

Summary Judgment

Another way to speed up the litigation process and to avoid the need for a costly trial is to file a motion for summary judgment pursuant to Fed. R. Civ. P . 56(c). This procedure allows the court to make an early ruling that decides all or part of the case in favor of one of the parties. Summary judgment can be granted if there is "no genuine issue as to a material fact" such that the court can apply the law to those undisputable facts and render a decision. Summary judgment is not appropriate if factual disputes exist that require a full hearing of the case with witnesses and other evidence.

Either party may move for summary judgment, and may do so at various stages of the litigation process. However, summary judgment motions are usually made after some significant discovery has taken place. The parties present their arguments with respect to summary judgment in both legal briefs and, often, oral argument before the court. The court can deny the motion, grant summary judgment, or grant partial summary judgment. A partial summary judgment does not obviate the need for a trial, but it does limit the scope of the trial.

The moving party has the initial burden of showing that no genuine issue of material fact exists.[22] If the moving party satisfies this requirement, the burden shifts to the nonmoving party to present evidence that there is a genuine issue for trial.[23] The nonmoving party must produce sufficient evidence to reasonably support a jury verdict in its favor.[24]

A motion for summary judgment of infringement or noninfringement is appropriate only if the issues genuinely in dispute relate to claim construction (i.e., how the patent should be interpreted), rather than as to how the accused game or device operates. A motion for summary judgment of literal noninfringement is based on the premise that the game or device is missing a required element of the claims. However, additional proof is needed to establish that there is no material dispute of fact with respect to infringement under the *doctrine of equivalents*. Under the doctrine of equivalents, an accused product or process that does not literally infringe a patent claim may nonetheless still infringe if, judged on an element-by-element basis, the differences between the accused product or process and the claim are insubstantial or, viewed alternatively, if the accused product or process "performs substantially the same function in substantially the same way to achieve the same result" as the patented invention.[25]

United States patents are presumed valid[26]; therefore, summary judgment of invalidity is more difficult to obtain. A summary judgment of inequitable conduct is a rare occurrence.

In the earlier cited Midway video game case, even though a preliminary injunction was granted, the defendants decided to continue the litigation. During the pre-trial phase, Plaintiff Midway took advantage of the option to file a motion for summary judgment. Midway prevailed, thereby obviating the need for a costly trial.[27]

The Markman Ruling on Patent Claim Scope

Determining the meaning of the patent claims is one of the most crucial events in a patent litigation. The claims of a patent establish the boundaries of the patentee's right to exclude. If the court defines terms used in the patent narrowly, infringement might be avoided. If claim terms are interpreted broadly, the odds of proving infringement go up, while the odds of the claim being found invalid also increase.

A court's construction of the claims can effectively dispose of the issue of patent infringement.[28] Thus, the parties should devote a great deal of attention from day one to this issue to achieve a correct claim construction.

In *JVW Enterprises, Inc. v. Interact Accessories, Inc.*,[29] JVW Enterprises sued Interact Accessories alleging that its racing wheel controllers infringed JVW's patent, United States Patent No. 4,494,754 (the '754 Patent). The '754 Patent described a particular apparatus for stabilizing video game controllers with a player's lower body weight. JVW claimed that Interact Accessories' racing wheel controllers infringed three claims of the '754 Patent. The parties' dispute crystallized around their disagreement about the meaning of the claim limitation "means for lockably receiving a video game controller in fixed position on said mounting member." You can see some of the figures from the patent filing in Figure 9.1.

Because a patent is written to be read by those practicing in the field of the invention at the time the invention was made, the trial court gives the patent claims their ordinary meaning to such persons of ordinary skill in the art at the time of the invention.[30] For example, if a patent involved in litigation is directed to a way of implementing a particular graphical effect in a video game, the court would interpret the meaning of the claims in the way that a software designer would understand the patent at the time the invention was made. To give the patent claims their ordinary meaning to persons of ordinary skill in the art, the judge typically relies on the patent

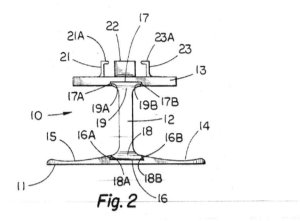

Figure 2 of U.S. Patent No. 4,494,754, the patent in suit in *JVW Enterprises, Inc. v. Interact Accessories*, showing a front view of JVW's video game controller holder invention.

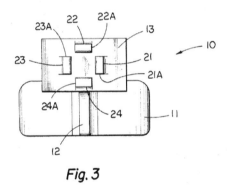

Figure 3 of U.S. Patent No. 4,494,754, showing the mounting member of claim 1 with "means for lockably receiving a video game controller in fixed position on said mounting member," a claim term that was the focus of the claim construction dispute between the parties in *JVW Enterprises, Inc. v. Interact Accessories*.

FIGURE 9.1 Figures from the '754 Patent filing.

itself and its prosecution history from the United States Patent and Trademark Office (Patent Office). In addition, the Court might consider expert testimony or written declarations, a tutorial on the technology, and attorneys' arguments. In the JVW case, the district court (and the Federal Circuit in review) relied on the '754 Patent, the attorneys' arguments, prosecution history, prior art, and dictionaries.

The court begins its claim construction process by examining the patent itself and considering the language of the claims in view of the patent as a whole; in other words, the claims in their entirety and the patent specification.[31] For instance, in *JVW Enterprises*, the district court, in rejecting defendants' definition for the term "video game controller," noted that the specification of the '754 Patent informs one of ordinary skill in the art that the proper construction for the term should be broader than that proposed by the defendants.

The court also considers the prosecution history of the patent, to attempt to understand how the inventor and the Patent Office understood the claims. If, during the prosecution of the patent, the inventor made a clear and unambiguous disavowal of a particular scope or meaning of a term in the claim, the court should exclude this scope or meaning from its claim construction.[32]

When the ordinary meaning of a claim, as understood by one of ordinary skill in the art, is not apparent from the claim language, specification, and prosecution history, courts can rely on extrinsic evidence; this is evidence not in the official prosecution records of the Patent Office, such as expert and inventor testimony, dictionaries, and technical treatises.[33] While extrinsic evidence may be considered, the court should give it less weight than the intrinsic record of the patent.[34] Among extrinsic evidence sources, courts have observed that dictionaries and treatises may be useful to claim construction and, in particular, technical dictionaries may provide the court a better understanding of the technology of the patent and how terms might be used therein. Extrinsic evidence may not be used to change the meaning of the claims in derogation of the language of the claims, the specification, and the prosecution history. For example, inventor testimony cannot be used to apply a new and different meaning to a claim term.[35] In *JVW Enterprises*, the district court adopted a dictionary definition to clarify its construction of the term "lockably" and construed the term to mean, "received in fixed position by the interlacing of fitting of parts into each other."

Definitions of intrinsic and extrinsic evidence are shown in Figure 9.2.

The crucial and sometimes difficult task of claim interpretation necessarily includes understanding the state of the art at the time of the invention, what specific claim terms meant at the time of the invention, and the problem the patent was intended to solve. As a result, many courts find that a hearing is necessary before rendering a claim construction ruling. These hearings are frequently referred to as *Markman* hearings.[36]

A *Markman* hearing is not required. Some courts have chosen to ascertain the meaning of the claims by relying solely on written submissions[37] and other courts have construed the claims only after hearing all evidence at trial.[38] But in the vast majority of cases, a *Markman* hearing is held by the court, typically midway through or at the end of discovery. In *JVW Enterprise*, a *Markman* hearing was held in district court 18 months after the filing of the complaint.

A district court's claim construction ruling is not immediately appealable.[39] Therefore, if a party believes that an erroneous adverse claim construction has been rendered that almost assuredly will lead to a finding of infringement, the nonprevailing accused infringer can concede final judgment on the question of infringement to proceed promptly to an appeal before the Federal Circuit. Without such a concession, the parties proceed toward trial. In *JVW Enterprises*, after the district court rendered its claim construction ruling, JVW and Interact Accessories proceeded to a bench trial

Evidence Used for Claim Construction

Intrinsic vs. Extrinsic Evidence

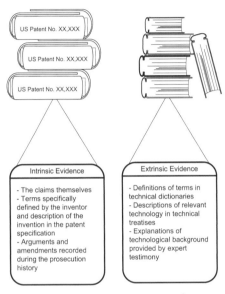

FIGURE 9.2 Evidence used for claim construction: intrinsic versus extrinsic.

(without a jury), where the district court found no infringement on the part of Inter-act Accessories. Thereafter, JVW appealed to the Federal Circuit from the district court's final judgment of noninfringement based on erroneous claim construction and infringement analysis.

When a decision is appealed, the Federal Circuit considers claim construction without giving any deference to the ruling of the trial court.[40] This effectively provides a losing party (with respect to claim construction) with a second chance to argue its case—this time before a Federal Circuit panel. The panel is likely considerably more experienced than the trial court at patent law and claim construction issues, and possibly more experienced with respect to the relevant technological issues.

The *Markman* hearing (and subsequent ruling) is often the most critical event in a patent litigation. Consequently, a party should put forth maximum effort toward achieving a favorable resolution of the claim construction issues. Effective discovery should be taken on each issue of claim construction; sufficient deposition time for claim construction issues should be allotted to experts, inventors and related investigators (who may provide evidence of the understanding of one of skill in the art); and trial-like investment should be made at all levels of preparation.

Furthermore, *Markman* briefs should be drafted in a way that clearly and concisely digests and presents the technical data and the testimony of experts. There may be serious and detrimental consequences if the briefs are unclear to the trial judge or if there are extraneous or ill-conceived claim construction positions taken in the parties' briefs. A court may even reject the proffered constructions of all of the parties, and instead, choose a claim construction of its own that it perceives as an appropriate middle ground.

In *JVW Enterprises*, the court's claim construction was the difference between a finding of infringement and a finding of noninfringement. The central dispute was over the construction of the claim language, "means for lockably receiving a video game controller in fixed position on said mounting member." The parties disagreed on a claim construction issue related to the function and the corresponding structure of the limitation.[41] While Interactive Accessories defined the function of "lockably" as "possessing the ability to lock and unlock," plaintiff JVW proposed that the term meant the ability to lock, but not requiring unlocking. The district court gave a construction that favored defendant Interactive Accessories and then rendered a judgment of non-infringement for both accused versions of its products.

On appeal, the Federal Circuit found that the district court erred in its claims constructions. Specifically, the Federal Circuit ruled that the lower court had improperly imported unclaimed limitations from embodiments disclosed in the specification and combined the task of defining the *function* of a means-plus-function claim with the task of identifying the *corresponding structures* of the claim. To remedy the errors, the appeals court construed "lockably" to mean "receiving and locking a video game controller into a fixed position on the mounting member for use," (no "unlocking" requirement); and the court found that one of the accused versions of Interactive Accessories' products infringed the '754 Patent.

To maximize one's chances in a *Markman* hearing, it is important to present a proposed claim construction in a way that is both understandable to a judge not necessarily trained in the technical area and consistent with the established understanding of one of skill in the art. In this regard, the expertise and input of the party's engineers is very important, as is the technical background of the party's lawyers. A technology company often has experience explaining its technology and can assist with explanatory graphics and other demonstratives to assist the court in reaching a proper claim construction.

Discovery

Discovery is the formal fact-finding stage of litigation during which all parties involved in the case can obtain information from others, including the opposing party and third parties not involved in the case. A party is entitled to request and receive relevant information that is likely to lead to the discovery of admissible evidence, a threshold that is fairly easy to meet. Discovery can be sought on "any matter . . . relevant to the claim or defense of any party" and need not be admissible at trial if "reasonably calculated to lead to the discovery of admissible evidence."[42] A party receiving a request is obligated to respond with facts or documents that are in its knowledge, possession, or control.[43]

In addition to being able to gather information, a party may be able to determine its opponent's theories of the case and the strength of its opponent's potential courtroom presentation based on the opponent's behavior during discovery. In particular, discovery can have the benefit of helping a party to better understand the relative strength of its position in the dispute and may lead to a litigation-avoiding settlement.

Protective Orders

Before discovery begins, the parties negotiate the conditions under which they will provide discovery of their confidential technical and business information. The negotiation process results in a court order known as a "protective order," which gives judicial enforcement to the protection of the confidential information. Typically, the parties create one, two, or even three levels of confidentiality, meeting the need for both companies to be fully informed and able to participate in the litigation strategy, yet preventing one's opponent from seeing sensitive competitive information. For example, a protective order might provide that correspondence can be viewed by the opposing party and its attorneys, competitive marketing information can be viewed by its attorneys only, and competitive financial information or trade secret technical information can be viewed by its outside counsel only.

Common Tools of Discovery

The first exchange of information in the case is termed the "initial disclosures." This is a limited exchange of basic information such as the name, address, and telephone number of individuals likely to have discoverable information, and a description of categories and locations of documents the disclosing party intends to use to support its claims.[44] Then the parties serve requests on each other for the production of documents (document requests), to answer written questions (interrogatories), and/or to admit or deny certain facts (requests for admission). The parties also ask oral questions of potential fact and expert witnesses (depositions).

Interrogatories to Parties (Fed. R. Civ. P. Rule 33)

Interrogatories are a written list of questions that must be answered by a party in the lawsuit. The purpose of these written questions is to obtain information relevant to issues in the case, such as the names of potential witnesses or an expanded explanation of the factual basis supporting a cause of action or defense alleged in the Complaint or in the Answer. The recipient can object to an interrogatory on grounds such as attorney-client privilege or lack of relevance. The answers are in writing and are given under oath, allowing them to be admissible at trial. Alternatively, the recipient of the written questions may respond by identifying and producing documents from which the requestor can ascertain the answer.

Interrogatories might also seek the identification of business records or financial data within control of the company served. Interrogatories are inexpensive and can be an efficient tool by which to quickly learn certain limited information. However, by statute, a party can ask no more than 25 interrogatories, although that number may be varied by local rules. Used in combination with depositions and other forms of discovery, interrogatories can be a very useful step in getting ready for trial.

Requests for Production of Documents (Fed. R. Civ. P. Rule 34)

A party can serve written requests upon another party, seeking to inspect or receive copies of financial, technical, or other business documents. The requested materials can be described generally (e.g., documents describing the structure of component X) or specifically (e.g., the software code for video game Y). Document requests and the production of documents in response thereto are very important parts of an IP case. The documents are needed to prove a case at trial, help to shape a party's theory of the case on the way to trial, and to prepare for the deposition of witnesses.

Requests for Admission (Fed. R. Civ. P. Rule 36)

To streamline a case, the statutes provide for a way to simplify proof where the parties can agree upon certain facts. Requests for Admission (sometimes called "requests to admit") are a series of statements that are sent to a party in the case, which the recipient must admit, deny, or object.

Depositions (Fed. R. Civ. P. Rules 30–32)

Depositions are a critical part of discovery and are used to shape proofs for summary judgment and trial. Depositions are oral testimony given under oath outside of the courtroom. The testimony is recorded by a stenographer, who makes a written transcript that can be used in the case. Sometimes, a deposition is also recorded on video, which may be played—under certain conditions—in the courtroom. If the witness is not at trial, the transcript and video are generally admissible into evidence; if the witness is at trial, they can be used on cross-examination to impeach a witness.

Depositions can be costly and time consuming, but they are necessary to assess the strength and demeanor of witnesses. In addition, they provide an opportunity for the parties to learn more information about the case than what can be gleaned through interrogatories and document requests. Depositions also allow parties to speak directly to witnesses without the opposing attorney filtering the witnesses' responses, although the attorney is present to represent the witnesses and to object to inappropriate questioning. In addition, depositions prevent a witness from changing his testimony before trial.

Depositions of Corporation (Fed. R. Civ. P. Rule 30(b)(6))

When parties need to obtain information from a corporation, the identities of individuals in the corporation who have valuable information relevant to the case may be unknown to the opposing party at the beginning of discovery. In addition, a party may want to know the official position of a corporation with respect to particular facts, as opposed to the belief of an individual who may not speak for the corporation. Therefore, the rules permit depositions of a corporation. Rule 30(b)(6) requires the party taking the deposition to specify the subject matter on which the questions will be asked. The opposing corporate party (or third-party corporation) must designate and produce an individual within the corporation who is sufficiently knowledgeable to testify on behalf of the corporation as to each of the subject matters specified.

One disadvantage of Rule 30(b)(6) depositions is that, when the deposed corporation is a party to the lawsuit, the individuals questioned are selected by the corporation. Therefore, the corporation usually chooses individuals who are least likely to do any harm to the corporate party's position in the lawsuit. On the other hand, Rule 30(b)(6) depositions provide an efficient way to obtain binding answers to key questions in the lawsuit, thus eliminating the uncertainty of whether answers provided by an employee or corporate officer bind the corporate party.

Third-Party Discovery

The law allows discovery to be taken of third parties who are not actually involved in the case. This is done by issuing a subpoena that commands a third party to produce documents (similar to the document request procedure described previously) and/or appear for a deposition. The subpoena, while ostensibly issued from a court, can simply be completed by an attorney and served upon the third party. Only if there is an irreconcilable dispute between the requester and the third party does the court become involved. In practice, while a third party has to respond to the subpoena, the burden imposed upon it is typically less than the burden would be if the third party were in the lawsuit. Courts generally recognize the need to balance the right of a litigant to obtain needed information with the imposition on a third party that has little or nothing to do with the dispute in the case.

Limitations on Discovery

The party on whom discovery requests are served does not typically have to produce information or documents that are protected by the attorney-client privilege or reflect attorney work product, unless the served party needs to rely on some of that information in its case.

If the served party has subsidiaries, such as sibling companies or a parent company, the issue arises as to the obligation of the served party to obtain documents from the related companies. The issue is further complicated when the related company is located overseas with no office in the United States.

The standard is whether the information sought is in the custody or possession of the served party.[45] Where a subsidiary is involved in litigation, and documents of its parent are sought in discovery, there are situations in which "control" sufficient to compel production may be found where (1) one corporation is the alter ego of the other, (2) one corporation is the agent of the other, (3) the litigant has access to the documents of the other corporation in the ordinary course of business, or (4) the subsidiary is the marketer and servicer of the parent's product and the parent's product is the subject of the lawsuit.[46] These decisions are typically fact-specific.

A court can limit discovery if it finds that the discovery request is unreasonably cumulative, duplicative, or obtainable from another source that is more convenient than the party from whom it is being requested. The court can also limit discovery if the burden or expense of obtaining the information outweighs the likely benefit it will have in the case.[47]

If discovery is sought from a foreign company that is not controlled by a party to the litigation, the party seeking discovery may proceed under the procedures of the Hague Evidence Convention[48] or seek letters rogatory from either a United States District Court or the State Department. These methods tend to be more time consuming and difficult than discovery from an American entity.

Protecting the Crown Jewel—Software Escrow

In the video game industry, software code is carefully guarded by its creators and owners because of its great value. Efforts are made to restrict access and to make reverse engineering difficult, if not impossible.

This need for secrecy of software code is in direct conflict with the philosophy of liberal discovery in federal court cases. While a protective order may limit the distribution of the code, limited distribution by itself is often not enough to allay the concerns of software companies. Even with a protective order, having extant copies of a company's valued video game code can lead to theft or inadvertent and unwanted disclosure.

When the code itself is accused, or a feature of a video game is accused, the code can legitimately be requested by the patentee during discovery. The patentee typically seeks to have an expert analyze the code to determine potential infringement. The patentee may also wish to have one or more in-house employees review the code; however, when parties are direct competitors, the patentee should not gain such access for its employees.

In addition to the code itself, the accused company generally has to disclose any existing annotations to the code, the tools necessary for use or analysis of the code (including decompilers), and any flow charts, schematics, manuals, or other technical documentation relating to the code.

One mechanism used to protect the code and this related information is to use a restricted software escrow system that carefully limits access. Such a technology was used in *American Video Graphics v. Electronics Arts, et al.*,[49] a case in which the use of a particular feature of a 3D graphics display was accused of infringing a patent.

In *American Video Graphics*, the companies that published the accused video games included most major video game publishers: Activision, Electronics Arts, Lucasarts Entertainment, Microsoft, Namco Hometek, Nintendo, Sega, Sony Computer Entertainment of America, Sony Online Entertainment, Square Enix, Take Two Interactive, Tecmo, Ubi Soft, and Vivendi Universal Games. Plaintiff and all the defendants agreed upon a list of games and documents to be produced, and the production was made to an intermediary escrow agent.

The escrow agent certified that it received a disk containing an electronic copy of each game with a label matching the listed games. The code was loaded on an access-restricted, stand-alone computer with no Internet connection, no wireless card, no ports, and no removable media drives. The computer was connected to a printer loaded with pre-marked paper with a confidentiality designation and sequential numbering. Only certain of plaintiff's experts—after pre-approval by all parties, and upon presentation of valid identification papers—could view the code, but they could not make electronic copies. Printing had to be tracked in a log, detailing the material printed and the page number range. No recording devices were allowed in the escrow room. Upon resolution of the case, the original disk and all printed copies had to be returned or destroyed.

While this did not provide perfect protection for the publishers' code, it represented a practical compromise that did as much as possible to protect the code while still complying with federal discovery standards.

Suggestions for Effective Preparation for Discovery

Document Retention

At the very beginning of a case, each party should promptly notify all employees who may have relevant documents to keep their files, including electronic files and emails. Evidence that is discarded inadvertently by a party may turn out to be essential in the case for that party. In addition, the court may impose severe sanctions for discarding evidence, even if it was done inadvertently or in compliance with a standard destruction policy.[50] If the court finds that the loss of the evidence occurred after the case started and that the loss prejudiced the opposing party, the court may order monetary damages or tell the jury they can make an adverse inference against the negligent party regarding the facts to which the lost evidence relates.

Document Collection

With the assistance of counsel, the party should carefully collect all potentially relevant files with a record as to the collection methodology. This strategy insures that evidence is preserved, and avoids repetitive searches for documents. While there may be situations in which a limited initial search is warranted (followed by a more complete search later), experience shows that repetitive searches can disrupt the normal work of important employees and lead to confusion as to whether documents have been collected, resulting in redundant or missed files.

Employee Witnesses

It is especially important for each party to identify and evaluate employees who are potential witnesses, especially employees who may be called as witnesses at trial. Counsel should interview potential witnesses early in the process, both to assess how comfortable a witness is in testifying and to measure the strengths and weaknesses of the party's case. The sooner witnesses can be familiarized with litigation procedures and their roles in the case, the more comfortable they are likely to be when called upon to testify in depositions or at trial. In addition, each party and its counsel can work together to determine which witness should tell the party's story at trial.

Expert Witnesses

Each party should retain technical expert witnesses as early as possible and can start the process by identifying non-testifying experts within its own organization who are familiar with the relevant technical issues. With the assistance of these in-house experts, counsel can better identify testifying experts outside of the corporate organization. Several factors should be taken into account when selecting testifying experts: education, academic or teaching experience, industry experience, publication history, communication ability, and prior testimonial and consultation experiences. These considerations help to ensure the selection of an effective and credible expert witness who can teach complex technical ideas to the judge and jurors. The expert's prior publications and former testimonies should be reviewed for any potentially damaging or inconsistent materials. After an expert is chosen, counsel—with input from the client—should thoroughly prepare the testifying expert to convey and defend his positions during direct and cross-examination both during his deposition and at trial.

Trial

Here is the most important piece of information in this chapter: if a patent litigation proceeds to trial, parties involved need to be well prepared to engage in the necessary battle and to win. Understanding the fundamentals of a trial is an indispensable start.

Jury Selection

The number of jurors in a civil trial is within the discretion of the court, as long as there are at least six jurors to begin the case. For a patent case, which typically takes longer than an average litigation, courts typically allow eight to twelve jurors to be chosen.

The jury is selected from a pool of jurors assembled by the court clerk's office. A party's only influence on this pool is the choice of jurisdiction, either by filing in or seeking to transfer to a jurisdiction with an advantageous demographic mix. For example, a company might choose to bring a case on its home turf, where jurors are likely to be familiar with or relate to the company.

In most federal jurisdictions, the judge asks questions of the potential jurors to determine if they are qualified to be jurors, although some allow the trial attorneys to participate as well (this is a common practice in state courts). Note that an individual qualified to be a juror is not necessarily qualified as to the technology involved in the lawsuit. After questioning, counsel can submit objections as to the competence of a potential juror to serve, such as bias. After the submission of objections, a party is given a certain number of peremptory challenges (three challenges is the statutory number) through which it may exclude certain jurors without even articulating a reason.

After the jury is selected and sworn in, the court reads preliminary instructions about the case, after which the parties begin the trial by offering opening statements.

Trial Format

Patent trials typically run for about two to four weeks. A trial begins with the plaintiff's opening statement, which gives the jury an idea of the plaintiff's theory of the case; and this is followed by the defendant's opening statement. The opening statement is a critical part of the trial because it helps to shape the way in which a jury listens to the evidence.

The plaintiff then calls its direct witnesses, typically including one or more experts, who explain the plaintiff's side of the case. Throughout the course of each witness's testimony, real or demonstrative evidence (such as pictures, records, and tangible items) may be presented to the jury. Each party has the opportunity to cross-examine the other party's witnesses. There may be subsequent re-direct and re-cross, if necessary. The cross-examination is limited to the scope of the direct testimony, and the attorney may use leading questions on cross-examination. On cross-examination, the opposing attorney generally attempts to attack the credibility of the witness, or the completeness or accuracy of his testimony.

After the plaintiff rests its case, the defendant has the opportunity to present its side of the case in the same manner. After the defendant rests, the plaintiff is sometimes allowed to have a rebuttal case. Thereafter, counsel for both parties give closing arguments to summarize the evidence and to explain their views on how the law should be applied to that evidence. The court then reads instructions to the jurors, including a description of their duties, the applicable law, and the rules of evidence, after which the jurors are sent to deliberate.

Once the jury retires to deliberate the fate of the parties, the only contact with them is through written questions and requests the jury makes to the court, such as asking for testimony to be read, or obtaining tangible evidence that was introduced in the courtroom. The court consults with the attorneys on potential responses to the jury. The jurors must be unanimous in their verdict unless the parties agree to be bound by a split verdict.

Remedies

If the jury finds no infringement or that the patent is invalid or unenforceable, there is no need for a damages decision. However, if the jury finds infringement of even one valid patent claim, they must assess damages.

The patent owner is entitled to be compensated for the loss it incurred as a result of the infringement, with a minimum entitlement of a reasonable royalty. If the patent owner can prove it lost sales to the defendant as a result of the infringement or had to reduce prices to compete with the defendant, the patent owner can be awarded the profits it lost as a result of those lost sales and reduced prices. Lost profits and price erosion damages account for the largest jury awards in domestic patent litigation. These awards can amount to tens or hundreds of millions of dollars. In *TiVo Inc. v. Echostar Comm. Corp*, TiVo was awarded over $32 million in lost profits for Echostar's infringement of its patent.[51] In *Advanced Med. Optics, Inc. v. Alcon Labs., Inc.,* $37.5 million in lost profits was awarded to Advanced Medical Optics for Alcon's infringement of its patent.[52]

In some cases, the jury is asked if the infringement was willful, meaning that the defendant did not take reasonable care to avoid infringement after becoming aware of it. If the jury makes that finding, it is up to the court to decide if the damage award should be increased. The court has discretion to treble the damages awarded by the jury. In addition, the judge can award attorneys' fees if the case was "exceptional." For example, the patent owner can be awarded its attorneys' fees when the infringement was willful and the defendant engaged in misconduct or bad faith tactics in the litigation.[53] The defendant can be awarded attorneys' fees when the patentee's case was wholly without merit.[54] An award of attorneys' fees is not common, but possible.

If the defendant is found liable for infringement, the court can issue an injunction prohibiting further acts of infringement. Courts are not required to issue an injunction, but prior to mid-2006, courts almost always did. In May 2006, the Supreme Court issued a ruling that gives trial courts greater discretion in deciding whether to issue an injunction by using a traditional four-part equity test under which a victorious patentee has to demonstrate: (1) that it has suffered an irreparable harm, (2) that remedies available at law, such as monetary damages, are inadequate to compensate for that injury, (3) that, considering the balance of hardships between the plaintiff and defendant, a remedy in equity is warranted, and (4) that the public interest would not be disserved by a permanent injunction.[55] How courts balance these four factors in the context of patent rights—which typically include the right to exclude—will be a developing area of law over the next few years.[56]

Post-Trial Activities

Following the verdict, the losing party still has several options. Either party can file post-trial motions with the trial court requesting that all or parts of the jury verdict be set aside due to error. These motions, known as motions for judgment as a matter of law, are based on an argument that either the jury misapplied the law or the jury's factual finding is not one that reasonably could have been reached. As a practical matter, the majority of jury verdicts are not disturbed by the trial court.

In addition, either side may appeal to a higher court if it is dissatisfied with the verdict. For patent cases, the appeal is heard in the United States Court of Appeals for the Federal Circuit, a specialized appellate court that hears the appeals of all patent cases around the country. The appellate court primarily reviews verdicts for legal error, but in some circumstances may overturn a factual finding made at the trial court level.

In patent cases, one critical aspect of the appeal is the Federal Circuit's review of claim construction. The appellate court reviews it *de novo*; in other words, they give the district court's construction no weight and simply begin anew. In a significant proportion of cases, the Federal Circuit reverses the claim interpretation, which can lead to a reversal of the decision on infringement.

For example, in *Alpex Computer Corp. v. Nintendo Co.*,[57] Alpex Computer patented a home video game system using removable, ROM-based cartridges. The patented system was commercialized in systems made by Atari, Mattel, and Coleco. Alpex sued

Nintendo, alleging that its Nintendo Entertainment System (NES) infringed one of Alpex's video display patents that was directed to a particular process for generating a video signal for each pixel based on information stored in RAM. This "bit-mapping" system provided greater control and flexibility compared to prior systems.

After trial, the jury issued a verdict in favor of Alpex, finding that Nintendo infringed the asserted patent and awarded damages of $250 million. The trial court denied Nintendo's post-trial motions and Nintendo appealed. On appeal, the Federal Circuit found that the claim construction was improper; therefore, the trial court should not have sustained the jury's infringement verdict as to either literal infringement or infringement under the doctrine of equivalents.

In theory, a decision of the Federal Circuit can be appealed to the United States Supreme Court, but the odds of the Supreme Court accepting the appeal are very small.

United States International Trade Commission (ITC)

The International Trade Commission (ITC) is an alternative forum to the district court in which patentees may seek to enforce their IP rights. The ITC is a Federal agency, located in Washington DC, that investigates and adjudicates complaints of unfair trade practices. While the federal agency is not a court, it has judicial functions, including the determination of whether there has been a violation of fair trade practice by the importation of articles that infringe United States patents.[58] If the ITC finds a violation, it can issue an order excluding the importation of the articles in question. The order is enforced by the United States Customs Service, which can prevent the articles from entering the country. The other type of ITC remedy is a cease-and-desist order that prohibits the further sale and distribution of infringing products that are already in the United States. A cease-and-desist order can only be directed to a party present in the United States such that the ITC has personal jurisdiction over that party.

Figure 9.3 shows the major differences between the U.S. District Court and the ITC.

In a proceeding initiated by Microsoft against Ultimate Game Club Ltd. (UGC) in June 2002 in the ITC, Microsoft asked the Commission to issue an exclusion order and a cease-and-desist order to stop UGC from importing into, and selling in the United States certain video game systems, accessories, and components.[59] Microsoft alleged that UGC's importation into, and sales within, the United States of video game accessories (X-Selector and X-Connection) infringed two Microsoft design patents.[60] Microsoft demonstrated that UGC's X-Selector and X-Connection are video game accessories that include an electronic housing and provide an interface between the Xbox™ video game system and other video game systems and components. Referring to samples of product photos and physical exhibits of the video game accessories in question, Microsoft asserted that UGC's products infringed the designs claimed in Microsoft's patents, because the products included an "X" design on electronic housings that is the same or substantially the same to the eye of the ordinary observer as the design claimed in the patents. The ITC found infringement of the Microsoft patents.

U.S. District Court v. ITC

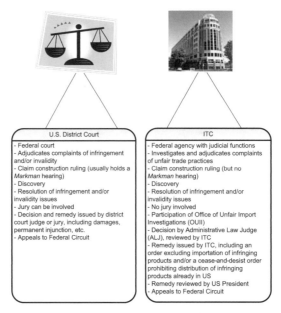

FIGURE 9.3   U.S. District Court and the ITC.

An additional requirement of the ITC is that the patentee must prove that the importation of the article covered by a United States patent causes harm to a domestic industry. To prove violation of 19 U.S.C. § 1337, an American company need not be involved for a domestic industry to exist. A foreign patent owner that has operations in the United States can be a domestic industry. A domestic industry can also be found to exist if a foreign patent owner has licensed the patent in the United States. The Administrative Law Judge (ALJ) found that while Microsoft's Xbox video game systems were not manufactured in the United States, a domestic industry nevertheless existed by virtue of the substantial activities relating to the Xbox video game system that were conducted in the United States, including Microsoft's significant investment in plant, equipment, labor, capital, engineering, and research and development activities relating to the Xbox video game console system. As such, the importation of the X-Selector and the X-Connection harmed that domestic industry.

Many of the same procedures found in federal court litigation are present in an ITC proceeding, including claim interpretation rulings (although not in a *Markman* hearing), discovery, and resolution of the infringement, invalidity, and unenforceability issues. In the Microsoft proceeding, because UGC failed to respond to the complaint, Microsoft's discovery requests, and a series of ITC notices and orders, the ALJ was directed by statute to presume Microsoft's allegations to be true,[61] thus obviating the need for claim construction rulings and other litigation procedures that are usually involved in a patent case. The determination of the ALJ is reviewed by the Commission, and if the Commission agrees that a violation has occurred, the Commission decides the remedy. In the Microsoft proceeding, the ITC determined that UGC violated 19 U.S.C. § 1337 by unlawfully importing and selling X-Selector and X-Connection in the United States. Therefore, the ITC issued a limited exclusion order prohibiting unlicensed entry of UGC's infringing video game accessories and a cease-and-desist order proscribing distribution and marketing of UGC's infringing video game accessories that were already in the United States. When determining whether to issue exclusion and/or cease-and-desist orders, the ITC considers the effects of the orders upon the following public interest factors: (1) the public health and welfare, (2) competitive conditions in the United States economy, (3) the production of like or directly competitive articles in the United States, and (4) the United States consumers.[62]

Additional differences between a patent case and an ITC proceeding are that, in the latter instance, no jury is involved, the decision is rendered by an ALJ instead of a United States District Judge, and a staff attorney of the Office of Unfair Import Investigations (OUII) is involved. The staff attorney advocates the public interest and takes a position on whether there has been a violation of 19 U.S.C. § 1337 and, if so, what the remedy should be. In the Microsoft proceeding, the OUII submitted a brief in support of a limited exclusion order and a cease-and-desist order against UGC.[63] In advocating that administrative proscriptions would not be in conflict with the public interest, the OUII in the *Microsoft* case reasoned that the products to be excluded were video games and accessories; therefore, they had no applications relating to public health and welfare. Further, the OUII argued that there was no reason to believe that the demand for such products in the United States could not be met by entities other than UGC. Finally, the OUII asserted, public interest also favored the protection of American intellectual property rights by excluding infringing imports.

After the Commission's decision, there is a period during which the United States President decides whether issuance of the remedy is consistent with United States trade policy. If the President does not reject the Commission's remedy, the remedy becomes effective. In the *Microsoft* case, compliance reports submitted by UGC in October and November 2003 indicate that it complied with the cease-and-desist order issued by the ITC. As with a patent case in federal district court, the losing party may appeal to the Federal Circuit.

ITC proceedings generally proceed on a more rapid schedule than federal court cases, with decisions rendered in 12 to 18 months, compared to federal court, which typically takes 18 to 27 months. The Microsoft decision only took six months, from June 2002 to December 2002. The case pendency was shorter than the average length of ITC proceedings due to the lack of response and failure of participation on the part of UGC.

Alternative Dispute Resolution

Companies resolve most intellectual disputes without resorting to litigation. In many cases, a patent holder forms a belief that a company is infringing its patent and notifies the alleged infringer. The alleged infringer disagrees but the parties meet, exchange the facts and theories that support their positions on infringement (and possibly validity), and may even produce some limited documentation to each other. The parties also discuss value: what the patent owner wants for use of its patent and what the accused infringer believes the patent would be worth, if it were used. If the parties can reach a compromise agreement, they sign a contract. If they cannot, they can agree to certain ground rules by which they hire a neutral party to mediate (i.e., give suggestions and opinions on a nonbinding basis) or arbitrate (i.e., take evidence and render a binding decision).

Many regard litigation as the alternative of last resort in the array of available dispute resolution processes. Arbitration and mediation, while each has its drawbacks, tend to be quicker and less expensive than a full-blown litigation. While the cost of arbitration can be less than litigation, the alternative resolution proceeding can still be a relatively expensive process. Therefore, one should also make strong efforts to negotiate a settlement even before arbitration.

The average cost of a large patent litigation is over $4.5 million; survey of patent infringement suits found that the average cost of litigation with less than $1 million at risk is $650,000, with risk between $1 million to $25 million, the total cost is $2,000,000, and with risk of more than $25 million, the inclusive cost is $4,500,000.[64] Advocates of alternative dispute resolution (ADR) contend that, if parties strategically select arbitrators or mediators trained in patent law, the cost of arbitrating or mediating patent disputes could save parties 50 to 90% of the cost associated with traditional litigation.[65] The average cost of typical arbitration and mediation range from $250,000 to $2,000,000.[66]

While many parties voluntarily agree to participate in arbitration or mediation, many courts (such as the District of Delaware and the Eastern District of Texas) also require parties to use certain types of ADR, such as mediation, as part of their local rules governing civil litigation. A court-ordered mediation can often help the parties get together when they are otherwise reluctant to be the first to suggest settlement talks.

Arbitration

Before entering arbitration, the parties must define the scope of issues that need to be resolved. To do so, a party's groundwork is to analyze the proof it possesses, and determine what additional evidence is needed from opponents or third parties. If discovery is needed from uncooperative third parties, the involved party may decide that litigation is a better choice because the arbitration panel has no authority over third parties. While arbitration takes less time than litigation, one should still devote sufficient time to do it properly.

Another factor in favor of arbitration is that it can handle a dispute of larger scope than can a single United States District Court. For example, if both domestic and international patent issues are at stake, while a United States District Court would not have jurisdiction to resolve both, an arbitration panel could be given the authority by the parties to resolve all issues.

Arbitration can be handled by either a lone arbiter or a panel of three arbiters. They are either agreed upon by the parties or are selected by the sponsoring ADR group. One method of arbiter selection is to have the parties rank a group of potential arbiters in order of preference: one for first choice, two for second, and so on; the arbiters with the lowest combined scores are selected. In some cases, each party chooses one arbiter and the two arbiters pick a third. The arbiters can be businesspeople, general commercial lawyers, patent lawyers, or even former judges or lawyers with specialized patent training. It is not necessary to have a panel, although a panel is likely to render a more comprehensive analysis than a single arbiter. Arbiters are paid an hourly rate comparable to a law firm partner, with the costs shared by the parties.

The panel acts as judge and jury, setting rules of procedure for discovery and hearings. In some cases, the panel orders written witness statements in lieu of direct testimony, but usually allows for live cross-examination. A panel typically issues a ruling 30 to 60 days after the hearing. Arbiters have the power to order damages, but their choices can be limited by agreement of the parties to range from full discretion, a limited range of choices, or baseball-style arbitration (pick the damages suggested by either side with no middle ground). Their decision can be converted into a judicial judgment for enforcement.

Mediation

Mediation is a dispute resolution process that is typically more business-focused (rather than legal-focused) than litigation or arbitration. Mediators often receive training in helping people with the decision-making process and in using different techniques to overcome sticking points. The mediator is empowered to communicate separately with each party.

The process is nonbinding; therefore, a party may withdraw at any time. Even so, mediation can still prove useful, since a party often adjusts its position after learning that a neutral third party does not agree with the party's position.

Mediation requires the presence of a business executive authorized to negotiate a resolution of the dispute. While each party is represented by counsel at the mediation, there may be situations where it is best to exclude counsel from a particular mediation session.

Typically, the parties prepare a written presentation for the mediator, including an explanation of the rationale for any settlement terms proposed. Mediators may make their own settlement proposals and may even give the parties an evaluation of the likely outcome of the case if it were tried to final judgment, subject to any limitations under any applicable mediation statutes or rules, court rules, or ethical codes.

Conclusion

Most companies that have gone through litigation agree that the process is costly, both monetarily and in terms of time invested, and should be avoided. However, it can be a necessary tool if a party feels it needs to make a strategic move to enforce or defend its rights and the other party is not willing to resolve a dispute in a reasonable business manner. Companies and individuals vary as to what is reasonable given their unique perspectives and commercial interests, but if one has to litigate, one needs to be proactive and well prepared. Litigation is stressful, but thoughtful planning can minimize the disruption and maximize the odds of a successful outcome (Figure 9.4).

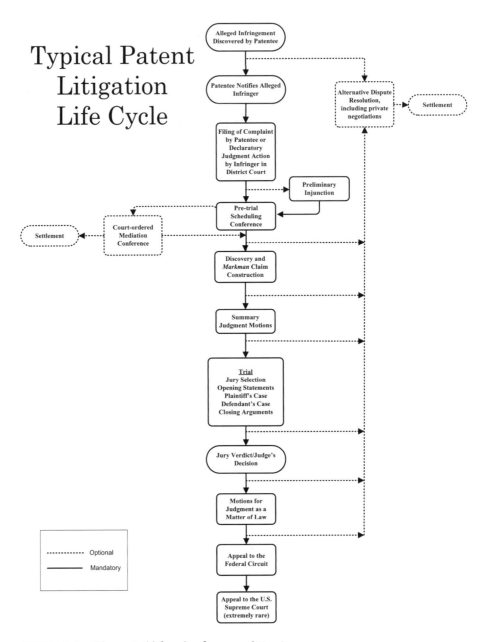

FIGURE 9.4　The typical lifecycle of a patent litigation.

Endnotes

1. This article is the result of the excellent work of Kenyon & Kenyon LLP attorneys Thomas Makin, Cecilia Zhang Stiber, and Grant Yang, and of members of the staff at Kenyon & Kenyon LLP.

2. *See* Top Patent Damage Awards: 1–25, 1980–2005, available at *http://www.fticonsulting. com/web/ip/presentations/ip_chart/slide0001_files/slide0195.htm* (showing recent patent damage awards ranging from $425,000,000 to $873,000,000); *see also* U.S. Courts Judicial Facts and Figures, Table 4.7 U.S. District Courts Copyright, Patent and Trademark Cases Filed, available at *http://www.uscourts.gov/judicialfactsfigures/Table407.pdf.*

3. *See, e.g.,* CBS News, Settlement Ends BlackBerry Patent Suit (March 4, 2006), *http:// www.cbsnews.com/stories/2006/03/03/tech/main1368894.shtml*; Andrew Pollack, *Lilly Loses Patent Case To Ariad*, N.Y. TIMES, May 5, 2006, at C1; *Rambus Wins Suit Against Hynix*, L.A. TIMES, Apr. 25, 2006, § 2, at 2.

4. *View Eng'g., Inc. v. Robotic Vision Sys., Inc.*, 208 F.3d 981, 983 (Fed. Cir. 2000). Unless otherwise cited, all subsequent discussions of the events of this case are taken from the reported opinion, at pages 982–983 and 985–986.

5. Federal Circuit cases show that, while the appeals court consistently requires a reasonable pre-filing claim construction, whether it requires a comparison during the pre-filing investigation of the accused product with the patented claims depends on the circumstances. *See, e.g., Antonious v. Spalding & Evenflo Cos., Inc.*, 275 F.3d 1066, 1075 (Fed. Cir. 2002) ("To be sure, when a number of different products are charged with infringement it is not always necessary for the plaintiff's attorneys to inspect each product separately to verify the facts on which the plaintiff bases its infringement allegations. At a minimum, however, the evidence uncovered by the patent holder's investigation must be sufficient to permit a reasonable inference that all the accused products infringe"). In cases involving method or process claims, the Federal Circuit has acknowledged the difficulty of obtaining information through reverse engineering, and has found mere attempts at reverse engineering to be a sufficient pre-filing investigation. *Hoffmann-La Roche, Inc. v. Invamed, Inc.*, 213 F.3d 1359, 1362-64 (Fed. Cir. 2000).

6. *See Q-Pharma, Inc. v. Andrew Jergens Co.*, 360 F.3d 1295, 1301-02 (Fed. Cir. 2004) (concluding that Q-Pharma's pre-filing investigations were sufficient because Q-Pharma's attorneys acquired a sample of the accused products, reviewed its advertising and labeling, and decided that a further chemical analysis was not necessary because the additional testing would not have changed its infringement analysis according to its reasonable claim constructions); *Hoffman-La Roche Inc.*, 213 F.3d at 1360, 1363-64 (finding sufficient pre-filing investigations when plaintiffs sought information from opposing parties and attempted to reverse engineer samples of accused products).

7. Declaratory Judgment Act, 28 U.S.C. § 2201.

8. 780 F. Supp. 1283 (N.D. Cal. 1991). Unless otherwise cited, all subsequent discussions of this case are taken from the reported opinion, at page 1286.

9. 391 F. Supp. 2d 695 (N.D. Ill. 2005). Unless otherwise cited, all subsequent discussions of the events of this case are taken from the reported opinion, at pages 697–707.

10. *See Idium Corp. of Am. v. Semi-Alloys, Inc.*, 781 F.2d 879, 882-83 (Fed. Cir. 1985).

11. *See, e.g., Zippo Mfg. Co. v. Zippo Dot Com, Inc.*, 952 F. Supp. 1119 (W.D. Pa. 1997).

12. *See* Fed. R. Civ. P. 4(k).

13. *See* 28 U.S.C. §§ 1404(a) and (b).

14. *See* 28 U.S.C. §§ 1332 and 1400(b).

15. *See* U.S. Courts Federal Judicial Caseload Statistic, Table C-3 Case Commenced by Nature of Suit and District (March 31, 2005), available at: *http://www.uscourts.gov/caseload2005/tables/C03mar05.pdf.*

16. *See Cybor Corp. v. FAS Techs., Inc.,* 138 F.3d 1448, 1455 (Fed. Cir. 1998).

17. *Amazon.com, Inc. v. Barnesandnoble.com, Inc.,* 239 F.3d 1343, 1350 (Fed. Cir. 2001), *aff'd in part, rev'd on other grounds,* 759 F.2d 1572 (Fed. Cir. 1985).

18. *Id.* ("[o]ur case law and logic require that a movant cannot be granted a preliminary injunction unless it establishes both of the first two factors, *i.e.,* likelihood of success on the merits and irreparable harm").

19. *Reebok Int'l, Ltd. v. J. Baker, Inc.,* 32 F.3d 1552, 1558 (Fed. Cir. 1994).

20. *Smith Int'l, Inc. v. Hughes Tool Co.,* 718 F.2d 1573, 1578, 1581 (Fed. Cir. 1983).

21. *See Midway Mfg. Co. v. Dirkschneider,* 543 F. Supp. 466, 479–90 (D. Neb. 1981) (copyright and trademark case). Unless otherwise cited, all subsequent discussions of the events of this case are taken from the reported opinion, at pages 482 and 484. A similar result was obtained in *Stern Electronics, Inc. v. Kaufman,* 669 F.2d 852 (2d Cir. 1982), in which a preliminary injunction was upheld by the appellate court after it was issued to protect the video game *Scramble.*

22. *See Celotex Corp. v. Catrett,* 477 U.S. 317, 325 (1986).

23. *See id.* at 322–23.

24. *See* Fed. R. Civ. P. 56(e); *Anderson v. Liberty Lobby, Inc.,* 477 U.S. 242, 248–49 (1986); *Matsushita Elec. Indus. Co. v. Zenith Radio Corp.,* 475 U.S. 574, 586–87 (1986).

25. *See Warner-Jenkinson Co. v. Hilton Davis Chem. Co.,* 520 U.S. 17, 41 U.S.P.Q.2d 1865 (1997)) and *Graver Tank Mfg. Co. v. Linde Air Prods., Co.,* 339 U.S. 605, 85 U.S.P.Q. 328 (1950).

26. *See* 35 U.S.C. § 282.

27. *See Midway Mfg. Co. v. Dirkschneider,* 571 F. Supp. 282, 286 (D. Neb. 1983).

28. *See Innova/Pure Water, Inc. v. Safari Water Filtration Sys., Inc.,* 381 F.3d 1111, 72 U.S.P.Q.2d 1001 (Fed. Cir. 2004).

29. 424 F.3d 1324 (Fed. Cir. 2005). Unless otherwise cited, all subsequent discussion of the events of this case are taken either from (1) this reported opinion, at page 1327, (2) *JVW Enters.,* No. 00-1867, 2003 U.S. Dist. LEXIS 16221, at *9–*11 (D. Md. May 8, 2003), (3) *JVW Enters,* No. 00-1867, slip op. at 2–4 (D. Md. May 9, 2002) (Supplemental Memorandum and Order Re Patent Claim Construction), (4) *JVW Enters.,* No. 00-1867, 2002 U.S. Dist. LEXIS 27885, at *9 (D. Md. Feb. 1, 2002), or (5) the patent at issue, U.S. Patent No. 4,494,754, at col. 1, ll. 35–59.

30. *See Phillips v. AWH Corp.,* 415 F.3d 1303, 1313 (Fed. Cir. 2005).

31. *Id.* at 1313.

32. *See Omega Eng'g v. Raytek Corp.,* 334 F.3d 1314, 1325, 67 U.S.P.Q.2d 1321 (Fed. Cir. 2003).

33. *Phillips,* 415 F.3d at 1317-24.

34. *Id.* at 1317.

35. *See Renishaw PLC v. Marposs Societa' Per Azioni,* 158 F.3d 1243, 1250, 48 U.S.P.Q.2d 1117 (Fed. Cir. 1998); *see also Phillips,* 415 F.3d at 1317, 1318–19.

36. The name being derived from *Markman v. Westview Instruments, Inc.*, 517 U.S. 370, 38 U.S.P.Q.2d 1461 (1996).

37. *See Interactive Gift Express, Inc. v. Compuserve Inc.*, 47 U.S.P.Q.2d 1797 (S.D.N.Y. 1998).

38. *See Lucas Aerospace, Ltd. v. Unison Ind. L.P.*, 890 F. Supp. 329, 332 n.3, 36 U.S.P.Q.2d 1235 (D. Del. 1995).

39. *See Schering Corp. v. Amgen, Inc.,* 35 F. Supp. 2d 375, 377 n.2, 50 U.S.P.Q.2d 1051 (D. Del. 1999).

40. *See Cybor Corp.*, 138 F.3d at 1456.

41. Paragraph 6 of 35 U.S.C. § 112 allows a patentee to claim a subject matter with "functional" language. That is, claim language that includes the phrase "means," a function, and no recitation of a structure that performs the function. In this way, a means-plus-function claim describes an invention in terms of what it does rather that what it is. According to the patent statute, a means-plus-function claim is construed to cover structure, materials, or act in the specification that correspond to the means for performing the claimed function. Therefore, a court interprets a means-plus-function claim with a two-step approach: (1) identification of the claimed function; and (2) identification of the corresponding structure, materials, or acts in the specification. *See, e.g, Cardiac Pacemakers, Inc. v. St. Jude Med., Inc.*, 296 F.3d 1106, 1113–14 (Fed. Cir. 2002).

42. *See* Fed. R. Civ. P. 26(b)(1).

43. *See, e.g.*, Fed. R. Civ. P. 26(a) and 34.

44. *See* Fed. R. Civ. P. 26(a)(1).

45. *See* Fed. R. Civ. P. 34(a).

46. *Glaxo, Inc. v. Boehringer Ingelheim Corp.*, 40 U.S.P.Q.2d (BNA) 1848 (D. Conn. 1996).

47. Fed. R. Civ. P. 26(b)(2).

48. Convention on the Service Abroad of Judicial and Extrajudicial Documents in Civil and Commercial Matters, Feb. 10, 1969, 23 U.S.T. 2555, 847 U.N.T.S. 231.

49. *See generally Am. Video Graphics v. Elec. Arts, Inc.*, Civil Action No. 6:04-CV-398 (E.D. Tex. filed Aug. 23, 2004).

50. *See, e.g., Rambus, Inc. v. Infineon Tech. AG*, 222 F.R.D. 280, 294–99 (E.D. Va. 2004)

51. *See, e.g., Tivo Inc. v. Echostar Comm. Corp.*, No. 2:04-cv-1-DF, Jury Verdict Form at 8 (E.D. Tex April 13, 2006) (US Patent No. 6,233,389).

52. *Advanced Med. Optics, Inc. v. Alcon Labs., Inc.*, No. 03-1095-KAJ, 2005 U.S. Dist. LEXIS 33369, at *9 (D. Del. Dec. 16, 2005) (US Patent No. 5,700,240).

53. *See, e.g., Golden Blount, Inc. v. Robert H. Peterson Co.*, 438 F.3d 1354, 1374 (Fed. Cir. 2006).

54. *See, e.g., Automated Bus. Cos. v. NEC Am., Inc.*, No. 4:98-cv-619-A, 1999 U.S. Dist. LEXIS 20962, at *12 (N.D. Tex. Feb. 8,1999), *aff'd*, 202 F.3d 1353 (Fed. Cir. 2000).

55. *See eBay, Inc. v. MercExchange, L.L.C.*, 126 S. Ct. 1837, 1839 (2006).

56. For example, in *z4 Techs., Inc. v. Microsoft Corp.*, the District Court for the Eastern District of Texas exercised the discretion granted by the Supreme Court and denied z4's request for a permanent injunction. No. 6:06-cv-142, 2006 U.S. Dist. LEXIS 40762, *6–*7, *19–*20 (E.D. Tex. June 14, 2006). There, z4 asserted two patents for methods of limiting unauthorized use of computer software and won a jury trial against Microsoft. *Id.* at * 2. The jury awarded $115 million in damages against Microsoft. *Id.* Thereafter, z4 sought for a permanent injunction against Microsoft, asking the court to (1) enjoin

Microsoft from making, using, selling, offering for sale, and/or importing its current software products that use the claimed invention, and (2) order Microsoft to deactivate the servers that control the use of the claimed invention and to re-design its Windows and Office software products to eliminate the infringing technology. *Id.* at *2–*3. In denying z4's motion for permanent injunction, the district court rejected the plaintiff's argument that the Supreme Court in *eBay* suggested a rebuttable presumption of irreparable harm when assessing a permanent injunction request in patent litigation. *Id.* at *6–*7. Instead, the Court explained that it must apply the principles of equity when balancing the four factors announced in *eBay*. *Id.* As such, the Court concluded that a permanent injunction was not appropriate in the instant case because z4 failed to show that (1) it will suffer irreparable harm in the absence of a permanent injunction; (2) money damages awarded by the jury were inadequate; (3) the balance of hardships weighed in its favor; and (4) public interest warranted the issuance of a permanent injunction. *Id.* at *19–*20.

57. 102 F.3d 1214 (Fed. Cir. 1996). Unless otherwise cited, all subsequent discussions of the events of this case are taken from the reported opinion, at pages 1215–1223.

58. *See generally* 19 U.S.C. § 1337, also known as § 337 of the Tariff Act. For further information, please see the ITC Web site at *http://www.usitc.gov/*.

59. *See generally In re Certain Video Game Systems, Accessories, and Components Thereof*, U.S.I.T.C. Inv. No. 337-TA-473 (June 21, 2002). Unless otherwise cited, all subsequent discussions of the events of this case are taken from reported briefs and orders found on ITC's Web site, at *www.usitc.gov*. On the same date its complaint was filed in the ITC, Microsoft also filed a patent infringement case in the District of Connecticut against UGC. *See generally Microsoft Corp. v. Ultimate Game Club*, No. 3:02cv1085-RNC (D. Conn. June 21, 2002). Court records indicate that in February 2003, the United States District Court for the District of Connecticut closed the case with an order granting a motion for final consent judgment and a motion for permanent injunction.

60. United States Patent No. D452,282 (filed Jan. 11, 2001); United States Patent No. D452,554 (filed Jan. 11, 2001).

61. 19 U.S.C. § 1337(g)(1).

62. *See* 19 U.S.C. §§ 1337 (d) and (f).

63. Brief of the Office of Unfair Import Investigations on Remedy, the Public Interest, and Bonding at 5-6, *In re Certain Video Game Systems, Accessories, and Components Thereof*, U.S.I.T.C. Inv. No. 337-TA-473 (filed November 6, 2002). Unless otherwise cited, all subsequent discussions are taken from the published brief at pages 5–6.

64. *See* Law Practice Mgmt. Comm., Am. Intellectual Prop. Law Ass'n., *Report of the Economic Survey* 22-23 (2005).

65. *ADR of Patent Disputes: A Customized Prescription, Not An Over-the-Counter Remedy*, 6 Cardozo J. Conflict Resol. 155, 169 (2004).

66. *See id.*

CHAPTER 10

Selling Internationally

Kellee McKeever

kmckeever@ncsoft.com

A game company considering selling internationally confronts dozens of variables. First, should the company even attempt to launch its games overseas? Is it better to employ an in-house salesperson or an agent? How does a company find an international partner? Finding and determining the correct partner in a specific territory or country is key to success. Once the partner is selected, how should the deal be set up: finished goods, licensing, or a distribution deal? In each case, the market, the distributor, the manpower available, and the expectation of profits will vary. Other questions we cover here are, which costs are borne by the distributor and which are borne by the publisher? Successfully launching a title or a publisher internationally requires significant forethought and planning, as this chapter details.

Considerations for Selling Internationally

Experience shows that expansion into the international market means additional sales and additional profit. However, the conventional wisdom that "If the U.S. amounts to 50% of the worldwide game sales, then you can make double by going international" is not necessarily true. In every case, achieving profit internationally depends on the level of commitment the company makes and the amount of profits desired. An important initial question is, "is the game/company right for international distribution?"

On one level, a developer or publisher with limited resources can be successful by using an English version to target English-speaking countries. A larger developer or publisher, one with resources to commit to multilanguage SKUs and aggressively pursue more territories, can sell more units and, with good planning, maximize their profit. Either way, the company must be ready to make the commitment required, including the sales personnel, an internal support system, and a separate financial budget. Success can be achieved in as little as a few months when searching for a local partner who is taking finished goods, or the process could take several years if a company is making a long-term commitment to localize and become a player in the international game industry.

Some of the primary benefits of selling internationally include expanding the consumer base, additional revenue, and prestige. Many companies that have reached success in the United States and Canadian markets feel the next step to growth is having products on the shelf in other territories. It may be that the timing is right to expand the product line to the international end user, or simply that someone at the top feels a need to conquer the countries outside North America. Someone who has worked in both scenarios will say that selling your product internationally may or may not bring added success. One thing is certain, however: international expansion will bring about numerous challenges. Unanticipated expenses, a lower price point, and possibly lower sales volumes than expected are all possible issues you may face. Some of these become hurdles; others are indicators that the timing may not be right to expand internationally.

The international market in the game industry may be the same size as the U.S. market, but as in the United States, the top five publishers are still making the majority of that money. Some hard questions need to be asked to see if selling internationally makes sense: How much risk is my company willing to take? Who is going to be responsible for making the actual sales? And will this be a sales agent or will you bring an employee in-house?

Sales Agent versus Employee

Deciding whether to hire a sales agent to sell products for a commission or hire an employee with a salary and benefits is something that needs to be analyzed before jumping into international business. An employee is riskier from a sunk cost point of view, but the financial return can be greater over time. The tasks are similar, but the job is different, depending on the publisher's needs. There may also come a day when it makes sense for the employee to use an agent to facilitate certain deals.

Hiring a Sales Agent

A sales agent is generally self-employed, has a track record brokering games, and has a long list of contacts in the game industry that he or she can use with dexterity to the advantage of the publisher. The sales agent licenses games for a fee. He or she essentially brokers a deal between a developer and a publisher, a publisher and a distributor, or a publisher and international distributors. The fee is generally 10% of the license. It is uncommon for a sales agent to sell finished goods, although not unheard of. The agent who helps take purchase orders (POs) is usually located in the country or territory where the sale is going to take place and helps facilitate the POs and the sales between the local partner and the publisher. The advantage of using a sales agent is reducing out of pocket costs. It costs nothing unless the agent makes a sale, and then it is only 10% of the gross revenue of the deal. The drawback is that the agent is not an employee, and although the agent may have good intentions, the product may not be as well represented as it would be by an employee.

Using an Employee

An in-house employee can focus solely on the titles owned by his or her employer. The cost of a salesperson is much more than a salary. Adding an employee means added taxes, employee benefits, and travel costs for any company's budget. If the 10% commission on one of the publisher's titles is nearly a major percentage of what it would cost to hire a salesperson, it may be wise to hire someone to focus exclusively on this growing segment of the business. The advantage of internal salespeople is that they are focused on expanding growth in a specific area, and can be an additional resource for other accounts in the United States, if necessary. As the cost of these employees is already included in the overhead, making good use of their sales skills while they are on payroll is key. Again, the decision will come down to out-of-pocket costs versus back-end costs. If there are only one or two games to be released or the games are in genres that won't make the cultural transition internationally, the employee probably won't be used to his or her fullest potential. On the other hand, one will never know if an agent will focus on all products he or she is handling equally. Hiring a person who is dedicated to international sales will increase sales if the product lineup has international appeal.

Considering Potential Revenue

The amount of revenue a company could see in international sales depends on a range of factors, such as the type of game, whether it is console or PC, the genre of game, the success of the game in the home market, whether it is a triple-A or a budget title, and so forth. A triple-A console game can bring in millions of additional dollars in revenue, whereas a language-intensive budget PC game may only see around $10,000 in incremental revenue from international sales.

A publisher with a hot shooter or racing game can be successful quickly, because of the ease of entry for a non-English speaker. A non-English speaker can jump in and play without knowledge of the language. However, a language-intensive Role Playing Game (RPG), although a successful genre worldwide, might not be successful due to the localization costs involved. On the other hand, if the title is highly anticipated, it is possible to team up with a local partner who will do the localization, resulting in a massive success. Despite the count of over a half million words for *Baldur's Gate*™ and over one million for *Baldur's Gate 2*, both games were highly successful games internationally, because Interplay brought in partners in the Asian territories, where RPGs are the number-one genre, who helped localize the game into nontraditional languages.

On the other hand, a small publisher with children's educational games or U.S.-centric genres that only has the budget to release their product in English may not sell enough units to justify an in-house person. For children's products, there are language issues, one of which are actual pronunciation changes among English-speaking countries which is highly relevant, because a good portion of the children's games have audio. Replacing audio would require resources that would not result in significant additional sales most of the time. There is also the issue of government apparals on children's products. This approval process is confusing and costly, and may require major revamping of the product to win approval. Each of these factors increases or decreases the amount it will cost a company to distribute internationally, and lengthens or shortens the time line in which the company will see a profit.

Finding an International Partner

After deciding if the product is worthy of venturing internationally, the next step is finding a partner in the chosen territory. A solid partnership is critical to international success, but it can be difficult to ascertain which potential partners to seriously consider. Most important is to hook up with an experienced partner who has established access to retailers. Knowledge of the game market in their territory is also crucial. Each segment of the industry is different. A particular partner may be an excellent choice for a single-player PC game, but have no knowledge of the console market or online gaming market. It may be necessary to go with more than one partner per territory, if there is more than one title or more than one platform.

One situation that arose at the start of a new job was a partner in Argentina who was not paying his advance. We had finalized the contract and were waiting on the advance payment to get the process started for local manufacturing. However, he was not paying. Calling upon a few friends, we gathered information on what was happening in the market with our products to have a better case when speaking to the partner. It turns out he was already in production on the title, *MDK,* and was selling it in pirate shops! He was also living in a van because he did not have enough money to rent an apartment! While he may have had knowledge of the local industry, he was far from a good partner. It is essential to do the homework to have a solid sense of who these partners are. However, there will still be times that the chosen international partner is not as solid as predicted.

In looking for an international partner, a good place to start searching is an industry trade or consumer show. There are different shows worldwide, usually promoting a specific territory or country; with the change in structure of the Electronic Entertainment Expo (E3), the consumer show in Leipzig, Germany will likely have the most international visitors. There are also shows in Tokyo, Japan; Taipei, Taiwan; Beijing, China; and Seoul, Korea that attract a large number of international visitors in their territory.

Types of International Deals

With a list of several potential partners in each territory, the next decision is what type of deal should you do? There are three basic deal types, although any of the basic characteristics from these three types can be customized to fit with the needs of the publisher and the international partner, starting with "what will be sold and what are the risks associated with the territory in which they will be sold?" Should it be finished goods, a license, or distribution rights only?

A *finished goods deal* is when product ships from the U.S. warehouse. Finished goods have the least amount of risk, because the partner generally pays the shipping and has no right to returns or marketing funds. The per-unit price is higher than a licensing deal, but the publisher pays the cost of goods and any handling costs at the warehouse. The distributor bears all the costs of shipping and potential loss or damage when they pick the product up. The risk to this type of deal is that a publisher may build units based on an order or anticipation of an order that may not come through, and then there is overstock in the warehouse.

A *license* or *royalty deal* requires all the art assets for the box, manual, and contents, all the art for the marketing, and the gold master to be delivered to the partner electronically or via courier. The local partner does all the manufacturing, marketing, and PR. They usually translate all the game assets into their local language. The price per unit is less than finished goods, but territory regulations and local pricing may make this the best scenario for a particular country. With a royalty deal, partners will factor in the cost of returns, bad debt, and marketing.

The international partner may have a person dedicated to the product. This person is usually the liaison between the publisher and the partner, speaks excellent English, and submits press releases, boxes, and manuals to the publisher for approval. On a console deal, this person will walk the product through submission with the first party, acting as marketing manager and producer.

The *distribution model* with international partners is similar to the retail distribution model in the United States. Finished goods are delivered to the local partner. This usually works best when a person from the publisher is located in the territory. The publisher has to pay the freight cost to get it to the local country if it is not produced there. Marketing and PR are the responsibility of the publisher, as are returns, Market Development Funds (MDF), and bad debt.

With a distribution deal, any localization, management of inventory, and all the costs associated with those items can be a full-time job for an international salesperson. The salesperson might manage the sales channel similarly to how a vice-president of North American sales might manage his or her team in the United States. It is a big job and can be even more daunting if the publisher is not located in the territory and is trying to manage more than one territory at a time. In addition, if it is sales of U.S. finished goods, the cost of returning them to the United States or destroying them at the end of the life cycle can be expensive. Occasionally, there are warehousing costs imposed by the distribution partner if the title sits in their warehouse for more than a specified amount of time, which is usually somewhere between three to six months for games. Although a distribution deal will bring in the most gross revenue of the three types of deals because of the high price point, this particular type of deal is very risky and requires continuous support and monitoring from the U.S. publisher, who must have an extensive knowledge of the territory where the deal is taking place.

Distribution techniques in Europe and Australia/New Zealand are the most similar to the U.S. market. The retailer expects marketing funds, returns, and support from the publisher. Since the retail channel is most similar in these territories, distribution deals in these countries would make the most sense if the publisher were looking toward that model. For example, a distribution deal may make sense if the employee is focusing solely on the United Kingdom and can be involved every step of the way—keeping track of local manufacturing, hiring a PR firm, and approving each marketing cost and each return at retail. If the in-house employee is trying to allocate time between a distribution deal in the UK, the rest of Europe, Japan, South East Asia, and Latin America, some details may fall through the cracks.

Deciding what kind of deal to make with which partner is going to be highly dependent on comfort level and how secure a publisher feels about its international business. Risk tolerance will vary from publisher to publisher and may change at one particular publisher over time. The deal is also dependent on whether you are shipping a single-player PC game, a massively multiplayer online game (MMOG), or a console product. A licensing deal is the only option for a publisher who wants to release a console title and is not a third-party publisher in Europe or Japan. A PlayStation, Nintendo, or Xbox product cannot be submitted unless it is done by an approved third-party publisher. If the U.S. publisher has not gone through the process of becoming a European or Japanese third-party publisher, they must use a partner to release their games in these territories. Local partner choices for a console game are then restricted to only those publishers who are approved third-party publishers. In addition to the United States, Europe, and Japan, Sony and Microsoft have offices in Korea and Taiwan where product needs to be submitted.

Europe and Japan are the largest territories in the industry outside the United States, and revenue potential is greatest in these markets. In addition to large numbers of consumers, these countries are both console and PC markets, where most, but not all, of the other territories are primarily PC. These territories also offer the broadest range of choices of partners, ranging from all the major European, U.S., and Japanese publishers to smaller publishers or local distribution companies. U.S. publishers can generally find a suitable partner in Europe and Australia/New Zealand quite easily. Japan is a more difficult market, not because of the lack of partners, but mainly because of the difference in taste between the cultures. The one genre that does well in both cultures is RPG. Japan is also mainly a console market; although it does have a PC market, it has gotten smaller and smaller over the years as consoles have taken over. Another difficulty in the Japanese market is that it is much harder to get a console game approved. Depending on the territory, some of the first-party publishers have strict "no bugs" policies. It can make the localization process much more difficult, because the title may pass in one territory with certain bugs in it and not in another. One time, there was a title for Japan that had passed in the United States, but the same version was in submission for over a year before it was finally passed in Japan!

Selecting a Partner in Smaller Territories

In the smaller countries, picking a local partner can be simultaneously easier and harder than it is in the major markets. It is easier, because the choices are usually limited. A short list of viable partners exists; others are new. The older ones usually have a list of major publishers they do business with or have dealt with in the past. The newer companies are usually young, gung-ho hardcore gamers with little experience in their local game industry. The benefit of the newer companies is that they know what they want and what other hardcore gamers in their country want. Whether the newer companies can get into the retail channel is something that needs to be confirmed by checking references or, even better, by taking a trip to the country to see first-hand where they are represented. It is hard to check companies out in smaller territories without a territory visit, because facts and figures are difficult to find and each partner has a different source and different data. A fact-finding trip is a good way to meet all the distributors and narrow the list by confirming who distributes in the major retailers. Making a visit to stores with each distributor is essential, because each will visit the stores that they have product in. This allows for visits to a broad range of stores. Believe it or not, even if two distributors visit the same retailer, they very rarely visit the same store. After visiting stores and talking to the store managers, a clearer picture of which distributor is actually important in the territory can be found. Confirming the market information and understanding what to expect can be very trying. Distributors in some counties will over-promise, while others will undersell themselves, sometimes due to cultural issues, and gossip about their competition. Some of it is based on fact; some of it is not.

Partnering with the Competition?

One of the oddities of international game sales is that sometimes the local partner may be a publisher that is competition in the United States. This can work to the publisher's advantage, because frequently the dominant U.S. publishers' local offices need additional revenue and are receptive to adding product to their catalog. One of the greatest factors for using a major game publisher is that generally they are in the key local retailers and maintain a local office. In a console market, they are also generally a third-party publisher. Some of the largest players in the game industry are Europeans, and their knowledge may make them the best choice as a partner in their home territory.

Deciding to partner with the competition is hard to swallow for some publishers and may not be right for everyone. In making the decision, some important things to analyze are: do they have a product or products in their catalog that are in the same genre or on the same release schedule as the one you are releasing? Are they going to focus on your product as if it were their own? Even when the publisher is a U.S. company in Europe, they have a local office and local employees who know the market. Look for the strongest publishers where your product complements their lineup.

The same holds true for smaller territories. If venturing into a country where there is lack of knowledge or contacts, or where there are valid concerns about the security of intellectual property (IP), a major U.S., European, or Japanese publisher may seem the most secure. Electronic Arts (EA) has offices in some of the smaller territories, where they feel local presence is either a necessity due to lack of local partners, or the growth potential is such that they need to invest early. EA has been a partner in at least six countries over the years in both large and small territories. In each case, EA was always a fantastic partner and supported the product as their own. Each office is its own Profit and Loss Center, and sometimes they need to find additional products to add to their bottom line. Many times, their lineup from headquarters is only partially suitable for the territory and they need to supplement their release schedule. EA Japan once told us they release one-half of the EA line up from the United States, and were eager to have more products to launch in that territory to meet their budget.

Another peculiarity in international game sales is that the local partner, even if it is not the competition, may handle titles for the competition. The reason is that in some territories, like Mexico, the retailer only has time to see one or two distributors. Many of the larger retail buyers in the smaller countries are not only buying games, they are buying DVDs, razors, televisions, and school supplies for their stores. If a local partner handles a top-tier publisher, it is assured, if that retailer stocks games, the distributor has a relationship with them. The flipside of this arrangement is that if the distributor is handling too many publishers, some titles may not make it on the retailer's purchase order. For example, Sam's in Mexico has approximately twelve slots for games; they have Distributor A who gets six slots, Distributor B gets four, Distributor C gets two, and Distributors D and E get nothing. If your game is with Distributor A, but they are also handling games from four of the top publishers in addition to your titles, you may not get any slots. This situation leaves your title off the shelf in an important retailer in Mexico. However, if you have the #1 title for Distributor C, your game would be in Sam's. Even a large company like EA may only get a slot for *FIFA* and *Need For Speed*. This is not exclusive to Sam's Mexico; it happens in many of the retailers that are handling other consumer products than just games.

The factors that go into deciding whether to partner with a competitor or someone who also represents your competitors are important to the success of a title in the territory. Questions that need to be asked are: do they represent too many triple-A games? Do they represent too many games in the same genre? What are the price points of the games that are in the same genre as yours? Will you get the support and bandwidth from the local partner or will they be focused on their larger publisher or publishers? Are those titles more anticipated or less anticipated? How much buzz is surrounding your title versus your competitors?

If a competitor with a local office or a local distributor with too much product from the competition has too many triple-A games, is solely focused on other titles, or has titles in the same genre as the rest of their catalog, the number-two distributor may be a better choice. Keep an open mind while choosing a partner. Consider the country in which the title will be sold, the maturity of the distribution channel, and the competition the title is selling against. A lot of hype surrounding the title helps international sales as well.

The PR machine in the United States has much more value than just a PR machine for gamers in the United States; international distributors and buyers scan the Internet and buy U.S. gaming magazines to see what are the biggest and most anticipated titles. Some of the local gaming magazines are partners with a large computer game magazine or website in the United States. The local game press reads everything from the U.S. to Europe and Japan on what the industry is talking about. A high score from a well-known computer game magazine or website is a sure way to have distributors knock at your door.

Local Manufacture and Pricing

The type of deal that is negotiated will depend on comfort level and where and what is being distributed. Some countries may be only able to take a few hundred units of a product, so it may not make financial sense for the partner to manufacture it locally. It makes more sense for the smaller territories to purchase goods from the United States and ship them to lower the costs.

Again, language is a factor. It may be that because of language, the publisher and the international partner sales will be negatively impacted if the title is not localized. Many times, the genre of the product itself will sway this decision. If a product is language-intensive, it may require, at the very least, that the box and manual be localized for it to make any impact in the territory. On the other hand, a racing game, which is very simple and has very few words, may not need any localization. Even certain English-speaking countries may want to manufacture locally depending on the title. It might make sense to produce a title that is expected to sell in Australia, for example. The quantity discount in the United States may be negated due to shipping costs to a territory as far away as Australia. There are also times when the local currency gives a better discount than the quantity discount the United States is getting.

Local laws in a given country may also make it necessary to manufacture locally. Take Brazil as an example. The government requires that all products on the shelves be in Portuguese. For imported foods, it makes sense to cover the label with a sticker. For software, the description, the system specs, and all the wording on the box would need to have stickers in Portuguese. The box would lose its sales effectiveness if it were covered with stickers.

Another important concept to consider when determining the type of deal is the needed local price. Many times, a partner can localize the box and the manual, and manufacture it cheaper than shipping an English finished box from the United States. All this can help bring the territory price into line with the local standard of living. There is price parity in countries. In currency exchange, one dollar in the United States doesn't equal one English pound or one Brazilian real; however, in the consumer's eye it is all relative. A soda may cost one Brazilian real in a Brazilian vending machine, one U.S. dollar in a vending machine here, and 100 yen in a Japanese vending machine. Each consumer see it as the cost of a soda, even though 1 dollar is equal to 2.15 Brazilian real and 120 Japanese yen. The most important price in a country is what the consumer can afford.

Piracy will invariably be a factor in the decision whether to license or ship finished goods. There are countries where common sense says, "ship finished goods because there is so much piracy," but in actuality, it may make more sense to license in that territory and use a model that can make the product more affordable in local terms to help fight piracy. For example, entering the territory with finished goods that can be priced excessively high due to purchase price, shipping, customs, duties, and markups along the way will send end users looking for the pirated version that is $2.00 versus the official version priced between $49.00 and $89.00. If a partner licenses the product and produces it in the territory, they can more realistically compete with the pirates. The distributor is also often willing to officially fight piracy with a letter from the publisher that states they are the local distributor. Over the years, end users are willing to pay a little more for the "official" version with a manual, but very few are willing to pay $30–$40 more. In some territories, $30–$40 is the entire disposable income for a person for a month or even longer.

Game Type Can Determine Deal Type

The type of title, such as a PC title or a console title, can also make a difference in what kind of deal to set up.

PC Titles

PC titles are usually the sole intellectual property of the publisher and have no first party (i.e., console manufacturer) to work through. PC titles follow most of the rules for deciding how to structure a deal set; pick which country, know their local laws, adjust pricing to local standards, and take into account the piracy rate.

Console Titles

Console games follow another model. The primary issue is that there are three different versions of the game depending on the type of television used: PAL, NTSC, and NTSC-J. The NTSC version is manufactured in the United States and works in North America, most Latin American countries, and some of the Asian territories. The PAL version is manufactured in Europe and works in Western and Eastern Europe, the Middle East, and North Africa. Due to dual machines, PAL versions also work in many Latin American countries. The NTSC-J version is for Japan, but will also work in some of the other Asian territories. Each of these versions can only have one publisher per territory, so if the U.S. publisher is not a Sony, Microsoft, or Nintendo third-party publisher in the territory, the game will need to be licensed and the partner may be the one who ships finished goods to other territories.

Online Titles

MMOGs are similar to the single-player games, with a few additional items to consider. The goal in launching internationally for a MMOG are threefold: expansion of current coverage, cultivation of strong relationships with local distributors, potentially laying the groundwork for future licensing agreements, and building a subscription base for in-country servers. With the right relationships, momentum toward expansion is inevitable. According to the research firm DFC Intelligence, the global market for online game subscriptions, downloads, and advertising is forecast to grow to $13 billion in 2011 from $3.4 billion in 2005.

Smaller MMOGs could sell their client as a download and require all subscriptions to be paid by credit card in any territory. Unfortunately, in this case, the consumers without credit cards or in countries where fraud prevents them from using their cards on international purchases would be left out. However, if the MMOG company is content with the revenue they have, then there is no reason to launch out internationally.

For larger companies, more planning may be involved. Among the clear advantages enjoyed by MMOGs is the true simultaneous worldwide launch. Shipments of the finished goods can be staged to meet the server date. The client can be manufactured and shipped in stages to reach international destinations at the same time. This allows each country to have product on the shelf the day the servers are to be turned on. This is advantageous, because it helps eliminates any gray market activity during the launch phase.

Other factors that need to be considered when deciding which type of deal to put together for MMOGs depends on the amount of security the publisher feels is necessary. If it is a license, how will the serial codes be delivered, and in what quantities? How will the monthly subscription be billed, or will there be a prepaid card of some type? Is it better to license the server code and proprietary technology and receive royalties from the box sales and the subscriptions? If the technology is going to be licensed, how will it be monitored to make sure the royalties are being paid correctly? Will the local server be secure enough to keep the code and the intellectual property safe? In some countries, credit cards will not work outside the home country due to fraud. Some countries do not have a high penetration of credit card users and use direct debits from bank accounts. In other countries, the online subscription rate is too expensive relative to their standard of living. Many of the countries with a lower standard of living have pre-paid cards available in smaller increments of time. This allows the end user to pay less at each purchase while the publisher still can make a good amount of money on the subscription over the course of a month.

MMOGs add a whole new set of questions to the issue of how to do business internationally. Many of the MMOG companies are still maneuvering through the uncharted waters with each company, asking, "Is this the best way? Is it secure?"

Do You Trust Your Partner?

Some of the biggest fears, when a company wants to expand internationally, are questions of security. A partner may be qualified, but how do we know he is trustworthy? Be conscientious about checking references with other publishers they have worked with. Evaluating and choosing a local partner that feels right is key to feeling secure and well represented in the country. There are times, when after choosing a partner, trusting that they were working in the publisher's best interests, you will still be disappointed in the end. It is the nature of the business.

Partner-Supported Piracy

In one instance, Interplay had a partner in Brazil that they had spoken to many times over many years at E3. They met with the partner while in their country and decided after three years to use them for a few titles. On a visit six months later to Brazil, they saw that their products were well marketed and deeply entrenched in the retail channel. The problem was not the titles that had been licensed to them, but the additional titles they took the liberty of pirating! The quality of the box was also not up to the standard of Interplay, because the art was not legitimate. In short, their rendition of our product made Interplay products look cheap and of poor quality. Moreover, to add insult to injury, Interplay never received a dime. It was easy for them to get the titles into retail, because the retailers assumed they had the rights to all the titles from Interplay. Interplay tried to sue them, but they filed bankruptcy, leaving Interplay with a large bill. Interplay got off easy in this situation; the same partner left another publisher with an unpaid bill of close to $1,000,000.

Gray Market Distribution

That was a problem of security on the licensing end, but there are also issues with finished goods agreements. Many smaller distributors ship gray market goods back to either the originating country or another third country. This is a problem when a partner in the territory has been shipped finished goods from the United States at a much more reduced price than other territories. An untrustworthy partner may ship the goods to an additional territory at a cost less than what that third territory is currently buying it for. The main reasons for this are either because the partner is greedy and wants the extra cash or, if a minimum guarantee is required and he was bidding against other distributors in his territory, he knew he could add additional units to his bid and not worry that he would be stuck with them. That partner could ship them elsewhere, make money, and please the publisher. Who will ever be the wiser? Sometimes, no one; it is very hard to track unless an end user or another territory is complaining.

This might not seem so much as a security issue as a trust issue with the chosen partner. It may be considered a breach of contract, depending on the way the contract is written, and the publisher can terminate the agreement, but, in actuality, it is not illegal. However, it can cause major headaches on the publisher's end when other territories start complaining that they cannot reach their minimum because someone else is buying it cheaper. Of course, they will also want to know why they are paying so much. It also can create major end user complaints if there was any type of security measures on the product.

For example, at one publisher, the product was copy-protected and the disks serialized, because they were having problems with gray market shipments. They thought they knew the culprit, but unless a buyer in the third country points out his source (and this generally will not happen because the buyer is getting a better deal), it is impossible to know for sure. When a user in Canada tried to download the patch for a version he bought at a swap meet, he received an error message telling him he had an illegitimate copy. This created a customer service nightmare, and the damage that occurred because of Internet forum postings was irreparable. In the end, the publisher caught the culprit, but had to serialize all the disks, which is costly, and then ask the complaining customers in Canada to return their "illegitimate" copy of the game and replace it with a new one.

The returned illegitimate copies had serial codes that matched a particular distribution partner, allowing us to cancel our distribution deal. This helped us figure out who was causing problems on some of our products; however, the customer backlash because of the territory coding killed the product very early in its life cycle and it never recovered. This is an exceptional, not to mention costly, way to find out if your partner is trustworthy. Gray market issues are generally more of a nuisance than a costly problem, and are more common in some territories than in others.

Intellectual Property

The level of fear for the security of your IP will change from country to country. Some countries have a higher rate of piracy than others, but the distributors are trustworthy to act on the publisher's behalf. Other territories have less piracy, but the entrepreneurial spirit drives the partners to find, shall we say, "extra sources of income." It is not possible to list specifically which countries are more prone to piracy or to gray market problems, since each territory is different. Over the course of a few years, changes in the standard of living or other factors can change attitudes.

The need to get your product to market as close to the U.S. and European launch is essential. Someone, somewhere, will pirate your game if it is good. In fact, in Russia, software pirates can hastily localize and get a game on the shelf in the pirate stores in as little as three to four days! While negotiating for the rights in Russia for *Silent Hill 4 The Room*™, a Russian language version was posted on a pirate site three days after the U.S. launch of the title. If your product is not on the shelf locally within a day or two of the U.S. and European launch, many "entrepreneurs" will get it to the end user regardless of the legitimacy in doing so. The key in these territories is speed and support from the publisher to help the partner fight the pirates. Your partner is competing against the other distributors and the pirates.

Legal Issues in Other Territories

It is unlikely that your partner will pirate your product, as in the Brazilian case described earlier. The partner has paid a minimum guarantee and usually wants the product on the shelf as quickly as possible to recoup their money and still follow their contractual obligations. It is mandatory that your contract include language that stipulates the partner's responsibility for knowing the local laws and regulations. Unfortunately, the cost of enforcing the contract in the case of a breach makes it unlikely that a smaller publisher would pursue legal recourse. In-house attorneys for larger companies frequently reject pursuing any claim less than $200,000. In those cases, the unscrupulous parties usually suffer no penalties, leaving bills unpaid.

While choosing a partner, it is important to cover the partner's responsibility if their local partners/retailers ship the product out of the contracted territory. Many distributors will argue this point in the contract, saying they do not have control over where the product goes after they sell it; however, depending on how important the particular deal is, it can be left in or taken out of the agreement. It is not necessarily illegal, but you always want the partner to know that you have brand integrity, and if he is dealing with unsavory characters, it is not OK. You are concerned enough about your product that you must support your other territories to the best of your abilities; this issue is something you should be willing to shut him down for. Let each partner know that they should sign a binding agreement with their retailers so they also can have some recourse if their local partner tries to ship the product to another territory.

Controlling Piracy

Now that we have a partner in a few territories and we are starting to see sales ramp up internationally, what happens when the partner complains of piracy and how it is affecting sales? First, all triple-A games get pirated unless the amount of disks makes it not cost-effective for the pirate. However, if the local cost of the game is so expensive that it forces people to go to the pirate, it will have an effect on the sales of the game. The wholesale price to the partner needs to be managed. The partner needs to keep their marketing and distribution costs in line, and then most end users will purchase the legitimate product with the manual and other extras rather than the pirate version, which may not work properly when they get home. In some territories, end users will purchase a product to try it, and if they like it they will go buy the legitimate version at their retail store. If you have a hot triple-A title, consumers will flock to get the "real" version with any extras provided. If they played the pirate version and thought little of the game, they will never buy the legitimate version.

Do not discount the effect of piracy on the industry. Informa Telecoms & Media estimates that in 2005, piracy accounted for $6 billion in lost sales in an estimated $17 billion market.

Helping the local distributors fight piracy locally is a small way to defeat it. Many times, the partner will ask for a power of attorney to fight the piracy on the publisher's behalf. Few lawyers will agree to this, but many will give a letter that states they are the local distributor for the territory to help their case. The local partner may have better access to, or be able to persuade, the proper authorities to file a complaint properly, especially if the U.S. publisher is not a member of Electronic Software Association or another trade organization that is already pursuing local action.

In Argentina in 1997, a distributor received a phone call from the local police on his way to dinner. The police were about to raid a pirate they had been watching for some time and were interested to know if he wanted to be there. He postponed dinner, witnessed the raid first-hand, and saw how local authorities responded swiftly to complaints made by the local software association against software pirates.

Another resource for fighting piracy is the Entertainment Software Association (ESA). The ESA has an anti-piracy workgroup that members of the association can join. The ESA also helps fight piracy on behalf of all its software members worldwide. They have a budget and the members vote on where they should spend that budget fighting piracy. In the past, they have conducted raids and searches against pirate organizations in Asia, Latin America, and Eastern Europe. They also target Internet sites that post downloadable versions of retail games. Most of the major U.S. publishers are members, and the ESA fights on behalf of the three major console companies as well. Most members have either a lawyer or an employee who, as part of his job, supports the ESA in their actions to fight piracy internationally.

Piracy has multiple fronts these days. It used to be small shops where a customer requested the game and waited while a guy copied the game and wrote on the floppy discs with a felt-tipped pen. Later, pirates operated in large rings that would copy tens of thousands of units in Asia and ship them to countries that had lax anti-piracy laws. Now, pirates are often online crackers who crack the copy protection and post the game on the Internet.

Another place to be careful when licensing a game that does not have serial codes is at the local manufacturer. It is important to know the manufacturer. Take a tour and ask questions at the manufacturing plant and the stores when visiting a country. While touring the plant, talk to the plant manager about their security. Most legitimate duplicators will have a system that doesn't allow employees to leave with anything, and they should have a method to account for every unit manufactured. Make approval of the manufacturer part of the contractual process with your partner. If visiting the country is not an option, call other U.S. and European publishers and see who they use locally. Someone on your reference list should be willing to collaborate and share information.

Localization

The translation of the game assets, such as text and audio, is the responsibility of the local partner unless the deal is a distribution deal. Some of the smaller countries will only localize text and not the audio due to high costs or lack of available resources for capturing audio. Many times, some of the more resourceful countries like Russia, China, or Taiwan are able to reverse engineer the game and localize it without help from the developer. Because of the cost of local labor, a partner may be willing to do this. It helps them because they can much more quickly translate and localize product without losing time sending the files back and forth electronically to have the developer re-integrate, recompile the code, and send it back to the partner for testing.

However, even the mention that a partner has the ability to reverse engineer the game will often send shock waves through the developer. It starts with the developer not believing it is possible and ends with anger that the partner would try. There usually ends up being a rift between the developer and the partner, which is counterproductive for everyone involved. In the past, there have been times when it was beneficial to have international partners reverse engineer the game. In the 1990s, very few American and European companies programmed in the double byte code necessary for many languages worldwide. Developers in those days always seemed to be amazed that a company could manipulate their code to get the Chinese characters on the screen. It was a tremendous amount of work, but many of the local companies realized they had to do this to capture the end user.

Many developers, especially if they are aware that the title will be localized into more than one language from the beginning, will set the product up so the localization process is straightforward. The best way is to program the game with Unicode support. This support allows more than the 26 Roman letters to be displayed on screen and the capacity to integrate Western alphabets, in addition to languages with specific character sets, such as Greek, Russian, and the Asian languages.

Each developer has their own method for making the re-integration of the local text as painless as possible, separating out the strings resources for easy translation and marking strings with identifiers for each language, such as F for French, I for Italian, and so on. The developer can then change the code to use the language resources needed for each version. Another method is to use language folders; the French folder has all the French text, the Japanese folder has all the Japanese text, and so on. The partner or localization company translates the folder and then the programmer directs the code to the correct folder for that particular version. Granted, localization is rarely as straightforward as planned, but at least everyone is on the same page if it is discussed from the beginning of the project rather than as an afterthought.

Once the localized text has been returned, the cost of re-implementing it is borne by the publisher and/or developer. It can take a few days for code that has folders set aside for text, or up to several months for an Asian translation if the code was double byte enabled, but the text was not segregated from the rest of the code. Once integrated, the local version needs to be tested by the local partner and the bugs need to be fixed by the publisher/developer. This is the same process for console games, except submission is added to the process once the local partner decides it is ready to be submitted to the first party.

Payment

The topic of payment should come up early in negotiations, around the same time as discussions for the number of units and the type of deal. However, knowing who should pay for what expense will make the process smoother. The burden generally falls on the distributors in the smaller countries because they are purchasing product for the cheapest per-unit cost. With the larger, more complex deals, the costs will be shared.

Most of the time, all payments are made in dollars; however, the more elaborate licensing deals can be a percentage of sales. Although the payments will be paid in U.S. dollars, the calculations might be done based on the local currency where the title is sold. For example, an Xbox 360 game licensed to a PAL publisher for a percentage of net sales, who in turn sold it to the different countries in Europe, will need to calculate the percentage of net sales based on the currency of the country in which the product was sold. They calculate all the different net sales per country and then produce a royalty report based on the contract amount. The royalty report will be in dollars, based on a converted rate from CNN.com or another reputable source for currency exchange rates.

Who Pays for What?

The more margin the distributor has, the less the publisher pays for. A distribution deal may bring the publisher 75% or more of the net receipts, whereas the royalty deal may only bring 25%. The publisher will need to bear the cost for much more on a distribution deal than on a royalty deal. A finished good deal will involve a set price per unit in U.S. dollars. The distributor will often pay in advance, especially for partners in smaller countries. The cheaper the price per unit, the more expenses the publisher will ask the partner to assume. For example, if a partner is buying a title for $8.00 compared to a $32.00 wholesale in the United States, you might ask him to pay for any Point of Sale (POS) material (e.g., standees, posters, shelf talkers, empty boxes) and pay the shipping costs. If the same title is sold in another territory for $21.00 a unit, you may give the partner the POS material and ship it for him. If it falls somewhere in between, you may give the partner the POS and ask him to pay freight. The scenario will also depend on how many units these distributors ordered.

Depending on the type of deal negotiated and the level of sophistication in the country or territory where you are working, which costs fall on the publisher and which fall on the distributor will vary. Every deal is different, and each cost sharing depends on the need of the country. Table 10.1 is an overview of some of the costs that are traditionally borne by which party depending on the type of deal.

Table 10.1 Cost Sharing

	Finished Goods		License		Distribution	
	Publisher	Partner	Publisher	Partner	Publisher	Partner
Asset Collection	X		X		X	
Cost of Goods	X			X	X	
Pick Pack and Shipping Costs	X			X	X	
In-Country Marketing and Press		X		X	X	
Freight		X		X	X	
Point of Sale Material		X		X	X	
POS Freight Costs		X		X	X	
Returns		X		X	X	
Bad Debt		X		X	X	
Currency Fluctuation		X		X	X	

A PC licensing deal in Taiwan with English software means the U.S. publisher will supply all the assets for the contents of the box to Taiwan, and once they translate the art and have approval, the Gold Master can be sent. The overhead for pulling all the files on CDs and the courier costs of getting the disks to Taiwan are the responsibility of the publisher, but the Taiwanese partner is responsible for everything else. This is why the net on the royalty payment is much less than that of a finished good. There is more work required on the publisher side if the CD is localized. A console title for Japan, with English software, is similar to the previous Taiwanese example; however, in addition to all the other costs, the Japanese partner is also responsible for getting the title approved by the first-party hardware manufacturer in Japan.

Show Me the Money!

Payments are usually made by wire transfer, usually the easiest method from a publisher's perspective. There are few costs involved, and depending on the bank's policy, the fee ranges from $15 to $50. Occasionally, if the U.S. publisher is set up to do so, it can also be made by credit card. However, the customer can contest the purchase for up to two years with some cards, and the credit card companies charge a small fee. It is wise to check with a credit card company before accepting them. Other costs such as currency conversion are generally borne by the partner if they are being billed in U.S. dollars. The only exception to this is in the instance of a distribution deal or licensing deal, as mentioned before, where the contract is based on a percentage-of-sales rather than a flat fee in U.S. dollars.

In addition to the standard fees when wiring money, several countries have withholding tax, a certain percentage of the sale that is kept by the government of the local country. This cost is borne by the U.S. publisher and becomes a tax deduction on their U.S. income taxes.

Let's Make a Deal

Let us say that a small U.S. publisher has a new triple-A racing game. They have limited knowledge of the international game industry, but want to find a partner or partners in several territories that can help them expand revenue. The new title, *Rocket Racer*, is getting some good press in the United States, so the publisher has had several inquiries from the large markets outside the United States. Additionally, a major international trade show is next week and the publisher will be able to look for other potential partners at the show.

At the conference, the company should talk to companies from Europe, Singapore, Mexico, and China. Each territory is going to come with its set of issues and barriers, so they will need to do due diligence with potential partners before settling on the type of deal and the partner.

Europe

The European company wants to license the title for the Western European markets. The most likely scenario after doing research is a license deal with the partner localizing the box into FIGS (French, Italian, German, and Spanish, in addition to English), which means at a minimum, the box and manual will need localizing. Localization of the product is not necessary since there is little in-game text. The prospective partner and the publisher decide on a royalty based on a percentage of net sales. This means a percentage of the wholesale price after returns and bad debt have been calculated. Since this is for more than one country, the percentage will be based on the wholesale price in each country times the number of units sold in that country, and then converted to U.S. dollars. The publisher might negotiate a deal for 50,000 units at 18% of net sales where the units are cross-collateralized across all territories. The publisher should also negotiate a minimum guarantee, a dollar amount the partner will guarantee to reach, regardless of the number of units he sells. They sign a contract and the publisher needs to deliver the art assets for the box and manual to the partner. They localize it into the languages agreed upon and send jpeg files back to the publisher. The publisher checks to make sure the brand integrity, service marks, logos, and any co-marketing partner logos are correctly laid out. The partner starts on press and marketing activities at the same time they are localizing and manufacturing the box. Along the way, the publisher approves all ads, press releases, and title-related material that they are releasing as "re-publisher." After the title ships, the partner provides samples, sell-in and sell-thru numbers, so the publisher can keep track of the progress of the title. At a designated time after the quarter ends, the publisher will get a royalty report with the price, units, and deductions, and a check or wire transfer.

Singapore

Another model is a company from Singapore that contacted the publisher. Singapore is a small market relative to many larger countries, but it is a quick finished goods sale. The publisher negotiates the per-unit price, and so that the product is on the shelf with a price equal to that of U.S. $49.99, the publisher sells it to them at $19.00 a unit. The partner has provided a list of their landed costs, marketing money, and retailer mark-ups that the publisher will need to help them arrive at the correct price. The only way to know if this is a relatively accurate estimate is to have several interested companies bid on the same title with the same breakdown of costs. Generally, when they are bidding against each other they are more careful to accurately reflect the actual costs. The pricing must be competitive because Singapore is such an international city that the product from the European partner may arrive there if it is priced lower. Singaporeans are very good at finding a way to make an extra dollar, and if a retailer realizes he can get it from a third party at a lower cost, he will do so.

Once the contract is in place and the purchase order is received, the Singaporean partner wires the funds and their order is processed for shipping. They pick it up from the publisher's warehouse, and at that point, it is their responsibility. To support the partner, the publisher might also give them art or ask them if they want to purchase any POS material at cost. If they want it, the publisher can ship it to them at their expense.

Mexico

Another finished goods distributor is in Mexico. The reason it is mentioned here is because although it is a Spanish-speaking country, distributors there generally prefer U.S. finished goods. Mexican end users generally do not like the European box, read the U.S. press and trade magazines, and want the U.S. product. This also avoids freight cost of getting product from Spain to Mexico, which is high due to customs and duties. NAFTA allows the product to flow from North America at minimal additional cost besides freight. The cost of manufacturing a Spanish box in the United States is high due to economies of scale. Relatively speaking, few units are needed for Mexico, so local production does not make much sense. The rest of the deal is similar to Singapore.

China

The last partner to approach the publisher is a Chinese company. China is one of the more difficult countries to do business in due to the barriers of entry placed on foreign entities doing business in China. From experience, it is not the actual regulatory process as much as knowing the process and getting to the correct department for the stamp of approval. Doing business in China requires a local partner who is well connected with the government. This is true not only in the game industry; the Chinese government can stop any product it wants to, from tennis shoes to game software. An outsider trying to maneuver the bureaucratic system will find it so cumbersome that it is all but impossible. So when the publisher is approached to sell *Rocket Racer* in China, they make sure to get a list of the other titles the company has released, and check those references. The partner must know the ropes for this deal to work. The process will be similar to the royalty deal in Europe; however, there will be a few more hurdles to overcome. The publisher will need to get *proformas* and other documents to the partner so they can wire the money out of China. The process will take longer, because in China, the government needs to review and give *Rocket Racer* approval before manufacturing can take place.

In reality, *Rocket Racer* would not sell in China. Currently, the market is an MMOG market. There are an estimated 65 developers of online games, 83 online game operators, and 153 online games in China. Along with the rest of Asia, China seems to have moved away from the single-player games. They are no longer trendy.

Conclusion

Not every publisher should strive to go international. While going to international markets can enhance revenue, the potential pitfalls are real and the hurdles are many. Connecting with adept in-country partners is helpful, but not the only consideration. A U.S. publisher must also closely monitor the partner and his progress. Visiting the country is a good way to make sure the publisher is being well represented in the territory. There are several ways to structure a deal depending on the needs of the publisher and in the territory. Deals are also different depending on whether the title is a single-player computer game, a console game, or an MMOG.

Finally, one thing is certain about international markets: the markets change frequently, and what was the case this year in a particular territory, such as Argentina, may not be the case next year. If India was a finished goods market in 2005, it may no longer be so in 2007. Territories become more sophisticated over time, and new territories pop up to take the place of the previously underdeveloped markets.

CHAPTER 11

Taxation

Peter H. Friedman

Peter@peterfriedmancpa.com

Taxation is never a popular topic, especially when it comes to business. However, as a new entrepreneur you need to be acquainted with certain terminology and concepts to run your business effectively. This chapter will help you navigate the treacherous waters of owning your own business and inform you of some common, and not so common, pitfalls. So let us begin our trip on the river of business ownership and see if we can avoid the rocks, tidal pools, and waterfalls that could sink your boat.

Entity Selection

The first choice in our journey is, what boat should you use? In tax jargon, instead of boat we would say, "What entity should you use?" Your choice in entities involves many factors such as professional fees, what will current and future investors require, how many people you want to be owners in the entity, limitation of liability for signed contracts, offsetting income against losses, and employees and their possible benefits.

What Are the Choices?

There are several different types of possible businesses. Depending on your needs, you can organize your company as one of the following types. One way to tell the different types apart is by which tax form you have to file.

A *Sole Proprietorship*[1] is the simplest form of doing business. It is owned directly by an individual who is running the business. All income and expenses are reported on the owner's Form 1040 Schedule C[2].

A *Partnership* is an entity that has at least two partners operating the business. It is treated as a separate entity for tax purposes and reports all income and expenses on Form 1065. Each partner's share of the income and expenses is reported on Form 1065 K-1.

A *Corporation* is an entity created under the laws of the state in which it has incorporated. All income and expenses are reported on Form 1120 and the corporation pays its own taxes. This type of organization is also sometimes called a C Corporation.

An *S Corporation* is a U.S. corporation created under the laws of the state in which it has been incorporated and has filed an election with the Internal Revenue Service (IRS) to have all its income and expenses be taxed at the shareholder level. All income and expenses are reported on Form 1120S. Each shareholder's share of the income and expenses is reported on Form 1120S K-1. Not all states allow this form of entity.

A *Limited Liability Corporation* (LLC) is an entity created under the laws of the state in which it was incorporated. It is treated like a partnership for tax purposes unless it elects to be treated as a corporation. All income and expenses are reported on Form 1065. Each unit holder's[3] share of the income and expenses is reported on Form 1065 K-1. An LLC is recognized in all 50 states and Washington DC.

Limited Liability

Limited liability is when the owners, shareholders, or unit holders of an entity are liable only to the extent of their capital contributed or any promissory notes they may have given to the entity. If a person is liable, that means that any debts incurred by the entity can be assigned to that person and be made liable for payment. On the other hand, limited liability means that the person cannot be held responsible for debts incurred.

Limited liability entities do not give you complete protection in startup companies. Startup companies have no financial track record, so banks, landlords, and leasing companies usually ask for the owners, shareholders, or unit holders to give their personal guarantees for any contracts or loans the company enters into. A personal guarantee means that if the company cannot pay, you will. This is called "piercing the corporate veil," and effectively renders the limited liability benefit null and void. As your company develops a financial track record, you should be able to negotiate the personal guarantees away, and the benefits of limited liability will be restored. In regard to payroll taxes not paid to the government, the government can always go after you to make them pay it whether or not the company has the money.

Sole Proprietorship—all owners are liable.

General Partnerships—all general partners are liable.

Limited Partnerships—all general partners are liable, but all limited partners have limited liability to the extent of the capital they contributed and any promissory notes they may have given to the Limited Partnership.

Corporation—all shareholders have limited liability.

S Corporation—all shareholders have limited liability.

Limited Liability Corporation—all unit holders have limited liability.

Pass-Through Entity

A pass-through entity passes its net income or net losses to its owners. Passing income through to the owners helps avoid double taxation. Double taxation is defined as income first taxed at a corporate level and then taxed at a personal level. An example of double taxation is net income taxed by a corporation, and when that income is passed to the owners, they also pay tax. Assuming a 35% tax rate for a corporation and a 35% tax rate for individuals, if the corporation had net income of $1,000 it would pay taxes of $350. If it passed the remaining income of $650 to its owners, they would pay $227.50. Therefore, on an income of $1,000, the total tax bill is $577.50 versus $350 if only the owners were taxed. Yet, what if the owners had to leave some money in the company so it can operate? Let's modify the previous example where the company needs to retain at least $200 for operation purposes after taxes. As a further modification, we will pay $650 salary to the owners. Income of $1,000 less $650 salary equals $350 net income. Tax on the corporate level would equal $122.50 ($350 at a 35% tax rate), and tax on the individual level would equal $227.50 ($650 at a 35% tax rate). Thus, the total taxes paid would equal $350.00. The potential benefit of this is that you are showing the corporation having income and establishing an income for yourself. This will help you establish a credit rating for yourself and the company. Remember, double taxation can be mitigated with good tax planning, and you can get additional financial benefits.

Sole Proprietorship—a pass-through entity, 100% to owner.

General Partnerships—a pass through entity. Partners can allocate ownership, income, and losses by different percentages as long as each category totals 100%. An example would be a General Partner who owns 10% of the partnership, gets 70% of any losses of the partnership, and gets 10% of any income of the partnership. All these allocations must be defined in the partnership agreement.

Limited Partnerships—a pass-through entity. Partners can allocate ownership, income, and losses by different percentages as long as each category totals 100%. An example would be a General Partner who owns 1% of the partnership, gets 1% of any losses of the partnership, and gets 50% of any income of the partnership; and the Limited Partners own 99% of the partnership, get 99% of the losses, and 50% of the income. All these allocations must be defined in the limited partnership agreement.

Corporation—not a pass-through entity.

S Corporation—a pass-through entity. The shareholders get whatever their percentage of ownership is to the whole entity.

Limited Liability Corporation—a pass-through entity. LLC members can allocate ownership, income, and losses by different percentages as long as each category totals 100%.

Ownership

Are there any restrictions as to who can own an interest in your entity or the amount of owners you can have? The issue of ownership is important because it can limit what entity you may be allowed to use, and where you may have to file in which state.

Sole Proprietorship—you can only have one owner and it must be an individual.

General Partnerships—no restrictions to ownership or amount of owners.

Limited Partnerships—no restrictions to ownership or amount of owners.

Corporation—no restrictions to ownership; you are restricted to the amount of owners you can have as it cannot exceed the amount of stock the state has authorized that you are allowed to issue. For example, say the state authorizes you to issue 1,000 shares of stock; if you issued one share of stock per owner, you would be limited to 1,000 owners. You can have multiple levels of stock. Some companies have one class in which every share of Class A has 1,000 voting rights[4] and every share of Class B has one voting right. No matter how many classes of stock you may have, it has no effect on the taxability of your corporation.

S Corporation—the requirements are that it must be a U.S. domestic Corporation, it can only have 100 shareholders; it can only have one type of stock; and only individuals, certain estates, trusts, and exempt organizations may be shareholders.

Limited Liability Corporation—no restrictions to ownership. However, you are restricted to the number of owners you can have: it cannot exceed the amount of units the state has authorized you to issue, similar to a Corporation.

Year Ends (Fiscal Year)

A *fiscal year* is your business's annual reporting period. The fiscal year is generally a 12-month period. A common exception is the initial fiscal year of your business, which may be shorter. A calendar year end is an annual reporting period beginning on January 1 and ending on December 31 of the same year. A fiscal year end is any annual (12 months) reporting period that ends on some period other than December 31.

Sole Proprietorship—must make the year end of the owner, which is usually the calendar year end.

Partnerships—must conform its tax year to its partners' tax year, unless any of the following apply: the partnership makes an election under Code section 444, the partnership elects to use a 52–53 week tax year, or the partnership can establish a business purpose for a different tax year.[5]

Corporation—establishes its tax year when it files its first tax return. The chosen year should reflect the cycle of business and does not have to be a calendar year.

S Corporation—must use a permitted year. A permitted year is one of the following: a calendar year, an election under code section 444, an election to use a 52–53 week tax year, or a different tax year for a business purpose established to the IRS.

Limited Liability Corporation—usually a calendar year unless you establish to the IRS a business purpose for a different year end.

Cost of Creation

When forming the company, there are some costs associated with forming the entity. Many of these costs will vary by state, or even regions within the state. The largest expense will probably occur if you need help from a professional, usually a lawyer, to file the necessary paperwork.

Sole Proprietorship—if you want to reserve your name in your state, you will be required to file a form with the state or the city in which you live. This form is commonly called a "doing business as" form. Depending on your region, this form can cost between $25 and $250.

General Partnerships—would require some help from a professional to file the articles of partnership in the state.[6]

Limited Partnerships—would require some help from a professional to file the articles of partnership in the state.

Corporation—would require some help from a professional to file the articles of incorporation in the state.

S Corporation—a corporation that elects for a pass-through ability for tax purposes. All you need to do is file Form 2553 with the Internal Revenue Service (IRS).

Limited Liability Corporation—would require some help from a professional to file the articles of incorporation in the state.

The major way to reduce costs of going to get help is to know what you and your other collaborators want. Look through these different aspects and put your requirements in writing; then have everyone sign off on it. Keep your presentation precise so you do not have to haggle in front of a professional who is charging you by the minute.

A Summary of Entity Types

A summary of the types of business entities is shown in Table 11.1.

TABLE 11.1   Business Entity Summary

Type of Corporation	Liability	Forms for Reporting Income and Expenses	Pass-through Entity?	Ownership
Sole Proprietorship	All owners are liable.	All income and expenses are reported on the owner's Form 1040 Schedule C .	Yes	Only one owner allowed.
General Partnership	All general partners are liable.	Partnership's income and expenses are reported on Form 1065. Each partner's share of the income and expenses is reported on Form 1065 K-1.	Yes	No restrictions.

$\rightarrow$

Type of Corporation	Liability	Forms for Reporting Income and Expenses	Pass-through Entity?	Ownership
Limited Partnership	All general partners are liable, but all limited partners have limited liability to the extent of the capital they contributed and any promissory they may have given to the Limited Partnership.	Partnership's income and expenses are reported on Form 1065. Each partner's share of the income and expenses is reported on Form 1065 K-1.	Yes	No restrictions.
Corporation (or C Corporation)	All shareholders have limited liability.	All income and expenses are reported on Form 1120.	No	Number of owners limited to shares of stock issued.
S Corporation	All shareholders have limited liability.	All income and expenses are reported on Form 1120S. Each shareholder's share of the income and expenses is reported on Form 1120S K-1.	Yes	Only 100 shareholders allowed, and types of shareholders limited.
Limited Liability Corporation (LLC)	All unit holders have limited liability.	All income and expenses are reported on Form 1065. Each unit holder's share of the income and expenses is reported on Form 1065 K-1.	Yes	Number of owners limited to number of units.

State Selection

The second choice in our journey is what river should we choose to sail our boat down? Or, in other words, what state should you set up your business in? Most people choose the state they reside in as the state they will do business in. This is done because of family, friend, and community ties, and people have already developed a source of income, which they can tap into while they are getting the company off the ground. Some individuals have the ability to move to any state and begin their business. Nevertheless, all companies should look into the following in determining whether they have the ability to move and start their business in another state.

States usually have two sets of tax structures for businesses: an income tax and a franchise tax. A franchise tax is a fee paid to the state for being registered in the state. An income tax usually is based on your federal income with certain modifications and multiplied by a fixed rate. Certain states may have an intangible tax, an inventory tax, or a tax paid on wages (other than state unemployment insurance and state withholding taxes). Before starting, call your state Department of Revenue and get a publication on the taxes your state will be assessing you and your company. To be forewarned is to be forearmed.

A later section discusses the tax and economic benefits that are offered to entice businesses to set up in a certain state. Remember, states want you because you will pay those taxes and hopefully employ their residents.

Accounting

The next choice in our journey is whether to go upstream or downstream; what methods of accounting will you be choosing to record your business's transactions, and what special issues might you have to deal with?

Methods or Basis

There are two general methods of accounting:[7] the cash method and the accrual method. The method you choose should reflect the matching of income to expenses within any given fiscal year. If you choose an accounting method that does not correctly reflect the matching of income to expenses, the IRS has the ability to adjust either income or expenses and move them into fiscal years other than when your reported them.[8] Issues relevant to the cash method are the claim of right doctrine and constructive receipt. For the accrual method, your central issues are the all events test and economic performance.

According to the claim of right doctrine, cash or property that is received in a given year will be reported as income if it is received by the company without any restrictions as to its disposition, even if the income must be repaid by the company at a later date.[9] An advance on royalties that can be used to pay current operating costs is income in the year received, if it is received without restrictions and even if it must be repaid in the future.

According to the theory of constructive receipt, if you are a cash-basis company and you have control of when you can receive either the property or cash and you choose to delay the receipt of that money until another fiscal year, the government has the right to reallocate those funds to the year you *could have* received the property or cash but didn't,[10] regardless of whether it was received. For example, assume a company has a calendar year (its fiscal year ends on December 31), and the company receives cash for work done in December. The company chooses to deposit the cash in January. The income must nevertheless be included in the month of December because the company chose not to deposit the cash in December (current fiscal year) and instead deposited it in January (next future year).

All Events Test

An accrual basis company includes income in its fiscal year when it has performed all the events that make another company pay for a product.[11] A game company is required to submit documentation to reach its milestone within a certain amount of time to get its next payment. If the game company completes everything it has to do and submits the required documentation in December, it has earned that income in December, whether or not it receives the income in a later month.

Economic performance for an accrual taxpayer is that prior to taking a deduction, all events must have occurred; the amount owed can be reasonably ascertained and economic performance has occurred.[12] For example, a company incurs a bill for software in December 2007 and pays for it in January 2008. When all events have taken place and the amount owed is known, economic performance has occurred. Another example would be when an independent contractor writes a program for your company and submits a bill; the company disputes the bill and refuses to pay. While all events have occurred, it is not possible to estimate what the exact amount is owed, so the company cannot take the deduction until it has resolved its dispute and determined how much it will pay.

If you use the *cash method* of accounting, all items of income, whether in the form of cash, property, or services are includible in income for the taxable year in which they were either actually or constructively received. Expenditures are deducted in the taxable year in which they are actually made. For example, assuming a calendar year, if you receive a check as income before December 31 and it clears in January, that would be income in December. Similarly, a credit card charge made in the month of December but paid in January is a deduction in the month of December.[13] In contrast, if you write checks dated December 31, and mail them in January, then that would be a deduction in January.

The purpose of the *accrual method* of accounting is to match income and expenses in the correct year. The accrual method is based on what is called the *all events test*. To record either a deduction or income, economic performance must have occurred, the amount is fixed and can be determined; a bill or invoice, however, does not need to be submitted.[14] If you therefore use the accrual method of accounting, it is not the actual receipt of payment that determines the timing of when you record the payment into gross income; rather, it matters when the right to receive payment has been established.[15] Thus, if you use the accrual method of accounting, it is not the actual payment of the liability that determines the timing of when you record the payment as a deduction or expense; instead, the timing depends on when the amount can be reasonably determined and when economic performance has occurred.[16]

No method or basis of accounting is permitted unless it clearly reflects the business operations of a company.[17] The simple rule of thumb is that expenses can be deducted when they have been incurred, and income is included when earned.

The differences between the two methods are compared in Table 11.2.

TABLE 11.2   A Comparison between Cash Method and Accrual Method

	Cash Method	Accrual Method
When is income counted?	Income is counted when payment is received.	Income is counted when it is earned, not when it is paid.
Advantages	Gives you a better idea of how much actual cash your business has.	Accurately shows the ebb and flow of business income and debts.
Employee bonuses	Can only deduct employee bonuses in the year they are paid.	Can record the bonus in December, and pay the bonus in December and in the next year.
Advance payments	Must be included in income in the taxable year in which they were received.	Can either be included as income in the year received or later, through the deferral method.

Revenue Recognition of Advance Payments

For Cash Basis, advance payments received by the taxpayer must be included in income in the taxable year in which they were received, as long as the payments were received without restriction and with no obligation to refund. An obligation that is not fixed but could happen—such as a reimbursement for upfront production money that must be refunded if the royalties earned on the software do not cover the advance on production expenses—does not qualify as a fixed obligation, and the income must be reported in the taxable year received.[18]

For Accrual Basis, advance payments received by a taxpayer can either be included as income in the year received or later, through the deferral method. Qualifying taxpayers generally may defer to the next succeeding taxable year the inclusion in gross income for federal income tax purposes of advance payments, to the extent the advance payments are not recognized in revenues in the taxable year of receipt.

To clarify, consider the following example: On January 1, 2007, Company O enters into and receives advance payments pursuant to a five-year license agreement for its computer software. Under this contract, the licensee pays Company O both the first year (2007) license fee and the fifth year (2011) license fee upon commencement of the agreement. The fees for the second, third, and fourth years are payable on January 1 of each license year. In its financial statement, Company O recognizes the fees in revenue for the respective license year. For federal income tax purposes, Company O must include the first year license fee in gross income for 2007, the second and fifth year license fee in gross income for 2008, the third year in gross income in 2009, and the fourth year license fee in gross income for 2010.[19]

Software Costs

Software Included in Hardware Purchases

If the software is not separately stated and is included in the hardware purchase, then it is expensed (depreciated) as part of the cost of the hardware. Usually, that would mean that the software/hardware will be depreciated over five years using the 200% declining balance depreciation method described in the depreciation section later. For example, a company purchases a new computer with an email program included in the price of the computer; the email program is not separately stated on the invoice. The email program is thus depreciated over the five-year life of the hardware equipment.

Separately stated software that is acquired is treated as a capital purchase and is expensed (depreciated) over 36 months using a straight-line method starting in the month the software is first used.[20] To qualify for this 36-month method, the software (1) must be acquired separately or be readily available for purchase by the general public, (2) is subject to a nonexclusive license, and (3) has not been substantially modified or customized.

Advance royalty payments to independent software developers are expenses for purchased software and were not deductible as research and experimental expenses because they were for the construction or manufacture of depreciable property by a third party, with the third party being at risk for the development of the property.[21] As long as it meets one of these two rules, it will not be subject to being expenses over 15 years.[22]

Developed Software

In the opinion of the IRS, the costs of developing computer software closely resemble research and experimental expenses; thus, these costs should both be treated using IRS section 174. Development costs must be treated consistently and can be expensed, expensed over 36 months, or expensed over 50 months.[23] If you are the sole person responsible for the creation and performance of the software project covered by the consulting contracts, the expenses for software developed by yourself are currently deductible. If, however, the costs are for the installation and modification of the software necessary to make it compatible with your business and the software cannot be operated without the add-on, the expenses are expensed over 36 months.[24]

Leased Software

If software is leased or licensed by you, the expenses are accounted for as if they are a lease or rental expense. Therefore, it is generally deducted over the term of the lease including options to renew.[25]

Remember, you must be consistent with how you treat software. Once you decide how you want to handle it, you must handle it consistently. If you want to change how you are expensing it, you must ask permission from the IRS by filing Form 3115 (Application for Change in Accounting Method) and printing at the top of the form "Automatic change filed under Section 8.01 of Rev Proc 2000-50." If you are electing to expense software over 36 months, you must attach a statement informing the IRS which taxable year you are choosing to make the change.

Depreciation

Purchases of property, equipment, furniture, and other physical assets cannot be deducted as ordinary and necessary expenses for a business; rather, they must be capitalized and expensed over time.[26] The term that describes the expensing of a capital asset over time is *depreciation*.[27]

The concept behind depreciation is that capital assets will need to be replaced over time as they are used up during business. Depreciation is a systematic way to recover the cost of the capital asset by an annual expense over the years the capital asset is supposed to last. The depreciation expense is calculated by taking the cost of the asset and dividing it by its theoretical standardized life.[28] The IRS has created these standardized life tables. These tables are called the modified accelerated cost recovery system (MACRS).[29] Once you check the MACRS tables and determine the "life" of the asset you purchased, you can then choose one of the three approved methods of depreciation.

First, the straight-line method of depreciation is calculated by taking the cost of the asset and dividing it by the life of the asset and taking the annual amount every year. For example, if an asset costs $10,000 and its estimated life is 10 years, the annual depreciation will be $1,000. This method is used when the company believes the asset depletes evenly before time.

Second, the 200% or double declining balance method of depreciation is calculated by taking the cost of the asset (less any previous depreciation) and dividing it by the remaining life of the asset and then multiplying by 2. For example, consider an asset that costs $10,000 with an estimated life of 10 years. The initial year's depreciation is $2,000 ($1,000 x 2). Second year's depreciation is $1,777 ($10,000 minus $2,000 divided by 9 years multiplied by 2). This method is used when the company believes the asset depletes faster in the beginning of its life.

The third method is the 150% declining balance method of depreciation. It is calculated the same way as the 200% method, but instead you use 150% (1.5 times) instead of 200% (2 times) of the declining balance. [30]

Section 179

Section 179 is an election[31] taken by a company to expense a certain dollar amount of a qualified Section 179 asset in its initial year of operation. In general, any newly acquired physical asset, such as equipment or furniture, used in an active trade or business will qualify as Section 179 property. Newly acquired does not mean it has to be new; used equipment will qualify if it is new to the company. For the years 2007 through 2009, the maximum amount the company can deduct under this election is $108,000, plus a Cost of Living Adjustment (COLA). For the year 2010, the maximum amount the company can deduct is $25,000.

To calculate depreciation expenses after taking the Section 179 expense is simple. The company takes the original cost and reduces it by the Section 179 expense. The company then treats that adjusted cost basis (original cost less section 179 depreciation) as the new basis and calculates the annual depreciation by choosing the method and life. For example, consider equipment that costs $10,000, and the company elects to take $5,000 of Section 179 depreciation. The company will be using the straight-line method of depreciation; the MACRS tables state the equipment has a 10-year life. Depreciation in the initial year is $5,500 (Section 179 depreciation of $5,000 and annual depreciation of $500). The depreciation deduction for years 2 through 10 is $500 per year.

Depreciation Recapture

A sale of a capital asset[32] such as equipment, furniture, computers, and so forth is treated for income reporting as either a capital gain or loss. If the company sells the capital asset at a gain, it may be required to treat some of the gain as depreciation recapture and that amount will be taxed as ordinary income. Gain is calculated as selling price less adjusted basis. Adjusted basis is defined as cost less any Section 179 expense and any depreciation deducted on the return. For example, a company purchases equipment for $10,000 in 2005. It takes the Section 179 election for $5,000 and takes a depreciation deduction of $500 per year for two years. In 2007, it sells the equipment for $6,000. The company's adjusted basis is $4,000 (original cost of $10,000 less $5,000 of Section 179 and $1,000 of annual depreciation). The gain is $2,000 (selling price of $6,000 less adjusted basis of $4,000). The gain is treated as ordinary income since the amount of the depreciation taken ($6,000) is greater than the gain of $2,000.

Consider the same facts, but now the selling price is $15,000. The gain is $11,000 (selling price of $15,000 less adjusted basis of $4,000). The gain is characterized as $6,000 of ordinary income (total amount of depreciation taken) and $5,000 of capital gains.

Consider the same facts from our first example, but now the selling price is $2,000. This sale results in a loss of $2,000 (selling price of $2,000 less adjusted basis of $4,000). This is treated as a capital loss.[33]

Employees or Independent Contractors

The next decision before launching your journey is, how are you going to hire the crew for your boat? Are you going to hire a crew that will only be working for you, or are you going to temporarily hire people as you need them?

For payroll tax purposes, *employees* are people working for the company, including any officer of a corporation. For withholding tax purposes, an employee is any individual who performs services at the direction and control of an employer, including an officer of a corporation.[34] For tax purposes, the company must withhold required taxes from an employee's payment, including income taxes, unemployment insurance, Social Security, and Medicare payroll taxes under the Federal Insurance Contributions Act (FICA), as explained later.

On the other hand, an *independent contractor* is someone who is hired for a specific task. They are treated differently than employees in terms of taxes, and are often treated differently within the company. For example, few contractors receive benefits such as health insurance. For payroll tax purposes, the company is not responsible for withholding any taxes from payment.

So, how do you tell an employee from an independent contractor? It is based on (1) 20 guidelines the IRS stated in 1987, (2) the perception of how you and your contractor believe your relationship is, (3) how you and the contractor present your relationship to outsiders,[35] and (4) other facts and circumstances.[36]

The 20 factors for being considered an employee are:

- Instructions
- Training
- Integration
- Services rendered personally
- Hiring assistants
- Continuing relationship
- Set working hours
- Full-time employment
- Work done on premises
- Order or sequence set
- Reports
- Payments
- Expenses
- Tools and materials
- Investment
- Profit or loss
- Works for more than one person or firm
- Offers services to the general public
- Right to fire
- Right to quit

If none of the preceding factors applies to an individual working for the company, the company can classify those workers as independent contractors and not employees. The more control the employer has over these factors, the more likely the worker should be considered an employee of the company.

If you erroneously classify an employee as an independent contractor and have no reasonable basis for doing so, your company will be liable for the back Medicare and Social Security taxes. Further, you may be held personally liable for a penalty equal to the amount of taxes that should have been paid. If you give fringe benefits to your employees, such as retirement plans and medical insurance, the newly classified employee could also be entitled to those plans retroactive to the date when he was determined to be an employee.

The independent contractor's reclassification also affects the independent contractor. He is only liable for the employee's share of Social Security and Medicare, which is a lower rate than the rate for self-employed individuals. Yet the independent contractor cannot deduct any expenses as a sole proprietor and must move those expenses to Form 1040 Schedule A itemized deductions. This will cause a higher income tax to be calculated, along with penalties and interest on the new liability.

There is a last type of worker, *volunteers*, who have been the subject of a few court cases. The first case is *Hallisey and Williams v. AOL, Inc.*, which was filed in May 1999 in U.S. District Court, Southern District of New York. In this case, Hallisey and Williams were part of a volunteer program set up by AOL to help other AOL users. Hallisey and Williams filed this action stating that they were really employees and entitled to a minimum wage and all the employee benefits that were given by AOL. The U.S. Department of Labor had investigated and dropped the allegations against AOL in regard to Hallisey and Williams's case in 2001. It should be noted that AOL dropped their volunteer program in June 2005. Another case in regard to this same issue was filed in September 2000 in the U.S. District Court District of Colorado entitled *Katherine Reab, et. al. v. Electronic Arts Incorporated and Origin Systems Incorporated civil action 00B1839*. This case was based on the same issue of volunteers stating that they were really employees of the company and entitled to compensation and benefits. In 2001, the court allowed this case to become a class action lawsuit. In February 2004, it was reported that this class action suit had been settled out of court.

The important lesson you need to remember is, free labor (volunteers) may not be so free. There is no established precedent for these types of workers, and it may end up costing you considerably.

Minimum Wage

The Fair Labor Standards Act (FLSA) establishes minimum wage, overtime pay, recordkeeping, and child labor standards affecting full-time and part-time workers. Covered nonexempt workers are entitled to a minimum wage of not less than $5.15 an hour. Overtime pay at a rate of not less than one and one-half times their regular rates of pay is required after 40 hours of work in a workweek.[37]

The regulations under the Fair Labor Standards Act help define the exemption from minimum wage and overtime pay for executive, administrative, professional, outside sales and computer employees. These exemptions are often referred to as the "white collar" exemptions. To be considered exempt, employees must meet certain minimum tests related to their primary job duties and, in most cases, must be paid on a salary basis at not less than $455 per week. The regulations state that exemptions do not apply to manual laborers or other "blue collar" workers who perform work involving repetitive operations with their hands, physical skill, and energy. Thus, for example, nonmanagement production-line employees and nonmanagement employees in maintenance, construction, and similar occupations such as carpenters, electricians, mechanics, plumbers, iron workers, craftsmen, operating engineers, longshoremen, construction workers, and laborers have always been, and will continue to be, entitled to overtime pay.[38]

The exemption for computer employees apply only to a computer employee whose primary duty consists of "(1) The application of systems analysis techniques and procedures, including consulting with users, to determine hardware, software, or system functional specifications; (2) The design, development, documentation, analysis, creation, testing, or modification of computer systems or programs, including prototypes, based on and related to user or system design specifications; (3) The design, documentation, testing, creation, or modification of computer programs related to machine operating systems; or (4) A combination of the above duties, the performance of which requires the same level of skills."[39]

Many states have adopted a higher minimum wage then $5.15 and tougher standards to be exempt from minimum wages than the Fair Labor Standards Act dictates. Contact your state Department of Labor and find out what you are required to do to meet your state's minimum wage laws and who qualifies as being exempt from those wage laws.

Payroll Tax Compliance

You now have a crew to man your boat. Now you are required to make sure you have life preservers, fire extinguishers, and floatable lifeboats to comply with boating regulations and to keep your crew happy and safe. It is your fiduciary responsibility to comply with the boating rules, and it is your fiduciary responsibility to collect and pay your payroll taxes. This is what we call *payroll tax compliance*.

You are required to report new employees to the state as a new hire. You are also required to verify that each of your new employees is legally allowed to work in the United States. The two forms an employee is required to fill out are the U.S. Citizenship and Immigration Services Form I-9 and the Internal Revenue Services Form W-4. In the past, you were required to send to the IRS any Form W-4 if the employee was claiming a complete exemption from federal withholding or claiming 10 or more allowances. This is no longer required.

Wages are what you pay to your employees. Employers generally must deduct and withhold taxes from wages actually or constructively paid to employees. Wages are constructively paid to an employee when they are credited to his account or set apart so he can withdraw them at any time without substantial limitations or restrictions.[40] Generally, *wages* refers to all remuneration for services performed by an employee for his employer unless specifically accepted by the IRS. Wages include but are not limited to salaries, fees, bonuses, commissions on sales or on insurance premiums, pensions, and retirement pay. The basis upon which the wages are paid does not matter in determining whether the compensation is really wages. Therefore, it could be paid on the basis of piecework or a percentage of profits, and may be paid hourly, daily, weekly, monthly, or annually. It also does not matter how the wages are paid. It can be in the form of cash, stocks, bonds, property, and benefits for a nonfamily employee, such as medical insurance for dependants of an employee paid for by the company. If payment is made for services and it is paid for other than cash, then the fair market value of that payment is the amount to be reported as wages. Payment for services rendered to you, unless such payment is excluded by the IRS, will be considered wages even though at the time payment was made, the employee was no longer employed by you.[41]

Social Security is one of the components of the Federal Insurance Compensation Act (FICA), and is withheld from your employees' gross wages. The amount withheld from the employee is matched by the employer. The employee Social Security withholding rate is currently .062 (6.2%). The amount you will pay the IRS is .124 (12.4%) (employees share is .062 and your share is .062, which equals .124). The rate is not dependant on the marital status of the employee or how many dependants he may have. Social Security for the year 2006 is limited to the first $94,200 of wages paid to an employee. In other words, once you have paid an employee $94,200, you no longer have to withhold Social Security. You should check if Congress has increased the ceiling on Social Security at the beginning of every year.

Medicare is the other component of FICA withheld from your employees' gross wages. The amount withheld from the employee is again matched by the employer. The employee Medicare withholding rate is .0145. (1.45 percent). The amount you will pay the IRS is .029 (2.9 percent) (employee's share is .0145 and your share is .0145, which equals .029). The rate is not dependant on the marital status of the employee or how many dependants he may have. Medicare for the year 2006 is not limited to any wage ceiling.

You must withhold *income tax* computed in accordance with the provisions of Internal Revenue Code 3402(a). You can withhold pursuant to the wage bracket method of withholding, the percentage method, or certain other methods as allowed by tax law. You can use different methods with respect to different groups of employees.

You are required to collect the tax by deducting and withholding the amount thereof from the employee's wages when paid. Wages are constructively paid when they are credited to the account of or set apart for an employee so they may be drawn upon by him at any time without any substantial limitation or restriction. You may use a third party to handle your compliance requirements in regard to withholding taxes. Nevertheless, the legal responsibility for withholding, paying, and returning the tax and furnishing such statements rests solely with you. The amount of any tax withheld and collected by you is held in a special fund in trust for the United States.[42]

Unemployment insurance is what pays for the unemployment benefits a worker can claim between jobs. The federal unemployment insurance was created under the Federal Unemployment Tax Act (FUTA), and works in tandem with state unemployment insurance to pay benefits to workers when they are unemployed. FUTA is imposed only on the employer and not on employees. Since both federal and state insurance funds work together, you are allowed a credit against your FUTA tax for the amounts paid for your state unemployment insurance. Many states borrow from FUTA during times of high unemployment, but these funds must be repaid. If a state has not repaid its loan within two years, the credit allowed to employers within that state against FUTA for taxes paid to the state program is reduced. The amount of the reduction increases up to a limit for years that balances remain outstanding.[43]

To calculate your FUTA tax, first determine if your state has any loans outstanding to FUTA. If it does not, then on a quarterly basis multiply the wages of your employees on an employee-by-employee basis (but not to exceed $7,000) by .008 (.8 percent) of wages. This will be your FUTA liability for that quarter. For example, you have two employees, and in the first quarter employee 1 earns $ 10,000 and employee 2 earns $5,000. Your FUTA liability for the first quarter is $96 ($7,000 × .008 for employee 1 and $5,000 × .008 for employee 2). In the second quarter, employee 1 earns $10,000 and employee 2 earns $5,000. Your FUTA liability is $16 ($0 for employee 1 and $2,000 × .008 for employee 2).

Depository Tax Requirements

As the company pays its employees, the company is withholding federal income taxes and Medicare and Social Security taxes[44] collectively called *payroll taxes*. The frequency of when the company has to pay a financial institution (commonly the company's bank) for the benefit of the IRS is determined by the prior amount of accumulated payroll taxes withheld over the last calendar year—the lookback period.

Payroll Taxes for the IRS

If you have paid $50,000 in federal payroll taxes or less for all your employees in the previous four-quarter period (July 1 of the second preceding year through June 30 of last year), you are considered a monthly scheduled depositor. That means the amount of money you have withheld from your employees and the amount you as the employer are required to match for FICA purposes must be paid by the 15th day of the succeeding month. For example, the payroll tax liability in the month January must be paid no later than February 15. There are penalties for depositing late, or for mailing payments.

If you have paid greater than $50,000 in federal payroll taxes in the previous four-quarter period (July 1 of the second preceding year through June 30 of last year), you are considered a semiweekly scheduled depositor. If your payday is Wednesday, Thursday, or Friday, you must make your deposit by the next Wednesday of the week. If your payday is Saturday, Sunday, Monday, or Tuesday, you must make your payment by Friday.

If you have accumulated $100,000 or more in payroll tax liability in any pay period, you must make a deposit on the next banking day. For example, if you accumulated payroll tax liabilities on Tuesday of $95,000 and $10,000 on Wednesday and your normal payday is Tuesday, you would pay the $95,000 no later than Friday, and the following Wednesday you must deposit the $10,000.

As a startup company or new employer, your payroll taxes in the lookback period are considered zero for any quarter your business did not exist. Therefore, in the first year of business, you are a monthly schedule depositor unless the $100,000 next-day deposit rule applies.

If your total payroll tax liability is less than $2,500, you are not required to make any deposits. You must pay the full amount of your liability when you file your quarterly payroll tax return.

The company must make deposits electronically (EFTPS)[45] for all depository tax liabilities for the current year, if (1) the company made more than $200,000 in aggregate deposits for all types of federal depository taxes in the year two years before the current year, or (2) the company was required to make electronic deposits in the previous year. If the company is required to make electronic deposits through EFTPS and fails to do so or makes deposits using a paper coupon, the company may be subject to a 10% penalty[46,47].

Federal Unemployment Insurance

When your FUTA liability exceeds $500 in any given quarter, you are required to make a deposit by the last day of the next month following that quarter. If your FUTA liability in the first quarter was $400, no payment is due in April. On the other hand, if you incur an additional liability of $200 in the second quarter, you are required to make a $600 ($400 from the first quarter and $200 from the second quarter) deposit no later than July 31.

State taxes and withholding vary widely across the country. Contact your state offices for filing requirements for withholding taxes and unemployment insurance.

Reporting Requirements

Note that filing dates are based on a calendar year and not on the company's taxable year.

Federal payroll taxes are reported on Form 941 and are due by the last day of the succeeding month after the quarter. The first quarter, which includes January, February, and March, is due by April 30.

Federal unemployment insurance is reported annually on Form 940 and is due by January 31 of the succeeding year. For example, Form 940 for the year 2006 is due by January 31, 2007.

Form W-2 is filed on an annual calendar year basis. A W-2 is used to summarize and report the employee's earnings and withholding taxes for the year. Your employees are to receive their Form W-2 no later than January 31 of the following year. You are required to report the W-2 wages to the Social Security Administration (SSA) using Form W-3. Form W-3 and the attached Form W-2 Schedule A for each employee are to be received by the SSA no later than February 28 of the following year. For example, for the calendar year 2007, your employees are to receive their W-2 by January 31, 2008, and the SSA is to receive the W-3 and attachments by February 28, 2008.

Information about wages for independent contractors is filed on Form 1099 MISC, an annual form used to report to the IRS. You must report a contractor with this form if you paid at least $600 in rents, nonemployee compensation (independent contractors for services), prizes and awards, other income payments, medical and health-care payments, and gross payments made to lawyers for a succeeding calendar year. The individual's copy of Form 1099 is to be mailed to the recipients by January 31, and mailed to the IRS by February 28. For the calendar year 2007, the 1099s should be mailed to the recipients by January 31, 2008, and to the IRS with Form 1096 (Annual Summary and Transmittal of U.S. information Returns) by February 28, 2008.

State withheld payroll taxes and state unemployment insurance are reported on a quarterly basis and are due by the last business day of the month following the quarter. If you have employees, many states require disability insurance and workman's compensation insurance. Contact an insurance agent in your state to determine if these two types of insurance are required if you have employees.

Table 11.3 is a summary of the deadlines for payroll tax compliance.

TABLE 11.3   A Summary of Payroll Tax Due Dates

Tax Requirement	Due By
Federal Withholding—Form 941	April 30, July 31, October 31, January 31
Federal Unemployment Insurance—Form 940	January 31
UI Deposits	April 30, July 31, October 31, January 31
Wage Reporting	
To Employees—Form W-2	January 31
To Contractors—Form 1099-MISC	January 31
To Government—Forms W-2/W-3, 1999/1096	February 28
State Withholding	April 30, July 31, October 31, January 31
State Unemployment Insurance	April 30, July 31, October 31, January 31

Fringe Benefits

Now you have your crew and you know your compliance needs for the government. However, all work and no play are going to make a disgruntled group, so you may want to give them a couple of perks to keep them happy. These perks are called *fringe benefits*. Some of these benefits are taxable and others are not taxable.

Taxable fringe benefits are included in the income of the recipient of the benefit. Examples of taxable fringe benefits include an employer-provided automobile, a flight on an employer-provided aircraft, an employer-provided free or discounted commercial airline flight, an employer-provided vacation, employer-provided discount on property or services, employer-provided membership in a country club or other social club, or an employer-provided ticket to an entertainment or sporting event.

On the other hand, nontaxable fringe benefits are excluded from the income of the recipient. Examples of nontaxable fringe benefits include qualified tuition reductions provided to an employee; meals and lodging furnished to an employee for the convenience of the employer; benefits provided under a dependent care assistance program; health insurance; long-term care coverage; Archer MSA contributions; health flexible spending arrangements (FSA); health reimbursements arrangement (HRA); health savings accounts (HSA); dental, life, and group insurance; legal assistance plans; adoption assistance; athletic facilities; and retirement benefits. Similarly, the value from an employee using an employer-provided transportation may be excludable from income if, for example, the transportation is provided for medical reasons.

The recipient of a fringe benefit is the person performing the services in connection with which the fringe benefit is provided. Thus, a person may be considered a recipient even though that person did not actually receive the fringe benefit. For example, if you provide an automobile to your employee's spouse, the employee is treated as the recipient of that particular benefit.[48]

The best benefits are the ones the company can expense and are not taxable to your employees.

Stock Option Plans

A special way to compensate your crew, if you and they qualify, is giving your crew an opportunity to own part of the boat itself. You can either give them an option to purchase part of the boat or actually give them a part of the boat if they perform services for you. This is called a *stock option* and *stock benefit* plan, and is the right to purchase your stock.

Incentive Stock Options

Incentive Stock Options (ISO) are designed to attract new employees and motivate existing employees. ISOs give the employee the right to purchase your company's stock in the future at its current value. If the company is successful and its stock increases in value, your employee can purchase shares of your stock in the future at a price below the future fair market value of the shares. By creating this potential "windfall," stock options motivate the employee to stay with the company and to work hard, hoping the company will succeed and the stock price will increase. These types of plans are more economically feasible in either publicly traded companies or companies planning to make an initial public offering.

Incentive Stock Options and employee stock purchase plans (ESPP) are considered statutory stock options. Other stock option plans in lieu of compensation are called *nonstatutory* plans.

To be granted an option, a person must be an employee of either the company granting the option, or a related company, from when the option is granted until at least three months before the option is exercised. Furthermore, the option must be nontransferable except at death. If an individual does not meet the employment requirements, or that person receives a transferable option, the option is a nonstatutory stock option.

The company's employees do not include any amount in their income either when the option is granted or when they exercise it. They will have either taxable income or a deductible loss when they sell the stock they bought by exercising the option. The income or loss is the difference between the amount paid for the stock (the option price) and the amount received when the employee sells it. The income or loss is a capital gain transaction, and the income would be taxed at the capital gain rates. Nevertheless, the employee may have ordinary income for the year when he sells or otherwise disposes of the stock and does not meet the holding period requirement. This usually occurs if he or she sells the stock within one year after its transfer or within two years after the option was granted.

If any employee holds 10% or more of the company's stock, the exercise price must be at least 110% of the fair market value of the company's stock when the option is issued and the option term cannot exceed five years. In addition, the total fair market value of stock subject to qualified options that can vest in one employee in one year cannot exceed \$100,000.[49] If an individual does not meet the holding period requirement and you have a gain from the sale, the gain is ordinary income up to the amount by which the stock's fair market value when the individual exercised the option exceeded the option price. Any excess gain is capital gain. If the individual has a loss from the sale, it is a capital loss and the individual does not have any ordinary income.

Nonstatutory Stock Options

If an individual receives a nonstatutory option to buy or sell stock or other property as payment for services, he usually has income when receiving, exercising, selling, or otherwise disposing of the option. In contrast, for most nonstatutory options other than those issued in lieu of compensation, there is no taxable event when the option is granted, and when the option is exercised, the fair market value of the stock received, less the amount paid, is included in income. The fair market value of an option that is not traded on an established market can be readily determined only if all of the following conditions exist:

- The individual can transfer the option.
- The individual can exercise the option immediately in full.
- The option or the property subject to the option is not subject to any condition or restriction that has a significant effect on the fair market value of the option.
- The fair market value of the option privilege can be readily determined.

If the fair market value can be ascertained, your employees will have ordinary income. This income will be taxed at the ordinary income tax rates when the employees exercise their options and the price they receive exceeds the price they paid. As an aside, nonstatutory plans are not subject to the \$100,000 limitation or to the requirement that they be employees.

Nonstatutory options issued to employees give the company an expense equal to the compensation aspect attributed to the employee upon the exercise of the option. The amount of this deduction is the same as the amount of income attributed and taxed to the employee when he exercises his option—the difference between the option exercise price and the fair market value of the shares purchased. Caution—for the company to be allowed the expense, the company must withhold payroll taxes.[50]

Generally, if someone receives property in exchange for performing services, he must include the property's fair market value in his income in the year he receives the property. However, if he receives stock or other property that has restrictions that affect the property's value, he does not include the value of the property as income until the restrictions have been substantially vested. The person can choose to include the value of the property in his income in the year it is transferred to him, as discussed later, rather than the year it is substantially vested. Property is substantially vested when it is transferable, or it is not subject to a substantial risk of forfeiture, meaning the individual does not have a good chance of losing it. Property is transferable if the individual can sell, assign, or pledge his interest in the property to any person (other than the transferor), and if the person receiving his interest in the property is not required to give up the property, or its value, if the substantial risk of forfeiture occurs. A substantial risk of forfeiture exists if the rights in the property transferred depend on performing (or not performing) substantial services, or on a condition related to the transfer, and the possibility of forfeiture is substantial if the condition is not satisfied.

Usually, the property is owned by the employer until it becomes substantially vested. Any income from the property, or the right to use the property, however, is included in the individual's income as additional compensation in the year he receives the income or has the right to use the property. When the property becomes substantially vested, he must include its fair market value, minus any amount he paid for it, in his income for that year.

Individuals can choose to include the value of restricted property at the time of transfer, minus any amount they paid for the property, in their income for the year it is transferred. If someone makes this choice, the substantial vesting rules do not apply and any later appreciation in value is generally not included as compensation when the property becomes substantially vested. The basis for figuring gain or loss when selling the property is the amount paid for it plus the amount included in income as compensation. If an individual makes this choice, she cannot revoke it without the consent of the IRS. Consent will be given only if one was under a mistake of fact as to the underlying transaction. If someone forfeits the property after having included its value in income, the loss is the amount paid for the property minus any amount she realized on the forfeiture. Individuals cannot make this choice for a nonstatutory stock option.[51]

Table 11.4 compares statutory and nonstatutory stock options.

TABLE 11.4   Comparison of Statutory and Nonstatutory Stock Options

	Statutory Stock Options	Nonstatutory Stock Options
Deduction for company	The company generally receives no deduction in the statutory stock option context.	The company obtains a deduction on exercise of a nonstatutory option equal to the income recognized by the employee.
Time of taxation	An employee receiving a statutory stock option realizes no income upon its receipt or exercise; instead, the employee is taxed upon disposition of the stock acquired pursuant to the stock option. A disposition generally refers to any sale, exchange, gift, or transfer of legal title of stock.	A nonqualified stock option is generally taxed to the employee at grant only if the option has a readily ascertainable fair market value at that time, which nonqualified stock options almost never do. If it does not have such a value at grant, it is taxed at the time of exercise.
Preferred type for employee	Arguably preferable for the employee because no income is recognized on the exercise of the option.	Arguably less preferable because income is recognized on the exercise of the option.
Limitations	Nontransferable, except at death.	May be fully transferable, and there need not be any restrictions on the amount of options that can be exercised in a single year nor when the employee can dispose of the option stock after exercise.
Requirements	For a stock option to qualify as an ISO (and thus receive special tax treatment under Code Section 421(a)), it must meet the requirements of Section 422 of the Code when granted and at all times beginning from the grant until its exercise. Employee stock purchase plans (ESPP) also must meet several requirements	There is no requirement that the option price of a nonstatutory option be equal to the fair market value of the stock at the time of the option grant.

Alternative Minimum Tax (AMT)

The U.S. taxing system actually has two methods to tax income. The first and more commonly known method is the graduated income tax calculation. Briefly, with this method, the more taxable income you have, the higher a percentage you will pay in income taxes.

The other method is called the Alternative Minimum Tax (AMT). It is a separate tax computation that, in effect, eliminates many deductions and credits, and creates a tax liability for an individual who would otherwise pay little or no tax.

The AMT starts with the individual's[52] adjusted gross income and then adds back income, disallows deductions, and either eliminates or reduces credits the graduated income tax computation took into account. Those items of income, expenses, or credits are considered preferential. After you make all those adjustments and subtract a statutory deduction depending on how you are filing your tax return, you arrive at your AMT taxable income. This AMT taxable income is then multiplied by 28%. This is called your AMT. Your AMT is compared to your graduated income tax you calculated in the first method. If the AMT is greater than your graduated income tax, the difference between the two methods is added to your personal income tax liability.

For example, assume your income tax for 2007 was $5,000 and your AMT was $7,000. Thus, your personal income tax liability would be $7,000 ($5,000 graduated income tax and $2,000 AMT). Also, if your income tax for 2007 was $5,000 and your AMT was $4,000, your personal income tax liability would be $5,000 ($5,000 graduated income tax and $0 AMT).

The adjustments and tax preference items include such things as standard or certain itemized deductions, taxable state and local tax refunds, accelerated depreciation of certain property, intangible drilling costs, certain tax-exempt interest and the difference between AMT and regular tax gain or loss on the sale of property, treatment of incentive stock options, and depletion allowances.[53]

The AMT has caused many people headaches; people in the technology sector after the stock market crashed in 2001 especially suffered. They received ISOs from their companies and large income tax liabilities without any means to pay the taxes, because their companies' stock was worthless. In fact, there is still a backlog of bills owed from 1999 to 2001 to the IRS because of AMT. While this is an unresolved issue, the IRS still attempts at times to collect these taxes owed.

Tax Incentives

As we check our map to begin our journey, we look for watering holes and places for collecting food or admiring the scenery. In the tax world, this refers to the ways you can offset your taxes by tax credits or incentives to locate in a specific region.

Federal Incentives

One of the federal tax incentives that directly relates to the computer gaming industry is the deduction relating to income attributable to domestic production activities. This deduction is allowed for certain qualified production activities. One of those activities is the manufacture of computer software. Computer software is defined to include the "machine readable coding for video games and similar programs, regardless of whether the program is designed to operate on a computer."[54] For tax years beginning in 2005, you can calculate your expense (deduction) as a percentage of your income derived from your computer game. Basic calculation is the lesser of the percentage multiplied by your income earned by the computer game (qualified production activities income) or your taxable income (gross income less gross expenses) for the taxable year. The deduction is further limited to 50% of the employee wages as reported on Form W-2 for the taxable year. The percentage is phased in starting at 3% for the years 2005 and 2006 and ending in years beginning in 2010 at 9%. This deduction is for manufacturing of a qualified activity whether or not your income is generated solely from the United States or internationally.[55]

Example 1—The company has taxable income in the year 2007 of $50,000 and has qualified production income of $100,000. The company has $250,000 of employee wages reported on W-2 for the year 2007. The company's deduction is $9,000 ($100,000 multiplied by 9%), which is not limited by the company's taxable income ($50,000) or 50% of employee wages ($125,000).

Example 2—Same facts as example 1, except that the company's taxable income is $8,000. The company's deduction is $8,000 ($100,000 multiplied by 9%), but limited by the company's taxable income ($8,000).

Example 3—Same facts as example 2, except that employee wages are $10,000 (this company relies heavily on independent contractors). The company's deduction is $5,000 ($100,000 multiplied by 9%) which is limited by the company's taxable income ($8,000) and further limited to $5,000 (50% of employee wages $10,000).

Example 4—Same as example 3, but the company had a taxable loss of $10,000. The company's deduction is $9,000 ($100,000 multiplied by 9%), but limited by the company's taxable loss of $10,000.

State Incentives

Most states offer economic and tax incentives to businesses operating within their borders. Some states facilitate low interest loans to companies that are located in a certain geographic area. Tax credits are also available in most states as an incentive for businesses to either locate in a state or invest in certain activities the state endorses. Tax credits can be used to offset dollar for dollar any tax liability you may owe to the state. Contact the State's Economic Development Department to see what incentives are available to your company.

The following paragraphs cover common tax credits that exist in most states.

Investment tax credit is a credit for purchasing certain qualified equipment that usually needs to be used in the production of a tangible item (personal property). Software in many states is defined as personal property, and therefore equipment such as computers and motion graphic machines could qualify for the investment tax credit. The credit is calculated by adding up all the qualified purchases made during your tax year and multiplying them by a fixed percentage set by the state. This credit is a dollar-for-dollar offset against your state income tax liability. Take caution, however, because many states require that if you take the credit and then sell the property before a specific amount of time, you will be required to pay back a pro rata share of the credit. This is commonly called *recapture*. Also, some states require that if you take the investment tax credit you must reduce the value of the equipment by the credit and only write off over time (depreciate) the reduced value.

Film production credit entices the film industry to locate and film in certain states. The credit is calculated by adding up all the qualified production costs for work that will be done in that state and multiplying it by a statutory rate. Usually, you have to apply to the state and they will determine if you qualify and how much of a credit you will receive. While some states may not allow the cinematic cut scenes of a videogame to qualify for this credit, some states will. The easiest way to find out is to find out if your state has an Economic/Business Development Office and ask.

Tax credits for expanding high-speed Internet service, usually to certain rural areas, does what it says. The software computer industry requires high-speed Internet service, and as your company grows, it may require that you bring high speed to you by laying, for example, T-3 lines. If you are located in a rural area or want to move to a rural area to set up your new production facility, wouldn't it be nice if you could share that high-speed Internet connection with your neighbors and the state would either give you tax credits or low-interest loans to do that? The cost of acquiring your dream facility just may have become affordable. Almost every state has some incentive to bring high-speed Internet access to rural areas.

Other Tax Issues

As you are getting ready to push off and start your journey, you look at your map and notice uncharted areas, rocks, whirlpools, and other dangers that can sink your boat. We are now going to address some of them.

Decoupling from the Internal Revenue Code

Within the last five years, the U.S. government has passed numerous tax code statutes that speed up deductions or defer income for businesses. Many of the states, being in a cash crisis, chose not to enact these statutes and retained their old laws. This concept is called decoupling the state tax laws from the federal tax laws. This means that if your state has decoupled from the federal tax laws, you will be required to keep two sets of books: one that conforms to the federal tax laws and one that conforms to your state tax laws.

Nexus

States are changing the rules in regard to who has the right to tax you. If the state can prove that you are doing business within its borders—and thus establish a nexus—they will have the right to impose taxes on you. The taxes could be an income tax and a sales tax. The issue here is not the state where you have set up and are doing business in; rather, a potential problem involves an adjacent state that is also asking you to pay it taxes. For example, one of the components that establish nexus could include having an employee or using an independent contractor in a state, having inventory in a state, or having sales in that state.

Some states have a minimum gross receipts level before they ask you to start paying taxes there. On the other hand, some states have a minimum tax regardless of gross receipts or net income.

The issue of nexus is important in e-commerce, where the Internet plays a strong role between your company and your customers. For example, you may want to use the Internet to distribute your game, have the Internet as a component of your game, or use the Internet to sell to the European Union.

Taxes in the European Union

The European Union (EU) has determined that digitally downloading software is becoming an alternative means of distribution, and some countries have begun to defend their traditional "bricks and mortar" businesses. In May 2002, the EU adopted a resolution that as of July 2003, digitally purchased and downloaded software will be subject to a *Valued-Added Tax* (VAT), comparable to sales taxes in many states. The issue of whether a company is a resident and physically located in an EU country is no longer pertinent: All digitally downloaded software will be liable for VAT tax, and the tax rate is dependent on the location where the software was downloaded. The EU will require companies that are not located in the EU to register for collecting VAT in an EU country of their choice. The additional compliance costs of registering in the EU, purchasing software that will track where the game is downloaded, and then computing the appropriate VAT tax of that locale will now need to be included in projected expenses. In June 2004, the EU required that the VAT rate between members be uniform in nature. As of this date, this has not been totally implemented yet. U.S. game companies have already started to charge their EU customers with a VAT tax on online gaming subscriptions.

On October 29, 2004, the European Commission proposed a "one-stop shop" system for applying and collecting value-added tax to simplify rules for companies operating in more than one European Union state. The plan would allow a company to use a single VAT number for all supplies made throughout the EU and to make VAT declarations to a single electronic portal, which would than be submitted automatically to the different states to which the trader supplies goods and services.

On July 20, 2005, the European Commission proposed legislation that would revise the rules for the way value-added tax is applied to services sold to consumers in an effort to reduce bureaucratic confusion and eliminate competitive distortions in the EU because of differing VAT rates. The new proposal would require the rate of the VAT to be applied based on where the consumer lives, instead of where the provider lives as under the current law. This proposed change also would put the VAT rules in line with the proposed changes the commission made in 2003 to require the VAT rate be applied based on the rate of consumption when it concerns business-to-business service transactions. The current rules cause what the commission called "distortions of competition" because companies often move their headquarters to member states where the VAT is lowest, such as in Luxembourg, where the VAT at 15% is the lowest in the EU.

Suppliers of digital products from outside the EU are required to charge VAT on sales to private consumers at the rate applicable in the member state where the consumer is resident. However, the current rule does not currently apply where non-EU suppliers establish themselves within the EU; nor does it apply to EU or non-EU suppliers of other services capable of being supplied at a distance, such as teaching. The commission admitted that the new proposal would create more administrative work for service providers but only if the EU member states do not approve the one-stop legislative plan put forward in 2004 to revise how the VAT levies are distributed to governments.

Both the proposal for revamping VAT rules when it concerns business-to-business service transactions and the one-stop-shop rules were due to be taken up in the Council of Economic and Finance Ministers under the British presidency of the EU, which began July 1, 2005, and lasted until the end of 2005. On October 17, 2005, the Council adopted a Regulation, agreed by unanimity, to ensure that all EU Member States apply some common VAT rules established in the Sixth VAT Directive (77/388/EEC) more consistently. Although the Directive provides the general framework for an EU-wide system of VAT, it does not contain rules for the application of the system. The Regulation covers VAT law relevant to the place of taxation of various types of services, the exception of specific goods and services from VAT, the amount to be considered the "taxable amount" for VBAT purposes, the definition of electronically supplied services, and accounting details for the special VAT arrangements for non-EU suppliers of electronic services. The Regulation entered into force on July 1, 2006.[56]

Taxes for Downloads in the United States

The U.S. Congress has been debating taking a position in regard to digitally downloaded software. There are two bills in place. The first bill, sponsored by Reps. Ernest Istook (R-OK) and William Delahunt (D-MA) on Sept. 25, 2003, unveiled long-awaited legislation (H.R. 3184) that would give states the right to require retailers to collect sales and use taxes on remote transactions if they simplify their sales tax systems. While this bill failed to pass in its initial year, it has been resubmitted every year for consideration in one form or another. Many states have not yet decided if downloading digital software is a taxable event in that state.

On October 1, 2003, Rep. Bob Goodlatte (R-VA), Rep. Rick Boucher (D-VA), and others introduced HR 3220, the "Business Activity Tax Simplification Act of 2003," a bill that would limit the state's ability to impose business activity taxes (BATs). It would require that a business have a physical presence in the taxing jurisdiction to be subject to a BAT. The bill was referred to the House Judiciary Committee. The Department of Treasury regulations that discuss foreign source income and foreign tax credits have taken a similar position as the EU.

On October 15, 2003, Senator Mike Enzi (R-WY), Senator Byron Dorgan (D-ND), and others introduced S 1736, titled the "Streamlined Sales and Use Tax Act," a bill to authorize state and local taxing entities to collect taxes from out-of-state remote sellers, including Internet retailers. Senator Enzi and Senator Dorgan also spoke in support of this bill. Also, on October 15, Senator Ron Wyden (D-OR) went to the Senate floor to warn that a version of the Internet Tax Nondiscrimination Act (INDA) being advanced by state and local governments would give state and local governments "explicit permission to tax what Internet users do once they get on line," including sending email.

The State Sales Tax Project (SSTP) has determined that downloaded digital software is a taxable event. As of October 20, 2003, the Streamlined Sales and Use Tax Agreement (SSUTA) is now in effect because more than 10 states with 20% of the total population of all states imposing a state sales tax have enacted the conforming legislation that complies with the SSUTA.

According to the California Legislative Counsel's Office, the following states plus the District of Columbia participate as voting members (implementing states) in the SSTP: Alabama, Arkansas, District of Columbia, Florida, Illinois, Indiana, Iowa, Kansas, Kentucky, Louisiana, Maine, Maryland, Michigan, Minnesota, Mississippi, Missouri, Nebraska, New Jersey, Nevada, North Carolina, North Dakota, Ohio, Oklahoma, Pennsylvania, Rhode Island, South Carolina, South Dakota, Tennessee, Texas, Utah, Vermont, Washington, West Virginia, Wisconsin, and Wyoming.

The following states do not have a sales tax and would not participate: Alaska, Delaware, Montana, New Hampshire, and Oregon. One of the components of the act states that for nexus/state taxation purposes, *any downloaded service is to be taxed by the state/locality where the end user's customer's billing address is located.* It is therefore easy for the states to expand this theory so that the service fees paid for PC online gaming are taxable in the state where the player is residing.

As of October 1, 2005, 14 states will start encouraging online businesses to collect sales tax just like brick-and-mortar stores are required to do. The 14 states are Indiana, Iowa, Kansas, Kentucky, Michigan, Minnesota, Nebraska, New Jersey, North Carolina, North Dakota, Ohio, Oklahoma, South Dakota, and West Virginia. The sunset provisions regarding the statutory amendments necessary to bring Rhode Island into compliance with the SSTP were extended from June 30, 2005, to June 30, 2006.

Conclusion

From payroll tax compliance to Incentive Stock Options, from choosing entities to choosing what state to set up your business, this chapter hopefully imparted to you a feeling of the complexities and niceties of taxation in running your business. Here is a final message to take to heart: the tax landscape is changing worldwide. Many of the concepts outlined here may become obsolete or be radically changed over a short period of time. Also, having read this chapter, you have been given a taste of what is involved; yet, you may not have gotten the full flavor of what will now be required of you. Instead of going by the adage "a little knowledge is a dangerous thing," please go by "to be forewarned is to be forearmed." We have given you guideposts in the copious endnotes so you can use them as a reference to do further research. Check out the IRS Web site (*http://www.irs.gov/*) as a source of information and publications to help you. Moreover, a good tax professional is a necessity when starting and running your business, and is highly recommended.

Good luck on your journey on the river of business. May you have smooth sailing and reach your desired designation without mishap or heartache.

Endnotes

1. Also referred to as proprietorship or schedule C.
2. Unless otherwise stated, all forms are from the Internal Revenue Service and can be found and downloaded at *http://www.irs.gov/*.
3. Owners of Limited Liability Corporations are unit holders, not shareholders.
4. This type of stock class structure is called super voting stock.
5. Internal Revenue Service Publication 538
6. It is understood that Web sites and stationery stores can sell you documents so that you can fill out the basic documents in forming these entities. I always find that individuals get in more trouble by not going to a professional and filing these forms themselves.
7. The third method is the Hybrid method, which is a combination of the cash method and the accrual method.
8. Internal Revenue Code §482 and Internal Revenue Code §269(A)
9. *James v. United States*, 366 U.S. 213 (1961)
10. Internal Revenue Service Regulations §1.451-2
11. Internal Revenue Service Regulation §1.451-1
12. Internal Revenue Service Code 461
13. Internal Revenue Service Regulations §1.446-1(C)(1)(i)
14. Internal Revenue Service Regulation §1.451
15. Internal Revenue Service Regulations §1.446-1 (C) 1(ii)
16. Internal Revenue Service Regulation §1.461-1(a)(2)(i)
17. Internal Revenue Code Section §446 (C)(1)
18. Internal Revenue Service Regulation §1.451-1
19. Revenue Proc 2004-34
20. Internal Revenue Service Regulations §1.167(a)-14
21. Internal Revenue Regulation §1.174-2(b)(2) and TAM 9449003
22. Internal Revenue Code 197
23. Revenue Procedure 2000-50 §§ 5.01 & 5.02
24. PLR 20023608
25. Internal Revenue Regulations §1.162-11(a)
26. Internal Revenue Code Section 263
27. For an intangible asset like software, the term is *amortization*.
28. Internal Revenue Code §168
29. The MACRS tables are used for assets purchased after 1985.
30. IRS Publication 946 *How to Depreciate Property*

31. Internal Revenue Code §179

32. There is depreciation recapture of equipment and other physical assets according to Internal Revenue Code 1245, and depreciation recapture of real property (i.e., buildings) according to Internal Revenue Code §1250.

33. IRS publication 544 Sales or Other Dispositions of Assets

34. Internal Revenue Regulations §31.3401 c-1

35. Revenue Ruling §87-41, 1987-a CB 296

36. Internal Revenue Regulations §31.3401 (C)-1

37. U.S. Department of Labor Web site *http://dol.gov/esa/*

38. Regulation 541.3(a)

39. Regulation 541 table 2-5

40. Internal Revenue Regulation §31.3402

41. Internal Revenue Regulation §31.3401 (A)-1

42. Internal Revenue Regulation §31.3401

43. Internal Revenue Code §3301

44. Medicare and FICA Taxes are usually referred to as Social Security Taxes.

45. *See* IRS Publication 966 for Electronic Federal Tax Payment System information.

46. *http://www.irs.gov/taxtopics/tc757.html*

47. *See* IRS Publication 15, *Circular E, Employer's Tax Guide*

48. Internal Revenue Code 61

49. Internal Revenue Regulations 1.421

50. Internal Revenue §83 and Internal Revenue §409A

51. Internal Revenue Publication 525

52. Corporations also have an alternative minimum tax. Internal Revenue Code §55

53. Internal Revenue Code §55

54. Internal Revenue Service Notice 2005-14, 2005-7 IRB 498

55. Internal Revenue Code 199

56. Council Regulation (EC) NO 1777/2005

CHAPTER 12

Exit Strategies

Greg Costikyan

greg@manifestogames.com

"Exit strategy" is a phrase most often used in the world of venture capital. Venture investors are not in the business of parking their money in a company forever; ultimately, they want to exit an investment, preferably making a large profit in the process. To a venture capitalist (VC), an exit is a "liquidity event," meaning that their illiquid investment in a private firm is liquidated into cash.

If you ever take investment capital, whether from VCs or angels, you will almost certainly need to exit eventually, because they will pressure you to find a way to liquidate their investment. Moreover, they typically have preferred shares while management has common shares. Preferred shares are usually structured to allow voting control over the company. The result of this voting control is they can force a sale if they wish. Although it is in theory possible to find investors who are interested in dividends rather than an exit—that is, in receiving cash out of your profits without forcing a sale of the company—the reality is that very few people invest on that basis.

Even if you are self-funded, or managed to bootstrap your company, you may still wish to exit at some point. Many developers enjoy the excitement of a startup rather than the maintenance of an established, and even very profitable, company.

Why Exit?

The first possible reason you may want to exit is because you need a liquidity event to satisfy the demands of your investors.

A second possible reason is that you find that you do not have adequate working capital. Even large independent developers rarely have more than a handful of projects under way at any given time, and one disastrous game or a failure to generate a hit over the course of several years can cause real cash flow problems for developers. Moreover, the trend has been toward ever-increasing development budgets; as late as 1992, the typical PC game had a budget of around $200,000, while today, triple-A titles for next-generation consoles are often budgeted in the $20 million range. Publishers are only willing to commit to financing an unproven project when it is already at an advanced stage of development, meaning that developers are often considerably out of pocket before a contract is signed. All of these factors mean that developers often find themselves with scarily depleted working capital—and one way out of the bind is a sale of the firm to someone with deeper pockets.

A third possibility is, shall we say, greed: an exit event may have been part of your plans since your inception. That is, whether or not you took investment capital, you may have been planning to build your company to develop games, but primarily to make a nice chunk of money by flipping it once it became worthwhile to do so. There is, in fact, nothing dishonorable about this, although an honorable entrepreneur will seek to ensure that any sale ensures the financial security of his or her employees—and, ideally, that the games the company produces will continue to be of high quality after any sale.

And, of course, a fourth possibility is that upper management is nearing retirement. They might like a nice nest egg to live on post-retirement, and sale of the company seems the most prudent way to effect this while preserving employability and continuity for the remaining employees.

How to Exit?

If you ask a venture capitalist, he will tell you there are really only two exit strategies: going public or sale to another company. Actually, there are some other possibilities (including the grim one of bankruptcy), but these are certainly the most common, and in most cases, the most desirable.

Initial Public Offering

An initial public offering (IPO) occurs when shares of the company's stock are sold on the public market. This is often called "going public."

Twenty years ago, it was not uncommon for even fairly small firms (for example, $10m in annual revenues) to go public via NASDAQ; today, it is rare for firms with less than $100m in revenues to do so. The main reason for the change is that regulation of publicly traded companies has become increasingly complicated and expensive, in terms of the cost of complying with regulations. Sarbanes Oxley, a law adopted after the Enron scandals to prevent such egregious fraud in future, has upped the ante even farther.

In other words, the likelihood that you will build an independent developer to the point that a public offering is feasible—at least on the major markets—is fairly remote. Not utterly impossible perhaps; in recent years, Jamdat (a mobile game publisher) and Funcom (a Norwegian MMO provider) have gone public (Jamdat was later purchased by EA; Funcom went public on the Norwegian stock exchange). And today, it appears that Elevation Partners, a private equity company that merged Pandemic and BioWare, is grooming the combined "superdeveloper" for an eventual public listing.

Of course, smaller companies can go public on smaller exchanges—the smaller European exchanges, for instance, or the "penny markets" (such as the Denver stock exchange) in the United States. If you are a non-U.S. developer, and your country has a reasonably well-developed exchange, this may be worth considering. U.S. penny markets, unfortunately, have a reputation for stock manipulation, and are generally the preserve of small investors and speculators—very few institutional investors will even look at penny stocks. As a result, IPOs on these markets tend to be small and thinly traded; not ideal characteristics if you are hoping to achieve a maximal value for your firm.

In an IPO, investors typically look for companies with major growth prospects—and assume that there will be continuity of management post-IPO. If you are planning to cash out and leave the firm, that will almost certainly be a negative.

A disadvantage is the cost of going public; in addition to the costs of preparing the offering, the lead underwriter (the investment bank that manages the offering and, typically, provides a base price, guaranteeing to purchase shares at that price even if the offering does not find enough takers on the public market) receives a substantial chunk of the money raised.

A public offering does have two big advantages, however. First is a high degree of independence; venture-funded firms in particular are pretty much under the thumbs of their investors. In an IPO, preferred shares are often converted to common and all become voteable, and most publicly traded companies' equity is widely dispersed among many investors. In effect, no individual investor (or small group of investors) can effectively dictate to management unless they own a controlling share of the public stock. In other words, once you are public, if you are careful about the composition of your board and maintain a controlling share of voting stock, you will have a high degree of freedom to act as you wish—it is rare for investors to manage to challenge management.

This may sound paradoxical; people often talk about how publicly traded companies are constrained by the need to hit quarterly targets, and analysts often claim the privately held companies have more freedom to plan strategically over the long term. There is some truth to that, but only because management, who typically have equity stakes and stock options themselves and who stand to profit personally by rising share prices, decide it is in their best interests to cater to the demands of analysts and the market as a whole. The point is that this is a decision, not an inevitability; the structure of the modern corporation favors management over investors heavily, and if you are willing to accept short-term hits to your share price, you do have great freedom of action.

Second is access to capital markets. Once you are public, it is much easier to raise additional capital by issuing additional shares. This of course dilutes the value of shares held by existing shareholders.

Sale of the Company

The far likelier path for most developers is sale of the company—typically to a publisher, although depending on the nature of your company there may be other potential purchasers as well.

In any sale, investors typically want to receive cash or, as a second-best, shares in a company that is already public (which can then be sold for cash). Deals are often structured so that management's shares are not exchanged for cash, or only partly for cash, but instead for shares in the larger company, whether or not public; part of the objective, of course, is to incentivize management to remain post-takeover. Depending on what you want to do after the sale, you may not want to achieve the highest possible price—but the highest possible price that gives you actual cash. The difficulty here is that this can produce a conflict with your investors—what is best for them is not necessarily best for you.

Similarly, you personally may be interested in taking a lower offer because you doubt the ethics of the company making the highest offer, because you wish to ensure the security of your staff, or because you want to ensure that future games your studio creates will remain high quality. Your investors, however, are almost certainly concerned mainly with achieving the highest possible return.

Thus, before embarking on the quest for a purchaser, it is wise to establish a solid working relationship with your board and your investors, and to achieve agreement on what the objectives are and what sort of purchase price is acceptable.

Leveraged Buy-Out by Management

A third, but rare, exit strategy is to take on debt to buy out existing investors. This is known as a leveraged buy-out (LBO).

LBOs are rare in an entrepreneurial setting; more commonly, they take place when an older company in a mature market has underperformed for some years. A private equity company takes over the firm, primarily with debt capital, installs new management, cuts costs, and works to turn the firm around. If they are successful, they pay down debt with newly higher profits, and then either sell to another private investor or make an offering on the public markets.

To put it another way, LBOs make sense when one group of people believes that value can be created in a company that current owners cannot unlock. For a venture-funded company, this is true only when management has much greater faith in future growth, and its ability to achieve that growth, than current investors. In other words, you can probably take this route only if you and the investors have very different beliefs about the current and prospective future value of the company.

There is another circumstance under which an LBO may make sense: you wish to retire, your colleagues want to continue as an independent firm, and they are willing to take on debt to buy you (and presumably your investors) out.

An LBO is difficult for most developers to accomplish under the best of circumstances; however, lenders like to see companies with stable and predictable cash flows, so they feel reasonably secure that the debt can be serviced and ultimately repaid. The game industry is hit-driven, software development is inherently difficult to schedule, and developers in general tend to see large swings in income from year to year. However, if you do have some sort of cash cow (a modestly successful subscription-based MMO, say), your investors want a liquidity event soon, and you think you have excellent future prospects, this option is worth considering.

Do keep in mind that if you adopt this approach, you are setting yourself (or your successors) up for years of additional hard work. You have undoubtedly worked long and hard to get yourself to your current level of success; you are setting yourself up to work equally hard in the future, scrambling for ways to service and repay the burden of debt you will need to take on to buy out your investors.

If you succeed, of course, your company will have achieved a high degree of independence; it will be out from under the thumbs of its investors, and privately held by management.

The Downside Strategies: Orderly Closedown or Bankruptcy

Any of the previous strategies assume that your company has real value that you can unlock in some fashion—and that you have enough capital to survive until you do so. In reality, of course, most companies fail. And sometimes they fail for reasons utterly beyond their control—Stainless Steel Studios went out of business in late 2005, for instance, because their publisher refused to provide additional funding to complete a title under development, despite high sales hopes on all sides for that game, and Stainless Steel just ran out of cash. They were forced to close the doors, despite a superb team and an excellent reputation in the field.

Shutting down a company is never fun, but it is an "exit strategy" of a kind—and there are smart and stupid ways to do this, too. This is discussed in more depth later.

Preparing for Purchase

What is your company worth? The only real answer to that is, "Whatever someone else will pay you." Typically, companies are valued on the basis of cash flow or net profits. In other kinds of businesses, it is fairly easy to look at a company's balance sheet, apply a price/equity ratio from comparable companies, and come up with at least a first-order approximation of the company's value.

That is not generally possible for game developers—first because so few developers are public (and so there are few bases for comparison), and second because game development is not a business that typically produces predictable cash flows or profits. As a result, valuing a game developer is an art, not a science—and what price you can sell for depends more on market conditions and the perceived needs of potential purchasers than anything else. To give a sense of how widely things can vary, in 2005 Jamdat (now EA Mobile) purchased Blue Lava Wireless, a mobile game developer that just happened to have a 10-year exclusive on the rights for Tetris for $137 million. Also last year, Take Two purchased Firaxis, Sid Meier's company and the owners of the rights to *Civilization*, for an undisclosed price that is rumored to be in the $20m–$30m range. Apparently, Tetris is worth an order of magnitude more than *Civilization*—more is the pity.

What Do You Have that Is Valuable?

Start by looking at what your company possesses and what value those assets have for others. Realistically, you have only four assets:

- The value of your back catalog and whatever future revenues (probably small) it is likely to generate
- Intellectual Property (IP)
- Games in development, and their likely future value
- Your team

In other businesses, fixed assets can also have value—but for most game developers, "fixed assets" mean rapidly depreciating investments in hardware and software, office equipment, and a lease on your office space. The total value of this is not going to be large. It is not like you own a state-of-the-art chip fabrication plant as other technology companies might.

Typically, your back catalog also has limited value. Games typically achieve 80% or more of their sales in the first two on-sale weeks, While an aftermarket in older titles is slowly developing via online distribution and some money can be achieved with "gold" versions, add-on packs, and budget compilations, these generally provide little real contribution to a developer's bottom line. But it is still worth looking at your back catalog and ascribing a value to it—particularly if you are lucky enough to own the rights to some beloved classic that can be ported to newer platforms like mobile or handheld devices. *Tetris* is apparently worth more than $100,000,000, remember.

The single thing purchasers are likely to value most highly is your IP—assuming you own any. If, for example, you own the rights to a franchise that has generated hundreds of millions of dollars at retail over the last few years, you are golden. The problem, of course, is that few third-party developers own the rights to the IP; publishers typically demand ownership of IP when they provide development funding. Stainless Steel Studios, for example, had to sign away the rights to *Empire Earth* to get funded; the Gollop brothers created the *XCOM: UFO* franchise—but signed away those rights a decade or more ago.

The lesson is that from the day you open your doors you must try to retain the ownership of your IP, however you can. If you are utterly reliant on funding from publishers, you will probably not be able to do so—but if you cannot retain rights to your IP, the likelihood is that you are building little value for your company. Beg, borrow, or steal the capital you need to retain your IP if there is any possible way to do so. We really cannot emphasize this enough.

While the rights to a franchise are the first thing that comes to mind when IP is mentioned, IP ownership can mean other things as well. If you have a good license, that is IP, and quite likely valuable to someone—Turbine landed $30m in venture funding in 2005 primarily on the basis of the MMO rights for *Lord of the Rings* and *Dungeons & Dragons*®.

Similarly, software infrastructure can be valuable IP. If you have the industry's best RTS engine, or a secure architecture for peer-to-peer multiplayer gaming, or something of the kind, that has value even in the absence of other IP.

The value of games in progress depends greatly on the degree to which the rights to those games are encumbered. Let us say you have a development contract with Midway for a triple-A title that has gotten a lot of buzz in the industry press; that is great. But if you sell out to EA, how eager will they be to spend capital to complete a game for a competitor? Not very, obviously—and Midway may be interested in making a bid, but the fact that you are locked into one publisher for that title means other publishers will be less interested, and you are likely to obtain a lower price as a consequence.

In other words, if you are contemplating a sale anytime within the next few years, it is worth trying to preserve your options in terms of an ultimate publisher for titles under development. If you can fund development, at least to some stage, without publisher funding, you should consider doing so. Even if publisher funding is needed, it is worth seeing if you can negotiate a clause that would allow you (or a future purchaser) to buy back the publication rights, perhaps at some reasonable premium over funding provided up to that point.

You probably view your team as your most important asset, and in some ways, it is—but it is not an easy asset to value. For one thing, it is an asset that walks out the door every afternoon, and if they are not happy with the purchaser, they do not have to come back the next day. They are not indentured servants, after all. Similarly, it is not uncommon for publishers to buy developers primarily for their IP, then gut them—closing the developer down, possibly moving some of the staff to other teams. Purchasers often do not view a developer's team with the same fondness and regard as the developer themselves.

Under what circumstances is a team valuable to a purchaser? Under two circumstances, generally: when the team is the best at what it does, or when it fills a gap in the purchaser's own mix of studios. If your team is the single best developer of sports titles in the world, or the best developer of multiplayer games on mobile devices, then it clearly has value. Similarly, if a publisher is primarily involved in home console development and eager to establish a larger presence in handhelds and your team has a lot of experience with DS and PSP, then you are filling a niche in the purchaser's studio lineup. In 2006, EA purchased Mythic Studios, the only large, independent developer of MMOs, precisely because EA felt it needed greater expertise in that rapidly growing game sector. (The sale price was undisclosed.)

Other factors that may be of importance include cost, proximity, and the strength of the local development community.

Cost is important because budgets continue to skyrocket and publishers are eager to find ways to develop at lower cost. If you are located in Bulgaria, paying Bulgarian wages, and still turning out triple-A quality work, that is a strong positive. More minor differences in cost are a plus, too; there is a reason why Austin, Vancouver, and Montreal have become major development centers in recent years—they may be far more expensive than Bulgaria, but salaries are still considerably lower in those cities than in Silicon Valley.

Proximity is important because upper management at all large companies spends far too much time on airplanes as it is. If they buy you out, people from their company are going to be spending a lot of time at your offices and it is a lot easier to deal with a studio that is within driving distance of corporate headquarters than one halfway around the world.

The strength of the local development community is important because it affects the sustainability of your studio. If you are located in a major development center, you always have access to a pool of talent—you can poach staff from other local developers, and in any event there is always some level of turnover and some availability of experienced people. If you are located in St. Louis, well, you may well have the best darn team in all of Missouri, but it is going to be hard to find good people if you need to expand—not many people from California are going to be interested in braving the Midwestern winter, even if you can get huge Victorian houses amazingly cheap in the Gateway City.

So, if you are a developer in New York City (high cost, small development community), negotiating with EA (a continent away), do not expect them to value your team very highly.

Who Will Value What You Have?

The usual answer is "the publishers," traditionally the main purchasers of developers; indeed, the proportion of games developed by third-party studios has declined precipitously over the last decade, as studios have been bought up and many have closed doors. There is some disagreement about whether this is a permanent trend; Bing Gordon of EA predicted last year that the age of the independent developer was over, but historically there have been periods in which the pendulum has swung back and forth.

A purchase by a larger developer (or merger with one) is also a possibility, but few developers have adequate cash to make purchases, and a merger with a private company is unlikely to provide the kind of liquidity event your investors presumably want.

Other possibilities do arise from time to time, but depend to a large degree on the fashions of the moment. For example, on a number of occasions in the past, large media conglomerates such as Time Warner and Viacom have been interested in acquiring assets in the game industry to establish a presence in an entertainment form where they do not currently participate except as licensors. Similarly, at present there is a high degree of interest in the game industry on the part of private equity investors (as evinced by the BioWare/Pandemic deal), and this may be an avenue worth exploring.

For developers in niche markets, a variety of other opportunities may exist. Mobile game developers will find that many mobile aggregators and nongame mobile content providers might consider an investment. Casual game portals such as Bigfish and Real might be interested in developers who provide the sort of games they carry. Advergame developers might be missing a good deal if they did not consider a sale to one of the major advertising agencies, almost all of whom do have some sort of game strategy at present.

In general, the more potential purchasers you have, the better off you are, and it is worth thinking about opportunities beyond the obvious publishers. What those opportunities are depend heavily on what sort of games you develop.

Researching Potential Buy-Out Partners

As with so many things in business, there is only one way to find a potential purchaser: network, network, network. You start, of course, with your own Rolodex; you already have business relationships with some publishers and other potential purchasers, and even if you do not know from the start who at those companies can make a buy decision, your contacts there can point you to the right people (and, ideally, serve as internal champions for the purchase).

As stated previously, however, you need also to look at nonobvious candidates, and here you will have to rely on second-order contacts. If you are venture-funded and want to investigate private equity purchasers, your VC investors can probably provide introductions. If you are an advergame company, even if you have worked directly with corporate clients, you can ask them what agencies they deal with, and in general, it probably is not too hard to find agencies with offices in your area.

More generally, it is worthwhile to ask trusted contacts for their suggestions, both because they may have ideas you had not thought of and because once the word starts to spread that your company is in play, potential purchasers you had not considered may show up unexpectedly.

Increasing Your Perceived Value

If you are contemplating an exit months or even years down the road, it is worthwhile looking for ways to increase your perceived value starting now.

Secure your own IP if feasible; look for ways either to recapture it from other partners, or negotiate clauses allowing a buy-back when finances allow. Consider purchasing licenses to IP to increase your perceived value if this is not too costly, even if you do not plan to exploit that IP in the near term. Also consider that IP includes the name and logo of your company. For more information, be sure to read the chapters on IP and IP licensing.

Consider embarking on new, high-profile, early stage development projects even without funding in place to complete them, and even if the announcement is largely smoke and mirrors; in other words, beef up your game pipeline, if you can.

Hire a PR agency—not to trumpet your availability for sale (you want to do that in a low-key way), but simply to get whatever coverage you can inside and outside the industry press, increasing your company's profile, so that the reaction of potential purchasers when you approach them is not "Who?" but "Oh yeah, I know them, they are supposed to be really good."

Make sure your business has as few problems and obligations as possible. Make sure your books are in order; any prospective purchaser will go over them carefully. If you have any pending lawsuits, tax issues, or other potential liabilities, try to settle them quickly.

If you are cash-poor, consider raising some interim capital. If you go into negotiations without enough money to carry you if (or when) those negotiations fall through, you are negotiating from a position of weakness—your negotiating partner can wait until you are on the brink and then low-ball you, knowing you have no real alternative but to fall into their arms to avoid shutting down. If you have reasonable prospects of selling, it should be possible to find investors—indeed, it's a pretty attractive investment to make, since it is a short-term investment. Of course, you sacrifice some equity, meaning you personally earn a smaller share of the ultimate selling price. However, the likelihood is that the sale price will be considerably higher in this case, because you will not be desperate for a deal, and some of the money can be used to improve your perceived value by, for example, securing IP.

Preparing for Life after Purchase

There are many questions you have to ask when selling your company. What are your personal objectives? What do you hope to gain by the sale? Do you simply want as much money as possible? Do you plan to continue managing your studio even after the purchase? Do you hope for a higher-level executive position at the purchaser? How much autonomy do you want once the sale is complete? Do you expect additional capital to expand operations beyond the sale price? Do you particularly care what happens to your staff, or to your games, after the sale?

You should also ask questions about the company purchasing your company to satisfy your needs. What is the corporate culture of your purchaser like? Is it a good match for the culture of your company? What do you need to work effectively with them? How likely is it that you will be replaced? What do they think they are buying? If they value you mostly for your IP and not for your team, is it likely that they will close you down and take the IP to another internal studio? How can you network to the purchaser's management hierarchy and persuade them to trust you and take you seriously? Are they going to pick up the whole company and move it to Florida (something that happened in 2005 to Hypnotix), and if so, are you willing to go, and how will your staff react?

Also consider what this means for your company and your career. What guarantees can you negotiate from the purchaser? What restrictions will they place on you personally? At a minimum, they will probably expect a multiyear noncompete—can you live with that? What employment contract can you negotiate for yourself? What about other team members? If the purchase is partly or wholly in stock rather than cash, what are the lockup periods and how rapidly can you liquidate your shares? (Yes, you want to do so; unless you are already rich, most of your net worth will be locked up in those shares after the sale, and even if you want to retain a stake in the purchaser, it is financially prudent to diversify.)

You *must* communicate frequently and openly with your board and your major investors during a purchase. Their interests may not be aligned with yours; they may simply want the highest possible price while you may be more interested in cash for growth and ensuring that life after the sale is comfortable; do what you can to reconcile your divergent interests and come to agreement with them. The last thing you want to do is present a divided front when it comes time to negotiate with your purchaser. Additionally, it is very likely that your investors have been through this stage of a company's life cycle many times, and are more aware of the opportunities, the pitfalls, and smart negotiating tactics than you; for VCs in particular, negotiating a sale is something they do all the time, and unless you are a serial entrepreneur, you probably have not been through this process before. While divergent interests can be a problem, there is also valuable expertise to tap here.

Think carefully about how to handle your staff. Any change in ownership, or potential change, is likely to be unsettling. The worst thing that can happen is for key team members to quit or raise a ruckus during negotiations. Consequently, you have a choice between keeping them in the dark or bringing them into the process from the inception. The first choice is not easy to sustain; if people from a half dozen publishers start showing up for lengthy behind-doors meetings, they will suspect that something is afoot. The second option increases the risk of problems, however. You may wish to consider granting key staff options exercisable on a buy-out to give them a personal stake in the sale. Additionally, if you are open with them, it is a good idea to get a sense of what they would like to see in a purchaser, and perhaps allow them to interact with people from the companies with which you negotiate to increase their comfort level with the process.

Downside Exits

Let us suppose you are running out of cash, your prospects of a sale are slim or nonexistent, and the likelihood of landing a development deal in the short term seems remote—not an uncommon situation for an independent developer. Remember that there is life after business failure, people tend to behave badly under pressure, and you still have responsibilities to your staff, your creditors, and your investors. Stay away from the damn bottle, pull yourself together, and get ready to make the best of a bad situation.

Your basic choice is between formal bankruptcy and an orderly close-down; an orderly close-down is vastly to be preferred if there is sufficient cash remaining to make it possible. Indeed, if you can bring yourself to do so, it is wise to keep a close eye on your cash, and pull the trigger before bankruptcy is the only option. If bankruptcy is where you need to go, you can pretty much forget about Chapter 11—developers don't generally have any stable cash flow, so relief of debts is not going to be sufficient for you to revive the company. Thus Chapter 7, liquidation, is the only option.

The first and most important objective (in either scenario) is to avoid criminal liability. Yes, this can be an issue; if you are liable for back taxes, they must be paid off, if at all feasible. Depending on their nature, officers of the company may be personally liable if they are not paid. Consult with your lawyers to determine the issues involved.

Second, if any of your staff has gone without pay for a period of time (not unusual in the circumstances), you may, depending on labor law in your state, be personally liable for back pay—and for payroll taxes on back pay. One possible option is to pay them minimum wage for the period; they will probably not be happy, exactly, but at least pleasantly surprised to receive anything. Make sure payroll taxes are paid on this as well.

Other expenses must be considered as well. Financial records will need to be stored for some time, in case of legal issues either with investors or with government agencies; retain enough cash to prepay storage for the necessary time. You will also need to find enough cash to pay legal bills for the paperwork necessary to close down the company.

Determine what cash remains, if any, and what debt is owed. The likelihood is that you do not have the resources to pay all remaining debts cleanly. Some liabilities can be shucked reasonably easily—if you are going out of business, you can probably negotiate your way out of your office lease. Pay off small debts in full; offer partial payment of larger ones. Return leased equipment and sell off any remaining assets.

It is unlikely that cash will remain once debts are dealt with; if any does, it will need to be returned to shareholders, or possibly a restricted class of shareholders.

Any IP the company retains at this point (including, say, game demos and concepts that were never funded) is probably not saleable—but you may want to obtain clean ownership of it personally (or with other founders). Your board may agree to this with the proviso that if any revenues are generated from these assets with the next few years, a portion is passed on to the remainder of the corporate shell. (This is not an option if you declare formal bankruptcy, as all assets, including these, will be administered by the bankruptcy court.)

Remember that even though all this sucks, you may work with your employees again—and may need to raise capital again for another venture. Try to retain as good relationships with investors and staff as you can. The reality is that you may have to "be creative" to creditors along the way—but do not lie to your employees or investors. Whatever you gain thereby will not be worth the loss of trust.

Other than for taxes and employees, try to minimize expenditures and maximize asset sales. Remaining assets will need to be returned to shareholders (or possibly a restricted class of shareholders).

Conclusion

Preparing an exit strategy requires you to start thinking differently about your business than you do at other times. Normally, your concerns are shipping the next game, keeping the doors open until you do, and landing the next development deal. However, if you are preparing to sell your company—either on the public market or to a private equity or corporate purchaser—your concerns need to be different. The questions you need to ask yourself are, what assets do we have? Who will value them? How can we increase our perceived value to potential purchasers?

Remember also that there really is no "accurate" valuation of your company's worth, so your sale price is ultimately based on the purchaser's needs and perceptions, rather than what your books say. As marketing people say, "all sales are emotional," and this is true whether talking about a $1 transaction or a $1 billion transaction. Consequently, you want to create an emotional environment that values your company highly, through selective publicity, connecting through people your targets are likely to trust, and perhaps associating yourself with brands with positive connotations (perhaps by acquiring licenses). Think of the process, in other words, as a marketing challenge—at a different scale, and with different potential purchasers than when selling a game, but a marketing challenge nonetheless.

CHAPTER 13

Virtual World Law

James Grimmelmann

james@grimmelmann.net

Virtual worlds are different. If you are making a single-player game, most of your work is done when the game ships. If you are making a virtual world, the work has barely begun. As Jessica Mulligan and others have emphasized, creating a virtual world involves running a *service*. That means taking responsibility for a large piece of server software. It means having an ongoing daily relationship with your players. And it means dealing with players' attempts to abuse the service. In this chapter, we explore the legal side of these issues by taking a close tour of the End User License Agreement (or EULA) that players agree to as a condition of being allowed to play.

Perhaps you are saying, "But I am not planning on having any legal problems with my virtual world!" Congratulations. You have put your finger on the best reason to read this chapter. *It is better to avoid legal problems than to have to deal with them.* This chapter will help you take concrete steps now so you will not have legal problems later.

Perhaps you are saying, "But I just want to focus on making my great design!" Congratulations again. You have put your finger on the second-best reason to read this chapter. *Design decisions have legal consequences, and vice versa.* As you make choices about how to make and run your world, those choices will shape your legal strategies. Moreover, legal problems are often just one symptom of design or customer-service problems that cause you all sorts of other trouble. Doing a legal audit, like doing a security audit, can help you flush out and fix small problems before they become big problems.

Perhaps you are saying, "But a EULA is an incomprehensible piece of legalese!" Again, congratulations. You have put your finger on the third-best reason to read this chapter. *The EULA is one piece of legalese it pays to understand.* Legalese can be like a new computer language: precise, powerful, and easier to learn than you would think. Because the EULA is the operative legal document that governs your relationship with your players, it is relevant to everything that happens in your world. This chapter will give you the basics you need to understand your own EULA and participate intelligently in drafting it.

After discussing some basics of how law fits into a world's various kinds of rules and of the drafting process, we will take a tour of the most common kinds of terms one sees in virtual world EULAs. Those terms will serve as an index to a great many of the design issues you will confront. For each term, we will try to identify three things. What potential problem does this term try to resolve? How does the new rule created by the term respond to the problem? And what spillover consequences can the rule have? You and your lawyer may or may not decide that this rule is the right way of dealing with the problem. But you deserve to make that decision consciously and with all the information you can accumulate.

When it comes time to talk about particular EULA terms, I am not going to give you specific legal language that would be usable in a real EULA. But as a way of anchoring the examples in reality, I will write out some legal pseudocode in a distinctive typeface, like so:

Author herein demonstrates the typeface for EULA terms.

Virtual Worlds Have Five Kinds of Rules

In games and in law, it is important to get the rules right. The choice of rules makes the game what it is. With different rules, chess would be dominoes. You as a designer are trying to make a game with satisfying rules, one that players enjoy. The key thing to understand here is that there are *different kinds of rules* in virtual worlds, and part of being a good designer is knowing how to use these different kinds of rules well together. We like to think of five kinds:

- The world's *software* establishes a baseline of what is and what is not *possible*. They are rules in the same way that the rules of physics are in the offline world.
- The *rules of conduct* tell players that some things, while possible, are still not *allowed*. These rules are enforced by your ability to punish players' avatars or to kick them out of the world.
- *Policies* are rules you *impose on yourself.* Doing things according to a consistent playbook makes life in-world more predictable for players.
- The *EULA* says that some things are forbidden in an even stronger sense. As a legal agreement between you and your players, it creates rules enforced by the *real legal system*.
- *Social norms* are the rules that *players create and enforce* against each other on their own. These rules are often not written down anywhere; they are just what players know about how to play well with others.

These five kinds of rules are your toolbox for keeping players in line and for protecting them from each other. If you understand their relationships to each other, you will understand which tool to pick up and when. Let us go through them in a little more detail.

Software

Most obviously, there are the rules of the software. Some virtual worlds are graphical; some are not. Some allow player killing; some do not. Some allow players to upload content; others do not. These design decisions are all decisions about the rules of the world. They are choices about what the software will allow players to do and what it will not. If the server software will not let your avatar walk through a wall or kill another avatar, that is a rule; it changes how you live in the world.

These rules of software are the basic substrate on which everything else builds. When players say that a world is or is not satisfying, they are thinking mostly of its software rules and its social norms. You need the other kinds of rules to fill in the gaps. But when the rules of conduct, the policies, and the EULA are working correctly, they should fade into the background, letting your perfect software-based world design shine in all its glory. Almost no one joins a virtual world because it has a fun EULA.

Rules of Conduct

Every virtual world—even the sadistically sexual *Sociolotron*—has some rules of conduct. These are rules, announced by the designers to the players, that forbid certain kinds of actions. What these rules have in common is that none of them can be enforced by the software alone. Take, for example, a rule against foul language. Anyone who has tried to write a spam filter knows that human *cre-8-ivitee* can always find a way past any given filter.

When players push too hard against the limits of what they can do and threaten to break your software or to ruin the experience for others, you have a reason to exercise your omnipotent powers over the virtual world to punish the evildoers. Your announced rules of conduct tell your players what behavior will make them in your eyes as "evildoers." Writing down the rules puts players on notice; with any luck, a few of them will be scared straight.

Something we will see repeatedly as we tour the EULA is that given the complexity of life in-world, you cannot hope to detail every last possible offense. Indeed, going into too much detail, listing the kinds of griefing or exploiting that are forbidden, will only cause some impressionable souls to start getting nefarious ideas. Two kinds of solutions come up again and again:

Fencepost rules: Sometimes, it makes sense to forbid more conduct than actually causes trouble. It is easier to enforce a rule against crossing the fence into the garden than to enforce one against picking flowers—even if all you object to is the flower picking. Fencepost rules keep people safely away from dangerous conduct.

General and specific prohibitions: It is common to give both a general prohibition on certain kinds of conduct ("No griefing.") and more specific examples of prohibited conduct ("No using sexually offensive terms."). The specific rules make it abundantly clear that certain core kinds of conduct are out of bounds; the general rule deals with loopholers trying to find something bad they can do that has not been explicitly forbidden. The specific rules make clear that the general rule does include certain important cases; the general rule makes it clear that the specific rules are not an exhaustive list. This combination also hedges your bets in case some court decides that the general version is not an enforceable term. This kind of cautious drafting is sometimes called "belt and suspenders" work, because careful lawyers do not take any chances that your pants could fall down.

Policies

The flipside of setting rules of conduct for your players is setting policies for yourself. The idea that you should write rules constraining yourself may sound silly, even paradoxical. But you are going to be writing these rules anyway, whether or not you show them to the players. If you get ten complaints of griefing a day, you will probably start following a consistent response pattern based on some mixture of habit and fairness. If you get 1,000 complaints a day, you are going to write that pattern down so your customer support staff has a consistent set of operating procedures. As your world and your staff grow, following consistent policies becomes not just sensible design practice but a business necessity.

Once you have a set of policies, the operative question is how many of them to explain to your players. This general problem of *transparency* is a recurring design issue. There are good reasons to be open or closed, depending on the context. Some reasons to explain policies include:

- It can save you customer-support work. Players will not come to you with problems that you have sworn you will not deal with, and they will come to you with issues you want to know about because you will respond quickly.
- It makes the world seem more understandable to players.
- It reduces players' suspicions about your motivations, because actions that might otherwise seem arbitrary are less objectionable if you are merely applying a well-known policy. If you suspend a player's account for a week for a specific violation such as corpse-camping, it is nice to be able to point to the section of your policies that says you suspend accounts for a week for corpse-camping.

Some reasons to keep policies secret include:

- It increases your flexibility. Some wiggle room can be useful in dealing with players who are determined to skirt repeatedly the edge of the impermissible.
- It avoids giving away the store. Policies that reflect details of your internal corporate structure or secrets of your operations are good candidates to keep under wraps.

The EULA

The job of the EULA is to make sure everything goes smoothly when the legal system interacts with your virtual world. The main way the EULA helps you is by putting legal muscle behind your world's *other* rules. A good EULA protects your world's rules in three ways:

It makes some violations of the other rules punishable with legal action. You want to be very serious about players not breaking certain rules. Yes, you can pretty much deal with foul language on your own. But if someone breaks into your servers, crashes the world, and starts deleting content, suspending that person's account is not going to cut it. You will want the Cyber Division of the FBI on the scene; you will want that perp behind bars; you will want a multimillion-dollar lawsuit to recover your damages. You should not expect to get all or even part of this list, but it helps to have an avenue that makes these consequences a possibility. When all your other rules fail, you want the law on your side.

It gives you the legal right to set the other rules. The last thing you need is some twerp telling you he has a First Amendment right to spam your chat channels with ads for discount OEM software and across-the-border prescription drugs, or some yokel suing you for nerfing her Sword of Infinite Pain into a Sword of Large but Finite Pain. The EULA makes clear that you run your virtual world, not the players—so they cannot go run and get legal intervention if they do not like the way you are running things.

It heads off legal issues that could threaten your entire world. The EULA can help you avoid getting dragged into legal trouble by your players. Governments do not like it when young kids play online games without their parents' consent. Copyright holders do not like it when people meet online to swap their copyrighted content. The EULA, together with appropriate policies and other design decisions, can help you keep third parties from getting angry—*lawsuit* angry—with you.

Social Norms

Social norms are a little different from the other four kinds of rules, because you as a designer have no direct control over them. They range from a guild's internal rules on sharing raid loot, to self-created "kid-friendly" play areas, to saying "hi" back when another player says "hi" to you. They can be incredibly complex and can change over time and from place to place in your world. They are rarely written down and new players learn them by example and experimentation.

You as a designer have no direct control over social norms. In fact, it would be a living nightmare if you did, if you could reach out into players' minds and *make* them behave the "right" way all the time. Instead, social norms are part of the natural and healthy life of a world. So, although some designs can encourage, discourage, or try to direct certain types of behavior, your players will remain independent-minded and generally do what they want. Players interact with your four kinds of rules and with each other and they develop a sense of who they are and how they relate to each other. Their social norms are a major part of what the world means to them. Designing and running your world in a way that helps foster your players' creation of thriving and fulfilling social norms is a difficult job.

For present purposes, just keep in mind that social norms are a key part of any virtual world. You will only confuse yourself if you try to understand the effects of other rule changes without accounting for the feedback effects of social norms. Sometimes, players solve their own problems through social norms that teach other players not to be jerks. To the extent that you can, you should make design decisions that help players create healthy and considerate norms.

How to Write a EULA

Do not even think about it.

Seriously. Do not write your own EULA. Find someone else—a lawyer—to do it for you. There are many jobs best done by trained professionals, and legal drafting is one of them. If you do it all by yourself, you are asking for 16 kinds of trouble. That does not mean you should not be involved. Your lawyer needs to understand what work your EULA will need to do, which means understanding the design and business model of your virtual world. And face it—the best person to explain your virtual world is you.

The rest of this chapter is a kind of checklist for you and your lawyer, with a list of topics the two of you should discuss. Your lawyer needs to ask you about them to understand what virtual worldly problems the EULA will have to solve. And you should know about them so you can understand the implications of the legal solutions your lawyer comes up with. You know virtual worlds; your lawyer knows law. If you are very lucky, your lawyer knows a little about virtual worlds and might even play in one. The two of you have to have a conversation in which you are absolutely certain that you understand each other's language well enough to know when you have come to an agreement.

This advice is particularly important for certain topics, the ones that don't fit under the blanket one-size-fits-all advice, because the details are too technical or situation-dependent. Lawyers have different ways of drafting particular clauses; virtual worlds have different issues. These are the topics on which you and your lawyer may have something important to tell each other—and are flagged here by "consult your lawyer."

Lawyers tend by nature to be fairly conservative. When it comes to drafting, conservative is good. If an issue could result in someone suing you, but the problem could be avoided by including a clause in the EULA, include it. You would feel incredibly stupid later if the absence of that clause were to come back and bite you hard. Lawyers are not cheap, but it is better to pay through the nose for a good EULA now than pay through the nose, mouth, ears, and tear ducts for a good litigator later.

Many clauses in a typical EULA are there to cover contingencies that might seem unlikely up front. They may give you rights you cannot imagine exercising all that often, even rights that may seem awfully overreaching. You can and should be much nicer to most of your players than the EULA, standing alone, would require of you. But the EULA is not there to protect you from your typical customer. It is there to protect you from your nightmare customer, the one who abuses everyone else, tries to crash the server, and then signs up again with a different name within minutes of being banned and starts the cycle of hate all over again.

On the other hand, more is not always better. Paradoxically, terms that seem too aggressive can be harder to enforce. Thus, for example, if your EULA says that you can repossess players' cars at will, well, good luck getting a court to enforce that one. It can also be bad business to have an overreaching EULA. Not that many players really join or quit a world because of its EULA. (Their concerns are more likely with play quality, community, and your customer service.) But a EULA with clauses that stick in players' craws can become a lightning rod for other discontents. (And players, being players, can usually find something to be discontented about.) Put on your player hat when you look over a EULA and ask yourself whether anything in it would make you outraged. (As we go along, we'll flag areas of particular concern.)

EULAs as Contracts

We begin with basic considerations. What does the legal system see when it looks at a EULA? The short answer is that it sees a contract between you and your players. We therefore begin by running through the contractual terms that help the legal system recognize your EULA and deal with disputes that arise under it.

Why EULAs Are Enforceable

Knowing why EULAs are enforceable gives us important information about what they can and cannot be used to do.

This Agreement shall bind the Company and the Player.

A EULA is a contract. Because your players freely agreed to its terms when they signed up to play, you can hold them to that agreement. In exchange, you give them the super-spectacular experience of playing in your virtual world. As a practical matter, you cannot actually *promise* that their experience will be super-spectacular. You will certainly try to make your world enjoyable, but legally guaranteeing that players will have the time of their lives would be arrogance verging on hubris. Instead, a typical EULA gives players more modest rights in return. Legally speaking, there are two sorts of rights involved.

Company grants to Player a limited license to copy the Software and Content.

First, players are using software you wrote to interact with a world you designed containing content you created. The software, the world, and the content are all protected by your intellectual property (IP) rights, especially copyright (see Chapters 6, "PR Plans and Programs for the Game Developer," and 7, "Intellectual Property," for more). Without some kind of license from the copyright holder (you), players would have little right to run the software. Thus, the name, "End User *License* Agreement."

Company grants to Player a limited license to connect to the Service.

Second, players are using your servers. The servers are your property. If you flip the power switch, the world goes away. And when the servers are on, no one can legally connect to them without your permission. Players need some kind of consent from you to make use of the service you provide by supplying the servers on which your world runs. Thus, the other frequent name: "Terms of *Service*" (ToS).

A EULA or ToS, therefore, consists of a bunch of restrictions you ask players to accept in exchange for certain specified rights to use your copyright-protected content or to access your service, respectively. The rights they give players are limited, but sufficient to participate in the world. These two perspectives are not mutually exclusive; some worlds have a EULA, some have a ToS, some have both, some have one document that uses both theories. Depending on your business model, one or the other may be more appropriate. Consult your lawyer.

In the absence of some kind of license, it is *illegal* for a player to copy your software or create an account on your servers. Such copying would constitute copyright infringement or a violation of the Computer Fraud and Abuse Act. These are serious, no-joking legal rules. They put a lot of muscle behind a EULA/ToS. The actual terms are contractual, but truly blatant EULA/ToS violators can be flirting with much more severe penalties. This legal force is something to help you sleep at night.

These harsh legal defaults, paradoxically, also provide a very good reason to have a EULA/ToS in the first place. You should not just assume that you can declare any player who displeases you a copyright infringer and ask the law to come down on him like a ton of bricks. A court is unlikely to decide that someone who just wanted to play in your world and would have agreed to any reasonable EULA is a copyright infringer just because you did not have a EULA for him to agree to. The court, instead, would probably find an "implied license." That means that the court will in effect *make up a EULA for you*, something that sounds reasonable to all concerned. That hypothetical EULA is likely not particularly sensitive to your concerns. In particular, it is not likely to include the swift justice you might have hoped for. If you have a clear EULA up front, everyone is happier. You can move quickly to fix problems, and players can be confident that they are on safe legal ground if they connect to your world and play nicely.

Finally, be warned that it is unclear exactly to what precise extent EULAs are enforceable. They are, in general, fairly enforceable. For example, clauses saying that you can exclude anyone for any reason are no problem. Similarly, clauses that prohibit players from hacking into or reverse engineering your servers have been doing well in court. Ditto for clauses saying that anyone who wants to sue you must do so in your home state. But no one thinks that *every* clause in a EULA would necessarily stand up in court. A clause forbidding Italian-Americans from playing would probably be struck down as against "public policy." Similarly, a clause that you could demand $10,000 from any player who fails to log in for a week could be deemed an unenforceable "penalty clause." It feels a little, well, *harsh* to the player, and that kind of gut feeling should signal to you that you might be getting onto shaky ground.

All in all, anything in a EULA that is genuinely important to your ability to create and market a successful world is highly likely to stand up in court. That category includes the vast majority of terms we will meet in this chapter. But it is only a matter of time before *some* term in *some* world's EULA is declared unenforceable. You may want to think a little bit about contingency plans for your more exotic terms. If you absolutely had to live without them, what would that do to your business model?

Terms Relating to Legal Process

Every EULA contains a few terms to make matters go smoothly in case the courts get involved. Because these terms deal with the legal process itself, they are not necessarily unique to games. They affect how and where you can sue and be sued, they deal with the interpretation of the EULA itself, and they affect what remedies a court could award. Use of them is part of a sensible strategy of legal risk management.

> **All suits under this EULA will be governed by the law of California and heard in a California court.**

We begin with two clauses that travel hand in hand in many contracts: *choice of law* and *forum selection*. Legal systems differ from place to place, both in terms of their procedure and in terms of the actual rules of law. These clauses manage the risk of being subjected to surprising law in an unexpected place by specifying what location's law will apply and where any suits must be brought.

Choice of law clauses are typically enforceable, as long as there is some not obviously strained reason to choose the place you do. The goal is more to select a particular known, stable source of law than it is to select the absolutely most advantageous law. It could be that some particularly egregious piece of doctrine would force you to choose the law of a different place, but more often, choosing the law of the state in which your offices are located is the most reasonable choice. Having your offices there is the textbook example of a nonstrained connection. Choosing your own state will also likely harmonize with your other legal connections to your home state, meaning that your lawyer will not need to worry much about multiple states' laws.

Because states themselves apply "conflicts of law" principles to figure out which state's law ought to apply in a given lawsuit, a clever subtlety seen in a number of EULAs is to insist that you are actually choosing *that place*'s law, not the law that place would choose to apply if it thought about it. (The possibility of infinite recursion, in which state A thinks that state B's law would apply but state B thinks that state A's law would apply, is called *renvoi* and is highly amusing to a small number of lawyers.) You will also occasionally see a EULA specifically exclude the application of a particular place's law, or of certain international sources of law (such as the Convention on Contracts for the International Sale of Goods).

Forum selection is slightly different—it involves choosing which court will hear the case. A federal court in state A, a state court in state A, and a state court in state B could all plausibly apply state A's law. The forum selection clause picks, in essence, which courthouse the lawyers will have to go to. Technically, "jurisdiction" only gets you down to the state level, and *venue* involves selecting a particular district within the state. Also be aware that federal and state courts use different districting systems.

Picking your home state is almost always a good idea; in case of a suit, it saves on travel costs, means not having to hire a local lawyer in addition to your own, and forces the other guy to come to you. It is important to get the wording of this clause right; you want the jurisdiction to be *exclusive*, so that your local court and *only* your local court can hear the case. You want to force them to have to sue you where you choose, not just give yourself the option to sue there. Forum selection clauses are also generally enforceable as long as the forum is not an unreasonable one. Choosing to be a "stay at home" litigant is usually reasonable.

If you elect this route, one legal subtlety that may be worth inserting is that the players waive any "personal jurisdiction" objection they may have to your chosen forum. That is another way of saying that they are not allowed to claim that they have so little connection to the place you have chosen that it would be unfair for them to have to be in a lawsuit there. This conclusion might be implicit in their agreeing to a EULA with you, or in their agreement to an exclusive forum, but it probably does not hurt to spell it out.

An important alternative—or perhaps, "qualification"—to a choice of forum is to select arbitration. Agreements to arbitrate are enforceable under the Federal Arbitration Act. Indeed, one of the rare pieces of virtual world litigation involved a virtual world EULA's arbitration clause being held enforceable.[1] Some virtual worlds choose arbitration in their EULAs; others do not. Arbitration is usually faster, cheaper, and probably more deferential to your EULA terms. Faster and cheaper could be good, or it could be bad (e.g., if you are relying on the high cost of litigation to deter suits). Consult your lawyer. The right answer may depend on the types of legal problems you deem most probable.

This EULA constitutes the entire agreement between Player and Company.

An *integration clause* basically says that the EULA means what it says, that there are no secret terms hidden in some other side agreement that isn't mentioned in the EULA itself. The *parol evidence rule* (nit-pickers be aware—the word is indeed "parol," not "parole") tells a court not to look beyond the EULA itself in determining what terms the parties agreed to. Anything not in the EULA does not exist. Including an integration clause is smart practice in drafting. It makes it more likely that the terms you inserted in the EULA will be upheld (by making it harder for someone challenging the terms to find a different "agreement" between the parties). It also reduces the cost of litigation (by narrowing the set of evidence relevant to interpreting the EULA). Similarly, another sensible term is one that dictates that only a written agreement may modify the EULA.

> **If any term of this EULA is held unenforceable, the remainder shall remain in effect.**

A *severability clause* tells a court what to do if some term in the EULA fails. Think of it as an exception handler that catches problems from other parts of the EULA. Good programs recover from the occasional memory allocation failure; good contracts recover from the occasional unenforceable term. The severability clause says that the loss of one term does not doom the EULA and that the rest should continue doing what it was doing before. Your lawyer will have the right wording.

> **Company will not be liable to Player for more than $100.**

An award of money damages is the normal remedy for breach of contract. Capping damage awards against you is one example of a limit on the *remedies* a player could obtain against you. "Remedies" is the term used to describe what things a court can and cannot do to set things right once it finds that someone has won a lawsuit. We will discuss this clause again in more detail later, when we take up the question of what harms your world could cause to a player.

> **Any breach of this EULA will cause irreparable harm, entitling Company to injunctive relief.**

There are also terms that affect the remedies you could obtain against players. This one is the most important; it appears in some EULAs. An injunction is a court order telling the losing party to do something *or else*. As discussed earlier, court orders are serious business, and getting an injunction can be much more effective than a damages award. That is especially true against people who may not have much money with which to pay an award. Against them, an injunction may be your only effective remedy. The part about "irreparable harm" is there so you will be able to satisfy the usual legal test for awarding an injunction. Courts are not supposed to award injunctions unless not awarding one would cause irreparable harm. Since proving irreparable harm can be difficult, getting players to stipulate to it might get you over a significant legal hurdle.

> **In any litigation under this EULA, the prevailing party shall be entitled to an award of attorneys' fees.**

In the United States, the normal rule for financing lawsuits is that each side pays its own lawyers. This rule can be modified by agreement. Some EULAs opt into the "English rule," in which the loser must pay for both sides' lawyers. This approach is designed to deter speculative lawsuits that have a small probability of success. These lawsuits against you (especially class actions) might be handled by lawyers on a contingent-fee basis—the lawyer will split any award with the clients, but take nothing if you win. Forcing the other side to pay for your lawyers is a way of creating potential downside for them and requiring them to take the risk of losing seriously. It can therefore deter some lawsuits. Of course, choosing the English rule also raises the stakes for you—if someone brings a successful suit against you, you could be on the hook for his or her legal fees.

Terms Ensuring that Players Play by the Rules

Now that we know why EULAs work at all, we can turn to the work they do. We start our tour with some basic "thou shalt nots." These are the terms governing what players will and will not do when they take part in your world. Most of them are essential to a virtual world's vitality. They keep players from acting in a way that could cause your world serious trouble. Here, the EULA is making absolutely sure that players have no legal right to do things that would destroy your world.

We slice those rules up into three categories. There are *ground rules* that make sure your players are real people who pay their bills and can be held accountable if they do something wrong. There are *game rules* that protect the world's software from being hacked or exploited. And there are *community rules* that make sure players play nicely enough not to ruin the experience for everyone else.

Ground Rules: Billing and Accounts

Even before players can enter the world, you need to make accounts for them. Assuming you charge your players at all, you only want to make accounts for properly behaved paying customers.

Player agrees to pay.

The term that confirms that players are obligated to play to pay may be the single most important term in your EULA. It can get quite complex in practice, because it is typically closely tailored to your billing model. If you sell monthly subscriptions, this term will explain that the payment is due every month on the same day. If you give out three months' access with the purchase of a starter kit, this term will explain that regular monthly billing will start for the fourth month. If you charge extra for access to additional in-world content, this term will explain the basics of your micropayment system.

Most EULAs do not specify the actual monthly fee or other prices; instead, they contain references to some other document containing the actual current rates you charge or some other clear description of "current prices." It is good enough if the

EULA explains the billing structure in enough detail that those who cared could easily find out how much playing will cost them. Whether you give refunds or not, your refund policy also typically goes in here.

Player authorizes Company to bill his credit card.

Something else you see in all EULAs is a term walking through the actual payment mechanics. Credit card is overwhelmingly the most common method of payment in the United States because of the good infrastructure and because it gives you some real-life information on your players to promote accountability. (With credit card information on file, you can, for example, reject registrations from a card associated with a known griefer, or more easily call the FBI on a hacker.) Thus, the most common payment mechanic term in an American EULA authorizes you to bill players' credit cards in accordance with the fees you have just explained. (Different systems, such as bank debits, are more prevalent abroad; this clause is regularly tailored to local conditions.)

This authorization is really important—consumers have extremely strong rights to reverse the charges on any payment they did not authorize, even if there is no dispute that they owe the underlying debt. Reversed charges suck for you, since dunning your customers individually is an enormous hassle, and exactly what using credit card billing is supposed to help you avoid. Ringing up "unauthorized" charges is also likely to violate your contract with the credit card empire.

If you read a lot of EULAs, you will often see a term that players are liable for any usage fees run up by their account, whether authorized or not. In addition to the accountability reasons for this term, it takes away some of the incentive for sneaky players to make false claims that "someone else" purchased all those elite items. As part of the basic mechanics of billing and making sure monthly charges go through properly, you will almost always see a term requiring that players keep their account information up to date and notify you promptly with any changes.

Player will keep his account secure.

It is hard to enforce user security. That is not to say you cannot try. EULAs regularly instruct players to follow basic security practices. Do not choose a weak password, do not reveal your password to someone else, and do not let someone else use your account. Reminding players that you and your employees will *never* ask for their password is, in this age of phishing, a sensible precaution. (That is a customer service commandment, too. Never ask your players for their passwords.) Interestingly, some EULAs actually warn players against using company-supplied features (such as password caching). This is not quite as crazy as it sounds; the idea is to emphasize that using features known to be riskier than normal is even *more* at the player's own risk than normal.

Everyone hates unauthorized account use, except for the blackguards who steal accounts; innocent players lose their stuff, their reputation, and sometimes their entire character. But without this restriction, you lose a lot of accountability. People called out for griefing can claim that their kid brother was using the account without permission. Are they lying? Telling the truth? You may have no way of knowing. When the line from avatar to player is muddled, it is hard to hold people responsible for the things they do in the world. It is hard for you, and it is hard for other players. Not that you or other players need to know who the actual player behind the avatar is; you just want to know that it is *consistently* the same person.

If you cannot actually make people keep their accounts to themselves, the next best thing is to make players responsible for *any* use of their account, whether it was them or not. Some EULAs explicitly state that players are responsible for any use of their account; some state that players are responsible for any harm flowing from various poor security practices on their part. Players who stand to lose out if they are bad about security might be scared into being maybe only mediocre about security. Good security happens only when the people with the power to undermine security have the right incentives not to.

A few types of account security breaches are worrisome enough that they often get their own terms. Sharing accounts with players who have been booted from the world is often a no-no. When you drop the banhammer, it should stay dropped. Helping a banned player back into the world is, for obvious reasons, itself a bannable offense. (Remember, on the Internet, you cannot easily tell if it is a friend helping Jack the Griefer get back in or just Jack himself with a different credit card.) This principle of collective responsibility often also extends to "related" accounts—if you ban someone, you may ban everyone using that name, credit card, IP address, or other specific information with them. Thus, many EULAs explicitly explain that all related accounts may be terminated for the sins of any. A clever little technique you see here and there is to cap the number of accounts per credit card or per person. The former is very easy for you to check—and few legitimate players need 20 accounts. If your world really does need players with that many alts, you should be billing them one large amount rather than in 20 small chunks.

Company or Player may terminate the account at any time.

All good things must come to an end. Sooner or later, your relationship with each of your players will end. A few terms in the EULA help you manage the breakup gracefully. As with a relationship, it is best if you can stay friends, but if they go crazy on you it is good to be able change the locks. Therefore, essentially all EULAs state that the company can end the relationship and terminate a player's account at any time, for any reason or for no reason at all. As a business matter, some of your customers will cost you more than they bring in. As a design matter, some players make the world worse. You want them out.

It is good practice to spell this possibility out in some detail. You should warn players both that you can terminate accounts at your unfettered discretion and about the consequences of termination. These warnings are aimed at heading off trouble from the "naïve" player who claims that he would not have cheated if he had known that you would wipe out his accomplishments and not refund the last two years of monthly fees. This section may also be a good place to state (or restate) your policy against using other accounts to regain access after being kicked out.

In addition to the general rule, you may also want to note some of the specific reasons why you can terminate an account. Violation of the EULA is A-number-1. Disruptive or illegal behavior is often worth a mention, too. In fact, you may see scattered throughout a EULA any number of clauses pointing out that such-and-such misbehavior is grounds for account termination, precisely because termination (or the threat of termination) is so often your best remedy for all kinds of trouble.

Your players have the right to go home, too. Some EULAs leave this possibility implicit, simply through the absence of terms requiring the players to keep playing. Other EULAs bring it up obliquely—they tell the players what to do if they no longer agree to the EULA (surprise, surprise: it involves not playing any more). Both are common enough that they are defensible, but you might want to be a little more explicit. Tell your players that they have the option to cancel their account and explain how. Remind them of the consequences of closing the account (the rules of conduct sometimes contain the appropriate warnings)—or tell them about a grace period within which they can change their minds and come back to the fold. A term pointing out a right that players enjoy is good for an overall tone of reasonableness.

Accounts are not transferable except as provided herein.

You may not want to allow truly unfettered account transfers. Front men opening accounts for other players create anonymity issues. If players can change accounts without warning, you will have people saying it was the *old* account holder going around being a jerk. Or, as mentioned before, you want to close off potential avenues for previously banned players to enter your game again. You may also want to avoid having players license out some of their rights to others; it may not be healthy for your business model or your design to have account brokers renting accounts out by the hour.

In general, you want to know whom you are dealing with. There are ugly contractual problems when third parties get involved—especially when some shyster of a player tries to give a third party more rights than he himself enjoys under the EULA. This kind of mess tends to cause trouble both for you and the third party, who may not have realized that the shyster was promising more than he could legally give. A EULA that clearly says "no assignment of rights" and "no transfer of accounts" can cut some of those issues off at the pass. As EULA violations go, unauthorized transfers are usually fairly harmless; banning them just gives you a foot in the door dealing with the small fraction of transfers that are troublesome.

That said, there are often very good reasons to allow transfers of accounts. If your world has a robust commercial economy and you look kindly on investors buffing up characters for sale, then you may not mind transfers. Allowing a transfer may also be a way of keeping a subscription even when the original player has had enough. Your best recruiters of new players, after all, are your current players. If a player's sister wants to step into his shoes, that might not be a bad thing from your perspective. Note that assignments of players' contractual rights that are not connected to an account transfer are almost invariably bad news. There has not been a compelling case for ever allowing them.

Thus, once you have set up a baseline of no transfers, you may want to insert a clause allowing *certain* transfers. You will probably want to set some limits on what kinds of transfers are allowed, based on your business and design objectives. For example, no transfers for any kind of compensation, or no more than one transfer per player, or no transfers of accounts to players formerly terminated by you, and so on and so forth. Consult your lawyer. You should not expect to get full compliance with whatever limits you set, but then again, you should not expect to get full compliance with anything in your EULA.

You will also need to set some procedural rules for transfers. A one-fell-swoop rule is typical and sensible. That is, the whole account, software, and password must be given from A to B in a single transaction that gives B everything and leaves A with nothing. Such a rule ensures that players do not use transfers as a backdoor to account sharing or account renting or other violations of the one-account-to-a-customer principle.

It is also a good idea to require players to tell you they are transferring an account. If nothing else, you probably need to update your billing records. It also gives you some ability to monitor the transaction to make sure things are on the up-and-up with respect to the things you care about. You should probably also require A to make sure B sees the EULA and notifies B that B must agree to it to play. That is mostly just another way of showing everyone that you take the EULA seriously. Further procedural mechanics of transfers are a good issue for you to consult with your lawyer.

Game Rules: Permissible Uses of the Software

Once you have the basics of account creation and maintenance down, you need to make sure an account can only be used in accordance with your overall design. Put another way, you need to guarantee the integrity of your software. Players should not be allowed to take unfair advantage of bugs in the software—and they certainly should not be allowed to introduce bugs deliberately.

Player will not hack or disable the servers.

Hacking is illegal. (Yes, the proper term for malicious hacking is supposed to be *cracking*. That linguistic war has been lost, and "hacking" is in more common use.) Even if you do not put a term in the EULA forbidding players from breaking in to your servers, the federal Computer Fraud and Abuse Act and various state laws forbid hacking. Violations of these laws can be punished with serious fines and even more serious jail time. That noted, your EULA still probably ought to say that hacking is forbidden and explain a bit what you consider hacking. Why? Because these laws generally punish the use of a computer system "without authorization." It is often up to you to spell out what uses of your service are and are not authorized. A good EULA here makes it crystal clear that no one is permitted to log on as an administrator except you.

Thus, you probably want to forbid breaking into the servers to change data or alter the nature of play. The definitions here can be a bit fiddly, so consult closely with your lawyer. Some EULAs try to define authorized access by requiring that players access the world only through the official client, which is not a bad way of excluding many different attack vectors. The prototypical offender here is the one who finds a security hole and starts teleporting everyone to the bottom of the ocean (as actually happened in *Shadowbane*®).

A EULA can (and probably should) also forbid denial-of-service (DoS) attacks on the world itself. The DoS offender is more often a script kiddie, acting out of sheer bored malice and trying to overwhelm your servers using standard tools. You may occasionally have to deal with more sophisticated attackers who craft attacks specifically at your world. (*Second Life*®'s scripting system has proven irresistibly attractive to attackers of this sort). Your first line of defense has to be technical—there is no time to run and get the law when the servers are crashing. But once the floodwaters are contained, you probably want the law to come down hard on the perps responsible.

Again, these things are often illegal even on their own, but it does not hurt you to be explicit that such attacks will not be tolerated. Many DoS attacks consist of taking something that would be legitimate if done once and doing it millions of times. Thus, it may be easiest to describe the forbidden conduct in terms of its scale or its effects on your service. "Unreasonable load" is a nice phrase you see in a number of EULAs—it captures the idea that no one should be doing anything that takes up far more than his or her fair share of your system resources.

Player will not hack the client software.

Well, that's half of the software out of the way. But the server is the easy half. There is still the client. You should, by the time you are drafting a EULA, have carried out a careful soup-to-nuts security review of your client-server architecture. That review will tell you how secure the client needs to be. Those needs, in turn, will dictate what your EULA should say.

At one extreme, you may not have any client security problems. If the integrity of your world does not depend on players using a particular client, then you can probably omit any discussion of hacking the client. Think of a game of online chess; it does not matter what board-visualization software the two players use to look at the pieces, because all they are sending back and forth are simple move notations and it is trivially easy to detect an illegal move. Similarly, in some text-based worlds, there is no client-side security issue because there is no possible way for anyone to gain an unfair advantage just by using a "hacked" piece of client software.

At the other extreme, you may be utterly dependent on having an honest client because the server completely relies on clients to keep track of state for it. If so, that is a bad place to be, because it is extremely hard to prevent someone determined from hacking a piece of software on a machine he controls. If you trust clients to keep secrets from a player, do not be surprised that some players can find out the secrets. ShowEQ is the classic example of modded client-side software; it displayed information the player was not intended to see. The Quake wallhack may be the best known.

Most worlds have requirements that lie somewhere in between. You should expect that some players will circumvent any expectations you make about using your client and only your client. Technical countermeasures remain your first line of defense. But for everything else, there is the EULA.

A few rules cover most of the common cases; select the ones that are appropriate to your world and your security model. You can require players to access your world using only your client software (this can be a good idea as a defense against incompetence and malice, as custom clients may well expose server issues). You can forbid players from modifying the client software. (A fencepost rule for this one is to forbid players from reverse engineering the client software.) If you are worried about interface overlays that reveal secret information to players, you can forbid players from monitoring or adjusting the flow of network traffic between the client and the server. If you are worried about gold farmers, you can forbid players from using "macro" programs that automate the actions their avatar takes. Having a term forbidding modified clients does not guaranteed that you will be able to recognize when a modded client connects—but if you do recognize a modified client you do not want to allow, it is better to have this term than not to have it.

There can be tricky complications here, depending on your design and your business model. If you want to allow clients modified in certain ways—perhaps to take advantage of your players' creativity in creating more usable interfaces or prettier skins—you do not want to forbid these particular modifications in your EULA. Note also that if your client includes open source software, you may not be legally allowed to restrict players from modifying it (only from accessing your servers using modified versions). This is one of the many reasons to be very careful about any use of open source software in a commercial game.

Player will not take advantage of exploits.

Hacking the software is not the only way for a player to get an unfair advantage. The sad truth is that there will be bugs in your design and implementation. A certain spell-weapon combo might one-hit-kill anything; a certain sequence of drops and trades might duplicate an item. The former bug can make a player unfairly powerful; the latter can make a player unfairly rich. Players taking advantage of these exploits can make the world quite unpleasant for everyone else—it is not much fun when jerks are strutting around ganking everyone in sight or when the economy is completely out of whack because of the influx of duplicated gold. Therefore, in much the same way that EULAs forbid hacking, they regularly forbid exploiting.

Anti-exploiting clauses are difficult, because exploiting occupies a conceptual middle ground—it is somewhere between in-world griefing-style misconduct and out-of-world hacking-style misconduct. This straddling makes it hard to draft these clauses precisely. Because an exploit is something that is allowed by the software, you cannot just define exploiting in terms of breaking or altering the software. Because if you knew what the exploit was, you would close it off in the software; you also cannot just define exploiting by specifying what exactly players should not do. The latest exploit will always be a moving target.

This is an area in which prohibitions that are too specific can backfire. Describing exploits in too much detail just encourages players to look for them and provides a helpful list of things to try. Since the main use of an anti-exploiting clause is to shield you from trouble if you close the accounts of exploiters, it should generally suffice if the clause is phrased in a way that puts players on fair notice of what they should not do. Telling them they should not use features of the world that obviously were not intentional is probably good enough.

You will also have to make difficult decisions about what to do with players who profit from exploits but do not take advantage of them. Simply deleting items you can trace back to a duplication bug may cause innocent players far downstream from the exploit to lose items they paid good in-game money for. On the other hand, there may be players closer to the exploit who were clearly complicit in it—they may have been gifted huge sums of cash for money-laundering purposes by the player who actually used the exploit. Distinguishing between innocent victims and conniving knaves is part of your customer service job (and one that comes up again and again). There is a lot of accumulated folk wisdom in the industry on how to do it, but you will still have to figure many of these issues out for yourself.

Finally, some—by no means all, but some—worlds' rules of conduct explicitly require players to tell the company if they find something they think might be an exploit. Now, yes, it would be great if all your players gave you that kind of feedback, but no, most of them will not. This rule is not there to punish everyone who never reported what might have been an exploit. It is there to provide a very easy-to-apply fencepost rule in case you know that a player was in on the exploit and helped keep it secret but did not actually *use* it personally.

Community Rules: Playing Well with Others

Now we cross from the technical to the social. The preceding rules might suffice for a contest or a single-player game—each player against the world. But since you are making a virtual world, you care about the interactions your players have with each other. You would like those interactions to be positive. So would your players. Most EULAs, therefore, contain a few terms specifically directed at reducing griefing.

Player will not engage in griefing.

As with exploiting, there is no single all-encompassing definition of griefing. In general, any feature you include that lets players interact provides a possible avenue for griefing. Players can grief by filling a chat channel with obscenity. They can grief by camping in fun spots and blocking anyone else from entering. They can grief by healing monsters other players are trying to fight. They can grief by cornering the market on particular items and refusing to sell at any price. They can grief by following other players around all the time, silently, just *looking* menacing. Things that are normal social interaction in one world may be griefing in another.

Therefore, a typical EULA contains a general-purpose anti-griefing provision. Sometimes this provision is folded in with other "you will not" rules; sometimes it is broken out as its own play-nicely-with-others rules. The rules of conduct or the EULA itself will frequently define many specific forms of griefing, too, but the general anti-griefing EULA term almost always reserves to the company complete discretion to define what is and what is not griefing.

You will also probably want to break out the details of some more specific forms of griefing in your rules of conduct or your policies. In some cases, clear and simple rules will work—for example, "Do *not* use language not suitable for a PG-13 movie." Simple rules are easy for your customer service reps to implement—there is little to argue about if they catch a player using slightly misspelled cusswords. (Where these rules are especially simple, you can even put them into your software.) Using software to screen offensive language can lead to unintentional, even amusing results. In some MMOs, the common "bastard sword" (a sword that can be wielded with one hand or with two) becomes the "@%$^&!! sword." For other cases, you will have to use vaguer standards—for example, "Do *not* ruin other groups' raids."

Your sense of what is and what is not griefing should be responsive to your player community's sense of what is and what is not griefing. If they honestly do not care about something, then ask yourself whether it is something you should care about. (Of course, if 35% of your players love a particular behavior that the other 65% abhor, it is not easy to say that the community does or does not approve of the behavior.) The stream of complaints to customer service will give you a good snapshot of what is bothering players inordinately.

Your players may also care vehemently about something you do not want to or cannot easily police. Players can be surprisingly effective in suppressing some kinds of unwanted behavior. (Check out the codes of conduct of some high-level guilds, for example. Chivalry is not dead.) With this possibility in mind, some worlds have tried to take a completely hands-off policy and let players sort out everything on their own. It rarely works. Players need to have substantial power over each other to deter griefing; but if they have that sort of power, your world may well be in the hands of vigilante mobs. *EVE-Online* and *A Tale in the Desert* have each gone some distance toward true community enforcement, but neither has been free from serious issues. The *Sims Online* remains legendary for the sociopathic chaos created by lax enforcement of anti-griefing rules.

Player will not cause grief by . . .

Several classes of griefing are serious enough that they regularly merit mentions in the EULA or rules of conduct of almost every world. For the most part, these types of griefing are serious enough to be causing a player real harm, not just the frustration of having a playing session spoiled.

Offensive statements: People who make offensive statements, such as those against a certain race, are abhorrent whether in the offline world or the virtual world. You probably do not want loudmouthed bigots in your world, and neither do your players. The same goes for statements insulting players for their religion, gender, sexual orientation, nationality, and so on.

Harassment: Sometimes, people want to be offensive to one person. That is pretty odious, too. There are jerks who will wage total and unceasing war on some innocent schmoe for the sheer jollies of it. These jerks are griefers.

Espousing evil: What should you do if you see a guild calling itself the "Mudville Anti-Semites?" Many European countries outlaw "hate groups" and do not draw much of a distinction between online and offline ones. Even if the Mudville Anti-Semites have not yet gone out and picked on any avatars with Jewish-sounding names, many Europeans would have a strong gut reaction that your world should not be endorsing a group like that. Some EULAs therefore forbid membership in hate-mongering groups.

Stalking: Not cool in offline life; not cool in virtual worlds. The creepiness of being followed and watched can be deeply disturbing—especially to players who have had prior bad experiences with unwanted attention. What is more, it is a distinct possibility that an in-world stalker may be looking to learn enough personally identifying details to become a stalker in the offline world as well.

Outing: As the stalking example indicates, linking up an avatar to an individual can cause serious trouble. In most worlds, players join with an expectation of privacy; they want to be free to take on a new character in-world, and they *do not want* someone they met online showing up on their doorstep or calling their employer to complain about what a jerk they are. Some worlds, that are otherwise extremely tolerant of player conduct, treat outing another player's real identity as a bannable offense.

Sexual abuse: Cybersex, like sex in the offline world, should be consensual. Unwanted in-world sexual advances can be highly unpleasant. The greatest piece of virtual world journalism ever, Julian Dibbell's article, "A Rape in Cyberspace," detailed the degrading consequences of an in-world description of a rape and the degree to which the rape was a blow against the world's entire community. Your world can and probably should be a safe space.[2]

Denial of service: Perhaps the most childish kind of griefing is slamming an open palm on the keyboard and filling everyone else's chat window with junk repeatedly. This same pettiness causes players to make thousands of the same item to slow down the server, to stand in doorways, to send unwanted party invites, to throw up the largest possible buildings to block views, and make any number of other pure peeing-in-the-swimming-pool moves. If its only purpose is to ruin things for others, it is griefing.

There is, it should be noted, such as thing as going too far. If you stamp too hard on griefing, you start stamping on fun, too. Blizzard was so zealous about its anti-harassment policies, for example, that it took action against a guild that had the temerity to call itself "GLBT-friendly." Why? The explanation Blizzard provided was that homophobes might have been so outraged by such a guild that they would go out and commit acts of harassment. The move was counterproductive—it made *World of Warcraft* less tolerant, not more, and made the world a worse place. Blizzard backed off once public attention shone on the incident. If you take your anti-griefing policies too far, you just wind up helping the griefers.

Player will behave honestly in all dealings with the Company.

If your world is like most worlds, you need to keep the lines of authority in-world clear. You are in charge and you will fix things if there is trouble. Players are not in charge, but they can come to you if there is trouble. Many EULAs and rules of conduct contain clauses designed to keep players from subverting that relationship through dishonesty. Here are four forms of subversion to watch out for:

A player could lie to you during an investigation. There is usually no good reason for a player to lie to you during an investigation of a legitimate misconduct issue. If you are investigating a possible duping bug or a harassment claim, you expect players to tell you honestly what they were doing.[3] Of course, you have records of everything (and you *do* have records of everything, right?), but it is typically going to be easier and faster to interview the witnesses. Lying to you is like punching a crossing guard.

A player could lie to you about another player's activities. That is like falsely telling the crossing guard that someone else is breaking into cars. At best, it is a waste of your time. At worst, if you did not properly check the reports against your records (and you *do* properly check reports against your records, right?), innocent players get punished for things they did not do. Lodging false accusations is a griefing issue—players who do it are using the complaint system as a griefing tool.

A player could impersonate you. That is like putting on a crossing guard uniform and luring kids into traffic. Jerks who do this cause other players fear and confusion. They also make it harder for people to come to you with legitimate customer-service issues because they are less sure who is the real you. You do not want players impersonating you, your customer service, or your in-world characters. (Related terms sometimes forbid players from falsely claiming that they have your endorsement or protection, and forbid players from naming their characters with names that would suggest some official connection.)

You could impersonate a player. No, seriously. To the extent that you have your employees running around in the world with alternate characters, players may be suspicious that the employees are rigging things to favor their own characters. That makes them treat you with more suspicion, which undermines the trusting friendly relationships that make things run smoothly. It can be good practice not to let your customer service people play characters on the servers they administer. There is a more general rule of thumb here: have policies in place so that people with positions of power over the world do not abuse that power.

Business Rules: Not Competing with You

A few miscellaneous "I promise not to" terms involve things players should not do because they threaten your ability to run the world successfully. We will talk about three:

You retain the IP rights beyond the ones players need to use the world at all. It is a EULA violation for a player to use your artwork and plot elements in a movie without permission, for example.

Similarly, you retain the IP rights over your software. It is a EULA violation for players to set up their own server and hack your client into connecting to it.

Players agree that you are not their employer. It is a EULA violation for them to claim that you owe them minimum wage for their many hours of play.

What do these terms have in common? Loosely speaking, they are all about what lawyers might call "unfair competition." When you invite players into your world, you are showering favors on them—giving them access to pretty pictures, space-age software, and unforgettable experiences. You are not inviting them to grab those resources and run to set up their own competing world, or to do something that would destroy your business. If they want to compete with you, they will need to put in the honest effort to create their own game assets, software, and customer support.

You neither can nor should forbid players from doing absolutely everything that might cause you trouble. *Project Entropia* has a term in its EULA forbidding players from spreading rumors about it. That is just plain wrong to require. If you are receiving criticism, stop it by fixing the problem or counter it by explaining your side of matters. The same game made headlines in 2006 by publicly and repeatedly accusing a respected Wharton Business School professor of slander for posting criticisms that questioned the newsworthiness of *Project Entropia*'s projects. Trying to silence your critics just creates even bigger PR problems.

> Company retains all IP rights not expressly granted to Player.

How would you like it if someone opened up a virtual world that copied your artwork, your geography, and your physics down to the last detail? Unless your goal was to build an open-source free software world, you would probably be pretty ticked off. You spent a lot of time creating those resources, and the law recognizes that effort and the substantial originality of your creations by giving you a copyright for them. Indeed, it gives you a copyright precisely so you can sue thieving scum who just copy everything you make wholesale and do not create anything original of their own. Just to make things clear, your EULA can explain that you will use that power of copyright to go after outright plagiarists among your players.

Similarly, players who use your trademarks on their own goods may not be doing you any favors. If another world starts up with the same name, new subscribers may get tricked into playing the wrong one. (That is called "infringement.") If the Internet is filled with sites that use that name to sell cars, t-shirts, discount Canadian pharmaceuticals, and other random junk, the virtual world at the core of it may get pushed aside in people's minds. (That is called "dilution.") And if that random junk is really terrible, people may start thinking that your world itself is shoddy. (That is called "tarnishment.") Your EULA can *remind* players that your trademarks are yours and that it is not cool to slap those trademarks all over the place without permission.

There are two distinct scenarios you should be thinking about here. First, there is the *competing world*: a world that tries to free-ride on your creativity and work. Now, as a designer, you would love nothing better than for hundreds of your players to be so inspired by your monumental achievement that they go out and pour their hearts into making virtual worlds—and in every interview, saying it was your brilliant design that inspired them. That is the community of designers building on its past successes with fresh innovation. That is a big part of how you are working, too—learning from past worlds, both what they did right and what they did wrong.

Now, legally ideas are not copyrightable, even if they copy many ideas from you. And even if their world copies a bunch of mechanics from yours, honestly, it is probably not hurting you that much. The reviewers will still say, "This has been done better before. Go play INSERT YOUR WORLD HERE instead." Your IP protection is a nuclear weapon, best dropped only in cases of obvious plagiarism with no offsetting creativity whatsoever. Like nuclear weapons, it can also be expensive to employ (as explained in the IP litigation chapter), but it is not one you should generally plan to be without, even if you have little expectation of needing to drop it.

The second core scenario is *merchandising*, T-shirts with your world's logo, action figures, novels explaining the world's mythology, such as the movie tie-in, the breakfast cereal, etc. Unlicensed merchandise siphons off a revenue stream you could profit from and can seriously hurt your reputation—or even your ability to protect your trademarks at all.

Once again, however, you need to be careful about overplaying your hand. Some merchandise is good merchandise; good licensing can pay you with publicity, not just with cash. If your world does not have an extensive network of fan sites, you are at a serious marketing disadvantage. Fan sites are a sign of deep engagement with the world; they allow players to create rich communities that build on their presence in the world. People wondering if they should join your world may judge it by the information they glean from fan sites.

One approach some EULAs take is specifically to create a "fan license" that lets players use your copyrights and trademarks for fan-like noncommercial purposes. It is generally better for people to be doing something with permission—from your perspective, there are trademark reasons why turning a blind eye to infringing uses is a bad strategy; from players' perspective, it is more secure to know that you approve of what they are doing and will not get angry.

One last note about writing EULA terms that allow or forbid various out-of-world uses of your IP: this may be the touchiest subject of anything in your EULA. You are dealing with people's creative engagement with something that is emotionally important to them. That means that they can get deeply, almost irrationally upset if their connection to it is threatened. Going after fan fiction is a surefire way to profoundly alienate some of your best players. Spelling out what players can and cannot do with your content in too much detail is also risky—you may come across as too corporate and legalistic. Again, there is potential PR trouble lurking. (More on these types of issues can be found under "Contingency Planning" in Chapter 6.)

It takes a deft touch to write these terms properly. Consult your lawyer, and your marketing and customer service gurus. Listening sensitively to player feedback, while always important, is also especially critical here. How you frame and phrase your policy matters as much as the rules of the policy itself.

Player will not misuse the client software.

Everything mentioned previously about unfair plagiarism of the world's content also applies to the world's software. In practice, you probably do not need to worry much about players ripping off your server software; they just do not have access to it. Players ripping off your client software, though, is another matter. What might they do on their own with the client that you would not like? They could *hack the client so it connects to their own private server*. If you are running on subscriptions, that is a direct attack on your business model.

How much you should worry about private servers depends on the nature of your world. The more content you supply, the harder it is for private servers to compete. The more stuff you automatically download to your client, the richer the experience that client-modders may be able to create on their own. The more that players depend on you and your top-notch community-building skills to create a fun and rich shared environment, the less attractive private servers become.

This end-run around your servers has a lot in common with other hacking-based techniques. It also involves modifying the software, but can be even more undetectable than other client modifications, because the private server user may never connect again to your servers. It also triggers similar legal countermoves on your end. There are copyright laws you might be able to invoke; there are aspects of the DMCA you might be able to invoke. Putting a term in the EULA lets you invoke contract law, which is a more direct route to the same end.

This happens to be one of the few litigated EULA issues for virtual worlds. A group of fans of Blizzard's computer games created their own server software, called "bnetd," to be compatible with Blizzard's own matchmaking service, Battle.net. (This was in the days of *Diablo* and *Warcraft*, before Blizzard's fabulously successful foray into true virtual worlds with *World of Warcraft*.) Blizzard sued the open source hackers behind bnetd and won.[4]

This also happens to be one of the most politicized issues in virtual world law. The bnetd hackers *loved* Blizzard's games and wanted to make the games even better. They just did not want to have their entire online experience with the games be entirely at Blizzard's discretion. They were not in it for profit, just for fun. And, all in all, they only made small modifications to the client software. All of these factors made them quite attractive to those people who think that companies have too much power over virtual worlds and that players should have more explicit rights. Being able to take characters and status and go off to another server would provide players with a major counter to developer control.

On the other hand, developers were almost uniformly equally strongly on Blizzard's side. If players can mod the client software in this way, the whole subscription business model could be in danger. It also reduces developers' control over their worlds when players have other ways to play in the "same" world. (Why should a player behave nicely when the developer can only kick them out of one version, not from all versions of the world?) And this vision of an open source virtual world that steals assets from an existing game can also be seen as an attack on the work of professional developers who get paid to create and run worlds. Little wonder why professional developers often do not like it.

This remains a complicated subject capable of arousing high passions. The relevant EULA terms, for now, are usually folded in with other anti-hacking provisions. You should be able to look at a term and know what kinds of hacking it prohibits—and you should be choosing to prohibit those that genuinely concern you. Even before you consult your lawyer, you need to think carefully through how your world works and what kinds of uses of the software are incompatible with your vision.

Player is not an employee of Company.

If you have employees, you probably already know about labor law. (If you do not—run, do not walk, to educate yourself about it. Read Chapter 11, "Taxation," to learn more as well. You can worry about your EULA later. Your employees are your first responsibility in development.) You have to pay your employees at least minimum wage; you may need to give benefits to full-timers; you have to allow them to unionize if they wish; and so on. Now ask yourself, what if your players were your employees? And you had to pay them, give them health coverage and workers' comp, and suchlike. Unless you are creating a very particular kind of virtual world (e.g., a virtual union hall), it would probably destroy your world.

Thus, it is essential that your players not be treated as your employees legally. Throwing a term in your EULA that they are not is a useful first step, but you also have to act like you mean it. You cannot treat your players—or even just some of them—like employees unless you mean it.

Back in 1999, a group of former AOL chatroom-monitor volunteers sued AOL, claiming that they had been *de facto* employees and were owed back pay. A few years later, some Ultima Online guides did the same to Electronic Arts. In each case, the former volunteers claimed that they were acting as junior customer service representatives, doing the work that would be done by employees, with the kind of supervision used for employees... but without the pay that would go to employees.

Both lawsuits settled, and the lesson for the industry was clear: volunteers are not substitutes for customer service staff. It is okay to give particularly enthusiastic and committed players some perks for being nice and good. (And it is okay to make the full leap and hire them on as real employees.) But you cannot turn around and start assigning them particular tasks with guidelines on how the tasks are to be done, schedules, and supervision. That could make them employees under federal law (or enough like employees to bring a very annoying class action lawsuit). Consult your lawyer on where to draw the line safely.

Terms Giving You the Power to Set the Rules

It is time to change gears. So far, we have been discussing all of the "thou shalt not" terms in the EULA. These terms are directed at players; they tell players what to do and what not to do. Now we are going to swing the camera around and look at *your* side of the picture. We are going to talk about what the EULA has to say about what *you* can and cannot do. Unsurprisingly, a typical EULA does not contain too many substantive limits on your actions. Instead, just as the previous terms were about keeping your players from ruining your world with actions, the terms here are about keeping them from ruining your world with lawsuits.

These terms are divided into three general categories. First, the EULA explains that there are *no warranties* with your world; you do not guarantee players that everything will always work as they expect. Second, it makes sure you have the power to *enforce your rules* against violators. Third, it protects your power to *make changes*.

You Are Not Required to Be Perfect

We begin with a family of terms that are genuinely universal in EULAs. Toward the tail end of almost every EULA, you will find two paragraphs mostly in all caps. The first is usually titled, "DISCLAIMER OF WARRANTIES," or some such; the second is usually something like "LIMITATION ON LIABILITY." Together, these paragraphs stand for the proposition that players cannot sue you if something goes wrong with the world. Or to put matters another way, you are allowed to screw up in your administration of the world without it being grounds for a lawsuit.

The language in these passages is generally extremely standardized. You are not likely to find a more stylized piece of legalese anywhere else in a EULA. Why? Because these terms have been battle-tested. Many businesses besides virtual worlds have needed to limit their liability with respect to the services they provide. These phrases have been carefully worked out by lawyers over the course of decades. Lawyers do not like to mess with success.

In part because these clauses are so standardized, you do not need to worry too much about the inner workings of them. If you want to start in on to *how this affects me*, just skip the next two paragraphs. If you are curious about the law involved, read them.

A "warranty" is a promise you make to someone buying something from you that the thing has a particular property. You could, for example, "warrant" that it will work, that it is been manufactured properly, or that it will not bring all life in the universe to a catastrophic end. Even if you do not explicitly make these promises, the law sometimes treats you as having implicitly made certain particular warranties merely through the act of selling. The DISCLAIMER OF WARRANTIES section runs through all of these warranties that lawyers can imagine, both explicit and implicit, and says that you *do not* make them. You are trying to supply a virtual world with the absolutely minimal set of warranties the law will let you supply.

Instead of talking about *causes* of trouble, the LIMITATION OF LIABILITIES talks about *results*. It states that you are not responsible for certain kinds of "damages," *damages* being the law's word for bad stuff that happens as a consequence of someone else's actions. As with warranties, there are many kinds of damages the law lets you say "not my problem" to. Thus, for example, you are not responsible for "lost profits"— the money someone lost when his business did not do as well as he'd hoped. As a backup in case a particular limitation does not hold up in court, these clauses also set a specific dollar limit—for example, $100, or maybe the amount a player has paid for the world in the last six months.

In addition to these fairly boilerplate cores, EULAs often provide additional specific disclaimers and warnings. These provisions tend to be scattered around a EULA, depending on the organizational choices its drafters made. But they share a common structure. The EULA points out something that could happen, something a player might consider bad. The EULA then says that it is *not your fault* if that bad thing happens. The player will not be allowed to bring a lawsuit against you on account of that bad thing.

Consult your lawyer to pick the exact list of things to warn about and deny responsibility for. In the rest of this section, we will catalog the most common specific bad things that EULAs flag.

Company does not provide all resources required to use the Service.

You would be amazed at what some people fail to understand about computers. In this age, as the popularity of virtual worlds explodes, the left tail of the normal distribution curve of cluefulness among players slides farther and farther to the left. Some of your players will be so unfamiliar with virtual worlds that they think that all they need to play in your world is to buy the software. They will forget about the part where they need to own a computer and connect it to the Internet. They will forget that they need to install the software. They will forget that you are not the same people as the retail store where they bought the software.

Thankfully, very few people are that clueless. Their numbers are probably greatly exceeded by the number of people who would be willing to claim they are that clueless for the sake of a good lawsuit. Therefore, EULAs regularly contain warnings about these basic facts. The point is not so much that you expect the clueless to read the EULA and suddenly become clued in. No, you are just putting a warning in a document they are legally presumed to have read, so they cannot later sue you on the grounds that you should have realized you would have players who did not understand aspects of virtual worlds that seem utterly obvious to you.

One warning that is more or less universal is that players need to supply their own Internet connectivity, and that such connectivity may cost them over and above your subscription fees. For people who are familiar with single-player games, the entire online world phenomenon *is* a bit of a mental shift. That is part of what makes virtual worlds special; it is what sets them apart. If you had never used a virtual world before, you might perhaps be forgiven for assuming that the virtual world subscription included the costs of the dial-up involved in playing. (That was, after all, how an older generation of gaming networks worked.)

Company does not guarantee that the Service will be error free.

Among the more flattering of the naïve assumptions players may make is that you are infallible. They expect your world to function perfectly, to be utterly bug-free, and to be accessible at all times without interruption. When this assumption breaks down, players can get incredibly frustrated. They *need* their fix of your world, and they *need* it now. A ten-minute outage is a disaster; a ten-hour outage is like unto a living death.

You therefore have a very good business reason not to make coding mistakes and not to let your server crash. Doing so frustrates players, breaks the sense of immersion, and can drive off happy customers. On the other hand, bugs and crashes are pretty much inevitable. The world will go down at times, and you will need to take it offline to patch severe server issues.

Thus, you hardly need a legal incentive to keep your world running well, and you do not want legal trouble when the bugs do hit you. These motives combine in the EULA term that warns players that the world may have bugs and may not always be available. You can warn them that the service may not always be available. You can warn them over and above that first warning that circumstances outside your control may make it impossible for you to keep the world running. The legal term for this is *force majeure*—some outside force that would overwhelm anything anyone could do.[5] You can reiterate that in neither case will you be legally liable for anything. Consult your lawyer on how strong and how unconditional the terms ought to be—some EULAs promise that you will take reasonable care, some promise nothing.

Typically, these clauses emphasize that you will not pay refunds for any periods when the world is inaccessible. Given your business model, you might agree to a pro-rated rebate for extended interruptions. Other worlds have been known to grant membership extensions for substantial interruptions. For example, eBay® extends auctions by the length of any outage—there might be an appropriate analogue for some virtual worlds. A few worlds do actually warrant that the software will meet users' needs to use the world. If you limit your liability to giving refunds, this can actually be a perfectly reasonable thing to do. (Note that these warranties still exclude cases in which the software has been hacked or modified between the company and the player.)

Sometimes, the outage clause also explains that you do not guarantee that the world will be bug-free. Sometimes, it is a separate clause. Either way, EULAs typically warn players that bugs happen, and that players' status, achievements, and in-world property may be affected or erased as a result. The details of such a term may, of course, need to be tailored to the types of stuff in your world.

Company does not guarantee that the Service will not harm Player's computer.

Software can fail in worse ways than simply not working. In light of the security problems in modern computers, it is entirely possible for a bug to cause system-wide instability, erase valuable data, or leave a computer vulnerable to hackers. You may not intend any of these results, but it is possible that they might happen. Let us not forget that your client software probably automatically downloads updates. Just contemplate for a moment what could happen if a hacker were able to sneak his own code into one of your updates.

Actually, the more common danger is not that your software *actually* damages some player's computer, but that a player *thinks* your software damaged his computer. Especially when the relevant computer is, by hypothesis, damaged, it can be quite difficult to reconstruct what caused a problem. Either complex software interactions among other stuff running on the computer or plain old user error could cause trouble for which you are (possibly unfairly) blamed. A EULA clause explaining that you are not responsible for damage to computers does the trick. Typically, this clause is folded in with your general disclaimer that you do not guarantee that the software will be error-free.

Three particular issues here deserve at least passing mention. First, "virus-free" is an increasingly common phrase in EULAs. That is a fairly sensible way of recognizing one common bug scenario—your software may be infected with a virus or backdoor of unknown provenance. A virus might sneak into your software via the reuse of bad code under license from someone else, a malicious employee, incompletely secured distribution servers, or rogue third-party sites distributing modified binaries. It is worth pointing out that you cannot 100% guarantee it will not happen. Any time users install any software at all on their computer, they need to evaluate the risk of malware. Virtual worlds are no exception.

Second, some kinds of software are riskier than others. *World of Warcraft*, for example, uses a client that aggressively scans the computer on which it is installed for evidence of cheating utilities. Some activists call the client "spyware" for its surveillance; be alert, however, that this kind of aggressive scanning is also riskier in a software-stability sense. If you try to take out cheat programs, you may take out legitimate ones as well. For this reason, Blizzard specifically discloses that its client software engages in this scanning and specifically disclaims any legal responsibility for the consequences. This is smart; if your software poses special risks, you should disclose those risks. Failure to do so can have serious legal consequences; just ask Sony/BMG, which was forced to settle a lawsuit after it installed software on users' computers to keep them from listening to its CDs using a music player of their choice. The techniques the software used to keep users from uninstalling it created security holes that made the computers more susceptible to viruses and other malware.

Finally, note that these disclaimers are closer to the fringe of enforceability than many EULA terms are. If your software completely toasts players' computers, you will be an unsympathetic defendant. (You will also have a massive public relations problem and will probably be having business issues attracting players anyway.) If it can be shown that you knew of the risk, or worse, knew but did not care that it would toast some players' computers, you may have an especially hard time. Some states simply do not allow you to disclaim responsibility under those circumstances at all. Consult your lawyer to understand how much protection the EULA buys you here.

Company does not guarantee that the Service will not harm Player.

For similar reasons, EULAs typically explain that you will not be responsible for harm that players themselves suffer as a result of playing. The issues are mostly the same as those posed by harm to computers, but since it may not be immediately obvious how a world could harm its players, a little discussion of some potential scenarios is in order.

One significant cause of harm—and one that many worlds warn players about in a dedicated clause—is that some players may be jerks. As jerks are wont to do, they may harass, defame, stalk, or grief other players. (In general, they may do any of the things you tell players not to do in a EULA.) Some of these forms of harm would be grounds for a real lawsuit, so it makes sense to tell players not to engage in them and to warn other players that some players may be jerks.

Another troubling issue is addiction. There are reported cases of virtual world players who have died during extended playing sessions without proper nutrition and rest. Some players may spend too much time in-world, to the detriment of their relationships with other people, their health, and their livelihood. No company has yet been held legally responsible for such addiction, but there are some rumblings suggesting it might some day happen. Designers do often deliberately try to make their games very engrossing—after all, "addictive" is generally a synonym for "fun" in game reviews. The moral responsibilities of developers (and other players) who make virtual worlds that are not just compelling but *too* compelling are still being worked out. Legal shifts may follow.

Virtual worlds, like other forms of entertainment, might occasionally cause health problems directly. Epileptics have had problems with rapid flashing graphics, and other neurological disorders may be triggered by the illusion of rapid motion through a 3D world. Heavy computer users have wrist and arm problems; also, the eyestrain of looking too long at a monitor is well documented. You are probably not at too much risk unless you have done something specifically and deliberately to exacerbate these problems. And you would not do that, would you?

Company does not guarantee that other players will not harm Player.

An especially important special case of the harm a virtual world may cause a player is the harm inflicted by other players. This possibility, sadly, is inherent in the nature of a shared virtual world. The best you can do is to remind/warn players that other players may be jerks.

There are many variations on the same basic idea; you often see many of them in the same EULA. Thus, anything a player does is that player's sole responsibility. You are not obligated to "supervise" what they do, or to "screen" what they say before they say it. (There are many synonyms. You do not "monitor," "censor," "filter," or "inspect," for example.) You do not guarantee that what players say is truthful, or that it is not offensive. Even though you are not obligated to monitor what players say, you may remove anything you find objectionable. (But removing something you find objectionable once does not obligate you to do so in the future.) These clauses together stand for the proposition that you can screen or not screen content at your discretion, and that whatever you do, none of the other players can complain to you.

Keep in mind that this does not guarantee that your players will not be doing things that could give them valid lawsuits against each other. Truly and profoundly offensive comments about a player's offline disability designed to make him or her collapse in tears could make the jerk liable for intentional infliction of emotional distress. The typical EULA is silent about this kind of lawsuit; it is purely between your players.

You May Take Action to Enforce Your Rules

If players do what they ought not, you need to be able to make the punishment fit the crime—both in the sense of giving players who misbehave what they deserve and in the sense of adopting the most cost-effective strategy to deter wrongdoing. The EULA does not sit in judgment of whether a particular reply is the most appropriate one; it just makes sure you have the full range to choose from.

There are three kinds of responses you might want to use. You will want to have the freedom to use at least some responses of all three kinds, even if you do not need the most severe from any category. In your privileged position running the world, you have the ability to take *in-world actions* against players—up to and including expulsion from the world. You also have the ability to design the world's *software* to your advantage—so that the server (or the client!) automatically takes action against jerks. In extreme cases, you may want to turn to the *legal system* to protect your rights and your powers as a developer. The job of the EULA is to protect you from legal trouble if you choose in-world or software responses, and to make sure the legal system will do what you need it to if you ask.

Company may take in-world action against Player up to and including expulsion.

If someone is a being a jerk, you can warn him, discipline him in-world, suspend him, or expel him. Your rules of conduct and EULA will lay out what kinds of actions are grounds for discipline; your policies will give some sense of what punishment will apply to what kind of wrongdoing. Your EULA should then contain a term making sure players have no legal recourse against you if and when you mete out those punishments.

Which term? It varies. This power is so central that EULAs have developed a handful of different ways to protect it. Many EULAs contain more than one. The EULA may, as suggested earlier, state that you may terminate an account at any time at your discretion. That discretion then obviously includes the choice to terminate accounts as punishment for violations of the rules. The EULA may also more specifically state that you reserve the right to punish violations of the rules (as determined solely by you) with termination. The EULA may state that players have no legal right to continue playing in defiance of your wishes. It may also imply that they have no such right by listing what rights the players *do* have and then stating that players have no rights beyond those stated. Reasonable lawyers may choose different solutions. For present purposes, though, remember this: *no court has ever forced a virtual world to continue providing service to a rule-breaking player.*

Company may use technical measures to enforce this EULA and the Rules of Conduct.

Some classes of jerks can be dealt with automatically. For starters, you have enormous design freedom to make a world that encourages or discourages griefing. If your world gives players good tools to avoid or deal with jerks, jerks may not flock to your world in such numbers in the first place. Similarly, you could try to write software that makes some kinds of jerky behavior impossible. Well-enough run servers will not be hacked. Cleverly designed chat systems can minimize harassment; Disney's *Toon-Town*™, for example, uses identity-management techniques to make sure players cannot spew their mouths at strangers in order to protect their younger audience.

These basic design freedoms are so fundamental that you rarely see EULA terms protecting them. Instead, they are treated as natural implications of other terms. If you can ban players for any reason, if players are free to quit at any time, if playing other than allowed by the software is forbidden, if you do not promise that the software will work, if players do not have any ownership rights in the world . . . all of these ifs naturally imply that players have no legal right to complain about your design decisions. Once again, reasonable lawyers will lean on different supports. Occasionally, a well-written EULA will make this freedom explicit, but many other well-written ones do not.

Technical measures that involve surveillance function a little differently. You could program your server software to monitor actions in-world and alert you to troubling conditions. Thus, you might keep track of players whose wealth suddenly spikes, as such spikes suggest the use of exploits. You might also keep track of players who are repeatedly triggering profanity filters (which would suggest they are looking for misspellings that will slip by). By simply detecting the wrongdoing at first instead of automatically disallowing it, you can gather more evidence of what they are up to, and perhaps avoid letting players know exactly what you can and cannot monitor. You might even wire this monitoring up to automated responses—for example, after ten unprovoked attacks, you will automatically suspend an account for unwanted PvP as soon as *any* other player complains about them. These techniques can involve interesting blends of human and automated response. They also may raise privacy concerns, so you should think about them in relation to your privacy policies.

You could also use your client software to monitor what else is running on the player's computer. Some call it "spyware," but it can also be a form of "digital rights management" if you are trying to prevent your software from being used in unauthorized ways. This kind of technical measure—especially if it takes automated action against players whom it catches using forbidden software—raises several issues. First, it risks damage to the player's computer, as mentioned previously. Second, it raises privacy concerns as discussed later. Third, it can be deeply unpopular with some of your players. Because of these issues, client-side technical responses virtually demand their own EULA term that discloses the issues and requires that players consent to such software's use.

Company may take legal action to enforce this EULA.

For the truly obnoxious jerks who cannot be dealt with any other way, there is legal action—or, at least, the threat of legal action. Lawsuits should not be anything but your absolute last resort. They are slow, risky, unpopular, and shockingly expensive. The process of going through one will probably be bad for business and worse for development and morale—it is *not fun* going through the discovery phase of a lawsuit and it is *not fun* doing the things your lawyer will tell you to do if you want to look sympathetic in court. In Charles Dickens' words, "Suffer any wrong that can be done you rather than come here!"

Still, sometimes there is no choice, and at least most jerks are not any more eager for a lawsuit than you are. You *must* have the option to call on the legal system for aid, and thus your EULA *must* make sure you have that option. Fortunately, this is not that hard. Most of the really important reasons for a lawsuit are either inherent in the nature of a virtual world or inherent in the nature of a EULA. Indeed, some EULAs do not contain any clauses specifically giving you the right to bring appropriate lawsuits. Some EULAs do; these clauses are often in the nature of warnings that particular violations could have particularly drastic consequences.

For misconduct that you need to stop immediately or has a demonstrably high price tag for you, a *civil lawsuit* is one possibility. This would be a "you vs. them" suit against the jerks. Picking your targets carefully is essential. As an example, the RIAA's lawsuits against file-sharing companies are much easier than its lawsuits against individual file-sharers; there are far fewer defendants, each of whom is more vulnerable to legal action, and each lawsuit produces more tangible results. If you have a problem that can only be solved through litigation, try to make sure you really are suing the jerk causing *the most* trouble. Finally, keep in mind that suing your customers may hurt your reputation, even if you are doing it to improve the overall quality of play.

For a few particular kinds of misbehavior, *criminal prosecution* is also a possibility. The FBI takes a keen interest in hacking and other computer crimes where substantial losses or national security are involved. The Secret Service and other federal agencies may also be involved. State law enforcement arms will also be attentive to large-scale fraud. Your lawyer will know whether particular misbehavior is potentially criminal and which agencies would be worth contacting.

Note that a criminal prosecution is under the government's control, not yours. That means that they will make the decision whether the case is worth pursuing; if they decide to let a case go because a particular jerk is small fry, that is the end of the matter. (They will not look kindly upon your wasting their time if the fry is obviously small.) That also means that the actual control of the case will be out of your hands once they decide to pursue it. Your cooperation may be essential (and necessary to convince them to file charges), but they will drive it, not you. Their top priority will be punishing your jerks to send a signal to other potential cyber-perps, not ensuring the maximum success of your world.

We will return later to further terms of the EULA that affect procedural details of the actual litigation process.

You May Make Changes

A virtual world is a service, not a product. The operations work is never done, and neither is the programming work. As your players' needs and business realities change, so too will your design. You will always be learning new things that can improve your world; you will always be making tweaks. Your EULA *must* preserve your freedom of action to modify your operations. That means you must be free both to make changes to the world and to the EULA itself.

Company may modify the Service at will.

Your right to make changes to the world resembles your right to use in-world punishments and technical measures to deal with misbehavior. Indeed, it could be considered the general principle from which those more specific rights are derived. The critical distinction is that you will need to be able to make changes even when no player has done anything wrong. Making design changes and fixing bugs is a normal feature of running a virtual world, even when everything is healthy and thriving. The right to make changes also includes the right *not* to make changes. A player may be upset that his character has lost key assets, or may just think that some other character class should be nerfed. You can refuse.

Most EULAs give you this right by way of a double negative; they *do not* give players the power to *stop* you from making changes. If players do not like the new shape of the world, they should stop paying and stop playing. Many common EULA terms are, however, relevant to your right to change the world. Your right to terminate access for any reason suggests that you have the right to change what players have access *to*. Explicit disclaimers of any player ownership over the world or its contents also imply that players have no right to stop you from making changes.

In some countries, designers' absolute control over their worlds is under assault. Chinese and Taiwanese courts have ordered virtual world designers to restore to players items lost through fraud or the designers' negligence. These rights, however, have tended to be quite particular—and aimed at restoring a player to the position he was in before some wrong was done him. So far, there has been no suggestion that a designer would not be free to remove certain content from a world entirely.

You should be careful with changes to the world that could lead to accusations of insider trading. Regardless of your legal rights, any suggestion of impropriety is bad for morale. If you buy and sell assets within the world to your players, changes that affect the value of those assets may alienate players. If you sell a player expensive content and then significantly change it, be prepared for claims that you deliberately concealed your plans to extract a premium from unsuspecting players. The more transparent your trading practices, the less the danger.

Company may make changes to this EULA.

EULAs need to change, too. New court rulings and laws will require new terms. Old terms may need to be updated with new terminology. Changes to your design and business practices may require modifying terms to track what you actually do. You may discover a bug in the legalese. Your EULA *must* allow you to change the EULA itself. Most EULAs therefore contain a term giving the developers the supposedly absolute right to make any changes they want to the EULA.

There are, however, some qualifications to this "absolute" right. A truly open-ended right to change would be both morally and legally problematic. A change to the EULA stating, "Player shall pay the Company $1,000,000 per second of playing time," would bankrupt some players if enforceable. Thus, all EULA-change clauses contain some provision giving players notice of any changes and an opportunity to opt out.

First, notice. Any changes to the EULA should be posted to the EULA itself. (And the EULA should explain that any changes will be posted there.) To make sure players read it, in theory if not in fact, the EULA will then require players to check the EULA periodically for any changes. A change log of modifications to the EULA is a sensible idea. More aggressively, it can be a good idea to email players that the EULA has changed, and tell them in what ways. You can even show players the new EULA when they log in again and require them to click on "I Agree" again.

Second, opportunity to opt out. You are not currently required to give players who do not want to play under a revised EULA anything more than the opportunity to stop playing. Many EULAs quite sensibly explain that players who do not like the new EULA can and should go through the normal account cancellation process. Another normal practice is to state that continued play after a revision constitutes consent to the new terms. The technique of showing players the new EULA and requiring them to click on "I Agree" has the advantage of getting players to agree directly to the new terms, instead of bootstrapping through the old ones.

Some major commercial institutions follow an even more cautious policy. They tell their users well in advance of upcoming changes—as much as 90 days in some cases. They then require the users to give affirmative consent to the new terms before the end of that period, or else their accounts will be automatically closed when the new terms take effect. These rollouts are often accompanied by FAQs that carefully explain the changes. If your world invites significant investment, you may want to consider this kind of deliberate, careful transition.

Terms Staving Off Legal Trouble from Third Parties

We come now to terms that do not directly deal with the relationship between you and your players. We have talked about duties you do or do not owe your players, and duties they do or do not owe you. The duties in this section are different—they are duties that you and your players may or may not owe to third parties. Failing to honor those duties could cause legal problems for you. Thus, the EULA will contain provisions that try to head off these third-party problems early. First, we will talk about what your players need to do to avoid trouble; then we will talk about what you need to do. As a finale, we will talk a bit about privacy issues—governments are taking an increasing interest in online privacy issues, so your treatment of your players' personal information can have significant consequences.

Players Are Required to Respect Third-Party Rights

Many laws that apply to conduct in the offline world apply to conduct online. Many of the things your players could do to harm others offline they can also do online. And some of the things your players could do online could open you up to liability from nonplayers seeking to hold you responsible for the misdeeds of jerks.

Now, there is some bad news and some good news here. The bad news is that nonplayers, by definition, are not parties to your EULA. They did not agree to take the risk that something bad would happen to them from playing in your world. They were just minding their own business when the world and its players came out of the blue and hurt them.

The good news is that because nonplayers, by definition, are not in-world, it is not usually as easy for players to do harmful things to them. Many of the obvious categories of harms are already prohibited by the terms in your EULA that keep players from doing harmful things to each other. (Thus, for example, telling players that they are not allowed to defame people includes defamation against both other players and nonplayers.) There is no particular reason to keep these EULA terms restricted so that they only protect other players.

In this section, we will talk about a few particular nonplayer issues in more depth:

Defamation: What are your responsibilities when your players insult or lie about nonplayers in-world?

Intellectual property: What are your responsibilities when your players violate third-party IP rights?

Criminal laws: What are your responsibilities when your players do things that could get them fined or jailed?

Indemnification: What can you do to recoup your losses if what one of your players does cause you third-party legal trouble?

All communications are made solely by players and are not the position of the Company.

You do not generally need to worry that nonplayers will be insulted, defamed, offended, distressed, or freaked out by things your players write in-world. It is not that your players will not sometimes try to insult, defame, offend, distress, and freak out nonplayers. No, it is just that legally speaking, such things are not your problem.

Thank Congress. *Section 230 of the Communications Decency Act of 1996* says that you will not be treated as the "speaker or publisher" of any information provided by an "information content provider." In effect, it means that when information flows through your system because someone else provided it, you will not be treated as having said it. That protects you from liability for "saying" the things your players say. But wait, there is more! The next part of Section 230 *also* immunizes you for any "good faith" censorship of objectionable material. Thus, you cannot be held liable for deciding to go ahead and remove pornography and harassing messages from your world. Thus, Section 230 protects you from liability both for too little screening and too much.

Section 230 could, however, fail you when *you* actually originated the objectionable content or when your filtering was actually in bad faith. If you republish the objectionable content yourself—say by quoting it in your monthly best-of-world newsletter—you could also be held liable. Avoiding such situations is mostly a matter of using basic good judgment (e.g., do not send broadcast messages to all players saying nasty, hateful things you know to be false) and having good supervision (e.g., do not let your employees broadcast these messages, either).

Player will not upload content that Player does not have permission to upload.

Welcome to the ugly world of IP infringement. (Section 230 is, by its own terms, inapplicable here.) Napster had to deal with it and failed. Google and Yahoo! have to deal with it on a daily basis. Now you have to deal with it. If your world has any facilities for content upload or player communication *at all*, you will have to deal with the possibility that players could upload or communicate something protected by IP. They could create IP issues by making their costume look like a trademarked logo, typing the text of a novel in as dialogue, or uploading a billboard texture that looks exactly like a copyrighted painting. If your world has rich multimedia, they could be introducing someone else's audio and video and thus infringing copyright, and so on.

The first thing you should do is tell your players not to infringe others' IP rights. A "do not upload infringing content" clause is standard, and it generally belongs with other "do not be a jerk" clauses. Indeed, it is sometimes phrased as a "do not infringe IP or other third-party rights" instruction.

Beyond that, the rules of IP liability are complex and shifting. They probably have changed in some respect between when this chapter was written and now. Realistically, you need to be prepared to deal with copyright and trademark issues. Of the two, copyright is far and away the more significant.

The Company will respond to DMCA takedown notifications as follows . . .

The Digital Millennium Copyright Act, or DMCA, contains a complex and interlocking set of immunities and rules dealing with the copyright responsibilities of online services. These "Section 512" rules provide, in effect, that you are guaranteed not to be considered a copyright infringer yourself as long as you follow certain "safe harbor" procedures. If you do not follow the procedures, you might or might not be liable, depending on the specific facts. It is much safer to follow the safe harbor procedures. Follow them.[6]

You have basically no copyright liability for anything that merely passes automatically through your systems and does not stay there (with the exception of some cached copies to transmit the content to all the users requesting it). The rules are that the transmission has to be automatic and you cannot modify the content. Thus, for chat channels, you are usually in the clear. The actual statute[7] is quite technical, so you should clear the exact details of your architecture with your lawyer.

Things are trickier when it comes to content that is stored on your systems. That category would include pretty much any uploaded content—something that becomes part of the virtual world, is stored on your servers, and can be accessed by other players.

Here, once again, you are generally not liable, but now the conditions are much more stringent.

First, as soon as you find out that uploaded content is infringing, you need to shut off access to it expeditiously. Second, you need to pass the vicarious infringement standard—see the next section to understand what that means. Third, you need to have a policy for dealing with repeat infringers. That means if you find out that someone is infringing copyrights repeatedly, you need to terminate his or her accounts (and you need to inform your players that you have such a policy).

The most important of the conditions is the notice-and-takedown rule. It requires you to maintain an address—both physical and electronic—at which copyright holders can send you notices of infringing content in your world. The address should be prominently displayed on your site, either in the EULA itself or in a corresponding DMCA page. You *must* actively monitor that address and act promptly if you receive a notification at it. (AOL lost the protection of the DMCA safe harbor in a copyright lawsuit brought against it by the author Harlan Ellison, in part because it let messages to its DMCA address pile up without paying attention to them.)

Loosely speaking, a valid takedown notice must contain enough information to make it possible to find the disputed content and a sworn statement that the content actually is infringing. Once you get a properly detailed notice, if you want to retain your safe harbor, you *must* disable access to the content. Leave the content up, and you are taking your chances with a copyright infringement suit.

At this point, you are also safe from a lawsuit by the uploader. To preserve that safety, you need to tell the uploader what you have done. The uploader now gets a chance to submit a counter-notification—basically a sworn statement that the content is *not* infringing. You then need to take *that* notification back to the original complainer. If the complainer does nothing, you put the content back online. If the complainer tells you that he, she, or it has filed suit against the uploader, you leave the content offline. (The DMCA has the full grisly details.)

What this process does is get the complainer and the uploader to play a game of chicken. If one of them backs down, you can do what the winner says to do. If neither of them backs down, the whole thing ends up in a lawsuit between the two of them, who are really the parties with something at stake. Either way, you are out of the picture. Play by the safe harbor rules and you will not get hurt.

Secondary Liability

Unfortunately for you, playing by the DMCA rules is not enough to shield you completely from IP trouble. That is because of something called "secondary liability," which is a legal term for what happens when you are not the one directly doing something wrong, but you are closely enough involved with it that the legal system will hold you accountable for it. Thus, for example, if a store clerk hits you, the store itself obviously did not hit you, but might be secondarily liable for employing the clerk, for having a policy encouraging clerks to hit customers, and so on.

You do not need to worry too much about most kinds of secondary liability. Secondary liability for defamation, for example, would require that you have acted to encourage a player to speak falsely or that you have directly profited from the defamation. Unless your customer service guides have decided to foment chaos, neither scenario is particularly likely. The usual wrongs that could be committed in-world are so obvious that you will typically be trying to stop them, rather than encourage them.

Intellectual property is different. Infringement can be loads of fun (and profit) for the people doing the infringement. Communities dedicated to lots of infringement can be very popular. In the early days, Napster was *busy*—people regularly left nice messages for the people whose MP3s they copied. If your world were to get a reputation as a place where players can just scoop up tons of great (if infringing) content, that would probably draw more players. It is not at all implausible that some virtual world would actively encourage players to infringe third parties' IP. That is exactly what happened to Napster Aimster, and Grokster—they were not copyright infringers themselves, but they got hit on *secondary* liability because their systems were designed and marketed to encourage copyright infringement. Some virtual worlds have relatively lax policies about IP infringement and may be next to fall under similar circumstances.

Copyright

There are two kinds of secondary copyright liability. The first is called *vicarious* copyright infringement. A vicarious infringer has (1) the *right and ability* to control users, and (2) a *direct financial benefit* from the infringement. The dangerous part about vicarious liability, from your perspective, is that you do not need to know about a specific act of infringement. The second kind is *contributory* copyright infringement. A contributory infringer (1) *knows* of the infringement, and (2) either *induced* the infringer or provided *actual assistance*. These are both high hurdles.

Two Supreme Court decisions, *Sony Corporation v. Universal City Studios*[8] and *MGM v. Grokster*[9], have provided further guidance on these standards as they apply to businesses like yours—those who make technologies that could be or are used by others to commit infringements. *Sony* created a test of "capable of substantial non-infringing use"—that is, if your technology can be used for things other than infringement, you cannot be held liable for secondary copyright infringement.

Grokster, however, indicates that this is not the end of the matter. First, the opinions in *Grokster* were multiple and murky; it is not clear how much non-infringing use is "substantial" and whether the technology must *actually* be used for such purposes or merely be *capable* of such uses. Second, there is another analytical prong, which makes liable "one who distributes a device with the object of promoting its use to infringe copyright, as shown by clear expression or other affirmative steps taken to foster infringement."

Where does this leave you? Consult your lawyer. In general, you should do your best to make sure of two things. First, you should protect yourself under *Sony* by making your world fun and useful for things that are not copyright infringement. That should not be too hard; presumably, that is why you are making a virtual world and not, say, a peer-to-peer file-sharing system. Second, you should protect yourself under *Grokster* by not encouraging your users to use the world to infringe copyrights. That means not marketing it in terms that even indirectly suggest infringement and not giving them easy instructions for committing infringement. Any further advice would have to depend on what your world actually enables.

Trademark

If you yourself do not put known trademarks in your world, you are probably not a direct trademark infringer. There have been attempts to argue that some features can amount to direct trademark infringement if they direct users to create characters or other content that resemble trademarks from outside the game. So far, however, these attempts have been defeated by lawyers representing developers of virtual worlds. The makers of *City of Heroes*™ won a judicial ruling that their character creation system— which could be used to create characters resembling familiar superheroes, among many others—did not infringe on trademarks held by Marvel Comics. For the time being, you are on generally safe ground as long the content you put in yourself does not itself come close to existing trademarks.

Trademark infringement also comes in secondary flavors, just as copyright infringement does. Honestly, however, you do not have as much to worry about here. The biggest direct trademark infringers are people who make counterfeit goods. The biggest secondary infringers are people who close their eyes to massive trademark piracy or actively encourage it; for example, the operators of swap meets at which many goods with counterfeit trademarks are openly and brazenly bought and sold have been held liable as secondary infringers. Without the massive direct trademark infringement of the sort that counterfeiters engage in, the danger of secondary infringement does not loom as large.

The most important thing for you to do is to respond appropriately if you receive reliable evidence that some player is infringing a trademark in-world. Opening a "McDonald's®" food stand in-world might be kind of cute, but when a player is using it to draw in other players as customers, and cashing in the profits for real money, then you are creeping into infringement territory. The blatant commercial for-profit trademark-infringing player should be stopped.

The legalities of other scenarios are not well defined. Players may or may not be committing trademark infringement if they use trademarks in-world but do not "cash out" any profits. Lawyers have varying opinions. It is probably safer on your part to stop them, but that would also constitute appeasement toward trademark holders, whose demands will only increase. Consult your lawyer if the issue arises.

Player will not violate any criminal laws.

This rule, like most other anti-jerk rules, is obvious as a condition imposed on players. The complications arise because being a jerk to the government is different from being a jerk to J. Random Bystander. The government is not a good third party to tick off. The government can squash you like a bug if there are criminal violations involved. Thus, in addition to this fairly basic EULA term, you should be careful not to get swept up in any criminal activity taken part in by your players.

Most of this should be complete common sense. If you find out that your players are conspiring to do something seriously illegal such as murder someone in the offline world or swap child pornography, you have a moral obligation not to turn a blind eye. Whether you should go to the authorities, disable their accounts, or take some other action depends on what they are doing, how dangerous they are, and whether you would be tipping them off. Absolutely, under no circumstances, should you *help* your players commit crimes.

You should also sanity-check your operations against several important classes of criminal laws:

Gambling is against most states' laws; precise definitions vary. Cautious evaluation may be necessary where your world contains both clear games of chance and the possibility of cashing out in items of real-life value.

Anti-pornography and anti-obscenity laws—although strongly hemmed in by the United States by the First Amendment—do have some bite. If you find out about obscene content uploaded by players, you may have affirmative obligations to remove it, depending on the details.

Stalking, harassment, and fraud are plausible player-to-player crimes, but it is hard to see how a company could be implicated in them without some significant wrongdoing by its employees. For privacy reasons as well as criminal ones, you should be careful with players' personal information; do not be an unwitting accomplice to stalkers and identity thieves, and especially do not let your employees turn into them, either.

Player will indemnify Company.

Your ace-in-the-hole countermeasure against players who get you into legal trouble is the indemnification clause. "Indemnification" means paying someone else's legal liabilities. Your car insurance company indemnifies you if another driver sues you. You require players to indemnify you for the lawsuits against you that they cause.

In an indemnification clause, the player promises to pay you back for anything you lose as a result of being sued because of the player's misconduct. Breach of the EULA is often one condition—if the player's breach causes you legal trouble, indemnification kicks in. But "use" (or "use or misuse") of the service is also a common trigger. That means *anything* caused by the players' conduct in the world that causes you legal trouble requires them to pay to fix the trouble.

Most indemnity clauses require the player to "defend, indemnify, and hold harmless" (in some order). "Defend" is the word with a surprising meaning—this means that the player will not just pay what you are ordered to pay by the court, but also pay for your lawyers, and even find and hire one for you.

For all of this, while a EULA indemnification clause is a sensible piece of good planning, it is more likely than not to be useless in practical terms. Like it or not, your company is richer than the average player. If a player who causes you legal trouble with a third party is rich enough to make good on the indemnification, well, you are exceedingly lucky. In fact, you will be lucky to recover enough from your average player to make it worth your while even to invoke the indemnification clause. Only in rare circumstances will the clause make a difference.

Company Is Required to Respect Third-Party Rights

You have an obligation to respect third parties' legal rights at all times. You cannot (usually) eliminate this obligation through the EULA. The point of dealing with your third-party obligations in a EULA is to make sure you are *able* to respect third parties' rights. You do not want to get caught between a rock and hard place, forced to choose between violating your obligation to your players and your obligation to third parties. EULAs typically contain several clauses warning players that you will do what you must to avoid infringing third parties' rights and requiring players to consent that anything you do for them is subject to those rights.

Many kinds of these third-party rights are folded in with your own rights. Thus, for example, if you have licensed IP to use in your software or your content, you will probably have had to agree to take reasonable measures to keep others who receive it from you from using it in unlicensed ways. The same clauses that require players to recognize your IP rights will also require them to recognize the IP rights of your licensors.

Some third-party rights, however, are not matters you would much concern yourself with were it just you. These rights impose more intrusive duties on you, duties that can affect your relationship with your players. In addition to a general statement, often implicit, that you will comply with all applicable laws, EULAs regularly contain specific statements about a few common cases. The most common come from those third parties par excellence, governments. In this section, we will talk about two of the most common: court orders and access restrictions.

Company will comply with court orders.

When a court orders you to do something, you *must* comply. (You can appeal, but unless you get a "stay" of the order, something you are not guaranteed to get, you must comply with the order while the appeal is pending.) Disobeying a court order is contempt of court, and the court will do whatever it takes to make continued disobedience less attractive than falling into line. That could include large and exponentially increasing fines, shutting down your world, and even jailing you until you obey. There are many procedural protections to make sure court orders are not entered lightly, but when the gavel falls, it *falls*. EULAs therefore regularly contain clauses indicating that the company will obey court orders. Players are on notice that their (limited) rights under the EULA are subject to court override.

While court orders could conceivably cover any topic in this chapter (or still others), the most likely scenario (and one frequently mentioned in EULAs) is an order demanding that the company turn over information about a player. That could include information about the player's offline identity or information about the player's in-world activities. These orders could be part of a criminal investigation, an outgrowth from a civil lawsuit, or an administrative procedure. Whichever they are, your privacy policy will have to yield to these orders.

This is not to say that you cannot protect players' privacy (or other rights) in the face of outside demands. The procedural protections involved depend on the sort of court order involved. Sometimes, you can tell the player about the order, sometimes you must, and sometimes you must not. Sometimes, a player can intervene to block the order; sometimes you can intervene on your players' behalf if you like; sometimes neither of you can. If and when you get notice of a search warrant, subpoena, or other such order, always consult your lawyer.

You can, in theory, choose to have your EULA commit you to taking steps to protect your players' rights to the extent you can. This tactic is not currently used by any major virtual worlds. It is much more common to remain safe by stating that you retain the unrestricted right to give information about players to any governmental agency or third party as necessary to resolve problems.

These are matters of choice. The ethics of when you should protect your players and when you should rat on them (or otherwise abandon them to their fate) are complicated. In many cases, protecting them is both the right thing to do and an attractive business move. In others—especially where they have been willfully abusing their place in your world to commit crimes or harm others in breach of the EULA—you do not owe them anything. Whatever your policy, you should set it at the highest level. This is not a matter to be decided by whoever opens the mail.

Company will respect local rules on access to the Service.

Governments, national and local, in the United States and around the world, have all sorts of different laws about access to certain kinds of content. It may be illegal for certain residents of certain places to access your world (or parts of it); it may be illegal for you to allow them to access it. Your EULA will contain several clauses telling these people to go away, that they are never licensed to enter your world.

The extent to which you must actually follow up on that restriction varies. You might just be required to ask players questions about their age, location, and so on. If they lie to you, it is not your problem. On the other hand, sometimes you might be expected to be more aggressive in using technical measures to check up on their answers—for example, to supplement an age question with proof of a credit card, or to supplement a location question with screening based on IP address. Consult your lawyer for details.

Here are the most common forms of governmentally mandated restrictions:

Age: In the United States, the Children's Online Privacy Protection Act (COPPA) generally makes it illegal to collect personal information from children under 13 without their parents' permission. In practice, this means that you will probably want to bar all players under 13 from signing up; if children want to play, their parents must open the account. Similar, although sometimes less completely restrictive, rules may often apply to children under 18, especially if parts of your world are zoned as unsuitable for children.

Location: You may make a world that is either entirely or partially illegal to play in some countries. Dr. Richard Bartle's examples of educational virtual worlds—worlds that force players to confront some of the great horrors of history to learn not to repeat them—although well-intentioned, might run afoul of some countries' hate speech laws. Adult-themed, sexually oriented worlds would not pass muster with official censors in other countries. You may not need to call out the particulars in your EULA, but you should include a clause stating that players cannot play if it is illegal to do so in their jurisdiction.

Export restrictions: Some countries go even further and make it illegal to join a virtual world from *other* countries. The United States, for example, currently designates Cuba, Iran, Libya, North Korea, Sudan, and Syria as state sponsors of terrorism and forbids exports to those countries of "dual-use items" that have both military and civilian applications. And yes, the advanced technology in a virtual world could sometimes be considered a dual-use item—typically, such technologies include strong cryptographic components. Certain EULAs, therefore, flatly forbid nationals of those countries from using the world or downloading the software (and forbid anyone else from doing it for them).

Privacy Policies

Information privacy law is a subject unto itself. There are entire *books* on it. It would be impossible to get into all of the relevant details here. Instead, we will focus on a few salient points:

- The sources of law are many.
- You should have an explicit privacy policy.
- Your privacy policy should cover certain standard subjects.
- Your privacy policy should adhere to certain standard best practices.
- You should comply with your privacy policy.

Information privacy is covered by a tangled web of laws. In Europe, the EU Data Protection Directive requires that individuals be able to access personal data you hold about them and that your use of the data complies with principles. The national legislation implementing the directive varies from country to country. In the United States, there is no overarching single piece of privacy legislation. Federal laws cover the use of personal information about children (COPPA), health care (HIPAA), financial services (GLBA), and other specific subjects. Some states have laws that penalize violations of stated privacy policies. California has a law requiring that you disclose privacy breaches affecting personal information. Your obligations under these laws vary based on what kind of information you collect and where you do business. This is absolutely a situation in which to consult your lawyer.

A prominent privacy policy is sometimes a legal requirement, but it's always a good idea. It increases player confidence to have one. It gives you a head start in case of privacy trouble. It forces you to model your use of data, to audit your actual handling of personal information, and to figure out your company policies on how you will work with player-provided information. All of these exercises are prudent system design points, which will improve your security, and help you understand your business better. The policy should be in clear English, not legalese. A number of organizations will certify members' privacy policies and privacy practices. The Entertainment Software Ratings Board's Privacy Online Program is designed for online game Web sites. Unfortunately, there are not yet any similar organizations specifically focused on virtual worlds.

Your privacy policy should discuss a standard basic set of issues. You should distinguish between personal information, nonpersonal information about a particular player, and aggregate information about players in general. You should discuss what information you collect about players, when you collect it, how you use that data, with whom (if anyone) you share the data, and how you protect the data. You should discuss players' ability to review and change personal information and what happens to their data when they quit. You should tell players what their options are (if any) to control how you use their information. You should tell players how to contact you with questions.

Some basic good practices are either required by most certifying organizations or are matters of respect for your customers. You should not collect information you will not reasonably use, and you should not use information you do not really need to. If you want to send marketing emails to players or to provide their contact information to third parties, you should give players the choice of whether to be contacted or to allow third parties to receive their information. Choices should be opt-in, not opt-out. You should have an employee whose job includes watching for privacy issues and responding to player privacy concerns. You should store personal information in a way that prevents your employees from accessing it without a valid business reason. You should audit your use of player information regularly to make sure you really are complying with what you think your privacy practices are.

Finally, if your privacy policy threatens to get out of sync with your business needs, look closely at the divergence. Perhaps your business "need" is less urgent than you think and you can keep yourself in full compliance. If that is not the case, then change your privacy policy to reflect the new needs. Be as open and candid about the change as you can. Do not, repeat, do not simply ignore your privacy policy. If you are caught breaching your own privacy policy, the PR fallout will not be pleasant.

Further Horizons

You should now be able to recognize about 95% of the terms in a standard virtual world EULA, understand approximately what they do, and know why they are there. This section is about the remaining 5%.

Some virtual worlds are pushing outward the frontiers of design possibilities. Innovative design decisions often require innovative EULA terms. Experiments in redefining the relationships through which a company and players create the shared social space that is a virtual world often require new terms that lay out the legal baseline for new kinds of interaction.

Unfortunately, to discuss the issues raised by these terms in anything approaching the level of detail we have used for the common-case 95% of terms would require another chapter as long as this one. The issues are often complex, controversial, and open ended; there are often many different legal answers (with different design consequences) to any given question. Moreover, these terms are less common and less uniform. Everything written here would pertain to fewer virtual worlds than the previous discussion.

Therefore, instead of going into the details of these active frontiers, this will be a brief overview of them. At the moment, four kinds of design questions can require new and innovative EULA terms, depending on the answers. If you are reading a EULA and you see a term you do not recognize, ask whether it maps onto one of these questions. If you are building a world that explores one or more of these questions, you are definitely in consult-your-lawyer territory.

First, there is *player-created content*. How, if at all, does the world deal with the problem of players creating content that is of low quality? How, if at all, does it deal with the problem of players creating content that is harmful to the world or to other players? Can players create content complex enough to qualify for IP protection? If so, what happens to the IP rights? Are players required to assign some or all of those rights to the company? Are players allowed to use IP rights to prevent other players from using the content in-world or in certain ways? If the players leave, what rights do they have to the content they created? Does the world contain an in-world IP system that uses different rules from what would apply outside?

Second, there is *virtual liberty*. How does the company reassure players that its power over the world will be exercised fairly? How does the company deal with criticism, both in-world and outside of the world? How, if at all, does the company help players resolve their disputes with one another? How does the company keep dispute-resolution mechanisms themselves from being used as griefing tools? What mechanisms does the world provide for players to form healthy communities and manage their own affairs? What control, if any, do players have to shape the world itself? Do players have any legal or technical control over the actual running of the world and the actions of the company? Is there even a company at all, or just a distributed group of players?

Third, there is what game designers call the *magic circle*. Virtual worlds are always partly connected to the offline world and partly distinct from it, but does this world emphasize the connection or the distinction? How, if at all, does the world encourage or require players to role-play? Does the world contain safe spaces? Does the world contain features designed to mirror certain aspects of the offline world? How does the world ask or tell players to manage the relationship between their real identity and their in-world character? To what extent does the world's internal economy resemble the offline world's economy?

Fourth, there is *virtual property*. What kinds of in-world resources can players' characters gain control over? What guarantees, if any, does the world provide that those resources will not be altered or deleted? How does the world encourage or discourage players from transferring or trading these resources in-world? How does the world encourage or discourage players from transferring or trading these resources for real-life money? Does the world have institutions that assist in trading in-world resources? Does it attempt to prevent the formation of such institutions? Are any of these attempts backed up by legal action, or just by in-world sanctions? How, if at all, does the world respond to disputes between players over particular trades gone wrong? How, if at all, does the world respond to differing player attitudes toward play driven by profit-making?

Conclusion

If this all seems like a lot, it is. There are many details to virtual world law, and it is all remarkably interconnected. Your consultation with the lawyer who drafts your EULA is going to have to touch on many topics. With any luck, though, thinking through the legal issues will help you clarify your world's design and your business plan. If you and your lawyer do your jobs well, your relationship should be a long, calm, profitable, and peaceful one.

Endnotes

1. *Blacksnow Interactive v. Mythic Entertainment, Inc.*, No. 02-cv-00112 (C.D. Cal. 2002). Mythic's ability to force the case into arbitration was sufficient to cause Blacksnow to drop the suit.

2. Adult-themed worlds, of course, may be another matter. The list of things that might happen to players is longer and more inclusive for some worlds than for others. That said, do not be a weisenheimer about treating players' willingness to join your world as consent to absolutely anything that happens in-world. Every world has some boundaries.

3. A nice consequence of such a term is that merely requiring players to *respond* when asked a question is a useful test for "players" who are, in fact, using automated scripts. Expecting players not to go AFK for too long while playing is an occasional rules of conduct device.

4. *Davidson & Assocs v. Jung,* 422 F.3d 630 (8th Cir. 2005).

5. "Act of God" is another common term for such things (although it seems unfair to attribute only the tornado to God and not all of the little things that go right). Why have both kinds of clauses? Belt and suspenders.

6. Actually, because the safe harbor procedures errs on the side of being overly censorious, there is a good ethical case that you *should not* always follow them. If you believe that you want to push back against overreaching copyright holders, consult your lawyer, and figure out exactly how and when you will stray from the safe harbor. But this is not a path for the timid or the unadvised.

7. 17 U.S.C. 512(a)-(b), for the lawyerly types in the audience.

8. 464 U.S. 417 (1984).

9. 125 S. Ct. 2764 (2005).

CHAPTER 14

I Wish I Knew

This chapter is one of our favorite chapters in the book. We asked some of the most experienced and respected people we knew in the game industry to give us their best advice for people starting out or surviving the business. They have decades of experience between them, and we even have a few people who helped create important parts of the industry. These authors have literally been involved with games that have collectively earned and lost billions of dollars; their advice is invaluable to people wanting to learn more about the business side of the game industry.

You may also notice that some of these people are giving advice you do not agree with; try to see why the person finds this bit of advice important instead of just discarding it. Some of them also seem to be giving contradictory advice. This is to be expected; different people arrive at success using different paths, and those individual paths are often quite different. Yet, the guidance can be very helpful in case you find yourself on a similar path.

The editors and publisher of this book have done only the bare minimum amount of editing required, because we believe that the best presentation of this chapter is the words direct from those experts. We hope you find these glimpses into the minds of some of the best developers as fascinating as we have.

Dave Ahl

Dave is the author of 22 how-to books, including *Basic Computer Games* (the first million-selling computer book), *Dad's Lessons for Living*, and *Dodge M37 Restoration Guide*. In 1974, he founded *Creative Computing* magazine, the world's first personal computing magazine. In 1967, he devised the first computer model for forecasting the success of new consumer products. He is also the author of more than 500 articles on technology, automotive restoration, marketing, logic puzzles, travel, market research, financial planning, and investment analysis. He created *Lunar Lander*, *Subway Scavenger*, *Orient Express*, and 50 other computer games. Dave holds an MBA from Carnegie-Mellon and an MS and BS in electrical engineering from Cornell University.

I Wish I Knew:

1. There is no fixed formula to achieving success. It's important to recognize the right strategy for different situations.

Success in computer games—or any field for that matter—most often comes from doing a job well, offering a better service, or making a product better than anyone else. Perfection equals success. But it can also come from narrowing your focus and specializing in a niche area. Or it might be important to broaden your focus and "draw large circles" to draw more people in. On the other hand, there may even be times when it's appropriate to do a job quickly and cheaply, when time and cost are more important than quality.

For example, at *Creative Computing* magazine we took a sort of whimsical, fun-loving approach in our articles and reviews. Our target audience was young people who were interested in personal computers, wanted to learn more, and were willing to experiment a little by typing in games and programs or by trying out unusual peripherals like plotters and sound cards. Over the years, I acquired seven other magazines, five of which I merged into *Creative Computing*, each time broadening our audience and scope.

However, two of the acquisitions, *Microsystems* and *Small Business Computers,* just didn't fit in with the *Creative Computing* readership. *Microsystems* was aimed at hardcore hardware experimenters and people that spoke assembly language. It had a tiny circulation (15,000) compared with *Creative Computing* (400,000), but by being the very best magazine in a niche field, we were able to charge proportionately higher advertising and subscription rates and it was very profitable.

Small Business Computers, on the other hand, was a small magazine in a large competitive field and more often than not had to compete by running discounted subscription promotions and offering "deals" on advertising. It was a bad acquisition that I had to kill off in less than two years because I didn't fully analyze how it fit into our product mix and what it would take to make it a success on its own.

2. Spend some time away from the computer and pay attention to what's going on in the real world and especially the business world. Read widely: *The Wall Street Journal*, a newsweekly, five or six monthly magazines in other fields, the Bible.
In 1969, Digital Equipment Corp. decided to sell computers, mainly its large PDP-10 time sharing system to schools and colleges. Although games didn't sell computers, they were a wonderful way to show an unknowledgeable administrator what a computer could do. One of the showpiece games, "Adventure," allowed players to get deeply involved exploring a vast underground maze of tunnels, meeting various creatures, finding magic spells, and collecting treasures. It was a wonderful way to show off a computer for schools with a million-dollar budget.

While there was no question that a PDP-10 could meet the current and future computing needs of most schools and colleges, I seemed to be a lone voice at DEC saying, "Read *The Wall Street Journal*, read *School Administration* magazine; schools don't have a million dollars to spend on a computer, even ten or twenty thousand is pushing it. Let's package up a bottom-of-the-line PDP-8 with a Teletype and some software, call it an EduSystem and see if we can sell some." The powers that be said, "Sure, go ahead, let's see what happens." So I wrote several simple little games like Lunar Lander (took 480 bytes of memory!), got some BASIC-language simulations from some other people, packaged them up, and within two years we were doing $14 million a year selling PDP-8 and PDP-11 computers to secondary schools and colleges. ($14 million may not sound like much today, but in 1972, it was quite impressive.)

3. Learn from the past; live for the future.

Every once in a while I read one of these lists of things of which college freshmen have no knowledge because they occurred before they were born. Things like vinyl records, Vietnam, Watergate, the Berlin airlift, drive-in theaters, and so on. Many young people seem to feel that if it didn't happen in their lifetime, it can't really be very important. But interestingly, if you go back 2,000 to 4,000 years to Biblical times, you find out that people then weren't very different at all from the way they are today. Some were greedy, they cheated on weights, teenagers rebelled against their parents, they killed, they committed adultery, they lied, they stole. Others repented, worshiped God, worked diligently, were kind to the needy, and loved their kids.

Reading the Biblical books of Judges and Kings makes you realize that human nature really hasn't changed very much and the broad flow of events repeat themselves over and over. Reading the Bible regularly has helped me keep things in perspective and almost anticipate the outcome of a new business approach without the need of market research or a consumer focus group. Oh, I'm not saying that market research isn't important—it is—but if you start off knowing how people responded to various situations in the past, you have a pretty good handle on how they'll respond today or in the future.

4. Etiquette and dress matter a good deal more than you think.

Creative Computing was a wildly successful new magazine and in 1978, I was invited to appear on the *McNeal-Lehrer* TV show as a featured guest. The atmosphere at *Creative Computing* had always been relaxed and casual. Shorts and t-shirts in the summer, jeans and sweats in the winter. So for the TV show I decided to wear one of our *Creative Computing* t-shirts so the TV viewers would remember the name. Big mistake. Two other publishers were guests on the show, one from the newly resurrected *Life* magazine, and everyone except me was in a jacket and tie. Looking at the tape afterward, I certainly stood out, but not in a positive way. Never again did I attend a business meeting, media event, or trade show in anything but appropriate attire.

Etiquette is equally important. In 1979, four companies were vying to develop the software for the learning games area at the Sesame Place amusement park. Two or three representatives from all four companies were invited to an all-day meeting where the specs were laid out and discussed. This was followed by dinner. It was both embarrassing and appalling watching some of the people at that dinner. No, you don't talk with your mouth full. No, you don't pick food out of your teeth at the table. You ask that the salt be passed, not reach across the table. You break your roll into small pieces and butter each one, not the whole thing all at once. You don't toss your napkin on the dessert plate at the end of the meal. In the awarding of the contract to *Creative Computing*, I think that dinner was equally—or more—important than our technical expertise, written proposal, or price quote.

5. Learn to speak confidently in public.

Jason, a nice young fellow whom I know quite well, graduated at the top of his class in engineering in both college and graduate school. He excelled in everything he set out to do. He was well liked by his peers and professors and had no trouble landing a good job. But unfortunately, his speech was so peppered with "like" and "you know" that after a short time his employer stopped sending him out to meet with clients, and instead of being on the fast track, he found himself on a siding.

Chris, another good friend, has a different barrier. A first-class engineer, Chris can speak confidently and make excellent presentations at department meetings of five or six people he knows. But ask him to make the same presentation at an inter-departmental meeting of 20 people or to customers he doesn't know, and he clams up, sweats, stutters, and fails miserably.

Another friend, Gary, plans his presentations to the nth degree, leaving nothing to chance, writing down every single word, and practicing in advance. He then reads his presentation to the audience word for word. Needless to say, Gary, too, is a public speaking disaster.

Fear of speaking in public is one of the top fears of scores of people. There are many ways of attacking the problem, including adult-education courses, practice, self-hypnosis, pretending you're in a room with just two other people, and so on. Find a method that works for you, apply it, and get up in front of a group whenever you have a chance.

Ralph Baer

I'm Ralph H. Baer, a television design engineer by profession and an inventor and developer of interactive games for the past 30 years. I hold some 150 patents worldwide. Among other things, I started the home videogame industry single-handedly in September of 1966. I was fortunate to have taken my own advice: As soon as the concept of playing games using an ordinary TV set percolated through my brain, I sat down and wrote a four-page document that laid the whole thing out in detail. Then I signed the pages, had another engineer initial those four pages also. A few years later, several patents were issued based on that initial concept and on the work we did in the lab cobbling up early videogames, ping-pong and light-gun games being two of them. Fifteen years of patent litigation and licensing activity later, $100 million had changed hands and mostly because we had no problem showing our track record.

I Wish I Knew:

A. that when I threw out those sketches of that fantastic game character and the notes that I had stapled to it, I was throwing a piece of my future irretrievably into the waste basket.

B. that when I showed that neat piece of code to some of my online friends I was blowing my chance to own that idea when it became valuable.

Why didn't anybody in school tell me to save yesterday's "obsolete" notes even if they contained just a rough idea and I had written a much better set of notes a couple of days later?

Why didn't somebody jump up and down and burn into my consciousness the need to treat novel ideas with respect and not blab about them carelessly.

Well, maybe they did tell you and you weren't listening. So why would we want to keep all those notes, like forever? Don't we have enough junk in our files already? This is supposed to be the paperless society!

Well, here are some reasons, for starters:

The next time your boss agrees that "you've got something there" and asks for your notes to try to get some patent protection for that great idea of yours, don't tell him you threw out all your early notes, schematics, flow charts, etc. He'll have cat fits! And the company's patent attorney, or an outside patent counsel, will roll his eyes and sigh.

Ah, yes! Patents! I won't lecture you on the need (or lack thereof) for obtaining patents. They made a huge difference in my life and maybe will in yours. If there is any chance that you may wind up pursuing one or more of them, you need to support them with copious quantities of documentation starting with whatever it was you generated on Day One.

One reason:

None of us is smart enough to know whether some of the creative things we do will become important some time in the future. Especially when we are young, we have only a limited sense of where and what we might be professionally a few years; hence, what's important, what isn't in the things we do. That's why you don't want some future opportunity to vanish just because you didn't keep good notes some time earlier—often years earlier. Keep decent notes, period! Take my advice: If you, or your management think that something you have come up with is original and potentially useful to the company or for licensing to others, then support that idea with decent record keeping. At a minimum, it'll earn Brownie points for you; at a maximum, it might become an important part of your history. You never know…

Another reason:

You don't want to look like an idiot if it should come to lawsuit after patents issue and get contested and you need to defend your invention in court….there is nothing like having a complete paper trail of an invention—preferably a day-by-day record—dated and initialed, every last sheet of it, so that when you are on the witness stand trying to convince the judge that it was really you who had that great idea, proving who-did-what is a slam-dunk!

Take it from me: been there, done that!

1. So, Advice Number One: Save all your notes, sign 'em and date 'em!

Patents should have an important place in your life. Learn about them yourself if you haven't been given a really useful introduction to their whys and wherefores. I have been in the interactive video and the electronic toy and game invention and licensing business for the better part of 40 years and I would be nowhere if I hadn't learned the ins and outs of patents. Get a good and enjoyable book like my friend Richard Levy's book, *The Toy and Game Inventor's Handbook*. It's an eye-opener written with tongue-in-cheek. You'll like it.

2. Advice Number Two: Learn something about the patent system from guys who have been there and made it work for them (it's in the book).

Document everything when you have a really great idea in the middle of the night or when one fell out of a piece of work you were doing on the job. Learn as much about the patent system as you care to absorb; check out your company's position with respect to patents and work within that system. Finally, there is the Disclosure Document service provided by the USPTO. For $10 you can send in a short description of an invention of yours and get a date-stamped receipt of your cover letter from the Patent Office. For $25 they send back copies of all of your pages, each date-stamped. If there is ever any litigation that involves the concepts you disclosed in that document, then at least you have a piece of paper that establishes the date of your invention. Easy to do—worth every penny. If nothing else, having expressed in a Disclosure Document what you think you invented and having done so in clear terms on a couple of sheets of paper does wonders for your understanding of your own stuff and your ability to communicate it to others who are entitled to know about it (like your manager, if you are employed). Then mail it off with a check. Better yet, have someone competent and trustworthy double-check it and add further inventive content, if possible. Then list him or her as a co-inventor and have that person initial each page alongside your own hieroglyphics.

3. Advice Number Three: Make use of the USPTO's Disclosure Document program.

Check into your company's position on that subject.

Enough said! The best of luck to you! Ralph H. Baer—*www.ralphbaer.com.*

Richard Bartle

Dr. Richard Bartle co-wrote the first virtual world, MUD ("Multi-User Dungeon"), while an undergraduate in 1978, and has thus been at the forefront of the online games industry from its very inception. A former lecturer in Artificial Intelligence and current Visiting Professor in Computer Game Design (both at the University of Essex, U.K.), he is an influential writer on all aspects of virtual world design, development, and management. As an independent consultant, he has worked with most of the major online game companies in the U.K. and the U.S. over the past 20 years. His 2003 book, *Designing Virtual Worlds*, has already established itself as a foundation text for researchers and developers of virtual worlds alike.

I Wish I Knew:

1. Suits are necessary.

Everyone not in game development who wants to get into game development actually only wants to get into game design. They see programming or animation or testing or production as a way of getting their foot in the door. They have ideas and they want them made. Consequently, development studios are packed with highly imaginative people, all trying to make their own mark, all wanting to get to create their own games.

Unfortunately, it takes more than a bunch of inventive geniuses to run a company. The reason why universities teach courses in Business Administration is that businesses need administrating. Pretty well every creative person who ever lived has a wild aversion to Process, and business administration is all about Process. Result: no one who wants to get into game development does so because they want to run their own company. They may want creative freedom, which they believe will come with running their own company, but they won't want to actually run their own company. They'll want someone else to do that.

Thus, game developers need suits. They may be staid, they may find boring things interesting, they may slap down a brilliant project because they say they can't resource it, but here's the thing: they know what they're doing and you don't. They're the real world, you're the world of the imagination; the bad news for you is that business takes place in the former, not the latter.

So accept the suits: you need them, whether they're accountants, lawyers, finance officers, marketing people, or venture capitalists. It's their job to let you do your job, so let them do it.

And if you find an MBA who's a gamer, chain them up and keep them in the cellar, they're rarer than a Black Lotus in Goldshire.

2. Game Programmers are not the *only programmers*.

Strange though it may seem to someone involved in the creation of games, computers do have other uses. They stop jets from hitting one another in the sky, they stop nuclear power stations from going KABOOM, they keep granddad's life support working while he has that triple bypass operation, they keep track of how much money you have (or haven't), . . .

Some of these programmers have skills that are desperately needed by the computer games industry. Come on, face it: games programmers will stay up until past midnight every night working on a graphics engine, but ask them to write a database and they'll tell you to use a commercial package. Some things they're interested in and some things they're not interested in. Make them work on them and you end up with code reluctantly written that operates only to minimum specifications and is entirely unmaintainable. The only comments in the source will refer to how miserable the author is and how you and your descendents for 10 generations should be damned for wanting it written.

Now, although game programmers are unhappy working on code that doesn't do anything interesting for gamers, that doesn't mean there aren't other programmers in other industries who might be more enthusiastic. In a client/server–based multiplayer game, most of the programmers want to work on the client, rather than on the back-end stuff the players never see. Besides, all that comms stuff is hard! Yet other programmers work on this kind of thing all the time. They write software to manage an office of 100 newspaper reporters, or 1,000 call center terminals, or a fleet of 10,000 trucks, and they like it.

Keep games programmers for programming games; for nongame stuff, hire people who like programming nongame stuff. That means looking to recruit from outside the 120 fresh-faced programmers who send you their CVs when you put a note that you're recruiting on an obscure part of your Web site. It probably means paying competitive wages, too.

3. Women are gamers, too.

I wouldn't recommend recruiting people merely on the grounds of their gender, but I would recommend imbuing your company with a culture that's not boys-only. Don't make implicit gender assumptions about who is going to do the development. If you want the best staff, you can't get by without the distaff.

The reverse also applies: men can make good administrative assistants, too.

4. You can't do everything.

Actually, you can; you just can't do them all at once.

When you start up a company, you may find that there are many roles and that you can fill them all. You can design, program, create the Web pages, place the magazine ads, negotiate with the bank manager, administer the database . . . These are all things you've done before, all things you know how to do, all things you're probably going to be better at than someone who comes to it cold. There are only 24 hours a day, though, and you have to spend 8 of those playing *World of Warcraft*, so that doesn't give you enough time to do everything else.

Use your understanding of the roles to direct and assist those you employ to fulfill them, but concentrate your efforts on the things only you can do. Don't spread yourself too thinly: delegate.

5. Don't be the players' puppet.

Players know nothing about game design. They know a lot about playing games, but they're not game designers. You're the game designer, not them; you get to decide how the gameplay works, not them.

This isn't to say you should arrogantly dismiss players' comments—far from it! Some of them are insightful, some enlightened, some simply brilliant. The other 99% (underestimate) you already thought of, or you didn't think of them because even your subconscious mind was smart enough to dismiss them out of hand.

"The customer is always right" is generally a sound dictum. However, when the customers are gamers, the chances are they're not making a suggestion or demand because there's an actual fault in your product; they're doing it as just another strategy in their attempt to win against it. Talking to the developers becomes part of the game.

The other thing is that every player wants to be a designer. You yourself were a player once, so don't deny it.

Listen to what players say. Assess their suggestions, and if they're good, hey, take them on board. If the same person consistently produces excellent ideas, hire that person! Just don't jump automatically to the will of the majority: it is indeed quite possible that the majority is actually wrong.

John Erskine

John Erskine has an extensive background in service and support operations, both inside and outside the game industry, and has worked on more than a dozen online games in various roles. He has been in charge of NCsoft North America's support operation since its inception, and his expertise has been central to both NCsoft's highly regarded support teams and his ever-expanding role at NCsoft. As Director of Studio Services, he oversees the operation of such organizations as Game Support, Customer Service, Localization, Quality Assurance, and Community Relations. John holds a BS degree in Psychology and an MBA with a specialization in Global Management.

I Wish I Knew:

Here are some bits of advice I would pass along based on my experience in the game industry. Most seem like common sense in retrospect, yet they are often overlooked. I hope they are useful as you get started, or progress in your career in the game industry!

1. Games are fun, but this is hard work!

Joining the game industry can be a great decision, and I do think it is fun, but it isn't really like the perception most people have about the industry! Making fun games is not all fun and games. It takes hard work, long hours, and lots of stress to make a great game (or even a bad one). And in the online game industry, the real work just begins when the game goes live.

2. Be prepared to start low and aim high as you get started in the industry.

It can be quite competitive to get started in the game industry; one popular way to do so is to begin on the ground floor. Testing and support are both great ways to get a foot in the door, learn about the industry, and build a network you can use throughout your career in the game industry. Many of today's top industry veterans started as QA Testers or Tech Support Representatives.

3. Treat every task as a learning opportunity, and make the most of it. Realize that the job you have today is the most important one of your career, but be open to and aware of new opportunities.

Every task is important, although it might not seem like it at the time. Build a repertoire of experiences that you can draw from. Recognize that experience is a great teacher, and often a hard one. Don't fall into the trap of dismissing the value of small projects today for the lure of glamorous projects in the future. Focus your energy on doing a great job in your present situation, and future opportunities will come your way.

4. Learn as many different things as you can about the game development process from start to finish.

Making a game today is more complex than ever before. Budgets are bigger, project management is more complex, and the technical complexity of the game itself is advancing at an amazing rate. It is a great asset to understand as much as possible about the entire process, so it would be wise to learn about as many different aspects of the game development process as you can. Some areas of focus should be design, art, technology and programming, business models, sales and marketing, distribution, manufacturing, support, testing, IT and network operations, legal issues, localization and globalization, and online community relations.

5. Build a strong network, and don't burn bridges.

Like most careers, "who you know" can be very important. Building a strong network of professional contacts, and building a positive reputation will be important factors for your long-term success in the game industry. The game industry is tightly networked; many people have worked together for years and at various companies, so your reputation will follow you as you move between positions and companies. Don't burn bridges because you may find that you need that bridge in the future.

6. Attitude is everything: keep an open mind and be ready to roll with the punches.

Most importantly, have a positive attitude, and be flexible! When I interview potential team members, or consider internal advancement opportunities, I feel that attitude is a key predictor of success. If the attitude is positive, even in the face of adversity, then things often have a way of working themselves out for the best. If the attitude is negative, then things will be sour even on a sunny day.

Matt Esber

Matthew Esber joined NCsoft Corporation in June 2004 as General Counsel. Prior to joining NCsoft, Matt was a corporate and securities attorney with Wilson Sonsini Goodrich & Rosati, where his practice focused on a wide variety of corporate and securities law matters for emerging growth companies. Matt holds a BA in Political Science and Sociology from Northwestern University, and a JD from UCLA School of Law.

I Wish I Knew:

1. How important the socialization/human connection aspect of gaming is.

Upon entering the gaming business, I did not fully appreciate the connection gamers have with their avatars and other players in the online community. The grouping aspect of MMOs versus the solo gaming experience really demonstrates the basic needs of humans to interact with one another. In an MMO, players are constantly interacting with NPCs and other players, which helps make MMOs an immersive experience. This interaction emulates the experience one would achieve in a real-world interaction and allows the players to achieve all the emotional aspects of a real-world relationship.

With this in mind, we must constantly focus on how the development of our games and the rules applied to the games (e.g., the user agreements) will affect the "human connection" experience of MMOs.

2. Search and register trademarks/domain names as early as possible.

It is extremely important to have your sales/marketing/development teams think of multiple names for your products as early as possible before the products introduction to the marketplace. Most people do not appreciate the need to conduct trademark searches and obtain domain registrations prior to product introduction. Discovering that someone else has registered, or is using, the name your company wants for similar goods and services can have dire consequences. To prevent a delay or loss of marketing momentum, a trademark search should be conducted immediately upon coming up with the product name.

Companies/individuals can conduct an initial search via the Internet. I would recommend searching both the United States Patent and Trademark Office (*www.uspto. gov*), for federal registrations and applications, and the Internet through one of the popular search engines. This initial search will help exclude some names early on in the process prior to incurring additional expenses. Once this initial process produces potential names, the company should conduct a more thorough search through a search company (e.g., CCH Coresearch).

F. Randall "Randy" Farmer

For more than 30 years, Randy Farmer has been a pioneer in connecting people with each other using computers as the mediating technology. He co-created one of the first online forums in 1975; the first Trek MUD in 1978; the first graphical MMOG, Lucasfilm's *Habitat*/QLink's *Club Caribe*, in 1998 with the first avatars and the first virtual MMOG currency complete with external rare object sales; the first virtual information marketplace, AMiX, in 1990; the first fully distributed virtual world platform, *EC Habitats*/*Microcosm*, in 1997; the first no-plugin Web session platform in 2002; and Yahoo!'s 360° social network in 2005. He's been a part of the development and operations of almost a dozen virtual worlds and platforms, including Fujitsu *Habitat* 1 and 2, *The Palace*, *The Sims Online*, and *Second Life*. He is presently applying the lessons of online gaming communities to Web 2.0 thinking at the Web portal Yahoo.com.

I Wish I Knew:

1. Design hubris wastes millions.

Read all the papers/books/blogs written by your predecessors that you can—multiuser game designers are pretty chatty about their successes and failures. Pay close attention to their failures—try not to duplicate those. Believe it or not, several documented failures have been repeated over and over in multiple games despite these freely available resources.

If you are going to ignore one of the lessons of those who went before, presumably because you think you know a better way, do it with your eyes wide open, and be ready to change to plan B if your innovation doesn't work out the way you expected. If you want to hash your idea out before committing it to code, consider consulting with the more experienced designers—they post on Terra Nova (*http://blogs.terra-nova.com/*) and talk to budding designers on the MUD-Dev (*http://www.kanga.nu/*) mailing list, among other places. Many of them respond pretty positively to direct contact via email—just be polite and ask your question clearly; after all, they are busy building their own worlds.

2. Beta testers != paying customers.

One recurring error in multiuser game testing is the problem of assuming that Beta users of a product will behave like real customers would. They don't, for several reasons:

A. Beta testing is a status symbol among their peers.

"I'm in the ZYXWorld Limited Beta!" is a bragging right. Since it has street-cred value, this leads the users to be on their best behavior. They will grief much less. They will share EULA breaking hacks with each other much less. They will harass much less. They won't report duping bugs. The eBay aftermarket for goods won't exist. In short, anything that would get them kicked out of the Beta won't happen anywhere near as often as when the product is released.

B. Beta testers are not paying.

Paying changes everything. During the Beta, the users work for you. When you release the game, you are working for them. Now some users will expect to be allowed to do all sorts of nasty things that they would never had done during the Beta. Those who were Beta users (and behaved then) will start to exploit bugs they found during the test period, but never reported. Bad Beta users save up bugs, so they could use them after your product's release to gain an edge over the new users, to dupe gold, or to crash your server to show off to a friend.

So, you're probably wondering, "how do I get my Beta testers to show me what life on my service will really be like and to help me find the important bugs/exploits/crashes *before* I ship?" Here are some strategies that worked for projects I worked on:

Crash Our World: Own up to the fact that Beta testers work for you and they do it for the status—incentivize the finding of crash/dup/exploit bugs you want them to find. Give them a t-shirt for finding one. Put their portrait on the Beta Hall of Fame page. Give them a rare in-world item that they can carry on into general release. Drop a monument in the world, listing the names of the testers that submitted the most heinous bugs. Turn it into a contest. Make it more valuable to report a bug than to keep it secret.

Pay-ta: Run a Paid Beta phase (after Crash Our World) to find out how users will interact with each other socially (or using your in-game social/communications features). During this phase of testing, you will get better results about which social features to prioritize/fix for release. Encourage and/or track the creation of fan communities, content databases, and add-ons—it will help you understand what to prepare for, and build word-of-mouth marketing. But, keep in mind that there is one thing you can never really test in advance: how your user community will socially scale. As the number of users grows, the type of user will diversify. For most games, the hardcore gamers come first and the casual players come later. Be sure to have a community manager whose job it is to track customer sentiment and understand the main player groups. How your community scales will challenge your development priorities and the choices you make will have you trading off new-customer acquisition vs. veteran player retention.

3. There are no game secrets, period.

Thanks to the Internet, in-game puzzles are solved for everyone at the speed of the fastest solver. Read about "The D'nalsi Island" adventure in Lucasfilm's *Habitat* where the players consumed hundreds of development hours in only tens of minutes.

The lesson? Don't count on secrets to hold up for long. Instead, treat game walk-thru Web sites as a *feature* to be embraced instead of the bane of your existence. "But," you'll say, "I could create a version of my puzzle that is customized (randomized) for every user! That will slow them down!" Don't bother; it will only upset your users.

The Tragedy of the Tapers

Consider the example of the per-player customized spell system in the original *Asheron's Call*® (by Turbine, Inc.): Each magic spell was designed to consume various types of several resources: scarabs, herbs, powders, potions, and colored tapers. The designers thought it would be great to have the users actually learn the spells by having to discover them through experimentation. The formula was different for every spell and the tapers were *different for every user*.

One can just hear the designer saying, "That'll fix those Internet spoilers! With this system, they each have to learn their own spells!" But, instead of feeling enjoyment, the players became frustrated with what seemed to be nothing other than a *waste of their time and resources* burning spell components as they were compelled to try the complete set of exponential combinations of tapers for no good reason.

What was interesting is that the users got frustrated enough to actually figure out the exact method of generating the random seed to determine the tapers for each user as follows:

Second Taper = (SEED * [Talisman + (Herb + 3) + ((Powder + Potion) * 2) + (Scarab − 2)]) mod 12 (Modified from Jon Krueger's Web page on the subject.)

The players put this all into a client plug-in to remove the calculation overhead, and were now able to correctly formulate the spells the very first time they tried. Unfortunately, this meant that new users (who didn't know about the plug-in) were likely to have a significantly poorer experience than veterans.

To Turbine's credit, they revised the game in its second year to remove the need for most of the spell components and created rainbow tapers, which worked for all users in all spells, completely canceling the original per-player design.

Hundreds of thousands of dollars went into that spell system. The users made a large chunk of that effort obsolete very quickly, and Turbine then had to pay for more development and testing to undo their design.

Learn from Turbine's mistake; focus on making your game fun *even if* the player can look up all the answers in a database or a plug-in.

Don't start a secrecy arms-war with your user. You'll lose. Remember: there are more of them than you and collectively they have more time to work on your product than you do.

Scott Foe

In September 2006, Scott Foe was called one of the world's "Top Three Under 30" game developers by *Escapist Magazine*. Foe is a pioneer in the networked console gaming space, having been a member of the Dreamcast Network product development team at Sega. Foe joined Nokia in 2003 and currently serves as Producer in the Nokia Games Business Unit, where he is responsible for pushing the limits of connected mobile gaming. As Producer of Sega's *Pocket Kingdom* ("The Ultimate Online Game"—*GameSpy*, "The Sleeper Hit"—*Penny Arcade*), Foe helped to bring massively multiplayer online gameplay to a handheld device for the first time.

Other titles that Foe has worked on include *Chu Chu Rocket!*™, *Phantasy Star Online*™, *NFL 2K1*, *Bomberman Online*™, and *Resident Evil Outbreak*®. Foe was also instrumental in creating Sega's SNAP network middleware technology and Nokia's N-Gage Arena global mobile community.

Foe is an active member of the International Game Developers Association, serving on the Mobile Game Development Special Interest Group Steering Committee, and leads the Academy of Interactive Arts & Sciences Cellular Peer Panel. He is a regular speaker at industry events, including Game Developers Conference, Harvard Berkman Center's State of Play, and Massachusetts Institute of Technology's Colloquium Series.

Foe earned Bachelor of Science degrees in both Mathematics and Computer Science from Antioch College in Yellow Springs, Ohio. In addition, Foe earned a certification in Japanese from Kyoto Seika University in Kyoto, Japan.

I Wish I Knew:

. . . what a producer is supposed to do.

. . . that a producer *is not a* game designer. The producer hires a game designer, usually as part of a team of professionals—artists, programmers, etc.—this team of professionals, hired by the producer, is commonly, collectively known as *the game*

developer. The producer has the money, and the producer has the vision; the producer uses the money to achieve the vision.

 . . . *that* responsibility *is the converse of* authority. The producer is not a game designer. Nor is the producer an artist, a programmer, a tester. Having ultimate *authority* over game development, the producer is, however, ultimately *responsible* for the production of the game.

 . . . *that gaming is a business, and as such, the production and promotion of games must be approached with a sense of economic responsibility.* The game product must be salable. Many producers will tell you that the primary role of the producer is to "*see that the product is finished on-time, under budget.*" That is the fallacy of production: You can go to the bathroom for less time, and for less money, than you ever thought possible, but at the end of the day, you still made a piece of s@#$. The primary responsibility of a producer is to create a product that is salable.

 . . . *what* profit *is.* We now live in a *knowledge-based economy*; that is, the world has become a place where a company's value is linked not only to how much capital that company has (or has the potential to have), but also to the *specialized knowledge* of the employees of that company—employee knowledge is a corporate asset, and the employee should be valued as such. *Profit* is not only the generation of wealth; *profit* is also the development of people. A producer must not only create a product that is salable; a producer must also develop people.

 . . . *that producers help people to develop their talents, not their weaknesses.* Whenever I am confronted with a staffing decision, I am reminded of a game programmer named Manny. Although quite gifted at math and sciences, Manny never wore shoes in the office. Others would come to complain to me, *He's walking around barefoot again! Make Manny put his shoes on!* To which I would always reply, *Are we paying Manny to write code? Or are we paying Manny to wear shoes?* Of course, we were paying Manny to write code. You see, a producer knows to place people in optimal position to trivialize weaknesses, develop talent, and generate wealth.

 . . . *that wealth is generated through* marketing and innovation; *everything else is just a cost. Marketing* is the act of convincing people to purchase a product. The producer is responsible for the game's development, and therefore the producer has more influence over the marketing of a product than any soul found in the marketing department. It is because of this unmatched influence that the producer must be disciplined in the art and practice of marketing.

 . . . *the difference between* invention *and* innovation. One could create a hardhat that dispenses toilet paper; it would be a neat little hardhat, and some people might even wear it—but how many? A creation that adds little or no value to peoples' lives is just an *invention*. Now, if one created a one-time-use pill that permanently increased the size of male genitalia by 12 inches, how many people would use it? A creation that adds *value* to the lives of many people is an *innovation*. A producer must be able to tell the difference between *invention* and *innovation*; a producer must always promote innovation over invention.

. . . *that "innovation" is not a line-item in a development contract.* Too often, producers find themselves in the position of having to choose whether or not to invest more than was originally planned in a game that, according to the schedule, should be done. A producer faced with this choice will either cancel the project, or spend more money, but in no circumstance will the producer approve a game that is not salable. The producer's motto: if the game's not fun, the game's not done. A good producer knows that *planning* is important but that *plans* are usually worthless; a good producer has planned for that.

. . . *mea culpa.* Perhaps because it is so frustrating and difficult a concept, no school of business—not even the most prestigious—offers a course in *mea culpa*: the ability to say, "*This was my fault, let's fix the problem and move on.*" Perhaps because no such course in mea culpa exists, narcissists are over-represented in corporate management. You can tell a narcissist by his or her tendency to hog credit and reject blame. A producer cannot afford to be a narcissist: No matter the problem, the problem is always, ultimately, the producer's fault; the producer is responsible for the game's development. The producer strives to be part of the *solution*, not a part of the *problem*.

. . . *to hitch my wagon to a star.* Producers must develop their own talents, and the best means toward that end is to pair with a respected *mentor*. A mentor is someone who has been around the industry long enough to show you the ropes. A mentor is also someone who likes you enough to show you more of the ropes than how to tie a noose for yourself. We will, quite literally, outlive most every company we work for, but the people we meet along the way can become lifetime co-workers, and even lifetime friends.

. . . *our reach.* Every person in the first-world under the age of 36 has played a videogame. Games are industry: people shelter and feed their families with income from games-related businesses. Games are serious education: there's no situation that cannot be simulated. Games are entertainment, a staple of culture equal to music, books, and movies. To bring joy . . . that is what a producer is supposed to do.

Steve Goldstein

Steve Goldstein is the Director of Business Development and General Counsel for Flagship Studios, Inc. Prior to joining Flagship in July 2005 Steve was an associate at the law firm of Stubbs, Alderton & Markiles, LLP, where he represented independent videogame publishers and developers, film studios and technology companies, including Flagship, NovaLogic, Inc., 1C Company, High Moon Studios, Revolution Studios, Interplay Entertainment, and Skype Technologies, S.A. Steve was the primary attorney for Flagship in negotiating its publishing deals with Namco Hometek Inc. and HanbitSoft, Inc.

In his role at Flagship, Steve has negotiated all of its co-marketing and ancillary properties agreements, including deals with Microsoft, Nvidia, Weta Workshop, TOKYOPOP!, Dark Horse Comics and Simon & Schuster, among others.

I Wish I Knew:

If someone just starting out in the video game industry asked me for advice, I don't think I'd have anything industry-specific to tell them. During the course of my career, probably the most important thing I have learned is that most business-related clichés are actually true. Rather than try to pretend that I'm clever enough to come up with something new and insightful, I'm just going to hit on a few that I've found to be true (or true enough).

1. Never delete a contact. You never know who he or she may wind up being.

I manage my Outlook contacts as if it were a game. I like seeing how many contacts I can build up. Every time I get a card, I put it into my Outlook, and I never ever delete a contact (in fact, I've got a few in there who have died, but who knows if you'll bump into them again). It doesn't matter who it is, or what they do, I'll add them to my contacts. The reason is that you never really know. The kid (such as yourself) you meet who is just starting out could very well be your boss or running a successful developer one day.

Case in point: Many moons ago, when I was in law school I interned in a large multinational professional services corporation. I worked for many of the partners in the particular department I was in. At one point, I was going to get a job at that company as opposed to taking the bar, but it didn't work out. However, when I left the company, I kept track of all the partners I had developed a professional relationship with, no matter how slight.

About six months ago, I cut a deal with a company relating to the game we're working on. One of the owners of that company is an extremely successful individual who used to be represented by the company I interned for when I was in law school. In fact, he was represented by one of the partners I had a direct relationship with (and had not spoken to for 10 years). So, using my new business deal as an entry point, I reconnected with him. We've now had several meetings together, and it may possibly lead to additional business later down the line.

2. Never take "no" as an answer, or "Never give up! Never surrender!"

A great line from *Galaxy Quest* turns out to be an outstanding way to look at business. You may hear "no" a lot of times in your career, but just don't accept it as an answer.

Actually, let me rephrase that. If you are looking for a job in the industry right now, and someone sends you a rejection letter, then don't show up at the office on Monday to start work. That rejection letter does mean "no"; however, most of the time it means, "not just right now." We get a ton of resumes from people who are really good, but they just don't have the requisite experience yet. So a "no" right now could be a "yes" after you've had a couple years under your belt. This goes back to point 1 above. If an HR person sends you a rejection at a company, don't lose her number. You never know when you may apply there again.

But back to not taking "no" as an answer. In almost all business negotiations, "no" is a way of saying, "let's try something else." People want to get deals done. They don't like rejecting them. Think about it. If your job is rejecting deals, then you have nothing to show for your work. If you get a "no," try to find another way to make the deal more palatable to the other side.

Case in point: We were putting an ancillary deal together in which a company was going to use the license of our game to create a derivative work (i.e., toys, books, movies, etc.). Our first position wasn't acceptable to them and they said "no." So I had to ask myself, why is this deal important to us? I realized that this particular relationship would be great for us in a manner that my initial offer didn't capture. So I went back to them with a new position that highlighted what we felt was important in the deal and at the same time addressed their concerns in getting involved with the venture. The "no" turned to a "yes." Again, a "no" doesn't always mean for you to go away. It means for you to come back with a different angle.

Brian Green

Brian Green, often known by the online pseudonym of "Psychochild," is an experienced online game developer. He is co-editor and co-author of this book.

Brian received degrees in both Spanish and Computer Science with a minor in Business. He started his professional career in 1998 working on the classic online RPG, *Meridian® 59* (*http://www.meridian59.com/*). He then left to work at the now defunct Communities.com on *The Palace*, a noted graphical chat product.

Brian later started Near Death Studios, Inc. with fellow former *Meridian 59* developer Rob "Q" Ellis II. In late 2001, the company had the opportunity to purchase *Meridian 59* and work on it again. In May 2002, *Meridian 59* was commercially re-launched. Brian has maintained *Meridian 59* and ran the business side of Near Death Studios, Inc. He is a frequent speaker at game industry conferences and shares his experiences in developing independent games and running a business.

I Wish I Knew:

1. It is important to know and understand business issues in order to develop games.

Business issues are important to nearly every developer. Only the junior level developers at large companies may be able to safely ignore business issues and still do their job. But once you get past that level, business issues will influence your career in many ways. Learning why your employer makes certain decisions can help you tremendously.

Of course, this lesson goes double when you want to start up your own studio. When people decide they want to start up a game studio, they worry about all the details of game development. What type of game should they make? Who will write the graphics engine? If business issues do get any attention, it is usually in the form of, "How will we spend all the money?"

Even people smart enough to know that business issues are important will claim that they don't have time. I definitely know how hard it is to develop a game on a tight budget with a small team and a seemingly unreachable goal. Game development is one of the most challenging things you can do. But, without understanding business issues, your development work could end up being all for nothing.

For proof, you only need to look around and talk to your peers. The industry is littered with the corpses of game development companies that had ambitious ideas but never really thought about the business side of things until it was too late. Many company closures could have been averted if someone had spent some time to plan the business side of things.

This is one reason why I wanted to help write this book: business issues will not go away if you ignore them, and I want to see more developers succeed.

2. Running a business isn't impossible.

I never saw myself as the entrepreneurial type. I wanted a nice, safe job with a steady paycheck when I was in college. Of course, then I got into developing games as a hobby and I was hooked. I got a job at a game company as soon as I could and loved it. Yet, I felt frustrated when I felt my project didn't get the attention it deserved. I'm sure many people reading this are nodding their heads, knowing exactly how that feels.

So, when I was happily working at a company getting a steady paycheck, it surprised me when I seriously considered starting a company. Looking back, I see how my attitudes had changed.

The most important thing is to learn from people who have done this before. I had attended some conference sessions about starting your own business, and was lucky when some of that advice helped save the company from a rough period at the beginning when one of the co-founders left. Having the proper agreements in place helped us tremendously. This book is full of the best advice we could find, so learn from it.

Once you are in the middle of running your own business, it is an exercise in common sense: don't spend more money than you have, don't take on more risk than you can tolerate, don't put off important things like taxes, learn to manage your time effectively.

3. The importance of finding a good lawyer and accountant.

This is the most practical advice I can give to a startup game development company. A good lawyer can help protect you and keep your company safe from outside harm. The only group of people your lawyer can't protect you from? The tax agency. That's why it is important to have a good accountant to take care of your taxes and check your bookkeeping. It may seem expensive initially, but the price of running into legal or tax troubles will be a lot more expensive. Ask people you know for information about a good lawyer, and a quality business lawyer should be able to refer you to a good accountant.

As I mentioned before, we had one of our co-founders leave the company under unfriendly circumstances. Because we had founder's agreements in place and overseen by the lawyer, our company was able to continue on with its goals instead of falling apart like other companies have under similar situations. The fees we paid to the lawyer were well worth every penny at that point.

William Leverett

Will Leverett is currently the manager of game support at NCsoft Corporation and a nine-year veteran of the massively multiplayer online games industry. He joined Origin Systems and Electronic Arts in 1997 for the launch of Ultima Online, and was personally involved in the creation of EA's support model, which is now used by every major MMO product today and considered standard among the industry. After establishing various additional revenue services and creating the groundwork for support for other EA products such as *The Sims Online*, *Motor City Online*, and *Earth and Beyond*, he rejoined several former coworkers in January 2004 to grow the service at NCsoft for a product line that currently includes *Lineage®*, *Lineage 2*, *City of Heroes*, and *Guild Wars®*. His experience and knowledge in these roles have led him to playing a key role in virtual world governance and intellectual property issues with all current and future NCsoft products.

I Wish I Knew:

MMO games are not games at all. They are professional Internet services in every respect, creating massive platforms from which virtual communities can grow and people of all walks of life are able to collaborate and socialize together, all in the name of entertainment.
And by the way . . . the world is flat.

I like to think that in my eight years of working specifically within the MMO service industry that I have, as much as anyone else, been able to capitalize and learn from the endless mistakes made by the industry. Mistakes made by companies I have worked for, by teams I have been part of, and most certainly from my own seemingly endless list of personal and professional blunders, trials, and tribulations.

So it makes me cringe that for all of the hardships endured, for all that I and others have learned, for every recreation of the wheel, and for all of my respected colleagues who in every way imaginable warn about this very specific lesson, almost all newcomers to the massively multiplayer online game industry—and even more perplexingly, a percentage of veterans who have not learned the lesson—frequently and tragically make the mistake that this is actually only about creating solid game content for players.

Shame, shame.

The global MMO industry has quickly found itself competing as a professional entertainment service that happens to use the Internet as a delivery system against the likes of cable/satellite television, the movies, music, print media, malls, coffee shops, bars, cell phones, iPods, Nintendo DS, Sony PSP, roller skating, and bowling. We're not just vying for the entertainment dollar but also for entertainment time, and with each year, the average person's 24-hour day seems to get shorter and shorter.

Is game content required? Absolutely! But enterprising MMO idealists who think that game content alone should be enough to meet the expectations and demands of players is at this point in time simply naïve. The various designs, instruments, and devices that empower players to create, populate, and network together in these massive worlds go beyond simple game content. These social mechanisms allow players to take what is a static void into a living, breathing environment.

Beyond in-game elements, players will experience the slew of technical and payment-related problems faced by any sort of commercial software purchase. But MMO games are fully reflective of human behavior. Put two people in the same room and over time they'll have problems. Put ten thousand in the same room and you'll have problems within half a minute. At that point, it's been our experience that natives become extremely restless and difficult to regulate.

Once the game commercially becomes "live," an army of technicians, engineers, game world administrators, and service representatives are required to oversee this evolving social construct. They are needed to identify, arbitrate, mediate, and resolve social, technical, and legal matters. They will assist, police, and pacify thousands on a daily basis. And sometimes, in order to maintain integrity of the service, they are required to do just as Captain Willard was instructed on how to handle Colonel Kurtz: "Terminate with extreme prejudice."

But don't let this apocalyptic horror depress anyone. The good news here is that we have also found ourselves on the cutting edge of commercial software production and operation, and that we are utilizing the global marketplace to our advantage to deliver these services.

I would not pretend to do better than Thomas Friedman in his excellent book, *The World Is Flat*, where he wonderfully examines the fusion of technological, cultural, and geopolitical events that have granted us these opportunities. As such, teams in Texas find themselves collaborating around the clock with those in Seoul, Seattle, Los Angeles, Denver, San Jose, Madrid, New Delhi, London, Taipei . . . as if they were in the very next room.

So, stay on your toes, and plan for that post-launch Day One. Within 24 hours, your baby MMO will have grown from a level-based dungeon crawl or space simulation immediately into a full-fledged professional Internet service.

Alexander Macris

Alexander Macris is co-founder, president, and CEO of Themis Group. In addition to providing the company's leadership and directing its key client engagements, he is the publisher of *The Escapist* magazine and served as editor-in-chief of its Themis Report series. Prior to Themis, he was founder and CEO of WarCry Network, a community destination for entertainment enthusiasts, which he grew to 1 million monthly users. A frequent speaker at both marketing and game industry events, Alexander is a graduate magna cum laude of Harvard Law School, where he authored a study on the effects of game design on community growth.

I Wish I Knew:

1. That networking yielded compounding returns.

Those of you who've invested in stocks or bonds will be familiar with the concept of compounding returns—that by getting a 10% return per year you can double your money in less than 10 years, and so on. It's the secret sauce of capitalist success.

Well, networking—the meet and greet, exchanging business cards, joining Linked In, getting your name onto forums—has compounding returns. The sooner you start doing it, the better off you are, and the longer you've been doing it, the more it's going to pay off. Why does networking compound?

In part, it's because every person you meet, every junior developer, intern, low-level designer, whatever they may be, is actively working on *their* career. In five years, the test lead you befriended at GDC may be a producer at EA. Even the most casual relationship can become suddenly valuable.

In part, it's because of the law of weak connectors. Research has shown that job leads, for example, often don't come from our close relationships, because we already know what they know and so they have nothing to offer. Rather, they come from our casual acquaintances, our friendly colleagues, our business associates. The more weak connections you have, the more powerful your network becomes.

And in part it's because of the implicit tit-for-tat of networking: the more actively you work to introduce people, make connections, offer help, and get involved, the more likely others are to do those things for you.

Add it all together and you realize that the sooner you start building your personal network, the better. Entering a new industry is hard, especially as you'll be coming in low on the totem pole, with few contacts or relationships in high places. The game industry is, perhaps, more difficult than most to penetrate, as it's relatively small and insular, and many of the industry's founders are actually still active in the field—it's harder to be the young radical when the old masters are still on hand. But don't get discouraged. The payoff for networking is worth it—it just takes time. I wish I'd started sooner. Like, say, college.

2. The importance of process.

There's an old military adage that says, "amateurs study strategy and tactics; professionals study logistics." And it's true. Starting out in any profession, whether it's military officer, or more relevant to this discussion, developer, lawyer, or executive, it's natural to be focused on just results; getting the job done, doing things. When I was just starting out, I was uncertain I could *get* the results, so I felt like it had to be my priority.

But a strict focus on results tends to make you hard to work with or work for—it leads to crunch time, miscommunication, sloppy code, slash-and-burn solutions. Professionals know what to do, but they also know how best to do it. The hallmark of professionalism comes when you can get great results in a clean, efficient way that makes it easy for others to follow your lead or be your team member. And that calls for an understanding of process—whether it's project management, software development methodology, or the AP stylebook, at some point you need to learn the rules.

3. The volatility of a startup.

When I launched *WarCry,* an online ad-funded game community, I thought I had an idea what I was in for. The reality of the risks and the wild volatility was far in excess of what I had envisioned.

It didn't help that I launched *WarCry* in April 2000, with what can only be described as colossally bad timing. Venture funding dried out simultaneously with the ad market crash. Nonetheless, we did have some funding from an angel round, and more importantly, some big ideas. Six months in, we had an office, a team of five, and functional technology. Six months after that, the company was basically down to a laptop, on a rug, in an empty bedroom. And three months after that, the company was in an office, with more funding, a new brand, and projects that pushed it into the black.

During those first, wild 18 months, I can't tell you how many times I was told to pack it in by people who assured me it was "game over." The day I was closest to quitting—I was literally freshening up the resume—the next round of funding came in. Five years later, still in business, I can recognize that as *the* single most important decision I ever made for the company; the decision not to quit. But it was a near-run thing.

So my advice there is that if you're going into a startup environment, like a new game studio, know what you're getting yourself into, accept that it's going to be a wild ride, and take a long view of the ups and downs.

Jessica Mulligan

Jessica Mulligan has been making online games since 1986 and has been involved in the design, development, or management of more than 50 of them, including such groundbreakers as *AD&D: NeverWinter Nights*™, *Ultima Online*, and *Asheron's Call*. A respected writer on industry issues, she wrote the popular "Biting the Hand" column on Skotos.net for over six years. Her most recent book, *Developing Online Games: An Insider's Guide,* with co-author Bridgette Patrovsky, has been published in 17 countries worldwide, including Korea and China, and is considered "the Bible" of MMO development.

Jessica is currently an online games executive consultant to major corporations and pens the "Outside, Looking In" column for Pacific Epoch at *http://www.pacificepoch.com/.* She can be contacted at *jessica.mulligan@gmail.com.*

I Wish I Knew:

1. 90% of the work in an MMO happens after launch.

You would think, after some 22 years of commercial online gaming, that the industry would have learned this lesson by now.

Apparently not. It doesn't seem to matter how much we talk about it, how many articles we write about it, how many times the phrase is tossed around at conventions; heck, my co-author Bridgette Patrovsky and I made it one of the keystones of our book, *Developing Online Games: An Insider's Guide*, published in 2003, and that book is widely recognized as a "must read" for executives and first-time MMO developers. No matter how much we talk about it and recognize it as a critical piece to MMOs, the meaning of that phrase is still misunderstood by pretty much every new entry into the marketplace.

Yet, this may be the single most important thing to understand about running a commercial MMO. The reason it isn't better understood is simple: most first-time MMO teams—and more than one experienced team, as well—continue to be almost blindly developer-centric. They are concentrated on initial game development, as if development suddenly ends when an MMO launches. They generally give short shrift to considering what happens in the years after the game launch. They should be as equally service-centric; it is the only way to understand what will happen after the launch.

If you don't understand that most of the work happens after launch before you begin development, you will most likely find at launch that you lack the necessary tools and manpower to actually service your game, because you won't have ramped them up during development. This has happened to virtually every first-time entrant into the MMO space; it has cost them dearly, because more people churn out of an MMO that is badly managed. Average churn rates for an MMO are around 4% monthly for a well-run game; they are twice that for a badly run MMO. And once a player leaves because of bad management of the service, you have less than a 5% chance of ever getting him or her back.

What the phrase "90% of the work happens after launch" really means is pretty simple: development of an MMO, for all that it can be a bloody war to the knife in the trenches, is the easy part. Getting ramped up for the launch and to be a service organization after launch, which means putting together a customer service organization, building coherent service and account management tools, hiring and training a network operations shop, ramping up a live development team to fix bugs and an expansion pack team to add content over time and then making all that work for years and years . . . that is the hard part.

In April 2006, I was invited to give a seminar at a university in Copenhagen, Denmark. One of my slides made the point that 90% of the work happens after launch and a member of the audience asked me what it really meant. After all, didn't three years of development mean tens of thousands of manhours of development? He'd worked on a couple standard videogames and it was grinding.

So I asked him if he had ever played the original *EverQuest* (EQ); of course, from launch day in 1999 to the present, he said. OK, I replied, do some simple addition: total up the manhours of three years of development by maybe 50 developers at peak, versus seven years of a Live Operations Team of about 200 people, including a customer service organization of over 100 representatives, several network operations people on a 24/7 schedule, several community relations people that have to monitor the forums, marketing and PR for seven years including setting up and running the EQ player conventions, a billing and account management team that had to bill and handle inquires from 450,000 subscribers at peak and over half-a-dozen expansion packs that pretty much doubled or tripled the content in the game. All this was geared, ultimately, at making the entire game experience, from log-in to log-off, as smooth and pleasing as possible to retain the highest possible number of subscribers.

Explained that way, he got it immediately. The importance of all this is simple, too: if you do it right, not only do you retain more subscribers past the free trial period, it creates great word-of-mouth advertising for your game and your current subscribers bring in new subscribers. Historically in the MMO space, we have acquired 80% of our customers after the initial surge of customers coming in during launch week through good word of mouth.

Now do you see why this is all so important?

Information about your players' in-game habits is your most important tool. *Ultima Online* in 1999 is a good example here. We were the first MMO to allow eBay transactions for real money, but this was causing real issues. By allowing sales of items and accounts for real money, we created an incentive to find and use bugs. Early that year, it became obvious to us that the game was rife with bugs, especially with duplication bugs that allowed some players to manufacture pretty much any object in the game. Normally, this was done by finding the boundaries between physical servers and causing a crash, which caused the player's inventory to be duplicated. Crash the servers while carrying 1000 gold and you ended up with 2000 gold, and so on, which would then be put up for sale on eBay.

So, not only was this was destroying the game economy; it was also causing our servers to go down constantly, preventing thousands of people from playing and creating a customer service nightmare. We were losing customers to the crashes, because we were seen as a technologically "unstable" platform. There was one group of such "exploiters" that was openly laughing at us on public message boards, daring us to stop them; they knew we probably couldn't. They were right.

It should have been simple to track these players; for example, we should have been able to run a database query to see which players had accumulated the most game gold or objects in a short period of time and investigate from there. However, we didn't have any way to track these attempts; our database was, simply, *the suck*. No one had ever anticipated problems such as these, because no one had ever had over 100,000 players in a single game before *Ultima Online*.

So, we had to spend the better part of a year retooling our database. As we added capabilities, it became incredibly easy to find players executing such bugs and exploits, track them for a while, and then cut them off at the knees. Having these capabilities cut our churn by a wide margin, because we were able to react in hours or minutes to problems, rather than days or weeks. It also cut our customer service response times by over 50% and our CS costs in half.

Incredibly, most MMOs today still haven't learned this lesson. Database tools for customer service, data mining, and security are still the low items on the totem pole, for the most part, when they should be designed and built along with the game itself, not as an afterthought.

2. Your Community Managers are not part of the Marketing staff.

Community Managers (CMs) are a unique breed; they have to be advocates on game matters for the players to the Live Team and developers, while at the same time understanding the needs of the business and being able to explain problems and tough decisions to the players in a way that won't sound like some Marketing puke making excuses. What players recognize, correctly or incorrectly, is that marketing is all about making things look good, not about what is best for the game and the players. And if there is one thing MMO players hate, it is some impersonal and anonymous Marketing puke trying to spin a problem or controversy to make a bad decision or problem look like a marvel of reasoning and customer service.

This creates a delicate high-wire balancing act without a net, and few people can negotiate it correctly without ending up as strawberry jam on the pavement below. It means that, for your Community Manager to have any legitimacy or personal connection at all with the players, he or she has to be considered a developer and a member of the Live Development team, report to the Live Producer or Executive Producer, sit with the developers and be a part of their discussions and decisions. Not only is this the only way your CMs will have full information to give the players and be able to react instantly when there is a crisis, it is the only way the players will ever trust the CMs. Sometimes, you have literally minutes to post about a crisis before it gets out of hand; an informed CM that reports to development can make those decisions in minutes, give the players the straight dope, and avert a PR disaster.

Since moving the CMs into the Marketing department makes such little sense, naturally the first thing many publishers want to do is just that. They defenestrate the CMs, move them out of the developer pit and into the marketing area, and have them report to the head of Marketing. In other words, they want marketing to control the message to the players on a daily basis. Marketing wonks don't like to move in minutes with any actual information; they want to let things settle out, so the message can be massaged and manipulated elegantly. So the first thing that marketing managers tend to do is make CMs clear every post with them before it is posted and to stop using their personal handle on posts. Then they rewrite posts to strip out any actual information, leaving only the "happy talk" phrases and familiar anodynes such as "We're experiencing technical difficulties" and "Thank you for your patience," signed as something brilliantly impersonal as "The <MMO> Live Team." All that is left is pretty much everything players hate about "marketing" messages, in other words. You remember those guys: the paying customers who hate marketing spin.

This whole concept of "CMs as members of Marketing" is so blindingly stupid that I am awed by its brainlessness. If the field of community management has a motto, it is "For players, instant gratification takes too long." When you can't react as the crisis is unfolding, you lose customers. Every customer lost to a commercial MMO is between $120 and $180 per year lost, forever. When CM is moved to the Marketing department, it is as if the senior executives got together and said, "Whoa! We're way too successful and making too much money; we need to figure out how to alienate our customers, right now!" As an enterprise, you lose that very important personal connection to the player; when you lose that, you are already half-way to losing the player, as well.

This all reads as very harsh toward marketing professionals and it is not intended to be; marketing is important to an MMO, it is just that it has different processes, goals, and long-term needs than those of the players and the Live Dev Team. Senior management has to understand that players want a personal connection to and actual information from the developers and act accordingly.

Jeff Vogel

For over a decade now, I have run Spiderweb Software. It's a small company, based in Seattle. With the help of two employees, I write fantasy role-playing games for Windows and Macintosh. They are then sold over my Web site using the marketing technique that used to charmingly be called shareware. In that time, I've made a lot of money selling my games. Nobody is more surprised by this than me. I have sort of a weird, mutant position in the computer game industry, serving a niche ('80s style fantasy RPGs) in my small, sincere, low-tech way. However, since writing games on your lonesome for a small, under-serviced clientele is a pretty darn decent way to break into this business, some of the things I learned might be of value. My advice is mostly aimed at small groups writing a game with limited resources.

I Wish I Knew:

It's difficult to write about the things I wish I knew when I started. Being an Indie game developer is painfully unforgiving. People who don't start out knowing what they need to know tend to be crushed. However, there are a few things I did learn, and I was saved from destruction by simple dumb luck.

1. Respect the 90/10 rule.

There are thousands of formulations of the 90/10 rule. My favorite one is, "10% of the job is 90% of the work."

What this means is that, when the game seems to be almost done, when you've been at it for months and months and you've poured your heart into it and it isn't much fun anymore and your energy is starting to flag, well, that's when you're about to be blindsided. Wham.

That is when the real problems will show up. The game mechanics that just don't work. The long, extremely unfun testing and bug-fixing period. The crashing bug that you just can't track down, even though you've gone through thousands of lines of code character by character and your eyeballs have filled up with blood.

The closer you get to shipping your game, the more you will be ambushed by the stuff you let slide, the stuff you didn't notice, or the errors that hadn't yet become visible. Be ready for this.

2. Comment your code.

Seriously. Someday you, like me, are going to return to a chunk of code you wrote and go, "I have no idea what's going on here." Help yourself out.

3. Don't neglect reality.

You're trying to start a business. That means you need a lawyer and an accountant. Don't be like me and wait until after I was actually pulling in money.

If you don't do your taxes right because you didn't understand the law, you will not get mercy. Your ignorance will only buy you a brief look of sympathy from the auditor before he DESTROYS you.

I was in business for years before I bought proper liability insurance. Don't think I ain't kicking myself about that.

4. Cherish your inner PR lizard.

Man, but I hate doing PR. Calling the magazines. Putting together the press kits. Looking up the Web site contacts. I wish I could spend that time writing games. Or smacking my face against the wall.

But if you neglect 10 hours of PR, your thousand hours of development might well be wasted. You have to get out there and let people know about your game. In the end, unless you have a kajillion dollars for advertising, word of mouth will make or break you. But you need to let that first group of people know about you.

And you'll have to be pretty patient. It took me years and several games to get noticed. Keep sending press kits across the editor's desk. It'll take a few before he or she notices you and believes you are serious.

Along those lines, learn how to write a good press release and put together a suitably professional press kit. Read a book on marketing. Scope out Web sites and try to find one with a reasonable rate for banner ads. Spend money to make money. And so on.

5. Play lots of games.

These days, I play games constantly. Being able to write games off is one of the great things about being in this business. But it took me a long time to realize that I needed to force myself to do it, even when I didn't want to.

You wouldn't try to write a word processor without scoping out the other word processors. You shouldn't make games without being up to date on the hippest and the hottest stuff available.

Plus, if you play games a lot, there is the slight chance that you may, sometimes, have fun. When you go from playing them to writing them, a lot of the fun goes away. It's good to get the occasional reminder of what the whole business is all about.

And if you ever play your own game and think it's fun? Keep doing what you're doing! You're getting there!

Gordon Walton

Gordon Walton has been authoring games and managing game development since 1977. He is currently co-Studio Director at BioWare Austin. Previously he was VP,

Executive Producer, and Studio Manager at Sony Online Entertainment in Austin, working on an unannounced product and *Star Wars Galaxies*®. Prior to joining Sony Online Entertainment, Gordon was VP and Executive Producer of *The Sims Online* at Electronic Arts/Maxis, and in the same role for Origin Systems managing *Ultima Online*™. He also served as Senior VP and General Manager of Kesmai Studios where he oversaw the development of several MMOGs including *Air Warrior*™ and *Multiplayer Battletech*™. Gordon has owned and managed two development companies and was development manager for both Three-Sixty Pacific and Konami of America, Inc. He has personally developed over 30 games and overseen the development of over 200 games.

Gordon has been a speaker at every Game Developers Conference since its inception in 1988. Gordon has also been a featured speaker at industry events such as E3, Austin Game Developers Conference, East Coast Computer Game Developers Conference, Kagan Conference, Japan Personal Computer Software Association Conference, and Jupiter's Conference.

Gordon is a founding member of the International Game Developers Association (IGDA) and a member of the Academy of Interactive Arts and Sciences (AIAS). Gordon holds a BS degree in computer science from Texas A&M University with a minor in electrical engineering.

I Wish I Knew:

1. Talent is common.
Talent is required to be in the games business, so it doesn't make you special at all. Having talent makes a person feel special and we want to be appreciated for having that talent. When you join a game company, you will find yourself surrounded by extraordinarily talented people. And at some point you will meet people who clearly surpass you in your area of expertise. Talent is expected of people wanting to be in the games business, so find and nurture your talent now, as it is one of the requirements for entry into making games. But don't come to the games business believing that your talent entitles you to special treatment.

2. How important being a team player was going to be.
When I started in the business, I believed that my talent and contribution would be enough for success. It didn't take me long to figure out that I needed a lot of other smart and talented people around me to achieve any success at all. But I also learned that having a bunch of great people together was necessary but not enough unless they worked as a well-oiled team. To get a team to work together well, I had to learn how to not only be a good teammate, but to help my other teammates succeed also. Being a good teammate means first doing your part, being completely dependable when it comes to your part of the game development. Also you should be willing to help your teammates when they have problems with their work. Coming to work

every day with a positive, can-do attitude not only helps you, but it will have a beneficial effect on your teammates. More than anything, you need to know your teammates as the humans they are. This insight will let you help your teammates become the best team they can be. Basically, all this boils down to setting the best example you can for your teammates.

To get a head start on being a good team player, do team projects before you get into the workplace. Whether it is something for school or an independent game, getting experience working with different teams is an extremely valuable learning experience. Get as much of this experience as you can before you get into the games business and you will stand out within your game team.

3. Making games is yet another game to play.

Playing games can be pretty darn fun for hours on end. Making games can be fun too, but it's at least 95% perspiration to about 5% inspiration. If you want to get into the games business, you need to recognize that it takes a tremendous amount of focused, mentally challenging work most of the time, and that most of that truly is work. Electronic games are at the intersection of high technology and consumer tastes. Both of these are evolving constantly, so keeping up with the market can be tough. Historically, this means we are always in a hurry to get our games done before consumer taste shifts or a competitor beats our game to market. You really need to love the process of making games so that the work involved ends up being more play than work for you. The best way to figure this out is to build games or mods of games yourself before you get into the business. See if you can get enjoyment from the process of making entertainment, not just enjoyment from consuming it.

4. How hard it is to finish what you start.

One of the hardest things game developers have to do is actually "finish" games. Finishing is a lot harder than it looks to most people. Getting a game kind of working is a lot easier than finishing it for market. Before I actually made commercial games, I underestimated how hard this was, and we see many new game employees have trouble with having the discipline to complete a game to the point that it is really ready for market. Even so, it is rare that a game is actually "finished," but there is a day it ends up being mastered for commercial release. So the goal here is to make the game the best it can be before that day comes, even if it takes a lot of extra effort. Preparing for the "finishing" aspect of making games requires completing things that are not all that fun. Good examples include finishing college, finishing school projects, and/or finishing small independent games. Part of the reason we hire people with game experience is that we want people who have been through the "finishing" process. So get as much experience finishing things as you can and play that up when it's time to get your first game job.

5. Ideas are cheap, execution is hard.

People outside of the industry overvalue ideas. I can't count the times I've had people (who don't make games for a living) try to sell their great idea to a company I worked for. The truth is there are extremely few unique ideas out there, and even those are not worth much unless they can be realized. Game companies are filled with talented and creative people, and most companies can only execute on a fraction of what those employees can come up with. Execution—that is, being able to actually build a team to take an idea from concept to a complete and fun-to-play product—is the rare quality in our business. Our people are expected to be creative, but those who find a way to execute are most valued and rewarded. When you look for a game job, show the potential employer situations where you have executed in the face of adversity and you will stand out from other candidates.

6. Learning how to welcome negative feedback.

When you do creative work, it's only natural to look for positive feedback. We all want to be liked and our work to be appreciated. When I started making games, I wanted to make games that were fun for me and other people. The challenge we have as game makers, though, is we need feedback, especially negative feedback so our games can get even better. You need a lot of negative feedback to improve your games. You can't let the negative feedback depress you, though; you have to embrace it. Listen to your potential customers and determine what would make them happier. Games get much better and you become a more professional game maker when you can take and integrate feedback, especially the negative kind. The best way to prepare for this is to really examine the negative feedback you get on almost anything in life. Look at that negative feedback squarely and rather than blame the feedback on the person giving it, figure out what you could change to get different feedback. Sometimes, that feedback won't be valid, but most of it will be from the person who is giving the feedback's point of view. You get to choose what feedback you integrate into yourself and into your work. The important thing is to actually hear and evaluate it all, not just dismiss the feedback you don't like to hear.

7. Terrible games take as much work as hit games.

Nobody starts out to make a bad game. Every game starts with the passion of a team along with someone enthused enough to fund its development, and the goal is always to make something great that people will love (and buy lots of). The truth, though, is that 90–95% of all games are destined to fail (i.e., not make a profit) even if they get finished and distributed to the public. This is one of the harsh realities of working in a creative, hit-driven industry such as electronic entertainment. And the work that the team puts into a game that fails is no less challenging than the work that goes into those games that are mega-hits. So once you get past your first job in the industry (which is hard enough to get that you shouldn't be overly selective), you need to take responsibility for picking places and games to work on that improve your chances of success. Looking at the track record of the company in the type of game they are building, evaluating the success of previous similar games, looking at the leaders and individuals on a given team are great places to start. Given all that, I still recommend you go where your passion is when you pick a game to work on, even if it is a risky proposition. Just do this with your eyes open, and recognize the risk level you are accepting by working on a particular game. You will still learn a lot even if the game fails; just don't take the game failure personally unless you single-handedly caused the problem!

8. "Making it" doesn't exist in the games business.

The games business is constantly evolving and changing and you will have to do that also to be successful. This means that you won't find a way to "plateau" or rest on your laurels in this business. What makes you successful now may not work as well only a few years later, so you will constantly have to be learning and improving your skills just to keep up. In my experience, you will be most successful if you cultivate a habit of "lifetime learning." Make sure you set aside time to learn more about game development and your core skills. And be open to learning things from both inside and outside of the games business. The games business doesn't have a monopoly on knowledge after all!

9. Remember your passion daily.

It is important to find a way to remind yourself of what brought you into game development daily. For each person, the reasons will differ. Some just want to exercise their creativity. Some like the feeling of being in "show biz." Some believe they will get rich and/or be famous. In the end, your motivation doesn't matter as much as finding a way to remind yourself of it on a consistent basis. This is because most games take a long time to accomplish, and because most of that is difficult work that is not inherently creative or enjoyable to most people. The last thing you want is for a job in the games industry to feel like a "real job," so make sure and find a way to remind yourself why you haven chosen this life on a daily basis if possible. It may mean playing games at least a little bit each day, or having reminders of things you have succeeded at in your office or cube. What is important is consistently getting in touch with the passion that got you into making games. Passion is critical for people in the business of creating entertainment.

These are a few things I have learned while making games over the last 27 years, which I wish I'd known at the beginning of my career. Not all of them may resonate with you, but I hope at least a few of them offer some value. Good luck in your gaming career!

Andrew S. Zaffron

As senior vice president and general counsel of Sony Online Entertainment (SOE), a subsidiary of Sony Corporation and Sony Pictures Digital Inc., Andy Zaffron brings over 15 years of experience to his position. Mr. Zaffron is responsible for all legal and business affairs of Sony Online Entertainment.

2003 marked Mr. Zaffron's tenth anniversary with Sony companies. Prior to joining SOE in 1999, Mr. Zaffron was director of legal and business affairs at Sony Computer Entertainment America—responsible for property licensing, litigation management, and providing legal and business affairs support to the sales, finance, operations, and customer service groups. Before joining Sony, Mr. Zaffron was a trial lawyer in San Diego, California.

Mr. Zaffron is a member of the California bar, has been admitted to practice before all state and federal courts in California, is a member of the American Corporate Counsel Association, and has spoken on numerous industry and professional panels. Mr. Zaffron received his Bachelor of Science and Juris Doctor degrees from the University of Illinois.

1. Avoid the "long, cold winter"; share your publisher's profits.

You have arrived—you've established your nascent game development operation, dreamed up an exciting novel game idea, created a vibrant visualization and pitch, and GamePubCo offers to fund your modest $5 million next-gen console game development budget as an advance against a 12% of wholesale receipts back end: it is so tempting to just close your eyes and sign! But as your hand irresistibly grabs that pen and moves toward that signature page—forcibly pull it back, pull out your spreadsheet, calculator, pencil and/or abacus first, and run the numbers: the winter after launch, will you be drinking Comte de Champagne or Cold Duck?

In the "good old days," it was so easy. GamePubCo advanced NewDevCo $200,000 to make that cutting-edge 8- or 16-bit cartridge game, against 8% of wholesale. Even if wholesale was $32, the royalty was $2.56/cartridge sold—so your abacus told you that at unit number 78,126, your cash register would start to ring. But in the last 15 years, development budgets have skyrocketed into the millions (and, for some development efforts, the tens of millions), moving that magical "cha-ching" unit number ever upward. So what if the royalty rate has edged upward to 12% or so, and "next-gen" wholesale is $40 by the time you get your game done? It doesn't take much manipulation of earth beads and heaven beads to figure out that if you are getting $4.80/disc and GamePubCo gets to recoup $5 million against it, GamePubCo needs to sell north of 1 million units before you see a dime (or 48 dimes). Might start buying that Cold Duck now.

What happened? Simply put, you spent your "old business model" royalties to get the game made.

Despite what you may read in *Variety*, why not take a paragraph out of Hollywood and share the profits instead? Why not go back to GamePubCo and offer to take a share of "net profits" instead? Once GamePubCo recovers the $5 million it paid you, the $1 million or so it spends on testing/internal production personnel/other hard development costs, the (let's be generous here) $5 million it spends on marketing, the $11/disc COGS and $2/disc other miscellaneous costs—the abacus tells you that on the same 1 million units sold, at 12% of "net profits," the $1.92 million check you receive from GamePubCo will buy a lot of Comte de Champagne. And your abacus will also tell you that, using the rough assumptions above, your "cha-ching" number is just north of 407,000 units. Who knows—you may even be able to nudge GamePubCo up to 15–18% of "net profits" on some sort of sliding scale.

Now doesn't that champagne taste good?

2. Play the right game(s).

This is the one industry in which gameplaying is not only encouraged, it is essential. You "overhead" types (e.g., finance, administration, corporate development, legal, etc.) out there—skip the corporate politics game, the head game, the mind game, and use all that stored-up energy to run or click your way to a store, buy some worthwhile games, and play the heck out of them. Do you want to join an MMO company? Go get and play *EverQuest* or *World of Warcraft*. Does your interest lie with a company developing neo-classics? Go get and play *Centipede*, *Asteroids*, *Tetris*, [fill in your favorite classic game here]. Sports? Don't just read some reviews—buy a few different annual versions of *Madden* and compare them.

You would be amazed how, in the game industry—once you really get into games—your advice becomes more relevant, your business judgment becomes keener, you can distinguish between something that really matters and a mere bagatelle, and your game knowledge gives you instant credibility. Taking the risk of paraphrasing the 1992 U.S. presidential campaign—it's the game, stupid!

CHAPTER 15

HUSTLE & FLOW: The Intangibles of Running a Game Company

Peter Lee and Eric Zimmerman—co-founders, Gamelab,
http://www.gamelab.com/

Many of the chapters in this book discuss the tangible, concrete problems of starting and running a game development studio. In addition to the thorny questions of legal structures and managing finances, there are equally important but less tangible issues game development entrepreneurs must face. How do you keep your employees creatively engaged in their work? What kind of company culture results in successful games? How do you interface with the outside world? These hard-to-define but essential-for-success intangibles often make the difference between a company that merely limps along and one that thrives and shines, both inside and out.

In this chapter, we try to make these intangible issues as tangible as possible by referencing our own experience with Gamelab, a successful seven-year-old independent game development company. Our approach to running Gamelab is based on four intangible principles:

- Make everyone an author.
- Design a company culture of research and play.
- Be process focused, not solution focused.
- Be an honest hustler to the outside world.

These issues are all intangible because each involves all of a company's departments and functions, and because each touches the daily experience of everyone on staff. They are part of the internal processes of how a company runs itself on a daily basis, and the way a company relates to the outside world. In our experience, the truly successful companies, the ones where we all wish we were working, are the companies that get these intangibles right.

Although we have identified four separate intangibles, the truth is that they all overlap and work together. A company culture of research encourages people to have discussions across departmental divides, which in turn engenders a focus on process. Involving staff in hustling the company makes them feel like an author of the organization's public image—and gives them a feeling of authorship over their day-to-day work. It is a tough problem to get these intangibles in place, but because they catalyze and strengthen each other, working on one part of the larger problem helps with other parts, too.

Before we dive in, one caveat: do not be fooled by the simplicity of the advice we offer. As with many aspects of starting and running a business, these complex questions have many correct answers and our solutions may not be right for you. We are not advocating that every company should be managed the way we run Gamelab. However, we hope there is something you can glean from our approach that can be useful for your own endeavors.

First Things First: Make Everyone an Author

If there is one overriding directive that infuses everything we do at Gamelab, it is the idea that everyone who works at the company is an author—our staff should feel as if they are the ones contributing ideas, working through problems, and creating great games. It is crucial that all employees at your company feel a sense of responsibility and authorship over what they do. If you can instill this key sensibility into your team, many of your other problems will begin to be solved as you find that your staff will solve them for you.

What exactly do we mean by a sense of authorship? Consider its opposite. If people do not have this attitude about their work, they will feel like wage slaves (even if they are well paid), clocking in at the start of each workday to tick off to-do boxes and complete tasks for someone else. Virtually every negative work situation stems from the fact that people feel like they are doing someone else's work, and so it does not matter to them how polished a game is or whether it gets finished. Such projects usually go over schedule and end up with lackluster results, or at their worst, crash and burn.

On the other hand, when staff have a genuine feeling of authorship over what they do, they are not merely workers anymore: they become collaborators. They take the extra time to diagnose obstacles with the overall development process. They will listen to critical feedback on their own work, and offer thoughtful comments to others. They will care very much about the quality of the final product and about the company as a whole.

Productivity will increase if employees are creatively engaged. It is easy enough for you—the owners and founders of a company—to be passionately engaged in what you do on a day-to-day basis. But how do you get your staff to care? Creative staff need to be personally invested in what they are doing. They require more than financial incentive; they need to be authors.

But what about financial incentives? Some companies use reward systems like bonuses or stock options to create a sense of ownership (or even genuine legal ownership) among its employees. These approaches can work to a certain extent, but for us, purely financial incentives can only go so far. Money without any genuine authorship becomes an empty gesture, a lure to keep talent from running off to another company. Make no mistake: financial incentives are important, but they are not enough. From our experience, the intangible benefits of an authorship-focused company generally outweigh any possible tangible financial gains. This may not be true in every industry, but it certainly is true of a creative field like game development.

So how do you impart authorship to your staff? The secret is that you cannot fake authority and responsibility. You cannot pretend to offer authorship, while still actually structuring your company as if most of the staff are minions that can't be trusted without extensive oversight and approvals. For them to feel authority and responsibility, they actually have to be given real authority and responsibility over what they do.

What does this mean in practice? At Gamelab, we do not have a single individual who plays the role of "creative director" or "vision leader" on any given project. If you are assigned to do character design on a game, then *you* are the one doing the character design. General decisions are made through team consensus, but there is no manager reviewing each of your designs, telling you that they do or do not measure up. You are given ultimate authority on the tasks assigned to you to solve.

In the real world, it is tricky to pull this off. In an environment without trust and communication among project team members, the danger is that staff become territorial and hoard their own authority while scoffing at others' attempts to tell them what to do. On the other hand, if you can keep trust and communication healthy, the opposite happens: team members become desperate for feedback from everyone else, and there is idea exchange and discussion across all disciplines.

Giving authority to your staff does not mean you cannot have internal hierarchies and structures. At Gamelab, the art director still supervises and directs the visual designers on a project, conceptually directing each individual designer through research and initial design explorations. However, every visual designer is ultimately given the autonomy to solve the problems he or she is assigned. And they are in large part responsible for making sure their individual work fits into the team's larger evolving vision for the game as a whole.

One result of this approach is that staff are always challenged to solve tasks in new ways. The experience of constant challenge is a key part of feeling like an author. If your team starts solving design and development problems in the same ways over and over, the spark will go out of their work. They will feel like zombies on an assembly line showing up each day to do someone else's drudgery. People feel like authors when they are given the creative freedom to solve problems in new ways—whether they are full-time employees or project-based freelancers. And a company full of motivated innovators will produce much better work than a company full of zombified assistants.

Creating challenges for your staff takes some strategizing, and a company that is interested in exploring new creative territory. For example, at Gamelab our goal is to always try to come up with new kinds of audio and visual aesthetics, new sorts of gameplay, and new directions for content on every project. For example, every downloadable game has certain interface elements in common, such as an options screen, a main menu, and so forth. On any given title, we try to express the game's narrative on these screens, finding different approaches each time. While at many game companies these common parts of games are all implemented in the same cookie-cutter style, our visual staff like the challenge of actually designing the interface themselves. That is why we hired them, right? It can be quite challenging to do this on every project, but it definitely motivates our talent—and it gives our games variety as well.

Relative to a more traditional, authoritarian approach, giving your staff a genuine sense of authorship by giving them real responsibility can feel scary. You and your senior staff probably know better how to solve many of the problems that come up and, in the short term, it is easier simply to tell people what to do. But if you proceed by treating the rank and file as extensions of the experienced staff, everyone will end up unhappy. Your supervisors will be overworked as they micromanage everything that happens under them, without the time to address their own tasks. The rest of your company will lose interest in the big picture as they simply do what they think their manager wishes without considering the larger game or the company as a whole.

Democratizing authorship has to come from the top down. Are you setting a good example for your staff? Do your processes instill the trust and communication team authorship requires? Are the people at your company given the freedom to solve tasks in the ways they see fit? To make everyone an author requires constant vigilance against the natural tendency to control everything that happens at your company. But making sure it happens is absolutely essential to success.

Playing at Work: A Research-Focused Company Culture

For us, company culture simply means the daily experience of the staff, both individually and collectively. The lived culture of a company should embody the values and philosophy of the company as a whole. Company culture is a prime example of a business intangible: it is difficult to perceive and to define, but it permeates everything at a game company and is essential to the success of the organization.

The culture of a company is both a cause and effect of everything the company does. If your group's culture is on the right track, then good work and healthy processes will thrive at your business and the culture will both reflect and positively impact the continued success of what you do. If there are problems with your company culture, these troubles are very likely symptoms of deeper problems and the unhealthy culture can easily compound into yet more problems.

Our main point about company culture must be conscious and intentional about it: you need to actively design the culture of your organization. Too often, the culture of a game company simply arises by default, as the business founders are too busy keeping things rolling financially to worry about the daily experiences of everyone on staff. But apathy or inattention will likely result in a lackluster organization. It takes experimentation and collaboration with your staff to figure out the kind of company culture that is appropriate for you and how to best achieve it.

One rule is to create the company you would want to work. Small efforts go a long way. At Gamelab, we have the best benefits packages for our staff that we can afford. We emphasize flexible hours to accommodate people's differing work patterns and needs. We consult with our staff on the computers, furniture, software, and supplies that they need. And the office manager always gets you a cupcake with a candle on your birthday. These simple gestures can make the difference between a company that feels like a place you would love to work and one that is just another paycheck generator.

Beyond these straightforward policies, we have a more particular focus for Gamelab's company culture: research. Our goal is to have a company experience in which research is integrated into the daily activities of the people at our company. We take "research" in the broadest sense of the word to mean finding connections between the company and the world outside. Research can be project-specific or quite general. It can include teaching, reading, playing, discussing, or traveling. And it should be fun.

Why is research important for a game company? Because game companies create culture—pop culture. Too often, game developers come from the insular and somewhat geeky world of hardcore gaming. But to create innovative games, the people making your games need to be inspired by art, entertainment, design, and other forms of ideas and culture outside of the narrow confines of the gamer lifestyle. By encouraging research, you increase the solution space from which your staff can draw as they tackle problems in their everyday work.

The culture of research we try to inculcate at Gamelab stems from very specific company activities and policies. A few are highlighted here.

Research Library

Every month, each Gamelab staff member can spend $50 on purchasing something for the Gamelab library. Purchases include books, videos, music, board games, magazine subscriptions, posters, toys, and—of course—video games. As the library grows, it comes to reflect the interests of the staff, even as it becomes a richer and richer resource for people to browse as they take a five-minute break from work.

Getting Academic

We actively encourage our staff to teach, lecture, and publish in game-related areas. Gamelabbers teach at New York University and Parsons School of Design. They speak at conferences from the Game Developers Conference and E3 to DiGRA and SIG-GRAPH. And they publish articles, books, and essays. These activities serve a number of purposes: relationships with the universities help us find new talent; speaking and publishing helps create PR buzz for the company; and the research required to put a class together or write an article certainly enriches the knowledge base at Gamelab.

Do More Together

For a game company, almost any field trip or activity is genuinely relevant research. The Gamelab soccer team learns about real-world gameplay and social interaction every summer. Visual designers have put together sculpt-with-clay evenings and comic book projects. Staff organize import anime movie nights and paper game events for Gamelabbers and their friends. All of these events serve as bonding experiences for our team, in addition to the research benefits. We empower the staff to organize activities, funding and facilitating them whenever we can.

Be Unique

Beyond these more typical activities, we try to invent research opportunities that dovetail with the company culture. Every year at the Game Developers Conference, Gamelab creates a social game that is played by thousands of attendees that serves as game design experimentation and guerrilla PR. A staff interest in community youth led to the Gamelab TEEN program, an ongoing mentorship program for high school students to learn about game design. These activities have concrete research benefits for the Gamelab staff who are involved with them, even as they create great hooks for media coverage of our company.

Outside the Bounds

Committing to a culture of research means supporting your staff's endeavors outside your company. Gamelabbers have organized and taken part in circus theater productions, street game festivals, robot art exhibitions, original graphic novels, cosplay extravaganzas—you name it. We make the utmost attempts to support and celebrate this work, even mentioning it in company press releases and bios. Your employees' lives should not be circumscribed by their work. The more interesting culture they consume and create outside of your company, the better games they will make for you.

Play Games!

In addition to all of these extracurricular research activities, the key research your staff undertakes is actually playing games. Everyone at your company should play games: old games and new games, games on digital platforms and games made out of paper, games that are your direct competition and games that have nothing to do with your company's business. Work tasks always take precedence over this kind of play research, but at Gamelab, staff generally end up spending several hours a week just playing. This kind of activity serves many purposes for us, including competitive market analysis, technological research, and general design inspiration.

Any office is a nexus for the exchange of ideas, and at Gamelab we encourage staff to share the insights from their informal play research. A section of our intranet is reserved for posting links and thoughts about new games and game sites—or just pointers to strange Internet culture. Furthermore, the open physical layout of our office lets us see what is happening on each other's screens, reducing the potential stigma of "playing at work" and encouraging discussions about games even as they are being played. The two of us make sure to join in these discussions and play games as well, so everyone can see that there is nothing wrong with playing and working at the same time.

So design your company culture. Our exact policies and activities might not be right for you. But however you decide to create your company culture, do so intentionally. You design experiences for game players. Design the experience of your company employees, too.

The Flow of Flow: Encouraging an Open Process

Whenever we give a talk about what we do at Gamelab and answer questions afterwards, inevitably one of the questions is, "Where do you get the ideas for your games?" This question is well intentioned, but as far as we are concerned, a bit wrong-headed. No game ever starts life as an idea and simply matures over time into a playable version of the original inspirational concept. Instead, games emerge through collaborative processes over time, growing and changing as they are implemented. In other words, a great game is *not* the result of a great idea. A great game is the result of a great process.

Because we are focusing on intangibles in this chapter, we are not going to discuss the details of the production phases of the development process such as writing a design document, getting from an Alpha to a Beta build, and so forth. Instead, we will identify the more fundamental attitudes that are needed to arrive at a healthy process. If you can instill a process-oriented ethic at your company—another key intangible for a successful game development business—then many common development problems tend to take care of themselves.

There are two aspects of continually improving processes at your company. On the one hand, process occurs on a personal level and each staff member needs to be given the space (and feeling of authorship) that lets him or her engage properly with the process at hand. The other aspect has to do with the more tangible problem of designing concrete procedures and selecting software tools that make the execution of the process possible.

A Process Attitude

Making games, on one level, is solving problems. What kinds of problems? There are game design problems, visual problems, technical problems, marketing problems—you name it. The key to a healthy process is realizing that finding the solution to each problem is actually not the most important thing that happens at your company. More important than finding solutions is finding the processes by which your staff identify, investigate, and grapple with these problems. Nobody should feel that his or her job is merely to find solutions. Instead, everyone's job is to take part in the process. The process solves the problems, not the individual people.

This might sound like just a rhetorical sleight of hand, but it is actually a crucial shift in emphasis from more conventional thinking about how people work. A process-focused company is a company in which everyone feels like an author. The feeling of being involved in the problem-solving process is a feeling of empowerment. In contrast, the feeling of being told a solution to a problem, or of feeling the singled-out pressure to solve a problem alone, is the opposite of employee authorship.

At any company, there will always be senior staff who know more about solving certain kinds of problems than less experienced staff. There is a strong temptation for these senior staff to simply dictate solutions to everyone else, and for less-experienced people to be afraid to ask questions because they think they will look inexperienced or stupid. It is important to resist this anti-process impulse at all costs, and instead involve everyone in the collaborative process of solving problems. One strategy for making sure this happens is to ask senior staff to set the example by admitting when they make a mistake or encounter a question they cannot answer by themselves. If the senior staff seek out advice from everyone else, they create an atmosphere of mutual respect where everyone is comfortable asking for help from others and engaging with the process *as a process*, rather than as a checklist of possible solutions.

Among the game designers at Gamelab there is a wide range of industry experience, from designers who have been in the industry for more than decade to those who are completely fresh. But each game designer has different areas of expertise: one is a former programmer and has strong mathematical skills, another has an incredible handle on pop culture and social games, another is a natural-born storyteller, and another is an incredible writer and editor. Game design on any given project involves all of these areas, and by encouraging the ability to ask questions and learn from each other, we create a healthy process. Each project has a lead game designer. But in the process of designing a given game, staff feel free to use the others as resources to help solve problems.

Just as important as these attitudes within a department are the inter-departmental relationships among the different divisions at your company. As much as you can, try to emphasize the importance of every development discipline so that none becomes too dominant. We have seen visual designers leave a technology-driven company and game designers depart from an animation-driven studio because they feel that their role was downplayed and disrespected. Even at Gamelab, a company with a strong emphasis on game design, we go out of our way to focus the importance of the project manager group, or the programming group, through departmental meetings and research activities. This drive to equal importance is more than just departmental politics: if people feel valued, they will feel more comfortable engaging with the process of working at the company.

Procedures and Tools

Once you have instilled a healthy process-based ethic, how are your staff going to actually enact their process? In addition to the big-picture general attitude, it is important to get the details right. For us, these details come down to procedures and tools. Procedures establish the overall flow and the specific steps of how certain tasks begin and end. And software tools are the means to help you execute these procedures.

Finding the right tools is very important, and there are many to choose from, including some that are freely available. A wiki is a good example of an open source community-based tool. We use our internal wiki to track and share the progress of each individual project by posting visuals and documents to a set of project-specific pages. Individuals on a project can quickly browse that project's wiki and see the state of many aspects of the game. Each project wiki can then also double as a way to share our progress with an outside publisher or partner.

Task-management and cost-tracking tools have also been important for us. We have found that most tools of these types are designed to work well for a very small group of users (less than half a dozen), or for very big groups (more than 100). It is surprisingly hard to find good process tools for a company that is somewhere in the middle. We have tried many over the years, from several different versions of wikis, to Track, Jira, and Timesheet. Our conclusion is that it requires some experimentation and creativity to find and modify tools to make them work. However, if you have established a process-centric attitude at your company, then everyone will acknowledge the importance of process tools, and you can tap the collective knowledge of your staff to strategize and improve on how you use your tools. And this process never really ends.

The thing about processes is that they are, in fact, processes—your goal should be to constantly improve them as you move your company forward. As your company changes, so will your needs for tools and procedures. With less than a dozen staff and a single small project, perhaps paper notes and yelling across the office will suffice. But as you grow, challenges of interaction dynamics and resource allocation become more complex. Without sacrificing the wonderful feeling of informally working fast and loose, you will have to implement more defined procedures to make sure all of the moving parts of your company are functioning smoothly.

Can you implement formal processes without erasing small team dynamics? It is difficult but possible, and it is important to keep this goal in mind when designing and improving your internal processes. The key is in recognizing the importance of process, and involving everyone in designing your processes and selecting your tools. If your staff feel like authors of their own process, they will not have any problem trying it out, evaluating it, and making sure it is under constant improvement.

The World Outside: Becoming an Honest Hustler

Part of running and growing a company is hustling the company. You have to hustle the company to reporters to get stories written about what you do. You have to hustle your strengths and connections within your industry to get more work. You have to hustle every contract negotiation to get the best outcome for your firm. You have to hustle everywhere you go to increase the profile of your company and attract talent.

Not everyone is a hustler. Over the years at Gamelab, Eric has been the primary hustler while Peter oversees the internal company processes. We are both fine with this arrangement. The important thing is to recognize the importance of hustling and to be as strategic and intentional (and playful) with your hustling as you are with everything else you do with your company.

We are choosing our language carefully here. We realize the word "hustle" has some negative connotations: it implies the deceptive manipulation of a swindle. But we like thinking about how a company relates to the outside world as a "hustle" because there is a liberating honesty in admitting that a company hustler is doing just that: jostling for best position and framing the company to best advantage. Acknowledging that hustling is important, and being honest with those you are hustling, are the keys to this somewhat intangible but absolutely essential company activity.

The first step in hustling your company is knowing exactly what it is you are hustling. From the outset, it is important to identify your company's core competencies and be able to articulate them to the world, as specifically as possible. Saying that your company makes "great games" or has "cutting-edge technologies" is not enough. What is great about your games? What is cutting-edge about your tech? Can you summarize your strengths in 10 words or less? Know your strengths and be prepared to hustle them. The materials you create about your company, from your logo and Web site to press releases and project proposals, should all communicate your distinctive competencies.

At Gamelab, we have stuck to a company vision based on experimentation and innovation. More specifically, we create games for broad audiences, exploring new ways for people to play, new kinds of content and aesthetics, and new forms of independent distribution. And that, in a nutshell, is our hustle. The trick is to keep your company description broad enough to communicate a clear central image but still have enough angles and hooks so you can emphasize different facets of your company depending on who you are hustling. When we are selling the company's game design consulting, we emphasize our track record of game design innovation and the academic credentials of our game design staff. When we are talking to a business reporter, we focus on the wide audiences our games reach and the ways we distribute games to our players online.

Just as important as communicating to the outside world is making sure that everyone inside the company is clear about what makes your firm special. Bring your staff into the process of defining who you are. Use your staff as resources to refine and polish your company image as it changes and evolves over time. If your staff feel like they are helping shape the company image, they will be more comfortable telling others about it as they move about in the world—because they in part will be authors of the company itself (yet another example of employee authorship). A clear company profile can also save you time in hiring. At Gamelab, everyone who comes into the company knows what we are about, so we never end up mistakenly hiring someone who only wants to make medieval RPGs.

With all of this emphasis on image, it might seem like we are advocating that you tell people just what they want to hear—whether or not it is actually true. But the key to great hustling is actually to be honest about what you are. Do not overhype and oversell before you actually get anything out into the world. Do great work, and then know how to showcase it to best effect. Little white hypes can work in the short term, but as your players, the press, and your industry colleagues begin to doubt your hustle, things can easily backfire. If you are starting a game company, you are in it for the long haul. Cultivating a reputation for honesty and integrity can do far more for your company image than an overreaching press release.

All of these guidelines for hustling also apply to PR opportunities and how you interact with the outside world in general. In publishing negotiations, in hiring staff, and in defining distribution and licensing relationships, be fair and honest above all. Our experience is that even adversarial negotiations benefit when you are direct and straightforward about what you want and what your positions are. Reputations stick. It is easy to get a bad rep, but a good reputation only comes from being staunchly consistent. It's OK to be known as a hustler—just be sure you are known for being an honest hustler. That intangible permeates through your own company, and throughout the sector of the game industry where you work.

Conclusion

As intangible as these intangibles are, they do not arise out of nothing. The attitudes and approaches we describe here are the result of concrete policies and procedures. Less important than designing one specific approach over another specific approach is being sure to design these intangibles in the first place.

Any game is defined by its rules: those mathematical guidelines that tell you when to roll the dice and move your piece, when to draw a card and place a bet, how to level up your character and go fight more monsters. Rules taken by themselves can be dry and formal. But for a player, rules ultimately do not matter. What really matters is the play that the rules make possible. As much as rules are logical and rigid, the experience of play at its best is spontaneous, creative, and unpredictable. Games are made up of rules. But they exist to create play.

Defining and designing how your company operates, for us, is a lot like creating a game. The policies you define, the tools you purchase, the way you lay out the workspace—these are the rules. The experience of your staff, and the products that emerge out of the functioning of your company are the play that come out of the rules you establish. The rules are important, but less so than what emerges out of them.

In any business field, there are a handful of leaders and dozens or hundreds—or even thousands—of imitators. And in a creative industry, being a leader means constant invention. The only way that is going to happen is when your company starts doing things and making things you could never have predicted in advance. We all know that the best games result in play patterns, game strategies, and fan cultures that none of us game developers could ever have predicted beforehand. And similarly, the best game companies also surprise us with the games that come out of them, games that shock us with never-before-seen gameplay and graphics, or incredibly elegant improvements on existing genres of play.

But great games like these can only emerge from a process of rules that was so well designed it surprised its creators. So design your company's intangibles. But design them for play, for results you cannot yourself imagine. Otherwise, you have taken the play out of work. And playing at work is why we all got started in the game business in the first place, right?

CHAPTER 16

Game Development Agreement Analysis

S. Gregory Boyd and Erik Smith

GBoyd@kenyon.com

It occurred to the editors that many people reading this book might not have ever seen a game development agreement before. In some ways, it is a little silly to spend so many pages talking about business and legal issues without actually having a development agreement to analyze. In many ways, this chapter is the culmination of several other sections of this book. Consequently, the chapter assumes you have read the rest of the book or, at least, have some familiarity with the topics it covers.

An attorney reading this chapter may cringe; the chapter attempts to walk through a game development contract and explain in simple terms what the contract means. Clearly, this is a Herculean task. There are inaccuracies inherent in the process of translating "legalese" to English, and we deliberately and repeatedly ignore the subtle nuances of certain clauses for clarity over perfect accuracy.

Yet, there are some benefits worth this cost. It is important to understand the motivation behind including these clauses in a contract. If you can understand some of the basic meaning of the clauses, even if you don't understand the legal reasons for them, you will learn more about what to look for in these agreements.

Again, please use an attorney to negotiate your game development agreement. Would you take out your own appendix even if someone gave you a book on how to do it? The same rule applies here. Again, this is merely a sample game development agreement; there is no way to anticipate what your agreement will look like and every situation is unique.

This is a sample in the sense that it is representative of many game development contracts. It has the majority of clauses that "standard" game development contracts contain. It also discusses game development in the form and structure that most development contracts use. It is *not* a "model" in the sense that it is an ideal contract from either the publisher's or developer's perspective, because there is probably no such thing as an ideal contract. Even if there were such a thing, it would be different for every deal and every party. How did we create this sample? The short answer is that we looked through a lot of game development agreements: agreements we had negotiated or reviewed in the past, agreements that were parts of past litigation; also some very generous clients even gave us more agreements just for the purposes of this chapter. Of course, we asked the clients before we used the agreements to help create the sample. Therefore, the agreement that follows is not representative of any one agreement; it is a mixture of many different agreements with all the names removed and every term changed into a form that can be used for educational purposes. It is our sincere hope that the sample agreement has been changed beyond all recognition. Its own mothers should not be able to recognize it.

Some may ask why this example agreement is so long. It is on the long end of the spectrum for game development agreements. There have been agreements as short as five pages, but this one is deliberately long so we could fit more sample clauses, and it works better for educational purposes. Do not worry if your agreement is not this inclusive, because they do not have to be. As a rule, agreements tend to become longer as more money is at stake, and the agreement tends to cover a longer period. For comparison on length and inclusiveness, some of the major details in this agreement are similar to a $45+ million development agreement to a 2008 launch "next generation" MMO game that involved a publisher, developer, and investors from different continents. If we can discuss a fictional long complicated agreement, the shorter ones should be easy.

Finally, a word about bargaining power. This agreement is very much in favor of the publisher. There are some minor concessions in it, but overall this is a traditional publisher-friendly game development agreement. Most game development agreements are very much in favor of the publisher because the publisher has the corporate size, money, and power that lead to a bargaining advantage. On the other hand, most developers do not have any real bargaining power until they develop a significant track record. For developers that have little experience or are untested with a particular publisher, there may not be much room for negotiation contract terms. This fact of life is no surprise, as the publisher is the one providing finances, and consequently is the one who calls most of the shots. However, more established developers might be able to negotiate terms more effectively since they have more leverage in the industry and there is more incentive to obtain their talent. It has been said that some developers are so sought after that they can get many sizable concessions in their game development contracts. Until that time comes for your development company, get used to reading the "publisher-friendly" development agreements because that is what the documents are going to look like for your first few game deals.

Also, leaving a company to start a new one can lower bargaining power; publishers and investors cannot be sure it was actually your talent that made the game sell so well or if it was something special about you being at the old company. In short, beware of your pride and ego before you make the leap to a new company or start a new development studio. As a rule do not expect publishers or investors to deal with your new startup company the same way they dealt with your old employer that cranked out two different top 10 games last year.

Now, let us examine the contract in detail:

GAME DEVELOPMENT AND DISTRIBUTION AGREEMENT

First comes the title of the agreement. This will usually say something generic like this title. It is not a term of the contract and is essentially something that the parties can read later to let them know what this stack of paper is and where it is filed. There should not be a great deal of negotiation over the title.

> This Development and Distribution Agreement (hereinafter, the "Agreement") is made and entered into as of this ___ day of _____ 200__, (the "Effective Date") by and between:
>
> **PUBLISHER**, a British Corporation, with offices at 10 St. Andrews Road, Manchester, M25 OAL, United Kingdom (hereinafter, the "Publisher"), and
>
> **DEVELOPER**, a Delaware corporation with offices at 15 Broadway, New York, NY 10004, USA.
>
> Publisher and Developer are sometimes hereinafter referred to jointly as the "Parties" or singularly as a "Party."

After the title, there is usually a date section and general provisions. This section will let you know important issues such as who the publisher and developer are. Also, notice the capital letters in some terms. Any word in an agreement that is capitalized is probably defined specifically for the contract. For instance, in the preceding section we see that this contract will be called the Agreement for the rest of the document. The publisher becomes the Publisher and the developer becomes the Developer. Letting the reader in on a little secret, there are two major purposes of assigning the names to parties in the agreement. First, to allow attorneys to recycle clauses in the agreement. Second, so the attorneys will not get confused later about which party is which. Whenever the contract discusses the developer or publisher individually or together they may be called a Party or Parties. The date we entered into the contract becomes the Effective Date. The main purpose of this section is to introduce the parties to the agreement and make certain there is no ambiguity in that regard.

RECITALS

> **WHEREAS,** Publisher is among other things, a developer, marketer and distributor of massively multiplayer online games, (hereinafter, MMOG);
>
> **WHEREAS,** Developer wishes to develop a new MMOG, tentatively titled ULTIMATE ORC-SLAYER and have it marketed and distributed by Publisher; and
>
> **WHEREAS,** Publisher and Developer wish to enter into an agreement to develop and publish a computer game and to provide related services;
>
> **NOW, THEREFORE,** in consideration of the mutual promises and covenants contained herein and for other good and valuable consideration, the receipt and sufficiency of which are hereby acknowledged, the Parties hereto agree as follows:

The next section in a development agreement may be labeled *recitals*. Sometimes, the section is also described as the collection of "whereas clauses." They are not in every contract, but if you find them, they will always come at the beginning. These serve to introduce the functions of the parties, foundational premises of the agreement, and introduce the purpose of the contract. Beware recitals that go on too long or state information too broadly. For instance, it is not hard to imagine that the claim, "Whereas Developer is the best game developer in the world" might be misinterpreted later and hurt the developer if something goes wrong with the contract. Also notice the recitals end with a clause that begins "Now, Therefore." This leads into the contract and acknowledges a very important concept: *consideration*. This means that something of value is changing hands in the contract and both parties agree that this is happening. This element is critical because contracts are invalid without consideration. A deeper discussion of consideration is not necessary for the purposes of this chapter, but suffice it to say that it drives many first year law students mad studying the development complexities of this topic. In short, explicitly writing that the contract has consideration removes all doubt and is the easiest way to go.

The definition section follows the recital section. Many of these definitions are common sense based, but in contract formation it is always advisable to define any terms that could be unclear or those where a question could arise later. These definitions make it explicitly clear what the parties are agreeing upon, which is helpful during contract formation and of crucial importance should litigation arise. Furthermore, the definitions section is helpful in defining industry-specific terms, like MMOG, RPG, source code, sequel, or software. In the absence of definitions written into a contract, a court interpreting a contract will do so with its own definitions. These interpretations may not be what you had in mind when signing the contract; therefore, it is best to have all important terms defined in this section. Lastly, many of these definitions are not explicitly discussed, but the sections that use them are discussed in more detail.

1.   DEFINITIONS

1.1   "Acceptance Date" shall be the date set forth on the Development Schedule on which the initial development of the Game is complete.

1.2   "Affiliate(s)" with respect to a legal entity (such as a corporation, partnership, or limited liability company), shall mean any legal entity that controls, is controlled by or is under common control with such person. For the purposes of this definition, the term "control" means the possession, directly or indirectly, of the power to direct or cause the direction of the management and policies of such legal entity, whether through the ownership of voting securities or by contract.

1.3   "Business Day" shall mean any day other than a Saturday, Sunday, or a legal holiday in the United States.

Notice the definition for Business Day before this paragraph. This definition is important in this deal because the agreement is international. Which country's norms do we follow and what days count as Business Days? Many items in contracts are counted using Business Days so it is easy to imagine how this becomes important. If your contract has currency clauses because of foreign interactions, consider if you need a business day definition.

1.4   "Commercial Launch" shall mean the initial date on which Publisher distributes the Game (which is not designated as beta or prerelease versions) to End Users for payment.

1.5   "<u>Customer Support System</u>" shall mean staff and infrastructure necessary
       to provide reasonable customer support after Commercial Launch. This in-
       cludes live in-game customer support, phone, and email customer support.

Remember derivative works from the copyright discussions in this book? Here is a definition that lays it out for this agreement.

1.6   "<u>Derivative Property</u>" shall mean any work(s), specifically excluding the
       Game and any authorized Sequels, based in any way upon any Intellectual
       Property related to the Game Content that is protectable by Intellectual
       Property Rights. Without limiting the foregoing, "Derivative Property"
       includes (a) works defined as "derivative works" according to the United
       States Copyright Act; (b) any work that has a substantially similar "look
       and feel" as the Game; and/or (c) any work which has as part of its name
       either the same or a similar name as that of the Game so as to potentially
       cause confusion as to the source of the work or that has the effect of di-
       luting the distinctive nature of the Game's mark. Derivative Properties
       include, without limitation, board games, toys, novelties, trinkets, sou-
       venirs, wearing apparel, fabric, foods and beverages, paper products,
       household items, publications of all kinds (hard- or softcover books
       whether pictorial and/or literary, comic books, and magazines) and Linear
       Programs.

1.7   "<u>Development Schedule</u>" shall mean the timetable for development of the
       Game, including milestones and an Acceptance Date, as set forth in Ex-
       hibit A. This Exhibit may be updated quarterly if both Parties agree and
       execute a signed revision.

1.8   "<u>Development Tools</u>" shall mean all software tools used to create the
       Game, not including items defined as part of the Engine.

1.9   "<u>End User</u>" shall mean an end user subscriber to the Game.

1.10   "<u>Engine</u>" shall mean the portion of the Software developed by or for Devel-
       oper that enables and handles the basic low-level operation of the Game,
       including all Source Code contained therein and software tools specifi-
       cally related thereto, and specifically excluding any Game Content.

1.11   "<u>Expansion Pack</u>" shall mean new Game Content that requires the original
       Game for an End User to participate in said new Game Content.

1.12   "<u>Extended Honing Period</u>" means a period of time up to six months beyond
       the development schedule specified in Exhibit A that is at the discre-
       tion of and recoupably funded by Publisher.

The *Extended Honing Period* definition in this agreement is a variation on a common
theme. It is also common to call this a *polish period*. More than anything else, it is a way to
build in slippage into the development schedule and is sometimes found in larger projects. As
a general rule, the more ambitious the project, the more difficult it is to predict the development schedule.

Even though you know what a game is, lawyers do not. So there has to be a definition. For the purposes of this contract, a Game and Game Content are defined in the clause following this paragraph.

1.13   "<u>Game</u>" shall mean the MMOG designed and developed by Developer pursuant to this Agreement, as further described in the Specification Exhibit B, including the Software and any documentation and other materials related to such MMOG.

1.14   "<u>Game Content</u>" shall mean all aspects of the Game, such aspects including the name, story line, characters, artwork, look and feel, and content related to the Game, but specifically excluding the Engine and Development Tools.

1.15   "<u>Initial Development Costs</u>" shall mean Developer's reasonable development costs and expenses, as mutually agreed upon by the Parties in advance, including, the costs and expenses (i) set forth in Exhibit A in connection with the Development Schedule and (ii) related to the localization of the Software.

This agreement contains separate definitions for what IP is and another definition for what IP Rights are.

1.16   "<u>Intellectual Property</u>" shall mean inventions, articles of manufacture, compositions of matter, methods, apparatus, improvements thereof, ideas, conceptions, formulas, data, programs, other works of authorship, derivative works, know-how, improvements, discoveries, developments, designs and techniques, technical or business information, names or marks, characters, other proprietary information, or any other intellectual property anywhere in the world, whether tangible or intangible.

1.17   "<u>Intellectual Property Rights</u>" shall mean all proprietary and intellectual property rights worldwide, including without limitation any and all utility patents, design patents, industrial registrations, copyrights, trademarks, trade secrets, moral rights, character rights, sui generis protection, rights of publication, rights of privacy, trade dress, state law right, and any other worldwide intangible or tangible right anywhere in the world that is related to Intellectual Property (including without limitation any pending registrations, applications, divisionals, continuations, derivatives, reissues, and reexaminations associated therewith).

1.18   "<u>Investment Agreement</u>" shall mean the Agreement attached in Exhibit C.

1.19   "<u>Key Personnel</u>" shall mean the key personnel assigned by Developer to work on the development of the Game, as listed in Exhibit D.

1.20   "<u>Linear Programs</u>" shall mean taped or filmed television shows, motion pictures and home video presentations without interactive gameplay.

1.21 "<u>Live Team Activity</u>" shall mean the "live team" development and maintenance activities related to the Game occurring after the Acceptance Date, including without limitation the continued development of additional functionality, enhancements, and maintenance related to the Game, as further described on Exhibit E.

1.22 "<u>MMOG</u>" shall mean a massively multiplayer online game.

1.23 "<u>Milestone Target</u>" shall mean any one of the various dates described in the Development Schedule, Exhibit A, by which Developer must complete the relevant development activities associated with such date. In order to satisfy or meet a particular Milestone Target, Developer must complete the relevant development activities to the satisfaction of Publisher by the respective date and provide a copy of the source code for the Game as it exists on the respective date.

1.24 "<u>Negative Sales</u>" shall mean any negative revenue caused after the recognition of the revenue due to return of the box product, refund, and other reasons. Negative Sales will be deductible from the gross revenue for royalty payment calculation.

1.25 "<u>Net Revenue</u>" shall mean the aggregate revenue actually recognized by Publisher in accordance with United States Generally Accepted Accounting Principles ("GAAP") less (i) normal and customary rebates, cash and trade discounts, and credits for returns and allowances, (ii) bad debt expenses, (iii) credit card chargebacks, (iv) commissions paid to third-party salespeople, sales agents, and distributors, (v) sales, use or other excise taxes and/or duties imposed upon Publisher with respect to such sales and licensing transactions (vii) distributor discount for box product and prepaid cards, and (viii) Negative Sales. Net Revenue shall not include any unused balances of any prepaid accounts. Unless otherwise stated, Net Revenue is calculated from receipts worldwide.

Behold, here is a definition of *Net Revenue*, usually one of the most contentious areas in the development agreement. Developers are often paid as a percentage of Net Revenue so they really care about how it is calculated. What is included and what is excluded are critical. Again, it bears repeating that this is just a sample, and actual development agreements vary this definition quite a bit. Just to show you how important it is, this definition of Net Revenue requires the use of another definition—see the definition of Negative Sales. There is no question that this is a battleground in negotiation and all that can be said within the scope of this chapter is the following. First, it can be calculated many different ways. Second, developers are often paid on Net Revenue, but payment can be calculated on gross revenue as well. Of course, payment on gross revenue leads to exciting discussions about what exactly gross revenue means, too.

1.26 "<u>Object Code</u>" means machine-readable form of computer programming code as opposed to the human readable form of computer programming code.

1.27   "<u>Open Source Software</u>" shall mean any software distributed under a license that mandates the redistribution of said software or a derivative work based upon said software must be made without charge or at a nominal charge, or that requires that the source code of the software be made available upon distribution of its object code.

Open source software is a growing issue in game development. Traditionally, many development agreements just had a "no open source" warranty clause that prevented open source from being used in the game. However, as open source software becomes more popular and the open source licenses are becoming better understood, there is a growing tolerance for the open source software as long as the open source license is compatible with the project.

1.28   "<u>Option Period</u>" shall mean the period from the Effective Date until December 31, 2012.

This Option Period clause will be used in a later section for purchasing the developer. If the publisher wants to buy the developer before the expiration of this date, the publisher has included an option in this agreement that allows for that purchase at a pre-set price.

1.29   "<u>Honing</u>" means additional development of the Game performed by Developer beyond the development activities specified in Exhibit A.

1.30   "<u>Platform Translation</u>" means a redesign of the Game to function on another platform besides the platforms on which at least one version of the Game presently operates or is under development to operate.

1.31   "<u>Sequel</u>" means a new computer, console, or similar medium game that is based on the Game Content.

1.32   "<u>Specification</u>" means the material contained in Exhibit B generally describing the Game.

1.33   "<u>Software</u>" shall mean the software that comprises the Game, both server-side and client-side, including without limitation the Engine and software representations of the Game Content, in both Source Code (and the software tools specifically related thereto) and Object Code format, unless expressly stated otherwise.

1.34   "<u>Source Code</u>" means the human-readable form of computer programming code or other work that is suitable for modifying computer programming code, including all the modules it contains, and any associated interface definition files, scripts, instructions, or other materials that are used to control compilation and installation of an executable based upon such human-readable form of computer programming code.

The next section outlines the scope of development activities and covers the breadth of what is expected of the developer.

2.   DEVELOPMENT SERVICES

2.1   <u>Development Work</u>. Developer shall be solely responsible for designing and developing the Game, including but not limited to the Game Content and

> all Software. Developer shall use its best efforts to design and develop
> the Game in accordance with the Development Schedule (Exhibit A) and
> Specification (Exhibit B). In furtherance of such effort, Developer
> agrees to appropriately staff such development efforts and to maintain
> adequate supervision to ensure the development is carried out in a pro-
> fessional, efficient, timely, and competent manner in accordance with the
> Development Schedule. Developer agrees to work exclusively on the Game
> for a period beginning as of the Effective Date of this Agreement and end-
> ing at the acceptance date of the last milestone described in the Devel-
> opment Schedule, Exhibit A. However, beginning six months before the end
> of this exclusivity period, Developer may enter into negotiations to de-
> velop games with persons other than Publisher.

This clause states that the Developer is the only party responsible for developing the game and that it must staff and work on the game appropriately. Additionally, it sets out that the Developer must make the game in accordance with the *development schedule* (sometimes called a *milestone schedule*) and the specification. The development schedule and specification are attached as an Exhibit at the end of the agreement.

The clause also allows for the developer to start seeking new work six months before the end of the development schedule. The period the developer signs this agreement and is working on the game until six months before the end of the development is referred to as an *exclusivity period*. In some agreements, the publisher wants the developer to work only on one project. In short, the publisher wants to make certain that milestone payments for this game are not going to finance production of some secret title. Clearly, the developer would rather have the freedom to work on other titles and the publisher usually desires to restrict the developer for as long as possible. Some agreements may have an exclusivity period and others do not. Obviously, they can vary in length and other circumstances as well.

> 2.2   <u>Personnel</u>. The Parties shall agree to a mutually beneficial staffing plan
> that is appropriate to meet the Development Schedule and cost con-
> straints. The Key Personnel (Exhibit D) shall be part of the full-time de-
> velopment team, and Developer will use all commercially reasonable
> efforts to retain the Key Personnel. Key Personnel shall not be reassigned
> to any other project without the prior written consent of Publisher. Such
> Key Personnel may only be replaced with personnel of equal or greater
> skills as determined in good faith by Publisher. Developer shall promptly
> notify Publisher (which notification shall be no less than fourteen days
> prior to any such proposed replacement) of any proposed Key Personnel re-
> placements and Publisher shall have the right to approve or reject any
> such replacements in its sole discretion. All development work related to
> the Game shall be performed either by employees or independent contractors
> of Developer, both of whom shall have entered into binding proprietary
> information agreements that (a) assign all of such individual's right,
> title, and interest in and to the Game to Developer; (b) waive such
> individual's moral rights to the extent allowed by law; and (c) ensure the
> confidentiality of the Game to at least the same degree as does this

Agreement. Developer agrees to update and provide to Publisher a full and correct version of Exhibit D at least on a quarterly basis.

The Personnel clause 2.2 highlights the importance of people in making a game. Development studies and people involved in game development are rarely interchangeable. Exhibit D at the end of agreement lists who the people are labeled as *Key Personnel*. Notice that this clause limits what those people can work on and limits how they are replaced. In some ways, this clause has a similar intention to the exclusivity period in 2.1. The publisher cares deeply about who works on the project and how much of their time is devoted to the project.

2.3　<u>Milestone Targets</u>. Developer shall meet the various Milestone Targets set forth in the Development Schedule, and time is of the essence with respect to such Milestone Target deadlines. Publisher shall determine in its reasonable discretion and with the reasonable assistance of Developer, whether or not Developer has satisfied a Milestone Target. Publisher shall notify Developer within fifteen (15) days after the due date of such Milestone Target as to whether Developer met the target. In the event of a dispute as to whether a Milestone Target has been met, Developer shall be given fifteen (15) additional days after being notified by Publisher to cure the non-compliance. After such fifteen (15) day period, Publisher shall again assess whether Developer has met the Milestone Target. If Developer fails to meet the Milestone Target at the end of such cure period, there shall be no further cure period. To meet any one particular Milestone Target, all work related to the previous Milestone Targets must be complete (regardless of whether the previous work was completed by the respective Milestone Target deadlines). In the event that, for whatever reason, Developer fails to meet any Milestone Target, or alternatively fails to timely meet the Acceptance Date set forth in the Development Schedule, then Developer shall be deemed to be in material breach of this Agreement. Publisher shall have the right to approve annual and quarterly budgets of the Developer.

This clause outlines the importance of *milestone targets*. As you probably know, milestone targets are game development production goals. A milestone target may state "develop functional user interface that includes the following . . . ." Developers are paid based on meeting milestones, which should be a measure of moving toward completion of the game.

Also notice there is a process for approving and rejecting the milestones. Clear milestone approval process descriptions are usually a good sign for the developer. Beware the contract that just calls for the submission of milestones. What happens after that? Who approves the milestones and using what criteria? How does the developer get paid and when? What if the milestone is not accepted? What if the milestone is submitted and there is no answer, is it approved or rejected by default? All of these are critical questions especially when meeting payroll depends on it. This clause is fairly publisher-friendly and leaves a lot of that information out. Ideally, for the developer, this clause would be much more robust and spell out the entire process exactly.

2.4　<u>Initial Development Costs</u>. Publisher shall pay or cause to be paid to Developer monies for the Initial Development Costs as set forth in Exhibit A.

This clause simply states that the publisher will pay the initial development costs of the game. These are recoupable costs the vast majority of the time, but in this agreement we have chosen to list the initial development costs as non-recoupable costs. Making the initial development costs non-recoupable means the publisher is planning to finance the initial development of the game without taking those costs back out of the developer's royalty. This is not explained in this clause, but will be explained in later clauses. Clearly, negotiating non-recoupable initial development costs is a rare treat reserved for established game development companies.

2.5   <u>Quality Control</u>. On each Milestone Target deadline set forth in the Development Schedule and as otherwise reasonably requested by Publisher, Developer shall provide Publisher with a copy of the Software on a mutually agreeable medium and any other necessary materials for quality control and analysis purposes. Within a reasonable amount of time thereafter, Publisher shall provide any feedback to Developer to aid Developer in the development of the Game, and Developer agrees to accommodate Publisher's reasonable requests. Monthly, Developer shall provide Publisher with the most recent game design documents and art.

This clause states that the Publisher has the ultimate say about whether the game content is acceptable. This also makes it clear who is in ultimate control of that content. Also, notice that the developer actually gives the code to the publisher monthly. Sometimes this may be done in escrow or reviewed at the developer's studio.

2.6   <u>Information and Assistance</u>. The Parties agree to keep each other informed with respect to the development activities (both financial and technical) related to the Game. To that end, the Parties agree to have regular telephonic or video conference meetings at least on a milestone basis to discuss financial issues, design issues, and other matters related to the development of the Game. Each Party shall disclose relevant problems and issues to the other Party in good faith and shall promptly respond to the other Party's request for reasonable information or assistance. Publisher shall appoint, at its sole discretion, an Associate Producer to act as a liaison between Publisher and Developer. Developer shall fully cooperate with and provide to Associate Producer all information reasonably requested by said Associate Producer.

This clause spells out that each party is going to do everything it reasonably should to meet the terms of the agreement. As a general rule, information and assistance clauses do not often add much to an agreement because the parties are assumed to cooperate to the extent necessary to get the project done. However, notice the Associate Producer in this clause. Here, the Publisher gets to appoint an Associate Producer to act as an intermediary. Who pays for this person? What is this person's position in the game development hierarchy? Does he or she work as part of the development studio or the publisher? Where is this person's office and who pays to provide that support? All of these are critical questions raised by this clause. In practice, this is probably a publisher employee, housed and paid for by the publisher, who will just call in to the studio a couple of times a week. To be safe, a developer should request that these details be spelled out in the agreement.

2.7   Audit Rights. Publisher or, at its choice, an independent agent of Pub-
       lisher shall have the right, at its expense and upon reasonable notice
       to Developer, to enter the premises of Developer and with the assis-
       tance of Developer, which assistance shall not be unreasonably with-
       held, obtain information necessary to verify Developer's compliance
       with the terms and conditions of this Agreement, including without lim-
       itation analyzing the development progress, performing quality control
       and analysis on the Software, and ensuring the protection of Confiden-
       tial Information in accordance with this Agreement.

This Audit Rights clause goes further to describe what the publisher is able to do to keep
track of the developer. Here, it explains the publisher may check on the game development
and check that any confidential information is being properly dealt with. Later in the agreement is a developer audit clause that is just as beneficial for checking on royalty calculations.

2.8   Sequels, Expansion Packs, and Platform Translations. At Publisher's dis-
       cretion, Publisher may decide to create Sequels, Expansion Packs, or Plat-
       form Translations. In the event that Publisher decides to create a Sequel,
       Expansion Pack, or translate the Game to a different platform (including,
       without limitation, consoles), Publisher shall send written notice of the
       same to Developer. Developer shall then have the right of first negotia-
       tion with Publisher to the development of such Sequel, Expansion Pack, or
       Platform Translation. If Developer agrees to develop such Sequel, Expan-
       sion Pack, or Platform Translation, Developer shall develop such Sequel,
       Expansion Pack, or Platform Translation on terms to be negotiated later in
       good faith. Publisher may develop the Sequel, Expansion Pack, or Platform
       Translation itself or contract with a third party for development of such
       Sequel, Expansion Pack, or Platform Translation if (a) Developer does not
       respond to such request within thirty (30) days of the date the written
       notice is received by Developer, (b) Developer declines the invitation to
       develop such Sequel, Expansion Pack, or Platform Translation, or (c) the
       Parties are unable to negotiate an agreement with respect to such Sequel,
       Expansion Pack, or Platform Translation after making a good faith effort
       not to exceed thirty (30) days following Developer's agreement to develop
       such Sequel, Expansion Pack, or Platform Translation and in any event if
       the Parties are unable to negotiate an agreement with respect to such Se-
       quel, Expansion Pack, or Platform Translation within sixty (60) days of
       the date the written notice is received by Developer.

This clause is driven by the IP rights. Since the publisher owns the copyright in the game,
the publisher controls the derivative works. This clause allows the developer to be the first to
bid on the sequels and expansion packs (often referred to as the *right of first offer*), but does not
guarantee the developer will be the company that works on these products.

2.9   Initial Expansion Pack. If Publisher selects Developer to develop the
       initial Expansion Pack, Developer develops and delivers to Publisher
       such initial Expansion Pack at a cost not greater than nine million dol-
       lars (U.S. $9,000,000) not later than 14 months after Commercial Launch.

The previous clause caps the maximum cost of the first expansion pack for the game. It also puts a limit on the timing of the expansion pack. This helps both parties plan and manages developer expectations.

2.10   Maintenance of Engine and Development Tools. In the event the Publisher
       engages another developer to produce a Sequel, Expansion Pack, or Plat-
       form Translation, Developer shall provide reasonable maintenance and
       support for the Engine and Development Tools at a cost not greater than
       one hundred thousand dollars (U.S. $100,000) per year.

This clause makes it clear that the developer will have to support the game engine and any necessary development tools if the sequel is given to another development studio. This also caps the payment. This is not the best-case scenario for any developer.

3.   MARKETING, PRODUCTION, AND DISTRIBUTION

The last major section discussed the developer's obligations. This section outlines the Publisher's obligations. Both of these sections should be laying out both rights and responsibilities. A right is a power to do something, and a responsibility is an obligation to do something. We would all like to live with as many rights as possible and as few obligations as possible. As a rule, the developer section will be laden with responsibilities for the developer and the publisher section will be filled with publisher rights. As you might imagine, the developer negotiating a contract would like to lock in more publisher responsibilities and more developer rights.

3.1   Responsibility. As between the Parties, Publisher shall have responsi-
      bility for and control of the marketing, production, and distribution of
      the Game in the United Kingdom (which, as used herein, does not include
      the Republic of Ireland), North America (which, as used herein, includes
      the United States of America and Canada) and other markets (hereinafter,
      "Other Territories"). Publisher shall make a reasonable effort to mar-
      ket, produce, and distribute the Game following the Acceptance Date;
      provided, however, that Publisher shall have the ability to cease mar-
      keting, production, or distribution activities related to the Game at
      any time and for any reason thereafter without liability to Developer.

This clause explains the role of the publisher and states that only the publisher has the responsibility for marketing, producing, and distributing the game. Note that the effect of this clause is to assign the publishing rights in certain markets. The purpose of mentioning specific countries is to ensure that there is no confusion over publishing activities in those markets. Also notice at the end of this clause that the publisher can stop marketing, producing, and distributing the game at any time with no consequences.

3.2   Developer Approval. Developer shall have approval rights for marketing
      materials in North America including packaging, promotional materials,
      and advertising content. Developer's trademark shall appear on the
      front of all packaging and promotional materials alongside Publisher's
      in approximately equal size and conspicuousness, and separately on the
      game's splash screens. The Developer will also have the right to a full
      credit list in the manual and Game.

This developer approval clause is a pleasant concession to the developer. This acknowledges that the developer wants to portray a certain image to the world and wants to have some control over how its product is marketed. It grants the developer the right to approve marketing materials in North America, and grants the developer equal size and conspicuousness for its trademark as the publisher has for its mark on game-related materials.

```
3.3   Expense. Unless otherwise agreed by the Parties, Publisher shall bear
      all costs and expenses related to the marketing, production, and distri-
      bution of the Game. Publisher shall spend at least $6 million on market-
      ing in North America prior to the date that is one year after Commercial
      Launch in North America.
```

Two items in the expenses clause are positive for developers: the publisher pays for the cost of marketing, and that cost has a lower limit. There have been some game development agreements where at least some marketing costs were covered out the developer's end. There have certainly been many game development agreements that did not list a lower boundary for marketing expenditures. This is a real benefit because it guarantees a certain level of marketing support for the title.

```
3.4   Software License and Subscription Fees. As between the Parties, Pub-
      lisher shall be solely responsible for determining, processing, and
      collecting all subscription fees related to End Users, and all such
      fees shall be paid to Publisher.
```

In any contract, look for the person who controls the money. What is paid first? Who controls the purse strings? In this contract, it is clear that the publisher will be "responsible" for the billing and collecting of subscription fees. May we all be so lucky to be so burdened with the "responsibility" of collecting money. From a drafting perspective, notice how clever it is to disguise this major benefit as a responsibility.

```
3.5   Complimentary Copies. Publisher will provide Developer with twenty-five
      (25) complimentary copies of the Product on first publication, and Devel-
      oper shall be entitled to buy a reasonable number of additional copies of
      the Product at Publisher's adjusted wholesale price at the time such
      copies are purchased; provided, however, that such copies, whether com-
      plimentary or purchased by Developer hereunder, may not be resold.
```

The developer gets 25 free copies of the game and can buy more at wholesale. The publisher generosity knows no bounds in this case. The developer may want more copies to give to employees, or to hand out as samples to other publishers they are trying to attract.

```
3.6   Press Releases. As part of its marketing activities, Publisher shall
      have the right to create and distribute press releases at its discre-
      tion. Developer may create and distribute press releases after obtain-
      ing Publisher's prior written consent.
```

This press release clause allows the developer to create and distribute press releases, but the publisher has to approve those. Notice that the publisher can create and distribute releases without any supervision by the developer.

3.7   <u>Trade Shows</u>. Publisher agrees to bear the cost of showcasing the game at
       E3 in 2007 and subsequent years until Game is released.

This trade show clause is in many game development agreements because the cost in terms of both money and hours for trade shows is substantial. It goes well beyond just renting a booth and taking some screenshots. Allocating these costs in the agreement may make sense for both parties so there is no ambiguity later. During the writing of this text, E3 announced that it will no longer be the public marketing extravaganza it once was. The purpose of the clause remains the same: there will always be big trade shows, and the cost to prepare for them will continue to be substantial.

3.8   <u>Community Development</u>. Publisher shall bear all costs related to the
       creation of a website associated with the Game including the mainte-
       nance of forums for the purposes of community development.

Community development has grown in importance as the world becomes more attached to the Internet. Was there a community development clause in the *Pac-Man* contract? Doubt-ful. Yet, community development clauses are very common in modern development contracts, particularly for online games that have the potential for a long lifespan.

4.   **OPERATIONS, SUPPORT, AND MAINTENANCE**

4.1   <u>Acceptance Date</u>. On or before the Acceptance Date, Developer shall pro-
       vide Publisher with a copy of the Software, and all other materials rea-
       sonably necessary for Publisher to begin operation of the Game. At the
       request of Publisher, Developer shall assist Publisher as necessary in
       the effort to install, setup, and configure Publisher's systems in
       preparation for the launch of the Game.

So what happens after this game is made? Does everyone go on vacation and bathe in truckloads of money? The answer is almost certainly no. In this agreement, the last milestone is the acceptance date. On that date, the developer has to give the publisher a copy of code and any other material necessary to run the game and must help the publisher set up the game for launch.

4.2   <u>Core Responsibility</u>. As of the Acceptance Date and except as set forth
       herein, Publisher shall be responsible for all operations and support
       related to the Game, including the operation and maintenance of servers
       and End User support. Publisher may fulfill its operations and support
       obligations however it deems fit, within commercially reasonable lim-
       its. Publisher will, using its commercially reasonable judgment, deter-
       mine which countries and markets in which to offer the Game. Publisher
       shall pay or cause to be paid to Developer all reasonable expenses as-
       sociated with all localizations of the Software. Publisher may localize
       the Software itself or contract with a third party for such localiza-
       tion if (a) Developer does not respond to such request within thirty
       (30) days of the date the written notice is received by Developer, (b)
       Developer declines the invitation to localize the Software, or (c) Pub-
       lisher and Developer are unable to reach mutually agreeable terms for

localization within sixty (60) days of the date the written notice is received by Developer. Should a third party localize the Software, Developer agrees to provide reasonable cooperation to Publisher and such third party with respect to such localization. All localization costs, whether performed by Developer or a third party, shall be recouped by Publisher.

This clause states that after the game is accepted by the publisher, the publisher will take on all responsibility for the operation and support of the game. The "live team" maintenance of an MMO does not have to be the publisher's responsibility. As with any clause in this sample, this clause can certainly be written other ways. In addition, this clause also covers localizing the game in various markets. The agreement provides that the publisher will offer the developer the opportunity to localize the game, but may use third parties. The clause also makes clear that the localization costs are recoupable costs.

4.3   <u>Maintenance of Software</u>. In the event that Publisher or an End User discovers a bug or other flaw that impairs the functionality of the Game, Publisher may at its option notify Developer of such bug or flaw. In such case, Developer shall use its best efforts to provide a patch that corrects the bug or flaw at issue and provide Publisher with a detailed description of such patch. Publisher will thereafter make a reasonable effort to make available such patch to all of the End Users. In the event Developer fails to provide an adequate patch for such bug or flaw in a timely manner, Publisher shall have the right to perform or have performed by another the necessary modifications or updates itself and to recoup the cost of such modifications from royalty payments to Developer. Developer shall provide a copy of the present state of the Source Code of the game to Publisher at the end of each quarter within ten (10) days of the end of the quarter.

This clause makes it clear that the developer is responsible for bug fixing on the software. If the developer does not respond, the publisher can outsource the bug fixes to a third party and recoup the cost out of developer royalties. Outsourcing the bug fixing is hardly practical, but the publisher wants this ability as a worst-case scenario and also wants the leverage it provides over the developer. The bottom line message is that the developer will fix the bugs or the publisher will pay someone else to fix them and take the cost out of the developer royalty payments.

4.4   <u>Security, Anti-Piracy, and Other Features</u>. Developer shall develop, incorporate into, and maintain reasonable computer security, anti-piracy and anti-cheating features for both the client and server copies of the Game, and for Game-related services and data. The computer security features shall be directed toward protecting the integrity and confidentiality of the Game, Game-related services, and data and defend against denial of service attacks. Anti-piracy features shall deter the creation and distribution of unauthorized copies of the Game, and deter the illicit creation and distribution of unauthorized derivative works of the Game. They shall also prevent unauthorized persons from gaining access to the Game, Game-related services, and data. Anti-cheating fea-

tures shall prevent cheating and prevent cheating mechanisms from affecting the Game.

This clause states that the developer must incorporate reasonable security, anti-piracy, and anti-cheating features for the game. Note that this clause may vary for games that antici-pate or want an active modification community; in such situations it is advisable to more specifically describe what is considered cheating and a violation of the game's security.

4.5   Live Team Activity. The division of responsibilities with respect to
       the Live Team Activity are set forth in Exhibit E. Developer shall use
       all commercially reasonable efforts to perform any Live Team Activity
       assigned to it, and any failure to perform such activities in a commer-
       cially reasonable manner shall be deemed a material breach of this
       Agreement.

The live team clause is critical for an online game. Anyone who has made an MMO will tell you that in many respects, the work begins after launch. The time leading up to launch is tough; the development work is hard and those people deserve great respect. However, just wait until you have several hundred thousand or several million people actively trying to hack, break, exploit, or even gently play the game. This agreement contemplates the live team activity after launch. The details for this sample agreement are in Exhibit E.

4.6   Expenses. Except as otherwise described herein, each Party shall bear
       its own costs and expenses with regard to the operation, support, and
       maintenance of the Game.

5.   ROYALTY

Clearly, the royalty section is going to be critical. Developers should look for similar structure and elements in this section of the agreement that they look for in the milestone section of the agreement. Specifically, look for concrete rules, days, and calculations. Even if everyone agrees on how much should be paid, there are still the issues of when it is paid, in what form, by what process, and who must make approval for those payments. There are more detailed comments on the royalty structure in Exhibit F.

This is also a good time to say a few words about the breadth of royalty payment struc-tures. They can look like almost anything. They can be based on gross or net revenue or some-thing in between. They can be flat or escalating or different by territory. There is literally almost no limit to the ways to calculate a royalty. The best way to go about it is to think about selling a certain number of games and run various models in an Excel spreadsheet so your development studio knows exactly how different scenarios will work out. Keep in mind all of the different revenue streams possible for your game. Make certain they are all accounted for in the agreement. For instance, make sure you know who gets money for items sales or in-game advertising or for selling extras such as special tokens for perks in the game.

Two royalty-related ideas we should point out are an *escalating royalty scale* and *phased recoupment*. An escalating royalty is a royalty that increases as game revenue increases. Perhaps the developer only receives 10% of net revenue for one tier of game revenue, but this increases to 30% of revenues that exceed a certain threshold. In Exhibit F of this sample agreement, you can see there is a two-tier royalty system that increases the royalty from 20% to 25% after subscriptions go over $500 million. Everyone has aligned interests in this model because everyone wants the game to sell well and there can be as many tiers as the parties are comfortable with.

A second idea is phased recoupment. That type of royalty structure asks the publisher to spread recoupment out over a longer period and send a small revenue stream to the developer during the recoupment period. In this sample agreement, the initial development costs are not recoupable, but keep in mind that those costs usually are recoupable, and even in this agreement there are other recoupable costs. By way of example, the developer may have a royalty rate at 20%. In many agreements, the publisher would recoup the game costs before paying that out, but the developer may be able to negotiate something like half of royalties toward recoupment and half paid to the developer. The advantage for the developer here is steady cash flow sooner after release. Under this type of recoupment model, the publisher may resist a phased recoupment because the publisher has to wait longer to recoup development costs.

5.1   <u>Royalty</u>. Subject to the terms and conditions of this Agreement, Publisher shall pay or cause to be paid to Developer on a quarterly basis the royalties set forth in Exhibit F for such quarter. Publisher shall provide Developer with a detailed report in accordance with Section 5.7 hereof within thirty (30) days of the end of each applicable quarter. Following delivery of such report, the initial royalty payment shall be made to Developer within fifty-five (55) Business Days of receipt by Publisher of an invoice from Developer. All subsequent royalty payments shall be made to Developer within twenty-five (25) Business Days of receipt by Publisher of an invoice from Developer. Publisher shall be under no obligation to make any royalty payment to Developer absent Publisher's receipt of an invoice from Developer. Publisher makes no warranty or representation as to the actual amount of revenue the Developer will derive hereunder. The royalties set forth in Exhibit F are gross royalties, and Publisher shall withhold the appropriate amount from such gross payments as required pursuant to Subsection 5.6.

5.2   <u>Objections</u>. Developer shall give Publisher specific notice of any objection to a royalty statement within twenty-four (24) months following the date Publisher first sent the statement to Developer, or such royalty statement will become conclusively binding and Developer waives any other right to object. In the event an audit reveals an undisputed underpayment by Publisher, Publisher shall immediately remit payment to Developer in the amount of such underpayment. In addition, unless Developer commences a legal or medial action within twenty-four (24) months following the date Publisher first sent a royalty statement to Developer, Developer waives its right to undertake any legal or remedial action in connection with such statement.

This agreement allows for a royalty report, described in 5.7. If the developer has any issues with the royalty report the developer may complain, but these complaints are limited to two years after the report. The clause following this paragraph also sets out that the developer has a limited time, two years in this case, to complain or the company loses its rights to complain.

5.3   <u>Overpayment</u>. If Publisher makes an overpayment to Developer, Developer
shall immediately return to Publisher such overpayment upon the earlier
of (i) receipt of Publisher's written demand together with documentation
supporting such demand, or (ii) Developer's otherwise becoming aware of
such overpayment. Notwithstanding the foregoing, Publisher may, at Publisher's sole discretion, deduct an amount equal to such overpayment
from any sums that may become due or payable to Developer by Publisher,
in lieu of Developer's reimbursement to Publisher for such overpayment.

Notice the contrast between the objections clause in 5.2 and the overpayment clause, 5.3.
The previous clause tells what to do if the developer is underpaid, and this clause tells what to do
if the developer is overpaid. Notice that the developer has to return any overpayment the publisher makes and furthermore there is no two-year limit on complaints in the developer objection
clause. Also, the developer has to return the money as soon as the developer or the publisher
notices the overpayment, whichever is earlier. Clearly, the clauses are very different and reflect
the standard difference in negotiating power.

5.4   <u>Expansion Pack, Sequel, Platform Translation, and Localization Recoup-</u>
<u>ment</u>. Recoupment shall not apply to Initial Development Costs. For Ex-
pansion Packs, Sequels, or Platform Translations described in 2.8 and
Exhibit F, and for localizations described in 4.2, Publisher is entitled
to recoup development costs. In the event Developer (i) develops an Expansion Pack, Sequel, or Platform Translation pursuant to Subsection
2.8, or (ii) localizes the Software for any particular market, Publisher
shall be entitled to deduct the actual total gross payments to such Developer for development costs from any royalties due to Developer until
Publisher has recouped the full amount paid for the development costs
for such Expansion Pack, Sequel, Platform Translation, or localization
in accordance with the following quarterly schedule:

5.4.1   In the first quarter after Commercial Launch of Expansion Pack,
Sequel, Platform Translation, or localization: Publisher will
deduct thirty percent (30%) in recoupment from royalty payments
to Developer.

5.4.2   In the second and subsequent quarters after Commercial Launch of
Expansion Pack, Sequel, Platform Translation, or localization,
Publisher will deduct fifty percent (50%) in recoupment from roy-
alty payments to Developer.

5.4.3   The deductions listed in this section 5.4 shall be made only
until the sum of such deductions is equal to the amount owed by
Developer to Publisher in recoupment for the cost incurred to
Publisher by Developer for the Expansion Pack, Sequel, Platform
Translation, or localization.

This preceding royalty clause shows an example of a phased recoupment model. It also
makes clear that the publisher has no intention of recouping the initial development costs for
the game before paying out royalties. This is not the normal course of business in the industry,
but it may be possible under some circumstances such as a well-established developer or a

developer that is partially or wholly owned by the publisher. Notice that the sequel costs are recouped, but the recoupment is a phased recoupment. As discussed previously, a phased recoupment is a situation where the developer still receives some royalties while paying back the cost of development.

5.5 Extended Honing Period Recoupment. Publisher may at its sole discretion agree to fund up to six months of additional development, which Developer shall perform at a cost to Publisher not to exceed 5 million dollars. The cost of this additional development will be subject to recoupment by Publisher in accordance with the following quarterly schedule:

5.5.1 In the first quarter after Commercial Launch: no recoupment.

5.5.2 In the second quarter after Commercial Launch: Publisher will deduct thirty percent (30%) in recoupment from royalty payments to Developer.

5.5.3 In subsequent quarters after Commercial Launch, Publisher will deduct fifty percent (50%) in recoupment from royalty payments to Developer.

5.5.4 The deductions listed in this section 5.5 shall be made only until the sum of such deductions is equal to the amount owed by Developer to Publisher in recoupment for the cost incurred to Publisher by Developer for Honing activities undertaken during the Extended Honing Period.

The honing or polish period is an example of some room for schedule slips built into the agreement. Also, notice that even though initial development costs are not recoupable in this agreement, this additional money is subject to recoupment and there is yet another example of a phased recoupment model.

5.6 Withholding Taxes. Any withholding or other taxes that Publisher is required by law to withhold and actually withholds and pays on behalf of Developer with respect to the royalties to Developer under this Agreement shall be deducted from gross payments and remitted to the taxing authority; provided, however, that for tax so deducted, Publisher shall furnish Developer with documentation of the taxes paid on its behalf which are reasonably required by Developer in seeking corresponding reductions available (in the form of income deductions or tax credits), if any, in the determination of Developer's U.S. income taxes. The Parties shall use commercially reasonable efforts to minimize withholding and other taxes.

Taxes are enormously complicated. This is a simple tax clause, but they can be much more elaborate. Pay particular attention to these clauses, because they are at least as important as the royalty clause. Do not be so proud of yourself for negotiating that extra 2% royalty if your company bears the tax burden on sales. All of that clever 2% negotiating just evaporated, and probably even more money along with it. This, like royalty payments, is not something to do by feel or guesswork. Get your accountant or tax attorney on the phone and run scenarios with different game sales. Paying a little money up front can save big headaches and a lot of money down the road. Obviously, when the agreement is international, this becomes even more complicated.

```
5.7   Royalty Reports. Publisher shall provide to Developer a royalty report
      substantially in the form set forth in Exhibit G (the "Royalty Report")
      within fifteen (15) Business Days of the end of each Publisher finan-
      cial quarter during the Term of this Agreement. Upon receipt of a Roy-
      alty Report, Developer shall promptly provide Publisher with an
      invoice.
```

The royalty report is critical for the developer. This is the revenue disclosure for the developer. Here, the developer can build in certain protections. For instance, how detailed is this report and what revenue streams are broken out for the developer? The developer wants this as detailed as possible, while the publisher may have some standard royalty report it uses for dozens of titles and it is not willing to make special arrangements.

```
5.8   Developer Audit Rights. Developer has the right to audit Royalty Re-
      ports and calculation of Net Revenue on business days, within normal
      hours of operation with 10 days notice. Cost of this audit is born by
      Developer except when a discrepancy of more than 5% is found in favor of
      Developer, then cost is born by Publisher. In the event that Publisher
      disagrees with the results of this audit, the Publisher may bear the
      cost of a mutually agreeable third-party accounting consultant to per-
      form an independent review. This final review shall be the final bind-
      ing calculation for the Royalty Report and Net Revenue. Developer may
      exercise this right no more than once per year and the result will be
      final and binding on both parties. The results of an audit for one year
      may not be recalculated in subsequent years.
```

The developer audit clause is a powerful and often overlooked clause. This clause allows the developer to check the relevant royalty accounting. Without this, the developer is paid on trust alone. This clause is the only way a developer has any control or oversight over publisher accounting. This is especially true if the publisher is a privately held company, because the accounting standards for privately held companies are not as transparent and rigorous as the standards for publicly held companies.

Keep in mind that this clause is working for the developer even if it is never invoked. The publisher knows that the developer has the right to look into the books and that gives the publisher an incentive to be especially accurate in accounting. Also, take note of the restrictions on this clause. The audit can only be performed once per year. It may make sense for this to be quarterly if a game is supposed to have a short lifespan, but yearly or twice yearly may make more sense for an MMO title. The developer has to give notice and perform the audit during normal business hours. The developer also has to pay for the audit unless there is a discrepancy of more than 5% in favor of the developer. Finally, notice that there is a built-in way to resolve disagreements. Of course, the publisher is going to disagree if the developer accountant believes the company is owed much more money. In that case, there is no need to run off to an expensive court proceeding because this clause is foresighted and provides for that consequence. If the publisher and developer disagree, the publisher pays for the cost of an outside accountant to come in and resolve the dispute.

6.   OWNERSHIP AND LICENSES

This section is critical. It describes in detail which party owns different parts and rights within the game. As a rule, this clause can be read as a land grab for the publisher. The general theme is that the publisher gets most everything and the developer gets to keep only as much as necessary.

This contract section is all about copyright and how that can be divided up. It bears repeating here that copyright is infinitely divisible, it is a great big bundle of rights that can be broken down in ways that are limited only by your imagination. This contract section shows some of those ways.

6.1   <u>Game</u>. Except for the express licenses granted or as otherwise set forth in this Agreement, Publisher shall have and retain all right, title, and interest in and to the Game (including the Game Content) and all Intellectual Property Rights thereto.

6.2   <u>Source Code</u>. Notwithstanding section 6.1 herein, except for the licenses granted in this Agreement, Developer shall retain ownership of copyright in and to the Source Code.

The source code clause is an interesting one because developers usually believe it has a great deal more meaning than it actually does. This clause states that the developer owns the copyright in the source code. If you ask developers about this, they will proudly exclaim that they own the copyright in the source code for their game. Ask them what that means in light of the rest of the development contract and there is much less to exclaim about.

From reading agreements and talking with experienced game attorneys, it appears that the developer has traditionally held ownership of copyright in the game source code. Furthermore, this ownership has been the subject of extensive debate in more than one game development agreement. This ownership is something developers fight for. However, remember that a license for something may be expressed as giving away the right to do a certain thing.

The insight here is that the publisher has the exclusive license to do everything with that source code. We will go out on a limb to suggest that the "ownership" of the source code copyright clause in this and many other agreements is a bit of sham to placate developer egos. Upon examination what does the developer really have? Can the developer make the game and sell it without the publisher? Can the developer make sequels to the game or other derivative works? Can the developer license out the game in any form whatsoever? The answer to all of these questions is "no." All of those rights are licensed exclusively to the publisher and they are almost always licensed exclusively to the publisher. All the substantial meaning and value in owning a copyright is given away in other portions of the contract. To say the least, having this ownership of source code copyright clause is not a robust victory for the developer.

6.3   <u>Development Tools and Engine</u>. Except for the express licenses granted in this Agreement, Developer shall have and retain all right, title, and interest in and to the Development Tools and Engine, including all Intellectual Property Rights thereto.

This next tools and engine ownership clause carries much more weight. This states that the developer retains the copyright in the development tools and engine for the game. Of course, the developer has to allow the publisher to use those tools to distribute the game, but otherwise, the engine and tools are developer property. This type of clause has made those developers a great deal of money. If your game studio is lucky enough to come up with the next Unreal or Source engine, then this clause is of critical importance.

6.4   Derivative Properties. Publisher shall have and retain all right,
        title, and interest in and to any and all Derivative Properties and all
        Intellectual Property Rights thereto.

The previous clause is a derivative properties clause. In other chapters in this book, we discuss that anything based on an original work under copyright is referred to as a derivative work. Practically speaking, this includes sequels, localizations, and platform translations. It also includes movies, cartoons, and cereal if your game is a mega-hit. In any event, the publisher owns the rights to make all of these. This is a major giveaway in the copyright structure described in this contract. It is commonly done, but it should be pointed out that this is a big chunk of copyright ownership that is contracted away here.

6.5   Designations. Publisher shall own all rights in and to any and all trade-
        marks, service marks, domain names, trade names and other designations
        that are associated with the Game, except for Developer's trade name.

Here again we see a clause that grants the publisher IP rights. The clause on derivative properties was for copyright and this clause is concerned with trademark. Everything except for the developer name goes to the publisher in this clause.

The database? Yes, the publisher owns that too, just in case there was any question on that front.

6.6   Database. As between Publisher and Developer, Publisher shall own all
        Intellectual Property Rights and other rights in and to each and every
        database associated with the Game, and to all data contained in such
        databases and its arrangement.

6.7   Source Code License. As to Source Code, and as to any other Intellectual
        Property Rights Developer may own in and to the Game, Developer hereby
        grants to Publisher an exclusive, worldwide, irrevocable, perpetual,
        sub-licensable, royalty-free, fully paid up license under all of Devel-
        oper's Intellectual Property Rights to make, have made, use, import,
        reproduce, have reproduced, distribute, have distributed, make deriva-
        tive works of, perform, and display the Game.

This source code clause is very tightly tied to clause 6.2. Remember previously that the developer "owned" the copyright of the source code? This states that any IP rights in the code, even potential patents, are licensed to the publisher. That license is exclusive meaning that the developer cannot grant those rights to any other party. The license is perpetual and irrevocable, which means the license goes on forever and cannot be cancelled or taken back. Finally, the license is good throughout the world and does not require any particular payments other than those discussed in this agreement.

6.8   Development Tools and Engine License. Developer hereby grants to
        Publisher a non-exclusive, worldwide, irrevocable, perpetual, sub-
        licensable, royalty-free, fully paid up license under all of Developer's
        Intellectual Property Rights to make, have made, use, sell, offer to

sell, import, reproduce, have reproduced, make derivative works of, distribute, have distributed, perform, display, disclose, use in commerce,
market, promote, and otherwise dispose of the Engine and Development
Tools. Developer will provide the Development Tools and the Engine, to
Publisher both in Source Code and Object Code form on or before the Acceptance Date and once per quarter thereafter for the duration of the
Agreement; and Publisher may make a reasonable number of archival copies
of the Development Tools and Engine for purposes of backup and recovery.

This tools and engine license is similar to the grant in 6.7. Reading this clause combined
with 6.2 really shows where the power and control is with the contract. The publisher essentially has all of the power and the control.

In clause 6.3, the developer was granted ownership of the tools and engine for the game.
This makes clear that the developer has to license the tools and engine to the publisher to the
extent necessary to market and distribute the game. Look at this license language compared to
the source code license clause language in 6.7. There is a critical difference in the exclusivity.
This license is "non-exclusive." That means the developer can potentially license the engine
and tools to other companies. As companies like Epic and Valve know, this is potentially a
major revenue stream.

6.9   <u>Game License to Developer</u>. Publisher hereby grants to Developer a non-
exclusive, royalty-free, fully paid up license for the term of this
Agreement under all of Publisher's Intellectual Property Rights to modify, make, have made, use, import, reproduce, have reproduced, and make
derivative works of the Game solely for Developer's internal use in
performing its obligations set forth in this Agreement, and then only
for the benefit of Publisher.

This game license clause really drives everything home if it is not obvious already which
party is in control. So much has been given to the publisher in this agreement, and in most
game development agreements, that it is now necessary to temporarily give something back.
To put it another way, so many rights have been granted to the publisher, it is necessary to
grant the developer a license back so the developer can fulfill its obligations under the agreement. Loosely speaking, the parties recognize the publisher now owns essentially everything,
and it is necessary to grant the developer a license back for some of those rights just to be able
to make the game.

6.10   <u>Assignment</u>. To the extent that each Party may own Intellectual Property
Rights that belong to the other Party as set forth in this Section 6,
such Party hereby irrevocably assigns to the other Party all such Intellectual Property Rights.

The preceding assignment clause may strike the reader as a little odd. It is really a house-
keeping clause just to make certain that some IP issues are totally covered, perhaps even
doubly covered. It is possible that the developer or publisher already owns certain IP rights
under this agreement, but those rights have been given to the other party somewhere in this
agreement. If that is the case, the party that currently holds those rights is agreeing to assign
them to the other party.

6.11   <u>Further Assurances</u>. Each Party agrees to use commercially reasonable efforts to protect the Intellectual Property it owns under this Agreement
and to assist the other Party in every proper way, at such other Party's
expense, in (a) securing such other Party's rights, including without
limitation the disclosure to such other Party of all pertinent information and data with respect thereto, the execution of all applications,
specifications, oaths, assignments, and all other instruments which the
other Party shall deem necessary in order to apply for and obtain, assign, or convey such rights; and (b) the enforcement of such other
Party's Intellectual Property Rights, including reasonable assistance
in initiating, carrying out, or defending any legal action against a
third party. Developer further agrees to waive any moral rights, to the
extent legally permitted, in any and all subject matter developed by Developer under this Agreement. Developer agrees to take all actions that
are necessary to ensure that any and all goodwill generated by Developer
in the course of performing its obligations hereunder and associated
with any designation (including any trademark, service mark, and trade
name) owned by Publisher shall vest in Publisher when and as such goodwill is generated, without any separate payment or other consideration
of any kind to Developer. Publisher shall have the right to sub-license
or transfer its rights under this Agreement to its Affiliates.

This further assurance may look like a benign boilerplate clause, but it actually carries
some heft if read carefully. Mainly it is concerned with each party doing everything it can to
help the other party secure IP. In this type of relationship, this usually means the developer
cooperating fully to help the publisher secure IP. Also notice this includes assisting with any
legal action (including litigation) if necessary to protect those rights.

7.   <u>CONFIDENTIALITY</u>

The confidentiality section is in every game development agreement. This outlines that both
parties have secrets and that some of these secrets will be shared with the other party while fulfilling this agreement. However, the party that learns the secret may not share it with others.
Those few sentences are expanded and explained in detail in the following section.

7.1   <u>Definition</u>. "<u>Confidential Information</u>" means any information of a Party
or third-party information under the control of a Party, including but
not limited to technical data, trade secrets, customer information,
know-how, research, product plans, products, services, customers, customer lists, markets, software, developments, inventions, processes,
feedback, formulas, technology, designs, drawings, engineering, hardware configuration information, marketing, business plans, finances, or
other business information disclosed by the disclosing Party either directly or indirectly in writing, orally, or by drawings or inspection
of parts or equipment. Without limiting the foregoing, Confidential Information expressly includes all information or materials related to
the Game, including without limitation the Software, details of operation, mechanics, and content.

Just to be clear about what the agreement is protecting, we need to know what confidential information is. As usual, this section is driven by IP; in this case, trade secret. The section starts with a definition of confidential information. If it were not at the top of this section, it would have been at the beginning of the agreement in the general definition section.

7.2   <u>Exclusions</u>. Notwithstanding Subsection 7.1, nothing received by a receiving Party shall be construed as Confidential Information which: (i) is now available or becomes available to the public without breach of this Agreement; (ii) is lawfully obtained from a third party without a duty of confidentiality; (iii) is known to the receiving Party prior to such disclosure; (iv) is, at any time, developed by the receiving Party independent of any such disclosure(s) from the disclosing Party and the receiving Party can reasonably show such independence; or (v) is necessarily disclosed to exercise a right granted to a Party herein.

This exclusions clause is a second part of the definition of confidential information. This explicitly discusses types of information that will not be considered confidential and lists those items within the clause.

7.3   <u>Non-Use and Non-Disclosure</u>. The receiving Party shall not disclose the disclosing Party's Confidential Information to any third party and may only use the disclosing Party's Confidential Information for the intended business purpose related to this Agreement and for the benefit of the disclosing Party. In no event may Confidential Information of the disclosing Party be used by the receiving Party to compete with or assist a third party to compete with the disclosing Party. Both Parties shall protect Confidential Information from disclosure or misuse by using the same degree of care as for their own confidential information of like importance, but shall at least use reasonable care. Further, Developer agrees to have each of their employees or independent contractors with access to any Confidential Information agree to be bound by an enforceable agreement that ensures the protection of the Confidential Information from disclosure to at least the same extent as does this Agreement. Each receiving Party agrees to promptly notify the disclosing Party upon learning of any unauthorized disclosure of the disclosing Party's Confidential Information, and shall provide reasonable assistance to the disclosing Party to remedy and contain such breach. It is understood that, except as otherwise expressly set forth in this Agreement, said Confidential Information shall remain the sole property of the disclosing Party.

Now that it is clear what confidential information is, the agreement goes on to set up some rules regarding that information. In short, do everything reasonable to keep the information secret and let the other party know if there is a leak. Specifically, the prior clause states that the parties cannot disclose the confidential information of the other party and measures such as non-disclosure agreements must be used when necessary to protect the information. Furthermore, if there is an unauthorized disclosure of information, the party must notify the other party of the unauthorized disclosure.

7.4   <u>Disclosure Required by Law</u>. Notwithstanding Subsection 7.3 above, a re-
      ceiving Party may disclose the other Party's Confidential Information if
      the information is required by law to be disclosed in response to a valid
      order of a court of competent jurisdiction or authorized government
      agency, provided that the receiving Party must give the disclosing Party
      prompt written notice and obtain or allow for a reasonable effort by the
      disclosing Party to obtain a protective order prior to disclosure.

There are occasions where parties are legally forced to provide confidential information to courts or administrative agencies. This can be in the form of a judicial order or an order from an administrative agency of the government such as the IRS or SEC. This clause makes it clear that complying with those demands is authorized and is not a breach of this agreement.

7.5   <u>Developer's Third Party Confidential Information</u>. Developer agrees
      that it will not, during the term of this Agreement, improperly use or
      disclose any proprietary information or trade secrets of any third
      party with which Developer has an agreement or duty to keep in confi-
      dence information acquired by Developer, if any, and that Developer
      will not bring onto the premises of Publisher or offer to Publisher any
      unpublished document or proprietary information belonging to such third
      party unless consented to in writing by such third party.

The prior clause is another protection built in for the publisher. The developer agrees that it may receive confidential information from third parties and that it will not send this information to the publisher. The publisher is trying to control its exposure and access to confidential information and therefore liability to third parties.

7.6   <u>Return of Materials</u>. Upon request of the disclosing Party, the receiv-
      ing Party shall within thirty (30) days of the receipt of said request,
      undertake reasonable efforts to deliver to the disclosing Party all of
      the disclosing Party's returnable Confidential Information that the re-
      ceiving Party has in its possession or under its control.

This previous clause is also relevant to control of confidential information and trade secret. If the party wants the information back, it should be able to get it all back. This clause makes it clear that the disclosing party can get any material back in 30 days.

7.7   <u>Confidentiality of this Agreement</u>. Except for the cases provided in
      Section 3 or Subsections 7.2 (i) and (v) hereof, neither Party shall
      disclose the terms of this Agreement or its existence other than to
      business, financial, or legal advisors, without the express written
      consent of the other Party. However, either Party may disclose the
      terms or existence of this Agreement as required under any applicable
      securities regulations, or in furtherance of a proposed sale, acquisi-
      tion, or merger of substantially all of such Party's business interests
      related to this Agreement as long as such disclosure is made under a
      duty of confidentiality. Either Party may disclose information to
      shareholders, analysts, and other parties as required in its judgment
      to fulfill its fiduciary responsibilities.

The agreement itself is confidential and has restrictions on discussing the deal terms. The deal terms between publishers and developers are some of the most sensitive pieces of information in the game industry. As the reader can see, this agreement sets out the exact terms and royalty structure payment in excruciating detail. Furthermore, the other deal terms contain sensitive information such as who is a key employee. The exceptions to this clause reference other areas in the agreement where some aspect of this agreement may be discussed such as in a legal proceeding or in certain marketing material.

8.   OPTION TO PURCHASE

There was a naïve time in the game industry where a publisher would buy a developer after that developer had a solid track record of making great games. Maybe the publisher and developer even had a history of working productively together as well. That can be a very expensive proposition. If the publisher waits until the developer is established, the developer is worth far more. A much better idea for the publisher is to lock in a nice low price when the developer is young and hungry. This is what this section is for. Before you can ask, yes, it absolutely does appear in many modern publisher agreements.

8.1   Option to Purchase Developer. Developer hereby grants to Publisher an exclusive, irrevocable right, at any time to purchase Developer during the Option Period for $[**As Little as Possible**], whether through merger, stock exchange, or sale of all or substantially all of its assets (the "Option"), on customary terms (including, without limitation, customary representations, warranties, covenants, conditions, and indemnification provisions, which shall include a holdback of at least 20% of the purchase price as security for Developer's indemnification obligations for a period of one year); the Parties shall negotiate in good faith to execute a definitive agreement with respect to the Option exercise on such customary terms. To the extent reasonably practicable, Publisher shall structure the transaction so it will qualify as a "tax free" reorganization.

Clause 8.1 is an option to purchase clause. This sets the price for acquisition of the developer. It is all up-side for the publisher in this instance. Another variation on this clause is a right of first refusal. In that clause, the publisher has the right to match a competing offer for the developer if another company wants to buy the developer. Sometimes, there is even a right of first refusal clause that includes the right to match the competing offer or purchase at the pre-set price, whichever is lower. Also notice this clause states that the option lasts until the expiration of an option period. This period is set forth in the definition section as ending on December 31, 2012. The goal of the publisher is to lock in a price on the developer until the game has had time to prove a success.

8.2   No Solicitation. From the execution of this Agreement until the expiration of the Option Period, Developer and the officers, directors, employees, or other agents of Developer and its affiliates will not, directly or indirectly, (i) take any action to solicit, initiate, or encourage any Transaction or (ii) engage in negotiations with, or disclose any nonpublic information relating to Developer to, or afford

> access to the properties, books, or records of Developer to, any person
> who has advised Developer that it may be considering making, or has
> made, an investment or purchase proposal.

This non-solicitation clause prevents the developer from entering into negotiations with other parties to purchase or invest in the developer. Therefore, not only does this section lock in a purchase price for the publisher, it prevents the developer from entering into meaningful discussions with other parties about purchase or investment.

9.   <u>TERM AND TERMINATION</u>

How long does this agreement last, how does it end, and what happens when it is over? All of these questions and more are answered in the very exciting term and termination section.

> 9.1   <u>Term</u>. This Agreement will commence on the Effective Date and will con-
> tinue until the earlier of (a) the date on which Publisher, at its dis-
> cretion, ceases operation of the Game, or (b) the date on which this
> Agreement is otherwise terminated in accordance with this Section 9.

Simply put, the term of an agreement is the period the agreement is in force. In this agreement, it starts on the *effective date*, which is defined at the head of the document as the date on the front of the document. The agreement ends when the publisher stops operating the game or if any of the other termination events set forth in this section of the agreement occur.

> 9.2   <u>Termination for Cause</u>. In the event that either Party materially
> breaches (including, but not limited to, the material breaches set
> forth in Section 14.9) this Agreement, the other Party may send a notice
> of breach to such breaching Party. The breaching Party shall have
> forty-five (45) days after receipt of such notice to cure such breach.
> After such forty-five (45) day period, if the breach remains uncured,
> the non-breaching Party may immediately terminate this Agreement by
> sending written notice of termination to the breaching Party. Any notice
> of termination of this Agreement shall be prominently labeled "Notice
> of Termination."

Termination for cause can be thought of as termination for a good reason. This is contrasted with *termination for convenience*. Termination for convenience is usually a termination based on a change in business needs and has nothing to do with the performance of the other party. The preceding clause covers termination for cause. As the clause states, termination for cause is due to a breach in the contract which is breaking a promise in the agreement. Some breaches are worse than others and the worst ones are called material breaches. There is a list of those in section 14.9.

This clause also discusses *curing* a breach, which usually means making up for the broken promise in some way. The cure is usually only available for a certain time. In the clause, the cure period is 45 days. The cure for a breach varies based on what the breach is. For instance, if the agreement is broken by not paying a royalty payment the way to cure the breach is to make the royalty payment. If the agreement is broken by not meeting a milestone, the developer must send in the appropriate milestone.

A list of the material breaches for this agreement is in section 14.9. Keep in mind that the list is not exhaustive and there can be termination for cause beyond even this list of material breaches. That can be derived from the "including but not limited to" language in this section. "Including but not limited to" is a favorite of attorneys all over the world looking for some wiggle room when making a list.

9.3   <u>Force Majeure and Termination for Convenience</u>. In addition, either Party may terminate this Agreement without penalty or liability to such Party, thirty (30) days after providing written notice thereof (i) in the event a Force Majeure Event persists and impairs or delays a Party's performance hereunder for a three-month period; and (ii) such event has not been cured by the end of the thirty (30) day notice period.

The preceding clause allows for termination due to a *force majeure* event. Do not fear the word *majeure*, it is merely French for "greater force." This type of clause is often called an "act of God" clause. The clause makes clear that the parties can terminate the agreement if an "act of God" gets in the way of the performance. These force majeure events are things such as war and natural disasters. The clause also allows for termination for convenience. This is termination without cause. The entire deal can be called off on 30-days' written notice with no penalty.

9.4   <u>Effect of Termination</u>. Notwithstanding any other provision of this Agreement, in the event this Agreement is terminated due to any uncured material breach of Developer, then Developer shall (a) cease all activities related to the Game, (b) promptly provide Publisher with the Engine and Development Tools (including all documentation, materials, Source Code, Object Code, content creation tools, authorizations, and assistance), (c) assign its agreements with third parties (together with the necessary rights and licenses) or grant proper sublicenses as requested by Publisher or a party selected by Publisher, to enable Publisher or a third party selected by Publisher to develop, maintain, and support, or have developed, maintained, and supported, the Game, and (d) upon the written request of a Party, the other Party shall return or destroy (at the direction of the requesting Party) and shall promptly cease to use all drawings, notes, memoranda, specifications, designs, devices, documents and any other material containing or disclosing any Confidential Information (other than the Royalty Reports, related financial information, and copies of this Agreement) of the other Party and erase such information stored in computer memory, provided that (i) if a legal proceeding has been threatened or instituted to seek disclosure of the Confidential Information, such material shall not be destroyed until the proceeding is settled or a final judgment with respect thereto has been rendered; (ii) any information held in computer, word processing, or other such systems shall only be destroyed to the extent reasonably practicable after using reasonable good faith efforts to destroy such information. Notwithstanding the return or destruction of any Confidential Information, or documents or material containing or reflecting any Confidential Information, the parties will continue to be bound by their obligations of confidentiality and other obligations under Section 7. Neither Party shall retain any such materials without the disclosing Party's written approval. The rights and remedies provided in this Section shall not be exclusive and are in addition to any other rights and remedies provided by law or this Agreement.

The end of the contract has certain effects. This clause describes those effects in detail. This can be thought of as how the agreement will be wrapped up. The game-related activities are stopped, the publisher gets a copy of all of the code, agreements with third parties are wound down, and confidential information is returned if requested.

9.5   Survival. Upon termination or expiration of this Agreement for any reason, all rights and duties of the Parties toward each other shall cease except for Sections 1 (Definitions), 5 (Royalty—only to the extent any royalties are owed prior to termination), 6 (Ownership and Licenses), 7 (Confidentiality), 10 (Representations and Warranties), 11 (Indemnity), 12 (Limitations of Liability), and 14 (General), which shall survive any such termination or expiration.

After the agreement is terminated, some clauses need to have a life beyond the contract. For instance, it would not be good for the parties to spill confidential information after the contract is terminated. Also, the ownership and licenses remain the same after the agreement is over.

9.6   Developer Purchase of IP. In the event Publisher terminates this Agreement without cause before Commercial Launch, Publisher may, at its sole discretion, permit Developer to purchase all Intellectual Property Rights in and to the Game upon payment to Publisher an amount equal to the total of milestone payments made by Publisher to Developer as of the date of termination, plus interest compounded annually at a rate of 20%.

The developer purchase of IP clause is a nice concession to the developer if the developer can get it. Many times a relationship between a publisher and a developer does not work out. The publisher may cancel a game even if the game is on schedule. It is also possible that a developer may be courted by another publisher or investor in the middle of the development cycle. If this happens, the developer may be able to negotiate the right to buy back the game IP. In the prior clause, this is allowed under certain circumstances. First, the publisher must terminate the contract for convenience, and second, the developer must pay the publisher milestone payments back with 20% interest. As with any other clause in this agreement, the specifics are negotiable, but being able to buy back the IP under any circumstances is a real boon for the developer.

10.   REPRESENTATIONS AND WARRANTIES

Representations and warranties is a section that describes what each party is telling the other party is true, its *representations*, and what each party will guarantee, its *warranties*.

10.1   Authority. Each Party represents that it is a business entity duly organized, validly existing, and in good standing in the jurisdiction in

which it is incorporated or where its principal place of business is located, and that it has all requisite corporate power and authority to
execute and deliver this Agreement and to carry out the transactions
contemplated by this Agreement.

Authority is critical for contracts. If a janitor at Electronic Arts (EA) signed your studio
game development agreement, would it be valid? Probably not. A person who signs an agreement has to be a representative of the company and has to have the authority to enter a binding contract on this subject matter. The reason why a janitor cannot sign the development
agreement is that a janitor does not have the authority to bind EA in those type of agreements.

On the other hand, can the head of marketing or a senior vice president for business
development bind EA to a development agreement? As we move up the hierarchy, the question becomes more complicated. This clause removes all ambiguity about the authority of the
person signing the agreement. The person could be committing fraud, but here the person
signing for both parties is explicitly representing that he or she has the authority to bind his or
her company in this agreement.

10.2   <u>No Violation of Laws and Regulations</u>. Each Party represents that it
       does not violate any law or regulation by entering into this agreement.

Contracts for services that are against the law are illegal. For instance, a contract involving
kidnapping would be unenforceable, and no court in the U.S. would allow it. This clause
makes it clear that the parties do not believe the subject of this contract is illegal, therefore
there should be no reason it is not enforceable in that respect.

10.3   <u>Development Work</u>. Developer represents and warrants that (a) it shall
       perform the development work described herein in a good and workmanlike
       manner with due diligence and in full compliance with the terms and con-
       ditions of this Agreement and all mutually agreed upon specifications;
       (b) the concepts and ideas related to the Game are original to the De-
       veloper and have not been taken from any third party; (c) it will not
       engage in any activity without the express written consent of Pub-
       lisher, which results in the creation or development of a Derivative
       Property that would be owned by Publisher under this Agreement or oth-
       erwise infringes or violates the Intellectual Property Rights of Pub-
       lisher; (d) the Game, including without limitation the Software, and
       any intended use resulting there from, does not and will not infringe or
       violate any third party's Intellectual Property Rights or any law or
       regulation; (e) the Game will be free and clear of any claims, liens, or
       encumbrances of any third party; (f) does not breach any duty toward or
       rights of any person or entity, and has not otherwise resulted in any
       consumer fraud, product liability, tort, breach of contract, injury,
       damage, or harm of any kind to any person or entity; (g) the Game will
       not contain any viruses, Trojan horses, backdoors, disabling code, or
       other such pernicious feature; (h) the Game will not contain any hidden
       code that will result in a change in the Entertainment Software Rating
       Board rating; (i) it shall include no Open Source Software in any por-
       tion of the Game that is to be reproduced, distributed, or modified; and

```
(j) it shall cooperate with Publisher to develop and implement effec-
tive anti-piracy measures to protect client and server copies of the
Game.
```

The developer makes certain warranties or guarantees in the preceding paragraph. It is useful to break out some of the warranties and examine them individually. Item (b) states that the ideas are original to the developer. This is an IP clause based on copyright and trade secret. This warranty assures the publisher that the game is not stolen from another source. Item (d) assures the publisher that the game does not infringe the IP rights of another party. Practically speaking, this is a tough warranty to make, especially in the patent area because patents are nearly impossible to be completely free of. One reason patents are hard to make a warranty for is that some patents are still pending. When those patents issue, the developer may find that they infringe the patent.

Item (h) is a new idea in game development agreements but a warranty that is growing in popularity. Since the Grand Theft Auto "Hot Coffee" scandal, publishers have feared hidden game code. It is now clear that the ESRB will change the rating of a game based on portions of the game that are not even accessible through most normal means. As the entire industry learned from that one event, hidden code can cost tens of millions of dollars in lost revenue. Now, developers often warrant that the game will not have any of this code just as they warrant it will not have any viruses in subpart (g).

10.4   <u>Right to Grant Licenses</u>. Each Party represents and warrants that it has
        the necessary rights to grant the licenses and/or assignments set forth
        in this Agreement.

The right to grant licenses clause is similar to the authority clause in 10.1. This merely states that the parties have the power to grant the licenses discussed in this document.

10.5   <u>No Other Warranties</u>. EXCEPT AS EXPRESSLY SET FORTH IN THIS AGREEMENT,
        THE PARTIES HEREBY DISCLAIM ALL OTHER WARRANTIES, EXPRESS OR IMPLIED,
        INCLUDING THE WARRANTIES OF MERCHANTABILITY, FITNESS FOR A PARTICULAR
        PURPOSE, AND THOSE ARISING FROM A COURSE OF PERFORMANCE, A COURSE OF
        DEALING, OR TRADE USAGE.

This is our first "all caps" clause. Clauses are put in all capital letters to draw attention to the clause and make it conspicuous. This clause makes it clear that there are no other guarantees in this agreement. This clause is necessary because many states have certain implied warranties that go into agreements between parties. Some of the common implied warranties such as the warranty of "fitness for a particular purpose" are even called out by name in this clause. In short, the parties guarantee what they wrote in this document, and beyond that, they make no other guarantees.

11.   **INDEMNITY**

Another word for *indemnity* is insurance, and that is an easy way to think about this section. If a party indemnifies another party that party insures the second party. The indemnity section often follows the warranty section in any agreement. In short, since the parties made all the guarantees in the previous section, now they back those guarantees up with money in case something goes wrong.

A good general idea regarding indemnities is to think about how much they are really worth at the end of the day. For instance, if a developer with $10,000 in assets and no insurance offers to indemnify Sony for $10 million, that indemnity is pretty worthless. Indemnification is nice to have if the other party has the resources to pay; otherwise, it is not worth very much.

11.1 <u>Developer Obligation</u>. Developer shall indemnify, defend and hold Publisher (and its sublicensees, stockholders, officers, directors, employees, and agents) harmless from any and all third-party claims, demands, reasonably incurred out-of-pocket costs and expenses (including attorneys' fees, costs, and expert witnesses' fees), liabilities, losses and damages directly arising out of or resulting from the infringement of any Intellectual Property Rights or other rights of third parties caused by the performance by Developer of its obligations under this Agreement.

Item (d) in 10.3 guaranteed that the developer did not violate third-party IP rights. This indemnification clause backs that up with money. The developer is guaranteeing to pay if the game does infringe third-party IP rights.

The third-party action clause explains in detail how the indemnification works, including how any litigation will be controlled and how payment of litigation expenses will be made.

11.2 <u>Third-Party Action</u>. If any third-party action shall be brought against either Party in respect of which a claim for indemnification (a "Claim") may be sought from the other Party hereto pursuant to the provisions of Section 11.1 or 11.2, the indemnified party shall promptly notify the indemnifying party in writing, specifying the nature of the action and the total monetary amount sought or other such relief as is sought therein. The failure of the indemnified party to provide prompt notice as so required shall not relieve the indemnifying party from any liability except to the extent that the indemnifying Party is prejudiced by such failure or delay. The indemnifying party may, upon written notice thereof to the indemnified Party, undertake to conduct all proceedings or negotiations in connection therewith, assume the defense thereof, and if it so elects, it shall also undertake all other required steps or proceedings to settle or defend any such action, including the engagement of counsel and payment of all expenses. The indemnified party shall have the right to fully participate in the defense of a third-party claim or liability at its own expense; <u>provided</u>, <u>however</u>, that the indemnified party shall have the right to retain its own counsel, at the expense of the indemnifying party, if such indemnified party shall have reasonably concluded by advice of counsel that representation of the indemnified party by the counsel retained by the indemnifying party would be inappropriate due to actual or potential conflicts of interests. The indemnified party shall cooperate with the indemnifying party in all reasonable respects in connection with the defense of any such action. The indemnifying party may not settle any third-party claim or action

that creates an affirmative obligation on the part of the indemnified
party (other than a monetary obligation that is assumed by the indemnifying party) without first obtaining the indemnified party's written
consent, which consent will not be unreasonably withheld, conditioned,
or delayed. The indemnifying party shall reimburse the indemnified party
on demand for any payments made or loss suffered by it at any time after
the date hereof, based upon the final and non-appealable judgment of any
court of competent jurisdiction or pursuant to a bona fide and final
compromise or settlement of claims, demands or actions, in respect to
any damages to which the foregoing relates.

12. LIMITATIONS OF LIABILITY

The limitation on liability section sets a cap on damages in the agreement. Practically speaking
this is a cap on money that one party can owe another. This means that the parties will not
ever owe an amount to each other that exceeds the amounts described in the clause. As a rule,
these sections are good to have in contracts because it does not make sense to enter into business agreements that incur more liability than potential profit.

12.1 Consequential Damages. EXCEPT FOR LIABILITY ARISING FROM SECTION 8
(CONFIDENTIALITY) AND SECTION 11 (INDEMNIFICATION) OF THIS AGREEMENT,
IN NO EVENT SHALL EITHER PARTY BE LIABLE TO THE OTHER PARTY FOR ANY SPE-
CIAL, EXEMPLARY, INCIDENTAL, OR CONSEQUENTIAL DAMAGES, INCLUDING BUT
NOT LIMITED TO LOST PROFITS, WHETHER ARISING OUT OF CONTRACT, TORT,
STRICT LIABILITY, OR OTHERWISE RESULTING FROM OR RELATED TO THIS AGREE-
MENT, WHETHER OR NOT SUCH PARTY KNOWS OR SHOULD HAVE KNOWN OF THE POS-
SIBILITY OF ANY SUCH DAMAGES.

Consequential damages are damages that result because of a breach. These damages do
not result directly from the breach, but follow later. An example would be the publisher stopping the game service and the developer losing profits from that cancellation. Notice that the
limitation on liability does not apply to breaches of the confidentiality provision and does not
apply to money owed under the indemnification provision.

12.2 Maximum Liability. IN NO EVENT SHALL THE AGGREGATE LIABILITY OF PUB-
LISHER TO DEVELOPER EXCEED AN AMOUNT EQUAL TO THE AMOUNTS PAID TO DEVEL-
OPER UNDER THIS AGREEMENT IN THE LAST 12 MONTHS.

This maximum liability clause is very publisher friendly. It states that the most liability
that can be incurred is equal to the amounts paid under the agreement in the last 12 months.
Read the clause carefully, though. The maximum liability cap is for the publisher alone. There
is not a maximum liability cap for the developer. So, the publisher can never owe more than
the last 12 months of payments to the developer, but the developer has no ceiling on damages.

13. INVESTMENT AGREEMENT

13.1 Investment Agreement Incorporated. This Agreement incorporates the
terms of an Investment Agreement attached as Exhibit C.

As it says in the clause, this agreement incorporates the terms of the attached investment agreement. In the case of this contract, the publisher had already purchased a portion of the developer and there were terms in that agreement the publisher wanted clearly in this one as well.

14.   GENERAL

Many people, especially non-lawyers, read right past these general provisions otherwise known as miscellaneous clauses. These are often boilerplate and given very little consideration. This really should not be the case. There is a lot of importance in these clauses. Each has a long history in contract law. As we will see later in the chapter, they also have consequences for every agreement. Like every other clause, they should be read with care and understood completely.

14.1   <u>Governing Law; Jurisdiction; Venue</u>. This Agreement shall be governed by
       and enforced in accordance with the laws of the State of New York, USA,
       exclusive of any laws or principles that would apply in the law of any
       other jurisdiction. With respect to any disputes arising out of or re-
       lated to this Agreement, the Parties consent to the exclusive jurisdic-
       tion of, and venue in, the state and federal courts located in New York,
       New York.

The clause that covers governing law is probably the most important general provision in a contract. This says what law should be applied to the contract. Is this contract under U.S. law? If it is, which state is it and how does that affect the interpretation of the rest of the agreement? In some ways, this single clause reflects back on everything else in the agreement. Knowing the legal trends for several states, particularly New York and California, are critical here. Which state is friendlier toward companies and which state has better laws for employees are all enormously important questions.

Along with governing law, there is usually a venue and jurisdiction clause. This clause shows where any case will be brought if there is a problem with this agreement. Will the case be in California, New York, another state, or another country? Also, is the jurisdiction exclusive or non-exclusive? This means is everyone agreeing that the case can be brought in New York and only New York or is it possible to be brought in New York and any other place legally found to have jurisdiction? In this agreement, the governing law is New York, and the exclusive jurisdiction and venue is in New York. Keep in mind that almost any combination is possible as long as the parties agree. It is possible to use French law in an Iowa court even though both of the parties are from California. This would be unusual, to say the least, but contracts are very flexible in this regard.

This venue and jurisdiction clause has real power. Imagine if one party is located outside the United States and the venue/jurisdiction is inside the United States. The foreign party is going to have great cost to litigate a case in a foreign country with unfamiliar laws. Now flip those circumstances and put the venue/jurisdiction in the foreign country. Now, the U.S. company has the substantial burden. The sports analogy would be the "home field advantage." From a business perspective, this weighs heavily on cost and the burdens of litigation.

Also, this is the clause where the parties make it clear whether they want traditional litigation or arbitration. Both of these are expensive and complicated, as explained in Chapter 9,

"Intellectual Property Litigation." However, arbitration is much cheaper and faster than litigation. In this way, it favors smaller parties such as a development studio. Does your development studio have an extra million dollars to do federal court litigation against your publisher? That is how an arbitration provision, especially a binding, non-appealable arbitration provision can be very developer-friendly here. Lastly, keep in mind this clause is working even when it is not invoked. If one party is aggravating the other, they can only do it to the extent that it will not provoke the other party to litigate. This clause sets that bar for litigation. It is possible to set the bar low enough that you cannot push the other party around too much before they bring the document before an arbitrator or a court.

Consider the following example. Imagine this clause said that the governing law was *Rock, Paper, Scissors* and the venue was the developer studio. Any disagreements over this contract would be finally decided by a best-of-three contest between the developer and the publisher. There would possibly be a disagreement over the contract every week.

Now imagine that the publisher and developer are both in California. The governing law is Japanese law with exclusive venue the federal courts of Alaska. In this second case, the litigation bar is much higher and the companies are much less likely to litigate. As a general rule, raising the bar higher crushes the little guy and merely inconveniences the publisher.

Efficient arbitration clauses bring the forced resolution process into the realm of possibility for a developer. Arbitration is still very complex and expensive, but it is usually much faster than litigation in federal court and ultimately cheaper as well. In this agreement, we have placed the publisher and developer in different countries, making dispute resolution very difficult. Negotiating the venue clause in this agreement is going to be critical.

The following clause makes it clear that the headings are just signposts used for reference. The real binding language is in the actual clause.

14.2   <u>Headings</u>. All descriptive headings used in this Agreement are for con-
       venience of reference only and are not to be used in interpreting the
       obligations of the Parties under this Agreement.

14.3   <u>Interpretation</u>. This Agreement was negotiated in the spirit of mutual
       cooperation whereby no clause should be necessarily construed against
       any one Party based upon the finding that such Party provided all or
       most of the contractual language contained within that clause.

There is an old legal tradition that is followed in some states where the contract should be interpreted against the drafting party if there is an ambiguity in the drafting. The prior clause is an effort to overcome that rule.

14.4   <u>Independent Contractor Status</u>. It is the express intention of the Par-
       ties that Developer is an independent contractor, and nothing in this
       Agreement shall in any way be construed to constitute Developer as an
       agent, employee, or representative of Publisher.

This clause is interesting because this makes the relationships clear. There are special obligations, rights, and responsibilities that attach once a person or entity becomes an employee, partner, or agent of a company. This clause clarifies all of that by putting the parties at arms length from one another and tries to minimize any ancillary obligations outside of the contract by making it clear that the developer is merely an independent contractor.

14.5   <u>Entire Agreement</u>. This Agreement, including all exhibits attached
       hereto, is the entire agreement of the Parties and supersedes any prior
       agreements, negotiations, or understandings between them, whether writ-
       ten or oral, with respect to the subject matter hereof. No waiver, al-
       teration, or modification of any of the provisions of this Agreement
       shall be binding unless in writing and signed by duly authorized repre-
       sentatives of each of the Parties hereto. This Agreement supersedes any
       conflicting terms and conditions on any work orders, invoices, checks,
       order acknowledgements, forms, purchase orders, or other similar com-
       mercial documents relating hereto and which may be issued by a Party
       after the Effective Date.

This clause is traditionally called an *integration clause*. The name means that everything else is integrated into this agreement. The phrase "entire agreement" sums up the concept as well, so many agreements use those words as the heading instead of the stuffy law school term. The practical meaning of this term is that all of your phone conversations, emails, and any promises made outside of this document are now meaningless. This document is the entire agreement.

14.6   <u>Severability</u>. If any provision of this Agreement becomes or is declared
       by a court of competent jurisdiction to be illegal, unenforceable, or
       void, portions of such provision, or such provision in its entirety, to
       the extent necessary, shall be severed from this Agreement, and such
       court will replace such illegal, unenforceable, or void provision of
       this Agreement with a valid and enforceable provision that will
       achieve, to the extent possible, the same economic, business, and other
       purposes of the illegal, unenforceable, or void provision. The balance
       of this Agreement shall be enforceable in accordance with its terms.

The severability clause is an attempt to make certain each clause is read independently, if necessary. It is possible that one of the clauses in this agreement could be found to be invalid or unenforceable, given the laws of a particular state or other circumstances. If this was found to be the case, this severability clause is an attempt to keep the rest of the contract together.

14.7   <u>Assignment</u>. Developer may not assign this Agreement, or any of its
       rights or obligations hereunder without the prior written consent of
       Publisher, and any such attempted assignment shall be void, except that
       Developer may assign this Agreement to a successor to substantially all
       of its business interests related to this Agreement without the written
       consent of Publisher, provided that such assignee agrees to be bound by
       all of the terms and conditions herein. Publisher may freely assign this
       Agreement, or any of the rights and obligations hereunder, by obtaining
       Developer's consent, such consent not to be unreasonably withheld.

Assignment refers to giving another person or company rights under the contract. For instance, if you have a contract with someone to mow your yard, that person may go on vacation and pay someone else to mow the yard. Usually this is not a problem, because your yard still gets mowed. However, imagine how much more complicated this becomes with a game development contract. If a publisher hires one studio to make the game, that studio is picked for very specific reasons and is not as interchangeable as one lawn-mowing service and another. In this assignment clause, the developer cannot assign the contract to another party without approval in writing from the publisher. The publisher also has to ask permission to assign rights under the contract, but the restrictions are not as significant as those placed on the developer.

14.8   <u>Currency</u>. All payments made hereunder shall be made in U.S. dollars. If any currency conversion shall be required in connection with the calculation of royalties hereunder, such conversion shall be made on the basis of the exchange rates of the last day of such month as payment is due as reported by the Barclays Bank based upon the 12:00 noon (United Kingdom time) buying rates of the International Monetary Fund.

The currency clause is always great fun. Someone with a superficial understanding may think it is enough to say that payments should be made in a certain currency. However, you are a hardened economic sophisticate who understands the high finance complexities involved in currency fluctuations. You eat quanto options for breakfast.

In all seriousness, this clause makes it clear that the payments are made in U.S. dollars. Furthermore, the exchange rate is based on the buying rate for the International Monetary Fund published by Barclays Bank at noon (U.K. time). If the companies in the deal are from different countries, such as the United States and China, this clause may take a bit of negotiating. If the companies cannot agree on a major bank in Beijing or New York, it is often an easy solution to pick a major bank in an independent country. The key here is that the exchange rate should be recorded and verifiable so there are no ambiguities down the road.

14.9   <u>Material Breach</u>. The occurrence of any of the following events shall be deemed a material breach of this Agreement, and upon any such occurrence, the Parties agree to act in accordance with Section 8 of this Agreement:

14.9.1   Developer fails to meet any Milestone Target, or alternatively fails to timely meet the Acceptance Date set forth in the Development Schedule;

14.9.2   Developer fails to use all commercially reasonable efforts to perform any Live Team Activity assigned to it and fails to perform such activities in a commercially reasonable manner;

14.9.3   Either Party breaches any of the Representations and Warranties set forth in Section 10 of this Agreement;

14.9.4   Either Party materially breaches the Investment Agreement attached hereto as Exhibit C;

14.9.5   Publisher breaches its payment obligations under Milestone Exhibit A or Royalty Exhibit F;

14.9.6   Either Party breaches the Confidentiality provisions set forth in Section 7.

When is the contract broken? A contract is broken in the event of a material breach. As discussed in this clause, a material breach is not breaking just any promise in the contract, but a fairly big promise like not paying for the game. This material breach clause goes through exactly what the parties consider a material breach. The clause lists items such as failing to meet milestones, failing to pay royalties, or leaking confidential information. If any of these items occurs, the contract has been broken, and the other party can seek a remedy from the appropriate court or arbitration authority.

14.10 <u>Injunctive Relief</u>. In addition to any other available relief, each Party agrees that any unauthorized disclosure of Confidential Information, trade secrets and proprietary information of the other Party will result in irreparable harm to such other Party, with damages that cannot be ascertained or compensated by monetary awards; and that, on that basis, each Party agrees that such other Party is entitled to, and may seek and obtain, without the requirement to post bond, any injunctive or immediate legal, equitable, administrative, or other relief available in the country, state, or other jurisdiction appropriate to such unauthorized disclosure.

Injunctive relief is a special kind of remedy that courts can provide. This remedy forces a party to stop doing something. Most people think of courts as sending people to jail or forcing parties to pay money, but courts can also issue *injunctions*. The clause states that leaking confidential information is one of the items that can be stopped by an injunction. It turns out that part of the legal test to apply for an injunction is establishing that an injunction is necessary. An injunction is a major exercise in judicial power, and the court must be persuaded that money damages or some other remedy is not enough. This clause makes it clear that both parties have agreed in advance that certain breaches of this agreement are enough to warrant an injunction.

14.11 <u>Waiver</u>. The failure of either Party to insist in any instance upon the performance by the other Party of any of the terms or conditions, or of the future performance of any of the terms, covenants, or conditions shall not constitute waiver and shall not relieve such other Party of its obligations with respect to such performance, and such terms and conditions shall continue in full force and effect.

As a rule, if a party does not complain over an issue or insist on performance of a certain contract element, that party may lose the right to complain later. The party that did not complain properly or early enough is said to have *waived* its rights to complain over that issue. The clause makes it clear that failing to complain in a timely manner about something in this agreement does not constitute a waiver. Furthermore, notice the clause is bilateral, meaning the developer or the publisher has the same rights under this clause. Either party can reserve the ability to insist on performance until a later period.

14.12 <u>Notices</u>. Any notice required or permitted under the terms of this Agreement or required by law must be in writing and must be: (a) delivered in person; (b) sent by first-class registered mail return receipt requested; or (c) sent by overnight air courier, in each case properly posted and fully prepaid to the recipient's designated address. Either Party may change its address for notice by notice to the other Party

given in accordance with this Section. Notices will be considered to
have been given at the time of actual delivery in person, ten (10) business days after deposit in the mail as set forth above, or two (2) days
after delivery to an overnight air courier service. If delivery is not
accomplished by some fault of the addressee, such notice will be deemed
to have been given when tendered. Notice shall be deemed given if sent
to:

DEVELOPER:	PUBLISHER:
New Developer	Mega Publisher
Attention CTO Mr. John Doe	Attention President
15 Broadway, New York, NY 10004	10 St. Andrews Road,
Telephone:	Manchester, M25 0AL,
Facsimile:	United Kingdom
(With a copy to the Legal	Telephone:
Department at the same address	Facsimile:
and facsimile)	

The notices provision tells the parties how to communicate with each other regarding the
agreement. If the developer has some complaint about the contract, which person should they
call or write to? This clause makes certain there is no ambiguity. This is also important because
time frames in agreements are often measured from notice of a problem. For instance, a developer may have a certain period after notice to correct a milestone. This clause explains exactly
what constitutes notice and where that notice should be sent.

14.13 Counterparts. This Agreement may be executed in one or more counter-
       parts, each of which shall be deemed an original, but all of which to-
       gether shall constitute one and the same instrument.

14.14 Telecopy Execution and Delivery. A facsimile, telecopy, or other repro-
       duction of this Agreement may be executed by one or more Parties to this
       Agreement, and an executed copy of this Agreement may be delivered by
       one or more parties to this Agreement by facsimile or similar elec-
       tronic transmission device pursuant to which the signature of or on be-
       half of such Party can be seen, and such execution and delivery shall be
       considered valid, binding, and effective for all purposes. At the re-
       quest of any Party to this Agreement, all parties to this Agreement
       agree to execute an original of this Agreement as well as any facsimile,
       telecopy, or other reproduction of this Agreement.

The two preceding clauses are meant to make signing the document easier. Traditionally,
contracts had to be original documents signed by both parties. This usually happened with the
parties in the same room, but this is not always practical in the global business environment.
The two clauses make executing the agreement easier. The counterparts clause makes it clear
that each party can sign different copies of the document and that will be enough for the contract to be valid. The telecopy clause makes it clear that a fax or .pdf of the agreement would
also be valid.

IN WITNESS WHEREOF, the Parties hereto have executed this Agreement as of the date first above written.

PUBLISHER:
MegaPublisher

By: _____
   (Signature of Authorized Representative)

Name: _____
     (Type or Print)

Title: ____ General Manager _____

Date: _____

DEVELOPER:
New Developer

By: _____
   (Signature of Authorized Representative)

Name: _____
     (Type or Print)

Title: _____

Date: _____

<u>Exhibits</u>:

Exhibit A—Development Schedule

Exhibit B—Specification of Game

Exhibit C—Investment Agreement

Exhibit D—Key Personnel

Exhibit E—Live Team Activity

Exhibit F—Royalty

Exhibit G—Royalty Report

This recognizable area is the signature block. Sometimes, this is put on a separate page instead of at the end of a document. As a rule, it is usually better to keep this on the same page as the end of the document or have very tight version control, marking, and perhaps initialing on every page of the document. Consider that many of these agreements are edited more than three times by two sets of attorneys. Furthermore, they can often be signed and sent around by .pdf. It makes some sense to not have a separate signature page that could be attached to most anything.

Unsurprisingly, the signature page is where the magic happens. Both parties sign on the line and we have an executed game development agreement. Now after all the really hard work negotiating, drafting, and editing the agreement is done, some other folks go off and actually make the game.

Exhibit A

Development Schedule

```
      Milestone      Date    Initial Development Costs*
0
1
2
3
```

    * Milestone payments will be paid upon acceptance by Publisher of each such Milestone.

Milestone Definitions

Milestone 1
Hiring
Design
Systems
Content
Miscellaneous

Milestone 2
Hiring

Design

Systems

Content

Miscellaneous

Milestone 3
Hiring

Design

Systems

Content

Miscellaneous

Milestone 4

Design

Engineering

Content

Miscellaneous

This is Exhibit A of the development agreement. This is the milestone list or development schedule for the game. Let it be said that probably no game in the history of the world has ever been completed entirely on schedule and had every milestone met on time. Yet, we still need to try to do the best we can predicting the schedule.

Another way of thinking about this is as a shopping list where the developer is delivering certain goods and the publisher has to pay if those goods conform to the milestone list. Experience has shown that it works well for both parties to make these as detailed as is practical. For instance, we cannot know the colors of hair available in the final build, but we can know that hair will have at least five styles and at least five colors. In short the detail helps both parties know if what is delivered is what was ordered. Invariably if these have very little detail, that equates to very little accountability. If a milestone reads "playable beta" delivered on this date, that is a recipe for disaster for the publisher. What is a playable beta? Walk around GDC next year and ask 50 people to list the elements of a playable beta and you will get at least 50 different answers. The developer does not know what to deliver and the publisher does not know what to pay for. Do everyone a favor and spend considerable time with this section to make it as clear as possible.

If the parties are uncomfortable committing to this amount of detail because it stifles the creative process, have the agreement allow for changing the milestone schedule through some agreed process. For instance, if both parties agree in writing the milestone schedule may be "updated" through an established process of submitting adjustments and securing approval.

Also notice that this agreement has developer areas such as hiring, design, systems, content, and miscellaneous. This organizational tool allows the parties to break down goals by area and by time.

Exhibit B

Specification of Game

1.　<u>Description of the Game</u>. The Game is a massively multiplayer online game ("MMOG") with the following features:

Feature

Feature

This is Exhibit B of the agreement. In this agreement, it is called a specification. In other agreements, it may be called a *vision document* or *design document* or something similar.

As a side note, some delusional egomaniacs have asked for $40 million, based on their stellar reputation with a previous studio and a hand-written half-page of paper. Those same delusional egomaniacs have then been metaphorically laughed out of the publisher's offices. Do not be a delusional egomaniac.

As a developer, it pays to be thoughtful and thorough here. Do as much as you can to be complete and be creative. If there are many possibilities to implement certain ideas then describe the possibilities that are most attractive. This is not as firm as the milestone agreement and is meant to be written in prose. These normally run from about 30 pages to about 200 pages depending on the scale of the project. As a rule, the more money you are asking for as a developer the more thorough this section should be.

Think about what you are asking for as a developer, weighed against this document. This sheet costs nothing but time to create and is usually written well before the contract is signed. This really should just be a version of what is pitched to the publisher. A developer can take a few months and hammer this out working with his development team. From a publisher or investor perspective, this document is the first sign of diligence and commitment. It is a first impression of what later documents and work will look like. Do your best with it. Being really good here can only help you down the road. It is an early sign of professionalism and competence that will pay dividends.

Exhibit C—Investment Agreement

Exhibit C in this game development agreement sample is an investment agreement. Sometimes publishers or other investors can come in to help fund and bear the risk of a large project. Sometimes these documents are entirely separate. Occasionally they are appended to the development agreement if the terms are relevant.

Exhibit D—Key Personnel

Developer agrees to staff the following Key Personnel in the capacity and responsibility shown.

Key Personnel   Capacity and Responsibility

The Parties shall negotiate in good faith to hire additional Key Personnel to
fill the positions set forth above which positions are not currently filled.

As the title states, this exhibit covers the list of developer key personnel. The document sets out special restrictions on the employment of these people. These restrictions can include what these people are allowed to work on, and restrict the hiring and firing decisions surrounding these individuals or the positions they fill.

Exhibit E—Live Team Activity

1.   Developer will manage and finance a Live Team responsible for the fol-
      lowing activities:

a. Live Team will provide in-game customer service. This includes re-
    sponding to in-game reports of bugs, player disputes, unacceptable
    player behavior, and other problems that require immediate in-game
    solutions.

b. Live Team will provide content, events, and fix bugs. The Live Team
    will fix any bugs, modify the Game to enhance service quality and
    user experiences, and further develop the Game. The Live Team is re-
    sponsible for regular updates, including additional content de-
    scribed in Section C and world events described in Section D. The
    Live Team is also responsible for emergency updates as described in
    Section E. The Live Team will also provide maintenance and enhance-
    ment to the Customer Support System as well as balance tuning as
    needed. The Live Team will initially consist of the entire develop-
    ment team, and future staffing will be mutually agreed upon between
    Developer and Publisher on a quarterly basis following Commercial
    Release of the product; provided, however, that Developer agrees to
    apply all of its company resources toward such activities for a pe-
    riod of one year following the Commercial Launch (the "Commercial
    Launch Period").

c. Live Team will provide additional content. New content such as
    items, weapons, vehicles, NPCs, quests, and map updates such as can
    be accomplished by 60 days of development (allowing for 30 subse-
    quent days of testing, final builds and localization) by a team of
    15 people, consisting of programmers, designers, and artists, and
    fit into less than a 50 Megabyte, downloaded patch.

d. Live Team will provide world events. Every 60 days, Live Team will
    co-operate with Publisher to develop world events consisting of
    player contests, promotions, item raffles, and other marketing
    events that take place in-game. Such events shall require no more
    than a team of five working for 30 days to develop and be delivered
    via download.

e. Live Team will provide emergency updates. Live Team will prioritize
    and may develop emergency updates for such bugs or balance issues
    that rise to the severity of negatively impacting the player expe-
    rience to the point of threatening the game's economy, subscription
    base, or stable and regular operations of the game service.

f. Publisher testing and localization. Publisher will provide local-
    ization, web support, and QA testing services for all updates de-
    scribed in this Exhibit. The expenses associated are recoupable by
    Publisher.

g. Publisher right to move Live Team. Publisher may determine, in its
    sole discretion, that it may bring the Live Team Activities in house
    or to move it to a third party. In that case, Publisher shall pro-
    vide notice to Developer that such activities will be moved in house
    or to a third party.

The live team exhibit reflects the importance of the live team activity to an online game. This sets out explicitly how often the live team will patch the game, develop additional content, and code world events. It also makes clear that the live team will cover customer service. It is critical to note the last section of this exhibit that makes it clear the live team may be moved in house by the publisher or handed off to a third party.

Exhibit F—Royalty

For the Game:

North America and other territories where Publisher directly publishes the game, except the United Kingdom

The Royalty is twenty percent (20%) multiplied by the Net Revenue actually received by Publisher for subscriptions to the Game before $500 million USD Net Revenue, twenty five percent (25%) multiplied by the Net Revenue received by Publisher thereafter.

United Kingdom

The Royalty is eighteen percent (18%) multiplied by the Net Revenue received by Publisher for subscriptions to the Game before $500 million USD Net Revenue, twenty percent (22%) multiplied by the Net Revenue received by Publisher thereafter.

Third-party publisher territories

Developer shall receive fifty percent (50%) of the Net Revenue received by Publisher from the third-party publisher. Such Net Revenue shall include, but not be limited to, the non-recoupable licensee fee paid to the Publisher by the third-party publisher.

For Derivative Properties:

The Royalty shall be ten percent (10%) multiplied by the Net Revenue received by Publisher for the Game (including, without limitation, revenue generated from in-game advertising), subject to recoupment of development costs per Subsection 5.2.

For Sequels Developed by Developer Pursuant to Subsection 2.8:

The Royalty is twenty-five percent (25%) multiplied by the Net Revenue received by Publisher for the Sequel (including, without limitation, revenue generated from in game advertising), subject to recoupment of development costs per Subsection 5.2.

For Non-PC-Based Platforms (e.g., consoles) of the Game Developed by Developer:

The Royalty is twenty-five percent (25%) multiplied by the Net Revenue actually received by Publisher for such Non-PC-Based Platform (including, without limitation, revenue generated from in-game advertising), subject to recoupment of development costs per Subsection 5.2.

Exhibit F is the royalty exhibit for this agreement. This explains in detail the elements that are discussed in section 5 of the contract. Notice that the royalty rate in this agreement is different in North America and other territories. The rate is also tiered so that there is an increase in the royalty rate after the game revenue grows over $500 million. The royalty rate is also defined for sequels and console ports. The royalty rate is rarely just one number and there are many different ways to divide it up.

Exhibit G—Royalty Report

The royalty report is filled with the relevant financial information the publisher and developer agree is relevant. Numbers would probably include gross sales, money actually received, and all the costs deducted from the definition of net revenue.

Conclusion

This chapter was not meant to side with either the publisher or developer when discussing the agreement. The authors of this chapter have represented both sides on the table, and this chapter is meant to represent both sides. The reality is that most game developers, especially studios without a hit title, have very little negotiating power. The bottom line here is that we cannot do very much about the lack of developer bargaining power, so we need to deal with the situation as it stands. It is best just to go into the negotiation process with your eyes open and your head full of understanding about the process.

As a practical piece of parting advice, beware of writing everything in the development contract. There is no way to write down enough detail to cover every contingency. You will also find that after a certain point, writing more tends to create conflicts and ambiguity within the document while driving up legal fees. Try to find the appropriate balance when negotiating your own game development agreement. Be careful with the cost-benefit analysis hammering out that ninth contract revision. Practically speaking, what are further revisions really going to buy for you? There is a time when you need to decide to walk away or just sign the document. There is also a point at which the other party will be fed up with negotiating and may just walk away from the table to deal with a more reasonable party.

Remember, your development agreement will not look like this one. There are potentially as many different agreements as there are deals. The terms in this agreement and the variations on those terms are not an exhaustive list. We hope this chapter can help you become an educated consumer of legal advice and an informed party in the negotiation.

CHAPTER 17

Wrapping It All Up

So, there you have it all in your hands: the secrets of starting and running a business in the game industry. Feel ready to tackle it all and make games for a living?

Well, thinking about all these issues can be a bit daunting. However, you have the advantage of reading works by experienced people who were gracious enough to contribute to this book. The one lesson you should take away from this book is that you cannot simply "make games" as a career without a business. Even creating games as a hobby can have you running into legal issues that are better to avoid. And, if you want to be independent, you will have to run your own company. In other words: ignore the lessons in this book at your own peril.

But, do not think the journey stops here. Entrepreneurs are still learning hard lessons about running a business every day, even in the game industry, no matter how many times they have started and run a company before. The people who contributed to this book just have a few more scars than other people have and were willing to share their experiences. Hopefully, the information will help you avoid some of the worst mistakes we have made over the years. Just the chapter on taxation is worth its weight in gold for the information you will not have to learn the hard way; the surest way to destroy your company is to run afoul of taxes.

However, we want to end with some words of encouragement to help those who might feel a little overwhelmed by this book. Many times, people get very excited about making games, and they want to take the industry by storm. They will show that you can create a fun game without all the waste and repetition that you see in the industry. "Innovation!" and "Originality!" are their rallying cries. Then they see something that shows them just how deep the rabbit hole goes, like this book, and get worried: all these issues to tackle, all these things to worry about. Is it worth it?

The answer is an emphatic YES! It may be considerable work to keep the bills paid, to keep your employees happy, to manage your external relationships with publishers and investors, and so forth. Some days, it can feel daunting just talking to a bank employee and trying to get a straight answer, as Spencer pointed out in his chapter. However, at the end of the day, you are still making a game. It is a truly magical feeling once you release your game and realize that people will be playing something over which you had some measure of control. It may not be the blockbuster-selling title you dreamed of, but it is still your game. And, once you have been around the block the first time, it becomes easier to do it again. And it becomes more alluring.

So, let us close with this bit of advice: Go out there and make great games. Keep the business and legal issues in mind, but do not forget to have fun. Despite what some people may say, games are an important part of our culture. Go do something great that will be remembered. Don't be afraid to take a leap of faith; you will almost certainly be able to pick yourself up, dust yourself off, and get back into the fray if you should stumble. If video games have taught us anything, it is that you always get another chance to conquer that obstacle.

We look forward to the games created by the new companies this book inspires.

S. Gregory Boyd
Brian "Psychochild" Green

For Further Reading

Contracts

Getting to Yes, Roger Fisher and William Ury

Getting Past No, William Ury

Contracts In a Nutshell, Claude D. Rohwer, Anthony M. Skroki

American Arbitration Association Web site, *http://www.adr.org/*

International Game Developers Association, Contract Walkthrough Nos. 1–3. Available at *http://www.igda.org/biz/contract_walkthrough.php*

Virtual World Law

Richard Bartle's book *Designing Virtual Worlds* (New Riders Games, 2003) is an essential handbook for any self-respecting game designer (even those not creating virtual worlds). Bartle breaks down all of the essential elements that go into creating a rich and satisfying play experience. He focuses on how design decisions affect players' experiences interacting with the world and with each other. You can learn what kind of design mistakes will make players unhappy (and possibly litigious) in one of two ways. The easy way is reading this book; the hard way is to making many mistakes that make players unhappy.

Jessica Mulligan and Bridgette Patrovsky's *Developing Online Games: An Insider's Guide* (New Riders Games, 2003) is equally informative but sadly out of print. Compared with Bartle, it has somewhat more extensive coverage of the management problems of developing a successful virtual world service, such as how to budget, how to build scalable systems, and how to transition from pre-launch to post-launch development. The case studies alone justify tracking down a copy.

Raph Koster, the design guru famous for *Ultima Online* and *Star Wars Galaxies*, has written extensively online about virtual world governance issues of the sort discussed in this chapter. He has distilled some of his more aesthetic ideas into the elegant *A Theory of Fun for Game Design* (Paraglyph, 2004), which also belongs on any game designer's shelf.

The single best piece of virtual world journalism ever is Julian Dibbell's *My Tiny Life: Crime and Passion in a Virtual World* (Henry Holt, 1999), an expanded version of a famous 1993 article he wrote for the *Village Voice* entitled "A Rape in Cyberspace." Dibbell's narrative makes profound points about the nature of griefing, its effects on player communities, and the limited techniques available to players and administrators in responding to it. Dibbell's more recent *Play Money: Or, How I Quit My Day Job and Made Millions Trading Virtual Loot* (Basic Books, 2006) is an equally entertaining look at the strange new economics of virtual worlds, with plenty of thought-provoking armchair speculation about the bizarre legal and social consequences.

Edward Castronova's *Synthetic Worlds: The Business and Culture of Online Games* (University of Chicago, 2005) is a comprehensive overview of what virtual worlds are and what they're likely to mean for the rest of society.

T. L. Taylor's *Play Between Worlds: Exploring Online Game Culture* is a sympathetic and insightful look at player culture in *EverQuest*. You need to read what she has to say about player motivations, communities, and creativity, even if you're making a single-player game. Her observations about the emotional relationships players form with each other and with the games they play should be internalized by every designer.

Dan Hunter and Greg Lastowka's article, "The Laws of the Virtual Worlds," *California Law Review* (vol. 92, issue 1), is deservedly the most influential academic article on the law of virtual worlds. They frame a number of long-term legal issues clearly and colorfully. Other interesting academic takes have been published in a special issue of the *New York Law School Law Review* (vol. 49, issue 1) devoted to law and virtual worlds.

An old and underappreciated article on law and virtual worlds is Jennifer Mnookin's "Virtual(ly) Law: The Emergence of Law in LambdaMOO," *Journal of Computer-Mediated Communication* (vol. 2, issue 1), reprinted in *Crypto Anarchy, Cyberstates, and Pirate Utopias* (Peter Ludlow, Ed.) (MIT Press, 1999). Mnookin traces the history of player attempts at dispute resolution in LambdaMOO and their real-life implications. She does not try to describe how real-life law has actually responded, but asks some deep questions about how it *should* respond.

Intellectual Property

Video Game Law, Jon Festinger, Lexis Nexis Canada, 2005.

IGDA IP Rights White Paper, 2004.

Public Relations

The New PR Toolkit: Strategies for Successful Media Relations by Deirde Breakenridge and Thomas J. DeLoughry.

Full Frontal PR: Getting People Talking about You, Your Business, or Your Product by Richard Laer.

Guerilla Publicity: Hundreds of Sure-Fire Tactics to Get Maximum Sales for Minimum Dollars by Jay Conrad Levinson, Rick Frishman, and Jill Lublin.

Business Management

The Mythical Man-Month, Fred Brooks

Good to Great, Jim Collins

Glossary

401(k) Plan: An investment plan offered by employers to their employees that allows the employees to invest part of their income and to defer all taxes on the investment until withdrawal.

1099-MISC: *See Form 1099-MISC.*

AAA title: *See triple-A title.*

acceptance: An agreement that an offer is satisfactory and a contract will be established.

accrual method of accounting: An accounting method where revenues are recorded and recognized in the period in which they incur. Even though cash may not be received or paid in a credit transaction, the cash is recorded because it is consequential in the future income and cash flow of the company.

adjusted basis: The value of an asset determining the profit or loss from a sale or exchange of property. This is the adjustment of the basis originally assigned to the asset upon acquisition.

advance: The payment of money before consideration is received. For example, money provided to a party of a contract before that party has produced anything of value.

advancee: The recipient of an advance.

advancer: The provider of an advance.

advergame: An interactive multimedia project that incorporates advertisements directly into the game-play or theme of the game. Advergames are generally funded by the company that sells the product or service advertised.

all events test: Under the accrual method of accounting, the time when the company can recognize income. This happens when "all the events" that establish your right to receive the income have happened, and when the amount of income you are to receive is known with reasonable accuracy.

alternative minimum tax (AMT): Tax rules to ensure that an individual pays a "fair" amount of taxes. This can affect employees who exercise stock options but do not realize a profit (sell the shares) during the same tax period.

ancillary and subsidiary rights: Rights of exploitation beyond, but related to, the principal focus of a license. For example, merchandising rights that tie into a particular intellectual property included in a license.

anti-time: *See negative productivity.*

appellate court: A court that reviews the decisions of lower courts.

arbitrary trademark: A mark not previously associated with the owner. A strong category of trademarks. For example, Apple (computers).

arbitration: A method of resolving disputes between parties by appointing an impartial individual or group to judge the differences at issue between the parties and issue a decision. The decision in arbitration can be legally binding if both parties have agreed to it before the decision is made.

art director: The individual who determines the visual aspects, including the style, look, and feel, of a video game production.

artist: An individual who creates all artwork associated with a video game production, including conceptual art, 3D models, textures, animations, and environments.

assignment: A complete transfer of all contractual rights or duties to a third party.

Assignment of Invention: A contract between an employer and employee that all work created by the employee during his or her term of employment belongs entirely to the employer.

avatar: The on-screen representation of a player's character in a game. Sometimes also referred to as a "toon."

basis: The amount you assign to an asset for later determining capital gain or loss. For assets purchased, the basis is the price paid.

boilerplate (PR): A block of standard text included in press releases and other documentation. For example, a "developer boilerplate" is text added to every press release issued by a video game development company explaining who the developer is.

boilerplate contract: A pre-made contract that is not tailored to a specific situation.

breach: A violation of a contract term. They are categorized into material and immaterial breaches.

build: A specific version of a video game during its development process. Examples include alpha build, preview build, review build, final (or "gold master") build, etc.

buzz: In public relations, the excitement, interest, and anticipation for a product.

C Corporation: *See Corporation.* (Pun not intended.)

cash method of accounting: An accounting method where revenue is recognized when cash is received and expense is recognized when cash is paid. In contrast, this method does not recognize promises to pay or expectations to receive money or service in the future.

cause of action: The violation of a legal right of the plaintiff that is the basis of a lawsuit.

Chapter 7 bankruptcy: The form of bankruptcy that involves liquidating all of a company's assets to pay off debt. This means the end of the company as an entity.

Chapter 11 bankruptcy: The form of bankruptcy that allows for a company's protection from debtors to reorganize the business and set a schedule for the repayment of debt.

Children's Online Privacy Protection Act (COPPA): (15 USC § 6501) A law requiring Web sites and online services to protect the privacy of children in the United States under the age of 13. It requires that the Web site not collect personally identifiable information from children and establish policies to ensure this does not happen. For more information, see *http://www.ftc.gov/bcp/conline/pubs/buspubs/coppa.htm.*

choice of law: Choosing which of several possible places' laws will apply in a given situation, contract term, or legal case.

choice of venue: A contract term that chooses the location where suit may be brought in the event of contract litigation.

claim construction: The legal process by which a court determines the meaning of the words of a patent claim.

claim of right doctrine: According to this doctrine, taxpayers must report a receipt that purports to be an income item for the period in which they have control over the item.

compensatory damages: Damages that fully recompense a party for the loss suffered.

complaint: The pleading that initiates a lawsuit and lays out the plaintiff's demand for relief and the plaintiff's assertions against the defendant.

consideration: Something of value that is exchanged in a contract. For example, money or services.

constructive receipt: Income is considered received when it is available to you, regardless of whether you actually take possession of it.

contract: An agreement between two or more parties that creates legally binding obligations as dictated by the terms of the contract.

contributory copyright infringement: Liability for copyright infringement committed by another, where the contributory infringer knew of the infringement and either induced it or assisted in it.

conversion rate: The number of customers who purchase your product after using a trial or demo version.

COPPA: *See Children's Online Privacy Protection Act (COPPA).*

copyleft: A licensing philosophy intended to remove restrictions on reproduction and modification of works as long as the derivative works are also licensed under copyleft. For an example, see *General Public License.*

copyright: The exclusive right to reproduce (that is, copy) or sell an author's original work. In legal terms, copyright law allows the owner to prevent the reproduction of his work.

copyright infringement: Making copies of a creative work without the permission of the copyright holder or otherwise interfering with the holder's exclusive rights to the work.

Copyright Office: The office that handles the registration of copyrights in the United States.

community: A group of people who discuss topics, usually online. Communities can have a focus, such as discussing a particular game, or games in general.

community trademark: A trademark that has been registered with the European Union and is valid anywhere in the European Union.

core operating hours: The main operating hours of a company during which employees are expected to be at work. These are the hours when most meetings are held within the company so all can attend.

corporation: An entity created under the laws of a state in which it has incorporated. All income and expenses are reported on Form 1120 and the corporation pays its own taxes. This type of organization is also sometimes called a C Corporation.

court order: A court-issued command.

Creative Commons: A standardized way to present a simplified IP license to people without formal agreement. The owner of the IP can specify which rights are given to licensees who choose to use the property.

creative director: The individual responsible for the overall creative design of a video game project and for ensuring that the overall vision of the game remains true to that design throughout the production life cycle. Sometimes referred to as imply the "director."

cross-collateralization: When profits from one project are applied toward the expenses of another project. For example, a publisher applying the profits from Game A toward recovering the advance paid for Game B.

cross-examination: The questioning of a witness who has already testified for the opposing side.

cross license: A license over a patent granted by one party in exchange for a license over the other party's patent.

crunch time: A period in which the production team of a development studio is "asked" (often implicitly required) to stay late and work long hours, often through the weekend, to meet a milestone or other project goal. This can result in negative productivity over extended periods of time.

cure: To fix an error made or breach that occurred in the course of fulfilling contractual obligations.

damages: Money granted by judicial decision as compensation for a party's injury or loss.

de novo review: Appellate review of a lower decision where the appellate court does not give any deference to the lower decision.

declaratory judgment: A judicial decision formally affirming a party's legal status or right.

declining-balance depreciation method: A method of depreciation where each period's depreciation amount is based on the previous year's value and the estimated useful life.

defamation: An intentional false statement that harms another's reputation.

defendant: The party against whom a criminal or civil action is brought by a plaintiff.

Denial of Service: An attack on a network that deprives users of a service they normally use, such as a Web site or a game server.

deposit schedule: In taxation, the frequency with which you have to deposit income taxes withheld from employee compensation. Common frequencies are monthly or semiweekly.

deposition: The recorded answers given under oath by a witness in response to written or oral examination.

depreciation: The decline in value of an asset over time as measured for tax purposes. Depreciation represents a cost of ownership and the consumption of an asset's useful life.

depreciation recapture: Taxing of part of the profit realized when an asset is sold at a gain. Some part of that gain is attributable to depreciation deductions taken in prior years and is taxed.

descriptive trademark: A mark that merely describes a source. The weakest category of trademarks, and often requires secondary meaning to qualify for protection. For example, Computerland (to describe a computer store).

designer: An individual who determines the functionality of different aspects of a video game, such as the specifics of gameplay.

developers: Artists, engineers, designers, quality assurance testers, and writers who make up the team that creates a game from inception to final product.

Digital Millennium Copyright Act (DMCA): A law that, among other things, forbids disabling security measures restricting access to copyrighted works. The act also provides a procedure for a copyright holder to instruct Internet hosting services to remove copyright material not authorized for distribution on that host. *See also Section 512 of the Digital Millennium Copyright Act.*

director of engineering: The individual who manages the software development and programming tasks for the engineering team of a video game production.

disability insurance: Health insurance that provides periodic payments when the insured is unable to work as a result of sickness or injury.

discovery: The procedure used by a party in a lawsuit to obtain information relevant to the suit that is held by the opposing party.

doctrine of equivalents: The act of infringing a patent when the differences between the accused product and the claims of the patent are insubstantial.

double taxation: Taxation of the same earnings at two levels. For example, the taxation of earnings at the corporate level and then again at the shareholder dividend level.

due process: The establishment of formal proceedings according to established rules and principles to protect fundamental private rights such as the right to a fair trial.

duping: From the word "duplicating." In a virtual world, using a bug or other exploit to create large numbers of an object, typically as a form of in-game wealth creation.

economic performance: For an accrual method taxpayer, economic performance has happened when all events have occurred and the amount owed can be reasonably ascertained.

employee: A person who performs services for a company, especially one where the employee must perform his or her tasks according to the employer's direct instruction.

End User License Agreement (EULA): A contract between the maker of a software product and a consumer, allowing the consumer to use the product on specified conditions. *See also Terms of Service.*

engineers: The programmers and developers who create the software engines that run a video game, such as AI engines, graphics engines, and physics engines.

enjoined: A party that is subject to the orders in an injunction.

equitable relief: Relief not concerned with money damages; for example, equitable relief could be in the form of an injunction.

European Registry for Internet Domains (EURid): A nonprofit organization that resolves disputes between trademark owners and domain owners. Also registers domains in Europe with the .eu suffix.

exclusive license: A license that is only granted to one party exclusively and not granted to any others.

exit strategy: A plan that allows for investors, entrepreneurs, or small business owners to cease or hand over operation of their business, usually with the intention of making a profit on investment.

exploit: An unintended feature in a software product or service that enables a user to take actions the designer did not intend. Exploits are sometimes the result of a bug in the game software or the result of limited design.

extrinsic evidence: Evidence gained from sources not directly connected with a specific patent, such as technical dictionaries and treatises.

fanciful trademark: A mark that has no meaning beyond that given by the owner of the mark. The strongest category of trademarks. For example, Xbox.

fan site: A Web site created by fans of a topic such as a specific game.

feature creep: The addition of functionality to a video game production not originally in the specification, particularly late in its production life cycle.

Federal Circuit: The United States Court of Appeals for the Federal Circuit ("C.A.F.C." or "Fed. Cir.") is located in Washington DC, and is the main court of appeals for all patent infringement cases.

Federal Trade Commission (FTC): A government-regulated agency that is responsible for protecting consumers against unfair trade practices.

Federal Unemployment Tax Act: The Federal Unemployment Tax Act (FUTA), authorizes the Internal Revenue Service to collect a federal employer tax used to fund state workforce agencies.

Fencepost Rules: Rules that forbid more conduct than necessary to ease enforcement.

fiscal year: A business's reporting period, generally 12 months, used for calculating annual financial reports. It can, but is not necessarily required to, coincide with the standard calendar year.

force majeure: Some outside force that would overwhelm anything anyone could do to prevent it. Sometimes referred to as an "Act of God."

Form 1099-MISC: The self-employed version of form W-2. A company that pays a self-employed person, such as a consultant or independent contractor, $600 or more in the previous year is required to report that payment, known as miscellaneous income, to the IRS via Form 1099-MISC.

Form I-9: A U.S. Citizenship and Immigration Services form to verify the citizenship status and employment eligibility of the employee.

Form W-2: IRS form that reports income paid and taxes withheld by an employer for a particular employee during a calendar year. Copies must be submitted to the employee, the federal government, and the state government.

Form W-3: Employers must file this form—Transmittal of Wage and Tax Statements—annually to the Social Security Administration in February. It is the form summarizing the W-2 forms submitted to the IRS.

Form W-4: The Employee's Withholding Allowance Certificate IRS form determines how much federal withholding taxes will be deducted from an employee's paycheck.

forum: A specific court of law or judicial body.

forum selection: Choosing which of several possible courts will hear a given case. *See also Choice of Law.*

fringe benefits: Amount paid by the employer for employee benefits such as retirement, health insurance, unemployment insurance, life insurance, etc. Some of these benefits are taxable.

game portal: A Web site that allows consumers access to a wide variety of games, usually casual in nature and generally organized by genre.

General Public License (GPL): A software license that requires, among other things, the source code for the software to be available to the end user. The license allows the creation of derivative works as long as the new work is licensed under the GPL and therefore has its source available to the end user. In other words, any software that includes GPL-licensed code must also have the source made available. Also written as "GNU General Public License" and "GNU GPL."

generic (trademark): Trademarks that are too common to be offered protection under trademark law. For example, Game (to describe a video game).

goodwill: A company's reputation, which can generally be converted into a monetary amount during the sale or auditing of a business.

gray market imports: Imports of products sold in one country into another country. This type of importation usually happens when the sale price of a product is lower in one country than another.

griefing: In a virtual world, deliberately attempting to make other players unhappy or taking pleasure from their frustration.

gross income: Revenue from raw sales before the deduction of expenses such as cost of goods sold, taxes, etc.

guerilla marketing: Unconventional marketing practices used to gain the maximum penetration for the least amount of money.

guild: A group of players who choose to associate with each other under a common identifier, sometimes officially recognized in the game. Typically formed to enable cooperation or for socializing. Also called "clans" in some games.

hybrid developers: Individuals in a video game production team who combine disciplines from multiple areas, often acting as a bridge between different production departments.

I-9 Form: *See Form I-9.*

immaterial breach: A violation of a contract term that is curable and does not prevent the contract from going forward.

impeach: To challenge the authenticity or veracity of a witness or item of evidence.

implied warranty: A warranty that is not specifically made, but is assumed to exist upon purchase of a product. For example, a warranty that the product in question is fit for the purpose for which it was sold.

incentive stock option: A stock option type that is not taxed when received or exercised. It is, however, taxed when the option stocks are sold.

indemnity: Holding a third party responsible for the reimbursement of all loss or damage incurred by an injured party. This typically refers to the responsibility of the third party to legally defend another party in a lawsuit.

independent contractor: A nonemployee who does work for a party via a contract, but is left to his or her own judgment as to the method of performance.

indicia: Other aspects of identity, in addition to name and likeness, for which an individual may be well known and recognized. This may include aspects such as voice, signature, or other personality characteristics.

Information Technology (IT): Individuals responsible for setting up and maintaining the internal technological infrastructure of a company, such as computer workstations and servers.

Initial Public Offering (IPO): When shares of a companies stock first become available for purchase to the general public.

injunction: A court order to perform or not perform a specific act.

integration clause: A clause in a contract that tells a court that there are no side agreements between the parties that are not included in the written contract.

intellectual property (IP): Intangible properties protected by copyright, trademark, patent, and trade secret law.

intent-to-use: The declaration that a registered trademark is intended to be used by the filer, even if the mark has not yet been used in commerce.

international sales agent: A broker between a publisher and a developer. Such agents are useful in finding interested parties and in helping to set up deals.

interrogatory: A written question submitted to the opposing party in a court case.

intrinsic evidence: Evidence obtained directly from the specification, claims, and prosecution history of a patent or patent application.

investment tax credit: A credit for purchasing certain qualified equipment that usually needs to be used in the production of a tangible item (personal property).

IP: *See intellectual property.*

IPO: *See initial public offering.*

judgment as a matter of law: A decision rendered by a judge against a party when there is no legal basis for a jury to find for that party on that particular issue at trial.

jurisdiction: A court's authority to hear a particular case or issue. Commonly refers to the area the court has authority over.

Lanham Act: Title 15 of the United States Code, which contains sections that pertain to the enforcement of trademark, copyright, and patent law.

leveraged buy-out (LBO): An exit strategy wherein a company will take on debt to buy the ownership of an investor or founder.

license: A contract granting any or all rights to use, distribute, or enforce intellectual property owned by another party.

licensee: A person or company to which a license is given.

licensor: A person or company who issues a license to a third party.

limited liability: Liability that is limited to a partner or investor's investment. A partner or investor therefore cannot lose more money than the value of their shares if the corporation runs into debt. In contrast, in sole proprietorships and general partnerships, the owner or partners are each liable for business debts.

Limited Liability Corporation (LLC): An entity created under the laws of a state in which it was incorporated. It is treated like a partnership for tax purposes unless it elects to be treated as a corporation. All income and expenses are reported on Form 1065. Each unit holder's share of the income and expenses is reported on Form 1065 K-1. An LLC is recognized in all 50 states and Washington DC.

liquidity event: *See exit strategy.*

literal patent infringement: The act of infringing every element described in a patent holder's patent claims.

localization: The process of changing a game's artwork and language for a particular country.

marketing: The art of getting customers interested in your product, usually through promotions and advertising. Related to, but a separate discipline from, public relations (PR).

markman hearing: A judicial proceeding through which a court obtains the facts and information required to render a claim construction decision.

Massively Multiplayer Online Games (MMOG): *See virtual world.*

market research: A method of determining what your target audience wants in a product, through surveys, test markets, or other means.

material breach: A violation of a contract term that involves elements essential to the performance of the contract itself.

media alert: *See news alert.*

mediation: A method of resolving disputes between parties by reaching a mutual solution through the assistance of a neutral third party. Unlike arbitration, no decision is officially made by the mediator.

Medicare: A component of Federal Insurance Compensation Act (FICA) withheld from an employee's gross wages. The amount withheld from the employee is matched by the employer.

merit bonus: A monetary award given by an employer to specific employees for performance and commitment beyond the employer's expectations.

milestone: Future dates when a specific stage of game development must be completed to the satisfaction of the publisher.

milestone bonus: A monetary award given to employees for successfully meeting a production milestone.

misappropriation: The fraudulent use of another's property for one's own use.

MMO: *See virtual world.*

MMORPG: *See virtual world.*

movant: The party that files a motion or requests a particular action in court.

multitiered management structure: An organizational hierarchy consisting of many vertical levels of management.

negative productivity: The reverse effect on productivity resulting from mistakes brought on by fatigue due to working long hours (over 40 hours per week) over an extended period of time. Also called "Anti-time."

net income: Income from sales after all expenses and taxes have been deducted. Deducted expenses can include salaries, operating costs, cost of goods sold, etc.

news alert: A prepared statement to the public that contains most of the elements of a press release but is less formal. Usually used to keep the name of a project in the news when smaller goals have been accomplished.

noncompete agreement: A contract between an employer and an employee preventing the employee from engaging in any activity that competes with the business of the employer for a specified period of time.

non-disclosure agreement (NDA): A contract that restricts the sharing by one or more parties of the agreement of the IP learned during meetings between the parties. Commonly used by companies to keep employees, visitors, and potential partners from sharing confidential information with competitors.

nonexclusive license: A license that is granted to one party but may also be granted to other parties.

Non-player character (NPC): An independent character in a video game not controlled by a player.

object code: The code of a computer program in a machine-readable format. For example, the result of compiling code written in a language such as C++ is object code.

offer: A signal that a party is willing to enter into a contract.

one of ordinary skill in the art: A practitioner of generally expected skill in the technological field of a patent at the time of the invention disclosed by that patent.

open source: A term used to describe various technical philosophies that encourage the sharing of the source code for computer programs. This includes, but is not limited to, the Free Software movement. *See also General Public License.*

operations: The department responsible for the everyday business tasks of a company. Sometimes called business operations.

parol evidence rule: A contract rule that tells the court not to look beyond a contract's written contents when interpreting the meaning of that contract.

partnership: An entity that has at least two partners operating the business. It is a treated as a separate entity for tax purposes and reports all income and expenses on Form 1065. Each partner's share of the income and expenses is reported on Form 1065 K-1.

pass-through entity: A pass-through entity passes its net income or net losses to its owners. Passing income through to the owners helps avoid double taxation.

patent: A federal grant of the exclusive right to make, use, or sell a novel, useful, and nonobvious invention for a specific period of time.

patent claim: The description of the patentable aspects of an invention used to define the scope of the subject matter protected by the patent.

patent infringement: The act of interfering with the exclusive rights granted to a patent holder.

patent specification: The written description of the invention covered by the patent.

patentee: The party that owns the rights to a patent.

personal jurisdiction: A court's authority over a particular party.

piercing the corporate veil: Occurs where a shareholder of a corporation is held personally liable for the debts of the corporation, despite the general principle that those persons are immune from lawsuits that otherwise would only hold the corporation liable. This can happen if the proper restrictions requiring separation of individual shareholder and company resources are not followed.

pitch: In public relations, suggesting a story idea to an editor or journalist of a publication.

plaintiff: The party that brings a civil suit to court.

policies: A set of rules that a service provider imposes on itself to make its actions more predictable to others.

PR plan: A pre-determined release schedule of PR assets, press releases, and previews/reviews.

PR assets: The multimedia, content, and information a video game company plans to distribute to the media to show off a game.

PR fact sheet: A basic overview of the game targeted toward editors of online and print publications.

pre-trial conference: A court-scheduled meeting with the parties in a suit to allow the court to obtain an overview of the case, assess the issues involved, and set a trial schedule.

press release: A prepared statement issued to the media to announce various major developments within a company. *See also news alert.*

profit-sharing: The payment of royalties or a percentage of an employer's profits, to an employee.

probation: A disciplinary technique where an employee whose conduct has become a problem is observed closely by the employer for a given period of time, during which the employer considers whether to terminate the employee's employment.

producer: The individual responsible for the business-related details of a video game project. This person ensures that a video game production project stays on schedule toward completion by creating and maintaining the overall schedule, budget, and team.

prosecution history: The documents relating to the filing and grant of a patent by the U.S. Patent and Trademark Office.

protective order: A court order prohibiting a party from committing actions that may aggravate or irritate another party.

public domain: Intellectual property that is now available for use without any license, often because protection has expired.

public relations (PR): The process of creating interest among editors and journalists toward a product or company. Related to, but a separate discipline from, marketing.

purchase order: A document that indicates a desired quantity and type of product, placed from a buyer to a seller. Such a document constitutes an offer for entry in a contract for provision of the goods in question.

quality assurance (QA) testers: Individuals who are responsible for testing video games and reporting any software bugs encountered during testing.

recoupable advance: A type of advance that is repayable only from the proceeds of the sale of the final product.

remedies: Those things a court can do to set matters right once it finds that one party has caused harm to another.

repayable advance: A type of advance that must be repaid without regard to the income generated by a product. If a product does not generate enough income to cover the advance, the developer must still pay back the advance. Also known as a recoverable advance.

request for admission: A statement prepared during discovery by one party and submitted to the opposing party who must admit, deny, or object to the factual assertions within the statement.

request for production: A party's written request that another party provide the documents and items specified within the request.

right of first refusal: The right to make an offer after any other offers. Someone who holds the right of first refusal is informed of the other offers and has the opportunity to exceed the best offer after all offers have been considered.

rules of conduct: Rules that forbid certain kinds of actions by the users of a service, such as an online game.

S Corporation: A U.S. corporation that has filed an election with the Internal Revenue Service to have all its income and expenses be taxed at the shareholder level.

screenshot: A still image of what is displayed on a player's monitor screen from a game. Also called "screens" in industry jargon.

secondary meaning: The additional meaning given to a descriptive trademark to associated it with a particular source.

Section 230 of the Communications Decency Act (CDA) of 1996: A law partially immunizing online service providers from liability for things said and done by their users.

Section 512 of the Digital Millennium Copyright Act (DMCA): A law creating an expedited system whereby copyright holders can ask online service providers hosting allegedly infringing content to take the content down. *See also Digital Millennium Copyright Act.*

serialization (of discs): Where each disc of a game has its own serial number, such that the discs can be individually tracked. Useful for tracking leaks or gray market trading in other territories.

service: In law, the delivery of legal process to a party in a legal action to place the party on notice of the action.

settlement: An out-of-trial agreement to end legal proceedings, usually with an agreement for one party to compensate the other without acknowledging any specific wrongdoing.

severability clause: A clause in a contract that tells a court what to do when interpreting a contract if a particular clause in that contract is found invalid.

shrinkwrap license: A license printed on the package of a software product that notifies the buyer that opening the package binds the user to the terms of the license.

Social Security: One of the components of the Federal Insurance Compensation Act (FICA), and is withheld from your employees' gross wages. The amount withheld from the employee is matched by the employer.

software engine: A computer program that handles specific technical tasks in a video game. A common example is a graphics engine that handles the presentation of the game graphics on the computer screen.

sole proprietorship: The simplest form of doing business, it is owned directly by an individual who is running the business. All income and expenses are reported on the owner's Form 1040 Schedule C.

source code: The code of a computer program written in a human-readable programming language—such as C++, Python, or Visual Basic—that defines the basic behavior of the program.

straight line depreciation method: The simplest and most commonly used method of depreciation. It is calculated by taking the price of an asset subtracted by the salvage value divided by the total productive years the asset can be reasonably expected to benefit the company.

stock option: A right issued by a corporation to an individual or an entity to buy a given amount of shares of company stock at a stated price within a specified period of time.

studio head: The individual in charge of the day-to-day operation of a video game studio, traditionally the founder of the studio.

suggestive trademark: A mark that suggests something about the source. One of the weakest categories of trademarks. For example, Electronic Arts.

sublicense: A transfer of specific contractual rights or duties to a third party.

subsidiary rights: *See ancillary and subsidiary rights.*

summary judgment: Judgment issued without the benefit of a full trial. Granted when there is no genuine issue of material fact regarding the claim.

synchronization license: A license granted by a music publisher or song writer that grants the use of song in conjunction with visual images.

termination: The end of a contract. Can specifically refer to releasing an individual from employment (i.e., ending the employment contract).

termination for cause: Termination of a contract for a specific reason related to a breach of the contract, the impossibility of performance, or other issues caused by the other party.

termination for convenience: Termination of a contract for reasons relating to the preference of the terminating party. For example, terminating a contract to take a more lucrative job would be a termination for convenience.

Terms of Service (ToS): A contract between a service provider and a consumer, allowing the consumer to use the service on certain conditions. *See also End User License Agreement.*

trade secret: Proprietary business information that is kept secret within a company.

trademark: A symbol that distinguishes one business entity's product over the products of others. Sometimes spelled "trade mark."

trademark dilution: The unauthorized use of a trademark on unrelated products, making it harder for consumers to recognize the distinctive qualities of the trademark.

trademark infringement: Using a trademark to identify goods or services without the permission of the trademark owner.

trademark tarnishment: A type of trademark dilution where the mark in question is being used in conjunction with poor quality or unsavory products.

treble damages: Damages that are three times the amount awarded by a jury meant to be punitive in nature.

triple-A title: A major game, generally with significant funding, that anticipates high sales.

unemployment insurance: A program for pooling funds paid by employers to be used for the payment of unemployment insurance to workers during periods of unemployment that are beyond the workers' control. These programs are generally run at the state level.

unfair competition: Deceitful or fraudulent business practices used to gain advantage in the marketplace.

Uniform Trade Secrets Act: A model law drafted to clarify and define the rights and remedies of common law trade secret.

United States Code (U.S.C.): The formal name for the codified United States federal law.

United States Patent and Trademark Office: The federal agency that oversees the granting of patents and trademarks used to protect intellectual property.

vicarious copyright infringement: Liability for copyright infringement committed by another, where the vicarious infringer profited from the infringement and could have stopped the infringement but did not.

viral marketing: Advertising campaign designed to spread interest in a product by individual word of mouth rather than through traditional direct public relations and marketing efforts. This usually involves something interesting or amusing that is shared between potential customers.

virtual world: Computer games that allow users to play and communicate between each other on the Internet. Also called MMOGs (Massively Multiplayer Online Games), MMORPGs (Massively Multiplayer Online Role-Playing Games, a specific game genre of virtual worlds), or simply MMOs.

volunteers: People who perform services with no compensation. The legal status of volunteers is undetermined at this time.

W-2: *See Form W-2.*

W-3: *See Form W-3.*

W-4: *See Form W-4.*

walkthrough: A guided tour of one or more stages/levels in a video game. Often provided to game reviewers to assist them in the process of playing and reviewing the game.

warez: Internet slang referring to unlicensed intellectual property, often software, movies, or music. Also spelled "wares."

warez sites: Internet Web sites where you can find warez available for download.

warranty: A promise made by a seller to a buyer that the item or service being sold will have certain desirable characteristics, such as not being unreasonably dangerous or performing up to standard.

worker's compensation: Benefits paid to a worker to compensate for losses caused by a work-related injury or illness. Also called "workman's compensation" in older texts, or "worker's comp" in informal speech.

INDEX

1099-MISC, 284–285, 464
3D Gamers, 148
"3D Squared," 5
401(k) accounts, 62, 459
50 Cent, 117

A

academics, company culture, 399
acceptance
  date, 421
  defined, 459
accounting
  game company startup, 17–18
  need for, 366–367, 379
  staying in black, 66–68
  taxation, 273–278
accounts, 401(k), 62, 459
accounts, ground rules, 322–326
accrual method of accounting, 273–275, 459
Activision, 123
activities, company culture, 398–401
actors
  audiovisual works licensing, 208
  individual rights licensing, 208–212
ad dollars, 102
AddictingGames.com, 122
addiction, 341–342
adjusted basis, 278, 459
administration necessity, 366–367
Administrative Law Judge (ALJ), 236–237
admission requests, 228
advancee
  defined, 79, 459
  publishing and developer contracts, 94
advancer, defined, 79, 459
advances
  contract terms, 78–79
  defined, 459
  revenue recognition, 275
advergaming, 120–121, 459
advertising. see also marketing
  ad dollars, 102
  false, 123
  in-game, 102
age
  demographic trends, 110–111
  government restrictions, 356
agents, patent, 187
agreements
  contracts. see contracts
  game development. see game development agreements
  licensing literary works, 202
Ahl, Dave, 362–364
ALJ (Administrative Law Judge), 236–237
all events test, 273–275, 459
allocation, money, 20
Alpex Computer Corp. v. Ninetendo Co., 234–235
alternative minimum tax (AMT)
  defined, 459
  stock options and, 289–290
American Arbitration Association, 83
American Marketing Association, 101
American Video Graphics v. Electronic Arts, et. al., 230
America's Army, 120
AMT (alternative minimum tax)
  defined, 459
  stock options and, 289–290
ancillary rights
  defined, 459

exploitation, 201–202
anti-exploitation clauses, 329
anti-griefing terms, 329–332
anti-obscenity laws, 353
anti-pornography laws, 353
anticipation, patent invalidity, 185
AOL, 280
AOL Games Channel, 122
appeals
  patent claim scope ruling, 225
  post-trial activities, 234–235
appellate court, 459
applications
  hiring paperwork, 58
  patent, 183–184
  provisional patent, 184–185
approval rights
  marketing, production and distribution, 419–420
  operations, support and maintenance, 421–422
arbiter selection, 239
arbitrary trademarks
  defined, 459
  IP, 179–180
arbitration
  clauses, 82–84
  defined, 459
  development agreements, 443
  forum selection and, 320
  IP dispute resolution, 238–239
architectural works, copyright, 163
art director
  defined, 459
  job allocation, 51
Articles of Incorporation, 14
artistic works, copyright, 163
artists
  defined, 460
  job allocation, 51–52
  salaries, 59
Asheron's Call, 373–374
assets
  depreciation, 277–278
  exit strategies, 303–306
  localization in international distribution, 259–260
assets (PR)
  defined, 468
  development, 142–145
  planning, 134–135
Assignment of Invention, 58, 460
assignments
  contract terms, 80
  defined, 460
  development agreements, 444–445
  IP licensing and, 91–93
  IP rights, 194
  licensing and trademarks, 198
  ownership and licenses, 429
at will employees, 90
Atari, 164–165
attitude
  importance of, 370
  open process, 401–403
attorneys. see also lawyers
  copyright and code, 171
  patent, 187
attorneys' fees
  drafting EULAs, 321–322
  trial remedies and, 234
attribution, trademark, 181
audience
  avoiding marketing mistakes, 127–128
  marketing to, 109–112
  pricing and, 104
  promotion and, 106–107
audio, localization, 259–260

audiovisual works, licensing, 207–208
audit rights, 418, 427
Austin Game Conference, 72
authority
  authorship and, 397–398
  contracts, 85
  game company startup, 8
  producers vs. developers, 375
  representations and warranties, 437–438
authorship
  company culture, 396–398
  independent contractors and, 89–90
  licensing literary works, 200–204
  public domain and, 168–169
avatar, 460

B

background checks, 58
bad games as hits, 391–392
Baer, Ralph, business advice, 364–366
Baldur's Gate, 247
bankruptcy, 303, 309–310
banks, company startup, 26–27
banned users
  rule enforcement, 343
  virtual world law, 324
bargaining power
  contract basics, 76
  development agreements, 408
  publishing and developer contracts, 93–97
Bartle, Richard, business advice, 366–369
basecamp, 134
Basic Computer Games (Ahl), 361
basis, defined, 460
BATs (business activity taxes), 294
Battle for Middle Earth, 167
Battlefield 1942, 169
behavioral market segmentation, 112
benefits
  fringe, 283–286
  independent contractors, 89
  prospective employees, 61–63
  stock option plans, 286–290
Beta-testing, 372–373
Beyman, Richard A., xv. see also licensing IP
The Bible, 362–363
bill paying
  daily issues, 24, 25
  electronic, 27
billing, ground rules, 322–326
BioWare, 388
Blizzard, 332, 336, 341
blogs
  Internet marketing, 121
  PR on, 149
boilerplate contracts, 78, 460
boilerplate (PR), 136–140, 460
Bonds, Barry, 211
bonuses
  accounting methods, 275
  money allocation, 20
  prospective employees, 60–61
  signing, 57
bottom line, business planning, 66
Boucher, Rick, 294
Boyd, Gregory S.
  about, 1, xv
  on development agreements. see game

development agreements
  on IP. see IP (Intellectual Property)
Boyer, Stephen, 218
Brando, Marlon, 209
brands
  marketing, 102
  in print marketing, 114
  trademarks and, 176–181
breach of contract
  contract terms, 80–81
  defined, 460
  development agreements, 435–437
  material breach, 445–446
Breakout, 164–165
Breen, Sean Michael, 166
briefs, markman, 226
Brooks, Fred, 69
Brookwood, Ted, xv. see also PR (public relations)
budgeting
  accounting. see accounting
  business operations, 67–68
  marketing, 129
bugs
  in demos, 148
  development agreements, 422
  exploits and, 328–329
  MMOs post-launch, 385
  rules and guarantees, 339–341
build, defined, 460
bullet points, fact sheets, 141
bureaucracy management, 33
burn rate, short-term survival, 23
business
  exit strategies. see exit strategies
  further reading, 458
  planning, 66–67
  regulations, 32–33
  rules, 333–337
  start-up tasks, 30–31
business activity taxes (BATs), 294
business advice, professional, 361–394
  Ahl, Dave, 362–364
  Baer, Ralph, 364–366
  Bartle, Richard, 366–369
  Erskine, John, 369–370
  Esber, Matt, 370–371
  Farmer, F. Randall, 371–374
  Foe, Scott, 374–376
  Goldstein, Steve, 376–378
  Green, Brian, 378–379
  Leverett, William, 380–381
  Macris, Alexander, 381–383
  Mulligan, Jessica, 383–387
  overview, 361–362
  Vogel, Jeff, 387–388
  Walton, Gordon, 388–392
  Zaffron, Andrew S., 392–394
Business Days, definition, 410
business entities
  company formation, 10–15
  taxation, 267–272
business operations, 41–74
  company culture, 63
  conclusion, 74
  crunch time, 45–49
  employee management, 41–45
  expanding, 73–74
  independence, 72–73
  introduction, 41
  measuring success, 69
  networking, 71–72
  opportunities, 71
  pitfalls, 69
  rewards and punishment, 64–66
  saving money, 69–71

staying in black, 66–68
who does what, 49–54
business operations, prospective employees
  benefits, 61–63
  bonuses, 60–61
  closing deal, 57–58
  in-person interviewing, 56–57
  independent contractors, 60
  interviewing, 55–56
  overview, 55
  paperwork, 58
  pay rates, 58–59
  performance, 60
Busta Rhymes, 117
buy-out partners, 306–307
Buy/Sell Share Agreements, 11
buzz
  defined, 460
  PR, 133–134
  promotion, 106

C

C Corporations, 10–15, 267–272
California Civil Code, 210
Call of Duty 2, 123
campaigning
  PR, 135–136
  viral marketing, 153–154
Candystand.com, 120
capital letters in contracts, 439
cash flow
  budgeting, 67–68
  game company startup, 21
cash method accounting
  defined, 460
  taxation, 273–275
casual games
  demographic trends, 111
  market segmentation, 112
cause of action, 80–81, 460
CD distribution, 105
cease and desist letters, 166
cease and desist orders, 235–237
celebrities
  individual rights licensing, 209–211
  marketing, 116–117
  publicity rights and, 187–188
cell phone market trends, 111
Chapter 11 bankruptcy, 309, 460
Chapter 7 bankruptcy, 309, 460
check processing, 18
Cheers, 210
Children's Online Privacy Protection Act (COPPA), 107, 460
China, international deals, 264
Chisum, Donald, 162
choice of forum, 319–320
choice of law
  contract terms, 82–84
  defined, 460
  in NDAs, 88
  virtual world law, 319–320
choice of venue, 460
choreography, copyright, 163
Christ, Roxanne, xvi. see also marketing
Circulars, 164
City of Heroes, 352
civil lawsuits, 345
claim construction
  defined, 460
  IP protection, 183
  scope ruling, 222–226
claim of right doctrine, 273–275, 460
click ads, 121
client software protection
  business rules, 335–336
  virtual world law, 327–328
close-down

downside exits, 309–310
exit strategies, 303
Club Caribe, 371
CMs (Community Managers), 386–387
Coca-Cola
  licensing and trademarks, 197
  trade secrets, 173–174
code
  documentation, 388
  as literary work, 163–164
  litigation and copyright, 171
  localization, 259–260
  protecting in discovery, 230–231
  saving notes, 364–366
Cohen, Yonatan, 166
commercial advertisement, 116–117
common law trademark rights, 177
communication
  daily issues, 31
  good managers, 42–43
community
  defined, 461
  marketing, production and distribution, 421
  rules, 329–333
Community Managers (CMs), 386–387
Community Trade Mark (CTM), 181, 461
company
  account termination. *see* rules, virtual world law
  boilerplate, 138, 141
  description, 403–405
  exit strategies. *see* exit strategies
  formation, 10–15
  marketing, 102
  policies. *see* policies
  third-party rights protection, 354
  Web sites, 38
company culture
  business operations, 63
  game company intangibles, 398–401
compensatory damages, 460. *see also* damages
competition
  business planning, 66
  international partners, 251–253
  virtual world business rules, 333–337
complaints
  defined, 461
  filing, 219
compliance, payroll taxation, 281–283
Computer Fraud and Abuse Act, 326
conferences
  marketing, production and distribution, 421
  networking, 72
  PR, 152–153
  trade shows, 112–114
confidentiality
  agreements. *see* NDAs (non-disclosure agreements)
  in development agreements, 431–434
Confidentiality and Non-Disclosure Agreement, 87–88
Congress
  copyrights, 163
  patent rights, 182
consequential damages, 441
considerations
  contract basics, 76
  defined, 461
  in development agreements, 410
console titles
  international deals, 250
  selling internationally, 254
construction, claim. *see* claim construction

constructive receipt, 273–275, 461
consulting, 31, 38
consumer market, segmenting, 112
consumer shows, selling internationally, 248
contact information, 139
contacts
  building, 30–31
  maintaining, 377
  pitching to, 145–147
  trade secrets, 174
contests
  fan sites, 150
  PR, 154
contingency planning, PR, 157–158
contract terms
  advances, 78–79
  assignments and sublicenses, 80
  choice of law, arbitration and equitable relief clauses, 82–84
  conversion rate and, 124–125
  cross-collateralization, 79
  gross and net, 79–80
  indemnification, 82
  staying independent, 73
  termination and breach of contract, 80–81
contractors, independent. *see* independent contractors
contracts, 75–99
  basics, 75–78
  conclusion, 99
  defined, 461
  development. *see* game development agreements
  employment, 88–91
  endnotes, 99
  EULAs as, 317–322
  further reading, 457
  independence, 73
  international deals, 262–264
  international legal issues, 257–258
  legal fees, 84–85
  licensing and assignments, 91–93
  musical composition licensing, 204–205
  NDAs, 85–88
  negotiation, 98
  publisher and developer, 93–97
  retailer distribution, 106
contributory copyright infringement, 351–352, 461
conventions. *see* conferences
conversion rates, 124, 461
COPPA (Children's Online Privacy Protection Act), 107, 460
copyleft, 461
Copyright Office, 164, 461
Copyright Office Circulars 61, 164
copyrights
  defined, 461
  derivative works, 167
  development agreements, 428–431
  examples, 164–165
  fair use, 170
  important points, 190–191
  in-game advertising, 120
  information, 165–167
  licensing IP, 194–196
  protection, 163–164
  public domain, 167–169
  questions, 171–172
  rights and, 164
  Scenes a Fair Doctrine, 169
  virtual world law, 351–352
core operating hours, 44–45, 461
corporations
  defined, 461
  depositions, 228–229

entities and taxation, 267–272
Costikyan, Greg, xvi. *see also* exit strategies
costs
  advice from Scott Foe, 375
  budgeting, 67–68
  business entities, 13
  copyright, 165
  development agreements, 416–417
  employees, 41
  employees vs. sales agents, 246–247
  entities and taxation, 270–271
  gross and net, 79–80
  legal definition, 412
  legal fees and contracts, 84–85
  marketing, 95
  patent litigation, 239
  patents, 183–184
  piracy and, 258
  selling internationally, 260–262
  short-term survival, 22–23
  software, 276–277
  trade secrets, 175
  trademarks, 178
counsel, IP, 188
counterclaims, 217
court orders, 354–355, 461
Creative Commons licenses, 172, 461
Creative Computing, 361–363
creative director, 50–51, 461
creativity
  authorship and, 396–398
  avoiding marketing mistakes, 128–129
  print marketing, 114
credit, 20–21
credit card authorization, 323
credit, tax, 291–292
credit unions, 26–27
Cribs, 117
criminal laws
  copyright infringement penalties, 166–167
  downside exits, 309
  prosecution, 345
  third-party rights protection, 248
  virtual world law, 352–353
cross-collateralization
  contract terms, 79
  defined, 461
  publishing and developer contracts, 93–94
cross-examination, 233, 462
cross-licensing, 200, 462
crunch time, 45–49, 462
CSI3, 118
CTM (Community Trade Mark), 181, 461
cultural lore, public domain, 168–169
cure
  breach of contract, 81
  defined, 462
  termination, 435–436
currency
  development agreements, 445
  exchange, 253–254
  international payment, 260–262
customers. *see* audience

D

Dad's Lessons for Living (Ahl), 361
daily startup issues, 23–25
damages
  breach of contract, 80–81
  copyright infringement, 166–167, 171–172
  defined, 462
  disclaimer of warranties, 338
  equitable relief clauses, 83
  licensing IP, 194
  patent infringement, 184
  trade secret infringement, 175

trademark infringement, 179
  trial remedies, 233–234
Darfur is Dying, 121
Dark Age of Camelot, 169, 177
database, ownership and licenses, 429
dating notes, 365
Davidson & Associates v. Internet Gateway, 92
de novo review, 234, 462
deadlines
  crunch time and, 45–49
  payroll taxes, 285
deals, international
  examples, 262–264
  types of, 248–250
debt
  downside exits, 309–310
  game company startup, 20–21
  liability protection, 11
decision making, 14–15
declaratory judgment action
  defined, 462
  IP litigation, 217–218
declining balance depreciation method
  defined, 462
  taxation, 277
decoupling from internal revenue code, 292
deductible expenses, 94–95
deductions, federal tax incentives, 290–291
defamation
  defined, 462
  third-party rights protection, 248
defendant, defined, 462
defense, fair use, 170
deferral, taxation, 275
definitions, development agreements, 410–414
Delahunt, William, 294
democratizing authorship, 396–398
demographics
  market research, 110
  market segmentation, 112
  trends, 110–111
demos
  contingency planning, 158
  Internet marketing, 122
  PR, 147–148
  press tours, 151–152
  releasing, 135–136
Denial of Service (DoS)
  anti-griefing terms, 331–332
  attacks, 327
  defined, 462
dental insurance, 62–63
deposit schedule, 462
depositions, 462
depository requirements, 283–285
depreciation
  defined, 462
  taxation, 277–278
depreciation recapture
  defined, 462
  taxation, 278
derivative works
  copyrights, 167
  legal definition, 411
  ownership and licenses, 429
descriptive text, asset development, 145
descriptive trademarks, 180, 462
design
  advice from Randall Farmer, 371–372
  advice from Richard Bartle, 366–367
  avoiding marketing mistakes, 128–129
  rule enforcement, 343–344
  specification of game, 450–451
  virtual world law and, 311
designations, ownership and licenses, 429
designers
  defined, 462

job allocation, 51–52
  salaries, 59
Designing Virtual Worlds (Bartle), 366
developed software, taxation and costs, 276
developer diaries, 134
developers
  contracts, 93–97
  copyrights and, 196
  defined, 462
  print marketing, 115
  vs. producers, 374–375
  understanding business, 378–379
Developing Online Games: An Insider's Guide (Mulligan), 383–384
development
  agreements. *see* game development agreements
  IP and, 161–162
  learning before you start, 370
  MMOs post-launch, 383–385
development schedule exhibit, 449–450
development services, 414–419
development tools
  maintenance, 419
  ownership and licenses, 428–430
  as trade secrets, 174
Dickens, Charles, 344
Digital Millennium Copyright Act (DMCA)
  defined, 462
  third-party rights protection, 249–250
digital rights management, 344
Dinner Dash, 4
director of engineering
  defined, 462
  job allocation, 51
disability insurance, 463
disclaimers, 337–342
disclosure. *see* NDAs (non-disclosure agreements)
Disclosure Document program, 366
discovery
  defined, 463
  overview, 226–227
  preparation, 231–232
  protective orders, 227
  tools, 227–231
dispute resolution, 237–239
distribution
  cost sharing, 261–262
  development agreements, 419–421
  gray market, 256–257
  licensing and trademarks, 197–198
  place and marketing, 105–106
  press release, 139–140
District Court vs. ITC, 236
DIY (do it yourself) PR, 134
DMCA (Digital Millennium Copyright Act)
  defined, 462
  third-party rights protection, 249–250
doctrine of equivalents
  defined, 463
  summary judgment, 222
document requests, 228
documentation
  company formation, 13–14
  contracts. *see* contracts
  disciplinary action, 64–65
  discovery preparation, 231
  protecting trade secrets, 175
  saving notes, 364–366
  taxation, 284–285
Dodge M37 Restoration Guide (Ahl), 361
domain names, registration, 371
domestic industry, IP litigation and ITC, 236
Doom, 167
Dorgan, Byron, 295

DoS (Denial of Service)
  anti-griefing terms,
    331–332
  attacks, 327
  defined, 462
double declining balance
  method of depreciation,
    277
double taxation
  defined, 463
  pass-through entities,
    268–269
downloadable demos, 122
downloads
  distribution, 105–106
  EU taxation, 293–294
  fighting piracy, 259
  selling internationally,
    254–255
  taxation, 294–295
Doyle, Matthew B.
  about, xvi
  on business operations. *see*
    business operations
drafting contracts. *see also*
    contracts
  basics, 77–78
  EULAs, 316–317
  legal fees, 84–85
dramatic works, copyright, 163
dress advice from David Ahl,
    363
due process, 463
duping, 463
duration, licensing, 199
dynamic ads, 119

E
e-commerce, nexus and
    taxation, 292–293
E3 (Electronic Entertainment
    Expo)
  live advertising, 112–114
  PR, 152–153
EA (Electronic Arts)
  derivative works, 167
  international partners,
    251–252
  marketing, 115–116
  protecting software escrow,
    230
  sports, 117
eBay, 385
EC Habitats/Microcosm, 371
economic performance
  accounting methods,
    273–275
  defined, 463
editors, marketing to. *see* PR
    (public relations)
Effective Date, defined, 409
EINs (Employer Identification
    Numbers), 32
Electronic Arts (EA). *see* EA
    (Electronic Arts)
electronic bill paying, 27
Electronic Entertainment Expo
    (E3)
  live advertising, 112–114
  PR, 152–153
Electronic Gaming Monthly, 114
eligibility forms, 58
employees
  advice from Scott Foe, 375
  authorship, 396–398
  company culture, 63
  defined, 463
  downside exits, 309–310
  exit strategies and, 308–309
  leadership, 14–15
  management, 41–45
  open process, 401–403
  players and, 336–337
  prospective. *see* prospective
    employees
  relations, 24
  rewards and punishment,
    64–65
  saving money on, 69–70
  selling internationally,
    246–247
  taxation vs. independent
    contractors, 278–281
  taxes and regulations,
    32–33
  team chemistry, 8

turnover issue, 38
who does what, 49–54
as witnesses, 231
Employer Identification
    Numbers (EINs), 32
Employment Eligibility
    Verification Form, 33
employment regulations, 32–33
Employment Stock Purchase
    Plan (ESPP)
  employee benefits, 62
  taxation and, 286
emulation software, 105
End User License Agreements
    (EULAs)
  defined, 463
  IP licensing and assign-
    ment, 92–93
  in virtual world law. *see*
    virtual world law
enforcing rules
  EULAs, 317–319
  virtual world law, 342–345
engineers
  defined, 463
  job allocation, 51–52
  salaries, 59
engines
  maintenance, 419
  ownership and licenses,
    428–430
  saving money on, 71
English speaking countries
  revenue potential, 247–248
enjoined parties, 83, 463
Enterment Software
    Association (ESA)
  demographic trends,
    110–111
  fighting piracy, 259
  market research, 110
entities
  company formation, 10–15
  selection and taxation,
    267–272
Enzi, Mike, 295
equipment, office, 25
equitable relief
  contract terms, 82–84
  defined, 463
  in NDAs, 88
errors
  bugs. *see* bugs
  rules and guarantees,
    339–340
Erskine, John, business advice,
    369–370
ESA (Entertainment Software
    Association)
  demographic trends,
    110–111
  fighting piracy, 259
  market research, 110
Esber, Matt, business advice,
    370–371
escalating royalty scale,
    423–424
Escapist Magazine, 374, 381
escrow agents, 230–231
espousing evil, 331
ESPP (Employment Stock
    Purchase Plan)
  employee benefits, 62
  taxation and, 286
etiquette, 363
EU (European Union),
    taxation, 292–294
EULAs (End User License
    Agreements)
  defined, 463
  IP licensing and assign-
    ment, 92–93
  in virtual world law. *see*
    virtual world law
EURid (European Registry for
    Internet Domains), 463
Europe
  deals, 263
  distribution, 250
European Registry for Internet
    Domains (EURid), 463
European Union (EU),
    taxation, 292–294
EverQuest, 118–119, 384
evidence
  document collection, 231

extrinsic vs. intrinsic,
    224–225
  trial format, 233
Excel, 18
exclusive licenses
  defined, 91–92, 463
  literary works, 200–204
exclusivity period, 415
execution, advice from Gordon
    Walton, 390–391
exemptions, minimum wage,
    280–281
exit strategies, 299–310
  conclusion, 310
  defined, 463
  downside exits, 309–310
  game company startup, 9
  how to, 300–303
  overview, 299
  preparation for purchase,
    303–309
  reasons to, 299–300
expansion
  business operations, 73–74
  going international. *see*
    selling internationally
expansion packs
  development agreements,
    418–419
  royalties, 425
expenses
  accounting, 273–275
  deductible, 94–95
  depreciation, 277–278
  downside exits, 309–310
  federal tax incentives,
    290–291
  marketing, production and
    distribution, 420
  operations, support and
    maintenance, 423
  software, 276–277
experimental uses, patent
    invalidity, 186
expert witnesses, 232
expired copyright protection,
    167–169
exploits
  defined, 463
  virtual world law, 328–329
export restrictions, 356
expulsion, rule enforcement,
    343
extended honing period
  legal definition, 411
  recoupment, 426
extra-curricular activities,
    398–401
extrinsic evidence
  defined, 463
  patent claim scope ruling,
    224–225

F
Facebook, 121
fact sheets, PR
  defined, 468
  development, 140–142
  planning, 134
Fair Labor Standards Act
    (FLSA), 280–281
fair use, copyrights, 170
fairy tales, Scenes a Fair
    Doctrine, 169
false advertising, 123
Fan Site Kit (FSK), 150
fan sites
  defined, 463
  merchandising, 334–335
  PR on, 149–150
  trademarks and, 181
fanciful trademarks
  defined, 463
  IP rights, 179–180
fans, 69–70
fantasy games
  in-game advertising, 119
  Scenes a Fair Doctrine, 169
Farmer, F. Randall, business
    advice, 371–374
fault, disclaimer of warranties,
    338
feature creep
  crunch time and, 47–48
  defined, 463
  pitfalls, 69

Federal Arbitration Act, 83
Federal Circuit
  defined, 464
  pre-filing requirements, 217
federal courts, lawsuit location,
    218–219
Federal Insurance Compensa-
    tion Act (FICA), 282
Federal Rules of Civil Procedure,
    216
Federal Tax Identification
    Number, 13
federal tax incentives, 290–291
federal tax laws, decoupling
    from, 292
Federal Trade Commission
    (FTC)
  advertising legal issues, 123
  defined, 464
  pricing, 104
federal unemployment
    insurance
  depository requirements,
    283
  payroll tax compliance,
    282–283
Federal Unemployment Tax
    Act (FUTA)
  defined, 464
  depository requirements,
    283
  payroll tax compliance,
    282–283
feedback, 391
fees. *see also* costs
  marketing, production and
    distribution, 420
  patent, 183–184
  trademark registration, 178
Fencepost Rules
  defined, 464
  virtual world law, 313
Ferrell, Will, 31
FICA (Federal Insurance
    Compensation Act), 282
field of use, 199
fighting piracy, 258–259
File Front, 148
File Planet, 148
filing lawsuits
  IP litigation, 219–220
  pre-filing requirements,
    216–217
film production credit, 292
finances. *see* money
financial help
  free, 16
  hired, 16–17
financial institutions, 26–27
finished goods deals, 248–249
firing. *see* termination
First Amendment, individual
    rights licensing, 210–211
fiscal responsibility
  financial institutions, 26
  staying in black, 66–68
fiscal year
  accounting methods and,
    273–275
  defined, 464
  entities and taxation, 270
Flock, John
  about, xvi–xvii
  on IP litigation. *see* IP
    (intellectual property)
    litigation
FLSA (Fair Labor Standards
    Act), 280–281
focus groups, 125
Foe, Scott, business advice,
    374–376
follow-up
  press release, 140
  story pitching, 146–147
for cause termination, 81
force majeure
  agreement termination, 436
  defined, 464
  rules and guarantees,
    339–340
forced dispute resolution,
    215–216
Form 1099-MISC
  defined, 464
  taxation, 284–285
Form I-9

defined, 464
  taxation, 281
Form W-2
  defined, 464
  taxation, 284–285
Form W-3
  defined, 464
  taxation, 284–285
Form W-4
  defined, 464
  taxation, 281
formats, screenshots, 143
forms
  hiring, 58
  registration. *see* registration
  taxation, 284–285
forum selection
  defined, 464
  virtual world law, 319–320
forums, online
  defined, 464
  PR on, 148–149
foul language, 313
Franchise Tax Registration, 14
franchise taxes, 272–273
Fraps, 143
fraud, 353
free labor, 280
free speech, 210–211
Friedman, Peter
  about, xvii
  on taxation. *see* taxation
Friedman, Thomas, 381
friends, working with, 8
Friendster, 121
fringe benefits
  defined, 464
  taxation, 283–286
FSK (Fan Site Kit), 150
FTC (Federal Trade Commis-
    sion)
  advertising legal issues, 123
  defined, 464
  pricing, 104
funding. *see* money
further reading, 457–458
FUTA (Federal Unemployment
    Tax Act)
  defined, 464
  depository requirements,
    283
  payroll tax compliance,
    282–283

G
Galaxy Quest, 377
Gamasutra, 55
gambling, 353
game company intangibles. *see*
    hustle and flow
game company startup
  accounting, 17–18
  business tasks, 30–31
  changing with times, 36–37
  checklist, 39
  company formation, 10–15
  conclusion, 38–39
  consulting trap, 38
  daily issues, 23–25
  debt, 20–21
  financial help, free, 16
  financial help, hired, 16–17
  financial institutions,
    26–27
  game making, 30
  government and, 32–33
  human resources, 34–35
  insurance, 5–39, 35–36
  marketing, 37–38
  money allocation, 20
  money overview, 16
  money rules, 21–23
  overview, 5
  before paperwork, 6–10
  paperwork, 19
  professional advice. *see*
    business advice,
    professional
  receipts, 19–20
  turnover issue, 38
  vendor relations, 27–30
game content definition, 412
game conventions. *see*
    conferences
game definition, 412
game demos. *see* demos

Game Developer Magazine, 59
game developers. *see* developers
Game Developer's Conference (GDC)
  networking, 72
  PR, 152–153
game development agreements, 407–454
  conclusion, 454
  confidentiality, 431–434
  definitions, 410–414
  development schedule exhibit, 449–450
  development services, 414–419
  game specification exhibit, 450–451
  general provisions, 442–447
  indemnification, 439–441
  investment agreement, 441–442
  investment agreement exhibit, 451
  key personnel exhibit, 451
  liability limitations, 441
  live team activity exhibit, 451–453
  marketing, production and distribution, 419–421
  operations, support and maintenance, 421–423
  option to purchase, 434–435
  overview, 407–408
  ownership and licenses, 427–431
  recitals, 408–410
  representations and warranties, 437–439
  royalties, 423–427
  royalty exhibit, 453–454
  royalty report exhibit, 454
  signatures, 448–449
  term and termination, 435–437
  title, 408
game engines. *see* engines
game making, 30
game marketing. *see also* marketing
  vs. company marketing, 102
  product, 103
game portals
  defined, 464
  distribution, 105–106
  Internet marketing, 122
game programmers, 367–368
game rules. *see* rules, virtual world law
game specification exhibit, 450–451
game testing, 369
game type and deal type, 254–255
game units, pricing, 103–104
"GameCamp!", 5
Gamelab. *see* hustle and flow
gamers. *see also* players
  advertising suspicion, 114
  not being their puppet, 368–369
gaming business introduction, 1–4
GarageGames.com, 71
Gasaway, Laura, 168
GDC (Game Developer's Conference)
  networking, 72
  PR, 152–153
gender
  demographic trends, 111
  women as gamers, 368
General Partnerships, 268–272
general prohibitions, 313–314
general provisions, 442–447
General Public License (GPL)
  copyrights and, 172
  defined, 464
generic trademarks
  defined, 465
  IP, 180
geographic market segmentation, 112

geographic scope, licensing, 199
goals
  business planning, 66–67
  contracts, 85
  game company startup, 7
  life after purchase, 308–309
  marketing, 102–103
  marketing success measurement, 124–125
  milestone targets, 416
  success measurement, 69
Godfather, 209
Goldstein, Steve, business advice, 376–378
Goodlatte, Bob, 294
goodwill
  defined, 465
  licensing and trademarks, 197–198
Google Video, 154
Gordon, Bing, 306
government restrictions, 355–356
GPL (General Public License)
  copyrights and, 172
  defined, 464
Grand Theft Auto: San Andreas, 123
graphic works, copyright, 163
gray market imports
  defined, 465
  selling internationally, 256–257
Green, Brian
  about, 1, xvii
  business advice, 378–379
griefing
  Beta-testing and, 372
  defined, 465
  rule enforcement, 343–344
  virtual world law, 329–332
Grimmelmann, James
  about, xvii
  on virtual world law. *see* virtual world law
Grokster, 351–352
gross income
  contract terms, 79–80
  defined, 465
ground rules, billing/accounts, 322–326
growth, business operations, 73–74
guarantees
  development agreements, 437–439
  game. *see* warranties
guerrilla marketing
  budget and, 129
  defined, 465
guilds, 465

H

Habitat, 371
hacking
  client software protection, 335–336
  virtual world law, 326–328
Hague Evidence Convention, 230
Hallisey and Williams v. AOL, Inc., 280
Halo, 117
Halo 2
  marketing success measurement, 124
  viral marketing, 153
harassment
  anti-griefing terms, 331
  virtual world law, 353
hardcore gamers
  advertising suspicion, 114
  market segmentation, 112
hardware problems, contingency planning, 158
Hawk, Tony, 117
headlines, press releases, 136–137
health insurance
  employee benefits, 62–63
  game company startup, 35–36
health problems, rules and guarantees, 342

Hector, Matthew
  about, xviii
  on contracts. *see* contracts
hierarchy
  authorship and, 397–398
  job allocation, 53
high-speed Internet service tax credit, 292
hire-out PR vs. DIY, 134
hiring
  contractors. *see* independent contractors
  prospective employees. *see* prospective employees
history, public domain, 168–169
holiday bonuses, 61
honest hustling, 403–405
honesty, 332–333
hours, operation, 44–45
human connection, 370–371
human resources, 34–35
hustle and flow, 395–405
  authorship, 396–398
  company culture, 398–401
  conclusion, 405
  honest hustling, 403–405
  open process, 401–403
  overview, 395–396
hybrid developers
  defined, 465
  job allocation, 52
hype, 403–405

I

I-9
  defined, 464
  taxation, 281
I wish I knew. *see* business advice, professional
ideas
  vs. execution, 390–391
  IP protection. *see* IP (Intellectual Property)
  open process, 401–403
identity, publicity rights and, 188
IGDA (Independent Game Developer's Association)
  Gordon Walton, 389
  IP protection, 191
  networking, 72
ilovebees campaign, 153
image, marketing, 128–129
images
  developing screenshots, 143
  licensing IP, 208–212
immaterial breach
  contracts, 81
  defined, 465
impeach, 465
impersonation, 332–333
implied licence, 318
implied warranty, 465
in-game advertising, 117–121
in-person interviewing, 56–57
in-world actions, 343
Incentive Stock Options (ISO)
  defined, 465
  taxation, 286–287
incentives
  authorship and, 396–397
  taxation, 290–292
income taxes
  AMT, 289–290
  payroll tax compliance, 282
  state selection, 272–273
indemnification
  contract terms, 82
  defined, 465
  development agreements, 439–441
  licensing and, 199–200
  licensing literary works, 204
  third-party rights protection, 248
  virtual world law, 353–354
independence, maintaining, 72–73
independent contractors
  copyrights and licensing, 195–196
  defined, 465

development agreements, 443
employment contracts, 89–90
  prospective employees, 60
  relations, 25
  taxation vs. employees, 278–281
Independent Game Developer's Association (IGDA)
  Gordon Walton, 389
  IP protection, 191
  networking, 72
indicia rights
  defined, 465
  licensing IP, 208–212
The Indie Games Con, 152–153
industry events
  finding partner, 248
  PR, 152–153
industry leaders, 4
industry research, 24
Informa Telecoms & Media, 258
information and assistance clause, 417
Information Technology (IT)
  defined, 465
  job allocation, 54
infringement
  third-party rights. *see* third-party rights protection
  trade secret, 175
infringement, copyright
  damages, 171–172
  defined, 461
  penalties, 166–167
infringement, patent
  litigation. *see* IP (intellectual property) litigation
  penalties, 184
infringement, trademark
  defined, 471
  penalties, 179
  virtual world business rules, 334
initial disclosures, 227
injunctions
  defined, 83, 465
  drafting EULAs, 321
  licensing IP, 194
  preliminary, 220–221
  trial remedies, 234
injunctive relief, 446
innovation vs. invention, 375–376
insurance
  employee benefits, 62–63
  game company startup, 35–36
insurance, unemployment depository requirements, 283
  payroll tax compliance, 282–283
intangible taxes, 272–273
integration clause
  defined, 465
  development agreements, 444
  virtual world law, 320–321
intellectual property. *see* IP (Intellectual Property)
intellectual property litigation. *see* IP (Intellectual Property) litigation
intellectual property rights. *see* IP (Intellectual Property) rights
intent-to-use, 466
inter-department relationships
  company culture. *see* company culture
  open process, 401–403
Interact Accessories, 222–226
Interactive Digital Software Association, 105
interactive product placement, 118
internal revenue code, decoupling from, 292
Internal Revenue Service (IRS). *see* IRS (Internal Revenue Service)

international demographic trends, 111
international distribution. *see also* selling internationally
  EU taxation, 293–294
  fair use and, 170
  sublicenses, 80
international sales agent, 246–247, 466
International Trade Commission (ITC), 235–237
international trademark law, 180–181
Internet
  connectivity rules, 339
  PR, 148–150
Internet marketing
  Ad Media, 102
  Web sites, 121–123
interns, 70
Interplay, 256
interrogatories
  defined, 466
  IP litigation, 227–228
interstitial gamers, 112
interviewing prospective employees
  in-person, 56–57
  by phone, 55–56
interviews, PR, 134
intrinsic evidence
  defined, 466
  patent claim scope ruling, 224–225
introductory paragraph
  fact sheets, 141
  press releases, 137
invalidity, patent
  declaratory judgment action, 217–218
  reasons for, 185–186
invention vs. innovation, 375–376
inventors rights. *see* patents
inventory taxes, 272–273
investment agreements
  development agreements, 441–442
  exhibit, 451
investment tax credits
  defined, 466
  state tax incentives, 291–292
investors
  budgets for, 67–68
  exit strategies. *see* exit strategies
  game company startup, 8–9
IP (intellectual property), 161–190
  company names, 12
  company value, 303–304
  conclusion, 191
  copyright and rights, 164
  copyright examples, 164–165
  copyright information, 165–167
  copyright protection, 163–164
  copyright questions, 171–172
  defined, 466
  derivative works, 167
  endnotes, 191
  fair use, 170
  further reading, 458
  importance of, 161–163
  important points, 190–191
  legal definition, 412
  legal problems, 2
  licensing. *see* licensing IP
  overview, 161
  partner trust and, 257
  patent information, 182–184
  patent invalidity, 185–186
  patent questions, 186–187
  patents, 181–182
  patents pending and provisional, 184–185
  public domain, 167–169
  publicity rights, 187–188
  Scenes a Fair Doctrine, 169
  sources, 191

strategy, 188–190
trade secrets, 172–176
trademarks, 176–181
virtual world business rules,
    333–335
IP (intellectual property)
    litigation, 215–244
    alternative dispute
        resolution, 237–239
    conclusion, 239–240
    discovery overview,
        226–227
    discovery, preparation,
        231–232
    discovery, protective orders,
        227
    discovery tools, 227–231
    endnotes, 241
    forced dispute resolution,
        215–216
    jury selection, 232
    lawsuit filing, 219–220
    location, 218–219
    Markman hearings,
        222–226
    overview, 215
    post-trial, 234–235
    quick knockouts, 220–222
    before suit, 216–218
    trial format, 233
    trial remedies, 233–234
    trials and ITC, 235–237
IP (intellectual property) rights
    developer purchase, 437
    development agreements,
        418
    in-game advertising,
        119–120
    indemnification and, 82
    independent contractors
        and, 89–90
    licensing, 91–93
    ownership and licenses,
        428–431
    staying independent, 73
    third-party rights protec-
        tion, 248, 249
IPO (Initial Public Offering)
    defined, 465
    exit strategies, 300–301
irreparable harm, 321
IRS (Internal Revenue Service)
    accounting methods and,
        273
    payroll taxes for, 283–284
    research, 10
    taxes and regulations,
        32–33
ISO (Incentive Stock Options)
    defined, 465
    taxation, 286–287
Istook, Ernest, 294
IT (Information Technology)
    defined, 465
    job allocation, 54
ITC (International Trade
    Commission), 235–237

J
Jackson, Peter, 167
Japan, distribution, 250
job allocation, 49–54
journalists, marketing to. *see* PR
    (public relations)
jpegs, screenshots, 143
judgment as a matter of law,
    466
jurisdiction
    choice of law clauses,
        82–83
    declaratory judgment
        action, 218
    defined, 466
    development agreements,
        442–443
    forum selection, 320
    IP litigation, 218–219
    jury selection, 232
jury selection, 232
*JVW Enterprises, Inc. v. Interact
    Accessories, Inc.*, 222–226

K
*Katherine Reab, et. al. v.
    Electronic Arts Incorporated
    and Origin Systems*

Incorporated civil action,
    280
Keir, Nathan, 122
key artwork, licensing, 208
key personnel exhibit, 451

L
language
    local manufacture and
        pricing, 253
    localization, 259–260
    selling internationally,
        247–248
Lanham Act
    defined, 466
    publicity rights, 210
laws
    contract terms. *see* contract
        terms
    contracts. *see* contracts
    IP. *see* IP (Intellectual
        Property)
    IP litigation. *see* IP
        (intellectual property)
        litigation
    minimum wage, 280–281
    selling internationally,
        253–254
    virtual world. *see* virtual
        world law
lawsuits
    filing, 219–220
    indemnification, 82
    IP litigation, 216–218
    virtual world law, 345
lawyers
    business operations, 67
    drafting contracts, 77–78
    IP strategy, 188
    need for, 366–367, 379
    staying independent, 73
    writing EULAs, 316–317
LBOs (leveraged buy-outs)
    defined, 466
    exit strategies, 302–303
lead designer, 51
leadership, 14–15
leased software, 276–277
Lee, Peter
    book content, 4
    on game company
        intangibles. *see* hustle
        and flow
legal fees, 84–85
legal issues
    company formation, 11
    false advertising, 123
    in-game advertising,
        119–120
    IP. *see* IP (Intellectual
        Property)
    IP litigation. *see* IP
        (intellectual property)
        litigation
    selling internationally,
        257–258
    virtual world law. *see* virtual
        world law
legal problems, 2
length, demo, 147–148
length of copyright protection,
    165–166
length of patent protection,
    182–183
length of trade secret protec-
    tion, 174
length of trademark protection,
    178
levels of management, 43–44
leveraged buy-outs (LBOs)
    defined, 466
    exit strategies, 302–303
Leverett, William, business
    advice, 380–381
Levy, Richard, 366
*Lewis Galoob Toys, Inc. v.
    Nintendo of America Inc.* ,
    217–218
liability
    company formation, 10–15
    development agreements,
        441
    entities and taxation, 268
    indemnification and, 82
    remedies, 321
licensed software, 276–277

licensee, 78, 466
licensing. *see also* contracts
    celebrity names/likenesses,
        117
    defined, 249–250, 466
    development agreements,
        427–431
    EULAs. *see* EULAs (End
        User License Agree-
        ments); virtual world
        law
    IP, 91–93. *see also* IP
        (Intellectual Property)
    marketing, production and
        distribution, 420
    MMOGs, 255
    right to grant, 439
    to stop piracy, 254
    terms. *see* contract terms
licensing IP, 193–213
    audiovisual works, 207–208
    conclusion, 212
    elements, 198–200
    endnotes, 213
    IP nature, 193–194
    IP rights, 194–198
    literary works, 200–204
    musical works, 204–207
    name, image, likeness and
        indicia rights, 208–212
licensor, 78, 466
life cycle, patent litigation,
    240
likenesses, licensing IP,
    208–212
limitations on discovery,
    229–230
limited liability
    defined, 268, 466
    development agreements,
        441
    virtual world law, 337–342
Limited Liability Corporations
    (LLCs). *see* LLCs (Limited
    Liability Corporations)
Limited Partnerships, 268–272
Linked-In networking, 30
liquidation, 309
liquidity event
    defined, 466
    exit strategies, 299
literal patent infringement
    defined, 466
    IP litigation, 235
literary works
    copyright protection,
        163–164
    licensing IP, 200–204
litigation
    copyright information,
        171
    IP. *see* IP (intellectual
        property) litigation
    patent, 184
live advertising, 112–114
live team activity exhibit,
    451–453
live team development, 423
LLCs (Limited Liability
    Corporations)
    company formation, 10–15
    defined, 466
    entities and taxation,
        268–272
local manufacture, 253–254
local networking, 37
local rules, 355–356
localization
    defined, 466
    recoupment, 425
    selling internationally,
        259–260
location
    government restrictions,
        356
    IP litigation, 218–219
logos
    fact sheets, 141
    trademarks and, 176–181
The Lord of the Rings, 167
lost sales, 233
Lunar Lander, 361

M
Macris, Alexander, business
    advice, 381–383

MACRS (modified accelerated
    cost recovery system),
    277–278
Madden Bowl, 117
Madden NFL 06, 118
Madrid Protocol, 181
magazines, marketing, 114–115
magic circle, 359
magic spells, 373–374
maintenance
    development agreements,
        421–423
    engines and tools, 419
    office equipment, 25
    patent fees, 184
Major League Baseball Player's
    Association, 211
management
    business issues, 2
    employees, 41–45
    further reading, 458
    open process, 401–403
    upper, 50–51
managing debt, 20–21
manufacturers, fighting piracy,
    259
MAP (minimum advertised
    price), 104
market research. *see* research,
    market
marketing, 101–132
    ad dollars, 102
    audience, 109–112
    avoiding mistakes, 127–129
    business operations, 54
    business planning, 66
    vs. CMs, 386–387
    communication, 31
    conclusion, 130
    costs, 95
    defined, 466
    development agreements,
        419–421
    endnotes, 130–132
    game company startup,
        37–38
    game vs. company, 102
    in-game advertising,
        117–121
    international distribution,
        249
    Internet, 121–123
    measuring success,
        124–126
    overview, 101
    phases of, 107–109
    place, 105–106
    vs. PR, 101. *see also* PR
        (public relations)
    price, 103–105
    print, 114–116
    product, 103
    promotion, 106–107
    saving money on, 70–71
    strategy, 102–103
    television, radio and movie,
        116–117
    trade shows, 112–114
markman hearings
    defined, 466
    IP litigation, 222–226
Marvel Comics, 352
Massively Multiplayer Online
    Games (MMOGs). *see*
    MMOGs (Massively
    Multiplayer Online Games)
master recordings licensing,
    204–207
material breach
    contracts, 81
    defined, 467
    development agreements,
        445–446
materials, marketing, 37
maximum liability, 441
McKeever, Kellee
    about, xviii
    on selling internationally.
        see selling internation-
        ally
Medal of Honor, 169
media alerts
    defined, 467
    PR planning, 135
media marketing, 116–117,
    133–134

mediation
    defined, 467
    dispute resolution, 238,
        239
    IP litigation, 220
medical insurance
    employee benefits, 62–63
    game company startup,
        35–36
Medicare
    defined, 467
    payroll tax compliance, 282
mentoring, 376
merchandising, 334–335
Meridian 59, 378
merit bonuses
    business operations, 61
    defined, 467
metrics, success measurement,
    69
Mexico, international deals,
    264
MGM v. Grokster, 351–352
Microsoft
    IP litigation and ITC,
        235–237
    trademark examples,
        177–178
Microsoft Project, 47
Microsystems, 362
Midler, Bette, 210
Midway
    infringement penalties, 166
    preliminary injunctions,
        220–221
milestone bonuses
    business operations, 60–61
    defined, 467
milestones
    defined, 467
    payments, 95–96
    schedule exhibit, 449–450
    targets, 416
minimum advertised price
    (MAP), 104
minimum wage, 280–281
minority groups, 111
misappropriation
    defined, 467
    trade secrets, 173–174
MMOGs (Massively Multi-
    player Online Games)
    advice from William
        Leverett, 380–381
    law. *see* virtual world law
    post-launch, 383–385
    Randall Farmer, 228–229,
        371
    selling internationally,
        254–255
    socialization, 370–371
mobile gaming, 111
mod-chips, piracy, 105
mod license agreements, 92–93
modified accelerated cost
    recovery system (MACRS),
    277–278
money
    accounting, 17–18
    advice from Andrew
        Zaffron, 393
    advice from Scott Foe, 375
    debt, 20–21
    financial help, 16–17
    game company startup, 8–9
    marketing, 129
    money allocation, 20
    overview, 16
    paperwork, 19
    receipts, 19–20
    rules, 21–23
    saving, 69–71
    selling internationally,
        potential revenue,
        247–248
monthly scheduled depositors,
    283
morale
    avoiding crunch time,
        45–49
    company culture, 63
Morris, Gary S.
    about, xviii
    on licensing IP. *see* licensing
        IP
motion pictures, copyright, 163

motions for judgment, 234
movant, 467
movie, marketing, 116–117
Mulligan, Jessica, 311, 383–387
multitiered management structure, 467
musical composition licensing, 204–207
musical works
  copyright protection, 163
  licensing IP, 204–207
MySpace, 102, 121
Mythic Entertainment, 177–178
Mythica, 169, 177–178
mythology, public domain, 168–169

N

names
  company, 11–12
  licensing IP, 208–212
  public domain, 169
Napster, 351
NCAA Football 07, 115–116
NCsoft, 369, 370, 380
NDAs (non-disclosure agreements)
  contracts and, 85–88
  defined, 467
  in development agreements, 432–434
  equitable relief clauses, 83
  hiring paperwork, 58
  IP protection, 188–189
  trade secrets and, 176
Neath Death Studios Inc., 1, 378
negative feedback, 391
negative productivity
  crunch time and, 46
  defined, 467
negotiations
  advice from Steve Goldstein, 377–378
  chronology, 98
  legal fees and contracts, 84–85
  prospective employees, 57–58
  publishing and developer contracts, 96–97
  selling internationally, 260–262
net income
  defined, 467
  legal definition, 413
net profits
  advice from Andrew Zaffron, 393
  defined, 79–80
net revenue, legal definition, 413
networking
  advice from Alexander Macris, 382
  advice from John Erskine, 370
  business operations, 71–72
  buy-out partners, 306–307
  game company startup, 30–31
  maintaining contacts, 377
  marketing, 37
New York Civil Rights Law, 210
news alerts
  defined, 467
  PR planning, 135
nexus, taxation, 292–293
niche gamers, 112
Ninjaneering. *see* game company startup
Nintendo, 218, 234–235
Nokia, 374
non-compete agreements
  defined, 467
  employment contracts, 90–91
  hiring paperwork, 58
non-disclosure agreements (NDAs). *see* NDAs (non-disclosure agreements)
non-English speaking countries, 247–248

non-player characters (NPCs), 467
non-solicitation, 434
non-use, confidentiality, 432
nonexclusive licenses, 91–92, 467
noninteractive product placement, 118
nonstatutory stock options, 286–289
notice
  breach of contract, 81
  filing complaints, 219
NPCs (non-player characters), 467

O

object code, 468
obscenity, 353
obviousness, patent invalidity, 185–186
offensive statements, 331
offers, 468
office equipment, maintenance, 25
Office of Unfair Import Investigations (OUII), 237
"on sale bar", 186
one of ordinary skill in the art, 468
online communities, 148–150
online job sites, 55
online titles, selling internationally, 254–255
open process, 401–403
open source
  defined, 468
  legal definition, 414
opening statements, 233
Operating Agreements/Bylaws, 14
operating costs, 41
operating hours, 44–45
operations
  business. *see* business operations
  defined, 468
  development agreements, 421–423
Operations department, 54
opportunities
  learning from, 369
  seeking out, 71
Option Period clause, 414
option to purchase, 434–435
options, stock
  defined, 470
  employee benefits, 61–62
  taxation, 286–290
oral contracts, 76–77
oral testimony, 228–229
organization
  company formation, 10–15
  levels of management, 43–44
Orient Express, 361
Origin Systems and Electronic Arts, 380
OUII (Office of Unfair Import Investigations), 237
outing, anti-griefing, 331
over-marketing, 129
overpayment, 425
overseas distribution. *see* selling internationally
ownership
  company formation, 11
  development agreements, 427–431
  entities and taxation, 269–270

P

Pac-Man, 165, 220–221
Pacino, Al, 209
packaging, 128–129
paid Beta-testing, 372–373
The Palace, 371, 378
pantomimes, copyright, 163
paperwork
  before, 6–10
  company formation, 13–14
  contracts. *see* contracts
  financial, 19
  prospective employees, 58
parody, fair use, 170

parol evidence rule
  defined, 468
  virtual world law, 320–321
partner-supported piracy, 256
partners, buy-out, 306–307
partners, international
  competition, 251–253
  cost sharing, 261–262
  finding, 248
  small territories, 250–251
  trust, 255–257
partnerships
  company formation, 10–15
  defined, 468
  entities and taxation, 267–272
pass-through entities
  defined, 468
  taxation, 268–269
passwords, 323
Patent Act, 182
patent claims
  construction. *see* claim construction
  defined, 468
patent infringement, 468
patent specification, 468
patentee, 468
patents
  advice from Ralph Baer, 364–366
  claim scope ruling, 222–226
  defined, 468
  important points, 190–191
  information, 182–184
  invalidity, 185–186
  IP overview, 163
  IP protection strategies, 190
  licensing, 198
  litigation. *see* IP (Intellectual Property) litigation
  overview, 181–182
  pending and provisional, 184–185
  questions, 186–187
Patrovsky, Bridgette, 383–384
pay rates, 58–59
payments
  billing/accounts, 322–326
  publishing and developer contracts, 93–94
  royalties, 423–427
  selling internationally, 260–262
payroll taxes
  compliance, 281–283
  for IRS, 283–284
PC titles, 250, 254
penalties. *see* damages
  copyright infringement, 172
  trade secret infringement, 175
pending patents
  IP, 184–185
  use of, 186–187
penny markets, 300–301
per-player design and secrecy, 373–374
perceived value, 307–308
performance reviews
  prospective employees, 60
  write-ups, 65
personal assets, infringement, 172
personal jurisdiction, 468
personnel
  development agreements, 415–416
  key personnel exhibit, 451
phased recoupment, 423–424
phone interviewing, 55–56
photocopying, receipts, 20
pictorial works, copyright, 163
piercing the corporate veil
  defined, 468
  limited liability, 268
piracy
  development agreements, 422–423
  distribution and, 105
  local manufacture and pricing, 253–254
  partner trust and, 256–257

selling internationally, 258–259
pitching stories
  defined, 468
  IP protection, 188–189
  PR, 145–147
plaintiffs, 468
planning
  advice from Scott Foe, 376
  avoiding crunch time, 47–48
  avoiding marketing mistakes, 127–128
  business operations, 66–67
  PR, 134–136, 468
  planning, contingency, 157–158
player-created content, 358
players
  not being their puppet, 368–369
  rules. *see* rules, virtual world law
  third-party rights protection, 347–350
players, banned
  rule enforcement, 343
  virtual world law, 324
Player's Choice Group Licensing Program, 211
playing games
  advice from Andrew Zaffron, 394
  advice from Jeff Vogel, 388
  at work, 398–401
Pocket Kingdom, 374
policies
  defined, 312, 468
  privacy. *see* privacy
  virtual world law, 314
polish period
  legal definition, 411
  recoupment, 426
pop-up ads, 121
pornography, 353
portals, game. *see* game portals
post-release marketing, 108–109
posting, online communities, 148–150
potential revenue, 247–248
PR (public relations), 133–159
  advice from Jeff Vogel, 388
  asset advice, 142–145
  conclusion, 158–159
  contests, 154
  contingency planning, 157–158
  defined, 133–134, 469
  demos, 147–148
  DIY vs. hire-out, 134
  fact sheets, 140–142
  further reading, 458
  honest hustling and, 403–405
  industry events, 152–153
  international distribution, 249
  vs. marketing, 101
  online communities, 148–150
  perceived company value, 307
  planning, 134–136
  press releases, 136–140
  press tours, 150–152
  program sample, 155–157
  saving money on, 70–71
  story pitching, 145–147
  viral marketing, 153–154
praise, business, 114–116
pre-filing requirements, 216–217
pre-release marketing, 108
pre-trial conference, 468
preliminary injunctions, 220–221
press releases
  defined, 469
  marketing, production and distribution, 420
  PR, 136–140
  scheduling, 135
press tours, 150–152

preview tours, 150–152
previews, 135–136
pricing
  marketing, 103–105
  selling internationally, 253–254
  virtual world law, 322–323
privacy
  individual rights licensing, 209–211
  policies, 356–357
  Web site promotion, 107
probation
  defined, 469
  disciplinary action, 65
problem-solving, 401–403
ProCD Inc. v. Zeidenberg, 92
process
  importance of, 382–383
  open, 401–403
producers
  advice from Scott Foe, 374–376
  defined, 469
  job allocation, 50
  salaries, 59
product
  boilerplate, 138
  business planning, 66
  marketing, 103
  sponsors, 119–120
product placement
  in-game advertising, 117–121
  marketing, 117
production
  development agreements, 419–421
  hierarchy, 53
professional advice. *see* business advice, professional
profile, company, 403–405
profit sharing
  advice from Andrew Zaffron, 393
  defined, 469
  employee benefits, 62
profits. *see also* money
  advice from Andrew Zaffron, 393
  advice from Scott Foe, 375
  pricing and, 103–105
program sample, 155–157
programmers
  advice from Richard Bartle, 367–368
  salaries, 59
prohibitions, 313–314
Project Entropia, 333
project time line, 45–49
promotion
  demo, 148
  marketing, 106–107
prosecution history
  defined, 469
  patent claim scope ruling, 224
prospective employees
  benefits, 61–63
  bonuses, 60–61
  closing deal, 57–58
  in-person interviewing, 56–57
  independent contractors, 60
  interviewing, 55–56
  overview, 55
  paperwork, 58
  pay rates, 58–59
  performance, 60
protection
  copyright. *see* copyrights
  IP. *see* IP (Intellectual Property)
protective orders
  defined, 469
  discovery, 227
provisional, patents, 184–185
PRWeb, 139
psychographic market segmentation, 112
public domain
  copyrights, 167–169
  defined, 469
public offerings
  defined, 465

exit strategies, 300–301
public relations (PR). *see* PR (public relations)
public speaking, 364
"public use", patent invalidity, 186
publicity rights
  IP, 187–188
  licensing, 209–211
publishers
  company value, 306
  contracts, 93–97
  cost sharing, 261–262
  development agreements. *see* game development agreements
  international deals, 249–250
  licensing musical works, 206–207
  sharing profits, 393
Pulp Fiction, 23
punishment
  business operations, 64–66
  copyright infringement, 166–167
  rule enforcement, 342–345
purchase order, 469

Q
Q&As (questions and answers)
  asset development, 144
  PR planning, 134
QA (quality assurance testers)
  Beta-testing, 372–373
  defined, 53–54, 469
  salaries, 59
Quake walhack, 328
quality control, 417
questions and answers (Q&As)
  asset development, 144
  PR planning, 134
QuickBooks, 17

R
racial demographic trends, 111
radio, marketing, 116–117
raises, 60
rates, conversion
  defined, 461
  marketing success measurement, 124
reading
  advice from David Ahl, 362–363
  advice from Randall Farmer, 371–372
  further, 457–458
Reagan, Ronald, 16
recapture, state tax incentives, 291–292
receipts
  financial issues, 19–20
  publishing and developer contracts, 94–95
recitals, development agreements, 408–410
record companies, licensing, 205–206
recoupable advances
  defined, 78–79, 469
  publishing and developer contracts, 94
recoverable advances
  defined, 79
  publishing and developer contracts, 94
recruiters, 55
redesign, unnecessary, 47–48
referrals, 55
registration
  business entities, 12–13
  importance of, 371
  patent, 183–184
  trademark, 178
registration, copyright
  licensing, 195–196
  process and cost, 165
  protected categories, 163–164
regulations
  employment, 32–33
  government, 32–33
relationships, importance of, 370–371
release marketing, 108

remedies
  defined, 469
  trial, 233–234
  virtual world law, 321
repayable advances
  defined, 79, 469
  publishing and developer contracts, 94
reporting requirements, 284–285
representations
  defined, 82
  development agreements, 437–439
requests for admission
  defined, 469
  IP litigation, 228
requests for production of documents
  defined, 469
  IP litigation, 228
research
  game company startup, 10
  industry, 24
  playing at work, 398–401
research library, 399
research, market
  audience, 110
  avoiding marketing mistakes, 128
  defined, 37, 467
  online forums, 149
responsibility
  company formation, 11
  marketing, production and distribution, 419
  operations, support and maintenance, 421–422
retail pricing, 104
retailers
  distribution, 106
  international distribution, 249–250
  licensing and trademarks, 197–198
retirement benefits, 62
revenue, potential, 247–248
reverse engineering
  localization, 259–260
  trade secrets and, 176
reversed charges, 323
reviews, marketing, 115
reviews, performance, 60
rewards
  business operations, 64–66
  crunch time, 49
right of first negotiation, 203
right of first offer, 418
right of first refusal
  defined, 469
  option to purchase and, 434
right of last refusal, 203
rights
  copyrights and, 164
  licensing IP. *see* licensing IP
  publicity, 187–188
  trade secret, 173–174
Roberts, Julia, 117
Robin Hood story, 168
Robotic Visions Systems, 217
Rockstar Games, 115, 123
Role Playing Games (RPGs), 247
Rolodex, 30–31
royalties
  development agreements, 423–427
  exhibit, 453–454
  publishing and developer contracts, 93–94
  recoupable advances, 78–79
  royalty report exhibit, 454
  trial remedies, 233
royalty deal, 249
RPGs (Role Playing Games), 247
rules, money, 21–23
rules of conduct
  defined, 312, 469
  virtual world law, 313–314
rules, virtual world law
  billing/accounts, 322–326
  business, 333–337
  community, 329–333
  software use, 326–329

terms for setting, 337
  types of, 312–317
running game company intangibles. *see* hustle and flow

S
S Corporations
  company formation, 10–15
  defined, 469
  entities and taxation, 267–272
salaries
  minimum wage, 280–281
  payroll tax compliance, 281–283
  prospective employees, 58–59
  saving money on, 69–70
sale of company, 301–302
sales agent
  defined, 466
  selling internationally, 246–247
San Francisco, 150–152
Saturday Night Live (SNL), 31
saving money, 69–71
saving notes, 364–366
Saving Private Ryan, 169
Scenes a Fair Doctrine, 169
scheduling
  development agreements, 449–450
  good managers, 43
  IP litigation, 219–220
  PR planning, 135
screenshots
  defined, 470
  developing, 143
  PR planning, 134–135
  in press releases, 139–140
scripts, press tours, 151
sculptural works, copyright, 163
sealed envelope copyright, 171
searching trademarks, 371
Second Life, 122, 371
secondary liability, 350–351
secondary meaning, 470
secrecy
  advice from Randall Farmer, 373–374
  NDAs, 85–88
  trade secrets. *see* trade secrets
Section 179, 277–278
Section 230 of the Communications Decency Act (CDA) of 1996
  defined, 470
  third-party rights protection, 248–249
Section 512 of the Digital Millennium Copyright Act (DMCA)
  defined, 470
  third-party rights protection, 249–250
security
  development agreements, 422–423
  partner trust, 256–257
  software, 326–329
  user, 323–324
Sega, 374
segmentation, market, 112
selling internationally, 245–265
  conclusion, 264–265
  considerations, 245–246
  deal types, 248–250
  dealing, 262–264
  development agreements, 419
  export restrictions, 356
  finding partner, 248
  game type and deal type, 254–255
  legal issues, 257–258
  local manufacture and pricing, 253–254
  localization, 259–260
  overview, 245
  partner trust, 255–257
  partnering with competition, 251–253

partners in smaller countries, 250–251
  payments, 260–262
  piracy, 258–259
  potential revenue, 247–248
  sales agent vs. employee, 246–247
semiweekly scheduled depositors, 283
sequels
  development agreements, 418–419
  licensing literary works, 203
  royalties, 425
serialization of discs, 470
server protection, 327–328
services
  defined, 470
  vendor relations, 27–30
  virtual world law, 311
services, development. *see* development
setting rules, 337
settlement, 470
severability clause
  defined, 470
  development agreements, 444
  virtual world law, 321
sexual abuse, 331
sexuality, 123
sharing accounts, 324
sharing costs, 261–262
short-term survival, 22–23
ShowEQ, 328
shrinkwrap licenses
  defined, 470
  EULAs and, 92
signature page, development agreement, 448–449
signing bonuses, 57
signing notes, 365
Silent Hill 4 The Room, 257
Simply Accounting, 17
The Sims, 118
The Sims Online, 371
Singapore, international deals, 263–264
slideshow presentations, 151
Small Business Administration, 10
Small Business Computers, 362
small businesses
  going public, 300–301
  IP protection strategies, 189
  over-marketing, 129
Smith, Erik
  about, xix
  on development agreements. *see* game development agreements
SNL (Saturday Night Live), 31
social norms
  defined, 312
  virtual world law, 315–316
Social Security
  defined, 470
  payroll tax compliance, 282
  tax information, 32
socialization, 370–371
Sociolotron, 313
SOE (Sony Online Entertainment), 392–393
software
  accounting, 17
  company value, 303–304
  costs, 276–277
  engine, 470
  escrow, 230–231
  game rules, 326–329
  maintenance, 422
  patents. *see* patents
  rule enforcement, 343–344
  rules, 312–313
  as trade secret, 174
Sole Proprietorships
  company formation, 10–15
  defined, 470
  entities and taxation, 267–272
Sony Corporation v. Universal City Studios, 351
Sony Ericsson, 166
Sony Online Entertainment (SOE), 392–393

sound recordings, copyright, 163
source code
  defined, 470
  as literary work, 163–164
  ownership and licenses, 428–429
source engines, 71
spam, viral marketing, 154
speaking in public, 364
specific prohibitions, 313–314
specification in patents, 183
Spiderman 2, 124
Spiderweb Software, 387
sports games, 119
spyware, 344
SSTP (State Sales Tax Project), 295
SSUTA (Streamlined Sales and Use Tax Act), 295
staff. *see* employees
Stainless Steel Studios, 303
stalking
  anti-griefing terms, 331
  virtual world law, 353
standard business formation documentation, 13–14
starting game company. *see* game company startup
State Comptroller Registration, 13
state law
  contracts, 75
  download taxation, 294–295
  publicity rights, 187
  trade secret infringement, 176
State Sales Tax Project (SSTP), 295
state selection
  lawsuit location, 218–219
  taxation, 272–273
state tax incentives, 291–292
state tax laws, decoupling, 292
Statute of Monopolies, 181–182
statutory stock options, 286–289
stock options
  defined, 470
  employee benefits, 61–62
  taxation and, 286–290
story pitching
  IP protection, 188–189
  PR, 145–147
straight-line depreciation method
  defined, 470
  taxation, 277
strategy
  asset development, 144–145
  marketing, 102–103
Streamlined Sales and Use Tax Act (SSUTA), 295
strength of protection, trademarks, 179–180
Stubbs, Alderton & Markiles, LLP, 376
studio head
  defined, 470
  job allocation, 50
subject line, 136–137
sublicenses
  contract terms, 80
  defined, 470
  IP, 200
subscription fees, 420
subsidiary rights
  defined, 459, 470
  exploitation, 201–202
  limitations on discovery, 229–230
Subway Scavenger, 361
success measurement, 69, 124–126
suggestive trademarks
  defined, 470
  IP, 179–180
summary judgment
  defined, 470
  IP litigation, 221–222
support, 369, 421–423
Supreme Court, appeals, 235
surveying

market research, 110
success measurement, 125–126
surviving the business. *see* business advice, professional
swag, 152
symbols, trademark protection, 179
synchronization licenses
defined, 471
musical compositions, 206

T
Take-Two Interactive Software Inc., 123
takedown notices, 249–250
talent, 389
tapers, 373–374
target market. *see* audience
tarnishment, trademark
business rules, 334
defined, 471
tax and worker eligibility forms, 58
taxation, 267–297
accounting, 273–278
conclusion, 295–296
decoupling from internal revenue code, 292
depository requirements, 283
download, 294–295
employees vs. independent contractors, 278–281
endnotes, 296–297
entity selection, 267–272
in EU, 292–294
fringe benefits, 283–286
incentives, 290–292
need for accountants, 379
nexus, 292–293
payroll compliance, 281–283
state selection, 272–273
stock options, 286–290
taxes
government and, 32
independent contractors, 89
withholding, 426–427
team
business planning, 66
company value, 305
team chemistry
company culture, 63, 398–401
game company startup, 8
importance of, 389–390
Team Play, Inc. v. Boyer, 218
tech, saving money, 71
technical measures, rule enforcement, 343–344
television, marketing, 116–117
tense, in press releases, 138
term
definitions, 410–414
development agreements, 435–437
termination
contract terms, 80–81
defined, 471
development agreements, 435–437
disciplinary action, 65
termination, account, 324–325
termination for cause
defined, 471
development agreements, 435–437
termination for convenience
defined, 471
development agreements, 435–437
terms, contract. *see* contract terms
terms for players' rules

business rules, 333–337
community rules, 329–333
game rules: software use, 326–329
ground rules: billing/accounts, 322–326
terms of service (ToS)
defined, 471
virtual world law, 318–319
Terms of Use (TOU), 92, 107
testimonials, print marketing, 115
testimony
depositions, 228–229
trial format, 233
testing
Beta-testing, 372–373
prospective employees, 56
quality assurance testers. *see* QA (quality assurance testers)
text assets, localization, 259–260
third-party discovery, 229
third-party rights protection
company, 354
confidentiality, 433
copyrights, 351–352
court orders, 354–355
criminal laws, 352–353
indemnification, 353–354, 439–441
local rules, 355–356
players', 347–350
privacy policies, 356–357
secondary liability, 350–351
trademarks, 352
Tiburon Studios, 115
time management
good managers, 43
money and, 22
timeline, goals, 102–103
title of game development agreement, 408
titles, 128–129
Tolkien, J. R. R., 167
tools, development
maintenance, 419
ownership and licenses, 428–430
Torque, 71
ToS (terms of service)
defined, 471
virtual world law, 318–319
tours, press, 150–152
TOUs (Terms of Use), 92, 107
The Toy and Game Inventor's Handbook, 366
trade secrets
defined, 471
important points, 190–191
IP, 172–176
IP overview, 163
trade shows. *see also* conferences
marketing, 112–114
marketing, production and distribution, 421
trademark dilution
business rules, 334
defined, 471
trademark tarnishment
business rules, 334
defined, 471
trademarks
defined, 471
EULAs and, 93
important points, 190–191
in-game advertising, 119–120
IP, 176–181
IP overview, 163
licensing, 197–198
registration, 371

virtual world business rules, 334
virtual world law, 352
transferability, account, 325–326
transparency, virtual world law, 314
treble damages, 471
trends, demographic, 110–111
trials
format, 233
ITC and, 235–237
jury selection, 232
post-trial, 234–235
remedies, 233–234
Tringo, 122
triple A title, 471
Turbine, 373–374
turnover issue, 38

U
U. S. Census Web site, 110
U. S. District Court, 236
UCG (Ultimate Game Club), 235–237
Ultima Online, 385
unauthorized account use, 323–324
unauthorized transfers, 325–326
unemployment insurance
defined, 471
depository requirements, 283
payroll tax compliance, 282–283
unfair competition, 471
Uniform Trade Secrets Act, 173–176, 471
United States Army, 120
United States Code (U.S.C.), 471
United States Constitution
copyrights and, 163
individual rights licensing, 210–211
patent rights, 182
United States ITC, 235–237
United States Patent and Trademark Office. *see* USPTO (United States Patent and Trademark Office)
unnecessary redesign, 47–48
uploading, 249
upper management, 50–51
U.S.C. (United States Code), 471
user security, 323–324
users, banned
rule enforcement, 343
virtual world law, 324
USPTO (United States Patent and Trademark Office)
defined, 471
Disclosure Document program, 366
registering/searching trademarks, 371
trademark registration, 178–179

V
Value-Added Tax (VAT), 293–294
value, company
assets, 303–306
perceived, 307–308
VAT (Value-Added Tax), 293–294
VCs (venture capitalists), 299
vendor relations, 27–30
venue jurisdiction
choice of law clauses, 82–83
development agreements, 442–443

virtual world law, 320
verbal warnings, 64–65
vicarious copyright infringement
defined, 471
virtual world law, 351–352
video trailers
asset development, 143–144
PR planning, 134–135
View Engineering v. Robot Visions Systems, 217
violating copyright, 166–167
violation of laws and regulations, 438
viral marketing
defined, 471
Internet, 121–122
PR, 153–154
virtual liberty, 358
virtual property, 359
virtual world, 471–472
virtual world law, 311–359
business rules, 333–337
community rules, 329–333
conclusion, 359
copyrights, 351–352
court orders, 354–355
criminal laws, 352–353
disclaimers and limited liability, 337–342
endnotes, 359–360
enforcing rules, 342–345
EULAs as contracts, 317–322
five kinds of rules, 312–317
further horizons, 358–359
further reading, 457–458
game rules: software use, 326–329
ground rules: billing/accounts, 322–326
indemnification, 353–354
local rules, 355–356
making changes, 345–347
overview, 311–312
privacy policies, 356–357
secondary liability, 350–351
terms for setting rules, 337
third-party rights protection: company, 354
third-party rights protection: players, 347–350
trademarks, 352
viruses, 340–341
Vogel, Jeff, business advice, 387–388
volatility of startup, 383
volunteers
defined, 472
players as employees, 336–337
taxation, 280

W
W-2
defined, 464
taxation, 284–285
W-3
defined, 464
taxation, 284–285
W-4
defined, 464
taxation, 281
wages. *see also* salaries
laws, 280–281
payroll tax compliance, 281–283
waiver, development agreements, 446
walkthroughs
asset development, 144
defined, 472
The Wall Street Journal, 362

Walton, Gordon, business advice, 388–392
WarCry Network, 381, 383
warez, 472
warez sites, 472
warranties
contract basics, 76
defined, 472
development agreements, 437–439
disclaimers, 337–342
indemnification, 82
licensing and, 199–200
licensing literary works, 204
Web sites
distribution, 105–106
Internet marketing, 121–123
launching and PR, 135
marketing yourself, 38
promotion, 107
research, 10
saving money on PR, 70–71
whereas clauses, 408–410
white collar exemptions, 280–281
White Paper, 191
White, Vanna, 210
wikis, open process, 402–403
willful infringement
damages, 171–172
trial remedies, 234
Wilson Sonsini Goodrich & Rosati, 370
wire transfers, 262
withholding taxes, 426–427
witnesses
employees as, 231
experts, 232
IP litigation, 228–229
women-as-gamers, 368
word-of-mouth PR, 70
worker's compensation, 472
The World is Flat (Friedman), 381
World of Warcraft
anti-griefing, 332
client software protection, 336
in-game advertising, 119
virus scanning, 341
World War II, 169
wrapping up, 455–456
Wright, Will, 115
Wrigleys, 120
write-ups, 65
writing EULAs, 316–317
writing press releases, 136–140
written contracts. *see* contracts
Wyden, Ron, 295

X
Xbox, 177
Xerox, 20, 93

Y
Yahoo.com, 371
Yahoo!Games, 122
Year Ends, entities and taxation, 270
YouTube, 154

Z
Zaffron, Andrew S., business advice, 392–394
Zimmerman, Eric
book content, 4
game company intangibles. *see* hustle and flow
Zuzolo, Spencer
about, xix
on game company startup. *see* game company startup